THIRD EDITION

Literacy & Learning

IN THE CONTENT AREAS

Sharon Kane

STATE UNIVERSITY OF NEW YORK AT OSWEGO

Holcomb Hathaway, Publishers
Scottsdale, Arizona

Library of Congress Cataloging-in-Publication Data

Kane, Sharon.
 Literacy & learning in the content areas / Sharon Kane. — 3rd ed.
    p. cm.
 ISBN 978-1-934432-06-8
 1. Content area reading.   2. Interdisciplinary approach in education.   3.
Literature—Study and teaching (Secondary)   4. Teenagers—Books and reading.
 I. Title.   II. Title: Literacy and learning in the content areas.
 LB1050.455.K36 2011
 372.47'6—dc22

                                                              2010037599

I dedicate this book to my sisters, Janie Trey and Ann Mazza.

Please note: The authors and publisher have made every effort to provide current website addresses in this book. However, because web addresses change, it is inevitable that some of the URLs listed here will change following publication of this book. The Kane Resource Site + Community, www.hhpcommunities.com/kane, may provide updates for broken links.

Holcomb Hathaway, Publishers, Inc.
8700 E. Via de Ventura Blvd., Suite 265
Scottsdale, Arizona 85258
480-991-7881
www.hh-pub.com

10 9 8 7 6 5 4 3

ISBN 978-1-934432-06-8

Printed in the United States of America.

brief contents

contents

4 THE ROLE OF KNOWLEDGE IN COMPREHENSION   87

5 METACOGNITION AND CRITICAL THINKING   125

6 VOCABULARY DEVELOPMENT AND LANGUAGE STUDY   151

7 WRITING IN THE CONTENT AREAS   189

8 SPEAKING AND LISTENING: VITAL COMPONENTS OF LITERACY   223

preface

Literacy and learning are essential and interconnected goals for students in the disciplines we teach. The third edition of *Literacy & Learning in the Content Areas* continues to share ways in which content area teachers can enhance student learning of subject matter and skills while also fostering their growth in the many facets of literacy.

Future middle school and high school teachers often enter the field expecting to teach the topics they love to students already proficient in reading and writing, and they may feel that literacy is a "requirement" that has been foisted upon them. Rather, literacy is key to learning in the content areas and to appreciating the rich treasure of knowledge in the various disciplines. Integrating literacy doesn't have to take a teacher's time or energy away from the teaching of math, art, history, science, or any other subject. We can teach our students every day how to use the language arts to become proficient in the subjects they study and to independently pursue curricular topics of interest.

This book will help provide readers with the knowledge, motivation, tools, and confidence for integrating literacy in their content area classrooms. It offers a unique approach to teaching content area literacy that gets readers actively engaged in reading, writing, viewing, visually representing, speaking, and listening—the very activities that they will use to teach literacy to their own students.

Research indicates a major problem with aliteracy in our society. Even young people who can read well often choose not to read independently. Neither future nor experienced teachers are immune to this aliteracy. Each semester, I begin my content area literacy class by asking students to answer the question, "Are you a reader and writer?" The answer is far too often a regretful "No" or "I used to be but now I'm too busy." I believe that content area literacy courses will not have a lasting impact unless these future and practicing teachers become readers and writers. *Literacy & Learning* works toward this goal through its interactive approach so that its readers will know how to reach this same goal with their students. Rather than passively learning about strategies for incorporating content area literacy activities, readers will get hands-on experience in such techniques as mapping/webbing, anticipation guides, K-W-L charts, and journal writing and reflection. For this third edition, the development of the companion website, the Kane Resource Site + Community (see p. xii for more information) makes the experience of reading this textbook more interactive than ever before. By encouraging future and practicing teachers to become active readers and writers, this book will help equip them with the motivation and skills to encourage their own students to engage in reading, writing, speaking, listening, and visual learning across the curriculum to improve learning in content area subjects.

Literacy & Learning also incorporates as a major theme the use of many different types of texts to teach literacy skills and strategies as well as to motivate interest in a subject area and enhance knowledge and understanding of content. Readers will learn not only how to effectively evaluate and use textbooks, but also how to integrate children's and young adult literature, primary sources, biographies, essays, poetry, online materials and websites, graphic novels, television, and film in their teaching. Each chapter of this book includes lists of resources that make it a valuable tool for content area teachers. In fact, readers who flip through the text and the Resource Appendix will find comprehensive book lists unparalleled by other content area books.

The book includes numerous concrete examples and teaching/learning scenarios for math, science, and social studies as well as others relating to music, health, art, and physical education. In this edition, the examples are labeled "Teaching in Action" followed by the subject to make it easy for readers to locate teaching examples in subjects of interest. At the same time, the book emphasizes interdisciplinary thinking, and readers are encouraged to make connections within and among fields.

Throughout *Literacy & Learning,* attention is given to the important issues of diversity, students with special needs, English learners, and teaching for critical thinking and social justice. Literacy is very much connected with the goals of positive change within our society. In this context, readers are offered opportunities to ponder how they can serve as change agents who can improve the scholastic lives of their students and, in the long term, help implement systemic change in schools and society.

Information on using technology for instruction is integrated throughout the book. Websites, various types of online communities, software resources, and strategies for incorporating technology with literacy in content area lessons are included.

Finally, *Literacy & Learning* demonstrates how wide and varied opportunities for reading, writing, listening, speaking, viewing, and visually representing can help students meet national content knowledge standards and benchmarks including the common core standards, showing that a standards-based curriculum can use literacy strategies not as add-ons, but as integral to content teaching itself.

New to This Edition

The many changes to this edition include the following:

- **Now available as a full-color ebook.** When adopting this book for use in your class, you may inform your students that the color ebook version can be purchased on our website, www.hh-pub.com. The ebook matches the print book page for page; this ensures ease of teaching if some of your students use the print book and some use the e-book. See p. xii for more information.
- **The Kane Resource Site (www.hhpcommunities. com/kane)** offers many teaching and learning tools. Some of these are discussed in the list items below; others include printer-ready versions of many of this book's handouts and forms, linked website URLs, additional Application Activities; and much more. You and your students can read more about the Kane Resource Site on p. xii.
- **BookTalks Online** (to supplement the many BookTalks in this text) can be found on the Kane Resource Site. Many of these are available as podcasts.
- The feature "**Websites**," at the end of each chapter, lists the websites from throughout the chapter for easy reference. All of these sites can be accessed through links on the Kane Resource Site.
- The new feature "**Teaching in Action**" helps readers quickly locate classroom teaching examples identified by discipline. Those who do or will teach science, for example, can look for *"Teaching in Action: Science"* for ideas tailored specifically to a science classroom (although all of the teaching examples will be helpful to all teachers!).
- At the suggestion of reviewers and adopters, and in order to streamline the text presentation a little, the in-text bibliographic figures have been shortened. Now, the text figures feature a limited number of select titles while numerous others are conveniently compiled in the **Resource Appendix**, by figure number. Thus, for example, if you want more suggested titles for Figure 9.3,

"Examples of graphic novels and texts in cartoon/comic format," you'll turn to Appendix Figure 9.3.

- As always, newly published titles in children's literature, young adult literature, and informational texts have been added to the extensive lists of resources in this book and will continue to be added to the Kane Resource Site.

The Book's Special Features

Embedded in each chapter are features that will help readers actively engage with issues, ideas, and suggestions. Throughout the chapters, you'll find the following tools:

- **BookTalks** and **BookTalks Online** introduce relevant books in many genres and subjects, encouraging readers to read the books for themselves and providing a model for booktalks in their own classrooms.
- **Activating Prior Knowledge** activities build on past experiences and stimulate critical thinking to prepare readers to learn theoretical and conceptual material about teaching, learning, and literacy. These activities also prepare readers to activate prior knowledge in their classrooms.
- **Action Research** activities encourage readers to improve the quality of their teaching through research, collaboration with peers, and observation and experimentation in the classroom.
- End-of-chapter **Application Activities** help readers apply what they've learned to their particular content area in concrete ways. As they modify the activities to fit their philosophy and the needs of their students, readers will create useful materials and strategies for their own content area courses. In the Kane Resource Site discussion forums, readers will be able to post and receive feedback on their own materials and access the teaching ideas of others.
- **In-text icons** are used to indicate related website features such as discussion forums, printable assessment forms and handouts, and podcasts.

The Voices and Stories in Our Teaching

Esteemed scientist E. O. Wilson (2002) says that science consists of millions of stories, which become science when they are tested and woven into cause-and-effect explanations. These stories can be "the key to helping the non-scientist understand the great ideas of science" (p. 10). What teacher wouldn't want to make such stories available to her students? Wilson explains that stories—both those that are stored in our memories and those that we generate while interacting with the world—are essential to learning and remembering. Luckily for us teachers, there are stories for every discipline.

This book makes use of stories to teach in-service and preservice content area teachers about the learners in their midst (including themselves), and about strategies for integrating literacy into their discipline-specific teaching. It employs stories of and by students; it includes stories of successful practices by caring teachers; it invites readers to construct stories of vital and stimulating classrooms full of literacy and learning.

The students in your classes have stories to tell. There are stories of struggling to learn, to comprehend, to read. There are stories of intense interest in and love for certain curricular topics, or authors, or genres of literature; stories of searching for ways to fit in socially and interact with peers and adults; stories about faraway homelands, other languages, different cultures, and the search for social justice; stories told through pictures, projects, and performances. One of the reasons teaching is so rewarding is that the stories are ever changing, ever being renewed. As we and our students grow more literate throughout the school year, a story of promise and potential is created. This book is meant to be a tool you can use to bring the story to fruition.

ACKNOWLEDGMENTS

T here are many people to thank as I complete this new edition. My editors at Holcomb Hathaway, Colette Kelly and Gay Pauley, believed in the project from the start and saw me through the publication process. My students believed in me even before the book's inception, requesting a textbook that would reflect what went on in our course. And my students ever since have been just as inspiring and helpful. Many contributed materials included in these pages as examples.

I wish to thank the following individuals, all of whose work made this a better book: Jane Partanen, University of Pittsburgh, whose thoroughness and generosity are unbounded; Jay Button, SUNY Oswego, who was once my professor for Content Area Reading and has been my colleague, mentor, and friend ever since; Nancy L. Hadaway, University of Texas at Arlington; Richard Mezeske, Hope College; and Jesse Turner, Central Connecticut State University.

I respectfully thank the reviewers of this and prior editions, whose constructive suggestions helped me to refine and improve the book: Jane Anderson, St. Mary's University of Minnesota; Thomas Cornell, Webster University; William Farr, University of Connecticut; Kathy Froelich, Florida State University; Cara Garcia, Pepperdine University; Naomi Garwood, Roberts Wesleyan College; Elizabeth Griffin, Gloucester County Institute of Technology; Lisa Hyland, Augsburg College; Donna W. Jorgensen, Rowan University; Diane Kern, University of Rhode Island; Maureen Mulvaney, Waynesburg University; Melissa Reed, Emporia State University; Regina Reese, Youngstown State University; Robert Reising, University of Central Arkansas; Ruth Sylvester, University of South Florida Polytechnic; Magdalene Tobias, Siena Heights University; Jeff Whittingham, University of Central Arkansas; and G. Pat Wilson, University of South Florida, Sarasota-Manatee.

A sabbatical granted by the State University of New York at Oswego and a grant from United University Professions helped my work on the first edition, for which I am grateful.

I wish to acknowledge and thank all the teachers who have allowed me to see their dedication in action and have shared strategies, ideas, success stories, and struggles. I especially thank Sharon Morley, who in my mind is peerless when it comes to managing a process classroom and bringing out the best in students; and team teachers Chris Leahey and Auddie Mastroleo, who took what they learned in my classes and ran with it, theorizing and constructing a collaborative content area project (described in Chapter 11) beyond what I could have foreseen. I also thank Juliana Bütz for allowing me to use a few of the scientific drawings she did in high school that show such talent and passion.

I thank my writing group, including Bonita Hampton, Mary Harrell, Tania Ramalho, Barbara Beyerbach, and Bobbi Schnorr; and especially Chris Walsh and Jean Ann for their challenging but kind responses to multiple drafts.

I appreciate the daily joy of working with my awesome colleagues in the Curriculum and Instruction Department at SUNY Oswego. In particular, I thank Claire Putala, whom I consider the newest sister to join my family, and Pam Michel, kindred spirit, who always reminds me that life is a joyful adventure.

I am grateful for the moral and spiritual support provided by my friends, including Dorothy Albert, Rosemary Brown, Ellen Bütz, Liz DePartout, Ellen Laird, Kathy Olson, Patricia Spencer, Lyn Spies, Alexis Stowe, Michael Williams, and especially Father Vincent Kilpatrick.

My sons, Christopher and Patrick, taught me much about literacy throughout their childhoods; their experiences in school confirmed for me how much impact teachers have on children's motivation, learning, and love for knowledge. I thank them for constantly broadening my horizons and enriching my world. Finally, I honor the memory of my parents, Marijane and James Goughary, who filled my childhood with many books and much love.

Thanks to all who saw me through.

about the author

I've received requests from some readers to provide a little information about myself. In addition, I've been asked to talk a bit about what audiences I envision for the text, and how I teach courses using my own textbook. So I'll do both things here.

I received a B.A. from Le Moyne College in Syracuse, New York; an M.S. from the State University of New York at Oswego; and a Ph.D. from Syracuse University. I taught reading in middle schools and high schools for nine years, then taught college writing courses for six. Since then, I have been in the Curriculum and Instruction Department at SUNY Oswego, where I teach Literacy in the Content Areas, as well as Adolescent English Methods and young adult literature courses.

It won't surprise you to hear that I spend a good deal of my time reading and writing for pleasure, and that I belong to both a writing group and a book discussion club. I also enjoy travel. In 2004 I went on a pilgrimage, walking a major part of the Camino de Santiago across northern Spain. In 2006 I went to West Africa, where I had the privilege of working with teachers in Benin. And in 2009 I visited schools and other educational institutions in Turkey.

Now, how do I use my book with my own classes? I use the book when I teach both undergraduates and graduates, both preservice and inservice teachers, and at both elementary and secondary levels. The book is also central to a course I've designed with a colleague, Pamela Michel, on literacy coaching. I tell my students in the courses, as well as teachers and coaches in workshops, that the book and I together will be their teachers. I also incorporate recently published books to introduce and reinforce the points made in the text. And importantly, I try to bring to class the literature cited as examples in the chapter activities, so the students have hands-on experiences that parallel what they're reading in the text.

I require students to read a minimum of four trade books over the course of our semester. During the first week, my classes read Lois Lowry's *The Giver,* as recommended in the Introduction, so they have a foundation as they begin the textbook. We have a whole-class discussion, and together go through some of the suggestions given in the Introduction. I often refer to *The Giver,* which we have as a common bond, as I explain concepts in the following several weeks. A few weeks later, around the time they're learning about using trade books and other non-textbook sources of reading, I ask students to choose a biography of someone famous in or working in the discipline they will be teaching. (You'll find suggested biographies in Figure 3.6, p. 72.) They meet in groups with classmates who share their discipline; they share responses and discuss ways they can use biographies in their future classes.

About halfway through the course, as I get ready to focus on the speaking and listening components of literacy, I facilitate literature circles, using novels that relate to the content areas they will teach. BookTalks and resource lists throughout the chapters, in the book's appendix, and on the Kane Resource Site offer fiction titles from which to choose. Finally, near the end of the semester, we have a final experience with literature circles, this time using texts and films that explore the dynamics between students and teachers. Figure 11.2 (p. 313) lists some of the books and movies that have proved helpful to my students as they reflect on the kind of relationships they want to have with their students and prepare to be teachers of literacy in their content areas.

I hope this gives you an idea of how I use this book in my courses (and you'll find many other resources in *Integrating Literature in the Content Areas* [Kane, 2008]). It probably doesn't surprise you that I use *Literacy & Learning* somewhat differently each time I teach a content area literacy course, since the composition of the class changes, and issues arise in the area schools and in our country and world that offer new opportunities for connections to and applications of the ideas in the text. That's one of the wonderful things about teaching.

The Kane Resource Site is dedicated to providing you with the tools to become confident as a teacher of literacy in the content areas. The site makes reading *Literacy & Learning in the Content Areas* a more interactive experience and provides additional information and resources beyond those in the book. The site's original URL was www.hhpcommunities.com/kane. Its new location is www.hhpcommunities.com/youngadultlit. Both addresses will access the site.

This online resource was created because we know that learning and growth do not end with the final word in a chapter or even a book. Thus, the Kane Resource Site offers opportunities to further explore content area literacy both while you are reading and when you are applying the concepts in your own classroom.

As you read *Literacy & Learning,* you will notice the following icons in the text, indicating ways to further enrich your experience with this book:

signals that a printer-friendly version is available for one of the many student handouts and assessments

indicates you can listen to a BookTalk in audio form

designates a discussion forum on a particular topic or question or indicates an opportunity to share and receive feedback for instructional materials you create

Also included on the website are step-by-step procedures for many of the books' literacy activities and strategies, literacy news, links to relevant professional and author websites, additional application activities, and new materials to use in your teaching.

We encourage you to return to the site regularly to find new book reviews and BookTalks, updated web links, updates on current news and events that impact teaching, and commentary from the author, Sharon Kane. In addition, the site's forums provide a community hub where you can connect with other readers and teachers, add your thoughts, share your work, and ask questions regarding material in the book or teaching strategies.

We hope that you find the Kane Resource Site a useful and engaging resource as you read and teach!

About the Ebook (available at www.hh-pub.com)

Interactivity is an important goal of both *Literacy & Learning* and the ideal classroom. For that reason this book is also available as an ebook to enhance your reading experience and provide seamless integration with the Kane Resource Site. Those reading the ebook will find the following interactive features:

- Linked icons that take readers to the Kane Resource Site for corresponding printable resources, podcasts, and more.
- Active web links for all URLs cited in the text.
- Instant access to cross-reference links between chapters; for example, readers can link directly to (and from) resources and booklists in the appendices as they are discussed.
- Active links to literature being discussed, allowing readers to learn more about the books, see what others have to say, and add books to their own virtual bookshelf.
- "Quick click" links that go directly to Blogger, where students can log in and instantly respond to the discussion questions throughout the textbook.
- Digital note-taking and unlimited bookmarking.

Introduction

"*I would make education a pleasant thing, both to the teacher and to the scholar. This discipline, which we allow to be the end of life, should not be one thing in the schoolroom, and another in the street. We should seek to be fellow students with the pupil, and should learn of, as well as with him [her], if we would be most helpful to him [her].*"

THOREAU, 1837

ear Readers,

Welcome to an exploration of how you can make literacy and learning come alive for the students in your content area courses. Because the teacher is the primary learner in any classroom, I hope that this book will add to your enthusiasm for reading, writing, and engaging in conversations about the topics you teach.

My voice will be present throughout the text, and I encourage you to grapple with what's here—to question, to argue, to rejoice, and to respond with exciting ideas of your own. Later, you will encourage your own students to do the same as they explore and learn.

Textbooks are philosophy-based, whether this is explicitly stated or not, and mine is no exception. The following are aspects of this text I'd like to note right away:

This text was designed as an interactive one. The book doesn't just *tell* and it doesn't just *show*; rather, it leads you to discover, construct, and reflect on knowledge. Passive reading won't work here; you are needed to make this text come alive. I've provided cues, questions, suggestions, and stimuli for experiences and activities throughout, and on the Kane Resource Site, to guide you to this more active kind of reading. Once you've become an active reader, you'll be better equipped to teach your own students, no matter what your subject, no matter what their grade level or reading ability or interests, to engage with text in a way that makes it their own. This will be exemplified by the way your instructor uses this textbook; there will probably be times when she modifies, ignores, or critiques the book's suggestions. Follow her instructions, of course, but also reflect on her rationale for making the changes; this, too, will teach you about decisions teachers make based on context, student population, instructional philosophy, and practical constraints.

You'll try things out for yourselves, get a feel for the concepts and principles, create various types of reading guides, and leave with practical examples of strategies you can use in your discipline-based classes. By the time you finish your active reading of this book, you will know *yourselves* well as readers and writers, thereby gaining confidence as you seek to understand and enhance your students' literacy. I encourage you to keep a learning log, either a notebook or computer file, where you record your responses to what you're reading, as well as the answers to the questions posed in the Activating Prior Knowledge, Action Research, and Application Activities features. You can write about ways that you can apply strategies and make connections to the content you'll be teaching.

There is much focus on listening to adolescents and preadolescents. This book calls for a student-centered philosophy, allowing young people to help us define adolescent literacy. Quotes from real middle and high school students help you understand, respect, and appreciate their perspective. I use young adult (YA) literature to help you understand teens. The voices of all kinds of readers shine through the chapters of this text.

I also quote from those who, next to the kids themselves, understand adolescents best—YA authors, researchers, and teachers. You'll encounter the real words of experts in the fields of literacy instruction and literature.

This book is literature-based throughout. We'll reconsider how textbooks are used and might be better used, and we'll explore and perhaps reprioritize the use of the wide variety of materials available. Nontextbook sources are not considered merely supplementary; rather, they are vital and integral to teaching and to students' reading. By the time you finish this book, you will likely know a lot more about primary sources and genres of literature than you did at the beginning, and this book can serve as a resource that will lead you to many others. I hope you'll look for trade books (those intended for the general public available through bookstores, online booksellers, and libraries) I refer to that might have the potential to enrich your own understanding of the subject you will teach. Now is a good time to begin a content area classroom library or at least a wish list for future reference. This text provides bibliographies and BookTalks to aid you in your quest for relevant materials for the curriculum in your discipline.

I have tried to attend to my students' wish for a reader-friendly textbook. Therefore, mixed in with the theories, strategies, and research results are anecdotes, literary tidbits, and personal musings. Each story is meant to demonstrate a point or make a connection or awaken some inquisitiveness on your part. I hope that I have created a textbook that is engaging and ultimately useful to your "composing a teaching life" (Vinz, 1996).

Many of the reading guides provided as models were constructed by preservice teachers using discipline-specific texts they selected. Thus, you will be learning from your peers; you can evaluate their examples and perhaps think of modifications and improvements, just as you may be doing with your own drafts and your classmates' work in progress. There is an emphasis on interdisciplinary guides, and readers are encouraged throughout to make connections within and among fields of study.

Throughout the book there is attention to issues relating to diversity and teaching for social justice. Literacy growth is a goal you must have for *every one* of your students, and literacy is very much connected with the goals of larger change within our society. It is our responsibility as teachers to serve as change agents; you'll be offered opportunities to ponder how you can be part of grassroots change that can improve the scholastic lives of your students and may eventually help implement systemic change in schools and society.

HANDS-ON AND MINDS-ON! AN INTRODUCTORY LITERACY EXPERIENCE BASED ON *THE GIVER*

This section affords you the opportunity to experience firsthand many of the concepts and aspects of literacy that are developed throughout this book. I created the following activities and guides for you based on Lois Lowry's novel *The Giver* (1993). Your instructor may substitute comparable activities relating to a different text, but the principles are the same. Even if you don't read *The Giver* right now as part of a course, the activities below will serve as examples to help you see how teacher-constructed guiding activities help readers as they comprehend texts and think about content and ideas. But I encourage you to read this popular, thought-provoking masterpiece for your own enjoyment and knowledge.

Pre-Reading and Reading Activities

Teachers can help students get ready, both cognitively and emotionally, to read a text by providing an *anticipation guide* constructed to activate their thinking on the topics that are dealt with in that text. Please complete the anticipation guide on page 3, created to be used in conjunction with Lois Lowry's young adult novel, *The Giver* (1993).

When you've finished filling in the anticipation guide, if you're in class, select a partner or join a small group of your peers and compare answers. Add others' examples of utopian literature to your own. I'll help out, too. My students provided *Utopia* (More,

FOR

The Giver

This guide will stimulate you to think about some topics in a way that will prepare you for reading *The Giver* by Lois Lowry.

1. Brainstorm to come up with words, phrases, people, and concepts you associate with the word UTOPIA.

UTOPIA

2. List any works of utopian literature, movies, or songs you have read, seen, or heard of:

3. Respond YES or NO to the following statements and think of a specific situation that exemplifies your position:

_____ Rules are made to be broken.   SHARE ONLINE

_____ Money is the root of all evil.

_____ In the interest of fairness, everyone should be treated equally.

_____ It would be a good thing to be able to totally forget bad memories.

_____ If I could eliminate pain from my life and the lives of those I love, I would.

_____ A government should have the right to enforce laws that will make society safer.

_____ A person has the right to choose to die if life has become painful or unproductive or just too long.

Now that you've answered these questions, you're ready to experience the world in which Jonas, the main character of *The Giver*, lives. So, open the book and enter!

1965), *Anthem* (Rand, 1995), *The Handmaid's Tale* (Atwood, 1986), *1984* (Orwell, 1949), *Animal Farm* (Orwell, 1954), *Watership Down* (Adams, 1974), *Lord of the Flies* (Golding, 1955), *Brave New World* (Huxley, 1932), *A Clockwork Orange* (Burgess, 1986), *Fahrenheit 451* (Bradbury, 1953), *Walden* (Thoreau, 1854), *The Hunger Games* (Collins, 2008), *Among the Hidden* (Haddix, 2000), as well as the movie *The Matrix* (Warner Home Video, 1999) and the songs "Imagine" (Lennon, 1971), "Somewhere" (Sondheim & Bernstein, 1957), "The Impossible Dream" (Darion & Leigh, 1966), and "If We Only Have Love" (Brel, 1968). Inevitably, whenever I use this guide in a class, a discussion ensues about the fact that most of the works mentioned are really about societies that *fail* or turn out to be horrible places rather than the ideal places represented by the words and phrases that the students supplied in Question 1. This is a perfect time for me to introduce the term *dystopia*, for some a new word to add to their vocabulary. I also show my students the resource *Encyclopedia of Utopian Literature* (Snodgrass, 1995), which gives many more examples, as well as a wealth of information about utopian authors, concepts, and historical background.

If you're reading this chapter outside class, please try to find another person with whom to discuss your responses to the exercise's statements, or share your answers online with the community on the Kane Resource Site. It's likely that you won't find total agreement, and discussion about the differences will be productive.

The next thing a teacher might do is to give a *booktalk*, a brief introduction that aims to entice the reader. BookTalk I.1 is my introduction.

Now read *The Giver*. Keep the anticipation guide you completed handy to see whether any of your answers change as a result of reading the book. Also, respond in a journal or learning log. Jot down things you think of as you read, then your reaction at the end of the story. What questions do you have for others? For the author? For your teacher? Read as actively as you can; instead of just absorbing information and plot, talk back, interact with this novel. Even talk to the characters if you wish.

Post-Reading Activities

The best way to start discussing a book is *freely*. Get in a large circle, or several smaller ones, with others who have read the novel. Use your journal responses to initiate the discussion and keep it going. Make sure everyone has the chance to talk; no one person (this includes the teacher) should dominate. This type of group is known as a *literature circle* or *literature group* (Johnson & Freedman, 2005; Short, Harste, & Burke, 1996), discussed further in Chapter 2.

BookTalk Online   I.1

"Memories
may be beautiful, and yet,
what's too painful to remember,
we simply choose to forget."
The Way We Were by Bergman & Hamlisch, 1973. Used with permission.

The anticipation guide you just completed caused you to think about whether you would erase painful memories if you could. You're about to read about a society that figured out a way to do just that. Its citizens also made other changes to eliminate many of the problems we experience today. Imagine a world where you'd never have to worry about losing a lover, deciding on risky career changes, being involved in a car accident, or going home to parents who fight. Welcome to Jonas's world. Welcome to Lois Lowry's *The Giver*.

On your own, please complete the worksheet on page 5. Once you have completed the worksheet, it's time to debrief. Did answering the questions on the worksheet add to your knowledge or insight? Did they guide your thinking? Did you have to look up any of the vocabulary words? I'm assuming your answers may reflect a rather negative reaction to this worksheet. Now, how would you like to be told you'll be answering similar questions for the next 22 chapters of *The Giver*? You may have read the book in one sitting, and you almost certainly would have resented the interruptions. My students and I generally agree to write "AVOID!" at the top of this worksheet, reminding us there *must* be a better way to help students comprehend a novel. Then, we set out to think of those possible ways.

ACTIVATING PRIOR KNOWLEDGE   I.1

Read the Literature Circle Guide for *The Giver* on page 6. Notice that it might lead to some redundancy if you discussed *all* of the questions in the order presented. Talk with your partner or group members again, concentrating on the topics your group didn't already address.

Some of you might remember that the worksheet approach was the way literature was dealt with when you were a middle school or high school student. Assigning comprehension questions might assure a teacher that a student read and comprehended the text, though you may have memories of

FOR

Chapter 1 of The Giver

VOCABULARY: Look up the following words in the dictionary (if necessary) and write their definitions.

distraught: _____

apprehensive: _____

release: _____

ritual: _____

transgression: _____

COMPREHENSION: Write your answers to the following questions in complete sentences:

1. During what month are jobs assigned in this community?

_____

2. What is the primary mode of transportation?

_____

3. Are certain genders preferred for certain roles in this community? Explain your answer by citing examples from the text.

_____

_____

_____

4. Define *released* as used in Chapter 1.

_____

_____

5. How did you feel about the telling of feelings at the dinner table?

_____

_____

6. Describe the setting of this story.

_____

_____

_____

FOR

The Giver

DIRECTIONS: In your circles, use your journal responses to help you discuss the book. The following questions may help you think about your reading experience. Use as many as you wish; you do not have to go in order.

1. At what point did you realize what *released* meant in this community? How did you figure it out?

2. At what point did you conclude that Jonas would defect?

3. What symbols can you find in this book? Do you think they're effective? In what ways might the characters' names be symbolic?

4. How do you think Lois Lowry feels about euthanasia? Assisted suicide? Would she say they are morally acceptable practices? Would she say they are good for individuals or for society?

5. The society in *The Giver* is very safe, but that comes about at the cost of freedom. There is always a tension between safety and freedom. Think of ways this plays out in our government and society today. What individual liberties have people given up in return for protection and security? What issues are currently being debated in this area?

6. Did any of you write any favorite sentences down or mark any passages you found significant? If so, which ones? What struck you about them?

7. Discuss Lois Lowry's crafting of this book, or her writing style.

8. The Newbery Medal is an annual award given by the American Library Association for the most distinguished contribution to children's literature published in the United States. Do you think this book deserved the 1994 Newbery Medal? Why, or why not?

9. What do you think of the cover art?

10. What would you say to or ask Lois Lowry if she visited your classroom?

11. How might this novel be used effectively in a social studies class? In a science class?

friends who were able to get by somehow without actually reading the book. They represent different levels of questioning, which we'll talk about in a later chapter. Teacher questioning is valuable and crucial to learning, but you will probably agree that completing this kind of worksheet is not a worthwhile use of your time. Such worksheets can reduce the enjoyment a novel can provide. Certainly Lois Lowry did not write this book for the purpose of having students write the answers to hundreds of questions in complete sentences! When I visit classrooms where literature is used this way, I look around at the struggling, bored faces of the students who will have the power of the novel diminished by the very fact that the book is being "taught" like this. I reluctantly conclude that what I see is, like the world of Jonas, a form of *dystopia*.

Are there alternatives to using these traditional worksheets? Many. In Chapter 2, you will read about the reading and writing workshops that are a part of many classrooms. For now, think about the literature circle you participated in on *The Giver*. Did others bring up ideas or pick up on details you hadn't thought of? Were there different interpretations of and reactions to the ambiguous ending of the story? Did the talk extend your thinking about the issues inherent in the novel? Once students get used to being allowed to talk about a text based on *their* responses, there may not be a need for *any* teacher-initiated questions at all. But a teacher *can* provide optional guide questions for the response groups, leading them to areas that might not otherwise get explored.

Throughout this book you'll be shown how to create *reading guides* that serve to aid the comprehension of and thinking about the texts you ask your students to read. That is a very different task from making up worksheets to assess your students' understanding of articles or textbook selections or novels. All of your guides should aim to bring your readers to the construction of thoughtful responses; your goal is to help them acquire knowledge and understand their own positions better.

ACTION RESEARCH   I.A

Now, find an article that explains how practicing teachers have used *The Giver* for instructional purposes or how a writer has analyzed the novel, and react to it. Do you like what the teacher and students have done? What educational benefits or curricular connections do you see at work? Do you see any drawbacks to the methods or activities described? Figure I.1 lists some of the many articles relating to *The Giver*.

FIGURE   I.1

Resources showing how teachers can use Lois Lowry's *The Giver*.

See more suggested titles in Appendix Figure I.1.

Albert, L. R. (2008). *Lois Lowry, the Giver of Stories and Memories*. Berkeley Heights, NJ: Enslow.

Gaines, L. (2005). Memories Matter: *The Giver* and Descriptive Writing Memoirs. www.readwritethink.org.

Johnson, A. B., Kleismit, J. W., & Williams, A. J. (2002). Grief, Thought, & Appreciation: Re-examining Our Values Amid Terrorism Through *The Giver*. *The ALAN Review, 29*(3), 15–19.

Mahar, D. (2001). Social Justice and the Class Community: Opening the Door to Possibilities. *English Journal, 90*(5), 107–115.

Whitelaw, J., & Wolf, S. A. (2001). Learning to "See Beyond": Sixth-Grade Students' Artistic Perceptions of *The Giver*. *The New Advocate, 16*(1), 57–67.

ACTION RESEARCH   I.B

Interview people of various ages about their reactions to and interpretations of *The Giver*. You will be amazed at the variety and the intensity of responses and even arguments. One of my students told her son that she thought Jonas and Gabe found a new community by sledding down the hill to where they saw lights on Christmas trees. He confidently retorted, "If you read it carefully, Mom, you can tell they *do* die. They were almost unconscious and were delusional. Jonas thought the moon and stars were colored lights." He tried to convince her further, "Well, Mom, think of this . . . Jonas and Gabe *really* saw heaven with all of the family memories they never had and the music, too. They died when they got on the sled. The sled trip was the trip to heaven. That's what *really* happened" (Margaret Carey, used with permission). His mother then showed him Lois Lowry's Newbery Medal acceptance speech to point out that the author herself says there is no *true* ending or *right* interpretation; rather, "There's a right one for each of us, and it depends on our own beliefs, our own hopes" (Lowry, 1994, p. 420). Lowry includes a few excerpts from readers who wrote to her. A sixth grader saw Jonas and Gabe traveling in a circle: Elsewhere was their old community, except now the people had come to accept memories and feelings. Another compared Jonas to Jesus, taking on the pain for everyone in the community so they wouldn't have to

(continued)

suffer; not surprisingly, he interpreted the Elsewhere at the end to be Heaven.

I've found, and I believe you will find as you talk with people, that some readers actually changed their thinking and their values as a result of being affected by what for them was a powerful book. Figure I.2 contains an example from a book called *Dear Author: Students Write About the Books That Changed Their Lives (READ Magazine,* Weekly Reader, 1995).

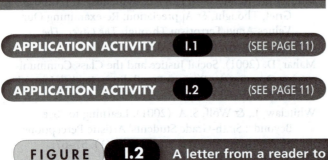

APPLICATION ACTIVITY   I.1   (SEE PAGE 11)

APPLICATION ACTIVITY   I.2   (SEE PAGE 11)

ACTIVATING PRIOR KNOWLEDGE   I.2

I invite you now to connect the idea of utopia to schools. First, take a few minutes to work alone or with a partner on the following: List the characteristics of "the perfect school." One way to do this is to think about the schools you went to, then highlight the good points and change or get rid of the bad. Imagine such power!

Activating Prior Knowledge I.2 is not merely a fantasy exercise that could never be realized. When a new school is opened, or when a new administrator arrives, or when restructuring within a district occurs, people think about *ideal* learning environments and teaching practices. For teachers or preservice teachers, each new school year brings with it great hopes

---

FIGURE   I.2   A letter from a reader to an author about a life-changing book.

Dear Ms. Lois Lowry,

Your book *The Giver* was very thought-provoking. It made me kind of sad and confused. Usually, I read a book two or three times, but I was so upset by *The Giver* that I returned it to the library the very next day.

I've given it a lot of thought, and I see now that *The Giver* made me really angry. I couldn't understand the hero's reluctance to intervene when he saw and understood all the injustices being done in the community. It was horrible.

The truth is, the giver in the story and I have a lot in common. I hold some strong views that I really believe in, but I rarely stand up for them. I'm just too scared to stick out or to expose my ideas to criticism. I can't be angry at the giver in the story for something that I myself do.

I live in a small town in Oregon, where I see bigotry, prejudice, and discrimination every day. We also have strong [proposed anti-gay legislation] here, something I'm firmly against. Still, I'm reluctant to voice my arguments, because some adults and friends of mine have different views.

I understand now that anything I can do is better than doing nothing. My voice is only one, but one voice can sometimes be just enough. As long as I am true to myself, I have nothing to be embarrassed or ashamed about.

From now on, I'm going to take sides on things I feel strongly about and won't let others intimidate me. I've learned, like the giver, that no thing or cause is hopeless, as long as people believe in it and stand up for their beliefs.

Ginger Bandeen, 16
Warrenton High School, Warrenton, OR
Teacher: Kay Rannow

and possibilities. But too often, we hear students referring to school as a jail, or worse. Much of the literature on schools, such as Jonathan Kozol's *Savage Inequalities* (1991) and *The Shame of the Nation: The Restoration of Apartheid Schooling in America* (2005), reports on atrocities within our educational system. Have some of our schools turned into dystopias?

On the other hand, some books aim for certain philosophical and educational ideals. B. F. Skinner's title *Walden Two* (1948) recognizes this utopian theme. Neil Postman's prophetic-sounding *The End of Education* (1995) has as its subtitle *Redefining the Value of Schools*. E. D. Hirsch, Jr. has convinced many policy makers and educators that what he proposes in *The Schools We Need and Why We Don't Have Them* (1996), *The Knowledge Deficit: Closing the Shocking Education Gap for American Children* (2006), and *The Making of Americans: Democracy and Our Schools* (2009) can turn around what has become a dismal situation. Mahiri's *What They Don't Learn in School: Literacy in the Lives of Urban Youth* (2004) is an edited collection of studies showing that many "perspectives and technologies are being appropriated by youth themselves to circumvent limits on learning that often seem imposed by schools" (p. 14). Mahiri poses the question, "Can societal structures and school curricula accommodate and incorporate youth desires for knowledge and the new kinds of knowledge they need for negotiating the literacy demands and possibilities of a new century?" (p. 15).

BookTalk **I.2**

When my students express disbelief about a society getting to the point of the one in *The Giver,* having given up so much freedom and choice and not realizing what is missing, or when they wonder how the Nazi regime was able to come into power, I read them the novella *The Children's Story: But Not Just for Children* by James Clavell (1989). It's an allegory that describes a morning when the new leaders of a conquered country replace the teachers in a school, and in under a half hour they are able to convince the children that the beliefs and values they've been taught by their parents are wrong. It's a simply told, chilling depiction of brainwashing. Clavell adds a note at the end telling about the day his daughter came home from school having been taught the Pledge of Allegiance but not its meaning, instigating his reflection and writing. I urge you to read this story to ponder the potential influence you'll have as a teacher, and the awesome responsibility that entails.

You can explore books and articles as you reflect on your ideal school, your educational utopia, and then use the information as you visit schools and classrooms, as you talk with teachers and administrators and students, and as you take other education courses. Aim for connections at all levels. This helps you develop a strong personal philosophy of education and grounds you as you explore what it means to teach literacy in your content area.

Throughout this book, you meet content area teachers who are striving for an ideal classroom that meets their students' needs in terms of both curriculum and literacy; you are introduced to some of the best practices of content area teachers. In the final chapter, we return to the concept of visionary schooling; for now, Allington's (2001) vision might help you as you begin your teaching career:

> In an ideal world every teacher would be a teacher of reading. Every history teacher would work to help students understand the typical structure of discourse in historical texts. They would model and demonstrate how historians think as they read and write texts. They would offer powerful instruction that fostered the development of historical vocabulary. And biology teachers would do the same sorts of things with the reading and writing expected in biology. They would help students learn to read, write, and think like biologists. In all cases content teachers would select texts for students that were well written and of appropriate levels of complexity given the students' prior knowledge as well as their levels of literacy development. If this were to happen we would experience a "win-win" outcome—students would develop not just better reading and writing skills but they would also learn more history and biology. (p. 143)

ACTIVITIES FOR YOUR STUDENTS

You could modify most of the earlier exercises to use with your students in middle and secondary grades, and you can adapt them to use with other texts relevant to the curriculum you'll be responsible for teaching. Throughout this book, you are introduced to trade books and other resources that you can use to teach the content of your discipline at the same time you enhance your students' literacy development. I am using *The Giver* as a model; you can apply the strategies to readings that work well for your classes.

The Giver can be used in an unlimited number of ways to initiate post-reading projects that lead to more learning, as well as enjoyment. Students who are dissatisfied with the ending might write a final chapter that they feel brings more closure to the story. Some can write poems or songs, or create dioramas, collages, or graphic organizers (diagrams illustrating relations among ideas). One of my students made a poster with the final scene, surrounded by actual blinking Christmas tree lights. Another came in with a list of meanings for all of the characters' names in the story.

Following are some examples of choices you could offer students as ways to further explore the issues raised in the book or their responses to the text. I encourage you to try out one or more yourself as a way of actively engaging with the pedagogical information in this textbook.

Teaching Suggestion 1. Ask your students to write a journal entry imagining how Lois Lowry might have come up with the ideas that came together for the creation of her utopian novel. Then read aloud and have the students respond to Lois Lowry's Newbery acceptance speech for *The Giver.* (It can be found in *The Horn Book Magazine,* July/August 1994.) She crafts her speech using, not surprisingly, *memories* that led to the writing of the book. They include family relationships, learning from special mentors, mistakes she made growing up, and personal reactions to problems within our society. She also acknowledges the ambiguity of the ending of *The Giver,* and shares some responses she received from her readers. Readers can see that they are part of a community of literary people who are all in this together. Perhaps some students will want to write to Lowry using her website, www.loislowry.com.

Teaching Suggestion 2. There are several readily available published reviews and critical interpretations of *The Giver.* For example, in her article "In the Belly of the Whale," Patricia Lee Gauch (1997) discusses the novel along with others in relation to the well-known archetype of the hero's journey. In contrast, John Noell Moore (1997) applies a type of literary criticism known as *deconstruction* to the book. Have students read one or more examples of this type of commentary and respond by connecting the information with their previous personal response to the book. Do these supplemental materials add to their insight and deepen their knowledge? What would they say in response to these writers and critics?

Teaching Suggestion 3. *The Giver* deals with topics related to science, government, English, and ethics; it is, therefore, ideal for interdisciplinary study or for exploration in a number of content areas. Encourage students to read further about a theme or topic dealt with in the novel and synthesize their new knowledge with that gained from the original source. Suggestions for exploration include memory, utopia, government control versus individual rights and freedoms, genetic engineering, capital punishment, infanticide, medical ethics, and surrogate motherhood. Figure I.3 contains sample bibliographies for the topics of memory and utopia. All of the suggested topics can be researched on the Internet.

FIGURE I.3 Sample bibliographies for exploring topics related to *The Giver.*

UTOPIA

Adlington, L. J. (2008). *Cherry Heaven.* New York: Greenwillow Books.

Block, F. L. (2004). *Ecstasia.* New York: Firebird/Penguin.

Bondoux, A. (2005). *The Destiny of Linus Hoppe.* New York: Delacorte Press.

Booraem, E. (2008). *The Unnameables.* Orlando, FL: Harcourt.

Child, L. (2002). *Utopia: A Novel.* New York: Doubleday.

Collins, S. (2008). *The Hunger Games.* New York: Scholastic.

Gonzalez, J. (2005). *Wings.* New York: Delacorte Press.

Levithan, D. (2003). *Boy Meets Boy.* New York: Knopf.

Lynch, C. (2008). *Cyberia.* New York: Scholastic.

More, T. (1965). *Utopia.* New York: Simon & Schuster.

Murphy, J. (1998). *West to a Land of Plenty: The Diary of Teresa Angelino Viscardi: New York to Idaho Territory, 1883.* New York: Scholastic.

Streissguth, T. (1999). *Utopian Visionaries.* Minneapolis, MN: Oliver Press.

Westerfield, S. (2005). *Uglies.* New York: Simon Pulse.

Whelan, G. (2002). *Fruitlands: Louisa May Alcott Made Perfect.* New York: HarperCollins.

MEMORY

Crew, G. (2004). *Memorial.* (S. Tan, Illus.). Verona, NJ: Simply Read Books.

di Pasquale, E. (2003). *Cartwheel to the Moon: My Sicilian Childhood.* Peterborough, NH: Cobblestone & Cricket.

Greenberg, J. (2003). *Romare Bearden: Collage of Memories.* New York: Harry N. Abrams.

Haddix, M. P. (2003). *Escape from Memory.* New York: Simon & Schuster.

Kurtz, J. (Ed.). (2004). *Memories of Sun: Stories of Africa and America.* New York: Greenwillow Books.

Rosen, M. (2005). *Michael Rosen's Sad Book.* (Q. Blake, Illus.). Cambridge, MA: Candlewick Press.

Rubin, S. G. (2010). *The Anne Frank Case: Simon Wiesenthal's Search for the Truth.* (B. Farnsworth, Illus.). New York: Holiday House.

Rupp, R. (1998). *Committed to Memory: How We Remember and Why We Forget.* New York: Crown.

Sacks, O. (1995). The Last Hippie. In *An Anthropologist on Mars: Seven Paradoxical Tales.* New York: Knopf.

Stevens, C. (2008). *Thirty Days Has September: Cool Ways to Remember Stuff.* (S. Horne, Illus.). New York: Scholastic.

BookTalk   I.3

Has *The Giver* piqued your interest in Lois Lowry's body of works or in utopian/dystopian literature? If so, consider exploring another futuristic society she created in *Gathering Blue* (2000). As in Jonas's society, people with differences and defects are not appreciated; they are eliminated. Kira has a twisted leg, so must fear for her life. Even as her gift for weaving is put to use by the Guardians controlling her fate, there are dark forces at work. As you read this book, note the recurring theme of the importance of memory. When you've finished, head for the concluding book of the trilogy, *Messenger* (2004), where the main characters from all three books join together to battle encroaching evil. Lowry's fantasy book *Gossamer* (2006) contains themes similar to those in the trilogy, including dreams, memory, and the healing power of love.

Teaching Suggestion 4. Check the Internet for websites containing information about Lois Lowry. Suggest that students join a chat room to discuss their reading of *The Giver* with readers from other places. It might be especially interesting to listen to readers from those countries with different types of governments and societal rules.

I hope that the variety of activities helped you realize the many ways a rich core text can be used in the classroom. You've expanded your background knowledge and constructed a base that will serve you well as you connect ideas from the following chapters to your personal experiences. That's why I wanted you to read a young adult book and try some of the suggestions before we got into the actual theories related to literacy. Now, it's time to do just that.

WEBSITES   INTRODUCTION   Access these links using the Kane Resource Site.

Lois Lowry
www.loislowry.com

Memories Matter: *The Giver* **and Descriptive Writing Memoirs**
www.readwritethink.org/lessons/lesson_view.asp?id=13

The Giver **as a Bridge to** *Animal Farm:* **Controlling Societies**
www.eric.ed.gov, http://www.eric.ed.gov/ERICDocs/data/ericdocs2sql/content_storage_01/0000019b/80/1a/3a/9a.pdf

APPLICATION ACTIVITIES

I.1 Did you come across any passages in *The Giver* that struck you as particularly effective or that evoked a strong emotional or intellectual response? Did you find yourself paying attention to the language itself at some points? Did any of your classmates underline a key sentence or copy a quote from the book to their journals? Many readers find a way to organize, record, and track text they find meaningful and memorable. I keep a folder that I call my "Favorite Sentence File." You can start one too or keep them in an electronic file; start gathering sentences from your personal reading for your unique collection. You may share some entries with others and compare what works for you with what others choose.

I.2 I also keep folders labeled with the titles of the books I use in my classes, as well as the topics within my curriculum. In them I collect articles that connect current events with issues inherent in the literature and in my lessons. For example, in my folder for *The Giver*, I have a newspaper article describing how Sweden sterilized a huge number of people—those considered undesirables—without their knowledge or consent, up until 1976. I also have an article about the Oneida Community that existed in Central New York in the late 1800s as a real utopian experiment. I have a review of the children's autobiography *Red Scarf Girl: A Memoir of the Cultural Revolution* (Jiang, 1997); it contains striking parallels with the society represented in *The Giver*. I have magazine articles on plans for new or renewed schools in New Orleans to replace those destroyed by Hurricane Katrina; these plans often represent ideal learning communities as envisioned by a wide variety of people working collaboratively. I also keep lists of relevant websites. Of course, these materials can be electronic and articles scanned and placed in the folder. I invite you to start your own folder system so that you will have interesting and relevant applications as you teach various topics. Read newspapers and magazines with a copier or scanner available; you'll be amazed at the connections you make once you start reading as a teacher on the hunt for knowledge to enhance your students' learning. Encourage your students to bring in news items and stories they find that connect to curricular topics.

chapter 1

Reading, Literacy, and Teaching in the Content Areas

This chapter helps you to think about and understand the term *reading,* then to consider the ever-broadening concept of *literacy.* You are asked to consider what it means for you to be a *teacher of literacy* in your chosen content area and are introduced to the concept of learning standards.

READING

Perhaps this is the first literacy education course you have taken, or perhaps when you were in earlier education courses, they focused on methods for teaching disciplinary concepts, procedures, and skills but excluded attention to literacy. Schoenbach, Braunger, Greenleaf, et al. (2003) note that

> few middle and high school teachers see their own abilities to read subject-area texts as a powerful resource for helping students approach these texts independently, confidently, and successfully. Because most secondary content teachers have not spent much time thinking about the mental processes by which they make sense of texts in their fields, this knowledge is invisible and therefore unavailable to most of them. (p. 134)

Entire books can be, and are, devoted to the subject of the process of reading. Researchers and theorists have made great progress defining the act called *reading* and explaining how it works. Smith (1985) writes: "Researchers are discovering that in order to understand reading they must consider not just the eyes but also the mechanisms of memory and attention, anxiety, risk taking, the nature and uses of language, the comprehension of speech, interpersonal relationships, sociocultural differences, learning in general, and the learning of young children in particular" (p. 3). There is not, however, universal agreement among experts as to how reading happens, how it is first learned, or the best way to teach it, as Smith's later works, including *Unspeakable Acts, Unnatural Practices: Flaws and Fallacies in "Scientific" Reading Instruction* (2003), demonstrate. We begin by exploring approaches to reading.

"Literature is my utopia. Here I am not disenfranchised. No barrier of the senses shuts me out from the sweet, gracious discourses of my book friends."

HELEN KELLER

Approaches to Reading

For many decades, scholars have presented various approaches to viewing reading and at times have fought so vigorously about the right way to teach reading that the field is full of talk about "reading wars" (e.g., Kim, 2008; Pearson, 2004). In the last couple of decades of the twentieth century, popular categories of reading approaches consisted of bottom-up, top-down, and interactive. Adherents of the *bottom-up* approach believed that readers first decode symbols and letters, then attend to words, phrases, sentences, and larger chunks of text.

The *top-down* approach to explaining literacy reverses this order. Readers go from the global to the specific, bringing their background knowledge and expectations to a text and applying strategies to *bring meaning to* the text, largely through prediction and confirmation. They still require vocabulary knowledge, of course, and they use phonics and a knowledge of word structure to decode as needed (especially when the text contains unfamiliar terms), but this isn't the starting place, or the most important part of comprehension (Goodman, 1967; Smith, 1985).

The *interactive view* purports that reading is neither strictly top-down nor bottom-up; rather, it is *interactive* (Adams, 1990; Anderson, Hiebert, Scott, et al., 1985; Rumelhart, 1976; Stanovitch, 1980). A sociocultural, transactional model of reading, it involves parts of both the bottom-up and top-down approaches, with part-to-whole and whole-to-part occurring as reading proceeds. Not all readers approach text or reach comprehension the same way, and an individual might stress the different components mentioned at different times, depending on the text type and the reading purpose. Some readers are very aware of the comprehension strategies they use as they construct meaning, while others may be very efficient readers but haven't analyzed what for them seems like a natural process.

Gee (2000) shows through an analysis of discourse and sociocultural studies that the long-standing dichotomies in reading theories and research no longer make sense. Reading is complex, and comprehension and response are based on the combination of many factors. Gee explains the reading process not as one thing but many, always situated in contexts and cultural communities; ultimately, "There is no 'reading in general,' at least none that leads to thought and action in the world" (p. 204).

Frank Smith and Kenneth Goodman, who have been very active in the scholarly, practical, and political aspects of the debates about reading for over 40 years, co-authored an article (2008) revisiting their early partnership and the history of the field. They have never wavered from their initial agreement with each other that "the key factors in learning lay with the child and the child's interaction with an informed and informative adult rather than in the particular materials used" (p. 62). And they presently argue "that the best instructional materials are the real-world ones: real children's literature, real print in the natural environment, and real nonfiction that provides the information for science and the social studies" (p. 64). Smith and Goodman have always promoted *authentic learning,* which will be a recurring theme throughout this book.

If there is no reading in general, let's turn to some particular cases. As you think more about how you read and as you observe and talk with your students, you will discover that there are numerous ways that individual readers process print and construct meaning from text. Varied examples of how people describe their reading processes are presented in Figure 1.1.

You can see that the way reading is thought of and talked about is dynamic. The field is always developing, and there are a number of ongoing philosophical and political debates. Throughout this book, various aspects of reading are explained and explored and teaching suggestions are provided. Skills and strategies are always presented in authentic contexts. For now, remember that reading is a meaning-driven process—readers must actively construct meaning and work toward fitting new information into the knowledge they already possess.

Although debates about how best to teach literacy continue, at present there is general agreement that certain components are absolutely necessary for a person to be successful at reading. Good readers must be competent at phonological processing, word decoding, and structural analysis. They are able to read texts fluently. They understand the meanings of words they encounter in texts and can comprehend fictional and expository texts; they use the information gained from the print and construct meaning as they apply the background knowledge they bring to the text. Of course, in order to accomplish all the tasks required while reading, they need to be motivated. Most of these concepts will be further developed throughout the chapters of this book. But because decoding and fluency have for some time been dealt with at the early literacy levels, and have recently become much more prominent in the literature on adolescent and content area literacy, the next section will introduce you to these crucial aspects of reading.

Decoding

In order to identify words in text, readers must have phonemic awareness, or the ability to understand that spoken words are composed of individual units of sound; they must be able to manipulate these units.

FIGURE **1.1** **Readers talk about their reading processes.**

After reading these examples, share a description of your own reading processes with the Kane Resource Site community.

"I'll read about a hundred pages of a book to get the big picture, then go back and read it a second time, for details."

—*Gerald Eisman in Rosenthal, 1995, p. 163*

"Right away, literally the second I start reading the first line, I begin formulating the 'movie' of the book. With girl characters, I am watching the 'movie,' but with boy characters, I am the star."

—*Forrest, a middle school student, in Atwell, 2007, p. 22*

"As an autistic, I think totally visually . . . I could have never memorized a whole bunch of words. Instead, I memorized the fifty phonetic sounds. . . . I assign a visual picture to each sound . . ."

—*Temple Grandin in Rosenthal, 1995, p. 187*

"I can't stand description since I don't visualize, but I absolutely love the dialogue. . . . I skip all the description. But when I get to the dialogue, I slow down and read at a luxurious pace, savoring every sentence. . . . I glance at everything and pick up two or three key words on a page in the boring parts . . . if I get lost, I do not go back."

—*Martha Lane in Rosenthal, 1995, p. 190*

"I stumble over every word with more than three letters and cannot answer the questions that she poses about the story. This encounter, in which the novice teacher who cannot control the class meets the reluctant reader unable to decipher the words on the page, is indelibly etched in my mind."

—*Jonathan G. Silin, now a professor, recalling being forced to read aloud in Silin, 2003, p. 261*

"When I'm in my reading zone, I feel like I'm a character in the book I'm reading . . . it's almost like a TV show or a movie. I can see it really well. I can feel, taste, see, smell when I'm in my reading zone. Everything around you disappears and all you care about are the characters."

—*Michael, a struggling middle school reader, in Atwell 2007, p. 21*

"I find reading a challenge. I need to read things twice, maybe three times, before I actually comprehend it. So it takes me a long time. I feel as if reading is a job, not a relaxing thing to do."

—*anonymous college student*

"I was so deeply inside the book that I could have been at the bottom of the sea. There was no way to quickly resurface without getting the bends."

—*Wilhelm, 1997, p. 4*

"What can you do? If you get confused, I guess you wait for the teacher. . . . I don't try real hard with it because sometimes I just don't get it and sometimes, it's like, what's the point? Most of it just seems boring and then some of it, sometimes it's just too hard."

—*Amy, grade 8, in Beers, 2003, p. 33*

"I was a very, very slow reader and couldn't read out loud or silently. . . . When I was a freshman in high school, . . . I became fascinated with nitrogen chemistry, so I got organic chemistry textbooks. And I read all the journals, various aeronautic journals. . . . [In history class] I'd actually stop and sit back and look away from the print. I'd imagine a sign with the date on it in front of me, and I'd see battles as they physically happened."

—*Daniel, in Fink, 2006, pp. 70–75*

Readers use phonics or the association between letters in written words and the sounds they make in speech. When students struggle with phonics, it's hard for them to decode (decipher the print and turn it into language sounds) multisyllabic words, and it affects vocabulary development, comprehension, and fluency. If you have students who are extremely weak in decoding skills, you'll need to recruit the help of a literacy coach or reading specialist; as a content area teacher, you probably don't have the expertise needed to best help these students develop skills in this area, while a literacy specialist has been trained to assess and apply intervention strategies. This is not to say that there is nothing you can do within the context of your subject area to help in word identification. You can look over course materials to identify words you think students might struggle with, and teach these words directly, modeling how you recognize patterns, notice prefixes or suffixes, pointing out syllables. More will be explained about structural analysis, or morphology, in Chapter 6.

O'Shea, Katsafanas, and Lake (2009) point out that secondary school students who struggle with the skills usually associated with beginning reading are often from families of poverty and from diverse cultural and linguistic backgrounds. The gap will widen between them and their peers if teachers don't intervene. The authors suggest explicit instruction using culturally specific materials, demonstrating for students how to sound out words; using materials and games that reinforce phonemic awareness and phonological processing; using choral reading; using connected, decodable text for readers to practice sound–spelling relationships; and using music, art, and movement to segment phonemes through a multisensory approach.

O'Shea, Katsafanas, and Lake (2009) offer instructional strategies for middle and high school teachers that will improve decoding and structural analysis skills. As a teacher, you can model ways to use phonics to sound out unfamiliar words. You can employ think-alouds to show how to break apart long words into meaningful chunks. (You'll learn more about think-alouds in future chapters.) You can supply dictionaries and help readers to look up culturally relevant, meaningful, interesting words, in both English and students' native languages. You can encourage student interest in word play and word investigation.

Fluency

Another crucial aspect of reading is fluency. You probably can recall a time when you listened to someone read and recognized that it was not smooth, but rather choppy and uneven. Perhaps you are not happy with your own ability to read with expression and a sense of rhythm or flow. These are examples of lack of fluency. In the following paragraphs, I've gathered what some experts have to say about the importance of fluency, especially with regard to those who are no longer considered beginning readers.

Rasinski (2008) explains, "Reading fluency is defined in two components—the ability to read words in print automatically, and the ability to read text with appropriate and meaningful expression (prosody). . . . Expressive or prosodic reading takes fluency to the next level in which a reader embeds prosodic features, such as pitch, volume, emphasis, and phrasing that make the reading sound like authentic oral language . . ." (p. 119).

Rasinski suggests an artful approach to teaching fluency, involving readers theatre, poetry, songs, and speeches, since "Fluency is best developed through assisted and repeated readings of texts. Repeated and assisted reading is best and most legitimately employed when readers intend to perform for an audience" (p. 137). His research found multiple benefits of using these texts, which

not only developed reading fluency, an area that has become a focal point for high-stakes testing of students . . . [but also] an appreciation of language . . ., deeper and more heartfelt or aesthetic understandings of the meanings authors intend to create through such texts, more varied responses to those texts, opportunities to write in various forms, opportunities to create a sense of unity among classmates, an appreciation of the differences that classmates bring to school, and, of course, greater opportunities to develop that internal confidence in one's own abilities that is essential to future growth. (p. 137)

Fink (2008) notes that her research "suggests that the more a student reads in one content area (such as science), the richer or better at reading the student becomes in that domain" (p. 36). This raises an intriguing question in her mind:

Should the concept of fluency be expanded to embrace a more flexible concept similar to the way Gardner (1983) expanded the notion of intelligence to a more dynamic theory that included multiple intelligences? Perhaps there are multiple fluencies. A more flexible, intraindividual concept of fluency could help teachers understand how children . . . read personally appealing texts at high readability levels with more ease and skill than they read other texts. (pp. 36–37)

McCollin and O'Shea (2009) address the challenge of addressing fluency with readers representing diverse heritages. They recommend using folktales and poetry, as well as websites devoted to cultural themes, that relate to students' particular cultural and linguistic backgrounds, as they practice repeated reading to increase their fluency. As we teach the content of our disciplines, we can employ strategies such as choral reading (which involves a group reading in unison as the teacher or another fluent reader leads), partnered reading, and readers theatre based on discipline-specific texts. For example:

A simple strategy to support fluency is to choose a familiar speech, skit, or poem and assign readers to roles/passages or lines. Advanced readers may begin the activity, modeling appropriate vocal tone and fluency. . . . Readers focus their attention to see and hear the speech-to-print correspondence in repeated readers' theater opportunities to present . . . aspects of various poems or stories with scaffolded materials, using poetry or stories from around the world, such as Dr. Martin Luther King's "I Have a Dream" speech. (p. 93)

We'll explore readers theatre more in later chapters, but one resource you might want to check out is *A Comprehensive Guide to Readers Theatre: Enhancing Fluency and Comprehension in Middle School and Beyond* (Black & Stave, 2007).

It's especially helpful for some readers who struggle with fluency to hear and see the text at the same time. So if you can have the combination of audio-books and print versions of titles that are not too difficult for your students, and can provide independent reading time or allow students to bring the materials home to practice, that could be very beneficial. The voices on computer programs and electronic readers that provide text-to-speech options are improving, also. Consider recording some of your required texts, so that students will be able to hear their teacher's expressive voice as they read along in their books or handouts. This could be especially helpful for your English learners, those whose first language is one other than English.

Reader Response Theory

This section introduces you to a particular way of thinking about readers and text called *reader response theory*. It often is discussed more in relation to literature than to other types of text, and you may wonder why you might find that helpful as a content area teacher. One reason is that you are encouraged throughout this book to use literature, as well as many other resources beyond the textbook, regardless of your subject area. Also, you can apply some aspects of this theory as you deal with all types of text, readers, subjects, and situations. A knowledge of reader response theory may help you as you ponder your own reading; it may answer questions that have puzzled you for a long time.

APPLICATION ACTIVITY **1.1** (SEE PAGE 26)

ACTIVATING PRIOR KNOWLEDGE **1.1**

Think of a book you have read at least twice. Perhaps you read a book as a child and became reacquainted with it recently. Maybe you have a favorite book that you return to often. My questions for you are: Did you have an identical experience each time you read it? If not, what was different? And what was the cause of the change? Write for a few minutes in your learning log or journal before continuing.

Obviously, the content of the text you selected in your reflection did not change. The same words appear in the book—*The Hobbit* (Tolkien, 1987), *The Bible, Chicken Soup for the Soul* (Canfield & Hansen, 1993), *Where the Wild Things Are* (Sendak, 1963), *Walden* (Thoreau, 1992), *The Da Vinci Code* (Brown,

2003), *Leaves of Grass* (Whitman, 1992), *Twilight* (Meyer, 2005)—each time you read it. But, inevitably, *you* changed. It's impossible for two readings of a text to be identical even if one occurs immediately after the other; the second time around, you know "whodunnit." Knowing the ending causes you to think differently about the ideas, events, and conversations that occur earlier in the text. If you read *The Giver* concurrently with this book's Introduction, I can say with certainty that if you reread the novel's first chapter now, you will agree that the experience is quite different from your first reading.

Significance of reader response theory

Reader response theory explains why two readers can have widely varying interpretations of a character's motives or a story's theme. It also calls into question the common educational practice of asking students what a poem *means,* or what a certain symbol represents, or what an author intended, as though there were only one correct answer that could be put into a multiple-choice test. Some of you may have memories of having had literature, or at least some genres or works, ruined for you because of this method of teaching and testing.

Louise Rosenblatt began championing what later came to be known as reader response criticism with her groundbreaking work *Literature as Exploration* (1938/1995). *The Reader, the Text, the Poem* (1978) expounded on her theoretical premises. She viewed the reader as transacting with a text to create what she called the *poem,* the meaning that emerges from the transaction at a given time. Feelings are evoked not just by the text, but by the text combining with the reader's prior experiences with life and literature, as well the reader's present mood and purposes. "The reader's creation of a poem out of a text must be an active, self-ordering and self-corrective process" (Rosenblatt, 1978, p. 11).

Examples of reader response theory in the classroom

Note: You may want to read *The Butter Battle Book* (1984) by Dr. Seuss (www.seussville.com) and *Snow White and the Seven Dwarfs* (1972) by the Brothers Grimm before reading the next section.

I'll use two examples from my own work to exemplify how reader response theory applies in the classroom.

Teaching in action: *Example 1.* A colleague and I set out to examine the responses of readers of different ages to Dr. Seuss's *The Butter Battle Book* (1984), an allegorical tale with multiple themes that is often used in social studies classes. We asked all participants to write a free response and then to state the main idea (theme, author's message, or moral of the story). We found that the third graders in our sample, in addition to drawing pictures in response to hearing the book read aloud, tended to have a literal interpretation of the story: there is a right way and a wrong way to butter one's bread. (This premise was the impetus in the story for the Yooks and Zooks to embark on an arms race.) A typical main idea statement was "Never trust a Zook that had toast with butter on the bottom."

We then asked students at the eighth-grade level to write the main point of the story. This age group was the first where the majority understood that the Yooks and Zooks represented nations, that the story was an allegory. One person lamented, "It's just showing that the wars of building weapons will keep on going."

Some of the most intriguing responses were the outliers, the unique answers, those we might perhaps call *wrong* answers, calling into question how reader response theory can work in our classrooms and what its limits are. A tenth grader wrote emotionally, "For stupid reasons we want to fight other people. We spend money and energy on weapons that we don't want to use. When we should use it for other useful things." Her response goes beyond the text, which never mentioned the economic aspects of the arms race, but we can certainly see the connection. What should we do with the tenth grader who wrote that the main point of the story is that the right way to eat butter is on the top of bread? Such a literal interpretation can be considered cute and appropriate from a third grader, but most teachers expect students by adolescence to understand allegory and symbolism. Another wrote, "The story conveys a feeling of hate for people who are different. I don't think children should be told to do this at such a young age." She might be considered to have misunderstood the author's intention, the text's purpose. As teachers, we should try to help these two readers read between the lines, to understand the genre of satire. We might model how we put pieces together to arrive at comprehension.

So, reader response theory does not say that *anything goes;* although idiosyncratic responses might be very interesting, the responses to a text must be plausible and defensible by using evidence within the text.

Teaching in action: *Example* 2. Another demonstration of reader response theory at work in the classroom involves an activity I created for my own teaching. Each semester, I form seven groups, then pass out copies of The Grimm Brothers' *Snow White and the Seven Dwarfs*. I particularly like the version translated by Randall Jarrell and illustrated by Diane

Burkholm (1972). I ask students to read the text with their group members, look at the pictures, discuss the story, and write a group response. As they read, I unobtrusively hand each group one of the following prompts:

- You are parents of preschoolers. You found this book in your child's nursery school classroom.
- You are six-year-old children.
- You are people who inherited the gene that causes dwarfism. You are under four feet tall and are politically active in the organization "Little People of America."
- You are feminists.
- You are librarians who are on the American Library Association committee that awards the Caldecott Medal to an illustrator for the best picture book of the year.
- You recently married someone who was divorced. You are a stepparent to your spouse's children who live with you.
- You are enrolled in a course called "The Bible *as* Literature and the Bible *in* Literature." *Snow White and the Seven Dwarfs* is a required text for this course.

When the groups finish writing, I ask a spokesperson from each to read their response to the fairy tale and I write key words I hear on the board. Not surprisingly, we often end up with seven quite different responses in front of us. The students playing the role of the Caldecott Selection Committee notice details about the illustrations and their relation to the text. The parents of preschoolers discuss age appropriateness and voice concern in terms of the violence, sexism, witchcraft and occult symbols, as well as word and concept difficulty. The group looking for biblical allusions usually has no trouble finding them: the apple as a symbol of temptation, the dying after disobedience, the rescue and resurrection by a savior. The group representing stepparents is outraged by the stereotypical depiction of the evil stepmother. Aren't their jobs hard enough without having to combat images in children's stories?

If you use such an activity in your classroom, you'll find that students use language that affects the voice and tone in their responses to help convey their message and their assumed identities. Anger and frustration are evident in this group's response: "The author is obviously uneducated and has no idea about the Little People of the world. He has us mining ore. This gives people the idea that we are ostracized from society because of our appearance. The author didn't even give the dwarfs names. He referred to them as 'the first one,' 'the second one,' and so on, dehumanizing them."

Another example also shows anger, but for a different reason: "Snow White was cast out of the castle because she was beautiful. This shows a lack of regard for her personality and her character. The dwarfs were male chauvinists."

In this exercise, I used a bit of manipulation to ensure that there would be major differences in the students' readings due to *interested* points of view; but to some extent every person's reading of every text is different. As noted earlier, an individual can't even read a text the same way twice at the same sitting. The first reading, along with many other factors, colors the second experience; one may recognize foreshadowing that wasn't noticed initially; having comprehended the main idea may free up one's energy to notice beauty of language or precision of organization.

Factors influencing reader response

A reader's stance or purpose for reading also affects his response to a text. Did you read *The Giver* for pleasure or for information? Do you read the newspaper for pleasure or for information? You may have said both, and that's fine, but if you had to say which was your primary purpose, you'd probably be able to decide. And for some texts the answer is easy—you read romance or detective thrillers almost totally for pleasure, not intellectual enhancement, and you read a required college chemistry text the day before the midterm almost totally for an understanding of the principles and facts. Rosenblatt categorizes the reader's relationship to the text, the stances a reader takes, as either *efferent* or *aesthetic*. With efferent reading, the reader's primary concern is to gain knowledge or information, to carry something away from the reading. She gives the extreme example of a mother reading a label on a bottle of poison because her child has just ingested its contents. With aesthetic reading, on the other hand, the reader's main concern is with what happens *during* the reading event. "Though . . . the reader of Frost's 'Birches' must decipher the images or concepts or assertions that the words point to, he also pays attention to the associations, feelings, attitudes and ideas that these words and their referents arouse within him. . . . *the reader's attention is centered directly on what he is living through during his relationship with that particular text*" (Rosenblatt, 1978, pp. 24–25).

The same text can be read by two people, or the same person at different times, for different purposes. Rosenblatt conceptualizes the two stances as being on a continuum, or a spectrum, involving complexity. We can switch from aesthetic to efferent stance, or vice versa, while reading. We can read informational text aesthetically and literary text efferently. We have a mix, but one is primary, and teachers can

make students aware of this. "Why not help youngsters early to understand that there are two ways of reading?" (Rosenblatt, 2005, p. 37). Galda and Liang (2003) explain how crucial the teacher's role is:

> If students know that they will be asked to recall facts in order to answer the teacher's questions, or questions on a computerized reading program, then they will learn to read for these facts. If students understand that the teacher's questions will focus on the students' lived-through experience of the story or poem, then they will learn to read aesthetically. (p. 271)

The authors explain why you can't simultaneously use a literary text for strategy instruction and goals that are response-oriented. They recommend letting students experience it first, then you can work on skills or teach content. After reading fiction in a content area, for example, you can use a variety of "activities that can include talking about the facts and about literary understanding, including critical evaluation, historical incidents, subjects, and settings—but the [aesthetic] experience must come first" (p. 274).

I also like visualizing the stances as intersecting circles. I read professional education journals to gain knowledge of new research, find out which theorists are debating, and learn about innovative practices teachers are developing. That's efferent reading. But I experience a great amount of pleasure doing this, and often let other duties slide when a new issue of the *Journal of Adolescent and Adult Literacy* or *The Horn Book Magazine* arrives in the mail. That's aesthetic reading. Ben Burtt, winner of four Academy Awards for his creation of the sound effects in *Star Wars* and other movies and producer of documentaries, states, "Reading to do research for a film is actually a form of entertainment for me" (Rosenthal, 1995, p. 169). You may read a book like Annie Dillard's *Pilgrim at Tinker Creek* (2000) because you love her writing style and the book relaxes you, yet find that you have picked up a lot of information about insects that you can carry over into your entomology class! About this example, I'd say that the two circles representing the efferent and aesthetic reading stances in a Venn diagram could be almost entirely overlapping.

One problem that occurs in schools is that the stances can get seemingly reversed. Most of us can name a classic that was spoiled for us because, instead of reading it for pleasure and for personal reasons, as authors intend, we were required to read it for school and were constantly tested to check our comprehension. Then, we were required to write an essay based on it, the purpose of which seemed to be to conform to what was already in the teacher's head. Ask a first grader what reading is, and she'll ask if you mean *home reading* or *school reading* (Michel,

1994). Ask a seventh grader about reading, and he'll also differentiate home reading and school reading (Worthy, 1998). Too often, home reading equates with pleasure reading and school reading is perceived as distasteful, or at least artificial. One of the aims of this book is to help you change that situation for your future students: to promote their natural curiosity, problem-solving ability, and general intellectual growth by providing real opportunities to interact with many types of text.

We explore reader response theory and its application to content area literacy throughout the chapters of this book; whether you teach math, science, art, history, or another subject, it will help both you and your students to understand that readers construct meaning from the texts they read based on their own purposes, background knowledge, emotional states, literacy abilities, and so on. This will become clearer as more discussion and examples, including nonfiction, primary sources, and textbook selections, are provided.

LITERACY

N ow that you've started thinking about reading, let's broaden the topic to that of *literacy* in general. How do the two concepts differ? What does literacy mean?

Defining Literacy (Or Should We Say Literacies?)

ACTIVATING PRIOR KNOWLEDGE   1.2

Imagine that you are being interviewed for a teaching position. An administrator interviewing you asks you to define the word *literacy*. What do you say?

As a follow-up question, the interviewer asks you to define literacy as it applies to the subject you will be teaching. How do you expand your answer?

Finally, another person on the search committee hands you a card that has "_____ literacy" on it and asks you to fill in the blank with as many appropriate words as you can. Take a moment to make a list of the phrases containing *literacy* that come to mind.

Figure 1.2 contains some of the phrases my students have contributed in response to the last question. These, combined with your own, indicate how widely used the word *literacy* is at present.

Traditionally, *literacy* has referred to the ability to read and write. In fact, the glossary of the *Standards for the English Language Arts* (NCTE/IRA, 1996)

FIGURE 1.2

Phrases showing some current uses of the term *literacy*.

cultural literacy	scientific literacy
media literacy	community literacy
civic literacy	computer literacy
critical literacy	functional literacy
mathematical literacy	digital literacy
geographic literacy	political literacy
Internet literacy	financial literacy
health literacy	global literacy
emergent literacy	adult literacy
adolescent literacy	

points out, "Until quite recently, literacy was generally defined, in a very limited way, as the ability to read or write one's own name" (p. 73). But the term has broadened to include "the capacity to accomplish a wide range of reading, writing, speaking, and other language tasks associated with everyday life" (p. 73). In the body of the Standards document is an even more expanded definition: "Being literate in contemporary society means being active, critical, and creative users not only of print and spoken language but also of the visual language of film and television, commercial and political advertising, photography, and more" (p. 5).

As it became increasingly obvious that the singular term *literacy* does not adequately express all the variations and complexities involved, scholars turned to the term *multiliteracies* (Cope & Kalantzis, 2000; Harste, 2003; Street, 2003; Paulson, 2005). Alvermann (2004) explains:

> The term multiliteracies refers to literacies that extend beyond print-based, alphabetic texts. . . . A pedagogy of multiliteracies broadens the meaning of text and relates textual reading to oral, aural, tactile, and digital modes of learning as well as to the social skills necessary for communicating and collaborating while engaged in such learning. (p. 227)

Alvermann, Hinchman, Moore, et al. (2006) deliberately choose to pluralize the word in the title, as well as the body, of their work; hence, *Reconceptualizing the Literacies in Adolescents' Lives*.

Leu, Mallette, Karchmer, et al. (2005) agree that it is necessary to talk about literacy as well as instruction in plural terms, since "there are so many new technologies requiring so many new literacies" (p. 4), and since new literacies are deictic; that is, "because literacy is regularly redefined by even newer technologies, learning *how to learn* may become just as important as learning particular technologies" (p. 4). The authors worry about the focus of beginning reading instruction, comprehension instruction, and assessment:

> If students are prepared only for the foundational literacies of book, paper, and pencil technologies, they will be unprepared for a future in which the new literacies are required by new information and communication technologies (ITCs). (p. 1)

Definitions and understandings of literacy are still expanding, as can be seen in articles with titles such as "The New Literacy Equation: Books + Computers = Multiplatform" (Hill, 2009) and "It's a Web 2.0 World: Expanding Perspectives of Literacy" (Carter, Ballard, & Vallée, 2009), which cites the definition of literacy formulated by UNESCO in 2003:

> "Literacy is the ability to identify, understand, interpret, create, communicate and compute, using printed and written materials associated with varying contexts. Literacy involves a continuum of learning in enabling individuals to achieve his or her goals, develop his or her knowledge and potential, and participate fully in community and wider society." (p. 114)

Now, think about the following definition of literacy (Victor & Kellough, 1997) relative to a particular content area:

> The scientifically literate person knows the social implications of science and recognizes the role of rational thinking in arriving at value judgments and solving social problems. The SLP knows how to learn, to inquire, to gain knowledge, and to solve new problems. Throughout life the SLP continues to inquire, to increase his or her knowledge base, and uses that knowledge to self-reflect and to promote the development of people as rational human beings. (p. 16)

If your answer to the interviewer's question in Activating Prior Knowledge 1.2 about literacy in your content area doesn't quite match the one discussed above, take comfort in knowing you are not alone. In 1999, the International Reading Association (IRA) disseminated a position statement on *adolescent literacy*. Noting that "adolescents entering the adult world in the 21st century will read and write more than at any other time in human history," and that "they will need advanced levels of literacy to perform their jobs, run their households, act as citizens, and conduct their personal lives" (Moore, Bean, Birdyshaw, et al., 1999, p. 99), the IRA's Commission on Adolescent Literacy offers seven principles for supporting adolescents' literacy growth, including "Adolescents deserve expert teachers who model and provide explicit instruction in reading comprehension and study strategies across the curriculum" (IRA, 1999, p. 104) and "Adolescents deserve teachers who understand the complexities of individual adolescent readers, respect their differences, and respond to their characteristics" (p. 105). Again, my goal is that this book will serve you as you strive to become the expert, understanding teacher called for here; I'll provide you with instructional strategies that can increase your students' multiple literacies.

Teaching Literacy as a Content Area Teacher

Moje, Ciechanowski, Kramer, et al. (2004) contend that content literacy learning and content learning are intertwined, and it is difficult to distinguish between them: "In fact, a critical aspect of learning in any discipline involves learning to communicate through oral and written language, among other forms of representation, in that discipline. . . . The opposite is also true: To be literate in a content area involves learning the content associated with the area" (p. 45). The authors show how complicated content area literacy is.

Whenever I supervise student teachers in math classrooms, I ask them, "Are you a mathematician?" They look at me with a puzzled expression; they've never asked themselves that question. But shouldn't the answer have to be yes? You wouldn't send your child to a violin teacher who didn't play the violin; neither would you take lessons from a yoga instructor who didn't practice the art herself. Maybe you won't ever be employed as a scientist or historian, but at some level you have to identify yourself as a practitioner in your field—at least as an active knowledge seeker and sharer. In other words, you have to be highly math literate, science literate, art literate in order to be an excellent teacher within your discipline. You have to belong to the discourse community. You have to read in your field in order to keep current. You'll have much more credibility with the students you're asking to read and write if they recognize that you are a reader and writer, also.

Numerous real-life examples illustrate academic ways of thinking and living within one's discipline. Gardner (1993) says of Einstein: "No matter what he was doing, science was always present in his mind. When stirring tea, he noticed the tea leaves congregating at the center and not the circumference of the bottom of the cup. He found the explanation and linked it to something unexpectedly remote: the meandering of rivers" (p. 127).

That's our goal: to help our students think like geographers, historians, economists, ecologists; to

BookTalk   1.1

A wonderful book illustrates the concept of subject area literacy. *Math Curse* (1995), by Jon Scieszka (www. jsworld.com) and Lane Smith (www.lanesmithbooks. com), is narrated by a child whose math teacher, Ms. Fibonacci, announces, "YOU KNOW, you can think of almost anything as a math problem" (unpaged). The student indeed looks at all aspects of her life mathematically from that point on; she thinks in terms of measurements, graphs, and percentages as she hurries to the bus, eats, and sits in social studies class. She finally breaks what she has come to think of as this math curse, only to have another teacher, Mr. Newton, the next week muse, "YOU KNOW, you can think of almost everything as a science experiment . . ." (unpaged). (This sets the reader up for the sequel, *Science Verse* [2004].) These books are for all who have ever wondered what math and science have to do with real life.

feel like they belong to the discourse communities related to the subjects they are studying. Wide and varied reading is the means to accomplish the goal. More reading correlates with better readers (Krashen, 2004; U.S. Department of Education, 1999). Adolescents broaden and deepen their content knowledge when they read more (Allington, 2001; Atwell, 2007), and, as they go through the grade levels, the gap widens between children who read a lot and those who read little (Stanovitch, 1986). It makes sense. The readers are getting practice time in; their skills are becoming automatic, like dribbling becomes for the kid who plays basketball hours each day, like finger movement becomes for the guitar player who chooses to spend significant amounts of time playing the instrument. So, literacy plays a crucial role in learning within the disciplines.

Many of your students will come to you unable to read well enough to learn from your course materials. Some may be new to the country and the English language; perhaps others didn't learn basic reading skills in the elementary grades due to sickness, emotional obstacles, inappropriate instruction, moving from place to place, learning disabilities, immaturity, social and economic disadvantages, or family turmoil. The list of causes is not as important as your realization that it is futile to blame students, teachers in prior grades, television, electronic games, or circumstances. It is your responsibility to accept each child as he comes into your class and help him to grow in learning as much as possible. This inevitably involves teaching literacy strategies.

Even if all 120 students you see each day are reading and writing on grade level, this does not mean you are free of the responsibility to teach literacy skills. For one thing, the construction of sentences and the vocabulary used increase in difficulty in upper grade and adult-level texts, as concepts and information become more complex. Also, reading really *is* different in specific disciplines. Children who had a wonderful background in the primary grades and who comprehend stories very well often falter when they have to tackle expository text. The expectations of readers by authors are different in various fields; therefore, reading behaviors and attitudes must change accordingly. Although there are generic reading skills and others that serve across a number of disciplines, some subject-specific reading skills do exist and must be taught.

APPLICATION ACTIVITY   **1.2**   (SEE PAGE 26)

Learning Standards and Teaching Literacy

Standards is a term that is proving to be almost as complex and multidimensional as *literacy*. If someone should ask you which camp you're in, the one *for* or the one *against* mandated learning standards, beware! What exactly does this pollster mean by *standards*? And whose standards, which standards?

Types of standards

Local, state, and national standards represent a variety of content areas. The major national professional organizations representing the core academic disciplines developed standards to serve as *guidelines* for content area teachers. It is important to note that the standards for every one of the subject areas recognize the importance of literacy. For example, the National Council of Teachers of Mathematics (NCTM) standards contend that problem solving and meaning take precedence over computation and expect students to become "mathematically literate" (Ravitch, 1995, p. 127). At every level, the NCTM standards stress mathematics as *communication*. In order to achieve the standards set forth by the National Council for the Social Studies, which center around 10 themes such as global connections; civic ideals and practices; and production, distribution, and consumption, students must exercise a great number of literacy skills. Similarly, the National Academy of Sciences, noting that the nation has established as a goal that all students should achieve scientific literacy, developed the National Science Education Standards (1996) in order to make that a reality in the twenty-first century. The Academy states:

All of us have a stake, as individuals and as a society, in scientific literacy. An understanding of science makes it possible for everyone to share in the richness and excitement of comprehending the natural world. Scientific literacy enables people to use scientific principles and processes in making personal decisions and to participate in discussions of scientific issues that affect society. (p. ix)

In 2010, common core state standards for English language arts and math, K–12, were released by the National Governors' Association and the Council of Chief State School Officers. They aim for clarity, consistency, quality, and rigor as they define skills and knowledge students must have in order to be ready for college, work, and participation in the global community. Most states were quick to adopt these standards, though there are critics who feel they are weaker than some individual state standards already in place; in addition, some worry about loss of local control, the impact on teachers, and/or the standards' effects on the teaching of English learners or students with disabilities, among other concerns. Now educators are working on how best to implement the standards, align the curriculum to them, and assess students accordingly. You can keep up with the latest developments regarding the common core standards through the official website, www.corestandards.org, and by reading articles in professional journals as people in your field continue the conversation. Add your voice!

Addressing standards

How can you address the literacy component of the learning standards for your content area in your long-term plans and daily lessons in a way that does not compromise your educational philosophy, yet meets the expectations of your school district, state, and national professional organizations? How can you ensure that your instruction is standards-based and still meet your individual students' literacy needs? The teaching strategies for attending to your students' literacy growth provided throughout this book should give you some answers. Be cautious of the ready-made materials publishers provide to give students practice with meeting the various learning standards. Rarely, if ever, should you have to take time from your content instruction to work on achieving standards or practicing skills out of context. For example, plenty of worksheets ask students to answer questions based on maps and timelines, skills students are expected to know to meet social studies standards. But you might prefer to provide your students with a book like Peter Sis's (www.petersis.com) *Starry Messenger: A Book Depicting the Life of a Famous Scientist, Mathematician, Astronomer, Philosopher, Physicist, Galileo Galilei*

(1996). This biographical picture book won a Caldecott Honor Medal for its artwork. It contains timelines and maps within the story and in the margins, as well as quotes from Galileo and graphic symbols within pictures. It is a multilayered story that invites a reader to consider many perspectives and to understand Galileo as a scientist, a religious man, a prisoner in his own home, a well-rounded person with a brilliant mind and profound feelings. Students can examine the language and the unusual and provocative writing techniques Sis employs; they can think critically about the relation of religion and science as they read about Galileo's conflict with the authority of the church of his time and his pardon by that church several centuries later.

As you use a rich text such as *Starry Messenger,* you can be aware of what standards are being addressed during the course of this exciting learning experience. For example, national science standards propose that students learn the history of science and its evolution (National Research Council, 1994). Galileo typifies mathematical literacy, as defined by the NCTM, involving "an individual's abilities to explore, to conjecture, and to reason logically, as well as to use a variety of mathematical methods effectively to solve problems" (1989, p. 6). The social studies standards (National Council for the Social Studies, 1994) cite skills such as reading maps and following a timeline and a sequence of events. Sis's biography encourages the development of these skills.

A simple test that you can use when you are designing a reading guide or selecting activities from published materials is to ask yourself whether the same type of activity is likely to be used in an authentic, out of school setting. Readers of novels, no matter what age, do not stop after every chapter to write out answers to questions in complete sentences. On the other hand, when we are learning a new skill because we are intrinsically motivated or because we know acquiring that skill might help us get something else we want, we are willing to practice, sometimes repeating steps over and over. It could be anything from aerobics to piano playing to calligraphy. If we apply this test of authenticity, students come to understand that we try not to make them do anything merely for the sake of using up time, or passing tests, or "meeting the standards." They will trust us when we assign something that we've thoughtfully chosen and explain why it was chosen.

APPLICATION ACTIVITY **1.3** (SEE PAGE 26)

It's beyond the scope of this book to go into depth about the standards movement, with the promises and hopes of its proponents and the worries and concerns of its critics. Figure 1.3 lists resources that you can explore to learn more and decide where you stand on this complex issue. The resources represent a variety of positions on the standards movement, so you can gather information, understand the arguments for and against the movement itself and certain methods of implementing the standards, and decide for yourself how standards-based teaching and curricula fit into your overall, emerging philosophy of teaching and learning. Chapter 10 discusses the connection between standards and the assessment of student learning.

Preparing to Teach Literacy in the Content Areas

At this point I'd like you to try your hand at preparing a strategy to use with students in your content area classrooms. Try giving a booktalk, perhaps modeled on the booktalks in the introduction and this chapter, to your peers or to a group of middle or high school students. Choose one of your favorite books or a book you consider important in the discipline you will be teaching. Decide on your target audience. Do you want to convince your fellow college classmates, or seventh graders, or the parents of your tenth graders to read this book? What can you say that will entice them, make them

want to go right home to start the book? You have a great deal of freedom for this experience; you can use props, ask for writing, invite dialogue, dance on your desk. In my classroom, I do insist on three rules for a booktalk:

1. Keep it short. Hold yourself to a maximum of three minutes if you don't require interaction from your audience. (Look back at my booktalk for *The Giver*—I didn't require you to actually answer any questions; I just talked to you at that point.) If you get the audience involved, as I model for you in Figure 1.4, use your discretion in deciding a time limit because there may be other objectives to accomplish simultaneously.

2. Do not start with the sentence, "The book I chose is _____." I know you can be more interesting than that. It's a good idea to get your audience thinking initially about a time, a place, an issue, a person, or a feeling, before you introduce the title of the book. They'll have something to connect the book *to* if you've already got them thinking.

3. Do not give a summary of the plot. Not only is this boring, it can actually *decrease* the listener's need and desire to read the book, which is exactly the opposite of your goal. And don't give away the ending; avoid spoilers. Most likely, the author can do a better job.

FIGURE 1.3 Resources relating to learning standards.

BOOKS

Carr, J. F., & Harris, D. E. (2009). *Improving Standards-Based Learning: A Process Approach.* Thousand Oaks, CA: Corwin Press.

Gregory, G., & Kuzmich, L. (2004). *Data Driven Differentiation in the Standards-Based Classroom.* Thousand Oaks, CA: Corwin Press.

Lachat, M. A. (2004). *Standards-Based Instruction and Assessment for English Language Learners.* Thousand Oaks, CA: Corwin Press.

Senk, S. L., & Thompson, D. R. (2003). *Standards-Based School Mathematics Curricula: What Are They? What Do Students Learn?* Mahwah, NJ: Lawrence Erlbaum Associates.

Squires, D. A. (2005). *Aligning and Balancing the Standards-Based Curriculum.* Thousand Oaks, CA: Corwin Press.

Zemelman, S., Daniels, H., & Hyde, A. A. (2005). *Best Practice: Today's Standards for Teaching and Learning in America's Schools.* Portsmouth, NH: Heinemann.

ARTICLES

Davis, O. L., Jr. (2005). The New Standards Are Set: Now What? *Journal of Curriculum & Supervision, 20*(2), 89–93.

Finn, C.E., Jr. (2010). Are National Standards the Right Move? *Educational Leadership, 67*(7), 2–26.

Gewertz, C. (2010). How to Move from Standards to Curricula? *Education Week, 29*(32), 1–22.

Long, R. (2010). Common Core State Standards Released: What Comes Next? *Reading Today, 27*(6), 26.

McClure, P. (2005). Where Standards Come From. *Theory into Practice, 44*(1), 4–10.

Newkirk, T. (2010). Standards and the Art of Magical Thinking. *Education Week, 29*(33), 29.

FIGURE **1.4** **Sample interactive booktalk.**

I've got some paper cups right here. And I've got this bottle of water. And I've got a promise. If you drink a single sip of my magic water, you will remain at your present age forever. You will never die. Take a paper cup if you want some. [Pass out cups.] I see some of you refused my offer. Why? People have searched for centuries for the Fountain of Youth! [Your remarks will depend on the answers you get, but the following are possibilities.] Oh, you don't want to survive all the people you love? Take enough for them, too. You feel that you're too young right now? Ok, take some for later; it will retain its magic for several years. Don't worry, it doesn't stop you from growing, learning, experiencing new things. It merely prevents you from *aging*. [Allow for more discussion.]

As you may have guessed, I've lied to you. I got the water from the drinking fountain outside the door. But the book I have here, *Tuck Everlasting* by Natalie Babbitt (2000), has a spring with the property I've tried to tempt you with. The 11-year-old protagonist, Winnie Foster, finds the spring and a family who drank the water—87 years ago. Now, she has a decision to make. If you've ever wondered why things have to die, if you've ever pondered the mysteries of the life cycle, if you've ever thought about the concept of "forever," read this book to find out if and when Winnie drinks the water.

CONCLUSION

A goal of this chapter was to stimulate your thinking about—and add to your knowledge of—literacy: What is literacy, and how does it relate to learning standards and other aspects of your teaching? The learner is anything but passive. Elliot Eisner (2002) explains:

> We tend to think that the act of reading a story or reading a poem is a process of decoding. And it is. But it is also a process of encoding. The individual reading a story must *make* sense of the story; he or she must produce meanings from the marks on the page. The mind must be constructive, it must be active, and the task of teaching is to facilitate effective mental action so that the work encountered becomes meaningful. (p. 581)

Throughout the succeeding chapters, we'll be dealing with literacy processes as *constructive*. You'll see how the concept applies to all genres of text and all aspects of learning through literacy in your discipline. And you'll be making meaning yourself as you engage with the text and apply its principles.

WEBSITES **CHAPTER 1** **Access these links using the Kane Resource Site.**

Common core standards
www.corestandards.org

Dr. Seuss
www.seussville.com

Jon Scieszka
www.jsworldwide.com

Lane Smith
www.lanesmithbooks.com

Peter Sis
www.petersis.com

APPLICATION ACTIVITIES

1.1 Think of ways to find out what reading means to your students. List some of these ways, or choose one and expound on how you might carry it out. If you're in contact with children or adolescents now, watch them in action and talk to them—get their ideas relating to reading, both in and out of school.

1.2 If, as the IRA's position paper on adolescent literacy says, teens deserve expert teachers who model and provide instruction in reading comprehension across the curriculum, you'll want to be one of those expert teachers. In writing, reflect about one or more ways you'll pay attention to literacy issues in your classroom. How will you establish credibility as a literate person in your field?

1.3 Ask teachers you know what they think about the various learning standards in your field. How has attention to standards helped and/or hindered their teaching and their students' learning? Or, choose one or more of the national, state, or regional standards established for the subject you expect to teach. Then select a book, as I did with *Starry Messenger* above, and reflect on how it might be used in addressing the standard(s) you chose. Share your book and ideas on the Kane Resource Site.

chapter 2

Affective and Social Aspects of Content Area Learning and Literacy

"A teacher who is attempting to teach without inspiring the pupil with a desire to learn is hammering on cold iron."

HORACE MANN

THE AFFECTIVE DOMAIN

Many factors affect student reading and learning in the content areas, including self-esteem, physical surroundings, emotional environment, sense of purpose, attitude toward learning, social conditions, self-determination, self-regulation, activation of interests, engagement in the learning process, and motivation. Self-efficacy, one's confidence about ability or performance in a particular sphere, is also important. For example, I might have a good level of self-esteem about my intelligence in general, but be afraid to tackle physics or technology because I believe I can't do the specific kinds of problem solving called for in those areas. Content area teachers can enhance both competence and confidence as they introduce and teach concepts and skills.

It's a given that content area teachers are responsible for the *cognitive* development of students; we help our students understand the concepts and knowledge base of our subjects, as well as teach them to analyze texts and think critically about course material and current events in the field. It's equally true that we must pay attention to our learners' interests, engagement, and motivation, which are considered to be in the *affective domain* (Krathwohl, Bloom, & Masia, 1964) of learning. As students grow in each of these domains, the other can be affected positively. You've probably listened to people talk excitedly together, sharing details and opinions about something you have little interest in, whether it be sports, computers, horses, or the stock market. Similarly, the subject you teach may not be inherently interesting to your September students, but by June they may belong to the discourse community you've helped create and have the attitude and motivation necessary to continue learning the subject independently. Your goal is to replace apathy and indifference with zeal and intellectual curiosity. Every chapter in this text involves both the cognitive and affective realms, often together, as we deal with various components of literacy and learning and develop teaching and learning strategies.

Interest, Engagement, and Motivation

No matter how good a teacher is, no matter how wonderful the strategies or the texts used, the results will not be good unless students are interested, motivated, and engaged (Guthrie & Wigfield, 2000). If students are bored by teacher-centered lessons that assume knowledge can be transmitted to passive learners, they will not learn. If students have turned their backs on school literacy, they will not learn. Teachers can't just transmit the necessary qualities to students, though there are ways to address these often intersecting issues. So, there is a call for culturally responsive teaching, which connects school, home, and community literacy practices (Lee, 2001), and for participatory approaches to teaching and learning, which are very concerned with content mastery, and which "actively engage students in their own learning (individually and in small groups) and that treat texts as tools for learning rather than as repositories of information to be memorized (and then all too quickly forgotten)" (Alvermann, 2002, p. 201).

Activating interest

Learning, wanting to know about the world, other people, and ourselves, seems to be as natural as breathing. When do these interests begin and how early do they affect a child's reading? Signs point to "very early." You may have known preschoolers who could tell you more about dinosaurs than you ever thought you wanted to know. Gallas (2001) describes a passionate six-year-old, Emily, whom she was convinced had started her life's work:

> Emily is a scientist. . . . During the year I taught her, in fine weather she spent all of her outdoor time pursuing insects, capturing them, and making containers to keep them in so that she could take them home with her for further observation. . . . She drew the insects and bugs she collected, wrote about them avidly, and offered a wealth of information about most of them to anyone who was interested. . . . At home she insisted on being read only nonfiction. . . . When she was left to herself, her interests in life were exclusively in natural science and/or things that were "real." (pp. 457–458)

If passion for learning is so common in youngsters, I wonder why so many of our students can identify with the following passage from the first page of Norton Juster's childhood classic *The Phantom Tollbooth*:

> "I can't see the point in learning to solve useless problems, or subtracting turnips from turnips, or where Ethiopia is or how to spell February." And, since no one bothered to explain otherwise, [Milo]

regarded the process of seeking knowledge as the greatest waste of time of all. (1961, p. 1)

I also wonder why it's so easy to find data from adults, even from authors, telling about their lack of learning, and specifically lack of reading, in school. See if you can think of someone you know who could identify with popular young adult author Chris Crutcher's words about his ninth grade experience reading *The Scarlet Letter*:

> The story wasn't about anything I knew. My teacher didn't give me anything contemporary with which to compare the complex issues addressed in the book, something that would have helped me relate those issues to my life. With that assignment, reading became something that was no longer fun for me. When it stopped being fun, I stopped doing it. (Monseau, 1996, p. x)

Crutcher read "a grand total of one book from cover to cover during my entire four years of high school, opting rather to invent titles for book reports, as well as stories to go with them" (p. 1).

ACTIVATING PRIOR KNOWLEDGE   2.1

In your learning log or journal, write about something that you have been passionately interested in learning about at some point in your life. It can be from when you were very young, a "passing passion phase," or it can be a long-lasting or present insatiable curiosity. What (or whom) did you want to investigate? Where did you find information about this topic? With whom did you talk about your interest? What initiated your delving into the subject? Share your response with others before reading on.

In "Successful Dyslexics: A Constructivist Study of Passionate Interest Reading," Fink (1995/1996) discusses research involving 12 case studies of adults who were very successful in their professions (e.g., a company CEO, a biochemist, a neurologist, a physicist) despite having had major difficulty learning to read. Eleven of the 12 reported learning to read between the ages of 10 and 12, and they "grappled with profound problems with letter identification, word recognition, and sound analysis" (p. 273). Each participant was interviewed extensively in order to learn how they managed to succeed despite their difficulties. The researcher's hypotheses were not confirmed. "I expected to discover extraordinary bypass and compensation strategies. Presumably, continual frustration with basic skills would lead dyslexics to avoid reading. To my surprise, I found that these dyslexics were avid readers. . . . they rarely circumvented reading. On the contrary, they sought out books" (p. 272).

The common theme Fink found was that in childhood each had "a passionate personal interest, a burning desire to know more about a discipline that required reading. Spurred by this passionate interest, all read voraciously" (pp. 274–275). Their passions included biography, math, religion, poetry, novels, business, history, and science. Fink expanded her study using 66 striving readers; the results reinforced her earlier findings about the role of passion in learning to read and excel. In *Why Jane and John Couldn't Read—And How They Learned: A New Look at Striving Readers* (2006), she explains how teachers can promote success with an interest-based model of reading, which can promote great gains in achievement in both reading and content knowledge. Key elements of the model include:

- A passionate, personal interest that spurs sustained reading
- Avid, topic-specific reading
- Deep schema knowledge
- Contextual reading strategies
- Mentoring support (p. 17)

Surely there are instructional implications of these studies—we can foster reading and learning if we acknowledge individual interests and build on them as we teach.

No matter your grade level or subject area, you can get to know your students' interests, letting them know you are interested in knowing them. Here is how one twelfth grader responded to her teacher's September survey about reading and writing practices:

> In the past, I have written research papers on such topics as the Great Depression, the Ebola virus, and capital punishment. After I begin researching, it is almost like I am so interested in the topic that I forget I am gathering information for a paper, and feel like I'm reading for enjoyment. For example, after I finished my paper on the Ebola virus, I became so interested that I kept reading all the books even after I finished writing the paper. *The Hot Zone* [Preston, 1994] is still one of my favorite books.

Galda and Liang (2003) remind us, "Literacy instruction should preserve and nurture pleasure, the idiosyncratic interests that feed curiosity, that keep us wanting to learn" (p. 265). However, Wilhelm and Smith (2006) (citing Hidi & Harackiewicz's [2000] caution that, while attending to individual interests has many benefits, it may be difficult to do in today's secondary schools) recommend creating *situational interest* within our classrooms. Situational interest is an individual's perception of the appealing characteristics of an activity, generated by certain conditions and/or concrete objects in the environment. That is, by paying attention to the environment and social

dimension of literacy and learning, giving students a sense of control and competence, and creating contexts where reading and writing have immediate payoffs in terms of the problems at hand, we can increase our students' motivation and engagement.

Engagement in reading

Csikszentmihalyi (1991) describes engaged reading as "flow," a state of total absorption, even to the point of a loss of self-consciousness, a feeling of being carried away by a pleasurable current. Most of us have experienced being lost in our work, or play, whether it involves writing, creating with paint or clay, running, working on a car engine, or another engrossing pastime. Fink (2006) reports that, for the striving readers in her study, "who became anxious in many reading situations, this feeling of flow while reading about a topic of interest was liberating" (p. 11). Wilhelm and Smith (2006) discuss ways teachers can encourage and help students achieve flow state in *Going with the Flow: How to Engage Boys (and Girls) in their Literacy Learning*. The value of engagement in reading is unquestionable; it is strongly associated with reading achievement (Guthrie & Wigfield, 2000), which is what we want for our students. Reed, Schallert, Beth, et al. (2004) describe a subset of engagement they refer to as *falling into involvement*, where:

> a person becomes totally absorbed by a task, so much so that non-task related emotions, motivations, or metacognitive thoughts are excluded . . . involvement tends to occur when a person undertakes a task that is at just the appropriate level of difficulty, appropriately challenging without being too difficult, something that requires concentration but is comprehended. (p. 260)

Motivation to read

Reading motivation, which is multifaceted, can be defined as *"the individual's personal goals, values, and beliefs with regard to the topics, processes, and outcomes of reading"* (Guthrie & Wigfield, 2000, p. 405, italics theirs). Motivation is what activates behavior, so you can see how crucial it is to learning. However, we need to carefully consider the type of motivation we rely on to encourage students. Deci, Koestner, and Ryan's (2001) meta-analysis of studies indicated that extrinsic, tangible rewards can have an effect that actually undermines intrinsic motivation or motivation that emanates from within a person. On the other hand, Alvermann (2002) notes, "Adolescents' perceptions of how competent they are as readers and writers, generally speaking, will affect how motivated they are to learn in their subject area classes" (p. 191). This makes sense; none of us feels

Examples of Books with Engaged and Motivated Learners

A wonderful place for students to meet passionate learners their own age is between the covers of a book. I'll introduce you to a few of them in the following booktalks, and the pedagogical strategies discussed throughout this chapter will help you think about how you can use these or other stories about passionate learning and action in your discipline with your students.

These books could be used together as a *text set,* which is explained later in this chapter.

BookTalk 2.1

Ally has long been passionate about astronomy; she dreams of discovering a comet someday. Bree and Jack arrive at Ally's family's campground not by choice, but eventually they join the passionate eclipse chasers who are there to get the best view of a total eclipse. Readers will learn some science while reading the chapters with three alternating teen narrators in *Every Soul a Star* (2008) by Wendy Mass. They may very well become motivated to explore the wonders of the sky through further reading, and possibly may become eclipse chasers (actual or virtual) themselves.

BookTalk Online 2.2

Nightjohn 1993 by Gary Paulsen explores the risks that one man took to teach slaves how to read and the consequences of a passion for learning. Hear more at the Kane Resource Site.

BookTalk 2.3

Meg Murry, the daughter of two scientists, is considered unusual among her peers because she is a girl who is gifted in math. Her little brother, Charles Wallace, is considered unusual in the community because he doesn't talk, at least not outside his home. His family knows that what is *really* unusual about him is his extremely high intelligence—we're talking genius-level intelligence. The siblings get the chance to use their gifts in a most unusual way. They must travel through time and space to rescue their father from the forces of evil on the planet Camazotz, where equality has been achieved by everyone being the same. Read *A Wrinkle in Time* (1962) by Madeleine L'Engle (www.madeleine-lengle.com) to join this physical, emotional, intellectual, and spiritual adventure. You'll never view *sameness* in the same way again!

BookTalk 2.4

Twelve-year-old Allegra faces a difficult choice. If she wishes to compete in the invitational Mozart competition, all other summer activities must be sacrificed. Her talent and passion for the violin determine her decision, but surprisingly, the areas in which she grows go far beyond the musical. And the people who end up being teachers and mentors to her go far beyond her dedicated music instructor. Is she the winner? Read Virginia Euwer Wolff's *The Mozart Season* (2000) to find out.

motivated to pursue and persist at tasks we're not good at. In any case, we must address the various aspects of student motivation if we want our students to succeed and achieve their goals, and our goals for them, in our content area courses.

Fink (2008) points out that her research as well as that of others, including Hidi and Renninger (2006) and Lipstein and Renninger (2007), demonstrates that motivation and skill performance go hand in hand, that cognitive aspects and motivational aspects of reading are equally important. "Students' interests play a pivotal role—both in motivating them to

read and in enhancing their reading levels" (p. 20). Atwell (2007) concurs. "Every measure that looks at pleasure reading and its effects on student performance on standardized tests of reading ability—and science and math—tells us that the major predictor of academic success is the amount of time that a student spends reading. In fact, the top 5% of U.S. students read up to 144 times more than the kids in the bottom 5%" (p. 107). She emphasizes, "Recently, the largest ever international study of reading found that the single most important predictor of academic success is the amount of time children spend reading books, more important even than economic or social status. And one of the few predictors of high achievement in math and science is the amount of time children devote to pleasure reading" (p. 130).

Fostering Interested, Engaged, and Motivated Reading and Learning

As teachers, our responsibility in the affective domain is twofold:

1. *To nurture our own passion for reading.* To accomplish this, we must read voraciously to extend our knowledge, refine our thinking, and join the literacy club (Smith, 1988) of our field. Lundberg and Lynnakyla's research (1993) indicates that teachers who are avid readers have students who have higher reading achievement than do the students of teachers who rarely read. Other scholars give added evidence of the benefits to students when teachers read for pleasure (e.g., Commeyras, Bisplinghoff, & Olson, 2003; Kane, 2008; Kolloff, 2002; Powell-Brown, 2003–2004).

2. *To share our passion for reading with our students, with a goal of sparking interest and fascination in them.* We must pinpoint or spark the passions of the students themselves, and help them use literacy to feed those passions and grow in wisdom.

ACTIVATING PRIOR KNOWLEDGE   2.2

"Are you a reader?" Ponder this question before you read on. Also, list some titles of books, magazines, poems, or short stories you have read for pleasure (not assigned for courses, not required for a job) over the past few years.

Nurturing our passion

You may or may not answer the question posed above in the affirmative. Certainly, some of my teacher education students can fill pages with titles of books they've read, but these students are the exception. Here are some admissions from others (and remember, I don't have a random sample in my class; these are people who are preparing to spend their careers in classrooms):

- *I must be pushed into reading a book.*
- *I am embarrassed to say I do not consider myself a reader.*
- *My first choice would not be to pick up a book and read, although I'd love to know all the information inside the book.*
- *All the way through school I got by reading as little as possible.*

- *To say that I am a reader would be a reach at best.*

There is ample evidence that *aliteracy,* the phenomenon of people who are able to read perfectly well choosing not to, exists at all levels of our society (e.g., Alvermann, 2004). It's not just the children, it's not just the poor, it's not just the less educated.

Nathanson, Pruslow, and Levitt (2008) wonder if the aliteracy of students is at least partly due to the lack of enthusiasm for reading that has been found in those very teachers who have been entrusted to nurture literacy habits in young people, and preservice teachers as well. Applegate and Applegate (2004) coined the term *the Peter Effect,* based on a biblical quote of the apostle Peter, who answered a beggar by asking how he could give what he himself didn't have. It's worth thinking about as we self-reflect: How much enthusiasm for ongoing reading and learning do we ourselves have to share with our content area students? And if we're not pleased with our conclusion, what goals can we set to assure that we'll have more to give in the near future and throughout the years as our career progresses?

During the semester that just ended for me, I attended lectures by two authors of nonfiction with whom I had not previously been familiar. Their fields are extremely different; Neil deGrasse Tyson is an astrophysicist, while Sarah Vowell is a historian. What they have in common is witty writing that makes learning a pleasure. Even their titles hint at humor: Tyson's (2007) *Death by Black Hole* and (2009) *The Pluto Files: The Rise and Fall of America's Favorite Planet;* Vowell's (2005) *Assassination Vacation* and (2003) *Partly Cloudy Patriot.* I could not contain my excitement once I started reading these books, and I gladly shared my enthusiasm with my classes. Several students took me up on my recommendations, and others put at least one of the titles on their "Someday Lists." Our students need to see us as readers, at least of texts within the disciplines we teach. Of course it's fine for them to see that our varied interests go beyond the subject we teach, too.

Commeyras, Bisplingfoff, and Olson (2003) grappled with the issue of teachers as readers (or as aliterate persons), noting, "Ask most any literacy teacher educator about the reading habits and interests of those preparing to be teachers. Most likely, you will hear that many do not like to read, have lost their love of reading, or rarely find time to read" (p. 2). Based on their experiences, they offer the following:

> our students appreciate and respond to knowing us as readers. We think developing genuine reciprocal reading relationships with students around reading may be far more significant and long lasting in regard to quality of life than reading performance reported through test scores. (p. 163)

You might be wondering at this point what all this has to do with you; you may be in an education program because you want to teach high school math or music or health or art or science. I'll assume you are passionate about, or at least interested in, continuing to learn in the field you plan to teach. If you're going to be a social studies teacher, I'll assume you read the newspaper, follow current events and politics, read history books, and so on. But try this out. Ask the other people in your class, those planning to teach subjects other than the one you have picked, whether they read anything that will further their learning in your chosen field. Even your colleagues are often less than moderately interested in your area of knowledge! Can you imagine how few of your high school geography students or middle school math students will initially desire the treasure you have to offer and come to your class willing to work for it?

So, it appears you have a double problem. Many of your students will care virtually nothing for the subject area you love, and they may be aliterate to boot. Am I trying to discourage you before your idealism has even been given a chance in the schools? Far from it. You hold the key to the solution to both halves of the dilemma.

Research shows that instructional practices can increase or contribute to a decline in students' reading motivation (Commeyras et al., 2003; McKool, 2007). Gaskins (2008) discusses 10 tenets to increase reading motivation, which are suggestions for teachers of struggling (and other) readers, including:

- explaining to students how learning works and how motivation impacts both present and future learning;
- presenting information and instruction in a way that is situationally and/or personally interesting;
- explaining the value and meaningfulness of what is taught;
- encouraging collaboration and sharing of talents;
- offering scaffolding and feedback; and
- providing choices to foster autonomy and internal control.

We face a huge challenge, but, as Milo discovered after rescuing the princesses Rhyme and Reason in Juster's *The Phantom Tollbooth,* "so many things are possible just as long as you don't know they're impossible" (1961, p. 247).

The first step toward a solution to student apathy or disinterest is to increase the breadth and depth of the reading and writing and learning that *teachers* and *preservice teachers* do. In a classic study (Rieck, 1977), 300 students of 14 content area teachers were asked whether their teacher liked to read: 20 percent said yes, 33 percent said no, and 47 percent didn't know. If you recall some of your own high school teachers and ask yourself that same question, you'll get some idea of whether the situation has changed over the years. My goal is to challenge, convince, and help you to become, if you are not already, a person who is such an avid reader that you cannot help but enthusiastically share the wealth with your students.

Sharing our passion

Teaching and promoting literacy is not about telling students to read and checking to see that they're doing it; rather, you can show them what you're reading and explain how you find and select material, make choices as you're reading, and work to comprehend and evaluate ideas.

Nell (1988) points out that there are certain preconditions that must be met before one becomes a person who chooses to read for pleasure.

1. The person must possess adequate reading skills and fluency, so that texts are not too tedious and slow to be rewarding.
2. There must be the expectation that reading will be a pleasurable experience.
3. The text selection must be appropriate.

Think about the teacher's role in relation to Nell's assertion. It is your responsibility to increase and enhance your students' reading skills and strategies as they read materials related to your curriculum. Your obvious love of reading and enthusiasm for particular genres or works can lead to the students' expectation that reading what you require or recommend will be worthwhile. As for the third precondition, you should select appropriate texts after determining the needs and interests of individuals and groups, as well as help the students develop and hone the skill of finding and selecting texts that will be worthwhile and rewarding.

There are many ways, both formal and informal, that we can learn about literacy practices our students enjoy and what they like to read for pleasure (e.g., Brautigam, Hart, & Swinde, 2002; Fink, 2006; Ivey & Broaddus, 2001; Johnson & Giorgis, 2002; Miller, 2009; Quintana, 2001). I listen carefully to my students as they enter and exit the classroom, and then sometimes surprise them with a book I've found with them in mind. "Jesse, I know you're interested in the ways DNA testing is affecting decision making in families. I came across this memoir, *The Test: Living in the Shadow of Huntington's Disease,* by Jean Baréma" (2005). Or, "Magda, since you're doing your internship this fall at ESPN, I want you to see my new book, *Saturday Shrines: College Football's Most Hallowed Grounds*" (Sporting News, 2005).

You can ask quick questions at the beginning or end of a class that give you data: How many like biographies? Who listens to audiobooks? Who has ever submitted a poem or essay for publication? How many read romance novels? What's the best travel book you've ever read? What kinds of how-to books do you read (car manuals, science experiments, cookbooks, scrapbooking)? Who reads e-books? How many of you have participated in an interactive or multiplatform book or series (e.g., books incorporating social networking, gaming, collectible cards)?

Sometimes I ask my students to talk with each other (as I eavesdrop) about their memories of childhood literacy, recalling favorite books parents or siblings read to them, or the first book they read independently. They work their way through the grades, sharing years of writing in a diary, reading all four volumes of Stephenie Meyer's *Twilight* series in a single summer, keeping a dream journal, reading sports magazines, collecting comics, playing video games, putting on plays in their backyards, belonging to a listserv on karate, exploring websites on religions of the world. If you help students discover the kinds of books that interest them, many of them may later credit you as the teacher who helped them discover the treasure in books and other texts.

Let me talk for a moment with the prospective math teachers in the class; if this is not your area, know that what I say can be generalized to your subject also. I chose math because my personal conversion to lifelong learning in this discipline has been the most recent and most surprising to me.

I was a fine math student in high school, not particularly math-phobic or math-anxious. I studied hard, I tested well, and, when I did think about math, it was as something separate from anything else I did. For a long time, I got along in my adult life with a minimum of mathematical activity. It wasn't until I began teaching college education courses in Content Area Literacy that I made a magnificent self-discovery. I love math! Math is enticing, beautiful, fascinating, aesthetically exhilarating! What caused this revelation? When I went looking for books to help my math education students see the value of teaching reading and having classroom libraries like the rest of the disciplines, I encountered math books that were written in words rather than in symbols and school-type exercises. I met people who devoted their lives to the love of the discipline; in books I met geniuses who had friends, enemies, ambitions, and failures. I bought myself a treat that proved to be the start of my personal math library, *Five Equations that Changed the World: The Power and Poetry of Mathematics* by Michael Guillen (1995). Such books changed my world, and my outlook on the world of math. No one had ever told me about the relationship of math to music, to art, to philosophy, to language. Figure 2.1 lists examples of books now in my class-

room library or on my wish list. I also recommend *The Journal of Recreational Mathematics*.

We hear so much about math anxiety and see evidence of innumeracy and math avoidance in our schools, but I rarely see a classroom library in a math teacher's room with books that could make an enormous difference in a child's life. If we all work together to enable our students to be wide readers, they'll come to you able to learn the math you are ready to teach them. If our students have technology teachers, economics teachers, earth science teachers, physical education teachers, and

BookTalk 2.5

Toward the end of the nineteenth century, a book was published that remains a mathematical classic and has been reissued many times: *Flatland* by Edwin Abbott (1963). The main character, A. Square, lives pretty comfortably in a two-dimensional world, not thinking beyond that until he's taken on a journey to other dimensions with societies of their own. It's a book that really exercises the brain while providing lots of playful situations, and it's a satire of Victorian society to boot. If you explore *Flatland,* you'll be able to join a contemporary community of fans who will delight you with their websites and their interpretations and puzzles. And now, more than a century later, a sequel has appeared. It seems that A. Square's great-great-granddaughter, Victoria Line, has come across his diary in her attic, leading her to an adventure through 10 dimensions. Read Ian Stewart's *Flatterland: Like Flatland Only Moreso* (2001) to travel through *mathiverse* with Victoria.

administrators who are readers themselves, of materials both within and beyond the confines of their disciplines, they will profit in ways we cannot even predict. We are models for our students; there must be no aliteracy among the faculty of the schools to which we send our children. Learning will come alive for all. Teacher burnout will become a virtual impossibility.

Teaching in action: *English.* Sharon Morley is a high school English teacher who lives this philosophy. She invites fellow teachers of various subjects, plus principals, her superintendent, and people from the community, to visit her classes and discuss their pleasure reading. Students might be surprised to know that their principal is a Civil War buff, that the gym teacher reads poetry. Morley explains, "Some presenters use 5 or 10 minutes; some use the entire period, spinning the book talk into an accompanying lesson about history, about life, or about what happens when one loves to read. A spontaneous dialogue usually emerges at the close of each book talk; students see the presenter as a fellow learner" (Morley, 1996, p. 131). Students keep track of their guests and the titles they recommend on a student-designed "faculty family tree" with each of the disciplines delineated and photos of the speakers on the branches. Morley tries to obtain the discussed books for the classroom library.

ACTIVATING PRIOR KNOWLEDGE   2.3

In your learning log, take a moment to respond to the following assertion: "Learning is social." What does that short statement mean to you? Do you agree with it? How does it relate to your own learning and to how students are taught in classroom settings?

THE SOCIAL NATURE OF LEARNING

Current theories of motivation recognize how learning is fostered by social interaction (Bowen, 2000; Stevens, 2003; Vaughan, 2002). Taboada, Guthrie, and McRae (2008) describe literacy social interaction as "student interchanges and dialogues in a literacy situation with the purpose of supporting students' reading motivation" (p. 158). Employ specific strategies, such as promoting open discussion of texts. English learners, as well as their peers, benefit when they actively participate in discussions and other literacy activities "in which both academic vocabulary and conceptual knowledge are at the core" (p. 159).

Psychologist Lev Vygotsky set forth a theory of learning and instruction predicated on the assertion that learners could not be separated from the cultural, historical, and social context of what they were learning, and that learning resulted from interactions.

He coined the phrase *zone of proximal development,* defined as "the distance between the actual development as determined by independent problem solving and the level of potential development as determined through problem solving under adult guidance or in collaboration with more capable peers" (1978, p. 86). Think about times when you were frustrated by a task because it was simply too difficult. Now, think of times, perhaps in school, when you had to complete assignments or solve problems that were extremely easy for you. Neither scenario is good for the learner. Vygotsky recognized that "what the child can do in cooperation today he can do alone tomorrow" (1962, p. 104). The teacher's responsibility is to assess where the student is and to *scaffold* instruction so that what is being taught is beyond the student's independent level, but not so far beyond that it can't be done with assistance. To understand the concept of scaffolding, think of the image of a scaffold on a building, providing support for as long as it is needed; you can help students stretch, grow, and accept academic challenges that are within their reach providing they have the resources to support their efforts.

Scaffolding is not an easy task, but when teachers teach to the middle, neither the high achievers nor the struggling readers are being taught in their zone of proximal development. When you provide a range of materials and options for students, and let them have some choice in selecting what materials they will use and how they will achieve goals, you can teach them to find materials that are within the range that is right for them (Fink, 2006; Roller, 1996).

There are many ways you can organize your courses and lessons to put Vygotsky's ideas into practice. Casey (2008/2009) describes a seventh-grade classroom organized around the concept of *learning clubs,* consisting of groups of students who have chosen to explore various topics within the curriculum and/or connecting to issues relating to the community in which they live. Often, "students are engaged in a conversation that invites critical thinking instead of a presentation focused on decoding and describing. This remains consistent for the struggling readers" (p. 289). Casey concludes, "Learning clubs have the potential to be a powerful vehicle for motivating engaged and interested learners across content areas to use literacy to build learning" (p. 293). Think about ways that potential can be fulfilled in your classroom!

You will be able to think of ways to use Vygotsky's theory as you design your courses and plan the instruction of your curricular content. Collaborative groups, peer tutoring, and projects involving social interaction are all appropriate and helpful. Many of the strategies and instructional methods introduced and developed in the next section stress the social nature of learning.

CLASSROOM PRACTICES INVOLVING THE AFFECTIVE AND SOCIAL DOMAINS

In *Beyond Numeracy: Ruminations of a Numbers Man* (1991), author John Allen Paulos, during what he calls a "mathematical stream of consciousness," made connections between what he saw while driving into New York City one day with mathematical concepts such as averages, logic, probability, and estimation. He concludes:

> For most non-scientists, what's most important in science education is not the imparting of any particular set of facts (although I don't mean to denigrate factual knowledge) but the development of a scientific habit of mind: How would I test that? What's the evidence for it? How does this relate to other facts and principles? The same, I think, holds true in mathematics education. Remembering this formula or that theorem is less important for most people than is the ability to look at a situation quantitatively, to note logical, probabilistic, and spatial relationships, and to muse mathematically. (p. 6)

The same principle holds true for English, social studies, foreign language study, music, health studies, business, technology, physical education, and art. We content area teachers have the challenge of helping our students think in ways conducive to learning our respective subjects long after they have left our classes and may have forgotten what element follows zinc on the periodic table. It is the practices in our classrooms that can help us achieve the goal for our students that Paulos helps us visualize. Schoenbach et al. (2003) encourage teachers to use the model of apprenticeship as they help adolescents in their subject area classrooms develop habits and thinking patterns of practitioners in the disciplines. Make visible and discuss the cognitive strategies you yourself use as you tackle new texts in chemistry, political science, or art history; encourage students to try out these strategies and verbalize their comprehension processes.

> *"It is easier to enhance creativity by changing conditions in the environment than by trying to make people think more creatively."*
>
> **CSIKSZENTMIHALYI, 1996, P. 1**

Activities to Determine Student Interests

How do your students feel about algebra, or economics, or learning a foreign language, or art history, or poetry? And what are their attitudes about reading and writing, particularly in your subject area? Both questions elicit information that is important for you to know. Perhaps you have some students who are interested in American history but tell you they couldn't care less about world history. Or students who tell you they find all science boring, but they love to read novels for English class. Some students may like to read but resist writing, or vice versa. Whatever your students tell you about their interests relative to your subject, you can capitalize on the positives they bring with them and accept the challenge to change some of the negative perceptions they have.

Interest inventories

In the first part of this chapter, I discussed the important role student interest plays in the learning process. How should you go about finding out about your students' interests? Quintana (2001) found by using an interest inventory that, not surprisingly, Mexican immigrant students at the middle school level preferred texts that reflected Mexican culture. You can create your own inventory, asking the questions you want to know about. It could be as simple as having your math students write out answers to these questions:

1. What would you like me to know about you as a math student? Tell me anything that might help me know you as a learner and provide what you need to enjoy this class.
2. If you like math, try to explain why or tell me what really interests you about it. If you don't like math or are afraid of it, try to explain why and relate any negative experiences you have had with math in the past.

Figure 2.2 is an example of a teacher-constructed interest inventory intended to be given at the beginning of an eighth-grade science course.

Published inventories are also available. For example, Kear, Coffman, McKenna, et al. (2000) developed a Writing Attitude Survey that can be used throughout the grades, and they explain how the information gained can be used to plan instruction so that "effective teaching strategies and engaging opportunities to write successfully can make real inroads in student perspectives" (p. 15). Examples of questions in the survey include: "How would you feel writing a letter to the author of a book you read?" (p. 16), "How would you feel writing to someone to change their opinion?" (p. 17), and "How would you feel writing about something you did in science?" (p. 17).

Listening questions

One strategy all teachers should use, whether or not you also create an inventory, is to listen carefully to the students. You might ask a question before each day's lesson that elicits their concerns and hopes. Bruns (1992) recommends:

FIGURE 2.2 Sample interest inventory.

Help Me Get to Know You

Mathematics

Welcome to eighth-grade ~~science!~~ I love the physical sciences, and I hope you'll enjoy playing the role of my apprentices as we explore our curricular topics throughout the year. To help me understand where you stand and how you feel about science at this beginning point in our journey, please answer the following questions.

A. Place an X on each continuum to show how interested you are in the topic or activity:

	Passionate	Quite Interested	A Little Curious	Bored	Don't Know
Stars and outer space					
Under the oceans					
Rocks and minerals					
The working of machinery					
Chemistry experiments					
Energy and light					
Conservation of natural resources					

B. If you could meet any scientist, living or dead, and interview her or him, whom would you choose and what questions would you ask? If you don't want to name a specific person, choose a kind of scientist (medical researcher, industrial scientist, astronomer, geologist, climatologist, physicist, etc.) for this question.

C. Tell me anything you want me to know about your past experiences with science. Have you enjoyed some experiments in previous classes?

Do you read any scientific magazines or other texts at home?

Do you have a particular interest?

How do you think I can help you do well in this course?

 Find a print-friendly, classroom-ready version on the Kane Resource Site.

There is probably no better way to convey interest and nurturance than through listening. Most teacher–student social exchanges are momentary—just a few words and a smile. But sometimes the opportunity presents itself to be with a student in a situation that has nothing to do with schoolwork. Exploit such opportunities to be attentive to remarks about the student's interests. The act of really listening is a tremendous compliment and a powerful tool in building a relationship. (p. 43)

In *The Child's View of Reading: Understandings for Teachers and Parents* (1994), Michel presents a model interview with a child and gives suggestions for conducting informal interviews using what she calls *listening questions*. The objective of this questioning "is to have a conversation and be a good listener, rather than to conduct a question-and-answer exchange. The interviewer is not merely acquiring answers but also learning what questions are important to ask and how to ask them" (p. 24). Michel recommends being nondirective, and suggests that the adult's questions should be based on the students' remarks to bring out more from them. If you informally interview students often as they work, taking cues from them and asking questions about the process they are using as they discover information, compose, solve problems, respond to literature, or comprehend reading material, they become comfortable talking about their

thinking, attitudes, and working processes. These conversations will lead to increased knowledge for you about what and how to teach. Figure 2.3 shows an informal classroom conversation that exemplifies a high school teacher's use of listening questions.

Activities to Foster Motivated Reading and Learning

ACTION RESEARCH   **2.A**

Interview a teacher in your content area to find out how he motivates students to read and write. The interview can be very open-ended, going in whatever direction the teacher chooses, or you could use specific questions such as: "Do you read aloud to your students? Do you use pre-reading activities or anticipation guides? Do you give booktalks? How do you encourage students to read beyond the textbook? What kinds of reading do you do for pleasure?"

APPLICATION ACTIVITY   **2.1**   (SEE PAGE 56)

What you do in class to set a purpose for reading a text and to activate the students' conscious awareness of their attitudes and values relative to the topic

FIGURE   **2.3**   **Using listening questions.**

The following is a conversation between a health teacher and a group of students who have been reading books and articles about child abuse. Notice how the teacher uses listening questions.

Jessica: Angelo and I read *Tangerine* [Bloor, 1997] and we've talked about it, but we can't come up with an idea for our wall poster showing what it meant to us.

Mr. Peng: Mmmm. Did it mean the same thing to both of you?

Jessica: Well, it's such a boy's book!

Mr. Peng: (laughs) A boy's book?

Jessica: Yeah, Angelo loved it; it had the football star, it had violence, it had sibling abuse, it had boys as characters . . .

Ryan: Well, Manuel and I read *When She Was Good* [Mazer, 1999], and that had wicked bad sibling abuse, and death! And it had two girl characters, and we loved it.

Mr. Peng: Oh, thanks for that input! So it's not just the sex of the characters that would make Jessica think that a book might appeal more to boys?

Jessica: Well, actually, I have to admit that I kind of liked *Tangerine,* too. And it did make me think about how sibling abuse would change the whole family. Like, how could those

parents not have told Paul the truth about what Eric did to him when he was little?

Mr. Peng: You found that unrealistic?

Angelo: No, think about it. If they admitted the truth, they'd have to report their own kid for a crime! And once they started the lying, it was harder and harder to get back to the truth. They probably rationalized that covering up would be better. Then Paul wouldn't grow up hating his brother, you know? I mean we as readers know they're wrong, but they're in the middle of a really messed up situation.

Jessica: I think I have an idea for our poster. You know Paul's thick glasses? I think they're kind of symbolic. I think Paul might actually be the *least* blind member of that whole family. The parents are choosing not to see the trouble Eric's in, everyone is blind to what a great kid Paul is and the talents he has. . . .

Angelo: Cool! I like it!

Mr. Peng: Sounds like you're building from each other's ideas. Go for it!

has enormous potential to enhance motivation and a willingness to engage with the author's ideas. Following are several strategies for preparing students to read and write.

Anticipation guides

Throughout this book, there are anticipation guide examples that can fulfill the purpose of engaging students' minds in preparation for content area reading and learning. They don't have to be elaborate. Imagine a teacher getting students ready for reading selections by popular young adult fiction writer Robert Cormier. She might have questions she asks students to reflect on in writing before they begin. Before assigning *The Chocolate War* (1986), she might ask them to respond to one of the following prompts: "Can there be evil, immorality, or unethical behavior within a school administration? What should students do if they discover this?" or, "Do I dare disturb the universe?" In another case, she could ask students to brainstorm situations where a person might have to start life over with a new identity (e.g., participants in a witness protection program or a person fleeing from the Nazis during the Holocaust), and then to imagine what it would be like to have to reject or hide your past and learn to live with a new name, family, country, and so on. This prepares the students to read Cormier's *I Am the Cheese* (1977).

Figure 2.4 shows an activity a preservice math teacher designed for her students to complete before they received their course textbooks and is another example of an anticipation guide. Chapter 4 contains additional samples and guidelines for creating other types of reading guides.

FIGURE 2.4 A reading guide for a lesson on life applications of mathematics.

RATIONALE: High school mathematics students often ask, "Why do we need to know this?" and "When are we ever going to use this outside school?" Many students believe that if what they are taught has no relevance to their lives, then there is no real reason for learning it. It is important that teachers help students make connections between mathematics and activities and contexts beyond the school setting.

DIRECTIONS FOR STUDENTS: You are to complete the mind map provided. Take a few minutes to brainstorm about ways math might be used outside of school settings before writing anything down. If you need help, refer to the following website:

www.maa.org/careers/index.html

I've also provided a word bank at the bottom of the page that may offer further ideas or suggestions for filling in the mind map. If you can successfully explain your answers, you do not have to worry about being wrong.

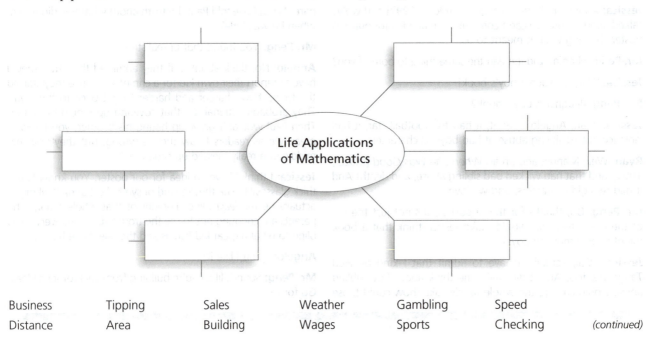

| Business | Tipping | Sales | Weather | Gambling | Speed |
| Distance | Area | Building | Wages | Sports | Checking |

(continued)

Oral reading

The following sections provide suggestions and guidelines for student and teacher read-alouds.

Student read-alouds.

ACTIVATING PRIOR KNOWLEDGE   2.4

Think for a moment about those times in high school or elementary school when your teacher may have instructed you to open to Chapter 5 of your science textbook. He began calling on people to read a few paragraphs at a time. Before your turn, what were you doing? After your turn, what did you do? How well did this classroom activity help you comprehend the material? Do you remember any amusing or embarrassing moments connected with this procedure? Reflect in writing for a moment.

At various times, I ask my education students to take turns reading orally. I use an encyclopedia entry on Africa, and I give no purpose for the reading or any background to set the stage. I simply start asking people to read. It's not long before I notice students trying to figure out my pattern of calling on people. They read a bit ahead to practice those hard names of places and rivers that are listed. After they have a turn, they relax and may start looking at the pictures or out the window; they're very surprised if I call on them again before everyone else has had a turn—that's against the unwritten rules of the game! Virtually everyone who has gone to school can identify with this: Linguist Stephen Krashen wrote, "I do remember reading ahead while the rest of the class was taking turns reading out loud, and so not knowing the place when the teacher called on me" (Rosenthal, 1995, p. 179).

After a few (usually deadly) minutes of this *round-robin reading,* I ask the students to write down

---

FIGURE   **2.4**   **Continued.**

Once you've finished the mind map, reflect on these concluding questions:

1. Did this reading guide help you to gain a better understanding of the uses of math outside the classroom? Explain.
2. Please give me some feedback on the type of graphic organizer, or mind map, used here. Did you like the use of this visual to increase your thinking and brainstorming skills? Were there any advantages to this approach? Disadvantages?

FOLLOW UP: Now check out some of the resources on our display table. Perhaps you'd like to borrow *Careers for Number Crunchers and Other Quantitative Types* (Burnett, 2002), *Cool Careers Without College for Math and Science Wizards* (Burnett, 2002), *Career Ideas for Kids Who Like Math and Money* (Reeves, 2007), or *McGraw-Hill's Careers for Geniuses and Other Gifted Types* (Goldberg, 2008). Or, explore the website www.maa.org/careers/index.html or explore another site about math careers to tell your classmates about.

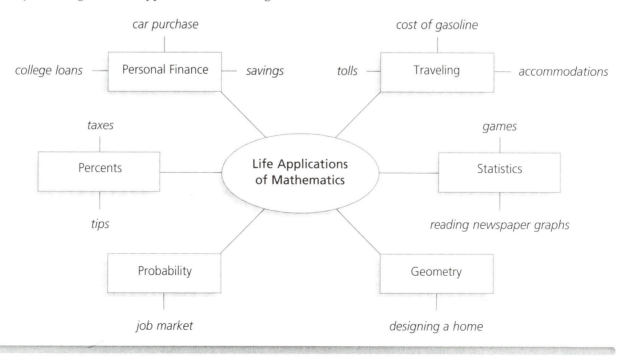

all they recall from the passage. The results are abysmal, but the mini-fiasco offers us an opportunity to debrief. Some students share that they were so anxious about being called on that they couldn't direct their energy toward comprehending the text either before or during their turn. Others got bored with classmates who stumbled or mumbled. The pace of the activity was right for no one. We couldn't think of anything good to say about this instructional method. So, why do teachers use it? We conclude that it's easy (though teachers will also admit to boredom while listening to students read) and it's what has come to be expected all too often.

This doesn't mean that student oral reading doesn't have its place in content classrooms. Good oral reading is a wonderful skill for people to cultivate. But in almost every setting where oral reading is required, with the exception of school, we do not expect people to read aloud in front of people from material they were just handed. Reading silently first is a help. Then, if a teacher or the students think the reinforcement of hearing the material might be beneficial, partners or small groups could form. Everyone gets more practice that way, and students can actually *hear* their classmates—not always the case when a class of 28 is participating in round-robin reading, especially if the desks are in rows and you can't even see the person who is reading.

Certain materials lend themselves to oral reading. Students may at times choose to read something aloud to the class, perhaps a text they've composed or selected. Certainly play scripts are meant to be read aloud, and students usually enjoy taking part and playing with their voices and roles. Poetry can be appreciated if it's read aloud to the whole class, with expression and appropriate tone. But for reading content area material in class, my usual recommendation is silent reading followed by partner reading. When pairs of students read aloud to each other, alternating turns, they can hear and help each other.

Teacher read-alouds. *Teacher read-alouds* are effective in terms of motivation and learning (e.g., Lesesne, 2006; Rycik & Irvin, 2005).

Teaching in action: *Math.* Imagine a math teacher beginning a lesson on word problems by rapidly reading this excerpt from *The Phantom Tollbooth:*

> If a small car carrying three people at thirty miles an hour for ten minutes along a road five miles long at 11:35 in the morning starts at the same time as three people who have been traveling in a little automobile at twenty miles an hour for fifteen minutes on another road exactly twice as long as one half the distance of the other, while a dog, a bug, and a boy travel an equal distance in the same time or the same distance in an equal time along a third

road in mid-October, then which one arrives first and which is the best way to go? (1996, p. 174)

The teacher, of course, reads the problem in such a way as to let the students know it's a *parody* of the word problems they will encounter. She laughs along with the students and assures them that no problem on a test will be that complicated and cumbersome; yet, she actually uses the problem to teach students how to discriminate between relevant and irrelevant data. In authentic contexts, situations can indeed be complicated and many-faceted, and problem solvers may have to consider a lot of input. Doctors, military leaders, teachers, inventors, lawyers, machinists, and parents can attest to that.

Richardson (1994) bemoans the resistance to read-alouds that secondary teachers exhibit, and shows how reading aloud can be fun and beneficial both affectively and cognitively. She measured her tenth graders' interest by noting their increased attention span and appreciative comments, and found that test responses to those questions based on the read-alouds were better than other responses. Richardson promotes the use of read-alouds that are integrated into lessons, not presented as an added, extraneous activity. Reassure high school students that read-alouds are not "baby stuff" by explaining the strategy in the context of their lesson objectives.

Richardson recommends that the major resource for finding read-alouds be the teacher's personal reading. She also suggests newspapers and magazines, as well as sources offered by librarians and professional organizations (e.g., International Reading Association). She has authored several articles that give concrete suggestions of materials and ways to use them as read-alouds (see Figure 2.5).

FIGURE 2.5

Resources for read-alouds in middle and secondary content area classrooms.

See more suggested titles in Appendix Figure 2.5.

Bircher, L. S. (2009). Reading Aloud: A Springboard to Inquiry. *Science Teacher, 76*(5), 29–33.

Laminack, L. L. (2006). *Reading Aloud Across the Curriculum: How to Build Bridges in Language Arts, Math, Science, and Social Studies.* Portsmouth, NH: Heinemann.

McDonnell, C. (2010). What Makes a Good Read-Aloud for Middle Graders? *The Horn Book Magazine, LXXXVI*(1), 66–73.

McQuillan, K. (2009). Teacher Reading Aloud. *Principal Leadership: Middle Level Edition, 9*(9), 30–31.

Trelease, J. (2006). *The Read-Aloud Handbook.* New York: Penguin Books.

Preservice and beginning teachers often venture out of their comfort zone when first reading aloud to students. I recommend the following:

- Start with a story or text you truly find interesting; this will be apparent to your students.
- Practice reading the text aloud to friends or family, or into a recorder, before you try it on the audience that matters.
- Aim for vivid expression, avoid a monotone, and be sure to make eye contact as often as possible with your listeners.
- Ask your students if your tone and your pacing are right for them. You may need to consciously slow down and enunciate.
- Don't be afraid to play if the text offers opportunities for using different voices for characters, or dramatic exclamations.
- Experiment with a variety of genres.

APPLICATION ACTIVITY **2.2** (SEE PAGE 56)

Literary field trips for the content areas

You probably entered the field you are teaching because of a love for or a fascination with your subject area. Your students, however, may not come to you with an inherent interest in the subject matter, and some may even resist learning any academic topics. So, as you plan to teach your curriculum, you'll have to figure out ways to pique their interest. There are many ways to motivate students, including hands-on experiences, guest speakers, and field trips—things that make a subject come alive and make the students part of the real experience. You probably can't take your students on too many field trips—you'll be constrained by geography, time, finances. But you can go anywhere in place or time with the help of literature, primary documents, and a strategy I call *literary field trips*. Figure 2.6 presents possible literary field trips for different content areas, and the following are guidelines for preparing a content area literary field trip:

1. Choose a place or location relevant to a content area lesson you are preparing.
2. Select book(s), websites, and/or other materials relevant to the lesson.
3. Brainstorm what a student might expect to find there.
4. Divide students into groups and have them prepare questions for their "tour guide."
5. Have the groups "tour" the location by reading.
6. Ask students to prepare a summary of the highlights of their tour, explaining what they

BookTalk Online **2.6**

Joyful Noise: Poems for Two Voices by Paul Fleischman (www.paulfleischman.net) and illustrator Eric Beddows (1988) offers students the chance to perform the poems with partners while learning about entomology. Read more at the Kane Resource Site.

learned about the location and its related content area subject.

7. Have students plot their journeys on a map and/or timeline.
8. Discuss where the students' inquiry can go from here, and what other resources they might "tour" next to learn about the topic in more depth and answer any remaining or new questions.

Teaching in action: *History.* Come along as American history teacher Ms. Maina applies the strategy. Ms. Maina is about to begin a unit on the Civil Rights movement. Last year she struggled with the first few lessons because her students were memorizing terms like *Jim Crow laws, desegregation,* and *bus boycott,* but not really appreciating the courage of the people who worked for justice and equality. So this year, she spent part of her limited materials budget to purchase 10 paperback copies of *The National Civil Rights Museum Celebrates Everyday People* by Alice Faye Duncan (1995). As an introduction to her Civil Rights unit, she announces to the class that they will be visiting the National Civil Rights Museum. She asks if anyone knows where it is located. Students guess Washington, DC; Atlanta; Montgomery. She affirms their hypotheses as logical possibilities, then asks them to brainstorm a list of things they might expect to see there. A student volunteer compiles a list as students call them out: Rosa Parks' bus, stuff from the March on Washing-

BookTalk **2.7**

The year is 1949. Two sixth-grade softball teams meet on the field. What makes this particular game unique is that on one team is a girl whose family spent the war years imprisoned in a Japanese internment camp. On the opposing team is a girl whose father was killed during the attack on Pearl Harbor. Multiple narrators tell their perspectives of the fateful game in Virginia Euwer Wolff's *Bat 6* (1998). This book could be read aloud in class, with students taking on the voices and personas of the players.

FIGURE **2.6** **Opening lines for literary field trips for various content areas.**

AMERICAN HISTORY: We're going to take a funny tour through pre-Revolutionary War years with Lane Smith's picture book *John, Paul, George, & Ben* (2006). Who can guess the last names of the title characters?

ENGLISH LANGUAGE ARTS: Henry David Thoreau, as we've learned, loved nature, loved simplicity, and loved to walk. Today we're going to walk with him as I read aloud *Henry Hikes to Fitchburg* by D. B. Johnson (2000). Get your pencils ready, because you'll be doing some calculating along the way.

ART: Now that you've learned a bit about photography and taken some pictures on our nature walk around campus, I invite you to take a literary walk with a great artist through this book I found: *Ansel Adams: America's Photographer* by Beverly Gehrman (2002). Get ready for some mental hiking—we're heading to Yosemite.

SENIOR HUMANITIES: You've done some exciting adventuring with Odysseus during his years of travel returning from the Trojan War. I offer this book to anyone who wants to travel again to that time, but with different companions—female companions. Let's go with Penelope, Helen, the sorceress Circe, and the goddess Athena. The adventure might look a little different with our new guides waiting for us in *Waiting for Odysseus* by Clemence McClaren (2000).

GLOBAL STUDIES: Ok, so we've heard the statistics and studied the graph about the rise of HIV and AIDS in sub-Saharan Africa. What does this mean for the children and for families? Two books are going to take us into this land, and into the hearts of the people. The first is a novel, *Chanda's Secrets,* by Allan Stratton (2004). Our narrator will tell us about the multiple worries of caring for a sick mother, raising her younger siblings, struggling to get an education, and dealing with the stigma attached to the disease. The second is the informational text *Our Stories, Our Songs: African Children Talk About AIDS* by Deborah Ellis (2005). You'll see photographs of the kids who will tell us their personal stories. Let's go meet Chanda first.

EARTH SCIENCE: Class, today we are going into the volcano, literally. Well, ok, what I really mean is that we're going literally *Into the Volcano,* with this book by Donna O'Meara that's subtitled *A Volcano Researcher at Work* (2005). Will it be a safe trip? I'll read you a few lines to give you an idea:

> I was sandwiched between a raging sea cliff on the right and a sacred temple on the left. If I hoped to find out what was causing the pink cloud, there was only one way to go. . . . I ran across the smoking tops of the lava tubes as if my life depended on it. Because it did! (pp. 19–20)

MUSIC: We've gone on a number of literary and audio field trips so far this semester. Last week, you found you liked going to the opera better than many of you thought you would when we looked through and read parts of *The Young Person's Guide to the Opera* (Ganeri & Barber, 2001). This week we're going to travel back to explore the origins, roots, and development of rap and hip-hop in C. Lonnel's *The History of Rap Music* (2001). Let's listen to an example of a rap song that's popular right now to get us psyched for the journey.

---

ton, drinking fountains with signs saying "White Only" and "Negro," a copy of the speech "I Have a Dream" by Martin Luther King, Jr.

Ms. Maina proceeds to ask her students what questions they might ask a tour guide at the museum. Students think they'd like to know what the beginning and ending dates of the Civil Rights movement are, what the museum contains on Malcolm X, and what it is like working at the museum. They are ready to head out.

Ms. Maina explains that they are going on a literary field trip and should stay with their groups of three. As they explore the museum and the Civil Rights movement through their reading, they can talk among themselves, ask new questions, and respond to the pictures and text freely. She passes out a copy of Duncan's book to each group and allows class time for the students to explore it.

After about 20 minutes, Ms. Maina directs the groups to take a sheet of paper, fold it in half lengthwise, and label the two columns "What we learned about the National Civil Rights Museum," and "What we learned about the Civil Rights movement." Students have no trouble filling up both sides of the paper. They learned, for example, that the museum is located in Memphis, Tenn., in the former Lorraine Motel, where Martin Luther King, Jr. was assassinated. It is designed as a hands-on museum: visitors can feel the bars of a replica of a Birmingham jail cell, crowd into a holding cell modeled after the ones where arrested protesters were kept, get in a bus like the one Rosa Parks rode. They can touch statues of strikers, marchers, and students at restaurant sit-ins. Visitors can stand on the very balcony where Martin Luther King, Jr. was shot. The readers in Ms. Maina's class saw photographs of students participating in an active tour through the museum and read captions about the exhibits. In the second column, they list many things they learned about the Civil Rights movement. They note the powerful photographs of Rosa Parks being fingerprinted after her act of protest, lunch counter demonstrators sitting peacefully as white customers poured mustard and sugar on their heads, a burned bus, bruised faces, attack dogs being turned on marchers, the Little Rock Nine walking into Central High and leaving later in caps and gowns.

Ms. Maina's room is noisy as students express disbelief and dismay at some of the knowledge they gained on their literary field trip. They are poised to continue with the unit. The strategy served to help the students begin to learn content at the same time it provided motivation for learning. Throughout the rest of the unit, Ms. Maina lectures and gives notes, guides them through a textbook chapter, encourages independent research, and uses a variety of other teaching strategies. One strategy includes visiting the National Civil Rights Museum's website (www. civilrightsmuseum.org) and taking a virtual tour via the Internet. They can then compare the information found there with that in the book and discuss what processes they used to navigate and comprehend each source.

Once students understand the concept of traveling through time and space via literary and Internet field trips, they can map where they've been—post maps and have the students pin strips of paper on the spots their reading material took them to. They can do the same on a timeline. For example, after reading *Hiroshima* (Hersey, 1946), students can make two strips listing the title and author, pinning one on the appropriate area of Japan on the map and the other at the appropriate point on the timeline they've made to record their literary journeys.

APPLICATION ACTIVITY   2.3   (SEE PAGE 56)

Learning centers

Learning centers offer a unique way for students to work independently or in small groups to explore resources and complete projects related to their curricular topics. The teacher designs the activities and assignments, then facilitates as students make choices, investigate texts, synthesize information, write up reactions and findings, and/or compose a creative piece. Rules and instructions are often posted on large charts, and materials (e.g., texts, paints, craft supplies, tools) are organized and displayed. There can be more than one center in operation simultaneously, and one advantage of centers is that they can free the teacher to work with individuals needing extra or different kinds of instruction while other students are engaged at the learning stations (Ford & Opitz, 2002). Figure 2.7 provides sample assignments that could be part of a learning center on Edgar Allan Poe for an American Literature class.

Following are suggestions for setting up a learning center:

1. Designate a certain area of the classroom as the learning center.
2. Provide a variety of fiction/nonfiction and print/nonprint materials in various genres and at various levels of reading difficulty that focus on a particular topic, theme, or author.
3. Offer students the option of working on suggested assignments or projects of their own.
4. Provide clear directions so that students can work on projects independently.
5. Allow one group to work in each learning center while you work with other students.

Types of learning centers appropriate for content area classrooms include:

- Listening center
- Viewing center: television and DVD player or computer with DVD capabilities, copies of movies, television shows
- Researching center: reference materials, note-taking suggestions, and computers with access to the Internet for website research
- Writing/publishing center
- Project/art center: materials for science experiments, solving math problems, creating collages or murals

Teaching in action: *History.* To see a learning center classroom in action, let's stay with Ms. Maina's class for a while. After the whole class experienced the virtual tour of the National Civil Rights Museum via the book *Everyday People,* she spent several days teaching structured lessons on the Civil Rights movement. Now, she feels the students are ready for some independent exploration. So, she introduces them to her learning center, which she set up in the back of her room at a circular table. There are books representing a variety of genres and levels of difficulty, and sets of directions for assignments. Students can choose from the suggestions or design an independent project of their own. Along the side of the room, there are several computers, and some of the requirements or options

FIGURE 2.7 Poe learning center sample assignments.*

This is our culminating activity for this unit; therefore, it is worth 50 percent of your unit grade. This is a great place to raise your grade with a fun assignment! For this center, you will choose from three options. First, however, you must decide if you prefer to work alone, in a small group of 2 to 3, or with up to 6 in a group. Please look over all of the choices before you decide, because there won't be time to change your mind later.

CHOICE 1. Found Poetry (if you wish to work alone)

Choose your favorite poem/work of Edgar Allan Poe and turn it into "Found Poetry" just as we did a few weeks ago. You must illustrate and/or decorate your final copy with the supplies on the table to receive full credit. Be sure your poem is creative and reflects the same tone as Poe. Also, make sure your decorations appropriately reflect the details in your poem. If you would like to use clip art please use http://office.microsoft.com/en-us/images. NOTE: Before you begin, please refer to the rubric (Figure 2.8) to make sure you complete the assignment as required.

CHOICE 2. Newspaper (if you prefer to work in a group of 2 to 3 students)

Form a small newspaper staff to create a two-page newspaper that reflects the time period in which Poe wrote.

Materials: Microsoft Publisher or Word, color printer, and Internet access. For clip art, please use http://office.microsoft.com/en-us/images.

CONTENT IDEAS:

- Pictures from time period (types of transportation, houses)
- Information on social activities in the community
- Seasonal highlights (weather, harvest info, health concerns)
- Advertisements
- Economic news
- Letters to the editor (example at center)
- Poetry/literary entry

NOTE: Please refer to the rubric (Figure 2.9) to ensure you include all required elements.

CHOICE 3. Pop-Up Book (if you prefer to work in a group of up to 6)

For this project, students will work in groups. Each group will select a subject for their pop-up book from the list on the following page, and each group member should be responsible for one page. Each student will complete his or her "page" individually before the next class. Students may stay after school with me if necessary to complete their page. Then, next block, groups will work together to put "finishing touches" on and assemble their book. When decorating the individual pages, use any of the supplies on the table: stickers, clip art (http://office.microsoft.com/en-us/images), markers, ribbon, glue, and scissors. Be sure to add details, research your information, and let your creative juices flow! NOTE: Please refer to the rubric (Figure 2.10) to ensure you include all required items.

Edgar Allan Poe's life timeline pop-up book

Visit www.poemuseum.org, http://bau2.uibk.ac.at/sg/poe/poe.html, or www.comnet.ca/~forrest/. On these sites you will be able to locate information about Poe's life and works.

Because there are inconsistencies in reports of Poe's life/death, it is important to know the order of events. If we know the order in which events occurred, we may be able to surmise how these events may have impacted Poe's works. Create at least one illustration to go along with each of the major events in Poe's life/career. Publishing date of popular titles may be marked in the same way. Be creative. All text should be typed for your page.

Edgar Allan Poe's literary work pop-up book

For this page, you can choose from the four works listed below. Choose the one that you feel you can write about and illustrate the best. For this page, be sure to include a brief narrative of the short story or poem, the theme, mood or tone, and the resolution. Make sure your illustrations and decorations on the page match these devices. Be sure to include in some way the names of major characters or other items significant to the story. All writing should be typed. Be creative and use the supplies to your advantage. Remember, color is important!

The Pit and the Pendulum   *The Tell-Tale Heart*
The Masque of the Red Death *The Raven*

* Created by Renée Warren.

FIGURE **2.8** Found poetry rubric.

	5 PTS.	4 PTS.	3 PTS.	2 PTS.
Creativity: Uses all supplies and resources with wide variety of color and texture	Uses supplies well. Includes wide variety of texture and color to enhance poem mood.	Uses many supplies with some variety of colors and textures.	Uses limited number of colors and textures.	Uses little to no color and very few supplies and textures.
Relates illustrations and graphics to "poem" chosen	Graphics are related to the theme/purpose of the poem, are of high quality, and enhance reader interest.	Graphics are related to the theme/purpose of the poem and are of high quality.	Graphics are related to the theme/purpose of the poem and are of good quality.	Graphics seem randomly chosen, are of low quality, OR distract the reader.
Represents or corresponds to original theme	Original theme and characters are represented clearly and enhance reader interest.	Original theme and characters are represented.	Original theme and characters are not represented. Not well thought out.	Only the theme OR characters are represented. Not organized.
Spelling, punctuation, and grammar	There are no spelling, punctuation, or grammar errors.	There are 1–3 spelling, punctuation, or grammar errors.	There are 4–5 spelling, punctuation, or grammar errors.	There are more than 5 spelling, punctuation, or grammar errors.
Narrative Poe style	Clearly imitates Poe's style through use of literary devices.	Uses many literary devices, does reflect Poe's work.	Some literary devices used, has minimal reflection on Poe's work.	Few if any symbols of Poe's work.

TOTAL X 2 =

FIGURE **2.9** Newspaper rubric.

	5 PTS.	4 PTS.	3 PTS.	2 PTS.
Connections to society —deals with all aspects of life	Includes representations from all aspects of life.	Includes many aspects of life.	Includes few different aspects of life.	Includes limited variation of aspects of life.
Creativity: Uses all supplies provided; includes COLOR	Has great balance of colors, pictures, variety of fonts, layout is pleasing to the eye.	Has good color, variations of fonts, some photos, is pleasing to the eye.	Minimal color and variation, one picture, balance and organization are off.	No color or pictures. Layout is awkward, obviously rushed.
Content: A successful paper has 6 items listed; others encouraged	Minimum of 6 items included, with extra topics also.	Only the 6 items are included.	3–5 of required items are included and no extras.	1–3 of required items listed and no extra topics.
Mechanics of grammar	There are no spelling, punctuation, or grammar errors.	There are 1–3 spelling, punctuation, or grammar errors.	There are 4–5 spelling, punctuation, or grammar errors.	There are more than 5 spelling, punctuation, or grammar errors.
Ability to work with peers	Worked equally on the project, worked cooperatively.	Project was completed but the partners did not work equally/cooperatively.	One partner did the majority of the work.	Did not work cooperatively, and with little participation.

TOTAL X 2 =

FIGURE   **2.10**   **Pop-up book rubric.**

	5 PTS.	4 PTS.	3 PTS.	2 PTS.
Creativity: Uses all supplies and resources with wide variety of color and textures	Uses supplies well. Includes wide variety of texture and color to represent page chosen.	Uses many supplies with variety of colors and textures.	Uses limited number of colors and textures.	Uses very little color and very few supplies.
Relates graphics to work chosen	Graphics relate to the theme/purpose of the book, are of high quality, and enhance reader interest.	Graphics relate to the theme/purpose of the book, are of good quality, and enhance reader interest.	Graphics relate to the theme/purpose of the book and are of good quality.	Graphics seem randomly chosen, are of low quality, OR distract the reader.
Major characters represented	The main characters are named and clearly described in text and pictures.	The main characters are named and described, but not pictured.	The main characters are named. The reader knows very little about characters.	It is hard to tell who the main characters are.
Spelling, punctuation, and grammar	There are no spelling, punctuation, or grammar errors.	There are 1–3 spelling, punctuation, or grammar errors.	There are 4–5 spelling, punctuation, or grammar errors.	There are more than 5 spelling, punctuation, or grammar errors.
Summary of work	Includes all of the important events that occur.	Includes most of the important events, but misses 2 or 3 points.	Includes most of the important events, but highlights unimportant points.	Includes some of the important events, but info is incomplete or not focused.

TOTAL X 2 =

for the center involve searching websites, including that of the National Civil Rights Museum. Figure 2.11 lists some of the resources at the learning center.

Project suggestions in Ms. Maina's learning center might include the following:

1. Read one novel by Mildred Taylor. Fill in the wall chart about the Logan family (see Figure 2.12) in the appropriate column. When we finish the chart, we will be able to trace the highlights of the Logan family's saga over the course of several years!

2. Read *The Story of Ruby Bridges* by Robert Coles (1995) and the memoir *Through My Eyes* by Ruby Bridges (1999), then watch the video *Ruby Bridges*. In a review intended for our school literary magazine, compare and contrast the artwork, the ways the information is presented, and the emotional impact of these three nonfiction works.

3. Choose several of Langston Hughes's poems and discuss them in relation to the things you learned about the civil rights movement from your textbook and other sources.

4. Explore Internet sites and recent issues of newspapers and magazines to find examples of

ongoing work for civil rights and social justice. Create a collage or other art project, or write a letter or story that represents your response to the issues and events you learned about.

FIGURE   **2.11**

Resources for a learning center on the Civil Rights movement.

See more suggested titles in Appendix Figure 2.11.

Adamson, H. (2009). *The Civil Rights Movement: An Interactive History Adventure*. Mankato, MN: Capstone Press.

Brimner, L. D. (2010). *Birmingham Sunday*. Honesdale, PA: Calkins Creek.

Mayer, R. H. (2008). *When the Children Marched: The Birmingham Civil Rights Movement*. Berkeley Heights, NJ: Enslow Publishers.

McMullan, M. (2010). *Sources of Light*. Boston: Houghton Mifflin.

Turck, M. C. (2008). *Freedom Song: Young Voices and the Struggle for Civil Rights*. Chicago: Chicago Review Press.

FIGURE **2.12** **Sample wall chart.**

	ROLL OF THUNDER	SONG OF THE TREES	LET THE CIRCLE BE UNBROKEN	THE ROAD TO MEMPHIS	THE LAND
What years are covered in the book?					
What is the status of the land?					
What conflicts do the family members face?					
How does a main character change or grow?					
What examples of racial prejudice are there?					
What examples of racial harmony and/or social justice are there?					

When you design a learning center, there are many possible ways to use it. Because the purpose is to encourage independent exploration, as well as creativity, make sure your directions are clear so the students can proceed with their reading, writing, and art projects without too much assistance (although you should certainly let them know that they can use you and their peers as needed). You can allow pairs of students or small groups to collaborate on the assignments. One group at a time could use the center while you work on different aspects of a unit with others. Or you could have more than one center set up at a time—the students can either choose a center in line with their interests or rotate through them according to your directions. The center could contain works of a single author instead of works around a theme. A center might be interdisciplinary, and perhaps be housed in a hall or library. A core team of English, math, social studies, and science teachers could create project ideas using a biography theme, with books representing heroes and masters from all of the disciplines. The English focus might be on the writing style and structure of the books, as well as on character development. Science, social studies, and math teachers can create questions to help students think about the inventions or accomplishments of the profiled people and draw attention to the content knowledge that can be gained and constructed as students read several choices.

Rewards and reinforcements as motivators

I find when I talk with teachers that the discussion of motivation very often gets intertwined with talk of an extrinsic reward system. This association of rewards with motivation is also evident in articles I read in my local newspaper every few weeks about schools where the students met the goals of a special reading program. One article reported that a principal kissed a pig after her students read an agreed-upon number of books, while other articles described a principal who ate a worm and one who took fourth graders (the class with the most books read) to McDonald's in a limousine. If you listen in on many classrooms on any given day, you may hear the teacher remind students of the consequences of doing (not doing) work. For example, studying hard should result in better grades, which should result in more options for college; understanding this math principle is crucial to understanding next week's topic; final exams are coming; standardized test results are crucial; if everyone's homework is handed in, we can go outside. The intentions behind reward systems are usually good. However, Alfie Kohn (1998) presents a somber warning about such rewards, along with the excessive use of grades, test scores, or competition, which can lead students to value reading less. He exhorts teachers to:

Steer clear of reading incentives, particularly in the form of corporate programs like "Book It," which attempts to train kids to open books by dangling pizzas in front of them. Worse still is something called "Accelerated Reader." Not only does it get kids to think that the objective of reading is to earn points and prizes, and not only does it limit the number of books that will "count," but it makes students answer superficial, fact-based questions about each text to prove they've read it, thereby changing—for the worse—not only why they read but also how they read. (p. 171)

What about praise? Is that a good motivator and reinforcer? It depends. Holt (1989) warns that continued praise, even when given with the positive intention of increasing self-esteem, can be destructive and actually decrease self-confidence. "I think of countless teenagers I have known who hated themselves despite having been praised all their lives. . . . Many children are both cynical about praise and dependent on it, the worst possible mixture" (p. 140). Warning that any kind of external motivation, positive or negative, submerges or displaces internal motivation, he advocates giving students thoughtful attention as they work rather than praise.

Internal motivators, on the other hand, are developed when people participate in goal setting and problem solving (Howard, 2000, p. 657). For example, Moss and Hendershot (2002) learned from a study of middle school students that some who had been unmotivated became motivated when they were allowed to select what they read, and when they could read nonfiction as opposed to fiction.

We'll deal with grades as motivators in Chapter 10, which focuses on assessment. For now, I'd like to encourage you to rely on internal motivators and on the interesting, sometimes enticing, texts themselves as much as possible. Many a reader can attest to reading being its own reward because texts give us the knowledge we seek and invite us deeper into the realms of intellectual treasure. Biochemist and Stanford professor Ronald Davis, discusses curiosity as a motivator for reading:

> You read science for how things are put together. . . . My interest in chemistry just came—it started with my interest in airplanes in grade school . . . that quickly converted to propellant systems in seventh and eighth grades. . . . I became fascinated with nitrogen chemistry. So the way to understand that was to start reading chemistry books. So I got organic chemistry textbooks. (Fink, 1995/96, p. 275)

Gambrell (1996) offers a "reward proximity hypothesis: the closer the reward to the desired behavior (for example, books to reading), the greater the likelihood that intrinsic motivation will increase." How sensible.

Motivating all students

You may find that you have students who seem to remain unmotivated and distant despite your best efforts at interesting them and inviting them into your field of study. There are many possible reasons for

BookTalk Online 🎙 2.8

The Passionate Teacher (2001) and *The Passionate Learner* (2001), both by Robert L. Fried, explore the philosophy that caring is at the heart of learning. Hear more at the Kane Resource Site.

such a case, and each student might require a different course of action on your part. If something outside school is causing the difficulty (e.g., problems at home, lack of sleep, or the need to work a part-time job), then your role might be listening to the student, sympathizing with her obstacles, and suggesting resources or support personnel who can help alleviate the situations preventing the student from committing energy to academic growth. At times a student's distaste for your subject area could be the result of an earlier failure or a boring year of study preceding your class. Again, talking to the student, reassuring and encouraging him, coupled with practical suggestions of techniques or materials that will help him catch up and regain confidence, is in order.

Some of the brightest students you teach will be a challenge because they stopped learning during school hours due to the cumulative effect of boredom in too many classrooms for too many years. Lloyd (1998) offers suggestions that engage students at the top of the ability range without leaving the rest of your class behind. She provides examples of role-playing activities, individual research projects, and interdisciplinary explorations that can reawaken and stretch minds and help the students learn to go as far as they can in content area courses, rather than merely completing the minimum requirements and then stagnating.

Another challenge awaits you. Bruns (1992) reports on a phenomenon he calls *work inhibition*, involving students who have the intellectual capacity and other conditions necessary for succeeding academically yet "have extreme difficulty engaging in the work of school" (p. 38). Neither outstanding teachers nor parental support make a difference. Bruns' research shows that up to 20 percent of students may fit this picture. He found in his study that nearly three of every four work-inhibited students were boys, and that most had good cognitive abilities and above average thinking skills and were generally not disruptive in the classroom. The personality characteristics he found to be fairly common among work-inhibited students included dependency (they did the work if a teacher was sitting next to them), poor self-esteem, and passive aggression. A passive-aggressive child might want to please, but hidden

Just how passionate can one be about the activity of reading? Well, the title of Daniel Pennac's book, *Better Than Life* (1994), gives his answer. This reflection on how the passion for knowledge, language, and literacy can be shared discusses the potential damage that can occur as a result of reading being institutionalized as a school subject. But Pennac recognizes the power of a teacher: "It does happen that a student meets a teacher whose enthusiasm helps turn mathematics, for example, into a field of pure study, practically into a branch of the arts. . . . It is in the nature of living beings to love life, even in the form of a quadratic equation" (p. 92). One of the most popular parts of the book is "The Reader's Bill of Rights" (pp. 170–171). Pennac recommends that we grant to our students the same rights we exercise ourselves as readers, including the rights to skip pages, reread, read for escape, and abandon books. A version of his advice, *The Rights of the Reader* (2008), is comically illustrated by Quentin Blake.

anger might cause him to forget to do assignments or take seemingly forever to accomplish a task. What can teachers do to turn this behavior around? Bruns suggests building a nurturing relationship, listening, teaching strategies for completing tasks in incremental steps, recruiting volunteers to assist the student, providing effective feedback, creating a climate of encouragement, and empowering the student by promoting autonomy.

What about the students in our classes who are behind their peers in reading abilities, weak in decoding and/or comprehension skills, or struggling in other ways? Roller (1996) shows through her research and experience that workshop settings are ideal for offering variable instruction to variable children. While recognizing the difficulty of creating an environment where all students' efforts are nurtured and respected, regardless of how wide the range of abilities might be, Roller shows how the structure of a workshop classroom can allow for differentiation. "The choice that forms the base of the workshop assumes that everyone will read different material and write different stories and approach classroom themes in their own way. Choice is a powerful mechanism for accommodating variability" (p. 135).

Atwell (1991) documents how students with special needs can flourish in a workshop setting. She relates the story of one eighth grader, Laura, who spent the previous six years in a special education class,

whose skills and motivation were greatly enhanced once she joined Atwell's community of learners.

Atwell credited Laura with showing her Vygotsky's theories in action. In eighth grade, with the help of teacher and classmates in a workshop setting, she read 31 novels and completed 21 pieces of writing, spanning many genres. Atwell concludes:

> The environment marched ahead of Laura and led her. . . . Laura was surrounded by people writing and conferring and publishing, by high expectations, by good children's literature, by energy, commitment, and a willingness on the part of her teacher to be patient and give the time and response that special writers need. (p. 36)

Activities Involving Social Interaction

Cooperative learning

Cooperative learning is a set of related instructional strategies where students are grouped into learning teams for a set amount of time or assignments with the expectation that all students will contribute to the learning process and outcomes. The instructional strategies share three common attributes: team rewards, individual accountability, and equal opportunities for success for all students (Slavin, 1983). During the last several decades, researchers implemented and studied a number of techniques for cooperative learning, where students are given roles and assignments that require the cooperation of group members to achieve a learning goal. Research confirms that thinking becomes deeper and responses grow more complex when students are encouraged to defend positions, ponder, and listen during a discussion (Almasi, 1995).

Cooperative learning has been linked to increased academic achievement at all ability levels (Jenkins, Antil, Wayne, et al., 2003; Stevens, 2003; Vaughan, 2002). Vermette (1998) provides evidence that supports the positive effects of cooperative learning on achievement, as well as motivation and self-esteem. This is true for both genders and all ethnicities, and includes those students with various disabilities. Cooperative learning outcomes include retention, application and transfer of principles and concepts, verbal abilities, problem-solving abilities, creative ability, divergent thinking, productive controversy, awareness and utilization of individual capabilities, and the ability to understand and take on others' perspectives (Johnson & Johnson, 1999).

Many teachers have students working in small groups, but in order to qualify as cooperative learning, the criteria represented by the mnemonic PIGSS must be met:

- Positive interdependence (students must be able to work together);
- Individual accountability (each student is still assessed on what he or she knows);
- Group processes (a structure exists for how students will work together);
- Social skills (particular social skills are emphasized during group work);
- Specific tasks (students work together to achieve a particular goal) (Lasley, Matczynski, & Rowley, 2002).

In cooperative learning, the teacher's major roles are to

1. Specify the instructional objectives
2. Make pre-instructional decisions
3. Communicate the task
4. Set the assignment in motion
5. Monitor the learning groups and intervene when necessary
6. Evaluate the learning and group interaction

Before putting students in collaborative groups, you can tell stories and provide resources about scientific advances that occurred as a result of teamwork. It's important that the students realize they are modeling their learning processes after the real thing. So, for example, a classroom library could contain a biography of the Curies; Richard Feynman's memoirs of working at Los Alamos with the team studying the nuclear bomb; James Watson's *The Double Helix* (2001), along with Francis Crick's reflective *What Mad Pursuit* (1988). Or a teacher could institute math or science "teas" to discuss principles and dilemmas, perhaps recalling the Princeton afternoons of the late 1940s as Einstein, Nash, Oppenheimer, von Neumann, Gödel, Wigner, Lefschetz, Church, Steenrod, and other brilliant teachers and students gathered to take part in mathematical gossip and share readings of papers, to participate in a true learning community. Collaborative strategies can create an atmosphere conducive to great discovery and contributions in any field.

Teaching in action: *Math.* As you read the following scenario, imagine how you can apply some aspect of cooperative learning to a curricular area you might teach.

Mr. Yang is a high school math teacher who sometimes uses examples involving gambling when he teaches concepts within the curricular topics of probability and statistics and as he teaches critical-thinking skills related to the national and state learning standards in his field. Mr. Yang designed an interdisciplinary, exploratory lesson focusing on gambling. He begins by asking his class to construct a *mind map*, a visual representation of their thoughts,

with "gambling" at the center. Anything that comes to mind is acceptable for this map. When students finish brainstorming, he helps them categorize their ideas. Based on the categories they develop, six groups form around the following self-selected topics: the mathematics of gambling, the economics of gambling, the psychology of gambling, gambling in literature, the moral and ethical dimensions of gambling, and the political aspects of gambling. Mr. Yang, with the assistance of the school librarian, has gathered books and other materials that the students can use. He also encourages them to use interviewing and to explore the Internet for information. After several days of facilitating the groups' investigations, discussions, and writing, he allows each group to share their research results and their positions and opinions on the aspect of gambling they read and learned about. On the class website, each group contributes a section of a class report on gambling, outlining the main points and synthesizing the groups' learning.

For a fuller understanding of how you might use cooperative learning strategies in your content courses, consult some of the sources listed in Figure 2.13.

Workshops

Some teachers choose to turn their classrooms into *workshops*. This seems sensible because through the centuries, artists had studios where interns and fledg-

FIGURE 2.13

Resources relating to cooperative learning strategies and social interaction of learners.

See more suggested titles in Appendix Figure 2.13.

English, R., Dean, S., & Luongo-Orlando, K. (2004). *Show Me How to Learn: Key Strategies and Powerful Techniques that Promote Cooperative Learning.* Portland, ME: Stenhouse.

Haenen, J., & Tuithof, H. (2008). Cooperative Learning: The Place of Pupil Involvement in a History Textbook. *Teaching History, 131,* 30–34.

McCafferty, S. G., Jacobs, G. M., & DaSilva Iddings, A. C. (Eds.). (2008). *Cooperative Learning and Second Language Teaching.* New York: Cambridge University Press.

McManus, D. A. (2005). *Leaving the Lectern: Cooperative Learning and the Critical First Days of Students Working in Groups.* Boston: Anker Pub.

Urbanski, C. D. (2006). *Using the Workshop Approach in the High School English Classroom.* Thousand Oaks, CA: Corwin Press.

ling artists learned alongside the masters, observing, experimenting, practicing the craft, asking questions, socializing. Picture your students studying your subject that way with you. A few of the elements common to all or most workshop classrooms include:

Student choice. A classroom workshop is student-centered. The teacher knows the students as individuals, so can suggest particular books and materials to fit their needs and match their learning styles. Seldom will you walk into the room to find all of the students reading the same thing at the same time. A classroom library containing a variety of genres of trade books, as well as reference materials and magazines, is arranged invitingly, because there is a relatively high association between the size of a classroom library and student reading achievement (Miller, 2009).

Talking and listening. Talk is valued and necessary in a workshop. Individual conferences between student and teacher are common, as are small group conferences among students. Students share information they've discovered, read drafts of their work to classmates, question each other, formulate projects, and talk out ideas. Literature circles, explained later in more detail, are a familiar occurrence in workshop classrooms. Social interaction is encouraged as a way for learners to develop. Chapter 8 focuses on these aspects in more detail.

Writing. As stressed throughout this book, the language components of reading, writing, talking, and listening are interrelated—good literacy education does not separate them or treat them in an isolated manner; neither is writing confined to English class. Although Chapter 7 focuses specifically on the topic of writing in the content areas, I hope that the book as a whole helps you see all aspects of literacy working together. Very often teachers refer to reading–writing workshop as one entity. Other teachers incorporate more writing than reading, or vice versa, which may be appropriate for their particular teaching situation. In any event, many types of writing occur in a workshop classroom for many purposes.

Structure. It might appear to an outsider that the structure of a workshop classroom is quite loose because some students might be walking around or talking, while others are writing, reading, listening to the teacher, or exploring the Internet. Actually, there must be consistency and an organization that matches the goals of the class. Students have to know what to expect from the teacher and their classmates and what is expected of them. Time blocks for various responsibilities and a list of rules are likely to be posted in the room; routines can be depended upon. Following represents a typical workshop routine:

1. Opening/teacher share time. During this period, a teacher may read a book excerpt aloud or give a booktalk.
2. Mini-lesson. In this period, a teacher might teach a specific skill or specific concepts or vocabulary. For example, in a science lesson, a teacher might introduce the topic of monomers and polymers by asking students to brainstorm other words they know that start with the prefix mono- (meaning one) and poly- (meaning many).
3. Student-selected reading/writing and response. This period should be the major part of the workshop. During this time, students should be reading and writing while a teacher conferences with individual students.
4. Closing/student share time. During this period, students share responses to the books they have been reading as well as their written work.

Perhaps the most widely read book on reading and writing workshops is Nancie Atwell's *In the Middle: Writing, Reading, and Learning with Adolescents* (1987), which describes the author's experience transforming her eighth-grade English classroom into an inviting place for young people to explore literacy. Atwell draws a picture of vibrant learning as students self-select books from various genres from the classroom library, choose to write for authentic purposes, talk freely with each other and their teacher, participate in mini-lessons, and grow in knowledge and skill. In 1998, Atwell updated her experiences in *In the Middle: New Understandings about Writing, Reading, and Learning.* The reading-writing workshop approach has been shown to work with other grade levels (e.g., Atwell, 2007; Miller, 2009) and other content areas, including science (Saul, Reardon, Schmidt, et al., 1993), social studies (Brown, 1994; Kneeshaw, 1999; Shafer, 1997), and math (Borasi & Siegel, 2000).

Teaching in action: *History.* Bennett (2009) describes renowned master teacher Chris Tovani using the workshop model with an eighth-grade American history class studying the 13 original colonies. In the opening structure, Tovani set a purpose and guiding questions, including, "How did the original colonists shape what we believe today?" (p. 168). After students brainstormed, she set a purpose for reading a text from *A History of US: Making Thirteen Colonies* (Hakim, 2005), and provided motivation by commenting about the author, "She writes about history kind of like the National Enquirer. She puts lots of juicy stories into it" (p. 169). Tovani read aloud and employed the think-aloud method. She then walked around conferring with students and helping as needed while they read. The class ended with debriefing, a time to synthesize information and look ahead to the following day.

Teaching in action: *Math.* In another example of the workshop approach, Robin Cox, an intermediate grade math teacher who wished to foster a spirit of mathematical exploration, wondered, "If I can develop a workshop time for reading and writing, why can't I do the same for math?'" (Whitin & Cox, 2003, p. 109). She found she could, with results that allowed students to achieve many of the standards promoted by NCTM. Students chose questions to investigate; chose tools, materials, and procedures to help them solve problems; and learned from and celebrated classmates' very different projects. One student set out to find out the number of heartbeats in a lifetime; some explored problems involving patterns using manipulatives; several got ideas from literature they were reading throughout the school day. Robin gave mini-lessons as needed. Whitin and Cox conclude:

> [The students] saw the relevance of their work because the skills and attitudes they were using were beneficial not only to the present task, but also to other problems that they would encounter. They were more eager to listen, as a community, to the work of others because of the diversity of investigations and the personal investment that was a part of all their projects. Last, their opportunity to choose put the focus on understanding. They were the ones who initiated the investigation and they were the ones who bore the responsibility for communicating their results to themselves and their peers. For these many reasons, we felt that math workshop helped us in developing a collaborative mathematical community. (p. 135)

An extended explanation of how she organized and laid the groundwork for the math workshop, along with examples of questions her students pursued and forms of evaluation she used, can be found in

A Mathematical Passage: Strategies for Promoting Inquiry in Grades 4–6 by David J. Whitin and Robin Cox.

Figure 2.14 lists resources that describe various ways teachers have implemented a literacy workshop in content areas.

It's true that teachers work within constraints, and that not every one of you could or should have a classroom turned totally over to a studio approach and a workshop setting. But there are all sorts of variations on the theme; some of you may choose to have a workshop once a week, or for one month out of the year, or for part of each class if you have block scheduling. There may be certain aspects of the studio classroom that you like and can apply to your particular style of teaching and the organization of your course.

Literature circles

The idea of reading circles has been prevalent in elementary schools for a long time. Blanton, Pilonieta, and Wood (2007) describe how teachers of adolescents can use what they call integrated literacy circles: "When applied to the middle- or secondary-level classroom, the circle concept provides a means for students to discuss the content under study while simultaneously learning how to apply a needed literacy skill" (p. 224). Many teachers use variations of circles as students explore literature and other texts related to their disciplines.

Literature circles can be part of a workshop approach or used on their own, giving students the opportunity to share responses to what they read as they learn from classmates' insights and reactions. They simulate the structure, atmosphere, and procedures that are seen in adult, voluntary book discussion groups. The teacher might or might not participate, and there may or may not be guide questions, depending on the purposes and needs of the participants. (Recall the literature circle guide questions I supplied for *The Giver* in the Introduction.) Questions about and suggestions for discussion topics can be very helpful to get the talk going in cer-

---

FIGURE 2.14 Professional resources dealing with a workshop approach and/or literature circles.

See more suggested titles in Appendix Figure 2.14.

Bennett, S. (2009). Time to think: Using the workshop structure so students think and teachers listen. In S. Plaut (Ed.), *The Right to Literacy in Secondary Schools: Creating a Culture of Thinking* (pp. 165–178). New York: Teachers College Press; Newark, DE: International Reading Association.

Daniels, H. (2006). What's the Next Big Thing with Literature Circles? *Voices from the Middle, 13*(4), 10–15.

Johnson, H., & Freedman, L. (2005). *Content Area Literature Circles: Using Discussion for Learning Across the Curriculum.* Norwood, MA: Christopher-Gordon.

Serafini, F. (2004). *Lessons in Comprehension: Explicit Instruction in the Reading Workshop.* Portsmouth, NH: Heinemann.

Urbanski, C. D. (2006). *Using the Workshop Approach in the High School English Classroom.* Thousand Oaks, CA: Corwin Press.

tain groups, especially for students who are new to learning via sharing and listening, but may be totally unnecessary or even impede the progress of veteran discussion group participants. Teacher decision making in terms of how much and what kinds of facilitation and guidance to provide is crucial.

The size of literature circles can vary, from the whole class to small groups of students. Usually, the circle consists of people who have read and responded to the same work of literature, and sometimes the group may then share its knowledge with the whole class. Sometimes, within groups, readers are assigned a role during the literature discussions, such as discussion director, vocabulary enricher, illustrator, questioner, and connector. However, teachers and researchers have found that these roles often become the focus of the group's interaction, and can actually impede natural discussion and deep thinking. Daniels (2006), the originator of the role sheets, now recommends not using them. He prefers what he saw good teachers do recently, which is to "have kids capture their responses in reading response logs, on sticky notes (the favorite tool by far), on homemade bookmarks (great for nonfiction), by using text coding, in drawn and graphic responses or in written conversations" (p. 13). Looking to the future, Daniels recommends more explicit instruction both in reading strategies and in guiding the group dynamics relative to literature circles; extending into nonfiction; and using written conversation as a mode of student-led discussion.

Guidelines for a literature circle. Following are some guidelines for teaching with literature circles:

PRE-READING

1. Prepare a text set of books, magazines, newspapers, Internet sites, or other sources on one topic or theme.
2. Prepare a study or discussion guide for the materials (optional).
3. Give booktalks to introduce each of the reading selections and important content concepts and to arouse interest in the readings.
4. Allow students to choose from the texts. Sometimes, a student will have to make a second choice if no one else chooses the same text. Groups should optimally have four or five members to ensure different perspectives and responses.

DURING READING

5. Have students read independently and record their responses in learning logs, listing important page numbers, drawing pictures, noting unknown words and concepts, making connections with their own lives, and noting questions they have about the material.

POST-READING

6. Have students meet with the others reading the same selection. Meetings should be scheduled regularly, daily or weekly and should last at least 30 to 45 minutes. Students should take turns leading the discussion, but all students should be involved.

The box on the following page offers an example from my own teaching to help you see how literature

---

FIGURE **2.15** **A text set containing fiction and nonfiction books about the experience of learning English.**

Aliki. (1998). *Marianthe's Story: Painted Words and Spoken Memories.* New York: Greenwillow Books.

Alvarez, J. (1992). *How the Garcia Girls Lost Their Accents.* New York: Plume.

Anzaldúa, G. (1987). *Borderlands = La Frontera: The New Mestiza.* San Francisco: Spinsters/Aunt Lute.

Brown, J. (2004). *Little Cricket.* New York: Hyperion Books for Children.

Cheng, A. (2005). *Shanghai Messenger.* New York: Lee & Low Books.

Cofer, J. O. (2004). *Call Me Maria: A Novel.* New York: Orchard Books.

Hoffman, E. (1989). *Lost in Translation: A Life in a New Language.* New York: Dutton.

Ives, D. (2008). *Voss.* New York: G.P. Putnam's Sons.

Khan, R. (2009). *Coming to Canada.* (N. Khosravi, Illus.). Toronto: Groundwood Books.

Kingston, M. H. (1976). *The Woman Warrior.* New York: Knopf.

Kopelnitsky, R., & Pryor, K. (1994). *No Words to Say Goodbye.* New York: Hyperion.

Little, J. (1987). *Little by Little: A Writer's Education.* Ontario, Canada: Viking Kestrel.

Medina, J. (1999). *My Name Is Jorge: On Both Sides of the River.* Honesdale, PA: Wordsong/Boyds Mills.

Na, A. (2001). *A Step from Heaven.* Asheville, NC: Front Street.

Paperny, M. (2005). *The Greenies.* Toronto: HarperTrophyCanada.

Rodriguez, R. (1982). *Hunger of Memory: The Education of Richard Rodriguez, an Autobiography.* Boston: D. R. Godine.

Sachs, M. (2005). *Lost in America.* Brookfield, CT: Roaring Brook Press.

Content Area Literature Circles in Action in Social Studies and English

I begin by giving booktalks, with the aid of a classroom wall map of Europe, for several books that take place during the time period we're studying. Notice how I work in some geography knowledge and map reading as I introduce the books:

> Look at this map of Europe and locate Denmark. If you were living in Denmark during World War II and needed to help a Jewish family escape the country, what might be a logical plan? The Danish people did what was reasonable given their geography; they hid people on boats and sent them north to Sweden. But of course the Nazis were logical and knowledgeable about geography, too, so this method became increasingly difficult and risky. *Number the Stars,* by Lois Lowry (1989), is a Newbery Medal winner that tells of one young girl's courage as she tries to help her best friend flee the country.
>
> Here's a different scene. *Waiting for Anya,* by Michael Morpurgo (1990), also involves helping Jewish children flee for their lives. But the action takes place in France, and the geography is different. See these mountains between France, which was occupied by the Germans during World War II, and Spain, which was not? There are children hidden in these mountains. There are border patrols to be evaded. Read this work of historical fiction to learn about the intelligence, skill, and bravery necessary for the rescue operations that really happened here.
>
> Tiny Holland. Picture one family here, the Ten Booms—Christians who are hiding Jews. Christians who get caught and sent to Ravensbruck. Exactly one member of the family leaves alive, and she subsequently writes *The Hiding Place* (1971). This is a nonfiction account of Corrie Ten Boom's experiences and her struggle to understand them in terms of her future, her religion, her humanity. You can learn from this humble woman if you'll enter her hiding place by reading this book.

> Then there's Germany itself; its Jewish citizens were trapped. *Four Perfect Pebbles,* by Lila Perl and Marion Blumenthal Lazan (1996), is a biographical account of the Blumenthal family's six and a half years in refugee, transit, and prison camps. Marion was nine years old when she arrived at Bergen-Belsen, the terrible concentration camp where Anne Frank and so many others died. If you choose this book, you'll learn how the child used her imagination and a game she made up to keep hope alive amidst the despair.

My students choose from these selections—the books represent a range in terms of difficulty and maturity level. After independent reading and responding in learning logs, I ask my readers to form circles in the four corners of the room to talk over what they have read and written. Without exception, students tell me they learned from listening to other readers. Reactions to the texts vary, but they are usually strong. Different parts of the stories have an impact on different students; some pick up details or nuances that others miss, some talk about their own discoveries and feelings during the reading process, some make connections with other works of literature or with information from their history textbooks.

As a follow-up activity to the discussion circles, I ask each group to select a member to role-play a character from the book its members read; we hold a "talk show" with the panel that sits in the front comparing and contrasting experiences while fielding questions from the audience. The result is that some of my students later read at least one of the other books from this text set on their own. All of the students end up understanding more about Europe during World War II, and come to a social studies textbook better able to comprehend the content of the chapter on World War II. They are willing to explore primary documents and other resources related to this segment of the curriculum. Literature circles cause ripples that last a long time.

circles can work in a history class that is studying Europe during World War II, and Figure 2.15 is an example of a *text set* (Harste & Short, 1988; Weaver, 1994)—copies of several related texts put together for the purpose of sharing and discussion-consisting of stories about or memoirs written by people who learned English as a second language. These books contain personal stories of struggles, triumphs, losses, and insights that can help all of the students in your classes better understand language, culture, and the human spirit. If you have single copies of these titles, a group can use them to read individually with the purpose of sharing the information with others. Figure 2.16 contains a text set for a health science class relating to medical ethics.

FIGURE **2.16** A text set for a health science class containing fiction and nonfiction books relating to medical ethics.

Baréma, J. (2005). *The Test: Living in the Shadow of Huntington's Disease.* New York: Franklin Square Press.

Cobb, A. B. (2003). *The Bionic Human.* New York: Rosen Publishing.

Crutcher, C. (2007). *Deadline.* New York: Greenwillow.

Egendorf, L. K. (Ed.). (2005). *Medical Ethics.* Farmington Hills, MI: Greenhaven Press.

Farmer, N. (2002). *The House of the Scorpion.* New York: Atheneum Books for Young Readers.

Hrdlitschka, S. (2008). *Sister Wife.* Victoria, B.C.: Orca Book Publishers.

Lovegrove, R. (2009). *Health: Ethical Debates in Modern Medicine.* Mankato, MN: Black Rabbit Books.

Moon, E. (2003). *The Speed of Dark.* New York: Ballantine Books.

Myers, W. D. (2004). *Shooter.* New York: Amistad/Harper-Tempest.

Nardo, D. (2007). *Biomedical Ethics.* San Diego, CA: ReferencePoint Press.

Pearson, M. E. (2008). *The Adoration of Jenna Fox.* New York: Henry Holt.

Picoult, J. (2004). *My Sister's Keeper.* New York: Washington Square Press.

Roach, M. (2003). *Stiff: The Curious Lives of Human Cadavers.* New York: W. W. Norton.

Shusterman, N. (2007). *Unwind.* New York: Simon & Schuster.

Simmers, L. (2004). *Health Science Career Exploration.* Clifton Park, NY: Delmar Learning.

Wagner, V. (Ed.). (2008). *Biomedical Ethics.* Greenhaven Press.

Werlin, N. (2004). *Double Helix.* New York: Dial Books.

CONCLUSION

This chapter was meant to get you thinking about your own and your students' passion for learning and motivation to participate in literacy activities that lead to knowledge and comprehension. The affective domain is intertwined with the cognitive, and you can go a long way toward helping your students achieve in social studies, science, math, art, language, music, business—any subject you can name—by sharing your enthusiasm; talking about your own reading and learning; using strategies that increase intrinsic motivation, intellectual curiosity, and engaged reading; and helping students discover the exciting world of learning.

The affective dimensions of learning continue to have an important role in subsequent chapters. Your own passion and literacy skills may increase as you learn more about the texts that are available to motivate your students and the instructional strategies that will improve your students' comprehension, knowledge, and thinking.

WEBSITES **CHAPTER 2** Access these links using the Kane Resource Site.

Clip Art for Microsoft Word
http://office.microsoft.com/en-us/images

Edgar Allan Poe Museum
www.poemuseum.org

Edgar Allan Poe's House of Usher fan site
www.houseofusher.net

Madeleine L'Engle
www.madeleinelengle.com

Meet the Author – Russell Freedman
www.eduplace.com/kids/hmr/mtai/freedman.html

National Civil Rights Museum
www.civilrightsmuseum.org

Paul Fleischman
www.paulfleischman.net

The Mathematical Association of America – Careers
www.maa.org/careers

APPLICATION ACTIVITIES

2.1 Look at a course syllabus or state or local curriculum guidelines for a particular course or subject you're interested in teaching. You might use a Teacher's Edition of a required course textbook. Then, create an interest inventory that will help you know the students and make wise decisions about how to engage and motivate them and accomplish the goals of the course.

2.2 Begin a file for "Content Exploration Through Literature." As you read books for your own purposes, keep an eye out for opportunities to connect story happenings or scene descriptions with concepts within your field. Once you start, you'll be amazed at the wealth of possibilities that exist. You can also use this file for professional articles and websites. Code those parts that you think might make good teacher read-alouds.

2.3 Select a book or other text in your content area and plan a literary field trip experience for your students. Using the example given in this chapter as a model, design pre-reading questions and a structure to guide them through the text and help them react to "being there" through reading. You can then add an invitation to take a virtual field trip to an Internet site related to the topic. Share your virtual field trip with others in your class or with the Kane Resource Site community. Refer to page 41, which provides some guidelines for your planning.

The Role of Texts in Content Area Learning

> "Many . . . textbooks, which were a weariness and a stumbling-block when studied, I have since read a little in with pleasure and profit."
>
> **THOREAU, 19 FEBRUARY 1854,**
> **JOURNAL VI:130**

As with the word *literacy,* the definition of the term *text* is constantly evolving and the word can be used to mean a number of things. In their article "The Role of Text in the Classroom," Wade and Moje (2000) define texts as:

> organized networks that people generate or use to make meaning either for themselves or for others. . . . Different views of what counts as text—whether they are formal and informal; oral, written, enacted; permanent or fleeting—lead to different views of what counts as learning, and consequently expand or limit the opportunities students have to learn in classrooms. (p. 610)

This chapter examines several types of texts that can guide you and your students as you strive toward your goal of content area learning, and provides strategies for choosing and using appropriate discipline-related texts as you teach.

APPLICATION ACTIVITY **3.1** (SEE PAGE 85)

Textbooks have historically been a central focus of most content area classes from elementary grades through college (Cuban, 1991; Gottfried & Kyle, 1992). Alvermann and Moore (1991) found that a class set of a single textbook was the primary reading material in subject area instruction, and these textbooks were rarely supplemented by newspapers, magazines, or library books; other research upheld their findings (DiGisi & Willett, 1995; Moje, 1996). Things are changing, however. An article entitled "The Day They Threw Out the Textbooks" (Ryan, 1994) describes a failing intermediate school in Alabama that the faculty restructured by virtually eliminating all textbooks except those used for math and as supplements in other courses. Eight thousand books were purchased and scattered throughout the school's classrooms, and another 8,000 were added to the central library. Teaching, of course, could not remain the same because materials to a large extent determine what and how content is taught. In another example, Dunn (2000) reports how four social studies teachers rely on the textbook as a supplementary tool, if at all, with great rewards for students and teachers alike. A school near me, where most students have laptops, is opting for software programs, e-books, and Internet resources more and more. In Indianapolis, 11 public schools have used funds normally reserved for textbook purchases to replace textbooks with digital content and provide professional development for teachers who will be teaching with videos, images, and games rather than the traditional textbooks (Barack, 2010).

I advocate the use of multiple texts and genres in every secondary classroom, but I recognize that textbooks, wisely selected and judiciously used, can play a vital role and hold much potential for helping students learn. The first part of this chapter explores the limitations of textbooks. Next, I offer suggestions for using them creatively and provide suggestions for evaluating and selecting textbooks for particular purposes. The second part of the chapter offers a parallel discussion of non-textbook sources, including several other types of texts that teachers can use to their advantage as they instruct students and lead them toward independent learning in the disciplines. Throughout the chapter and the rest of the book, we explore strategies to help students comprehend all types of texts and use them with purpose and with increasing independence.

TEXTBOOKS

As consumers of textbooks, students are in some sense the most qualified to judge their usefulness, quality, and ability to promote and enhance learning (and this includes you as a current university student or member of a professional development group). Therefore, your own experience using textbooks is a good starting place for thinking about the topic of teaching with textbooks.

ACTIVATING PRIOR KNOWLEDGE　3.1

Think about how you interact with your textbooks. Do you always read assignments? Why, or why not? Do your teachers actually show you how best to read and use your textbooks? Is it necessary to read the textbooks in order to do well in the classes? Do your teachers know when a significant percentage of students doesn't read the assigned material? If so, what is their reaction? Do they do anything about it, or try to find out why the text wasn't read? Are there consequences? What will you do if your students don't read the textbook assignments you give?

Textbook Limitations

In general, high school students are not reading much from the textbooks that are so prevalent in their courses. Some middle and high school teachers have given up expecting students to read the textbooks for their courses. Perhaps the text is too difficult; there is a discrepancy between its readability level (explained later in this chapter) and the actual reading ability of at least some of the students. Often textbooks must stay in the school building because there are not enough to send home with all students taking the courses. Or maybe the students are in a community where extracurricular activities or jobs take up their late afternoon and evening hours. Again, some teachers have changed their teaching as a result. They may outline the chapter during class or give the information from the book in the form of a lecture. I've had students tell me that they don't bother to read their textbooks for some courses because they don't have to: "Mr. Dugan puts everything on the overhead projector, and we copy down what he writes. The tests come right from the notes." Many secondary teachers feel they can cover the content more quickly through lecture or demonstration (O'Brien, Stewart, & Moje, 1995). And when students realize they can rely on teachers' recitations to learn the content, they see little need to read the textbook pages they've been assigned (Hinchman & Zalewski, 1996; Moje, 1996).

Teachers and students too often concentrate on the minimum that must be learned for an assessment, and the textbook really does become unnecessary for that goal to be achieved. So, what happens the next year? Students have not practiced reading a textbook and expect that the course material will be given to them in some other way. They are less prepared and less able to handle the textbook, the difficulty of which has increased because they are in a higher grade. A downward spiral throughout the years can result.

Moss (2003) points out several other limitations of textbooks. They usually contain technical and abstract vocabulary, are often poorly organized, and can use complex, nonlinear arrangements, making them difficult or inaccessible to readers who struggle. They cannot go into any depth, since there is so much to cover, and the information provided can be outdated and/or inaccurate. Of great concern to educators who understand the importance of engagement of learners is the interest factor:

> Content area texts are typically not motivating for children to read. Despite the increased visual appeal of recent textbooks, the writing continues to be boring—it lacks the life that skilled authors can bring to virtually any subject. In addition, textbook publishers seek to avoid controversy, which

also contributes to bland, lifeless writing that may offer little to entice today's young readers. (p. 8)

In other research, Abd-El-Khalick (2002) points out that secondary students' understanding of the nature of science is not strong, largely attributed to the format and content of science textbooks, which often

> present science as a body of facts to be memorized; the accompanying science instruction is mainly didactic and coupled with cookbook verification activities. Such instruction seldom presents science as a process or a way of thinking and rarely involves students in posing questions and seeking evidence-based answers. (p. 122)

Should textbooks have a point of view? Should we as readers be told the textbook authors' opinions about issues, or should the material be presented in an objective, neutral, or balanced manner? Schallert and Roser (1996) note, "perhaps because textbook authors are so concerned with their task of mentioning all the necessary topics, they seem to forget to make their prose interesting and to shy away from expressing any particular point of view toward their topic. Textbook language easily takes on a didactic, impersonal tone, the expression of a reasonable, all-knowing intellect, removed from any emotional commitment to the topic or to the audience" (p. 33). However, when textbook authors do express an evaluation, teachers must help their students recognize this and encourage them to read their texts critically. A student might bring up in a class discussion, for example, "Our textbook refers to John Brown's 'crackbrained scheme' (Bailey, Kennedy, & Cohen, 1998, p. 432) to invade the South secretly. Isn't that a bit judgmental?" The teacher or peers could then give their opinions about whether the textbook's use of that phrase is justified and appropriate.

Some textbooks deal with controversial issues by recognizing competing positions and allowing disparate voices to be heard, at least a little. For example, *The American Pageant* (Bailey et al., 1998) includes boxes labeled "Varying Viewpoints," offering a forum for dealing with such questions as "Where Did Modern Conservatism Come From?" (p. 1021) and "The Sixties: Constructive or Destructive?" (p. 961). Opinions and their sources are offered for thought and discussion, as well as for further exploration. Political cartoons representing satiric views are included. Primary and secondary sources listed at the ends of chapters offer more in-depth information than a textbook itself can provide.

Despite the problems mentioned previously, the textbook still holds a central place in the curriculum in most schools and some teachers consider the textbook the "expert" on subject matter, defining curriculum purpose and instructional guidelines.

BookTalk 3.1

Steve Sheinkin is a former textbook writer who has found an alternative; he now writes a series of non-textbooks! In a confessional letter to his readers in his book *Two Miserable Presidents: Everything Your Schoolbooks Didn't Tell You About the Civil War* (2008), he pleads, ". . . as you've probably noticed, textbooks are filled with charts, labels, lists, names, dates, review questions . . . there isn't any room left for the good stuff. . . . I kept telling myself, 'One of these days I'm going to write my own history books! And I'll pack them with all the true stories and real quotes that textbooks never tell you!' . . . If you can find it in your heart to forgive my previous crimes, I hope you'll give this book a chance" (unpaged 2008). He also presents "history with the good parts put back in" in *King George: What Was His Problem?: Everything Your Schoolbooks Didn't Tell You About the American Revolution* (2005).

Familiarity and comfort level can also be factors. As Hynd explains, "Traditionally, high school history teachers have felt successful teaching history as a story. Typically, teachers use a single textbook, follow its sequence, and embellish it through skillful storytelling" (1999, p. 429).

Suggestions for Using Textbooks Creatively

How can you begin to make sense of the seemingly conflicting views on textbook use, weigh the disadvantages and advantages, and decide whether and how to use textbooks? Remember, it is still the teacher who is in control, and a creative teacher can make a less than perfect textbook situation beneficial, for herself and her students. Forsten, Grant, and Hollis (2003) advocate teachers help students negotiate their textbooks through strategy instruction before, during, and after reading the material. Following are some other more specific guidelines for helping students use their textbooks.

Provide a preview guide

You can prepare students by giving them a guide to preview and help them become familiar with the main textbook they'll be using. Figure 3.1 shows a sample of what I mean. If teachers introduce a textbook well and show students how to use it effectively and efficiently, the students benefit and will grow toward using textbooks independently. Chapter 4 discusses preparation and use of preview guides in more detail.

FIGURE 3.1   A textbook preview guide for *The American Pageant*.

Dear Students:

Welcome to our American history course and to your textbook, which will be a constant companion to you, along with lots of supplemental materials, throughout the year.

Treat this activity like a puzzle or a treasure hunt; it will help you become familiar with some of the features of this book. Use your knowledge of the structure of textbooks to answer the following questions. Your answers will help me determine how to best teach you. If you don't know how to find an answer, make an X on that question to let me know. I'll conduct mini-lessons as needed.

1. State two ways the maps of the United States on the inside front cover and the inside back cover are different.

2. What documents can be found in the Appendix?

3. On what page could you find information on James Baldwin? Where did you look to get your answer?

4. What kind of information will you find in the "Makers of America" sections of the text? Give a specific example.

5. Write the page number where you located an example of each of the following:

- a political cartoon
- a photograph
- a treatment of varying viewpoints about a topic
- a chapter title
- a sub-heading within a chapter
- an introduction to one of the major parts (1–6) of this textbook
- a primary source

6. After the table of contents, you'll find two helpful lists. What are they?

7. After perusing this book, what is your initial reaction? What do you think you'll like about it? What scares you or puts you off? What questions do you have for me about the book or how we'll use it?

8. Do you think the book will be too easy, too difficult, or just about right for you?

Plan to interact with this book; I'll be teaching you ways to read the material actively rather than passively. As we progress, please tell me about any areas of difficulty. If you don't understand something about a topic or about how to use this textbook effectively, let me know.

Use multiple textbooks

Textbooks can be used as direct sources of instruction or as learning tools in innovative ways. For example, instead of having everyone in your class read the same text, you could make several options available. Then, students could explore, compare, and contrast. How does one science book compare with another on the topic of evolution? How do different publishers and authors treat the era of the Vietnam War? A standard junior high school American history text can be read alongside *Now Is Your Time!: The African American Struggle for Freedom* (1991) by Walter Dean Myers, as well as *We Were There, Too!: Young People in U. S. History* (Hoose, 2001), *Tell All the Children Our Story: Memories and Mementos of Being Young and Black in America* by Tanya Bolden (2001), Joy Hakim's *Freedom: A History of US* (2003), *Girls: A History of Growing Up Female in America* (2000) by Penny Colman, and *We Are the People: Voices from the Other Side of American History* by Nathaniel May, Clint Willis, and James Loewen (2003). You can have books in your classroom that specifically discuss differences among and controversies about the way history is portrayed, such as Lindaman and Ward's *History Lessons: How Textbooks from Around the World Portray United States History* (2004) and Moreau's *Schoolbook Nation: Conflicts over American History Textbooks from the Civil War to the Present* (2003). With tools like these, you can teach students how to think about subject matter and about critically evaluating sources of information. Edwards (2008) helps students analyze old and new textbooks on various historical events in order to grapple with the problem of historical interpretation. Using multiple textbooks can turn drudgery into fascination as students explore to find differences and even contradictions.

If you're teaching math concepts, for example, students with various learning styles might require the unique approaches presented by different textbooks. If a student doesn't understand the principles of probability theory, send her to another textbook that might explain it more to her liking or might contain an example that causes the principles to click for her. Textbooks can complement each other, so having several editions produced by various publishers on your classroom shelves makes sense. You can pull versions as needed or have students search independently for alternative explanations and additional examples.

Encourage students to think critically about their textbooks

A teacher's assignments and guidance in terms of using the text as one resource along with many others may change the way students perceive and use their textbook. For example, supply students with books and articles that point out flaws in textbooks, such as potential bias or omissions, as well as errors found in textbooks, and help students explore and analyze their own textbooks to see whether they can find examples of problems or even outright misinformation. Thought-provoking books to start with are Loewen's *Lies My Teacher Told Me: Everything Your American History Textbook Got Wrong* (1995), his *Rethinking Our Past: Recognizing Facts, Fictions and Lies in American History* (2004), and *Teaching What Really Happened: How to Avoid the Tyranny of Textbooks and Get Students Excited About Doing History* (2010). Students can use the Internet, a bookstore, or a librarian to seek out similar resources dealing with textbooks in other areas.

Textbooks aren't going to go away, and in many places, they are mandated. Thus, we should learn to use them creatively, in ways that entice our students to read them. The good news is that textbooks are improving in many ways; publishers listened to consumers. Perhaps in response to threats from process- and literature-based classrooms that have shown textbooks are not necessary for learning to occur, as well as to the reality that it is now much easier, and possibly cheaper, to access up-to-date information from the Internet, publishers are making textbooks more attractive and user-friendly. We can take advantage of the improved versions, though we still must know how to use them well, without becoming slaves to them or surrendering our curriculum to them. Teachers must help students become active, engaged, critical readers of their textbooks. Schallert and Roser remind us, "It is the teacher, not the textbook, who is responsible for guiding the process of learning, even of learning from the text" (1996, p. 31).

Evaluating and Selecting Textbooks

Textbooks are big business; school districts spend a lot of money on them and expect them to be used. Earlier, I pointed out the potential advantages and limitations of textbooks in general. In reality, there is a huge range in terms of the characteristics and quality of particular textbooks, as well as the cost, another factor that comes into play. How are textbooks selected? You may have the wonderful opportunity and important responsibility of evaluating textbooks or a series for your classroom or district at a time when you actually have a voice in determining the outcome of the selection process. At other times, you may be teaching within the constraints of being expected to use a textbook that was chosen for you, perhaps even at the state level—far removed from your students and you. In any case, it is extremely important that you gain expertise in evaluating textbooks. Once you know their strengths and flaws or weaknesses, you can teach

with those in mind and instruct your students on how to achieve the most from the materials.

Resources for evaluating textbooks include the professional educational journals in your field, which publish reviews of recent textbooks. These reviews, usually written by other instructors, are a valuable resource. They discuss both the strengths and weaknesses of the materials.

ACTION RESEARCH   **3.A**

Go to the website of a textbook publishing company, such as Scott Foresman, Houghton Mifflin Harcourt, Holcomb Hathaway, or Merrill. Read what information is available on a textbook appropriate for the grade level and subject area you wish to teach. If outside reviews are not available, write the company via e-mail and ask whether the textbook has been reviewed in any educational journals. If possible, read the reviews themselves. Respond in your learning log.

APPLICATION ACTIVITY   **3.2**   (SEE PAGE 85)

Performing Your Own Textbook Evaluation

Textbooks may be examined according to many criteria and using a variety of methods. I discuss four methods, but urge you to use a combination approach because no one procedure is complete in itself.

1. Use your own judgment

You will be, if you are not already, an avid reader and an expert in the content area you teach. Therefore, as you read through and subjectively respond to a textbook, you can learn a lot. Notice your thoughts and feelings as you peruse the book. After you've made an initial judgment, you can use the following questions to guide and refine your evaluation:

- Do you find the information intriguing and enticing?
- Do the authors make your job easy by organizing the material in a coherent manner? Are the chapters and subsections well-organized? Do the chapters contain introductions and summaries?
- Do the pictures, graphs, and charts work well with the text itself? Are they clear and meaningful? Are captions present and helpful?
- Do you like the questions asked of the students before, during, or after the chapters? Are they

stimulating, thought-provoking? Do they call for mere literal recall, or do they stimulate students to think critically, apply concepts, and synthesize information?

- Does the material's presentation encourage readers to engage in higher-level thinking skills?
- Does the publisher supply supplemental materials such as workbook exercises, and, if so, do they require the students to do things that will actually further their practice of a skill or their knowledge of a subject? Do you consider them a valuable use of your and your students' time or just busywork?
- Are suggestions and resources given for further exploration using primary and secondary sources, and websites?
- Are technical terms highlighted, defined well, and explained adequately?
- Is there a glossary? an index? bibliography? appendices?
- Does the text presume an appropriate amount of background knowledge in relation to what you know about your students?
- Do the illustrations and examples represent race, ethnicity, gender, and class fairly? Are the representations of people nonstereotypical?
- Do the authors use nonsexist language throughout?
- Are the examples ones that students can relate to?

If you are answering in the negative, be as specific as possible in identifying the potential problems. This will help if you have to instruct the students on using the text. You'll know which sections might require that you supply more background knowledge, which parts should be complemented or supplemented with other sources, what information you might challenge in your lectures.

2. Apply a readability formula

A readability formula is a ready-made procedure used to approximate the difficulty level of printed material that consists of connected prose. There are several available, including the Flesch "Reading Ease" Formula and the Dale–Chall Readability Formula. The Fry Readability Graph (Fry, 1977), shown in Figure 3.2 and widely available on the web, is one of the most popular. The resulting scores are represented as grade levels, and they reflect the level at which a child should read with the assistance of a teacher. You might actually have a readability formula available as a tool on one of the software programs on your computer. An advantage to apply-

ing formulas is that they are easy and quick to use. Yet, caveats must accompany any recommendation to use such formulas, for, although they have their place, they have been misused. A readability formula provides no more than a rough guide. It usually uses sentence length, number of syllables, and word difficulty or length as criteria to determine difficulty. We know, however, that many more variables, including a reader's background knowledge, interest in the topic, and motivation to succeed, may play an even more important part in determining how well a student can handle a text. The formulas do not take into account syntax, the use of specialized vocabulary, or the abstractness of the concepts being taught. They are absolutely not intended to be used as guides to writing.

A widely used system for matching students with appropriate texts is the Lexile Framework for Reading. Thousands of books have been leveled and indexed using this guide. Scores range from 200L (for beginning readers) to 1700L for advanced texts. You can find a score by searching www.lexile.com by title, author, or key word. For example, I searched the key word *astronomy* and found numerous books on the topic. Some students in a middle school science classroom might be comfortable reading Janice VanCleave's *Astronomy for Every Kid* (1991), which has a lexile score of 920, while others will thrive on the challenges of *The Story of Astronomy* (Motz & Weaver, 1995), having a lexile score of 1470.

A readability formula does provide a good and easy way to estimate the appropriateness of a text in terms of difficulty. However, in individual cases, your professional judgment can and should override the formula's rating. If, for example, after applying the other evaluation procedures explained here, you prefer a certain ninth-grade textbook over the other options, even though the formula indicated that it has a tenth-grade readability level, you can still choose the textbook—just remember, you'll have to provide more help to make the text accessible to your students. By listening carefully to your students as they use the text, and by actively seeking their feedback, you'll know whether they're struggling and in what ways they're finding the text hard to comprehend.

3. Listen to the students

Lester and Cheek (1997/1998) surveyed students in grades 9 through 11 to find out what they thought about their textbooks in various subjects. The students indicated that they liked math textbooks the least and English texts the most. They offered recommendations to improve the textbooks, including

FIGURE **3.2** **Instructions for using Edward Fry's Readability Graph.**

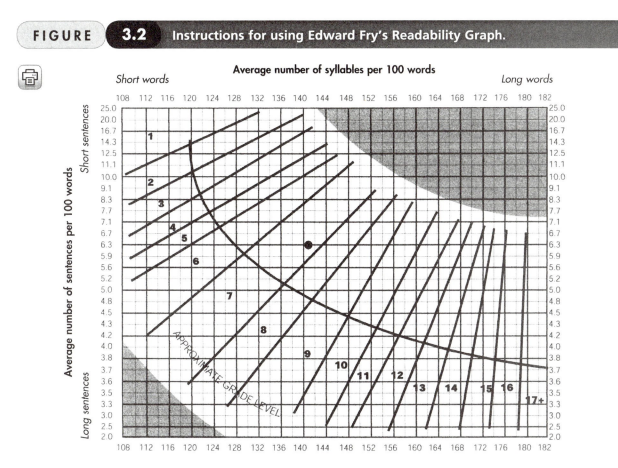

DIRECTIONS FOR WORKING READABILITY GRAPH

1. Randomly select three (3) sample passages and count out exactly 100 words each, beginning with the beginning of a sentence. Do count proper nouns, initializations, and numerals.

2. Count the number of sentences in the hundred words, estimating length of the fraction of the last sentence to the nearest one-tenth.

3. Count the total number of syllables in the 100-word passage. If you don't have a hand counter available, an easy way is to simply put a mark above each syllable except the first in each word, then when you get to the end of the passage, count the number of marks and add 100. Small calculators can also be used as counters by pushing numeral 1, then push the 1 sign for each word or syllable when counting.

4. Enter graph with average sentence length and average number of syllables; plot dot where the two lines intersect. Area where dot is plotted will give you the approximate grade level. For example, the dot on the graph above indicates a reading level of seventh grade.

5. If a great deal of variability is found in syllable count or sentence count, putting more samples into the average is desirable.

6. A word is defined as a group of symbols with a space on either side; thus, *Joe, IRA, 1945,* and *&* are each one word.

7. A syllable is defined as a phonetic syllable. Generally, there are as many syllables as vowel sounds. For example, *stopped* is one syllable and *wanted* is two syllables. When counting syllables for numerals and initializations, count one syllable for each symbol. For example, *1945* is four syllables, *IRA* is three syllables, and *&* is one syllable.

Fry's Readability Graph: Clarifications, Validity, and Extension to Level 17, *Journal of Reading,* 21 (December 1977), 249. Reproduction permitted.

using more graphics and illustrations, dealing with more topics that interest teens, presenting vocabulary in a student-friendly way, and using larger print. Lester and Cheek conclude: "Students are experts because they have consistently been exposed to textbooks as an integral part of their learning process. . . . It is critical to view your students as decision makers in this collaborative process. Their ideas incorporated with yours will result in a more productive learning environment" (pp. 290–291).

ACTION RESEARCH   **3.B**

If you have access to adolescents through a practicum connected to your course work or some other avenue, listen to what the current consumers of secondary textbooks have to say about the products. As Lester and Cheek did in their study that was reported in "The 'Real' Experts Address Textbook Issues" (1997/1998), ask one or more students the following questions:

1. Is a textbook available for each of your classes?
2. How often do you use your textbook?
3. Which is your favorite textbook and why?
4. Which is your least favorite textbook and why?
5. If you were writing a textbook, how would you set it up? (p. 284)

Listen carefully to student input, and compare your answers with those of others in your class, if possible. You might be surprised at the wealth and depth of the data you collect. Your middle and secondary students can tell you how they are interacting with their textbooks, what they like and dislike about them, what parts they find particularly confusing or difficult, and how the structure and organization help or hinder their comprehension and ability to retain information.

It's likely you'll be using the same textbook for several years, so the information you gain from paying attention to your students can help you in subsequent years. Keep notes, perhaps right in your Teacher's Edition of the textbook, to remind yourself of the valuable input you get from your student readers.

Figure 3.3 shows excerpts from a preservice teacher's evaluation of a textbook that she has seen used in courses she hopes to teach some day. The textbook is often a necessary component in education, but it is virtually never sufficient alone.

Textbook Adaptations for Students with Special Educational Needs

As noted in Chapter 2, a number of factors cause students to have difficulty with reading. You will have struggling readers in your subject area classes, so you must find ways to help them be successful. Middle grade students with learning disabilities are, on average, reading at a level three years behind grade level (Schumaker & Lenz, 1999). So, your eighth-grade science textbook will be difficult or impossible for those students without some accommodations. Fortunately, there is much you can do. You can order audiobooks for students with particular learning dis-

FIGURE   3.3

Excerpts from a preservice teacher's review of a content area textbook.

The textbook I chose to use, a standard across New York State, is *Course I, Integrated Mathematics,* 3rd Edition, by Isadore Dressler and Edward P. Keenan (New York: Amsco School Publications, Inc., 1998). I applied Fry's Readability Graph to the book, which is commonly used in eighth or ninth-grade classrooms. I chose three random hundred-word passages. . . . The average ended up being a seven sentence passage with 153 syllables, which places it at a ninth-grade reading level, exactly where it's supposed to be. As far as the usability of this book, I have concluded that it is an excellent book that I would be more than happy to use in my classroom.

Obviously, vocabulary is a big part of the math curriculum. Each year introduces a new set of words for students to learn. This book has every vocabulary term italicized, and it is defined within one or two sentences of the word's initial use.

Each chapter's main ideas or purposes for reading are explicitly stated in the beginning. The first chapter begins with a review of the definition of whole numbers, their uses and where they're found, and why we have them. The chapter ends with a discussion on number lines and graphs. The authors present an organizational structure to guide the student while reading/studying. Each topic is presented along with several examples, which the authors work out, explaining every step along the way. After the topic has been covered, there is a page of exercises for the students to attempt for themselves.

The Table of Contents is excellent, showing a logical development of subject matter. There are lots of graphs, tables, diagrams and pictures, with clearly written captions.

[One weakness is that] there are no outside resources listed as available to the students, or projects for the students to attempt.

So, my overall rating for this textbook is: EXCELLENT.

—*Vanessa Dudley*

---

abilities or vision loss; some students' individualized education plans (IEPs) will require that the text be read to them—there is technology available that can "read" books out loud. Also, it is not necessary that everyone use the same textbook all of the time—textbooks written at an easier level might be a good place for some students to start, and you can fill in any additional information or help students read specific parts of the class textbook that you're using.

Some students must have direct instruction and practice to recognize the textbook's structure and features. For example, you might model how you preview a chapter by looking at the headings and subheadings and reading the topic sentences. Ask your students how they're handling the textbook, and identify the specific areas of difficulty from their answers and by watching them. Monitor them as they read, and note where comprehension breaks down in order to determine what strategies might work. Assure them that they will get the support they need in order to comprehend the textbook material.

Textbook publishers will be happy to talk with you about how to adapt and supplement their materials for learners with special needs or who are struggling in any way. Some companies have websites and/or software that offer extra graphic organizers, study guides, practice tests, visuals, and other aids. The Teacher's Edition will also likely have suggestions for helping students get the most from the textbook.

Textbooks certainly have their place in content area classrooms, and you may use one or more either as the backbone of your instruction or as a supplementary resource. However, textbooks are not enough. Thus, we now explore materials beyond the traditional textbook, concentrating on several types of trade books and primary sources. Other materials, such as digital and electronic resources and film, are discussed in subsequent chapters.

TRADE BOOKS

Some of the students' complaints about textbooks listed previously (e.g., the book is not interesting, the information is too compacted) can be alleviated or corrected by using *trade books* in subject area classes. Trade books are any books other than textbooks or reference books. Think of the books people buy from bookstores or borrow from libraries; think of children's and young adult literature. Trade books can be narrative or expository, and they span all genres: fiction, poetry, essays, biography or other information books, and so on.

The use of trade books in classrooms is growing in popularity; hundreds of articles by teachers at all grade levels describe increased student interest, understanding, and enthusiasm, as well as an increased ability in writing and reading, as trade books replace or supplement textbooks. The use of trade books throughout the curriculum has many proponents (e.g., Atkinson et al., 2009; Ebbers, 2002; Fink, 2006; Hoyt & Therrialt, 2003; Johnson & Freedman, 2001; Kane, 2008; Moss, 2003; Raham, 2004; Wenze, 2003). Trofanenko (2002) points out that trade books are typically more compelling than textbooks and have the potential to help students understand the past and develop historical consciousness. Walker and Bean (2003) note that it makes sense to use multiple texts, since no one text is capable of meeting the needs of diverse students.

In some cases, trade books are a better match to individual reading levels, abilities, and learning styles than the standard grade-level textbook chosen by the district or state. As a rule, trade books are also superior to textbooks in their ability to tap into the *affective* realm, discussed in Chapter 2. When students' emotions and values become involved, they are more likely to be engaged with the material and remember it longer. Recall from Chapter 1 that Rosenblatt (1978) classified reading as having either an *efferent* (the reader is primarily concerned with extracting information from a text) or *aesthetic* (the reader is engaged with the material and experiences emotions as she reads and responds) purpose. Trade books can be used for either purpose or for both. BookTalk 3.3 relates to texts that teach historical information while telling engaging stories or otherwise involving the reader.

In order to have credibility as you recommend trade books to students, you have to foster your own growth by reading children's and young adult literature. Fortunately, you will find this a rewarding adventure. Here are two reflections from preservice teachers who discovered this during an education class on content area literacy:

> The first couple of weeks into this class, I was hesitant to believe that any books besides the biology textbook I would use for my class have any space in any of my lesson plans. But I am convinced now that any kind of books in the classroom can and will stimulate students' minds. . . . over the semester my role as a teacher/reader has changed, too. I was put off at first about using children's or young adult books in a classroom setting. . . . But then you pulled out a book [*Standing Up to Mr. O* (Mills, 1998)] in which the storyline was about a child's dislike of dissecting and I thought how well that could be used. . . . I guess my resistance was futile. . . . I can honestly say that when I go to a bookstore or the library, I look for children's or young adult books about biology.
>
> —*Marty Hudson*

BookTalk Online 3.2

A Wrinkle in Time by Madeleine L'Engle is a classic novel that teaches us time travel is simple compared to the larger problem of good versus evil. Hear more at the Kane Resource Site.

Looking back I would have to say that I was the stereotypical math education student. I saw that I had to take a reading course, and said to myself, "John, you're going to teach math. What could reading possibly mean to you as a math teacher?" I walked into class on the first day with skepticism, but on that very day, a change started to occur. Each and every subsequent Monday and Wednesday, I was being transformed into a teacher of reading above all else.

The opportunity to read full books contributed to my transition to a teacher of reading. For the first time ever, I would sit down and read an entire book, not because I could not read before, but because I now had the desire to read. Where did this motivation and desire to read come from? It came from these wonderful things called booktalks. These sensitive renditions from [my classmates'] personal experience with reading a book gave me a desire to read.

. . . I now uncover the mystery and wonder that is found on every page of a book. . . . I am very happy to have found this alternate world and plan on continuing with my pleasure reading into the future.

—*John Turbeville*

The next subsections will help you understand how you might use particular genres of trade books to teach content, as well as enhance your students' literacy.

BookTalk Online   3.3

Debate has continued for over half a century about the necessity and morality of the first wartime use of the atomic bomb. Several picture books can help us understand the consequences to those most immediately and directly affected. *Shin's Tricycle,* by Tatsuhari Kodama (1995), shares the true story of an innocent three-year-old victim of the bomb; you'll see photographs of Shin and of the tricycle he was riding when the bomb fell (on display at the Hiroshima Peace Museum). *Hiroshima No Pika* by Toshi Maruki (1980) and *My Hiroshima* by Junko Morimoto (1990) tell of the happenings of August 6, 1945, from the perspective of the city's citizens. *Sadako,* by Eleanor Coerr (1993), relates another true story of a girl dying from leukemia, the "atom bomb disease," a decade after the war; the book includes paintings of the memorial statue of Sadako. The powerful text and illustrations in all of these books will stay with you for a long time. Take a look at these books—reading about wars in your history textbooks will never be the same.

Picture Books

ACTIVATING PRIOR KNOWLEDGE   3.2

Make a list of your favorite picture books, stretching as far back as your memory will take you. What made them so good in your mind? Would you still enjoy them today? Now, think of picture books that relate to academic subjects. Do you know of any picture books that are aimed at adolescents or adults rather than children? Brainstorm a list with others in your class or with the Kane Resource Site community.

The term *picture books* can refer either narrowly to the books that require illustration in order for the text to be understood, or to those books whose words could stand alone, but whose pictures are integral to the total experience (Brown & Tomlinson, 1993; Miller, 1998; Pearson, 2005). The close connections between the pictures and the words ensure that the meaning readers derive from the book goes beyond that conveyed by either element individually. In picture books, the illustrations help readers absorb the plot of a narrative story or the information in an expository text. As Pearson (2005) says, "The illustrations in picture books interact with the story, making the whole greater than the two parts. . . . The best picture books are a meld of both story and pictures" (p. 91). Students might not realize how much meaning can be constructed by carefully studying and reflecting on the illustrations. In fact, sometimes the text alone is not meaningful or only partially able to be understood; the pictures are essential, and therefore must be "read."

The artwork or photographs in a book can be the first thing that entices a student to become engaged. Pearson points out: "Perhaps the most important function of picture books is the emotional content. . . . When students' emotions are involved, the lessons are more memorable, and the level of understanding is broader and deeper. . . . Using these stories can add a completely new dimension to any unit" (p. 105). Knowing this, many content area teachers display picture books and have them accessible for students to use freely.

As middle or high school teachers, you may not have been exposed to the array of wonderful texts in this category—so you might think that using picture books with secondary students is inappropriate because they are too easy or the students may feel insulted by their use. During the past couple of decades, however, many sophisticated and beautiful picture books filled with information and thought-provoking prose were published. Content area teachers can use these books to enhance vocabulary growth; present the facts, theories, and background necessary for new lessons; clarify discipline-related concepts; and show how content knowledge is applied in real life (Bloem & Padak, 1996). Perhaps most important, having picture books in your classrooms can lead to an increase in the *volume* of reading done by your students, as they peruse your classroom collection during free moments at the beginning or end of class or while waiting for others to finish an assignment.

Perhaps you can visualize having picture books in your classroom for students to enjoy as an extra, but you're having difficulty thinking of how you could really *teach* from them. The following teaching suggestions and examples may help.

Teaching in action: *Social Studies.* You may consider using any of the numerous picture books that have political messages to stimulate discussion in a social studies course. Think of *The Butter Battle Book* (Seuss, 1984) discussed in Chapter 1. *Faithful Elephants* (Tsuchiya, 1988), *Hiroshima No Pika* (Maruki, 1980), and *My Hiroshima* (Morimoto, 1990) all take place in Japan and give a specific perspective on World War II events. They produce a more visually powerful effect than any social studies textbook could. *Shin's Tricycle* (Kodama, 1995) tells of a young child riding his toy when the atomic bomb fell—they were buried together, but the tricycle was later exhumed and put in the Peace Museum in Hiroshima. You won't find many students telling you such books are too babyish for them.

The same holds true for picture books with environmental themes, such as *Aardvarks, Disembark!* by Ann Jonas (1990), *The Great Kapok Tree* (1990) and *A River Ran Wild* (1992) by Lynne Cherry, and *The Lorax* by Dr. Seuss (1971); or for those conveying social messages about such topics as homelessness, as in *Fly Away Home* by Eve Bunting (1991) and *We Are All in the Dumps with Jack and Guy* by Maurice Sendak (1993). The latter book was shared with fifth graders, and the children responded favorably, for reasons ranging from "'I like books that need a sharp reader and have hidden messages in the pictures' to 'I loved the significance and the pictures. But the story about being poor is sad'" (Norton, 1999, p. 222). The students discussed the parts of the illustration they felt were symbolic, such as the rats, the stars, and the newspaper headlines, and they verbalized what they thought about the book's themes.

Actually, you might wish to present a book that *is* biased in favor of one side of an issue and balance it with another that represents the opposing viewpoint. Students can apply their analyzing, comparing and contrasting, evaluating, and persuading skills as they discuss or write about particular texts.

Miller (1998) points out that picture books can be used to increase vocabulary, help students appreciate the diversity of cultures, introduce abstract topics, and provide appealing, quality literature for our students' pleasure reading no matter what the subject area.

Most of the picture books I've mentioned are fictional, though they do deal with topics taught in subject areas. There are also nonfiction picture books, classified as informational books, that can be very helpful and interesting. Bucher and Hinton (2010) suggest questions teachers, librarians, and students can ask when evaluating such books, including:

- Is the content accurate, current, and clear?
- Is there an unbiased presentation and perspective?
- Does the writing have a didactic or preachy tone?
- Is there a distinction between fact and conjecture or opinion?
- What are the qualifications of the author?
- Is there evidence of research—bibliographies, notes, suggestions for further reading, and mention of Internet sites or key words for searching? (p. 278)

Students need instruction on how to read illustrated informational text. Perhaps you can recall picking up a book or magazine at some point and going through it the first time interacting with little other than the headings, pictures, and captions. I've done that often, and the method has resulted in my learning a lot in a short amount of time. I then go back to read the parts that most interest me (and sometimes that means the whole text). Students can be taught to read in the same efficient manner.

Teaching in action: *History.* Picture this scenario. Mr. Grace shows students the front cover of Diane McWhorter's *A Dream of Freedom: The Civil Rights Movement from 1954 to 1968* (2004). It's a close-up of the face of an African American boy, and in his sunglasses is the reflection of the American flag and the Washington Monument. He invites students to talk about the choice of this photo, the impact it has, and the symbolism involved. Then he asks students to peruse the book with him, paying attention to the photographs and captions; he takes them on a picture walk (Richards & Anderson, 2003) through the text. History comes alive in his classroom as students comment on photos of robed Klansmen, a child in a black rural classroom in Alabama with no desks, Coretta Scott King and her three young children packing a picnic basket to bring to Martin Luther King, Jr. in jail, demonstrators kneeling and praying in Birmingham, a police dog attacking a 15-year-old African American, four young girls who were murdered in a Birmingham church. They read quotes such as Eldridge Cleaver's "You're either part of the solution or part of the problem" (p. 140) and John F. Kennedy's "We are confronted primarily with a moral issue. . . . It is as old as the Scriptures and is as clear as the Constitution" (p. 89). They react to powerful captions, such as, "Lynchings like this one of 32-year-old Ruby Stacy in Fort Lauderdale, Florida, in 1935 had the atmosphere of a community picnic, children welcome" (p. 21).

After students have transacted with the visuals, Mr. Grace tells his class they'll use the Jigsaw II approach to learn about what McWhorter's text has to say about the civil rights movement. The class often uses cooperative learning, so they're not surprised when members of base groups are assigned various sections to read. The following day, Mr. Grace allows time for students to meet in "expert groups." The individuals who read the section involving the Montgomery bus boycott meet together to talk to each other about the main points of the text and how best to teach those points to their base groups. Those who read about the march on Washington do the same, as do the students who are responsible for the section on Malcolm X. The next day, students meet in base groups once again, teaching and learning from each other. Mr. Grace observes great enthusiasm; his readers have embraced the project and feel deeply about the content of the book. Several students say they are going to bring the book home to read it in its entirety. Mr. Grace feels that the initial work with the pictures in the book was well worth the time he devoted to it.

Dean and Grierson (2005) report on the benefits of giving middle and high school students guided practice in reading and writing combined text/picture books, those "that unite multiple genres of expository and narrative writing" (p. 456). They give examples of science and social studies–related books that fit this category, such as Virginia Wright-Frierson's *An Island Scrapbook: From Dawn to Dusk on a Barrier Island* (2002), and show how teachers can help students "read" the illustrations, explore patterns within the text, examine and compare textual differences, and then create their own texts combining genres such as prose and poetry. The authors recommend asking students to reflect on their practices of reading and writing during this kind of scaffolded instruction, so that "students can begin to translate their skills into strategic behaviors that can be used for future reading and writing activities" (p. 487).

The style, colors, perspective, tone, form, use of space, and medium an illustrator uses in a book all make important contributions to understanding and increase the book's impact on a reader. You can explore and choose picture books that motivate and extend your students' understanding of academic subjects. They can analyze perspectives and values conveyed by both the illustrations and the text. At the same time, you can teach them to notice the quality of the artwork and ponder the relation between the text and pictures. The pictures may stay in the readers' memories and affect their thinking and behavior long after they leave your class.

I encourage you to go to bookstores and libraries to explore the genre of informational picture books, and to enthusiastically recommend your favorites to your students. Figure 3.4 lists picture book titles appropriate for various subjects at the middle and high school levels.

Poetry

You might be surprised at how much poetry exists that is accessible to young adults and relevant to school subject areas. Although many students and teachers tend to think of poetry as belonging exclusively in English courses because that's where it's typically taught, there's no need to limit it. Poetry is ideal for all areas because there are ways to use it without taking up much instructional time. You may use a collection of poems to start your lessons as a motivational strategy.

Teaching in action: *Science/Health.* For example, a science or health teacher might use the following humorous poem at the beginning of a lesson on communicable diseases.

The Germ

A mighty creature is the germ,
Though smaller than the pachyderm.
His customary dwelling place
Is deep within the human race.
His childish pride he often pleases,
By giving people strange diseases.
Do you, my poppet, feel infirm?
You probably contain a germ.

Copyright © 1935 by Ogden Nash, renewed. Reprinted by permission of Curtis Brown, Ltd.

Teaching in action: *English.* An English teacher might use the following poem as a mini-lesson to emphasize the importance of punctuation before she hands back some student papers that were a bit lacking in that area:

Call the doctors Call the nurses Give me a breath of air I've been reading all your stories but the periods aren't there Call the policemen Call the traffic guards Give me a stop sign quick Your sentences are running when they need a walking stick Call the commas Call the question marks Give me a single clue Tell me where to breathe with a punctuation mark or two

Reprinted with permission of Simon & Schuster Books for Young Readers, an imprint of Simon & Schuster Children's Publishing Division from *If You're Not Here Please Raise Your Hand* by Kalli Dakos, Text copyright (c) 1990, Kalli Dakos.

Teaching in action: *Physical Education.* A physical education class can enjoy such poems as "Casey at

the Bat" (Thayer, 2000, p. 282) along with sequels: "Casey's Revenge" (Wilson, 1936, p. 284), "Casey—Twenty Years Later" (McDonald, 1936, p. 286), and "Casey's Daughter at the Bat" (Graham, 1988, p. 42).

Teaching in action: *Music.* Music teachers can open classes with recitations of poems from Jaime Adoff's *The Song Shoots Out of My Mouth: A Celebration of Music* (2002).

Chapters 1 and 2 addressed the affective realm of learning, and poetry is a perfect way to help students invest emotionally in the topics they study. For example, compare this textbook excerpt (from

FIGURE 3.4 Examples of picture books appropriate for teaching concepts in middle and high school disciplines.

See more suggested titles in Appendix Figure 3.4.

ART AND MUSIC

Aaseng, N. (2001). *Wildshots: The World of the Wildlife Photographer.* Brookfield, CT: Millbrook Press.

Brennen, B. (Selector). (2000). *Voices: Poetry and Art from Around the World.* Washington, DC: National Geographic Society.

Davies, A. (2000). *The Encyclopedia of Photography: An A-to-Z Visual Directory, with an Inspirational Gallery of Finished Works.* Philadelphia: Running Press.

Greenberg, J., & Jordan, S. (2008). *Christo & Jeanne-Claude: The Gates and Beyond.* New York: Roaring Brook Press.

Rubin, S. G. (2000). *Fireflies in the Dark: The Story of Friedl Dicker-Brandeis and the Children of Terezin.* New York: Holiday House.

ENGLISH/LANGUAGE ARTS

Aliki. (1999). *William Shakespeare and the Globe.* New York: HarperCollins.

Lyon, G. E., & Catalanotto, P. (1999). *Book.* New York: DK Publishing.

Truss, L. (2006). *Eats, Shoots & Leaves: Why, Commas really do make a difference!* (B. Timmons, Illus.). New York: G.P. Putnam's Sons.

Truss, L. (2008). *Twenty-odd Ducks.* (B. Timmons, Illus.). New York: G.P. Putnam's Sons.

Wisniewski, D. (1996). *Golem.* New York: Clarion Books.

HISTORY/GEOGRAPHY/SOCIAL STUDIES/CULTURAL STUDIES

Ambrose, S. E. (2001). *The Good Fight: How World War II Was Won.* New York: Atheneum.

Carey, C. W., Jr. (2000). *The Emancipation Proclamation.* Chanhassen, MN: Child's World.

Corey, S., & McLaren, C. (2000). *You Forgot Your Skirt, Amelia Bloomer!* New York: Scholastic.

Macaulay, D. (2003). *Mosque.* Boston: Houghton Mifflin.

Smith, L. (2006). *John, Paul, George and Ben.* New York: Hyperion Books for Children.

MATH

Ball, J. (2005). *Go Figure! A Totally Cool Book About Numbers.* New York: DK Children.

Barasch, L. (2005). *Ask Albert Einstein.* New York: Farrar, Straus & Giroux.

Ellis, J. (2004). *What's Your Angle, Pythagoras?: A Math Adventure.* Watertown, MA: Charlesbridge.

Milbourne, A. (2007). *How Big Is a Million?* (S. Riglietti, Illus.). London, U.K.: Usborne.

Neuschwander, C. (2003). *Sir Cumference and the Sword in the Cone.* Watertown, MA: Charlesbridge.

PHYSICAL EDUCATION

Forten, F. (2000). *Sports: The Complete Visual Reference.* Buffalo, NY: Firefly Books.

Hoyt-Goldsmith, D. (1998). *Lacrosse: The National Game of the Iroquois.* Photos by L. Migdale. New York: Holiday House.

Wilson, S. (2000). *The Hockey Book for Girls.* Toronto, Canada: Kids Can Press.

SCIENCE

Aulenbach, N. H., & Barton, H. A. (2001). *Exploring Caves: Journeys into the Earth.* Washington, DC: National Geographic Society.

Craats, R. (2000). *The Science of Sound.* Milwaukee, WI: Gareth Stevens Publishing.

Henderson, D. (2000). *Asteroid Impact.* New York: Dial Books for Young Readers.

Riley, J. (2005). *The Nervous System.* Minneapolis, MN: Lerner.

Skurzynski, G. (2000). *On Time: From Seasons to Split Seconds.* Washington, DC: National Geographic Society.

The American Pageant) on the topic of Reconstruction with the poem narrated by a former Southern soldier that follows it.

Teaching in action: *History.* Consider how a history teacher might use the two genres together.

> Beaten but unbent, many high-spirited white Southerners remained dangerously defiant. . . . Conscious of no crime, these former Confederates continued to believe that their view of secession was correct and that the 'lost cause' was still a just war. (Bailey, Kennedy, & Cohen, 1998, p. 489)

The Rebel

> . . . I won't be reconstructed! I'm better now than them;
> And for a carpetbagger, I don't give a damn;
> So I'm off for the frontier, soon as I can go,
> I'll prepare me a weapon and start for Mexico.
>
> I can't take up my musket and fight them now no mo',
> But I'm not goin' to love 'em, and that is certain sho';
> And I don't want no pardon for what I was or am,
> I won't be reconstructed and I don't give a damn.

Time, or the lack of it, is one of the biggest problems teachers face. Learning content takes time; introducing, practicing, and reinforcing literacy skills take time. Of course teachers want, and try, to work in time for pleasure reading, including the enjoyment of poetry. The opportunity for teaching skills plus content is present when you use poems that fit the curriculum. For example, an American history teacher can use a poem or song within a story to help students understand slavery and the Underground Railroad. By reading *Follow the Drinking Gourd* (Winter, 1988), students get invested in the story of Peg Leg Joe, the legendary conductor who taught slaves a seemingly harmless folk song:

> When the sun comes back, and the first quail calls,
> Follow the drinking gourd.
> For the old man is a-waiting for to carry you to freedom
> If you follow the drinking gourd.

From *Follow the Drinking Gourd* by Jeanette Winter. Copyright © 1988 by Jeanette Winter. Reprinted by permission of Alfred A. Knopf Children's Books, a division of Random House, Inc.

Students can be taught that there are "hidden meanings" in this poem—the directions for escape had to be kept a secret from the masters. "The drinking gourd" is the Big Dipper (some science content as an added bonus); the first line refers to spring. Three additional verses contain similar "coded messages" or symbols. When students encounter other poems with symbols, the concept of symbolism may be easier for them to understand because they have understood this song.

The class can discuss the techniques the poet used to make this simple poem so powerful, and they might try to model some of their own writing after this and other favorites. They can experiment with rhyme, repetition, and rhythm, using conversations and questions. Language arts skills are handled very naturally in an authentic context.

We do have to be careful not to overemphasize the skills as our students read poetry because the focus takes away from the enjoyment and wonder. To check ourselves, we might well keep in mind this poem composed and narrated by the character Kate, a middle school-aged child:

> I used to like "Stopping by Woods on a Snowy Evening."
> I liked the coming darkness,
> The jingle of harness bells, breaking—and adding to—
>   the stillness,
> The gentle drift of snow. . . .
>
> But today, the teacher told us what everything stood for.
> The woods, the horse, the miles to go, the sleep—
> They all have "hidden meanings."
>
> It's grown so complicated now that,
> Next time I drive by,
> I don't think I'll bother to stop.

"After English Class," a selection from *Hey World, Here I Am!* Text copyright © 1986 by Jean Little. Reprinted by permission of HarperCollins Publishers.

Figure 3.5 lists some resources you can explore as you use poetry to enhance your curricular content and your students' understanding of the people, con-

BookTalk   3.4

Do you think there are "boy books" and "girl books"? How about "boy poems" and "girl poems"? What might be some characteristics that make certain texts appeal to one gender or the other? No matter how you feel about the issue of gender and reading preference, I suggest you investigate two collections: *A Fury of Motion: Poems for Boys* by C. Ghigna (www.charlesghigna.com) (2003) and *A Maze Me: Poems for Girls* by Naomi Shihab Nye (2005). See which poems you think could be used in either collection; read what the authors themselves say about targeting one gender for their poems. Share some of the poems from each with young people you know. You could use these books when you model reading intertextually, showing your students how your juxtaposition of the two texts helps you think about each in relation to the other.

| FIGURE | 3.5 | Sources of poetry for the content areas. |

See more suggested titles in Appendix Figure 3.5.

MATH, SCIENCE, AND TECHNOLOGY

Franco, B. (2006). *Math Poetry: Linking Language and Math in a Fresh Way*. Tucson, AZ: Good Year Books.

Harley, A. (2008). *The Monarch's Progress: Poems with Wings*. Honesdale, PA: Wordsong.

Nelson, M. (2004). *Fortune's Bones: The Manumission Requiem*. Asheville, NC: Front Street.

Tang, G. (2005). *Math Potatoes: More Mind-Stretching Brain Food*. New York: Scholastic.

ENGLISH LANGUAGE ARTS

Atwell, N. (2006). *A Poem a Day: A Guide to Naming the World*. Portsmouth, NH: Heinemann.

Carroll, L. (2007). *Jabberwocky*. (C. Myers, Illus.). New York: Jump at the Sun/Hyperion Books for Children.

Holbrook, S., & Wolf, A. (2008). *More Than Friends: Poems from Him and Her*. Honesdale, PA: Wordsong.

Mora, P. (2010). *Dizzy in Your Eyes: Poems About Love*. New York: Knopf.

Nelson, H. (Ed.). (2010). *Earth, My Likeness: Nature Poetry of Walt Whitman*. Berkeley, CA: North Atlantic Books.

SOCIAL STUDIES

Bryant, J. (2008). *Ringside, 1925: Views from the Scopes Trial*. New York: Alfred A. Knopf.

Carlson, L. (Ed.). (2008). *Voices in First Person: Reflections on Latino Identity*. Photography by M. Rivera-Ortiz. (F. Morais, Illus.). New York: Atheneum Books for Young Readers.

Engle, M. (2008). *The Surrender Tree: Poems of Cuba's Struggle for Freedom*. New York: Henry Holt.

Hopkins, L. B. (Ed.). (2008). *America at War*. New York: Margaret K. McElderry/Simon & Schuster.

Nelson, M. (2008). *The Freedom Business: A Narrative of the Life and Adventures of Venture, a Native of Africa*. (D. Dancy, Illus.). Honesdale, PA: Wordsong.

FINE ARTS

Greenberg, J. (2001). *Heart to Heart: New Poems Inspired by Twentieth-Century American Art*. New York: Harry N. Abrams.

Greenberg, J., & Jordan, S. (2008). *Side by Side: New Poetry Inspired by Art from Around Our World*. New York: Abrams Books for Young Readers.

Myers, W. D. (2003). *Blues Journey*. (C. Myers, Illus.). New York: Holiday House.

Nye, N. S. (1998). *The Space Between Our Footsteps: Poems and Paintings from the Middle East*. New York: Simon & Schuster.

Rubin, S. G. (2008). *Whaam!: The Art and Life of Roy Lichtenstein*. New York: Abrams.

PHYSICAL EDUCATION

Carney, G. (1993). *Romancing the Horsehide: Baseball Poems on Players and the Game*. Jefferson, NC: McFarland.

Glenn, M. (1997). *Jump Ball: A Basketball Season in Poems*. New York: Lodestar.

Korman, G., & Korman, B. (1996). *The Last-Place Sports Poems of Jeremy Bloom*. New York: Scholastic.

Macy, S. (Ed.). (2001). *Girls Got Game: Sports Stories and Poems*. New York: Henry Holt.

Smith, C. R., Jr. (2001). *Short Takes: Fast-Break Basketball Poetry*. New York: Dutton Children's Books.

FOREIGN LANGUAGES

Ferrer, R. (2008). *Cascarita de Nuez (Little Nutshell)*. (T. Lewis, Trans.). Asunción, Paraguay: Fausto Ediciónes.

---

cepts, and events important in your discipline. You'll find many more titles and suggestions for using poetry in your discipline in Chatton's *Using Poetry Across the Curriculum* (2010).

Biographies/Autobiographies

Biographies and autobiographies are powerful ways to build enthusiasm for learning because they use the stories and words of actual people in fields of study. Very often geniuses are eccentric, and anecdotes about the way they work will fascinate your students. For example, math teachers can pass along the legacy of Paul Erdös, a brilliant man who forsook having his own family and home for the sake of mathematics. They can have students read excerpts from *The Man Who Loved Only Numbers* by Paul Hoffman (1998). Erdös traveled all over the world, staying at other mathematicians' homes, prodigiously publishing proofs that had stymied the best in the field for years or centuries, thinking about math for 18 hours a day. Yet, he had difficulty tying his shoes, cutting grapefruit, following directions, accomplishing mundane tasks. Science teachers can show some of the new biographies about Charles Darwin concurrent with the 200th anniversary of his birth, including *Charles and Emma: The Darwins' Leap of Faith* (Heiligman, 2009), *One Beetle Too Many: The Extraordi-*

nary Adventures of Charles Darwin (Lasky, 2009), *What Mr. Darwin Saw* (Manning, 2009), *Darwin's Paradox* (Munteanu, 2007), *Young Charles Darwin and the Voyage of the HMS Beagle* (Ashby, 2009), and *What Darwin Saw: The Journey That Changed the World* (Schanzer, 2009). Figure 3.6 lists other biographies of outstanding practitioners who show an extraordinary passion for their fields, as well as some who became activists to further their causes.

BookTalk Online   3.5

A Beautiful Mind: A Biography of John Forbes Nash by Sylvia Nasar explores the brilliance and illness of a mathematical genius. Hear more at the Kane Resource Site.

BookTalk   3.6

Some of your students will love trees. They will also love Julia Butterfly Hill (juliabutterflyhill.wordpress.com), the young woman whose memoir, *The Legacy of Luna: The Story of a Tree, a Woman, and the Struggle to Save the Redwoods* (2000), tells of her two-year stay atop a giant redwood to protest the destruction of the environment. After they read about her life on a platform 18 stories off the ground, writing and receiving hundreds of letters weekly from youthful supporters around the world, fighting with industrialists and politicians, they may be motivated to pursue more knowledge about nature and to take action in their own communities where nature is at risk.

ACTION RESEARCH   3.C

Choose one of the biographies listed in Figure 3.6 or mentioned in the preceding section or the booktalks, or another you find about a practitioner in the discipline you will teach. Read it, responding in your learning log about your own reactions, as well as any thoughts and ideas the text may stimulate in terms of your own teaching. What can you take from this book that will help your students grow in their knowledge of your subject?

Other Nonfiction

The number and quality of nonfiction trade books have increased enormously over the past several years. Take advantage of this abundant treasure throughout

FIGURE 3.6

Stories of and by passionate practitioners and activists, some in picture book format.

See more suggested titles in Appendix Figure 3.6.

Bardhan-Quallen, S. (2008). *Up Close: Jane Goodall.* New York: Viking.

Bryant, J. (2008). *A River of Words: The Story of William Carlos Williams.* Grand Rapids, MI: Eerdmans.

Demi. (2009). *Rumi: Whirling Dervish.* Tarrytown, NY: Marshall Cavendish.

Grimes, N. (2008). *Barack Obama: Son of Promise, Child of Hope.* (B. Collier, Illus.). New York: Simon & Schuster Books for Young Children.

Krull, K. (2008). *Hillary Rodham Clinton: Dreams Taking Flight.* (A. J. Bates, Illus.). New York: Simon & Schuster.

your curricular units. Students can examine topics in depth while employing critical-thinking skills to synthesize and evaluate the information, and still enjoy the ideas and presentation. A classroom library rich in nonfiction texts also encourages students to practice reading expository text, a skill that will serve them throughout their lives. Attractive and entertaining nonfiction books are tantalizing and motivational; they bring curricular topics to life in a way that textbooks cannot.

Figure 3.7 lists some of the many nonfiction books available for incorporation into your content area teaching.

Evaluating and Selecting Trade Books

As is true of textbooks, trade books vary greatly in quality. Select them wisely. Be aware that many trade books, especially older ones, contain inaccurate information or biased presentations of groups. For example, the popular *Little House on the Prairie* series, by Laura Ingalls Wilder (www.lauraingallswilderhome.com), has come under attack from many critics because of the negative way it depicts Native Americans (e.g., Kuhlman, 2001; Mowder, 1992; Romines, 1997; Segal, 1977). Some people recommend avoiding the use of such texts altogether, not having them available in classrooms and school libraries. Others see materials like these as potential teaching tools to motivate student thinking, discussion, and research. For example, teachers could use the Wilder books along with excerpts from Miller's *Laura Ingalls Wilder and the American Frontier: Five Perspectives* (2002), which contains chapters repre-

FIGURE **3.7** **Examples of nonfiction books that connect to content curriculum.**

See more suggested titles in Appendix Figure 3.7.

SCIENCE AND MATH

Highfield, R. (2002). *The Science of Harry Potter: How Magic Really Works.* New York: Viking.

Kelly, E., & Kissel, R. (2008). *Evolving Planet: Four Billion Years of Life on Earth.* New York: Abrams.

Macaulay, D. (2008). *The Way We Work: Getting to Know the Amazing Body.* Boston: Houghton/Lorraine.

Odifreddi, P. (2004). *The Mathematical Century: The 30 Greatest Problems of the Last 100 Years.* (A. Sangalli, Trans.). Princeton, NJ: Princeton University Press.

Wells, D. (2005). *Prime Numbers: The Most Mysterious Figures in Math.* New York: Wiley.

HISTORY/SOCIAL STUDIES

Aronson, M. (2008). *Unsettled: The Problem of Loving Israel.* New York: Atheneum.

Bartoletti, S. C. (2005). *Hitler Youth: Growing Up in Hitler's Shadow.* New York: Scholastic.

Brown, D. (2008). *All Stations! Distress!: April 15, 1912: The Day the Titanic Sank.* New York: Roaring Brook Press.

Gay, K. (2008). *The Aftermath of the Chinese Nationalist Revolution.* Breckenridge, CO: Twenty-First Century Books.

Getzinger, D. (2008). *Triangle Shirtwaist Factory Fire.* Greensboro, NC: Morgan Reynolds Publishing.

FINE ARTS

Beckett, W. (2000). *My Favorite Things: 75 Works of Art from Around the World.* New York: Abrams.

Carroll, C. (1996). *How Artists See the Weather.* New York: Abbeville Kids.

Rubin, S. G. (2004). *Art Against the Odds: From Slave Quilts to Prison Paintings.* New York: Crown.

Sayre, H. (2004). *Cave Paintings to Picasso: The Inside Scoop on 50 Art Masterpieces.* San Francisco: Chronicle Books.

Sills, L. (2000). *In Real Life: Six Women Photographers.* New York: Holiday House.

HEALTH, WELLNESS, AND PHYSICAL EDUCATION

Armstrong, L., & Jenkins, S. (2000). *It's Not About the Bike: My Journey Back to Life.* New York: Putnam.

Gottlieb, L. (2000). *Stick Figure: A Diary of My Former Self.* New York: Simon & Schuster.

Hirschfelder, A. (2001). *Kick Butts!: A Kid's Action Guide to a Tobacco-Free America.* Lanham, MD: Scarecrow Press.

Kent, J. C. (1998). *Women in Medicine.* Minneapolis, MN: Oliver Press.

Walsh, M. (2008). *Does This Book Make Me: Look Fat?* New York: Clarion.

ENGLISH LANGUAGE ARTS

Cary, P. (2005). *Wrong About Japan: A Father's Journey with his Son.* New York: Knopf.

Greenblatt, S. (2004). *Will in the World: How Shakespeare Became Shakespeare.* New York: W.W. Norton.

Truss, L. (2003). *Eats, Shoots & Leaves: The Zero Tolerance Approach to Punctuation.* New York: Gotham Books.

Wolf, A. (2006). *Immersed in Verse: An Informative, Slightly Irreverent & Totally Tremendous Guide to Living the Poet's Life.* New York: Sterling.

---

senting a variety of viewpoints, including that of an elementary school teacher; and *Constructing the Little House: Gender, Culture, and Laura Ingalls Wilder* by Ann Romines (1997), which could help students investigate aspects of the books they hadn't consciously thought of before. Additional resources include two biographies called *Laura Ingalls Wilder,* one by Berne (2008) and one by Sickels (2007), as well as *Laura Ingalls Wilder, Farm Journalist: Writings from the Ozarks* (Hines, 2007) and *Writings to Young Women from Laura Ingalls Wilder* (Hines, 2006). Kuhlman (2001) purports:

> . . . we must present our students with reasons to go beyond the surface and ask critical questions of the author and text that involve perspective and power structures. Additionally, we must provide multiple perspectives through other pieces of literature when possible. A companion book to any of Wilder's *Little House* books is *The Birchbark House* by Louise

Erdrich (1999) that tells a young Ojibway girl's family experience for one year in 1847. (p. 397)

Erdrich has since written sequels, *The Game of Silence* (2005) and *The Porcupine Year* (2008).

APPLICATION ACTIVITY **3.3** (SEE PAGE 85)

Guidelines for selecting trade books

As with textbooks, use several procedures to evaluate trade books. To assess difficulty, use the cloze procedure (discussed in Chapter 10) or a readability formula to get an idea of a book's appropriate grade level. But remember, a score derived this way is not smarter than the teacher. Let's say you have a student named Chaneta in your eighth-grade English class who has severe reading difficulties; reliable assessment instruments (more on these in Chapter

9) determined Chaneta's reading level to be at about the third grade. She has a passionate interest in biographies of people who have overcome disabilities. You have a book in your classroom library, *Dear Dr. Bell . . . Your Friend, Helen Keller* by Judith St. George (1992), and the back cover indicates that it has a fifth-grade readability level (it doesn't say which formula was used). You appreciate the rough estimate that was supplied, but decide to recommend the book to Chaneta anyway, offering assistance should she need it. She still has the right to abandon it and find a different book if she chooses.

In addition to assessing difficulty, ask yourself a few questions, such as the following, when choosing trade books:

- Do I like this book?
- Does it connect to one or more of my curricular topics?
- Does it have the potential to build background knowledge for topics in my course?
- Does it assume background knowledge my students might not possess?
- Is it accurate and up-to-date?
- Do I detect any biases or stereotypical treatment of people?
- Are issues relating to diversity represented well?
- Will my students find it attractive and appealing?
- How easy or difficult will it be for various students?
- What do I think of the style and tone?
- How might my students react to these?
- What do I know about the author or publisher?

Fortunately, we do not have to tackle the formidable task of reviewing every trade book that sounds like it might be a profitable addition to our classroom or school library. There are excellent sources of reviews done by experts. Although we won't necessarily agree with each one, they provide an excellent starting place and can help us stay abreast of the recent releases. Figure 3.8 lists some of these resources for teachers, librarians, parents, and students.

When students or in-service workshop participants see my personal traveling library of trade books, I'm often asked whether I spend half my salary at bookstores. There are many ways you can build your personal or classroom collection of discipline-related trade books quite inexpensively. Libraries often sell withdrawn or donated books; I do check out the sale tables at bookstores. Following Figure 3.8 are the web addresses or phone numbers of several book clubs that cater to the curricular needs of middle and secondary teachers or that are related to disciplines taught in schools.

FIGURE 3.8

Resources for selecting and reviewing trade books.

See more suggested titles in Appendix Figure 3.8.

Bodart, J. (2010). *Radical Reads 2: Working with the Newest Edgy Titles for Teens*. Lanham, MD: The Rowman & Littlefield Publishing Group.

Kane, S. (2008). *Integrating Literature in the Content Areas*. Scottsdale, AZ: Holcomb Hathaway.

Pearl, N. (2007). *Book Crush: For Kids and Teens—Recommended Reading for Every Mood, Moment, and Interest*. Seattle: Sasquatch Books.

Sandmann, A. L., & Ahern, J. F. (2002). *Linking Literature with Life: The NCSS Standards and Children's Literature for the Middle Grades*. Silver Springs, MD: National Council for the Social Studies.

Schall, L. (2009). *Genre Talks for Teens: Booktalks and More for Every Teen Reading Interest*. Westport, CT: Libraries Unlimited.

The following journals and periodicals are also extremely helpful for reviews and commentary on relevant trade book issues:

The Horn Book Magazine

The Horn Book Guide

The ALAN Review (The Assembly on Literature for Adolescents of the National Council of Teachers of English)

Books for the Teen Age (New York Public Library)

English Journal (National Council of Teachers of English)

Journal of Adolescent and Adult Literacy (International Reading Association)

Book Links

The New Advocate (Christopher-Gordon Publishers)

KLIATT

VOYA (Voices of Youth Advocates)

School Library Journal

TAB: The Teen Book Club, www.scholastic.com/tab

Arrow Book Club (for middle grades), www.scholastic.com/arrow

The History Book Club, 1-800-348-7128

Your school librarian can become your greatest ally as you implement the use of trade books in your content units and projects. Librarians are usually eager to be called upon and are happy to share their expertise and their enthusiasm for content-related literature. They can gather titles and actual books for the teacher, and give booktalks to students.

Special populations and the selection of trade books

Gender considerations. Recent attention has been paid to the specific reading preferences of girls and boys. Books such as *"Reading Don't Fix No Chevys": Literacy in the Lives of Young Men* (Smith & Wilhelm, 2002), *Out of this World: Why Literature Matters to Girls* (Blackford, 2004), *To Be a Boy, to Be a Reader* (Brozo, 2005), and *Reading for Their Life: (Re)building the Textual Lineages of African American Adolescent Males* (Tatum, 2009) give reasons for addressing students' literary preferences and needs with gender in mind. Children's author Jon Scieszka initiated a nonprofit literacy program, Guys Read, and a related website, www.guysread.com. He also edited *Guys Write for Guys Read* (2005), which he describes as a "bunch of pieces by a bunch of guys . . . about being a guy . . . [which are] funny, action-packed, sad, goofy, gross, touching, stupid, true, and all very short" (p. 11).

Fink (2006) notes that in her study of 66 striving readers, the women in general preferred novels, while the men preferred nonfiction texts, though there were exceptions. We must ask ourselves, as Fink does, "How can we engage boys and girls in reading through their preferred interests and genres without promoting gender stereotypes?" (p. 118). She suggests using gender-balancing activities, including having students think about how stories would have been different if certain characters' genders were reversed; by giving voice to minor characters in books; and by selecting books containing sensitive, nurturing males and/or active females. I sometimes use the nonfiction adventure book *Shipwreck at the Bottom of the World* (1998), noting that its author, Jennifer Armstrong (www.jennifer-armstrong.com), is a female. Keep gender issues in mind as you build your classroom library and make assignments and suggestions relating to trade books. In addition, try to broaden your own reading interests and let students know what new areas you're exploring.

English learners. You'll need to pay special attention to the students in your class whose first language is one other than English. It's important to recognize that there will be a gap between those students' facility and verbal skills in everyday settings and their ability to handle language tasks in content areas such as math, social studies, and science. We'll explore this topic in more depth in Chapter 6, but for now, you can begin thinking about how you can ensure there will be appropriate materials in your content classroom for students reading at all levels and whose fluency in English will be at varying levels. Vardell, Hadaway, and Young (2006) cite research demonstrating that students in classrooms having libraries read 50 percent more than those without (Morrow, 2003), and that access to classroom libraries might be even more crucial for those learning English (Chambliss & McKillop, 2000). Essential elements to consider when choosing literature for this population include content accessibility (familiarity with the topic will help), language accessibility, visual accessibility, genre accessibility, and cultural accessibility. Vardell et al. conclude:

> With such variety in the classroom and library and time to pore over these books, English learners will notice the many powerful ways the written word can be used—to inform, to entertain, or to persuade. In short, they can discover the power and pleasure of their new language through good books. (p. 740)

Internet sites provide access to trade books in many languages. Begin by checking out the International Children's Digital Library (www.icdl.org).

PRIMARY SOURCES

According to McElvaine (2000), primary sources are:

> the raw material of history. . . . Using primary sources allows us not just to read about history, but to read history itself. It allows us to immerse ourselves in the look and feel of an era gone by, to understand its people and their language. . . . And it allows us to take an active, hands-on role in (re)constructing history. (p. 8)

Trofanenko (2002) recommends teaching students about how authors research sources as they construct particular ways to present the stories they've chosen to tell, and teachers should not limit themselves to trade and textbooks, but use primary documents also. Primary sources are those that provide direct testimony or evidence about a topic. They are created by witnesses or recorders, either at the time when historical events occurred or afterward, in the form of a memoir or oral history. Primary sources are characterized by their content, regardless of whether they are available in original, digital, or print format. They may include letters, manuscripts, diaries, journals, newspapers, speeches, interviews, memoirs, maps, documents produced by government agencies, photographs, audio or video recordings, and objects or artifacts. Trafanenko states, "Using primary source documents allows the student not just to read about the past, but to see how the past is constructed as history through such sources. It allows students to immerse themselves into the language, events and individuals and to take agency in reconstructing his history" (p. 132).

In all subject areas, the use of relevant documents can add interest to your lessons, as well as information that will benefit your students as they seek to acquire knowledge in and understand the foundations of the discipline. There's just no substitute for the real thing. For decades, social studies teachers were trained to teach about people, events, ideologies, social movements, and historical eras using published instructional materials. Science teachers taught about the major revolutions precipitated by the discoveries of Copernicus, Newton, Einstein, Darwin, and Watson and Crick the same way. However, current national standards for many content areas now call for students to be exposed to and taught to read and analyze primary sources in the disciplines. They are expected not only to comprehend various texts, but also to react to them; to synthesize information from several places and compare and contrast information from disparate voices. Happily, it is very easy to find documents that support your teaching and your students' scholarly explorations. Figure 3.9 lists titles that history teachers might provide students or use as material for lessons.

Newspapers, scholarly journals, government files, Internet sites, autobiographies, and library archives provide fascinating and detailed accounts of events and people's thinking about the topics you teach. This section, by way of example, highlights two types of primary sources, or adapted primary sources,

---

BookTalk 3.7

History textbooks summarize, highlight, and paraphrase important documents. That's their job. But your classroom library can also give students the real words of the people who played roles throughout American history. *Words that Built a Nation: A Young Person's Collection of Historic American Documents,* by Marilyn Miller (1999), provides the complete text or excerpts from such varied pieces as the "Statement on the Causes of Wounded Knee" by Red Cloud, Jane Addams' "Twenty Years at Hull House," Malcolm X's "The Ballot or the Bullet," Cesar Chavez's "Speech to Striking Grape Workers," and *Silent Spring* by Rachel Carson. Students can compare the farewell addresses of George Washington and Ronald Reagan, experience Richard Nixon's letter of resignation, and travel back to 1954 as they read from the U. S. Supreme Court decision in the case of *Brown v. Board of Education of Topeka.* The book offers margin notes that provide context and relevant photographs. It provides a literary field trip to pivotal times and events in our nation's history, and brings together diverse voices on crucial issues.

---

that contain modernized spelling and language and are usually easier to find: letters and personal journals. Speeches, biographies and autobiographies, and other types of documents are introduced throughout later chapters.

Letters

It's likely your students will be familiar with *epistolary* writing, though they may not know this term and they may not have considered it a real genre or connected to their academic learning. We can change that by using their comfort with writing to their friends and relatives, perhaps via e-mail or a social networking site, as a bridge to other areas of this important category. Encourage students to explore the preserved letters from real people and examine them in terms of formality, style, and content. They can read aloud selected relevant excerpts from correspondents within the discipline, perhaps along with commentary from others.

Teaching in action: *Physics.* For example, a physics teacher could read a letter written by Richard Feynman to a layperson who had written with a question similar to the questions inherent in her lesson for that day, selected from the letters his daughter organized and published for the sake of continuing

---

FIGURE 3.9

Examples of documentary resources for history teachers.

See more suggested titles in Appendix Figure 3.9.

America's Words of Freedom: Speeches, Documents, and Writings That Moved Our Country. (2007). Nashville, TN: Ideals Publications.

Finkelman, P., & Lesh, B. A. (2008). *Milestone Documents in American History: Exploring the Primary Sources That Shaped America.* Dallas, TX: Schlager Group.

Frader, L. L. (2006). *The Industrial Revolution: A History in Documents.* New York: Oxford University Press.

Lowenstein, F., Lechner, S., & Bruun, E. (2007). *Voices of Protest: Documents of Courage and Dissent: Martin Luther King, Jr., Tiananmen Square, Jesus, Communisto Manifesto, the Boston Tea Party, Rachel Carson, the U.S. Bill of Rights.* New York: Black Dog & Leventhal Publishers.

Panchyk, R. (2009). *The Keys to American History: Understanding Our Most Important Historic Documents.* Chicago: Chicago Review Press.

the wonderful teaching he did during his lifetime (Feynman, 2005). Another day, the teacher might read from *The Born–Einstein Letters: Friendship, Politics, and Physics in Uncertain Times: Correspondence between Albert Einstein and Max and Hedwig Born from 1916 to 1955, with Commentaries by Max Born* (Born, 2005). Students who hear such moving conversation will understand the dynamic nature of scientific, as well as political and philosophical, thought and development. You can determine other ways to use these books in your classroom.

Teaching in action: *Art.* Art teachers can use the letters written by Frank Lloyd Wright and Georgia O'Keefe found in *Letters of a Nation* (Carroll, 1997), and one from Vincent Van Gogh to his brother, Theo, found in *Famous Letters: Messages and Thoughts that Shaped Our World* (McLynn, 1993). The personal glimpses into the artists' minds help students bring more background knowledge and curiosity to the study of their works.

Teaching in action: *Social Studies.* Social studies teachers may have the largest selection of easily accessible letters that will help students get inside the minds of famous leaders and people who initiated, or were affected by, policies and social movements. Letters available in Carroll's *Letters of a Nation* include Meriwether Lewis and William Clark to the Oto Indians (on the purpose of their journey), Abigail Adams to John Adams (exhorting him to "remember the ladies" in their deliberations on the Declaration of Independence), Frederick Douglass to his former master and to Harriet Tubman, Franklin D. Roosevelt's secret cable to Winston Churchill the day after the bombing of Pearl Harbor, John F. Kennedy to Nikita Khrushchev on resolving the Cuban Missile Crisis, Malcolm X's letter to his followers about the possibility for peace and good will between blacks and whites, and Elizabeth Cady Stanton to Susan B. Anthony. Other relevant books are Schomp's *World War II (Letters from the Battlefront)* (2004), *Searching for Anne Frank: Letters from Amsterdam to Iowa* (Rubin, 2003), *George Washington the Writer: A Treasury of Letters, Diaries and Public Documents* (Yoder, 2003), and *Dear Mrs. Roosevelt: Letters from Children of the Great Depression* by R. Cohen (2002).

Teaching in action: *Science.* Science teachers might share the following letters from *Famous Letters* with students: Galileo Galilei to Belisario Vinta, Louis Pasteur to his family, Albert Einstein to Franklin D. Roosevelt. Biology classes might appreciate two intriguing books by Jane Goodall: *Africa in My Blood: An Autobiography in Letters: The Early Years* (2000) and *Beyond Innocence: An Autobiography in Letters: The Later Years* (2001).

Here is an excerpt from a letter written by Albert Einstein to a sixth-grade student who had asked him in a letter whether scientists pray:

> . . . everyone who is seriously involved in the pursuit of science becomes convinced that a spirit is manifest in the laws of the Universe—a spirit vastly superior to that of man, and one in the face of which we with our modest powers must feel humble. In this way the pursuit of science leads to a religious feeling of a special sort, which is indeed quite different from the religiosity of someone more naive. (Carroll, 1997, pp. 404–405)

Teachers might use that letter as if it were addressed to all sixth graders, or to their class, and to ask for their response, discussion, and thoughts about science and religion and about a man as important as Einstein taking time to answer a child's letter. Preserved letters are an educational gold mine, treasures just waiting to be put into students' hands.

Journals and Diaries

Lest students think that journals are things dreamed up by teachers to be imposed on students, and nonexistent in the real world, we can assure them that this is not the case. In every field, there are wonderful examples of information we would not have now if practitioners had not kept logs. Darwin kept one during his voyages on *The Beagle*; Malcolm X kept one while in prison. Abraham Lincoln poured out his soul in his journal as the Civil War raged. Beatrix Potter created an illustrated journal that led to some very famous children's books. I was in awe when I saw in a museum the open journals of Leonardo da Vinci on display, showing a record of his creative genius and his unique handwriting. Journals allow us into the minds of people as no other source can. On July 15, 1868, Louisa May Alcott wrote in her journal, "Have finished *Little Women*, and have sent it off—402 pages. . . . Hope it will go" (Cheney, 1995, p. 139). Of course, she couldn't have known it would still be in print and in theatres a century and a half later. How lucky we are to have her recorded private thoughts, as well as her published masterpieces.

Students can learn about additional work that resulted from the original journals of people in a

BookTalk Online   **3.8**

Famous Love Letters: Messages of Intimacy and Passion, edited by Ronald Tamplin, makes the connection between academic texts and romance. Read more at the Kane Resource Site.

variety of disciplines, and the value that people's journals have to future generations. Use this knowledge about authentic journals to help your students view journal-keeping as potentially valuable to *their* real worlds as opposed to a school assignment that simply must be endured. Students can use published journals as models, for both ideas and formats. In all subject areas, students can get to know people in the field who kept journals to record data, to ask important questions, to reflect on the meaning of life, to gain knowledge through writing. The journals of real people can serve as inspiration to young writers who might be reluctant at first to put their thoughts on paper. Journals can serve as an inspiration for teachers who wish to introduce their classes to the best mentors fledgling journal-keepers could ever have (Kane, 1995).

Journals have the potential to help students learn content, too. They'll remember the horrors of World War II after reading *Anne Frank: The Diary of a Young Girl* (Frank, 1952) or *War Diary 1939–45* (Cavendish, 1995), with excerpts from soldiers' and military leaders' accounts written as the battles raged. Students can meet Lewis and Clark as real people, rather than just as names to be learned for a test on westward expansion, as they read firsthand records of the dangers they faced. In the Rocky Mountains, on May 29, 1805, Lewis wrote, "Last night we were all alarmed by a large buffalo . . . that ran up the bank in full speed directly toward the fires, and was within 18 inches of the heads of some of the men who lay sleeping" (Bakeless, 1964, p. 153). On June 16, he worried:

> Found the Indian woman extremely ill. . . . This gave me some concern, as well for the poor object herself—then with a young child in her arms— as from the consideration of her being our only dependence for a friendly negotiation with the Snake Indians for horses to assist in our portage from the Missouri to the Columbia River. (p. 188)

What an opportunity that provides for students to think about how Native Americans were used and viewed by white settlers! On August 18, Lewis was feeling philosophical:

> This day I completed my thirty-first year, and conceived that I had, in all human probability, now existed half the period I am to remain in this sublunary world. I reflected that I had as yet done but little, very little indeed, to further the happiness of the human race, or to advance the information of the succeeding generation. (p. 246)

And on November 7, "Great joy in camp. We are in view of the ocean, this great Pacific Ocean which we have been so long anxious to see, and the roaring made by the waves breaking on the rocky shores . . . may be heard distinctly" (p. 277). This primary source is very different from the textbook account students usually encounter, which simply cannot convey the emotion that a journal entry can.

Figure 3.10 lists books that contain journal entries of real people. Students will find in these examples a wonderful variety of formats and styles, as well as interesting information and glimpses into mathematical, scientific, artistic, political, and poetic minds. The journals can serve as models and as inspiration. More specifically, Figure 3.11 lists resources a social studies teacher might use to give students firsthand accounts of and perspectives on the various wars in which the United States has been involved.

FIGURE 3.10

A bibliography of journals relevant to content area learning.

Carter, J. (1989). *An Outdoor Journal: Adventures and Reflections*. Norwalk, CT: The Easton Press.

Cheney, E. D. (Ed.). (1995). *Louisa May Alcott: Life, Letters, and Journals*. New York: Random House.

Columbus, C. (1987). *The Log of Christopher Columbus*. Camden, ME: International Marine Publishing.

Darwin, C. (1989). *Voyage of the Beagle: Charles Darwin's Journal of Researches*. New York: Penguin Books.

Potter, B. (1966). *The Journal of Beatrix Potter from 1881 to 1897*. (Transcribed from her code writing by Leslie Linder). New York: F. Warne.

FIGURE 3.11

Firsthand accounts of war.

See more suggested titles in Appendix Figure 3.11.

Beah, I. (2007). *A Long Way Gone: Memoirs of a Boy Soldier*. New York: Farrar, Straus and Giroux.

Dennes, D. J. (1992). *One Day at a Time: A Vietnam Diary*. Portland, OR: University of Queensland Press.

Filipoviác, Z., & Challenger, M. (Eds.). (2006). *Stolen Voices: Young People's War Diaries, from World War I to Iraq*. Toronto: Doubleday Canada.

Humbert, A. (2008). *Résistance: A Woman's Journal of Struggle and Defiance in Occupied France*. (B. Mellor, Trans.). New York: Bloomsbury.

Zullo, A. (2009). *War Heroes: Voices from Iraq*. New York: Scholastic.

USING MULTIPLE GENRES TO STUDY A TOPIC

Whenever you are planning your instruction of a particular topic, ask yourself whether there are materials representing different genres, and, if so, which might benefit your students. Before beginning a math unit on geometry, you might gather historical accounts of its beginnings and the mathematicians who developed and flourished in the field. There are puzzles containing geometric principles and books relating to construction, such as David Macaulay's (www.david macaulay.com) series *Cathedral* (1973), *Castle* (1977), *Pyramid* (1975), *Unbuilding* (1987), *Ship* (1993), and *Mosque* (2003), as well as cartoons relating to the subject and novels involving the topic, such as *A Higher Geometry,* by Sharelle Byras Moranville (2006). Using these materials gives the exercises in the math textbook a context and your students a big picture so that the proofs and skills they're learning won't seem isolated or irrelevant. Following is an example of a history lesson on John Brown using multiple texts. To prepare you for the lesson, I invite you first to reflect on your own knowledge of this historical figure.

ACTIVATING PRIOR KNOWLEDGE | **3.3**

In your learning log, write down what you know of John Brown. For what is he most known? What places are associated with his name? What causes? When did he live? How did he die? What did your teachers and your American history textbook tell you about this man? Compare your memories and knowledge with that of others before proceeding.

Perhaps your reflection on and discussion of John Brown reveal only a sketchy knowledge—he was an abolitionist, he's connected with Harpers Ferry, he was executed for his violent ways of promoting his cause, he caused dissension before the Civil War. Or there might be some disagreement over whether he was a righteous hero, a murderer, a misguided religious fanatic, or a crazy person. If you had to teach middle school or high school students about John Brown, where would you look for the information to pass on to your students, what materials might you have them explore?

Example Genre/Text Selection

I am no expert on the subject, but I decided to see what genres and texts within those genres might help me should I be responsible for teaching about this man and his proper place in history. Here's what I now have in my "John Brown" file.

1. Textbook treatments

These treatments include excerpts from several textbooks, representing different levels of difficulty and somewhat different perspectives. I have written marginal notes or highlighted particular passages or language I want my students to notice. For example, sentences from *The American Pageant* (Bailey et al., 1998), such as "The fanatical figure of John Brown now stalked upon the Kansas battlefield," and "[Brown and his followers] literally hacked to pieces five surprised men, presumed to be proslaveryites. This fiendish butchery, clearly the product of a deranged mind . . ." (p. 423), give a different picture to readers than other textbooks that portray Brown in a more sympathetic light. I also include pages from *Lies My Teacher Told Me* (1995), with Loewen's commentary that of 12 recent textbooks he examined, only three used any quotes from John Brown himself. "Our textbooks also handicap Brown by not letting him speak for himself. . . . Brown's words, which moved a nation, therefore do not move students today" (p. 171).

2. Encyclopedia entries

Students can compare and contrast versions, including some from reference works published long ago. For example, look at how excerpts from two different encyclopedias portray Brown:

> . . . this early abolitionist had all the piety, uprightness, and willingness to die for a cause that marked his Puritan ancestors . . . always brooding with the fervor of an Old Testament prophet on the sin of negro slavery, against which he swore eternal war. . . . In a famous battle at Osawatomie, with only fifteen men, he held off 500 pro-slavery Missourians . . . His bearing at the trial produced an extraordinary impression of heroic simplicity and purity and grandeur of character. . . . his tragic end took on historic significance. (*Compton's Pictured Encyclopedia,* 1931, p. 516)

> John Brown . . . was one of the most radical opponents of slavery in antebellum America. A devout Calvinist, Brown combined an exemplary life of Christian humility and charity for others with uncompromising, often ruthless acts to eliminate the stain of slavery from the nation. . . . Despite imprisonment and the certainty of execution he spoke out unwaveringly. . . . Brown refused any attempts to be rescued by supporters, and many noted abolitionists, such as Henry David Thoreau and Ralph Waldo Emerson, compared his execution to the crucifixion of Jesus. (*New World Encyclopedia,* www.newworldencyclopedia.org/entry/John_Brown, retrieved 9/21/09)

3. Letters and speeches

This section includes copies of letters from John Brown to his pastor and to his children. The first-person narrative is powerful and has the potential to help students understand the humanity of the names they learn about in their textbooks. These letters can be found in *The Life and Letters of John Brown* by F. B. Sanborn (1969), as well as on the Internet. I also have this excerpt from the speech he made to the court just before being sentenced to die:

> I did no wrong but right. . . . now, if it is deemed necessary that I should forfeit my life for the furtherance of the ends of justice, and mingle my blood further with the blood of my children and with the blood of millions in this slave country whose rights are disregarded by wicked, cruel and unjust enactments, I say, let it be done. (Loewen, 1995, pp. 167–168)

4. Biographies and other nonfiction sources

Here, too, in my selection of adult and juvenile biographies, students see variety in how this controversial historical figure is portrayed. My sources include *To Purge This Land with Blood: A Biography of John Brown* by Stephen B. Oates (1984), *John Brown: A Cry for Freedom* by Lorene Graham (1980), and *John Brown: Militant Abolitionist* by Robert R. Potter (1995), which is part of the *American Troublemaker Series*. There is a very easy text, written at a primary level, Streissguth's (1999) *John Brown*, and a powerfully illustrated book, *John Brown: One Man Against Slavery* (Everett, 1993). Jacob Lawrence's paintings are worth examining. Stein's (1999) *John Brown's Raid on Harpers Ferry in American History* goes into much more depth than a textbook or encyclopedia could, as do *John Brown: Abolitionist: The Man Who Killed Slavery, Sparked the Civil War, and Seeded Civil Rights* by David S. Reynolds (2005), *Patriotic Treason: John Brown and the Soul of America,* by E. Carton (2006), and *John Brown's Raid on Harper's Ferry,* by J. Glaser (2006), which uses a graphic novel format.

5. Historical fiction

The young adult novel *Mine Eyes Have Seen* by Ann Rinaldi (www.annrinaldi.net) (1998), narrated by a daughter of John Brown, can help students imagine how others saw Brown. It is well researched and tells the story in an imaginative way. *Lightning Time,* by Douglas Rees (otterlimits.org/doug) (1997), is told from the perspective of a young follower of Brown, and Russell Banks' adult-level novel, *Cloudsplitter* (1998), is narrated by Brown's only surviving son years after the event. Cummings' novel *The Night I Freed John Brown* (2008) is set in present-day Harpers Ferry, and the main character grapples with mysteries involving the historical John Brown at the same time he is figuring out some of his family's dark secrets. I could ask my students to use one or more of these books as models as they write a portrait of Brown, or some other historical figure, from the point of view of someone else watching the events and behavior. I also located Bruce Olds' novel, *Raising Holy Hell* (1995), which uses an unusual collage-like structure consisting of songs, folktales, poems, diary entries, scriptural citations, eyewitness recollections, speeches, interior monologues, newspaper articles, and more. As with the biography and nonfiction, the difficulty levels of the texts represent a large range, ensuring that the needs of the students are met.

6. Documentary and secondary source information

Students can make connections among people and begin to get a big-picture view of events by reading what other people were saying at the time of Brown's life and death. One example is from Victor Hugo: "The gaze of Europe is fixed at this moment on America. . . . [Hanging Brown] will open a latent fissure that will finally split the Union asunder. The punishment of John Brown may consolidate slavery in Virginia, but it will certainly shatter the American Democracy. You preserve your shame but you kill your glory" (Loewen, 1995, pp. 168–169). Another example describes the interpretation of John E. Dangerfield, who was taken prisoner at Harpers Ferry: "During the day and night I talked much with John Brown, and found him as brave as a man could be, and sensible upon all subjects except slavery" (Colbert, 1997, p. 199).

7. Internet sites

The entire text of Thoreau's "A Plea for Captain John Brown" is available at www.msstate.edu/Archives/History/USA/Afro-Amer/johnbrown.thoreau. The tone of this 13-page work of art is as passionate and accusing as the voices rising against the death penalty today, as is evident in this excerpt:

> Who is it whose safety requires that Captain Brown be hung? Is it indispensible to any Northern man? Is there no resource but to cast this man also to the Minotaur? If you do not wish it, say so distinctly.

8. Songs

John Brown's Body
(sung to the tune of Battle Hymn of the Republic)

John Brown's body lies a-mold'ring in the grave,
John Brown's body lies a-mold'ring in the grave,

John Brown's body lies a-mold'ring in the grave,
His soul goes marching on.

Glory, Glory! Hallelujah!
Glory, Glory! Hallelujah!
Glory, Glory! Hallelujah!
His soul is marching on.

I could make a poster of these words to display in the classroom as we study the Civil War. In a way, John Brown will still be present, showing just how true those words carried into battle were!

Can you see how my planning and researching enable me to bring this history lesson to life and to encourage critical thinking and debate from my class? My file will grow as students bring in more information that they've found in additional resources as they investigate the enigma known as John Brown.

Intertextual Reading Instruction

Of course, supplying variety in materials is not beneficial unless you teach the students how to use and think about them. Most students do not naturally read intertextually, comparing and contrasting sources and viewpoints. This type of reading strategy must be taught, even at the high school level (Perfetti, Britt, Rouet, et al., 1994; Stahl, Hynd, Britton, et al., 1996). So, for example, a teacher presenting several of the materials listed above relating to John Brown might point out clues students can pay attention to as they evaluate the authors' positions. Even the title of Reynold's *John Brown: Abolitionist: The Man Who Killed Slavery, Sparked the Civil War, and Seeded Civil Rights* is telling. A teacher could ask students to determine the author's stance and be ready to point out evidence from the text as she reads the following excerpt about Brown's capture and arrest after the Harpers Ferry uprising from Joy Hakim's *Freedom: A History of US* (2003):

> Brown is caught and brought to trial. He pleads not guilty to treason and murder. The fiery abolitionist has the skills of a brilliant actor, and, thanks to the telegraph, his captors give him a worldwide audience. Reporters write of his every word and action, and Brown puts on a performance few will forget. Often he lies, but he knows how to make people believe in him, and there is truth in the cause he argues. (p. 119)

Then the teacher might say, "Now let's look carefully at Thoreau's 'A Plea for Captain John Brown.' It's a speech he gave on the eve of Brown's execution. I've given you a copy, and I'd like you to make a mark next to the lines that let us know how Thoreau views John Brown as a person, and then underline lines that let us know what he thinks about the actions of the U. S. government. After that, I'm going to ask you to find a source that represents a negative or positive stance toward the actions of John Brown, and to explain how you determined that stance."

Afflerbach and VanSledright (2001) studied fifth graders who read from two textbooks on the topic of the Jamestown Colony: a traditional history textbook and a more innovative text that had an imbedded poem and excerpt from the Jamestown governor's diary. They found that the embedded texts benefited some students by eliciting an emotional response of empathy, but created obstacles for others who had difficulty shifting from one text type to another, or had trouble understanding the diary's archaic vocabulary and complicated syntax. The researchers concluded:

> . . . the think-aloud protocol of our readers suggests that much additional work remains to determine how reading multiple texts can be a productive experience for students. . . . Embedded texts and sources may create opportunities for students to develop historical thinking, to have enriched interactions with text, and to foster strategies for critical reading practice. However, these interactions and ways of thinking are learned, and many students may need coaching and modeling from teachers and knowledgeable peers around how the texts can be understood as part of a much larger historical evidence chain from which history is constructed. (p. 705)

APPLICATION ACTIVITY 3.4 (SEE PAGE 86)

As you read more within your field, you'll find that gathering resources and modeling how to read and synthesize multiple texts on a topic becomes easier, and you can develop other folders for future use with students. You can begin now to organize a set of empty file folders for various topics within the disciplines that you are likely to teach or that you have a special interest in, so that as you come across things in your own reading, you'll be ready with a place to put them. For example, language arts teachers might start folders labeled Reading Lists, Grammar, Letter Writing, Themes in Literature, Censorship, Stories about Authors, Satire and Irony, Journals, Articles about Language, Examples of Metaphors and Similes, and Blogs and Interviews of Authors of Young Adult Literature. Over time, you'll fill these folders with samples of all of the types of texts discussed in this chapter. You can add newspaper and magazine articles, student papers on the topic, Internet addresses, and a list of trade book titles along with where to find them (e.g., your personal collection, the school library, public library). Figure 3.12 provides an example from a teacher's math files.

FIGURE 3.12 An example of curricular file contents for intertextual reading.

PROBABILITY AND STATISTICS

A. Textbook reading:

"The Probability Formula," pp. 95–101 in Bellman, A., Bragg, S. C., Chapin, S. H., Gardella, T. J., Hall, B. C., Handlin, W. G., & Manfre, E. (2001). *New York Math A: An Integrated Approach*. Upper Saddle River, NJ: Prentice Hall.

B. Titles of resources to introduce, teach, and reinforce the topic:

- *Conned Again, Watson: Cautionary Tales of Logic, Math, and Probability* by C. Bruce (2001). New York: Perseus.
- *Calculated Risks: How to Know When Numbers Deceive You* by G. Gigerenzer (2002). New York: Simon & Schuster.
- *Probability with Fun and Games* by L. Bussell (2009). Pleasantville, NY: Weekly Reader Books.
- *Practicing Sabermetrics: Putting the Science of Baseball Statistics to Work* by G. B. Costa, M. R. Huber, and J. T. Saccoman (2009). Jefferson, NC: McFarland & Company.
- *The Unfinished Game: Pascal, Fermat, and the Invention of Probability* by K. Devlin (2008). New York: Basic Books.
- *The Manga Guide to Statistics* by S. Takahashi, Trendpro Co. (2009). San Francisco: No Starch Press.
- *Probability* by M. Cohen (2010). New York: Crabtree Pub.
- *Digital Dice: Computational Solutions to Practical Probability Problems* by P. J. Nahin (2008). Princeton, NJ: Princeton University Press.
- *Socrates and the Three Little Pigs* by T. Mori & M. Anno. (1986). New York: Philomel Books.
- *Against the Gods: The Remarkable Story of Risk* by P. L. Bernstein (1996). New York: Wiley.
- *The Universe and the Teacup: The Mathematics of Truth and Beauty* by K. C. Cole (1998). New York: Harcourt Brace.

C. Newspaper articles:

1. (June 10, 1998) My Summary: Three boys in Central New York, injected with the same batch of chemotherapy medication, became paralyzed, which is normally an extremely rare side effect. It was anywhere from a one-in-a-million to a one-in-a-billion chance for all of the boys to become paralyzed as a known side effect of the drugs. The medical mystery has baffled the National Cancer Institute and the Food and Drug Administration because experts say there was no way a mistake was made at the pharmacy where the drugs were mixed, and there is no evidence of impurities or overdoses. The conclusion is that it was a strange coincidence, a statistical fluke.

TEACHER'S NOTE: I'd like my students to grapple with this mystery. The parents of the victims say that the chances of the three cases being coincidental are so astronomical they won't even consider the possibility. Yet, that's what the medical, governmental, and legal establishments are asking them to accept. I believe this case will help students deal with related issues, such as how this incident might affect future decisions about the treatment of children with leukemia, and how doctors and patients weigh the risk factors of using such medications and treatments against risk factors of *not* using them to fight progressive diseases. Students will see how probability and statistics are used in authentic situations, which will help them understand the more abstract concepts of our unit, and they'll be on the lookout for other examples of statistics at work.

There was another article on January 18, 2001, with an update on the boys' condition and the story of a settlement involving a $6 million payment to the boys. There's definitely more grist for the mill in that story.

2. *Herald American*, 8/2/98, Study: It's Happier and Healthier at the Top. "According to the first international research study examining the links between social rank and mind-body health, every increase in socioeconomic status brings an elevation in physical health and sanity. In other words, a corporate CEO is invariably healthier in body and mind than his middle manager. An administrative assistant is bound to be less fit and more frazzled than the boss, but far more likely to be in better physical and mental shape than a factory worker."

TEACHER'S NOTE: I'll ask students to analyze these opening sentences and apply what we have studied in statistics so far to identify the error in them.

D. Internet addresses:

- gasbone.herston.ug.edu.au (AIC: Statistics Introduction)
- www.learningchoices.com (information on resources)

E. Favorite sentences:
(enlarged and put on overhead transparencies)

1. For a coin to land on heads 50 consecutive times, it would take a million people tossing coins 10 times a minute for 40 hours a week—and then it would happen once every 9 centuries! (found in a seventh-grade math classroom posted on a wall).
2. "The probability that a student, guessing randomly, could get 9, four-choice multiple choice answers correct is less than 4 in a million" (Smith, 1994, p. 218).

MATCHING STUDENTS AND TEXTS

Matching materials to students is an important challenge teachers must meet, and collecting resources will help. Times change, students change, and teachers and materials must change. If you are wide readers yourselves, your files will be current and will match your students' needs. Thank goodness!

Of course, matching texts with students requires that you know your students well; this is not easy for secondary teachers, who often have well over 100 students in their multiple daily classes. Yet, there are many reasons why students need their teachers to know them as individuals, so listening to them; talking informally before and after school and between classes; and paying close attention during a reading or writing workshop, small group work, and whole class discussion are crucial. You might keep a class list handy and jot down notes about things you hear from your students that will help you recommend or supply relevant texts. You might quietly place a book on volcanoes or a newspaper article about a tornado on the desk of a student you know is interested in natural disasters. Or you could write a short note to a student, saying something like, "Reggie, I know you like Gary Paulsen's books. I just got *Guts: The True Stories Behind Hatchet and the Brian Books* (2001) and *Mudshark* (2009), which looks like a really quick adventure/mystery, along with a biography called *Gary Paulsen* (2007), by James Blasingame,

for our classroom library. If you want to be the first to take them out, let me know today before I put them on the shelves." An efficient way to learn your students' interests is to ask them to fill out a survey. Figure 3.13 has some sample questions, and you can add others relating to particular curricular areas (see Chapter 2 for examples).

A very short read-aloud has the potential of capturing even the most resistant student. Imagine Mario, a student who is discouraged with school and thinks he has absolutely no interest in biology, especially this second time around. Now, picture him perking up when he hears his teacher reading the incredible prose Annie Dillard (1998) uses to describe her observation of a praying mantis and its mating habits:

> I lay on the hill this way and that, my knees in thorns and my cheeks in clay, trying to see as well as I could. I poked near the female's head with a grass; she was clearly undisturbed, so I settled my nose an inch from that pulsing abdomen. It puffed like a concertina, it throbbed like a bellows; it roved, pumping, over the glistening, clabbered surface of the egg case, testing and patting, thrusting and smoothing. . . .
>
> The male was nowhere in sight. The female had probably eaten him. . . . The mating rites of mantises are well known: a chemical produced in the head of the male insect says, in effect, "No, don't go near her, you fool, she'll eat you alive."

FIGURE 3.13 An interest survey for a content area class.

Dear Student,

In this course we will be doing a lot of reading beyond the textbook. You'll find a great classroom library from which you can borrow books. I'll be able to supply you with other resources once I get to know you better. This survey will help me to know what kinds of reading you already do and to learn something about your interests. Please answer the following questions, and then add anything else you'd like me to know.

1. What is your favorite subject?
2. What interests and hobbies do you have?
3. Please list the names of any magazines or newspapers you read.
4. What kinds of books do you enjoy reading outside of school?
5. When you go to a traditional or online bookstore, what section(s) do you head for?
6. List any of your favorite books or authors.
7. Which course topics interest you most? What would you like to learn more about?
8. What websites do you use to find out information? What kinds of searches are you likely to do on the Internet? What are some topics you've researched lately?
9. What games, if any, do you play on the Internet?

At the same time a chemical in his abdomen says, "Yes, by all means, now and forever yes."

While the male is making up what passes for his mind, the female tips the balance in her favor by eating his head. (pp. 58–59)

Mario asks for the book *Pilgrim at Tinker Creek* (1998) and becomes increasingly hooked. His teacher has more Annie Dillard, and other books on insects and pond life, as Mario asks for them. Thoreau waits in the wings. Teacher and student keep talking about texts, about ideas.

Susan Nelson Wood is a teacher who was willing to admit that motivating her reluctant readers was wearying work. According to her article "Bringing Us the Way to Know" (2001), her attitude changed to "Truthfully, I was leaping out of bed in the mornings, eager to get to school" (p. 67) after she introduced her students to author Gary Paulsen. They could not get enough of him (fortunately, he's written more than 240 fiction and nonfiction books, so the supply did not run out). She witnessed astonishing changes, such as the one in Brad, who was "finishing his fourth year in our two-year school; not prone to talking, much less reading, he was more at home in the school hallway picking a fight than in the library picking a book" (p. 67). Brad was so enthralled with his newfound hero–author that he searched out Paulsen's home phone number. It ultimately resulted in Paulsen visiting the school and sharing stories with Wood's previously resistant eighth-grade readers. The success stories are mounting, and yours can be added to the testimonies of students being turned on to reading when teachers match them up with texts that meet their needs.

CONCLUSION

In terms of instructional materials, it's a great time to be a teacher. We've never been better off. There are considerate, up-to-date, and multicultural textbooks; a proliferation of trade books at low prices; online journals; audiobooks on CDs or DVDs, books that can be downloaded to e-readers and mp3 players; primary sources; TVs; DVRs; and movie rentals. We have access to the Internet and educational software. Students can create their own texts by using desktop publishing. One of my students had this to say in his learning log at semester's end:

There is no better way to open up this story-world [of history] than by reading stories about the times. I could not possibly convey the struggles faced by Jews during World War II as well as Anne Frank could. I couldn't give an account on slavery as accurately as Frederick Douglass would. It would be impossible to explain the despair of the Chinese immigrants on Angel Island without sharing the poetry they had written on the detention center walls. One cannot explain history without the voices of the people who lived through it. . . .

Stories, whether fiction or nonfiction, can magically give a reader the feelings of an experience. Books are like time machines that transport us through time and space. They can pull at our heart strings, fill us with anger or remorse, and make us laugh or cry. These are the experiences I want my students to have. I want them to know what it was like so that they can not only have the knowledge, but also treasure the wisdom. . . .

I also believe that history is an exploration from which each individual can form a perspective. As a teacher, it will become my job to give my students as many resources as possible for them to formulate their own sense of the world and its events. They cannot rely on the textbook alone.

Make it a goal to become a collector of interesting texts of all sorts on the topics in your curriculum, and begin to work toward that goal immediately. Your students may catch your enthusiasm for seeking out information and opinions, and then you can take advantage of the opportunity to teach them how to

- find materials that will enrich their learning
- gain independence
- collaborate with others
- and develop a lifelong love for learning through reading

No matter what texts are used, teachers help students comprehend by what they do before, during, and after the reading. By helping students deal with vocabulary, background knowledge, organization, concepts, and so forth, they make reading and learning enjoyable experiences. Future chapters expand on the strategies that teachers and students can use to aid comprehension and expand thinking.

WEBSITES CHAPTER 3 **Access these links using the Kane Resource Site.**

AIC: Statistics Introduction
gasbone.herston.ug.edu.au

Ann Rinaldi
www.annrinaldi.net

Arrow Book Club (for middle grades)
www.teacher.scholastic.com/clubs/arrow

Charles Ghigna
www.charlesghigna.com

David Macaulay
www.davidmacaulay.com

Douglas Rees
otterlimits.org/doug

Guys Read
www.guysread.com

Henry David Thoreau's "A Plea for Capitan John Brown," full text
www.gutenberg.org/etext/2567

History Book Club
www.historybookclub.com/

Information on Resources
www.learningchoices.com

International Children's Digital Library
http://en.childrenslibrary.org/

Jennifer Armstrong
www.jennifer-armstrong.com

"John Brown" entry, New World Encyclopedia
www.newworldencyclopedia.org/entry/John_Brown

Laura Ingalls Wilder
www.lauraingallswilderhome.com

Lexile Framework for Reading
www.lexile.com

TAB: The Teen Book Club
www.teacher.scholastic.com/clubs/tab

APPLICATION ACTIVITIES

3.1 Imagine that you are being interviewed for a teaching job in your content area. The search committee, consisting of a principal, a curriculum coordinator, and several teachers, informs you that the school you hope to work in has a policy of using no textbooks! They ask you to surmise what the philosophy underlying this decision might be, and ask you what kinds of materials you would use and how you would teach under these circumstances. Write in your learning log, thinking through how you might envision your job and answer your interviewers.

3.2 Start a file now for book reviews, including textbook reviews. You'll find reviews in professional journals, and you can search for reviews of particular materials on the Internet. Be sure to note who the reviewer is. Whether the commentaries you find are positive, negative, or mixed, they can help you think about curricular and pedagogical issues as you assess materials and design instruction for your courses.

3.3 Jean Fritz is an award-winning author of historical biographies for children and young adults. She is respected by many experts in the fields of library science and education, and is the winner of the Laura Ingalls Wilder Medal. In 1983, Fritz's *The Double Life of Pocahontas* was published. The biography has several pages of notes and references, as well as a bibliography of scholarly sources and an index.

The book was chosen as an American Library Association Notable Book, and it won the Boston Globe–Horn Book Award, both prestigious achievements. A college content area textbook, in a chapter encouraging the use of trade books throughout the curriculum, considers Fritz's work exemplary. "More than a few high schoolers have had their interest in American history piqued by the style and wit of Jean Fritz, who makes such historical figures as Sam Houston and Pocahontas alive and human without sacrificing accuracy in the telling" (Schallert & Roser, 1996, p. 35). If possible, read this book and think about how you feel about its overall quality and how you think it might work with secondary students, especially those who are struggling readers needing materials that are interesting but not difficult.

Now, read the following review of Fritz's work from *Through Indian Eyes: The Native Experience in Books for Children* (Slapin & Seale, 1992).

> Although most historians now acknowledge that John Smith lied when he told of having been saved by Pocahontas, the popular conception remains unaffected. Jean Fritz's "biography" will do nothing to change this. She reproduces the standard version, intact, with enough chunks of history of the Jamestown colony thrown in to make it book-length. There is plenty of speculative padding: "she would have" and "she must have" are common phrases. John Smith is portrayed as a hero, and there is more about him in this book than there is about Pocahontas. . . .

There is considerable emphasis on the trickery, savagery and childish naiveté of the Native people:

" . . . other Indians were not one bit friendly. Once they killed an English boy and shot an arrow right through President Wingfield's beard. Often they lay in the tall grass . . . waiting for someone to come through the gate. . . . Not even a dog could run out safely. Once one did and had forty arrows shot into his body."

And surely it should not *still* be necessary to point out that there has never been such a thing as an Indian king, queen or princess?

It would serve no useful purpose to go through this book page by page, separating fact from fantasy. Suffice it to say that Fritz has added nothing to the little already "known" about Pocahontas, and that this little is treated with neither sensitivity nor insight. (pp. 157–158)

From B. Slapin and D. Seale (Eds.), *Through Indian Eyes: The Native Experience in Books for Children.* Los Angeles: UCLA American Indian Studies Center. Reprinted with permission.

What is your response to this review? As a teacher, what would you do if confronted with its information and opinions? Should Fritz's biography of Pocahontas be removed from our shelves? Write an argument in favor of this, or write about some ways you could use both the book and the review with students.

3.4 Choose a curricular topic in your subject area and begin a file in which you collect text titles representing the various genres' treatment of the topic. You might research several current or past textbooks to see how they handle the topic, then check the library for fiction and nonfiction sources, as well as reference materials. Explore the Internet, also. You may wish to start with a topic about which you have read widely or a topic you have wondered about and want to investigate more thoroughly. Share the contents of your curricular file on the Kane Resource Site. Enjoy!

chapter 4

The Role of Knowledge in Comprehension

We've considered many issues relating to literacy, motivation, readers, and texts thus far. In this chapter, we explore the reader's role in comprehension—what the reader brings to the text and does before, during, and following the reading is crucial. You, as a content area teacher, play a huge role, too: you can activate and build prior knowledge, procedural knowledge, and discourse knowledge.

PRIOR KNOWLEDGE

ACTIVATING PRIOR KNOWLEDGE 4.1

Fold a piece of paper in thirds, and label the columns K, W, and L. For the next few minutes, write down in the K column things you **know** about the topic ROBOTICS. (If absolutely nothing comes to mind, free associate about the word ROBOTS. What do they look like? What are they used for? Who programs them? Have you seen any in movies? In real life?) If you're in class or with other people, share your ideas and build on others' knowledge. Maybe there is a previously unidentified robot whiz among you who can be the hero of the moment.

My students, after the initial "You're kidding, right?" are usually able to start the column with some simple stuff like R2-D2 and C-3PO, then add some things they've learned from science class, novels, newspapers, or conversations. Once in a while, a student amuses the others with an anecdote, such as knowing a pharmacist who works alongside a prescription-filling robot.

The next part of the activity is often the trickiest for teachers. In the next column, which you've labeled W, write down what you **want** to know about robotics. Now, you can imagine that seventh or eighth graders, when asked by a teacher or textbook what they want to learn about almost any topic—cells, the Industrial Revolution, fractals, Impressionist painters—might feel inclined to answer, "Nothing." And I can understand how you

> "A man [woman] receives only what [s]he is ready to receive, whether physically or intellectually or morally. . . . We hear and apprehend only what we already half know. If there is something which does not concern me, which is out of my line, which by experience or genius my attention is not drawn to, however novel and remarkable it might be, if it is spoken we hear it not, if it is written we read it not, it does not detain us."
>
> THOREAU, JOURNAL XIII: 77–78

might say the same about this topic; if you were interested in the subject of robotics, you would have explored it on your own. So, I'm going to help you out.

Imagine the following scenario. You have just been informed by your doctor that there is something seriously wrong with you. You have two options. You can have major surgery that will require you to miss school and work for eight weeks. Or, you can agree to having a tiny robot inserted into your body to fix the problem. You will be an outpatient and can resume your normal activities the following day. In the W column, write the questions you want answers to before making your decision.

I'll bet you didn't leave the column blank or answer "Nothing" to the implied question of what you want to learn this time. Typically, my students are suddenly very inquisitive about this robot and the medical procedure. "How big is it?" is often at the top of the list. "Will it hurt?" they want to know. How expensive is this new operation, and will insurance cover it? How many times has it been performed before? How is the robot removed? What are the risks? You've probably listed additional questions.

The third step of the K-W-L strategy (Ogle, 1986) is to read an assigned text and fill in the third column, under L, the things you've **learned.** Have your questions been answered? Was there information you didn't know before? The box on p. 89 contains the reading I assign my students.

Some teachers add a fourth column to the exercise, changing the name to K-W-L Plus (Carr & Ogle, 1987), when the class maps out what they have learned by creating some kind of graphic organizer. Other teachers use K-W-L-S (What do I STILL have to learn?) (Sippola, 1995). In the fourth column, the reader lists additional questions generated by reading. For example, something a text says might contradict something you thought was true. You might have to look further to clear up any confusion. Other teachers add an H column so students can become aware of and verbalize HOW they plan to or how they did get their questions answered.

At this point, I also ask my students to notice the information's source. They realize that the Steve Nadis article, while sounding a bit futuristic to some, is actually quite dated, so they wonder what advances have been made since 1994. A few of my students have observed that although *Omni Magazine* was noted for reporting on scientific breakthroughs, it often featured articles on

UFOs and the paranormal, so caution on the reader's part might be advisable.

In this particular situation, I've had students bring in articles from various sources on nanotechnology that confirm, update, or extend the information we've read together. For example, a student presented us with a newspaper article about a hospital using a robotic surgical arm, controlled by a surgeon's voice, that holds and moves a camera around inside a patient during an operation. Another brought in an article on magnetic devices implanted in patients that can reduce or eliminate seizures. We've read of a camera within a pill that can photograph the small intestine. (You'll notice that I've followed my own advice from Chapter 3 about keeping file folders on topics I teach; I have a growing "Robotics" file. My favorite subset within this file contains articles and websites about Robobama, the life-size audio-animatronic figure at Disney World that recites a speech in the president's own voice.)

Students might realize they know more for that first column than they originally thought; perhaps they just never thought about pacemakers being connected with the field of robotics. My students usually discover that they're more interested in robotics than they had initially thought, and the little bit of information they've acquired enables them to learn more easily when they do encounter new material on the topic.

The simplicity of the K-W-L-S strategy makes it a natural for students to use independently. Some students, after an explanation and some practice in a content area classroom, may find that it's a portable, transferable strategy that helps them manage and comprehend all kinds of texts. But there's a danger. It can become artificial, another one of those "workbook" type, please-the-teacher techniques, or simply a way of assessing whether students have read and understood, or busywork. We have to help students experience the real help a strategy such as K-W-L-S can give them as readers of authentic materials. And we have to use our teaching skills as we're planning assignments. Teachers are constantly constructing new ways to adapt this flexible strategy to work for their curricula and contexts (e.g., Hershberger et al., 2006; Laverick, 2002; Ogle, 2009; Sampson, 2002; Szabo, 2006). So, add a Teacher (T) column for us as we apply the strategy, asking, "What will make K-W-L-S work with this *particular* text, and with our *particular* students?"

Fantastic Voyage: Traveling the Body in Microbiotic Style

by Steve Nadis

Researchers at MIT's Artificial Intelligence Lab have plans to go where no man, woman, or "mobot" has ever gone before—into a dark, slimy, and winding tunnel known as the large intestine, or colon. The microbot—named Cleo and little more than an inch in width, breadth, and height—was devised by 22-year-old MIT senior James McLurkin, who admits to having "always liked small things." Cleo is about the smallest thing on two treads going these days and it's also among the smartest. It can find a path between obstacles, move toward or away from light, avoid hills, and grasp objects with a small claw. All these actions can be initiated by a person operating a joystick. Cleo can also function on its own, untethered, making its way through a plastic colon maze, for instance, by bumping into a wall, backing up, and shifting its direction ever so slightly.

Cleo is the fourth so-called "ant" created by McLurkin—and the product of an effort certainly disproportionate to its modest size. To gather all its miniature parts, McLurkin pored through catalog after catalog, making a million phone calls, always asking the same question: "Do you have anything smaller?"

The project is funded by the Advanced Research Projects Agency (ARPA) in the Department of Defense which is looking to remote surgery as a long-term goal. According to this vision, [one day] remote manipulators (robot arms) might perform surgery on U.S. soldiers around the world, guided by physicians back home. For the nearer term, the agency regards colon examinations and surgery as the most immediate applications. "A diagnostic task such as looking for cancer is the main motivation," explains ARPA surgeon Richard Satava.

The technology allows the microrobot to work in conjunction with light and a camera; if something unusual is spotted, the controlling physician might take a sample (a biopsy), or possibly snip off little growths or polyps and stop intestinal bleeding with lasers or electricity. "We can do all these things today in a procedure called colonoscopy, but that involves pushing a long tube into a person, which is extremely uncomfortable," Satava says. "A small instrument like a microrobot has the potential to be much less painful and much less dangerous." He predicts that robotic colon surgery could be possible within five to ten years.

Robotic surgery is not altogether new. "Robodoc," for instance, is used during hip replacement surgery to bore a precision hole in the hip bone for an artificial replacement part. Robots have also helped neurosurgeons determine the exact position of brain tumors. But Cleo is among the first to be designed to go *inside* the human body. . . .

It may be quite a few years before anything as futuristic as this high-tech version of the 1966 classic *Fantastic Voyage* is in common use, but McLurkin is optimistic about the future. "This is not pie-in-the-sky," he insists. "Sooner or later, one way or another, robotic surgery is gonna happen." Now that really will be a fantastic voyage.

Omni Magazine, Winter, 1994, p. 9.

Donna Ogle (2009) describes how a teacher structured a lesson using the K-W-L strategy (which Ogle developed) with a class with a Latino population. The teacher allowed students to brainstorm what they knew about the Asian Indian culture in preparation for reading Gloria Whelan's novel *Homeless Bird* (2008). Students wrote down whatever they could alone, then worked in small groups, and finally shared as a whole class. After that, the students had authentic questions for the W column; they really did want to know whether the people pray to one god or many, why there are arranged marriages, and why so many believe education for women isn't important. Ogle suggests that the teacher, in addition to the comprehension instruction she provided, might want to keep collecting textual and visual materials about India and help students make new connections.

Figure 4.1 shows a preservice teacher's application of the K-W-L-S strategy. In the next section, I will discuss the role of prior knowledge in reading comprehension to help you understand the importance of activating your students' prior knowledge through strategies such as the K-W-L-S.

The Role of Prior Knowledge

Stanovitch (1986) coined the term *Matthew Effect* with respect to learning and reading. Readers who come to a text with a rich background in a subject area have a much easier time learning the new information. Think about a hobby or an interest you have, and consider how you could comprehend an article on the subject compared to a person uninitiated in the field. Whether we're talking sports, computers,

BookTalk 4.1

If you found the article on robotics interesting, you might wish to read Isaac Asimov's *Fantastic Voyage* (1966), to which the article referred. Another related work of fiction is Madeleine L'Engle's second novel about the Murry family, whom readers come to know so well in *A Wrinkle in Time* (1962). *A Wind in the Door* (1973) tells of the mysterious illness of Charles Wallace, the baby of the family, and the courageous voyage his sister Meg and her teammates make into his body to battle the forces trying to kill his mitochondria.

Eager (2004) and its sequel *Eager's Nephew* (2006) by Helen Fox are novels about a family that interacts with robots that have been programmed with characteristics such as emotion, which we think of as human; and so the interactions, decisions, and locus of power become complex. Finally, nonfiction books such as *Robotics Demystified* by Edwin Wise (2005) and *Rise of the Thinking Machines: The Science of Robots* by Jennifer Frelland VanVoorst (2009) can answer a lot of questions raised by some of the other books!

art, the stock market, gardening, manga, or cooking doesn't matter. The rich get richer; the poor give up or turn away. This is extremely important for teachers to understand. Young adult novelist Richard Peck (1994) calls the age of six "late in life. Most of what we'll be is already decided before we ever see school. Formal education doesn't build foundations; it builds upon them" (p. 6). Think of the diversity of children entering first grade, a crucial year in terms of learning to read. Some have spent literally thousands of hours listening to family members or others read to them; some have spent virtually none.

> *"Whoever has will be given more, and he will have an abundance. Whoever does not have, even what he has will be taken from him."*
>
> **MATTHEW 13:12**

By the time those students get to the upper grades and are members of content area classes, the range has widened. But you can't just despair or blame the elementary teachers, parents, television, or society. Despite what Peck says, sometimes teachers

FIGURE 4.1 K-W-L-S guide for science.

EBOLA			
K	**W**	**L**	**S**

Answer the first two questions before watching the movie *Outbreak* (1995).

1. WHAT WE KNOW: Write down everything you know about Ebola and similar deadly viruses in column 1 (K).
2. WHAT WE WANT TO FIND OUT: What should you know if people in the community you live in came down with one of these viruses, and authorities quarantined your town with you in it? Write your questions in column 2 (W).

Now watch the movie, noting if, when, and how your questions are answered. Then, answer the next two questions.

3. WHAT WE LEARNED: What did you learn from watching the movie about the outbreak, how the virus is spread, and other interesting facts? Write your answers in column 3 (L).
4. WHAT WE STILL WANT TO KNOW: Write down any new questions you've come up with as a result of watching this movie in column 4 (S). Tomorrow, we'll search the Internet together for current information about the status of the Ebola virus in the world today. I predict many of our questions will be answered. For those that aren't, we'll discuss what steps to take next in our inquiry.

—*Brian VanArsdale*

do have to build foundations, or repair or strengthen them, in order to introduce new curriculum. That's a crucial part of teaching. Marzano (2004) emphasizes, "In fact, given the relationship between academic background knowledge and academic achievement, one can make the case that it should be at the top of any list of interventions intended to enhance student achievement" (p. 4). Schools and teachers can provide both direct experiences, such as field trips, and indirect experiences in the classroom to build background knowledge. Marzano advocates reading as a straightforward and powerful way to help our students fill the sensory memory with images that can later aid in gaining new knowledge and increasing levels of achievement. "In working memory, the virtual experience of the camping trip is for all practical purposes the same as the direct experience" (p. 36). Reading can help our students from diverse cultures narrow the gap between their experiential base and the texts they encounter in mainstream classrooms (Nathenson-Mejia & Escamilla, 2003).

The importance of background knowledge, or prior knowledge, to reading comprehension and to learning in general cannot be overstated. Researchers have found that readers spend up to 70 percent of their time interpreting the author's ideas and deciding how those ideas relate to their own prior knowledge on the subject. They engage in an ongoing dialogue with authors as they read (Harste, 1986).

Schema Theory

When we learn, we naturally connect new information to information we already possess. It's much harder to understand and remember facts in isolation. Research has indicated that there are networks of concepts that seem to trigger each other. *Schema theory* demonstrates how a person's knowledge affects the way new information is comprehended and remembered. A reader actually constructs new knowledge by combining textual material with information already possessed. A schema is a set of mental slots used for storing concepts in memory (Rumelhart, 1981). We have *schemata* for many types of knowledge. When I asked you in Chapter 1 to brainstorm a list of words you associate with the word *utopia*, your schema for that concept was activated. You'll probably recall that you and your classmates shared many of the same associations, maybe phrases like "an ideal place," "a place of peace," "a place with no worries or problems," but some specifics may have been different—one person may have known that the term was coined by Thomas More and means "no place," another may have just read *The Handmaid's Tale* (Atwood, 1986), and so on. By having you look at each other's lists of associations,

I hoped to increase your background knowledge as you began reading *The Giver*. In general, the richer your background knowledge, the more success you will have understanding new material.

Assimilation

One way that readers use prior knowledge during reading involves the concept Piaget (1952) called *assimilation,* the process by which the reader recognizes and remembers some facts and not others. There is a base upon which new information can be added and comparisons made. For example, middle school students have learned some things in science and social studies about the food chain, the balance of nature, and endangered species. If they read the novel *Who Really Killed Cock Robin?* (George, 1991), they learn more details about how environmental pollutants can cause a chain reaction that upsets the balance of nature. In addition, they learn how politics can affect decisions that are made regarding industry and the environment. Their now-expanded prior knowledge is even more helpful when they encounter related newspaper articles, encyclopedia entries, Internet sites, or other works of literature whose plots involve environmental concerns, such as Carl Hiaasen's *Hoot* (2004), *Flush* (2005), and *Scat* (2009). Knowledge breeds knowledge. Stahl, Hynd, Glynn, et al. (1996) explain, "One must view each fact as embedded in a fabric of other related information. To learn a fact, it is not enough to memorize it; it should be learned as part of an overall schema" (p. 140). A statement by chemist Linus Pauling exemplifies assimilation:

> Whenever I see something that seems to me to be new, or new so far as my memory goes, I ask myself, "Does this fit into my picture of the world that I've developed over ninety-three years?" If it does, that's fine. If it doesn't, then I ask, "Well, why doesn't it? How can it be interpreted to fit into my picture of the world?" (Rosenthal, 1995, p. 152)

Accommodation

A second element of schema theory involves *accommodation,* the process by which schemata are used to interpret and reconstruct information from the text and the reader's mind to form new concepts. Accommodation involves creating new slots in the reader's storage system and sometimes dissolving existing ones.

New material challenges what we thought we knew. In the science area, children often have mistaken theories (e.g., plants get their food from the soil, heavy objects fall faster than light ones, winter jackets make one warm by generating heat). Sometimes the mistaken "knowledge" has actually been taught by parents or by teachers. Fill in the following blank:

BookTalk Online   4.2

Shocking Science: 5,000 Years of Mishaps and Misunderstandings by Steve Parker and John Kelly (1996) teaches scientific principles while exploring the many mistakes that happen in science. Read more at the Kane Resource Site.

BookTalk   4.3

Since my discovery of the internment during World War II of Japanese Americans, I have found sensitively written accounts that have helped my knowledge grow. *Baseball Saved Us* (1993), by Ken Mochizuki (http://kenmochizuki.com), is a picture book that tells a story of daily life within the camps. Jerry Stanley's nonfiction account, *I Am an American* (1994), includes emotion-provoking and thought-provoking photographs. Equally interesting are some books that tell about Japanese Americans after the war. *Snow Falling on Cedars,* by David Guterson (1995), is a best-seller that tells of lingering racism through a story of a Japanese American accused of a terrible crime and brought to trial. The young adult novel *Bat 6* (1998), by Virginia Euwer Wolff, relates through various narrators a story of two girls' softball teams in 1949. On one team is a Japanese American girl who had been in an internment camp; on the competing team is a girl whose father was killed in the Pearl Harbor attack. Read this book to find out if such differences can be reconciled. Eve Bunting's *So Far from the Sea* (1998) is narrated by a child telling of her family in 1972, revisiting Manzanar, where her father had lived as a child and where *his* father is buried. A lesson has been learned at a very great price.

Kira-Kira (Kadohata, 2004), winner of the Newbery Medal, is narrated by a young girl whose family endured internment; *Music for Alice,* written and illustrated by Allen Say (2004), takes place during the same time period, as does *All the Way Home: A Novel* by Ann Tatlock (2002). Students will find relevant information in *Remembering Manzanar: Life in a Japanese Relocation Camp* by M. L. Cooper (2002) and *Japanese American Internment During World War II: A History and Reference Guide* (Ng, 2002).

"Never start a sentence with _____." Chances are you immediately wrote "because" or "and," which indicates that some helpful teacher most likely taught you that rule so that you would not use a sentence fragment in a composition. At some point you notice that some excellent published writers break the rules, and you accommodate that new information by recognizing that the rule you had to follow in fourth or seventh grade does not generalize to all sentences in all circumstances. By using the process of accommodation, you are no longer just a receiver of knowledge; you are a constructor of knowledge. Teachers can help students construct new knowledge by making them aware of any discrepancies between long-held ideas and new ideas and by providing some explicit hands-on experimentation or demonstration when possible.

Accommodation is an intellectually demanding task, and a teacher must take steps to help students make the conceptual change. This chapter provides a number of instructional strategies that teachers can use to activate students' prior knowledge and curiosity, and also help them recognize what they do not know or are unsure of so that they approach the text prepared to learn.

Of course, there may be times when incoming information conflicts with the student's schemata and the text is actually wrong! For example, for a few years after the collapse of the Soviet Union, many students were using social studies textbooks that were quite suddenly outdated and no longer accurate. Literacy skills are necessary to deal with the barrage of information in daily newspapers and on the Internet that may challenge a reader's thinking so that inaccuracies and faulty reasoning in text don't cause accommodation that actually lessens knowledge. We must teach students how to check the validity of all text sources, especially those they find on the Internet. Also, you can include books in your classroom library that explicitly deal with misconceptions, such as *Lies Across America* by James Loewen (2000) and *Yes We Have No Neutrons: An Eye-Opening Tour Through the Twists and Turns of Bad Science* by A. K. Dewdney (1997).

The principle of *scaffolding*, as you learned in Chapter 2, involves a teacher starting with a student's knowledge or skills base and building on it. You'll determine how much and what kinds of supports your students need. For example, you might use the tree diagrams and the humorous story of a wolf trying to determine his best chance for nabbing a pig in Mori and Anno's *Socrates and the Three Little Pigs* (1986) to prepare students for a lesson on probability.

Vygotsky (1978), as mentioned in Chapter 2, called the range where a student could not function independently but could learn with the help of a teacher or other competent mentor the *zone of proximal development*. He emphasized the social nature of learning, which constructivists have built on ever since. It only makes sense that we assess where our students are, activate their prior knowledge, and then provide supporting structures to take them further on their learning journey. As students improve a skill, such as reading, and are capable of more independence, some of the supports can be removed, and new guidance offered at a higher level.

PROCEDURAL AND DISCIPLINE-BASED KNOWLEDGE

According to schema theory, the facts, terms, concepts, events, and theories we've just discussed belong in the category of *declarative knowledge* (Ruddell & Unrau, 1994). Another type of knowledge relates to knowing *how* the disciplines work and how people within a discipline think and work; *procedural* knowledge has to do with strategies for using and applying knowledge (Ruddell & Unrau, 1994). It makes sense that we want our students to understand how people who practice our discipline think, what they do to gain knowledge and learn. For example, what does a scientist do? Shanahan (2004) asked a laboratory scientist about literacy activities related to his job and was told that he spent 99 percent of his time at work reading and writing. (His childhood reading of biographies of great scientists originally led to his interest in the field.) Shanahan also points out the importance of reading and writing about science for those who wish to be informed consumers and engaged citizens; and this must involve a multitude of genres, for:

> textbook dominant classes keep students from engaging in more authentic scientific reading and writing. . . . Textbook reading should be balanced with laboratory experimentation and a variety of reading and writing activities that show students what it is like to engage in the processes of science, as well as to learn the body of knowledge that scientists have created. (p. 76)

Shanahan offers a number of ways teachers can help students take on the dispositions of scientists, including critically thinking about the information they consume from sources such as scientific research articles, issues-oriented essays, and editorials. She recommends supplying texts that refute intuitive understandings (which are often inaccurate) and providing opportunities to engage with scientific principles in different formats, including trade books, the Internet, and textbooks. Teachers can model good questioning techniques during reading and can teach students to create graphic organizers tailored for science texts and scientific thinking.

Did you learn to think like a historian when you were in middle and high school? In the field of history, Stahl and Shanahan (2004) distinguish between *history,* "a narrative of a people's political and social changes over time" (p. 96), and *historiography,* which involves comparing perspectives and understanding who produced texts and for what reasons. Teachers who value disciplinary knowledge will teach historiography as they teach the history curriculum, "teaching the processes of history, focusing on the critical analysis of the various narratives that exist about any particular event or cluster of events" (p. 96). The authors offer strategies for doing this, using multiple documents, group processes, graphic organizers showing compare–contrast, and writing, among other things.

As *Math Curse* (see BookTalk 1.1) shows in a humorous way, people in certain fields really do observe events, interpret data, and talk to others in ways consistent with their work. You'll find that this is true in education. I can't read the newspaper anymore without scissors in hand because I know I'll find something of interest to bring into my content area reading classes. Professional conferences in every field can be stimulating and invigorating because people belonging to the same *discourse communities* enjoy listening to and sharing with others in their fields. I encourage you to join local, state, national, or international educational organizations in your discipline and to take advantage of the opportunities they provide for enriching your knowledge, as well as for meeting others who love the field you love. The names and addresses of several professional organizations are listed in Figure 4.2.

Stahl, Hynd, Glynn, et al. (1996) discuss the rich disciplinary knowledge that students need in addition to topic knowledge. "Although we are interested in the ways readers learn what historians and scientists have discovered, our interest is also focused on ways readers learn to think like historians and scientists. Developing such knowledge involves texts, but it involves using those texts differently than when students read and study primarily for the goal of passing a test" (pp. 139–140). Disciplinary knowledge includes knowing how inquiry takes place within a field. Students can learn that scientists use a method actually called the *scientific method,* and that they evaluate hypotheses through research; they measure claims by collecting data and examining evidence. Historians also weigh evidence and draw conclusions. Mathematicians follow steps to test maxims, algorithms, and theories. Professionals often collaborate and sometimes compete with colleagues to arrive at proofs.

Students also can be taught to understand that throughout history, new understandings replaced prevailing theories that no longer worked. The principles of assimilation and accommodation, discussed earlier, can apply to entire fields, as well as to individuals. Constructing knowledge is not a totally *linear* process, always moving forward;

FIGURE   4.2   Professional organizations.

National Council of Teachers of Mathematics
1906 Association Drive
Reston, VA 20191
www.nctm.org

National Art Education Association
1916 Association Drive
Reston, VA 20191
www.naea-reston.org

National Council of Teachers of English
1111 Kenyon Road
Urbana, IL 61801-1096
www.ncte.org

Council for Exceptional Children
1110 North Globe Road, Suite 300
Arlington, VA 22201-5704
www.cec.sped.org

American Council on the Teaching of Foreign Languages
6 Executive Plaza
Yonkers, NY 10701
www.actfl.org

National Council for the Social Studies
3501 Newark Street NW
Washington, DC 20016-3167
www.socialstudies.org

National Science Teachers Association
1840 Wilson Blvd.
Arlington, VA 22201
www.nsta.org

The National Association for Music Education
1806 Robert Fulton Drive
Reston, VA 20191
www.menc.org

American Association of Family and Consumer Science
400 North Columbus Street, Suite 202
Alexandria, VA 22311
www.aafes.org

International Reading Association
P.O. Box 8139
Newark, DE 19714-8139
www.reading.org

---

rather, it's a *recursive* one, as new knowledge gets absorbed and debated based on what is already known. Your students can see disciplinary thinking as evolving, yet sometimes involving leaps, and understand that there are various approaches to knowledge. When a new discovery or theory so shakes the foundations of a discipline's knowledge that a totally new way of thinking results, a *paradigm shift* occurs (Kuhn, 1996).

DISCOURSE KNOWLEDGE

ACTION RESEARCH   4.A

Write in your log for a moment answering the following "Forced Choice" questions, giving a reason for your choices.

You must take a required course in your major or the content area you plan to teach. There are two sections offered by different teachers. Teacher A is very knowledgeable in her content area, but is weak when it comes to pedagogical skills. Teacher B is very strong in her knowledge of teaching and motivational strategies, but is weak when it comes to content. Which would you choose: Teacher A or Teacher B?

How about if you were a parent and had to choose one of these teachers for your middle school child: Teacher A or Teacher B?

How about if you were an administrator (a principal, curriculum coordinator, or department chair) and had to hire one of these teachers for your high school: Teacher A or Teacher B?

Discuss your answers with your classmates or with the Kane Resource Site community.

Then, read the following two quotes, and see if your thinking changes at all:

As a recent graduate of a teacher education program, I can tell you the profession is in danger of being overwhelmed by hordes of candidates who are well schooled in innovative methods of instruction, brimming with creativity, idealistic and sensitive to students' feelings, but who know little about what they are teaching. (T. R. Burns, 1995, p. 2)

More important than the information a teacher acquires about science is a teacher's knowing how to inquire, how to find answers, how to use material and human resources, and how to model these in a science classroom. (Yager & Penick, 1990, p. 663)

How Early Can Children Deal with Varied Genres?

A literacy textbook asks, "Are you surprised that the reading materials first grade children are introduced to are stories? Can you imagine passing out science books and welcoming children to their first readers?" (Brozo & Simpson, 1999, p. 32). My answer to the latter question is a resounding YES! It's true, as the authors say, that "We begin teaching children to read with stories because they are already familiar with the structure of stories" (p. 32). But many are also familiar with, and may even have a preference for, nonfiction of various sorts. Children will pore over toy catalogs; Turtle, a toddler in Barbara Kingsolver's *The Bean Trees* (1988), is very attached to seed catalogs! I've known youngsters who had short attention spans when it came to stories, but who could attend to texts on manatees, baseball statistics, cars and trucks, or black holes for an unlimited amount of time. As teachers, we can encourage children's parents to provide varied experiences and reading materials, and we can continue at all grade levels to introduce and supply nonfiction texts and help students actively engage with them. The book *Informational Picture Books for Children,* by Patricia J. Cianciolo (2000), has recommendations and annotations of books exemplifying expository writing ranging from the primary level to books appropriate for teens, as does every issue of the *Horn Book Guide,* published semiannually.

I suspect you and your colleagues found this a hard choice because you would surely prefer in each of the three scenarios to choose a hypothetical Teacher C, who is strong in both areas. Now that you've been reminded of the ideal combination and maybe recommitted to becoming that Teacher C, I'd like you to look more carefully at the construction of the quotes I supplied. Each takes the teaching components of pedagogy and content knowledge and relates them in some way. I went a step further by juxtaposing them, hoping to provide you with somewhat contrasting statements on the topic.

This next section discusses the type of comprehension requiring *discourse knowledge,* that knowledge of organization and connections that enables us to understand text beyond the single sentence level (Beck, McKeown, Omanson, et al., 1984; Leu & Kinzer, 1999). That's what helped you know that there was a relation between content knowledge and pedagogical knowledge in each quote, as well as a connection between the two quotes as used in this section. Those readers who can decode and recognize the meaning of every word in those quotes will still have great difficulty with comprehension if their discourse level knowledge is not adequate. Discourse knowledge in literacy involves knowledge of different genres, text structures, and patterns of organization.

Genre

As you learned in Chapter 3, your students must understand that there are different types of texts and recognize into which type a particular piece of writing falls (e.g., Fletcher-Spear, Jenson-Benjamin, & Copeland, 2005; Roller, 1990). Writers of various types of texts have differing expectations of readers, and readers must approach different types of texts in the most effective way. Texts can first be divided under two major headings: (1) *expository,* or explanatory, and (2) *narrative,* using a story form. Typically, children in the primary grades are taught to read primarily through the use of narrative text, but that is changing. Some say that expository text is more demanding than narrative text, but actually, I've found that varies depending on a number of factors. Some nonfiction pieces can be quite straightforward, while some narratives are quite complex, having perhaps several strands that intersect. A sixth-grade teacher I know told me her class wouldn't be able to comprehend the novel *The View from Saturday* (Konigsburg, 1996) because the story line was not linear; the four or five interconnecting stories would be too confusing. As this example indicates, the sequence of events in narrative texts may be recorded in a nonlinear way, with flashbacks, changes in verb tense, dream retellings. Some narratives are told from more than one character's point of view. In fact, Paul Fleischman's *Bull Run* (1993) has 16 narrators; *Bat 6,* by Virginia Euwer Wolff (1998), has 21; and Walter Dean Myers' *Here in Harlem: Poems in Many Voices* (2004) has numerous narrators.

The categories of expository and narrative are not mutually exclusive. Especially recently, there have been a number of books published that combine the two. *The Magic School Bus* series, by Joanna Cole and Bruce Degen (www.scholastic.com/magicschoolbus), takes readers on imaginary adventures with Mrs. Frizzle and her class as they explore the human body, the solar system, the age of dinosaurs, and hidden mysteries beneath the earth's crust. Explanations of facts and scientific principles, whole lessons, are embedded in the story. Smolkin and Donovan (2004) offer research-based advice for teachers as to how to read and use these hybrid texts with students. Recommended strategies include:

- look carefully at books before reading them aloud
- read running text first, followed by speech balloons and separated reports
- work to deepen students' understanding of how science operates in our surroundings
- bring a sense of wonder to the scientific aspects of trade books read aloud
- question the students as you read
- help them transfer knowledge gained from a book to other situations
- stress scientific terms
- make science tangible

David Macaulay's *The New Way Things Work* (1998) uses a similar format. As another example, in the middle of a very informative article on sponges in the *Smithsonian Magazine*, Genthe (1998) invites, "To best understand them, come with me on a scuba dive. Let your imagination take over. Shrink to microscopic size and roll off the dive boat's gunwale into the warm waters washing over a coral reef somewhere tropical. Exhale, sink down and swim over to that bright red sponge" (p. 54). A combination of narrative and expository styles helps make this information-packed article an enjoyable read.

Within the major categories of expository and narrative, there are several genres, each with its own characteristics and conventions and demands upon the reader, though categories can overlap or a certain text may break some of the genre's rules. It's crucial that we help our students recognize, appreciate, and interact appropriately with particular genres and text structures. Expository writing is not all alike, nor is it always accurate or "true." A daily newspaper contains editorial essays, human interest stories, movie reviews, and political cartoons in addition to "the news." Biographies and autobiographies differ; memoirs often combine elements of expository writing and narrative. Technical reports are common in all fields, from science to business to politics. Students also should know that fiction consists of short stories as well as novels, and that there are further subdivisions such as fantasy, realistic fiction, historical fiction, horror, satire. When readers are aware of the conventions of various types of writing, comprehension is aided. Students who approach the comprehension of all genres and formats in the same way, on the other hand, can find themselves in trouble.

Even textbooks vary their formats and structures. Some are totally formal, while others may contain anecdotes and vignettes, letters from experts, cartoons. As a

literature-based and primary source–based teacher of your content area, you should create many opportunities for students to do wide reading within and across many genres, and guide them in that reading. Introduce them to examples of different text structures, and teach them how to actively engage with them.

ACTION RESEARCH   **4.B**

Is satire within the fiction or nonfiction category? Is it narrative or expository writing? What examples of satire can you think of? Compare your answers with your classmates'.

Now, read the following paragraphs, the beginning of a newspaper editorial.

SUMMER READING REQUIREMENT:
How Cruel Can Teachers Get?

Corporal punishment is no longer allowed in public schools. But that doesn't mean school officials have no alternatives for indulging their brutal instincts and inflicting misery on their vulnerable charges.

Take the heart-breaking case of the poor waifs at Cicero-North Syracuse High School. After huffing and puffing to the finish line of the school year, they were looking forward to a well-earned 10-week break.

Not so fast, said their tormentors, with a sinister laugh borrowed from Snidely Whiplash. The kids' vacation would not be entirely their own. [They] would be required to perform a painfully arduous task before returning to class after Labor Day. Or else.

They have to read a book. . . .

How in the world are these disciples of the Marquis de Sade allowed to get away with such torture? Why haven't higher authorities intervened? There oughtta be a law.

One 11th-grader explained . . ., "You're not supposed to have to work over vacation. [Reading] . . . takes too much time."

How much time? Well, to get through a 200-page book during the course of a summer, a student would have to read at the pace of nearly three pages a day. Oh, the inhumanity!

Teachers and administrators . . . want to improve students' performance on college entrance and Regents exams.

Those are noble goals, but at what cost? Are they worth the trauma being inflicted upon the tender sensibilities of these young scholars? Why, they might have to miss the rebroadcast of an episode of "Seinfeld" in order to meet the requirement. . . .

(continued)

At what point did you realize that the editors did not mean for this text to be taken literally? What clues or signs did they give the reader? What techniques were used to create a satiric text? Now, think what would happen to comprehension if a reader did not possess the discourse level knowledge that enabled her to appreciate the spoof. How and where and when does this skill or ability develop, and whose responsibility is it to teach and reinforce it? This section helps you think about and begin to answer these questions and understand the higher-level thinking skills necessary for reading and evaluating various content area–related materials.

Patterns of Organization

Regardless of what overall genres authors use, all texts also structure the ideas within them in certain ways; sentences relate to each other according to discernible patterns of organization. That's what makes paragraphs and chapters *coherent*. It's important for readers' comprehension to recognize organizational structures and patterns in the text (Alexander & Jetton, 2000; Goldman & Rakestraw, 2000; Harvey, 1998; Hoyt & Therrialt, 2003; Massey & Heafner, 2004). This section addresses five major types of relations in expository texts: time order or sequence, cause–effect, compare–contrast, problem–solution, and description. Moss (2003) explains:

BookTalk 4.4

Some books have more than one story going on at a time. *Walk Two Moons,* the 1995 Newbery Medal Winner by Sharon Creech (www.sharoncreech.com), uses a journey motif to tell the story of Salamanca coming to terms with the fact that her mother left her. As she and her grandparents retrace the route across the country her mother took when she left, she fills the time by telling them about her friend Phoebe, whose mother also disappeared, but for very different reasons. This embedded story is a mystery, complete with a suspicious stranger, notes seemingly written in code, and the girls' adventures as sleuths trying to put all the pieces together. The "story within a story" structure is fascinating; readers can appreciate the crafting even as they become emotionally involved with these two very likeable teenaged characters who have lost their mothers and have the courage and imagination needed to do something about it.

Understanding text patterns helps children recognize how expository text is constructed. It provides them with a map that guides them as they travel through a text. The greater children's awareness of the various expository text structures and organizational patterns, the better they can follow the thread of the author's message. . . . Research tells us that children who are aware of and understand these patterns comprehend and recall exposition better than those who don't. (p. 99)

In the following sections, I give examples of each pattern from various genres and offer ways you can guide your students to use their knowledge of the patterns to comprehend and remember information. Keep in mind that these categories are not necessarily discrete; rather, they can overlap. Authors can use more than one simultaneously; in fact, good writers almost always do.

Sequence

I'd be surprised if any teacher in any subject said sequence was not important. It may be most immediately apparent in history, where dates and timelines come with the territory. But math teachers point out that the order of operations is crucial to arriving at correct answers; science teachers tell of disasters that occur if experiments are done with the steps out of order, or cite the importance of time in geological and archaeological discoveries and theories. Artists do some things before others as they create; so do cooks, market researchers, attorneys, computer programmers. Teachers plan, thinking through objectives, examining materials, assessing students' prior knowledge, before they instruct. Fiction writers pay great attention to sequence. They either tell a story chronologically or deliberately manipulate time through flashbacks, time travel, or other literary devices. Readers must pay attention to clues that let them know when things are happening, how much time is passing during the story, how time relates to other aspects of the story.

Writers use any number of words to alert readers to sequence, including the following: *first, second, then, finally, after, before, following, subsequently, previously.* Your reading guides, your instruction, and your questioning during the reading of texts in your class can help students pay attention to clue words and important points about time and sequence. You might be surprised to learn that the students in your class have less knowledge and understanding of time issues than you might have expected. For example, in the classic study "What Do Our Seventeen-Year-Olds Know?" (Ravitch & Finn, 1987), a wide survey of students found, among many other things, that only 35 percent of the sample could place the Civil War within the correct 50-year time period given in a multiple-choice question. It's up to you as a teacher to help your students comprehend their texts and your subject relative to sequence issues.

Some texts are very explicit in their treatment of time order. The table of contents in the book *Extraordinary Women of Medicine* (Stille, 1997) consists of a chronological list of names, birth and death dates, and fields of influence, accompanied by photographs of the women highlighted in the chapters. There are other types of sequence also, such as step-by-step instructions for assembling something or completing a procedure. In *Why Greenland Is an Island, Australia Is Not—and Japan Is Up for Grabs* (Davis, 1994), the author outlines a sequential strategy for readers to follow in order to become geographically literate:

Step #1: Immediately identify the geographical issue . . .

Step #2: Study closely all maps reproduced in or accompanying the reading material you're using . . .

Step #3: Compare the maps you're given with more *detailed* maps in an atlas . . .

Step #4: Compare the maps you're given with *large-area* maps showing how the area in question fits into a broader geographical context . . .

Step #5: Combine what you now know about the geography with the other facts involved in the situation . . .

Step # 6: Close your eyes and try to picture the scene you've been studying. (pp. 21–22)

Davis is just as considerate to the reader in terms of time order in the section under the subtitle "What Exactly Happened to the USSR?" She uses phrases such as "As you read through this sequence of events" and "This scenario, presented in chronological order," and then recounts:

Event One: *Lithuania* makes a declaration of independence from the USSR on March 11, 1990 . . .

Event Two: *Georgia* begins to seek independence in late 1990 . . .

Event Three: A coup is attempted by military leaders on August 19, 1991, against USSR President Mikhail S. Gorbachev . . .

Event Seven: On December 21, 1991, eleven of the twelve former republics of the USSR . . . join the Commonwealth of Independent States.

Event Eight: The USSR is formally dissolved on December 25, 1991. (pp. 24–25)

Other texts are not so explicit and reader-friendly; for texts that do not use a clearly discernible time sequence, teachers have to help students do more of the constructing of the events' times and sequences. Making timelines to be posted in the classroom is an ideal strategy to accomplish this purpose or to help students who have to visualize the sequence of events in any text.

No matter what your subject area, you might begin a discussion of time issues with your class by having them brainstorm the titles and lyrics of songs that deal with this popular theme. Or you could make a class chart of proverbs and common sayings about time to stimulate discussion and activate thinking about this important concept.

Figure 4.3 lists examples of texts about time that cross various disciplines. You and your students can add to this chart as you make new discoveries in your reading.

Cause–effect

Purposes for actions and consequences of actions have been with us since early childhood in all aspects of our lives; it's almost impossible to get through a day without thinking or speaking in terms of cause and effect. We wonder why things happen or people act the way they do, and we explain our thoughts and actions starting with "because." Science teachers help students understand why certain reactions occur, and can predict or debate what the results of particular behaviors and actions will be. In fact, Duke, Pressley, and Hilden (2006) point out that good readers make inferences based on their background knowledge as they read, and "The most salient inferences that readers make, at least with narrative text, are causal ones" (p. 503).

Readers apply their knowledge of cause–effect in order to understand characters in fiction, as well as the heroes and villains of biographies. Math teachers must be ready to answer such student questions as "Why do

FIGURE 4.3

Books about time and sequence.

See more suggested titles in Appendix Figure 4.3.

Bober, N. (2001). *Countdown to Independence: A Revolution of Ideas in England and Her American Colonies, 1760–1776*. New York: Atheneum.

Bray, L. (2009). *Going Bovine*. New York: Delacorte.

Kent, P. (2010). *Peter Kent's City Across Time: From the Stone Age to the Distant Future*. New York: Kingfisher.

Raum, E. (2009). *The Story Behind Time*. Chicago: Heinemann Library.

Stead, R. (2009). *When You Reach Me*. New York: Wendy Lamb Books.

BookTalk 4.5

When I ask my students what happened in 1492, I get an immediate poetic response: "In fourteen hundred and ninety-two, Columbus sailed the ocean blue." When I follow this with, "What else?" I draw silence and blank or quizzical stares. That's when I introduce *The World in 1492* by Jean Fritz et al. (1992). This collaborative effort by a number of popular children's authors and illustrators gives a global perspective of that particular point in time. Katherine Paterson tells of Asian nomads who belonged to the most sophisticated army in the world; Patricia and Frederick McKissack describe the art, religions, and storytelling traditions flourishing in Africa at the time. Margaret Mahy depicts the rich family life of aboriginal people of Australia, and Jamake Highwater recounts the accomplishments and lifestyles of the Aztecs, Incas, Plains Indians, and other cultures already present in the Americas at the time of Columbus's "discovery." Your students can learn much information from this book, then use the same procedure and format for doing research and making their own books or posters covering other points in time. Cooperative learning groups might produce texts about the world in 1776, 1865, 1929, 2010. You can show them *1968* by Michael T. Kaufman (2008) as a model.

we have to do it that way?" and "Why do we have to know this, anyway?" and "What would happen if we solved the problem this way?" Psychology texts deal with why people behave certain ways under certain circumstances, and what the consequences of various medicines, nurturing styles, stresses, and heredity are.

Chris Leahey, a first-year teacher in a workshop I led, challenged the group to name any event and promised he could make a cause–effect poster of it. A veteran teacher called out, "The bombing of Nagasaki," and Chris wrote it in the middle of the paper. He drew lines upward and wrote causes as the rest of us called them out, and then did the same downward as we contributed results. I was impressed both with the teacher's confidence and with how pervasive the cause–effect pattern is. But what really stimulated us was his showing us that the causes we listed could be clustered into categories that he labeled *political, social, ideological, scientific,* and *economic;* the results fell into the same categories. He uses this strategy with his social studies students; although they consider it a game, it aids them in understanding the content, reading texts, and studying and remembering connected details. It organizes their knowledge.

You can apply the cause–effect strategy to literature, also. Choose a crucial happening or decision by a character. Then, depict the causes leading to it and the results stemming from it. Categorize them if appropriate. Or create a graphic organizer to map out the connected ideas in a cause–effect relationship. Figure 4.4 shows an example of a visual representing the cause–effect pattern running through the plot of Chris Crutcher's *Ironman* (1995).

FIGURE 4.4 A graphic organizer depicting a cause–effect pattern in the novel *Ironman* by Chris Crutcher.

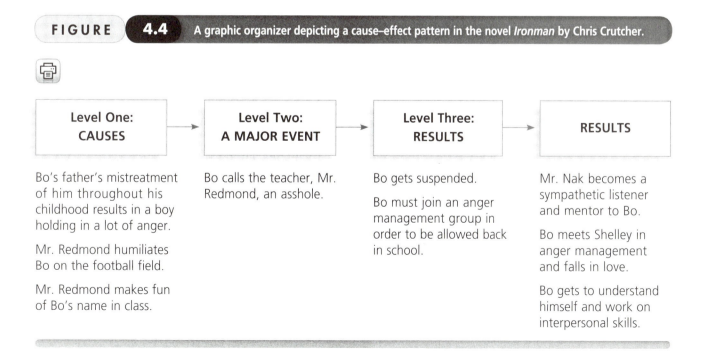

Level One: CAUSES	Level Two: A MAJOR EVENT	Level Three: RESULTS	RESULTS
Bo's father's mistreatment of him throughout his childhood results in a boy holding in a lot of anger. Mr. Redmond humiliates Bo on the football field. Mr. Redmond makes fun of Bo's name in class.	Bo calls the teacher, Mr. Redmond, an asshole.	Bo gets suspended. Bo must join an anger management group in order to be allowed back in school.	Mr. Nak becomes a sympathetic listener and mentor to Bo. Bo meets Shelley in anger management and falls in love. Bo gets to understand himself and work on interpersonal skills.

Many texts are much easier to comprehend, and react to, if you zero in on the cause–effect pattern they rely on. Good readers do this naturally, paying attention to clue words and understanding that some sentences connect to others using this relationship. But some of your students may treat each sentence as an entity separate from those before and after, losing much of the paragraph's message. Good teaching and guidance on your part can capitalize on this discourse level of comprehension. You can also have a chart posted listing clue words to the cause–effect relationship, such as *because, therefore, why, thus, as a result, so, consequently,* and so on.

One straightforward strategy that aids comprehension involves readers asking themselves why the facts in a text are sensible. You might try this out yourself as you read this text or the curricular materials you use in your content area. Then, create and take advantage of opportunities to show your students how you ask the why-questions and how they lead to understanding.

Figure 4.5 shows a preservice teacher's reading guide prepared to facilitate students' understanding of the cause–effect patterns during their reading of a text.

BookTalk 4.6

If the birds from your community disappeared, wouldn't you wonder why? Wouldn't you worry? What might you do to find out the cause? A group of youngsters decides to investigate their town's diminishing bird population in Jean Craighead George's (www.jeancraigheadgeorge.com) 1991 environmental mystery *Who Really Killed Cock Robin?* The result is a further mystery: why won't the town's mayor cooperate with them? Join your efforts to theirs as they solve the mystery and battle the dire consequences that greed and corruption can cause. The author has two more environmental mysteries: *The Missing Gator of Gumbo Limbo* (1992) and *The Case of the Missing Cutthroats* (1996). You and your students can exercise your cause–effect and problem-solving skills as you vicariously experience the mysterious circumstances and clever solutions of fictional characters.

FIGURE **4.5** A "during reading" text pattern guide focusing on cause–effect.

DIRECTIONS:

Some Native Americans believe that one's actions affect the people and the environment for seven generations. As you read "Plenty Kill," Chapter One of Luther Standing Bear's autobiography, *My People, the Sioux* (1983), fill in what you think are the causes for these cause–effect relationships. After you've finished, reflect on the questions with honesty and sincerity. We will be discussing them in class tomorrow, and your thoughts and opinions are anticipated.

1. Cause: _____

   Effect: "White man" could take control of land and push Native Americans out easily.

2. Cause: _____

   Effect: Native Americans did not fear "white man."

3. Cause: _____

   Effect: Members of the Sioux Nation thought they could get water at the railroad station.

4. Cause: _____

   Effect: A council was called, and members of the Sioux Nation decided to take action.

5. Cause: _____

   Effect: A train was derailed.

6. Cause: _____

   Effect: Beads were introduced to the Sioux culture.

   Effect: Tensions grew between the Sioux and "white man."

ANTICIPATION QUESTIONS:

1. Form a hypothesis about how you think these relations, which affected members of the Sioux and the dominant culture in the late 1800s, made an impact on today.

2. Thinking ahead to the next few chapters: "White man" killed buffalo (an animal that the Plains Indians relied on for food, clothing, and shelter) for sport, not really thinking of the end result until it was too late. Think about the following items and how your attitude and actions toward them may affect generations to come:

water	pesticides	violence in film
trees	urbanization	

—Branden Wood

Compare–contrast

In Roald Dahl's (www.roalddahl.com) *Matilda* (1988), the novel's gifted title character (who is treated as an outcast by her family) meets two educators on her first day of kindergarten, and I'd like you to meet them too:

> Their teacher was called Miss Honey. . . . She had a lovely pale oval madonna face with blue eyes and her hair was light brown. Her body was so slim and fragile one got the feeling that if she fell over she would smash into a thousand pieces, like a porcelain figure. . . .
>
> Miss Trunchbull, the Headmistress, was something else altogether. She was a gigantic holy terror, a fierce tyrannical monster . . . you could almost feel the dangerous heat radiating from her as from a red-hot rod of metal. . . . When she marched along the corridor you could actually hear her snorting as she went. (pp. 66–67)

Dahl makes his use of contrast explicit by using the phrase "something else altogether." Teachers and students can also notice—and judge—particular traits the author uses in his comparison. Some astute readers might be bothered by Dahl's use of stereotypes; the nice teacher is pale, slim, blue-eyed, and young, while the mean Headmistress is overweight and animal-like. Here's an opportunity for teachers to help students recognize and consider the effects of the use of such devices.

When we try to explain something to another person, we often compare a new idea to something familiar to our listener. Writers do the same, sometimes very beautifully, through the use of analogies. I'd like to suggest that you and your students start an "Analogy File," collecting examples from texts you read in your discipline. Comparisons can be as short as a phrase, as in a simile, or a sentence such as the following from a novel: "The air was so humid that the backyard felt as if God had turned on a giant vaporizer for a world full of asthma sufferers" (Konigsburg, 1993, pp. 37–38). Thompson (1996b) employs a comparative structure to make a point about the basic grammar of a sentence:

> When Crick and Watson were searching for the secret of life in the structure of the DNA molecule, they let their search be guided by the strong conviction that the guiding molecule of life would not be an ugly, amorphous molecule, a misshapen tangle, but would be something beautiful—and so it was. The double helix with its twin spirals is both a biological and aesthetic miracle, a gorgeous secret to the vast biological complexity of our planet. In a precisely similar way, the vast complexities of human thought structures have in common the beautiful subject/predicate nucleus which, if it is understood and appreciated, yields understanding of the very essence of clarity. (p. 155)

Students can learn, as a result of your instruction and modeling, to recognize when writers are making comparisons or contrasts, to ponder the aptness of analogies, and to pay attention to helpful cues. An author or character may make an extended analogy. Note the comparisons used in Granddaddy Opal's explanation of a black hole to Miracle, the protagonist in *Dancing on the Edge* by Han Nolan (http://hannolan.com) (1997):

> "You know what a star is, don't you? . . . Did you know stars can run out of gas?"
>
> "Like a car, you mean?"
>
> "Kinda. . . . The star just gets so hot and gives off all that gas until it uses it all up and then guess what? . . . See, what happens is the star, once it loses all its fuel, starts to cool off and shrink, like the light on your TV set, and then once it shrinks enough, gravity pulls on the star. . . . Now here's where it gets interesting. The gravity is pulling on the star so much that the light, instead of being sent out in the universe so's we can see it, gets turned inward, like pulling on a sock and turning it inside out. See, and if you pull that sock inside out and all the light was on the outside of the sock and now it's on the inside, well, then you have a black hole, because without the light you can't see it, and the light can't escape back out the hole. It's invisible. Just like staring into a TV set when it's off." (p. 87)

You can have your students contrast the explanations and analogies in various nonfiction texts, such as *Black Holes and Baby Universes* by Stephen Hawking (1993) and *Death by Black Hole* by Neil deGrasse Tyson (2007). (Sometimes the titles of books imply

BookTalk 4.7

Are there patterns other than those we've been exploring in this chapter? Leonard Mlodinow's *The Drunkard's Walk: How Randomness Rules Our Lives* (2008) discusses how we often mistakenly perceive causal patterns when events are actually random; the author insists that chaos is actually a more fundamental conception than causality. This is an entertaining, informative, interdisciplinary text that can supply great excerpts for teacher read-alouds. Math teachers can read stories that explain concepts of probability theory; social studies teachers can use stories related to political polls and famous trials; science teachers can employ excerpts relating to chaos theory, medical screening mistakes, and the position of planets. Students can cite Mlodinow when debating about grading systems or explaining happenings on television game shows.

that a comparison–contrast approach will be used; *George vs. George* by Rosalyn Schanzer (2004) and James Cross Giblin's *Good Brother, Bad Brother: The Story of Edwin Booth and John Wilkes Booth* (2005) are examples.) Here's an excerpt from the nonfiction book *Star Crossing* by Judith Herbst (1993); notice both cause–effect and compare–contrast relationships at work:

> Black holes do not sit idly by minding their own business. They can't. Their gravity is much too intense and has disastrous effects on everything in the neighborhood. Careless stars that stray too close are gobbled down whole, while those a little farther away are held captive like flies in a spider web. As the prisoner star orbits the black hole, it slowly loses material to the black hole's deep gravity well. The star's gas is sucked down into the black hole, similar to the way crumbs and other debris are pulled toward a vacuum cleaner nozzle. The gas spirals around the perimeter, forming a glowing ring called an accretion disk, before it vanishes forever into the black hole's hungry jaws. (p. 146)

It's easy to see how reading well-written text and noticing, delighting in, creative language that exhibits patterns of relationship such as compare–contrast takes students a long way toward true and lasting comprehension. The information they learn in your

BookTalk Online 4.8

Star Crossing: How to Get Around in the Universe (1993) by Judith Herbst teaches physics and astronomy while raising questions about everything from space travel to cryogenics. Hear more at the Kane Resource Site.

classes need not be spewed out onto a test and then sucked forever into a black hole.

Textbooks and nonfiction books use compare–contrast to teach concepts and make points. Student readers can be taught to notice this pattern and use it as an aid to comprehension. Rather than learn all of the facts about the North and the South before, during, and after the Civil War as separate entities, if they compare each side in terms of society type, population, positions on slavery, position on states' rights, they will have an easier time understanding and remembering the issues and information. Sheinkin's *Two Miserable Presidents* (2008) does a masterful job with this. You can teach students to be alert to clue words indicating the pattern is at work, including: *like, on the other hand, differ, in contrast, but, similarly, however, contrary to, more than, less than, fewer than.* Figure 4.6 depicts a preservice teacher's construction of a reading guide to aid

---

| FIGURE | 4.6 | Compare–contrast guide for a historical novel. |

DIRECTIONS:

The book *Nightjohn,* by Gary Paulsen (1993), takes place on a plantation in the American South prior to the Civil War. In Columns A and B, write down all of the aspects of slavery and the Southern plantation system that you can recall. Think about the lifestyles that differentiated the lives of the slaves and their owners. To help you begin, think about the food, living arrangements, level of education, and material possessions that each group might have had.

A. LIFE OF A SLAVE

_____

_____

_____

_____

B. LIFE OF A PLANTATION OWNER

_____

_____

_____

_____

Now that you have filled in the chart, read the book *Nightjohn*. When you have completed the book, go to Columns C and D and write down any new information that you learned in these categories. Did anything surprise you? What new ideas or facts did the book introduce you to that you had not thought of before?

C. LIFE OF A SLAVE

_____

_____

_____

_____

D. LIFE OF A PLANTATION OWNER

_____

_____

_____

_____

—Kevin Palkovic

comprehension of a work of historical fiction using the compare–contrast pattern. Figure 4.7 shows a semantic map prepared by a preservice teacher to help students relate ideas after reading two novels.

One way you can help your students become increasingly aware of compare–contrast relationships is to use the pattern in your teaching, drawing their attention to your use of clue words as you do so. Listen in as Ms. Beyerbach gives booktalks in her seventh-grade humanities class:

> This week in reading workshop you'll have your choice of reading one of two novels that have several similarities yet several differences. I've made a Venn diagram to illustrate this. First, they're both Newbery Medal winners. *Walk Two Moons,* by Sharon Creech (1994), won the gold in 1995, and *Holes,* by Louis Sachar (1998), won four years later. Both contain a story within a story and both contain surprises. You'll find some humor, some sadness, some symbolism, much friendship, and some mystery, no matter which you pick. However, *Walk Two Moons* has a female main character, while *Holes* has a male. The settings are very different—while Salamanca Tree Hiddle travels across the country to find answers about life, Stanley Yelnats' adventure takes place in a juvenile detention facility called Camp Green Lake (though it isn't green and it has no lake). So, look at the diagram I've shown you, examine the books, sign up to read one of them, and then participate in a literature circle. Enjoy!

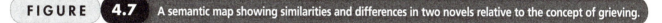

FIGURE 4.7 A semantic map showing similarities and differences in two novels relative to the concept of grieving.

Mick Harte Was Here, by Barbara Park, and *Bridge to Terabithia* by Katherine Paterson.

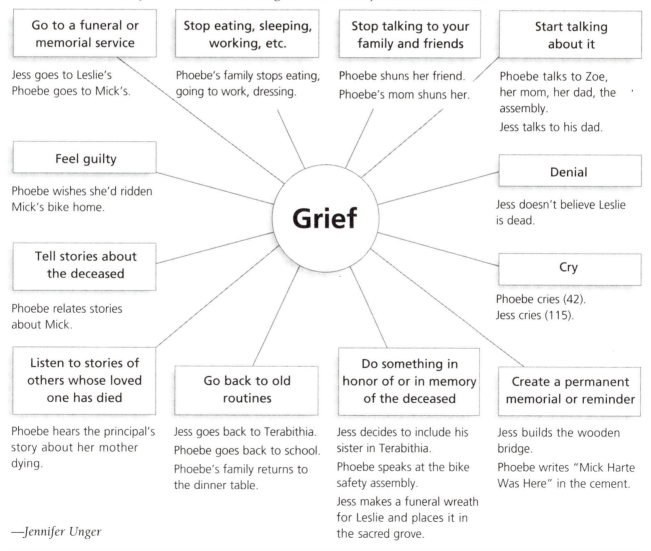

Go to a funeral or memorial service

Jess goes to Leslie's Phoebe goes to Mick's.

Stop eating, sleeping, working, etc.

Phoebe's family stops eating, going to work, dressing.

Stop talking to your family and friends

Phoebe shuns her friend. Phoebe's mom shuns her.

Start talking about it

Phoebe talks to Zoe, her mom, her dad, the assembly. Jess talks to his dad.

Feel guilty

Phoebe wishes she'd ridden Mick's bike home.

Tell stories about the deceased

Phoebe relates stories about Mick.

Grief

Denial

Jess doesn't believe Leslie is dead.

Cry

Phoebe cries (42). Jess cries (115).

Listen to stories of others whose loved one has died

Phoebe hears the principal's story about her mother dying.

Go back to old routines

Jess goes back to Terabithia. Phoebe goes back to school. Phoebe's family returns to the dinner table.

Do something in honor of or in memory of the deceased

Jess decides to include his sister in Terabithia. Phoebe speaks at the bike safety assembly. Jess makes a funeral wreath for Leslie and places it in the sacred grove.

Create a permanent memorial or reminder

Jess builds the wooden bridge. Phoebe writes "Mick Harte Was Here" in the cement.

—*Jennifer Unger*

BookTalk   4.9

The books in the series *Scientists in the Field,* produced by Houghton Mifflin, provide authentic examples of how scientists operate in the problem–solution mode. Take, for instance, *Once a Wolf: How Wildlife Biologists Fought to Bring Back the Gray Wolf* by Stephen R. Swinburne (www.steveswinburne.com) (1999). This book, containing exquisite photographs, details how the deliberate killing of the wolves and altering their habitat caused an upset in the balance of nature (problem), then gives a fascinating account of scientists tracking and studying wolves, rethinking the importance of predators in ecosystems, educating the public, and diligently working for years to bring wolves back to roam free in Yellowstone National Park for the first time since 1926 (solution). "Wolf biologists believe that their work with the wolves is about fixing what humans have destroyed in the past, righting a long-standing wrong" (p. 44). That's problem–solution at its best, but biologist Doug Smith insists, "All credit is due the wolves. They are supremely adapted to life in the wild. Our plan was good, but once the wolves hit the ground, they did it. Wolves are great at being wolves" (p. 43). This book is great at helping us appreciate that. Readers can find out what has transpired in the decade since by reading works including *When the Wolves Returned: Restoring Nature's Balance in Yellowstone* by Dorothy H. Patent (2008), *Gray Wolves: Return to Yellowstone* by Mersh Goldish (2008), and Jean Craighead George's *And the Wolves Came Back* (2008).

Problem–solution

Literature is based on conflict; if a protagonist does not have to come up against some force, human or otherwise, there simply is no story. So, the most common story structure is that of a struggle building, reaching a climax, and being resolved in some way. Math students, as well as math textbooks, refer to the work they have to do as "math problems"; they search for "solutions," although there have been problems, such as Fermat's last theorem, that took centuries to solve. History is often relayed through explanations of problems and at least attempted solutions, though one group's solution doesn't always please another, which can lead to more problems. Artists, athletes, and scientists encounter problems in their projects, as well as in their lives. Paying attention to the problem–solution patterns in a text can aid comprehension; in fact, readers can predict the solutions to problems and read to confirm or disconfirm them.

Your reading guides, your modeling, and your instructions regarding reading will teach students to recognize and to think using this important pattern. They can also react to the problem solving evident in their curriculum. For example, Josten (1996), in an article aptly titled "Students Rehashing Historical Decisions—and Loving It!" explains a structured strategy she teaches her students called concerns and decision making (CAD) so that they can discuss and evaluate the real decisions they learn about in their textbooks. The article illustrates how students used the question, "Did the Continental Congress make a good or a poor decision when it adopted the Ordinance of 1785 and the Northwest Ordinance of 1787?" (p. 571). After reading and discussing the data, they agreed with the decision. Imagine using this strategy to think about recent U.S. Supreme Court decisions, presidential acts, or decisions made by scientific research organizations or by characters in works of fiction. As students repeat the strategy in several disciplines with a variety of text samples, they will rely less on teacher guidance and become independent thinkers about political decisions of leaders. Asking questions about decisions and analyzing data can also help them as they confront problems, academic and otherwise, and seek viable solutions. Josten (1996) offers the following template for CAD.

1. Ask students to fill in the blanks in this question:

   "Based on _____'s concerns, did _____ make the right decision when _____ decided to _____?"

2. Have students inquire and think about the concerns by following these steps:

   - Searching for _____'s concerns (as a purpose for reading)
   - Identifying _____'s concerns
   - Verifying through discussion of the reading material
   - Verifying through discussion of accumulated prior knowledge
   - Prioritizing the concerns (p. 568)

3. Involve students in making decisions and drawing conclusions by doing the following:

   - Identifying alternatives
   - Predicting consequences of each alternative
   - Comparing consequences with relevant concerns

■ Tallying numbered consequences to determine the appropriate decision (p. 568)

By giving students ways to grapple with problems in texts and problems in their lives, as well as in your field of study, and to recognize and utilize the problem–solution pattern, you enable them to become active constructors of knowledge. You open up new worlds to them within and beyond the texts they're reading. Figure 4.8 depicts what a literature circle's analysis of a biography using this relationship might look like.

FIGURE 4.8

A problem–solution timeline.

Timeline based on *Restless Spirit: The Life and Work of Dorothea Lange* by Elizabeth Partridge (2002).

PROBLEM: 1936. Dorothea knows she has to help the starving migrant workers at the pea-pickers' camp at Nipoma, California.

SOLUTION: She brings her photos to the *San Francisco News*, and they are published. "Seeing the desperate, helpless mother unable to feed her children shocked Americans. . . . The federal government acted immediately, shipping twenty thousand pounds of food to the California fields" (p. 5).

* * *

PROBLEM: 1942. Dorothea is conflicted about working for the War Relocation Authority, since she disagrees with Executive Order 9066, which calls for the forcible removal of people of Japanese descent living on the West Coast, taking away basic freedoms guaranteed by the Bill of Rights.

SOLUTION: Though she hasn't the power to provide a real solution, she decides, "The best she could do was to photograph the process, so there would be a clear record of what was actually happening" (pp. 83–84).

* * *

PROBLEM: 1964. Dorothea is diagnosed with incurable cancer of the esophagus. She longs for the peace and care that her doctor recommends, and must decide how to spend her final months of life.

SOLUTION: She chooses to do a retrospective show at the Museum of Modern Art in New York, covering her lifetime of photography. "In this show, I would like to be speaking to others in the sound of my own voice, poor though it may be . . . I don't care how wide I lay myself open, this time" (p. 108).

Description

On the first page of Barbara Kingsolver's *The Poisonwood Bible* (1998), one of the five female narrators describes the jungle of the Congo in 1960 by listing vivid details that help the reader visualize the setting:

> Every space is filled with life: delicate, poisonous frogs war-painted like skeletons, clutched in copulation, secreting their precious eggs onto dripping leaves. Vines strangling their own kin in the everlasting wrestle for sunlight. The breathing of monkeys. A glide of snake belly on branch. A single-file army of ants biting a mammoth tree into uniform grains and hauling it down to the dark for their ravenous queen. And, in reply, a choir of seedlings arching their necks out of rotted tree stumps, sucking life out of death. This forest eats itself and lives forever. (p. 5)

The final sentence goes beyond description or enumeration; it contains the hierarchical (overarching) idea that all of the previous sentences exemplify. The more typical order is for a broad concept to be stated before specific facts. Kingsolver uses an inductive approach, and the reader is expected to understand the implicit connection between the ideas. You probably did this without being conscious of it, but your students may require instruction and guidance with this discourse level of comprehension.

Often an author uses a more direct approach, such as this pair of sentences from *Brain Surgery for Beginners*: "The human brain is the most amazing bio-computer. It can think, remember, predict, solve, create, invent, control and coordinate" (Parker & West, 1993, p. 12). The list of functions explains and emphasizes the main point. Again, you as a teacher can help your students comprehend text where the author has determined that enumeration is necessary, and you can guide them to connect those lists with other sentences so that the text as a whole is coherent. You might use a think-aloud procedure while reading a passage using this pattern, calling attention to the textual features, such as a colon before a group of examples of a point, a numbered list, bullets, or repeated words or phrases, that alert you to the organization. Note how the following quote by Saunders Redding from a biography of poet Langston Hughes uses strings of words and phrases—in other words, enumeration—to drive home points that involve the compare–contrast pattern:

> There is this difference between racial thought and feeling: what the professors, the ministers, the physicians, the social workers think, the domestics, the porters, the dockhands, the factory girls, and the streetwalkers feel—feel in a great tide that pours over into song and shout, prayer and cursing, laughter and tears. More than any other writer

of his race, Langston Hughes has been swept with this tide of feeling. (Meltzer, 1997, p. 221)

You could read this example aloud, using emphasis and pauses to highlight the structure of the sentences. Students can then appreciate the power of the language and the structure the author used as they ponder the meaning of the passage. They can be guided to pay attention to enumeration cues, such as a colon followed by a string of words or phrases separated by commas, and to use the organization to comprehend the texts they read. They can bring in examples they find in magazines and newspapers. Your goal is that, eventually, your students gain automaticity, so that they recognize and use this pattern along with other organizations of connected ideas without conscious effort.

Description can go beyond the word or phrase level. In the following text, also from Meltzer's biography of Langston Hughes, you can help students respond to the rhythm of the sentences, as well as understand that they work together and are tied together by the final abrupt conclusion. Try reading this out loud:

> Somebody in Washington wants to put Dr. Du Bois in jail. Somebody in France wanted to put Voltaire in jail. Somebody in Franco's Spain sent Lorca, their greatest poet, to death before a firing squad. Somebody in Germany under Hitler burned the books, drove Thomas Mann into exile, and led their leading Jewish scholars to the gas chamber. Somebody in Greece long ago gave Socrates the hemlock to drink. Somebody at Golgotha erected a cross and somebody drove the nails into the hands of Christ. Somebody spat upon his garments. No one remembers their names. (Meltzer, 1997, p. 206)

I hope you can see by these examples that description can be an important pattern of organization that enhances arguments, clarifies and exemplifies assertions, and adds to the force and beauty of narration and exposition. If your students get in the habit of recognizing and paying attention to its use in texts, they will strengthen their discourse knowledge and increase their comprehension abilities. Writing and spoken discourse can improve, also; we deal with these further in Chapters 7 and 8.

INSTRUCTIONAL TECHNIQUES FOR ACTIVATING AND INCREASING PRIOR, PROCEDURAL, AND DISCOURSE KNOWLEDGE

Block (1999) uses metaphoric language to explain comprehension, calling comprehension a crafting process and students sculptors, rather than molds to be filled. "Thus, if students are to craft a more

enriched understanding they must be taught how to experience a broad continuum of thoughts, bordered on one side by authors' intended meanings and on the other by their personal applications of text to their lives" (p. 99). However, Durkin's classic study (1978/1979) showed that, although teachers recognized comprehension as important and talked about it, there was little explicit teaching of how to do it. That is often still the case (Ross & Frey, 2009). This book attempts to give you a repertoire of ways to guide your students to process text beyond the word and sentence level and to respond actively and thoughtfully, giving students strategies to analyze, synthesize, and critique texts of all sorts. Content area teachers can learn how to follow Block's advice to demonstrate how students can use authorial clues and comprehension strategies interactively to craft meaning.

Teachers should explain and model strategies, perhaps by thinking aloud as they implement them using authentic texts; monitor the students' practice; scaffold instruction based on students' needs; and reduce feedback and instruction as students become independent. Teachers also should show students how to transfer the use of strategies to various learning contexts and types of text. Pressley (2000), in his review of the research on comprehension instruction, emphasizes, "Teaching to stimulate the development of comprehension skills must be multi-componential and developmental. . . . Comprehension instruction can be enhanced by long-term instruction that fosters development of the skills and knowledge articulated by very good readers as they read" (p. 557).

Pre-Reading Strategies to Activate and Build Prior Knowledge

There are many ways teachers can assess, activate, and supply background knowledge to provide support as students read relevant texts. This section discusses several pre-reading strategies that you can employ in your content area classes.

Brainstorming

Brainstorming to call to mind what we know about topics can be done individually or in groups. I used this strategy with you earlier in this chapter in the robotics exercise. Sometimes, I structure whole-class brainstorming sessions by putting up pieces of poster paper with category labels. For example, before discussing the trade books about war introduced in Chapter 3, or a textbook chapter on the same topic, I ask the students to fill in posters that have the following headings: EVENTS, DATES, PEOPLE, PLACES, CAUSES, and RESULTS (WHO, WHAT, WHERE, WHEN, WHY could also be used). I vary the posters as needed for different topics. For example, when I begin my sixth-grade Bible Study class each fall, I explain to my new students that I can teach them better once I know what they already know. I ask them to walk around with markers and fill in information on posters labeled PEOPLE IN THE BIBLE, BOOKS OF THE BIBLE, BIBLE VERSES I KNOW, and so on. As the course progresses, the students add information to these posters, and the evidence of new knowledge becomes visible.

List–group–label

For the brainstorming strategy mentioned previously, I provided labels that structured the answers I wanted to elicit. Taba (1967) approached brainstorming a different way. She modified the strategy by asking the students to free associate first, and then to examine their list to see whether the words could be placed into logical groupings—she called the activity List–Group–Label. Students may find that their schema for a topic includes facts that are hierarchical. For example, they may realize that, in preparation for a geography reading assignment, they have brainstormed names of countries, names of states or provinces or regions within those countries, names of cities within those regions, and finally, names of specific sites within the cities.

Before my class read Diane Stanley's (www.dianestanley.com) beautifully written and illustrated biography *Leonardo da Vinci* (1996), I asked my students to call to mind whatever they associated with the name of this famous man. Answers included: "The Last Supper," "helicopters and flying machines," "Mona Lisa," "He wrote backwards," "machine guns and grenades," "He did dissections of human bodies even though they were illegal," "self-portraits," "submarines," "He competed with Michelangelo," "engineering," "Renaissance Man," "He drew that, you know, that human body with all the arms and legs in a circle." Students were able to group their answers into categories representing Leonardo as *inventor, artist, mathematician*, and *scientist*, as well as one containing *personal characteristics*. Further discussion revealed that the categories couldn't be seen as discrete; sometimes a work was both a scientific and artistic achievement, for example. This activity prepared the students intellectually and affectively to delve into the text in order to clarify and extend their knowledge of Leonardo. They loved the book and were amazed at all they learned.

Graphic organizers

Because we know from schema theory that our prior knowledge is somehow organized in our minds, that the bits of information we have are connected to each other, instructors can make great use of visual representations of connected ideas to activate the knowledge that students can bring to their reading and learning. You may have experienced these in your own education and might know them by various names, including *graphic organizers, semantic webs, clusters, structured overviews*, or *visual maps*. These organizers have many other instructional uses, as you will learn in the next few chapters, but right now we'll look at how they can be used as a type of structured brainstorming to activate the schemata of individuals and groups in preparation for reading.

You might supply the structure and category labels for the students, as exemplified in the pre-reading organizer for an interdisciplinary inquiry into the topic of gambling in Figure 4.9.

You can find out what students already know, identify misconceptions, and have students share their ideas and learn from others. They should then be ready and motivated to read the chapter to gain new information, and their minds will be keyed in to the superordinate categories of *causes* and *effects*, which can aid comprehension. After the reading, students can go back to change any information that conflicts with their new knowledge (unless they want to dispute the text and research further) and add more details to the categories.

At times, it might be more appropriate to have the students themselves generate the categories for a class graphic organizer in preparation for a unit of study.

Teaching in action: *Art.* Figure 4.10 shows a wall chart that students in an art course might make on the first day of class, representing their combined thinking on the discipline the teacher asked them to brainstorm: art history. Using this chart, you will get a good idea of what the students already know and will be able to use appropriate "hooks" on which to hang the new information they will gain from reading, viewing, and listening to your lessons. As the weeks proceed, they might consciously or unconsciously look for the characteristics and concepts they addressed on the poster. Again, at intervals during the course, students can add or revise information on the chart, representing their knowledge growth.

APPLICATION ACTIVITY **4.1** (SEE PAGE 122)

Anticipation guides

You're already familiar with anticipation guides from earlier chapters. Pre-reading guides are very helpful in activating schemata, challenging beliefs and commonsense notions, provoking differences of opinion among classmates that lead to productive dialogue, and modifying misconceptions about a topic.

FIGURE   4.9   A pre-reading graphic organizer for a chapter on gambling.

DIRECTIONS: Before we start our chapter on gambling, I'd like you to brainstorm what you already know (or hypothesize) about various aspects of the topic. Please place information in whatever categories you can. If you're not sure about some ideas, place a question mark after what you write.

CAUSES OF/REASONS FOR GAMBLING

psychological: _____

_____

mathematical: _____

_____

moral/ethical: _____

_____

social: _____

_____

financial: _____

_____

EFFECTS OF GAMBLING

psychological: _____

_____

mathematical: _____

_____

moral/ethical: _____

_____

social: _____

_____

financial: _____

_____

Alvermann and Phelps (1998) provide concrete steps to help teachers create anticipation guides.

1. Analyze the text to identify key information and major concepts.
2. Find "points of congruence between text ideas and students' prior knowledge" (p. 179), anticipating ideas that might be controversial or counterintuitive, especially possible misconceptions students might hold.
3. Devise several statements that address students' existing prior knowledge.
4. Write an introduction to the assignment, and write directions for the students.
5. Have the students complete the guide after you give a short introduction to the topic.
6. Provide time for small groups to discuss their answers before and after reading.

Alvermann and Phelps warn of a mistake teachers can make when creating an anticipation guide—including statements that are too passage dependent. I often see this mistake on my preservice teachers' early attempts. When I write in the margin, "How would I have any idea about this before I read the text?" they say, "Oh, yeah," and eliminate or change the statement. For example, one student asked students to agree or disagree with statements such as "Abner Doubleday created baseball in 1839 at Cooperstown, New York" and "In 1887, all black baseball players were banned from all white teams, and the ban was not lifted until 1946." If students had the

FIGURE **4.10**   **A graphic organizer showing whole-class brainstorming in art.**

WHAT WE ALREADY KNOW ABOUT ART AND ART HISTORY

Genres of Art We Know:

sculpture	painting	glass blowing/stained glass work
drawing	photography	crafts (maskmaking, jewelry, quilting, etc.)

Types of Painting We Know:

Impressionism	cave drawings	modern art
cubism	surrealism	pop art

Artists We Know:

Picasso	Matisse	Van Gogh	Dali
Michelangelo	Andy Warhol	Jackson Pollack	Monet
Mary Cassatt	Leonardo da Vinci	Georgia O'Keefe	Grandma Moses

Illustrators We Know:

Maurice Sendak	David Wiesner	Leo and Diane Dillon	Allen Say
Barbara Cooney	Chris Van Allsburg	David Diaz	Susan Jeffers
Christopher Myers	Faith Ringgold	Jan Brett	Patricia Polacco

Famous Works of Art We Know:

The Mona Lisa	Starry Night	The Sistine Chapel	Whistler's Mother
The Persistence of Memory	The Thinker	Michelangelo's Pieta	David

level of knowledge necessary to answer these detailed questions, they'd have no need to read the chapter for which the guide was supposedly preparing them.

Figures 4.11 and 4.12 are examples of anticipation guides created by my education students. You can find additional sample anticipation guides, including a printable version, online on the Kane Resource Site.

APPLICATION ACTIVITY 4.2   (SEE PAGE 122)

"What would you do?"
Pre-reading thinking activity

Imagine you receive the following two letters from friends. How would you reply to them?

> Hi! You'll never believe what happened to me! I found a baby! She's so cute, and I'm taking really good care of her. I can tell she trusts me. I know you'll find this hard to believe because I'm so independent, but I want to keep her. What do you think I should do?

> Hello from your traveling friend! Don't tell a soul, but I'm on a really important mission. I'm trans-

porting some illegal immigrants to a place of safety. It's scary, but exciting and rewarding. I believe in this cause! What do you think?

The "What Would You Do?" pre-reading activity prepares students to reflect actively on ideas, using prior knowledge of events and relationships in their own lives. It often involves students' values as well as their decision-making skills. The main character in Barbara Kingsolver's *The Bean Trees* (1988) gets involved in situations like the two described. In preparing to read the novel, your students' knowledge and opinions relating to abandoned babies and illegal immigrants were activated, as well as their values related to each. This readies readers for engagement with, comprehension of, and response to the story. Your students' opinions might change as they read, and their knowledge might grow. In every subject area there are stories, real or fictional, that involve situations you can ask students to think about prior to reading.

Figure 4.13 shows a preservice Spanish teacher's guide designed to activate knowledge and thinking before reading the autobiography *When I Was Puerto Rican* (1994) by Esmerela Santiago.

FIGURE **4.11** **An anticipation guide for geography.**

DIRECTIONS: As you know, we have been studying the climate and geography of various regions of the world. Please answer the following questions in preparation for our next assigned reading.

1. What comes to your mind when you think of Alaska? What do you think it would be like if you visited there? How would you describe it? Climate? Environment? Plant and animal life? What would you pack if you were planning a trip there? Write down any concepts or words that come to mind.

2. Imagine you are standing deep within a tropical rain forest. How would you describe it? What does it look like? Where on the earth might you be? List any words or concepts that come to mind when you think of a tropical rain forest.

3. Have you ever heard a person claim that it was raining or snowing on one side of the house, but not the other? Do you think this is possible? Why or why not?

4. If you were planning a vacation for your family, and one parent wanted to go mountain skiing, while the other wanted to hike through a rain forest, what would you do if you could choose only one destination? Where might you go?

For homework, please read the article "Winter Green," by Jill Shepherd, found in the magazine *Alaska*, February 1999, beginning on page 34. When you finish, review your answers to the questions above. In a different color pen, add information you learned from your reading.

—Palmyre "Pam" Charron

FIGURE **4.12** **An anticipation guide for mathematics.**

DIRECTIONS: Before reading Chapter 1 of *The Broken Dice: And Other Mathematical Tales of Chance* by I. Ekeland, answer the following questions.

1. How many possible outcomes are there if two dice are rolled? How did you arrive at your answer?

2. To the best of your ability, draw a tree diagram that would represent the possible outcomes of rolling two dice, along with their probabilities. If you're not sure, draw something anyway to see if you discover anything.

3. What are some uses of dice?

4. For what purposes do you, personally, use dice?

5. What is meant by the phrase *loading the dice*? What is the effect of loading the dice?

6. What would happen if a die broke while in use? For example, if two faces of a die are facing up, should both numbers count?

Now you're ready to read the chapter. After the reading, we'll have a class discussion of the story, and we'll solve a problem that involves issues of the accuracy of the methods discussed in the story. Then, we'll look at different ways to represent the use of dice to solve problems.

—Author unknown

FIGURE **4.13** **A "What Would You Do?" guide for Spanish class.**

In preparation for *When I Was Puerto Rican* by Esmerela Santiago.

1. Brainstorm words, phrases, and people that you associate with the term *imperialism*.

2. List any titles of works of literature, movies, or songs that deal with imperialism that you have read, seen, or heard of.

3. Imagine that you are 10 years old. People from another country come to yours and force their customs, beliefs, and ways of life on you. How would you feel?

4. Imagine also that these people speak another language, eat different foods, listen to different music, and practice a different religion from yours. Would you accept this and change, or would you speak out and try to resist?

5. Now imagine that you were being pressured to move to these people's country in order to help your single mother raise your seven younger siblings. Would you fight to stay with your father and his new family, or would you go along and help your mother?

Now read *When I Was Puerto Rican* to see how Negi reacts to these challenges. Does she do anything that you would have done also? What does she do differently?

—Kelly Gorman

Previews

Everyone is familiar with the effectiveness of movie previews, letting us in on coming attractions. You can use a similar strategy—read aloud a script you compose to get students ready to read a narrative or expository text that is challenging. This activity provides the scaffolding that enables them to comprehend at a higher level than they could do independently. Previews have been used effectively with second-language learners (Chen & Graves, 1996).

Ryder and Graves (2002) provide helpful instructions for constructing a preview:

- Read the text selection yourself several times to become familiar with important characters, ideas, or events.
- Ask yourself how you might make the information relevant to your students by linking it to their background knowledge.
- Write an introduction to the text, ending with a question that draws upon students' prior knowledge.
- Write a summary of main ideas and supporting details following the order used in the text, being careful not to give away the ending of the story.
- Ask purpose-setting questions.
- Tell students about anything they should watch out for in terms of structure or potentially troublesome parts of the text.

Figure 4.14 shows a preview activity for an American history class. Now you try. Choose a text that you think is demanding for the grade level you're targeting and compose a preview that will activate or build on prior knowledge, summarize the selection, set a purpose, and provide guidance for your students.

Short readings as preparation for main readings

When students read two articles on the same topic, their comprehension of the second improves (Crafton, 1983). This should not surprise you, given what you know about the importance of activated prior knowledge. So, one way to prepare your students for a chapter in their textbook or another text is to provide related readings.

Teaching in action: *Social Studies.* For example, a social studies teacher introducing the novel *Maniac Magee,* by Jerry Spinelli (1990), with a title character who is a homeless boy, might bring in a recent article from a local newspaper quoting statistics on homeless teens in the area. Or she could have students peruse picture books on the topic, such as *We Are All in the Dumps with Jack and Guy* (Sendak, 1993), *Fly Away Home* (Bunting, 1991), or *A Day, A Dog* (Vincent, 2000), and then ask the students to discuss the topic of homelessness.

The strategy works equally well before a textbook treatment of a major topic. Before students read a chapter from their history text on the Civil War, you can offer them Jennifer Armstrong's *Photo by Brady: A Picture of the Civil War* (2005), and read aloud Lincoln's Gettysburg Address or excerpts from soldiers' diaries, official papers dealing with buying and selling slaves, or quotes from Southern and Northern newspapers of the times. You can start a file now that matches these short readings with longer ones.

Keene (2007) shows how she used "way in" texts—picture books and short pieces of text students can use to build background knowledge (schema)—to provide a "way in" to understanding more abstract, concept-, and vocabulary-laden texts. She used Toni Morrison's photo essay *Remember: The Journey to School Integration* before students encountered a series of complex essays on *Brown v. Board of Education.* Here's her think-aloud showing her comprehension process for Morrison's photo essay:

> "One of the first things I think is important here isn't the concepts in the text; it's the way it's written—the narration of the book itself. It's fascinating to me the way Toni Morrison has chosen to narrate this book as if she were the subject in each photograph. I have to believe that she chose this very personal form of narration because readers like us who never experienced the effects of school segregation would be able to feel it very personally." (p. 30)

Prior knowledge and English learners

You are aware that the students in the middle and secondary grades come to your subject area courses with varying types and levels of prior knowledge, and that this affects their ability to read and understand the new material that you require. The variability is even greater when you have students who are just learning English or who have a limited proficiency in the English language.

Imagine moving to a country you know little about—Cambodia, perhaps, or Brazil, Russia, Iran, Uganda. Now, place yourself in a secondary math, history, literature, or science class there. A large part of your difficulty meeting the expectations of the class has to do with your limited skills in the new language, of course. But you also should notice that you just don't have the background knowledge that the native speakers possess. No matter how knowledgeable you are in your native culture, there are gaps in your knowledge about the new culture that interfere with learning. The support of your teachers

FIGURE   4.14   Preview activity for an American history class.

MS. LIDELL: We're about to read this book called *Countdown to Independence* by Natalie S. Bober (2001). Now, you already know a lot about the colonists and their being upset by the way the English government was treating them. We've read in our textbook about the Stamp Act, the Boston Massacre, the Boston Tea Party, and so on. We've read picture-book biographies of Patrick Henry, Benjamin Franklin, and Samuel Adams. But this book here is going to give you a whole new appreciation for what was going on in the years preceding the American Revolution. What can you tell from the title and the front cover about the patterns of organization that will be used?

BRUCE: The years from 1760 to 1776 are listed down the side. Plus the word countdown is a clue. She's going to tell things chronologically.

CHRISTY: But the subtitle is "A Revolution of Ideas in England and her American Colonies: 1760–1776." Sounds like we might be in for some compare–contrast.

MS. LIDELL: You're both astute. Remember that we've been finding a combination of organization patterns in most of what we read. These two will indeed be used by Bober as overarching ways to organize her material. Would you predict there will be others?

SUZANNE: There's always cause–effect when we learn about wars—even wars today, sad to say.

WOODRUFF: And how about problem–solution? We learned from our textbook that the colonists tried to solve some of their grievances diplomatically, but it didn't work.

MS. LIDELL: Oh, good background knowledge to bring in. Let's check out the first few pages of this book. Lots of writers add an Author's Note at the end of a book, but Bober has put one right up front. You can read the whole thing on your own later if you want, but I'm going to point out one thing now, because I see this as her way of inviting us into her research process. She was a questioning child, especially about this topic, because her grandmother lived in England and her stories didn't quite match what Natalie learned in school about the villains, including King George III of England. Later, when she traveled to England, she found out that the history teachers there hardly mentioned the loss of the colonies. Where was the truth? She decided to study what was happening on both sides of the Atlantic during the 15 years leading up to 1776. Here's what she tells us about her process:

> The biographer is a portrait painter who sets her subject against the canvas of history. In fact, biography has been described as the human heart of history. Now I would attempt to portray history through the eyes of the people who made it happen. I would ask the question: What forces were at work that swept these people into a

conflict that ultimately precipitated a shocking revolution and severed the ties between Britain and her American colonies? (p. viii)

SUZANNE: Cause–effect—told you so!

MS. LIDELL: No argument there. I want to read you one last sentence. "Four years of research and writing, in both England and America, have resulted in this book." See how she's letting us in on how a historian works? Now, let's skip a few pages and look over the Table of Contents. Take a minute, and then you can volunteer to share observations.

SALVATORE: Most of the chapters are in quotation marks, "A blot on the page of history"; "Give me liberty or give me death"; "Seduced into war." We'll probably see those quotes somewhere in the chapters.

MEGAN: I see Chapter XIII, "A study in contrasts." There's an obvious pattern of organization.

PATRICK: Chapter XVII is called "Firmness is the characteristick of an Englishman." I see a different way of spelling.

MS. LIDELL: All good things to note. Now turn the page, where you'll see a Chronology. The main events of each of the years are listed succinctly, so this could be a good reference to return to later to remind yourself of the big picture. The same will be true of the next pages, which list the "Main Characters in the Colonies," followed by "Main Characters in England." After that comes a sentence from some correspondence the author considers important enough to set apart on its own page. Melynda, will you please read us p. xix?

MELYNDA: Sure. "As to the history of the Revolution, my ideas may be peculiar, perhaps singular. What do we mean by the Revolution? The War? That was no part of the Revolution. It was only an Effect and Consequence of it. The Revolution was in the Minds of the People, and this was effected, from 1760 to 1775, in the course of fifteen Years before a drop of blood was drawn at Lexington." John Adams to Thomas Jefferson, August 24, 1815.

SUZANNE: Cause–effect—told you so!

MS. LIDELL: So, we have key people reflecting much later in their lives on the meaning of the Revolution they had been involved in—they're thinking about history. Ok, now I'm going to give you a few minutes to browse the pages of this book. Look at the portraits and photographs, and read some of the captions. Tomorrow we'll start reading some key sections, and comparing Bober's treatment of events to what your textbook and some primary documents have to say. We'll be historians, too. I'll give you a purpose-setting question to mull over tonight. Why do you think it's important for us to understand what was happening in *England* during the 15 years before the American Revolution?

and your peers is necessary to help you meet your educational goals. The same is true, of course, for the English learners (EL) in your classroom.

When you have students who are learning English, do all you can to make them comfortable and able to learn. By your words, nonverbal expressions, and attitude, express your confidence that they can learn and that you will be patient and helpful as they do so. Get to know them and assess what their educational background is like in their native language. Some students are very literate in their own language, and others didn't have the opportunity to become so. Some Limited English Proficient (LEP) learners grew up in this country, perhaps speaking Spanish at home, while others are coming from far away where their cultures and lifestyles were extremely different. Your role differs depending on factors like these.

No one expects you, as a content area teacher, to be an expert on second language acquisition issues; rather, you should collaborate with an English as a Second Language (ESL) teacher or use resources your district provides to teach and support the English learners. There are some things content area teachers can do to help build the background knowledge base that these students require in order to be successful. For example, you learned in Chapter 3 about the value of your students using many types of texts, representing a variety of genres and levels of difficulty. Mundy and Hadaway (1999) documented the benefits of using informational picture books with secondary ESL students to help them understand content concepts, as well as to learn new vocabulary.

Thinking of a particular student and course may be helpful here. Imagine that a student named Hao, whose family recently immigrated from China, has joined your eighth-grade American history class. The following strategies may help Hao succeed:

1. Allow Hao to self-select books about the U. S. government and American history from your classroom library. Picture books, such as Jean Fritz' *Shhh! We're Writing the Constitution!* (1987), *House Mouse, Senate Mouse* (Barnes & Barnes, 1996), and Alice Provenson's *The Buck Stops Here: The Presidents of the United States* (1997), provide basic information about how our government came to be and currently runs. (By the way, your library should also contain enticing books about other cultures and types of governing. They will benefit all of your students.)

2. Use audiovisual resources, such as films, to provide context and background knowledge before reading assignments. Literary field trips via the Internet (see Chapter 2) are very helpful to second language learners. Remember, they might need more time to explore or opportunities to revisit sites in order to comprehend what is offered; that's the beauty of interactive programs that allow for unlimited, untimed, and varied ways of navigating the material. Hao can explore the White House, Congress, and the U.S. Supreme Court at the computer along with his classmates and on his own.

3. Provide as much direct experience and as many authentic contexts as you can, such as conducting experiments and going on field trips.

4. Use visuals. For example, show objects and use maps, charts, pictures, and graphs to make the learning concrete and meaningful (see Chapter 9).

5. Consider using simulation games as pre-reading activities to benefit English learners (Peregoy & Boyle, 1997). The games build background knowledge, provide opportunities for enjoyable social interactions, and help motivate students to read. Having students simulate oral arguments in front of the U.S. Supreme Court before reading about *Brown v. The Board of Education* helps the material come alive. See Chapter 8.

6. Provide peer support whenever possible. When Hao is involved with other students in a cooperative learning group that is researching the Trail of Tears, about which he may have no previous knowledge, he can listen and watch the others, ask questions, and learn in a safe, comfortable environment. He'll have knowledge and stories that can enrich the other students, also—encourage him to share. Cooperative learning is discussed in Chapter 2.

7. Have students write in learning logs, reflecting on content and their own learning processes. You can learn from Hao's entries not only about his writing progress and needs, but about how he's thinking of the material he's encountering, and you'll be able to determine what further scaffolding you should supply. You can also respond in writing to his entries, explaining concepts he shows confusion about, suggesting new resources or strategies, and providing words of encouragement. This shows your interest in and respect for the knowledge he brings with him. See Chapter 7 for more discussion of writing in the content areas.

You may be thinking that these suggestions seem like they'd be good for all students, not just for ESL students, and you're correct. Many of the things you do for second language learners are simple extensions or adaptations of what excellent teachers do for all. Because you'll get to know all of your students and their strengths and needs, you'll be used to modifying instruction, learning about how to address new challenges, and collaborating with experts in your district to provide whatever students need. You'll find that the English learners in your class can make many valuable contributions, and you'll benefit from providing background knowledge and literacy strategies to them. Other issues related to learners with limited English proficiency are addressed in subsequent chapters.

You may have noticed that I've used different terms and acronyms to denote people learning English: EL, LEP, ESL. All are used in the literature, sometimes differing slightly in meaning. The most current and widely used at present is English learners (EL), though you may also hear English language learners (ELL).

ACTION RESEARCH   **4.C**

Picture using the novel *The Giver* with a class that has a very diverse student population, one in which many of the students remember life in another country, or at least have heard their parents talk about the cultures they were a part of before coming to the United States. How might the background knowledge of these students affect their understanding of and response to the novel? Write for a few moments in your learning log, noting specific aspects of the book that might elicit unique responses from your students. (I realize that some of the readers of this text also fit this category of "diverse learners" and might have background knowledge and experiences that make this thinking exercise an easy task, and can share valuable contributions with others.)

After completing Action Research 4.C, read this next section to discover one teacher's experience in having a diverse group of students read *The Giver*. Enriquez (2001) conducted research in two intermediate ESL writing courses during a summer school enrichment program. Her teenage students came from 11 different countries. Enriquez asked her students to explore the thematic question, "What does it mean to belong to a culture?" (p. 15) as they read *The Giver*. Her analysis of the data revealed that the students generally engaged in the following sequence as they generated meaning from the book:

1. They identified information about Jonas's culture that was unfamiliar to them and unique to Jonas's world.
2. They used prior knowledge to make sense of Jonas's culture.
3. They reflected on the unique characteristics of their own cultures.
4. They identified the unique characteristics of Jonas's culture.

The students used personal experience as they talked about the text, comparing and contrasting facets of Jonas's community with their own, such as arranged marriages, government control of society, and the rule that each family unit can have only two children. One student wrote, "'In my society we are watched, too, but not by the Elders but by Allah, God, the creater [sic] of heaven and hell. We Muslims . . . believe that God is watching us" (p. 18).

Enriquez found that her students began by using their own cultures to make sense of the fictional one, and then examined their own cultures, often coming to a new appreciation for them. We can learn from the insights provided by this study as we think about reader response theory and issues relating to background knowledge.

Building Discipline-Based and Procedural Knowledge

It should come as no surprise that I recommend your encouragement and modeling of voluminous, wide, and yes, passionate reading as the best way to help students increase their new content knowledge and procedural knowledge, and to help students learn to think like a practitioner in your subject area. How does one think like a practitioner? It varies. Whitin and Cox (2003) delineate through chapter headings some of the habits of mathematicians: posing problems, keeping records, being skeptical, going beyond the data, solving problems, discovering patterns and relationships. Henry Petroski, an engineer who has written books helping laypeople to appreciate engineering marvels from the pencil to world-famous bridges, shares that reflection on failure is crucial to his practice, as is his curiosity. Even as a child, he took things apart and couldn't always put them back together (Ryan, 2005). Schoenbach et al. (2003) encourage content area teachers to make explicit for students how they read in their disciplines through think-alouds and metacognitive questioning. They are the practitioners, inviting students to become the apprentices. So ask yourself the question: "What does it mean for me to think like a practitioner" (a scientist/science teacher; a historian/history teacher, a musician/music teacher, etc.)?

Teaching in action: *Science.* Consider the following scenario where a science teacher reinforces the concept of thinking procedurally with her students.

> **Ms. Trey:** We've been talking about methods of doing good science research, no matter what the special area might be. What are some of the habits we've acquired this year as we've consciously taken on the role of scientists?
>
> **Augie:** We observe everything really closely.
>
> **Stacy:** And we remember that the smallest detail might turn out to be very significant.

Christopher: We're patient and respectful of what we're observing or interacting with. Do not kill ants!

Patrice: We make hypotheses and stay open to revising them as the data gets collected and analyzed. At some point, we draw conclusions and then ask new or related questions.

Ms. Trey: Ok, that's a good list to start with. Now, I've chosen excerpts from two books about scientists. *The Tarantula Scientist,* by Sy Montgomery (2004), is about an arachnologist. *Into the Volcano,* by Donna O'Meara (2005), is about volcanologiss. I want you to read the texts I'm giving you, and see if you find similarities in how they use procedural knowledge. I also want you to compare what you're reading with how we conduct ourselves as experimental scientists. Look up at the screen now. Here's the first excerpt.

> Volcano watching . . . takes a keen eye, an open mind and a lot of patience. Field assistants sit for hours in shifts to photograph, videotape and record in journals the onset of each eruption, the type of the eruption (ash, lava or steam) and the height of the eruption, estimated volume, intensity and duration. Back in the office, the data are entered into computers, and graphs are made to look for patterns or correlations or anything different or unusual. These detailed observations will someday be used to help unravel the secrets of how volcanoes work. (O'Meara, p. 32)

Ms. Trey: Ok, here comes the second; read it, and then we'll talk. I'm glad to see you jotting notes in your science journals as you read.

> [Sam] decided to compare desert tarantulas and rainforest tarantulas: Which ones were more energetic, and why? How did different temperatures affect the different species? He went to Arizona to catch desert tarantulas. He traveled all the way to Venezuela in South America to catch rainforest tarantulas. He captured about a dozen of each species and set up tanks for them at his college. The tarantulas were so happy and comfortable in Sam's tanks, some even had babies there.
>
> Sam set up his own laboratory. He even designed special machines to measure how much oxygen each tarantula breathed, and at what rate, and at what temperature. . . .
>
> "I got so into this, and then I realized: I love research! And I realized science really is a process. It's not the knowledge the process generates," Sam says. "Once I understood that anybody can do the process, it's very simple— scientific research is just a way of asking a question and answering it. That was the thing

that totally changed my life." (Montgomery, pp. 24, 26)

The class continues their discussion, based on the data the two texts supplied. Throughout the year, Ms. Trey can continue to offer information about scientists in the field, and to encourage students to bring in texts they find that contain specific examples of scientists doing what scientists do.

Madeleine L'Engle, author of *A Wrinkle in Time* and several other works of fantasy, warns, "A child denied imaginative literature is likely to have more difficulty understanding cellular biology or post-Newtonian physics than the child whose imagination has been stretched by fantasy and science fiction" (Bloom, 1998, p. 72). Annie Dillard, author of the Pulitzer Prize–winning *Pilgrim at Tinker Creek* (1998), a book full of fascinating scientific knowledge, illustrates L'Engle's point. As a child, she read many genres. "Books swept me away, one after the other, this way and that; I made endless vows according to their lights, for I believed them" (Dillard, 1987, p. 85). A favorite that she reread every year was Ann Haven Morgan's *The Field Book of Ponds and Streams* (1930), which led to her desire for a microscope, which led to her beginning to do work in science and gain knowledge experientially, as well as from continued reading. She had joined the discourse community. Similarly, Linus Pauling, the scientist quoted earlier in this chapter, explains:

> My eldest son says that I'm successful because I have an extraordinary memory, I'm curious so that I often begin reading about a new field in science on my own, and I make the effort to connect the great body of knowledge I have of science as a whole with what I read about in the new field. The result is that I often make an important discovery in the new field. (Rosenthal, 1995, p. 152)

Cunningham and Stanovitch (1998) showed that "the very act of reading can help children compensate for modest levels of cognitive ability by building their vocabulary and general knowledge . . . ability is not the only variable that counts in the development of intellectual functioning. Those who read a lot will enhance their verbal intelligence; that is, reading will make them smarter" (p. 14).

Imagine that! You can promise your students that reading will make them smarter. Who wouldn't be

BookTalk Online 4.10

Starry Messenger by Peter Sis explores the life of Galileo through rich illustrations. Hear more at the Kane Resource Site.

happy to know that increasing intelligence is an achievable goal? And you can easily see how this can occur.

Teaching in action: *History.* If your students read several of the World War II books that were booktalked in Chapter 3, they learned many, many facts about the war. For example, Lowry's *Number the Stars* (1989), within the context of the story of two families, tells of King Christian of Denmark ordering that his whole fleet be destroyed rather than allow it to be used by the Nazi conquerors. The stories in the books help students understand which countries were fighting which other countries, who some of the political and military leaders were, causes of conflict, significant dates, how ordinary citizens handled problems and relationships, and how events were interconnected. The knowledge gained can help them in future reading of textbook material, historical documents, and reports of current events that are affected by the past. In addition, those students may search for other books about World War II, about refugees, about courageous escapes; or they may look for other books by the authors, including Lois Lowry's subsequent Newbery winner, *The Giver.* They'll be acquiring content knowledge plus procedural knowledge in terms of research.

Figure 4.15 lists books appropriate for a classroom library that can provide much procedural knowledge, an understanding of discipline-based inquiry, and background knowledge in various subjects. They can be used as reference tools, or students can peruse them at their leisure. Many are written in a style meant to be enjoyable, intriguing, or humorous.

Of course, just having books and other sources available isn't going to magically increase your students' procedural knowledge. Teacher modeling is a great instructional strategy for the purpose of developing discipline-based inquiry skills. You might demonstrate how *you* go about learning science, history, or an artistic skill, talking aloud as you go through the process, and connecting your process to those of others in the field, especially those your students have already read about. Reading guides that use questions specifically about procedural knowledge also are helpful with particular texts.

Figure 4.16 gives a sample reading guide that a science teacher could use to help students use procedural knowledge and think like a practitioner.

Building Discourse Knowledge: Combining and Applying Patterns of Organization

Graesser, McNamara, and Louwerse (2003) call for all teachers to teach students to become aware of the patterns of organization, the coherence relations within texts, not just for a day or two, but regularly, and with much practice, since "The process of identifying and interpreting such relations will need to be *overlearned* to the point of being automatic" (pp. 95–96). Moreover, the different patterns should not be taught as though they occurred discretely; combinations of sequence, cause–effect, and compare–contrast can appear within a text. Sweet and Snow (2002) give helpful suggestions for teaching skills at the discourse level. "Research has indicated that specific instruction, for example, prereading, can improve poor comprehenders' understanding of a difficult text" (p. 38). They advise building background knowledge, using graphic organizers and story structures, implementing pre-reading and post-reading writing, for all these things provide instructional scaffolds that help them comprehend.

Teaching in action: *Interdisciplinary.* The following scenario shows a teacher, Ms. Ramalho, guiding her students before, during, and after their reading of an information book as part of a middle school interdisciplinary unit.

> As you know, you've been learning in all of your subject areas about the topic of disease. As mathematicians, you've looked at the numbers involved in various epidemics and worked with those numbers to ask questions and solve problems. You've flagged our classroom timeline across the top of the wall and our world map at points when and where plagues have occurred. You've played the role of scientists as you investigated how certain diseases affect victims and how they spread. Now, we're about to begin a fascinating book called *When Plague Strikes: The Black Death, Smallpox, AIDS* (1995) by James Cross Giblin. Most of you are familiar with this author of informational books;

FIGURE 4.15

Books providing procedural knowledge.

See more suggested titles in Appendix Figure 4.15.

Baker, R., & Zinsser, W. (1995). *Inventing the Truth: The Art and Craft of Memoir.* Boston: Houghton Mifflin.

Christolow, E. (1999). *What Do Illustrators Do?* New York: Clarion Books.

Montgomery, S. (2009). *Saving the Ghost of the Mountain: An Expedition among Snow Leopards in Mongolia.* Boston: Houghton Mifflin.

Panchyk, R. (2005). *Galileo for Kids: His Life and Ideas: 25 Activities.* Chicago: Chicago Review Press.

Turner, P. S. (2009). *The Frog Scientist.* Boston: Houghton Mifflin.

FIGURE **4.16** Reading guide for *The Stargazing Year: A Backyard Astronomer's Journey Through the Seasons of the Night Sky* by Charles Laird Calia (2005).

DIRECTIONS: We've read the chapter in our textbook about astronomy. Now it's time to join a practitioner who shares his process, knowledge, and reflections through this book. The author uses a structure that can help you comprehend what he's teaching if you pay attention to it. This guide will help you to do just that.

BEFORE READING:

1. Think of times you've looked up at the stars at night. Do you have a favorite memory? Are there certain things you look for, or favorite times to stargaze? Since the beginning of our unit, you've kept a journal of what you've seen in the sky when you stepped outside your home each night and looked for five minutes. Write a couple of sentences about a discovery you've made (about the stars or about yourself).

2. Open the book and look at the title page and the photograph of the sky opposite it. Turn the page and read the two quotes the author included there, one by Oscar Wilde and the other by Meister Eckhart. Write a response to the one that speaks more to you, or respond freely to both if you wish.

3. Flip through the book's pages. Though there is no Table of Contents, notice that the author chose a chronological order; his four major sections are labeled with the names of the seasons, and the chapters correspond to the months of the year. Look at the illustrations showing constellations and see if any are familiar to you based on what you've learned from your textbook reading, our lessons over the past two weeks, and your own stargazing. Write down things you notice or questions you're wondering about.

4. Read Calia's Introduction where he tells us a bit about his childhood and adolescence, and explains how he got into this yearlong project. Write one or two sentences when you're done—note something that struck you, or address the author, telling him what he got you thinking about, or how his life was like, or unlike, your own.

5. Here are a few of the first sentences from various chapters. Indicate the pattern of organization the author used.

   a. There is no peace like the peace of a starlit evening (p. 1). _____

   b. The idea came as many ideas do, unexpectedly, like a bright meteor across the night sky (p. 15). _____

   c. Geometry rules the winter night. First the angles of snowflakes, intricate and original configurations that all children know, and then the stars (p. 41). _____

   d. Twilight drops like a slow curtain (p. 89). _____

   e. Spring also carries miracles, and nobody knows this better than the farmer (p. 107). _____

   f. October boasts some of the clearest nights of the year (p. 209). _____

   g. The stars of November foretell a future chill. Winter is coming (p. 227). _____

   Now you're ready to begin the book. Pay special attention to the author's use of compare–contrast, sequence, and cause–effect. Be ready to converse with the author as you read his words and conduct your own observations.

DURING READING: Use your science notebook to respond to each chapter you read. Write a brief summary of the main points, state which pattern of organization you think the author used the most, and write your thoughts and feelings while reading the chapter, working in thoughts from your own continued nightly observations. Copy any sentences from the chapter that you love, and create one or two sentences yourself in your role as "Backyard Astronomer."

AFTER READING: Complete one of the following:

1. Write a letter to Charles Laird Calia, telling him some of the main things you learned from the book, or describing the chapter you liked the best, or discussing his writing style, or comparing the way he thinks about the night sky to the way you've been thinking since your study of your backyard sky began several weeks ago and since we've experienced our Astronomy unit.

2. Write out at least 10 sentences or paragraphs from the book that use a particular pattern of organization. Tell how the sentence or paragraph structure can help a reader's understanding of and remembering the important material.

3. Write an outline of how you could tell the story of your "Stargazing Month." How can you get across to your readers the discoveries you made about the sky and about yourself? What will you do to interest your readers and make them want to come along on your journey into the wonders of the night? What will be your major pattern of organization? You might include a poem you compose, or songs or famous quotes.

many of you have taken out *The Mystery of the Mammoth Bones* (1999), *The Riddle of the Rosetta Stone* (1990), *Did Alexander Rescue Winston?: A Research Puzzle* (2008), *The Many Rides of Paul Revere* (2007), and *Good Brother, Bad Brother* (2005) from our classroom library.

You also know that I've encouraged you to look for patterns of organization in the texts you read, to use them to help you understand, study, and remember information, and also to use them in your own writing to organize your thinking and help your readers. *When Plague Strikes* uses all of the patterns of organization, and it is a really powerful book that I think you'll find intriguing and thought-provoking. I've created a chart for you to fill in as you go along, or at the end of each section—whichever is the best comprehension strategy for you as a reader. Let's look it over first so you know what you'll be particularly looking for.

Across the top I've put categories that I considered important as I read the book. Giblin deals with each of these topics in each of the three sections of the book. The first category has to do with CAUSES: How did the epidemics start? The second will involve INFORMATION—fill in the boxes in this column with statistics, facts about the plagues that you found important or interesting. The third has to do with HUMAN NATURE AND THINKING. In every epidemic described in this book, people looked for scapegoats to blame when they couldn't understand the reasons for such magnitude of suffering. We'll be comparing, contrasting, and critiquing people's reactions to crisis. The final column will help you organize what you learn about the EFFECTS of each epidemic. Find out the political, social, and economic impact they had, as well as the advances in science and medicine.

You can write free responses in your dialogue journal as you read. Write whatever you want, in whatever format you want. In addition, as usual, I also want you to monitor your comprehension; be metacognitive. Ask yourself and the author questions, make predictions, note where your hypotheses get confirmed or disconfirmed, note places where you have difficulty understanding what the text is saying. In short, be an active reader. And let me know if you're confused and could use a bit of help. When we finish the book, we'll go over our compare–contrast chart, have a discussion, and see where our reading and thinking will lead us next.

Ms. Ramalho allows some class time for silent reading; during this time, she's available for those with questions or experiencing difficulty. She might have an audiobook version for certain students; she may read aloud to a small group, or have partners reading

off in corners. Students are allowed to collaborate as they fill in the chart. After the students have read the book, filled out the chart, discussed what they learned from the book, and given their response to and evaluation of the book itself, Ms. Ramalho gives a follow-up project:

You'll all do independent reading having to do with one of the plagues discussed in Giblin's book or a different one. You can use the categories from our chart to help you think about and organize the information you learn. You can choose to read one of the following books: *Fever: 1793* (2000), by Laurie Halse Anderson, which is a fictional story about a family, as well as a well-researched account of an epidemic in America during its early days; *The Hot Zone* (1994), a popular book by Richard Preston about the Ebola virus; *Swine Flu/H1N1: The Facts* (2009), by T. Stephenson; or *Flu: The Story of the Great Influenza Pandemic of 1918 and the Search for the Virus that Caused It* (1999), by Gina Kolata, a recent nonfiction selection that represents the continuing fascination with this historical event. You'll learn science and medicine, statistics, history; you'll ponder ethical questions and look at noble and not so noble examples of human nature in times of crisis. You'll come away from your book changed.

Some of you may prefer exploring reference materials and the Internet for information about a particular disease that has caused or is causing havoc among populations, families, and individuals. That's fine. Ms. Bresnahan, our librarian, and I will be here to help you develop questions and search for answers. The chart will probably work for you too; though if it doesn't, we'll come up with new ways to organize your thinking and the information you're finding. All of you will have the opportunity to share what you've learned so that we all learn from each other and our knowledge of the big picture will grow.

Remember, as you read, look for clue words and phrases that alert you to the author's use of sequence or time order, cause–effect, compare–contrast and problem–solution. They help comprehension.

APPLICATION ACTIVITY 4.3   (SEE PAGE 122)

APPLICATION ACTIVITY 4.4   (SEE PAGE 123)

Teaching in action: *Social Studies.* To make the concepts of reading at the discourse level and teaching comprehension clearer, I'll use Carmen Agra Deedy's *The Yellow Star: The Legend of King Christian X of Denmark* (2000) as a second example. In this book, the reader is let in on a series of decisions the king has to make after his country is conquered. When the Nazi flag is hung at the palace, the king sends a Danish soldier to remove it. Subsequently, when a Nazi officer threatens to shoot the next man who takes down the flag, the king counters with a warning that he himself would be that man. "The Nazi flag did not fly from the palace again. The missing flag became a powerful symbol of resistance . . ." (unpaged). The reader is expected to comprehend that the flag did not fly because of what the king said; the cause–effect relationship is implied, rather than stated directly.

What follows is a transition sentence that can help a reader make connections and predictions and be ready to comprehend what comes next. "Yet it was only a small victory; the king and his people's greatest test was still to come." The next few pages tell of the edict ordering all Jews to sew a yellow star onto their clothing. There is a picture of the king deep in thought, with images of war surrounding him, and the text helps us visualize the problem-solving process he uses:

> If King Christian called on the tiny Danish army to fight, Danes would die. If he did nothing, Danes would die. . . ." If you wished to hide a star," wondered the king to himself, where would you place it?" His eyes searched the heavens.
>
> "Of course!" he thought. The answer was so simple. "You would hide it among its sisters."
>
> The king summoned his tailor. (unpaged)

The book never says directly what the king requested of his tailor, but the picture on the next page shows him riding alone on a horse through Copenhagen, wearing a yellow star. "As they watched him pass, the subjects of King Christian understood what they should do." The following page shows Danish citizens, all wearing a Star of David.

Comprehension of this text is dependent on the reader being able to read beyond the words. A teacher could teach and model the skill of making inferences using this story as an example, putting together text and picture cues to reach understanding. She could then draw attention to the Author's Note following the story, where Deedy provides the dictionary definition of the word *legend* and explains that in her research she found only unauthenticated references to King Christian's legendary defiance. Yet, she defends its telling, noting that among the Nazi-occupied countries, Denmark was the only one that rescued the overwhelming majority of its Jews.

Asking "What if . . . ?" is a good way to get students' imaginations actively engaged in a topic. The author's final words to the reader are a perfect example of this thinking prompt:

> What if it *had* happened? What if every Dane, from shoemaker to priest, had worn the yellow Star of David?

And what if we could follow the example today against violations of human rights? What if the good and strong people of the world stood shoulder to shoulder, . . . saying, "You cannot do this injustice to our sisters and brothers, or you must do it to us as well." (unpaged)

You might choose to have the students read the story first, and then point out things like the connection between sentences, as well as the convention of the Author's Note at the end, which supplies more historical statistics and leaves the reader with questions. Or you might tell them what to watch for before they begin and help them connect what's coming with the background they have from previous lessons or from your introductory lecture on the topic. You could supply an anticipation guide, or a K-W-L-S exercise, or stop students at predetermined points to illustrate how a reader "reads between the lines." You might employ one instructional strategy with some students and a different one with others. There are no magic answers to teaching comprehension; you decide based on the assessed needs of individuals in your class. But what you *won't* do is just leave comprehension to chance or assume that if the students can decode words and know their meanings, comprehension will naturally follow.

STUDENTS WITH SIGNIFICANT COMPREHENSION DIFFICULTIES

It is certain that you will teach some students who have great difficulty reading. Some might even be considered beginning readers, and this will most likely make learning in the subject areas very hard. Some will not be able to decode words easily and fluently, thus keeping them from understanding texts. But others will be capable of normal word recognition, and still not comprehend the ideas in the text. Duke, Pressley, and Hilden (2006) remind us that there is no single explanation for comprehension difficulties. There are several different possible causes, and "there is a very real possibility that multiple causes are at work simultaneously" (p. 506). They offer a number of questions teachers can ask to determine the causes of the problems, so that the right help can be given. These questions include:

- Is the student struggling with word recognition and decoding?
- Is the student struggling with fluency?
- Does the student have poor short-term or working memory?
- Does the student have difficulty with oral language?
- Is the student an English language learner?

- Does the student struggle with particulars of written language?
- Does the student think actively the way that good readers think?
- Is the student engaged in reading? (pp. 506–511)

The authors conclude:

> Our view is that experience matters, and that comprehension can be improved greatly by providing students with experiences that increase their word-recognition competencies, vocabulary, world knowledge, and comprehension skills. (p. 515)

If your building or district has a literacy coach, ask him to give you suggestions for helping your students with severe comprehension problems. Let him know what topics and concepts the class is studying, and give as rich a description as possible of what kinds of difficulties the students are encountering (preferably after listening to the students themselves telling you where comprehension is breaking down). Perhaps the coach will work with one or more of these students while you watch and learn specific strategies he uses with them.

CAVEATS ABOUT COMPREHENSION INSTRUCTION

More of something good is not always better. Cognitive scientist David T. Willingham (2006/2007) points out that although a compilation of research studies provides evidence that strategy instruction improves comprehension, this is true only after students are able to decode fluently. His analysis found that "Reading strategy programs that were relatively short (around six sessions) were no more or less effective than longer programs that included as many as 50 sessions" (p. 44), so he recommends that teachers keep their instruction in reading comprehension strategies brief. In addition:

> Acquiring a broad vocabulary and a rich base of background knowledge will yield more substantial and longer-term benefits. . . . This knowledge must be the product of years of systematic instruction as well as constant exposure to high quality books, films, conversations, and so on, which provide students with incidental exposure to a great deal of new vocabulary and knowledge. (p. 50)

Many other teachers and scholars concur that too much comprehension instruction can backfire and do more harm than good. Block, cited earlier in this chapter, warns, "No matter how well students engage in comprehension strategies, if they do not have the opportunity to read what they want, they may never fall under the spell of wonderful texts" (p. 100). Atwell

(2007) abandoned much of her comprehension strategy instruction when her students let her know their application of strategies was actually interfering with their engagement and interaction with texts; after listening to them, she realized: "A reader could become as proficient as hell [with comprehension strategies] but *never ever enter the reading zone*—never become immersed in a great story, experience the life of a character, escape from his or her own life, dream, laugh, despair, celebrate, understand, wonder, or fall in love" (p. 54). She concludes, ". . . I think that directing story readers to activate comprehension strategies may hurt their comprehension" (p. 56).

Miller (2009) concurs. "The fact is that scores of the children who enter our classrooms are students who like to read or once did, before years of traditional reading instruction focused on comprehension worksheets . . . the drudgery that surrounds reading continues, year in, year out" (pp. 32–34). She cites Stephen Krashen's (2004) meta-analysis providing evidence that no one literacy activity has a better effect on students' comprehension than free voluntary reading.

So, content area teachers can be knowledgeable about the usefulness of multiple comprehension strategies, watching students carefully to determine which strategies are helpful and providing modeling during the reading of excellent, authentic texts.

Teaching in action: *Art.* Lapp, Fisher, and Grant (2008) provide an example of an art teacher's thinking aloud to show how he tackles comprehension as he previews a biographical profile of Vincent Van Gogh:

> "I think that this is going to compare and contrast the life of Van Gogh before and after his time in the asylum. I see that the author has provided us some information about Vincent and is starting to use some signal words that I know are used when comparing things. I see here in this paragraph that he used *in comparison, nevertheless,* and *in contrast.*" (p. 382)

The teacher conducted a shared reading of the song "Vincent (Starry, Starry Night)" by Don McLean; the students were seeing the text while a recording of it played. The teacher paused the recording to say:

> "This line, 'now I understand what you tried to say to me, how you suffered for your sanity' reminds me of the asylum from the biographical sketch. . . . I've made this connection between the song and the fact in the biography we read. Van Gogh had to live in an asylum for treatment." (p. 381)

It seems that the students in this class got brief, relevant instruction that did not overly interfere with their engagement with their texts.

Teachers and researchers also note that comprehension instruction will not work if conducted without knowledge of the students involved. Bakken (2009) recommends that, in order to be culturally responsive, teachers use materials and pedagogies that recognize students' *social identities,* individuals' "sense of self in relation to others" (p. 132), and their identification with certain groups, so that they will be more willing to engage and learn. Anders and Spitler (2007) combine what they call vintage comprehension instructional practices that have proven their worth with findings about the social nature of learning from the field of sociolinguistics and from a sociocultural–historical theory of learning and instruction. Spitler describes her classroom as she uses this reinvention of comprehension instruction for adolescents. One of her high school juniors commented, "This class was designed to help us realize and examine who we are as individuals and as part of the American society. In the curriculum of this class there were many pieces of literature we read and many strategies that we used to analyze and understand them on a deeper level. Through this class and the new reading strategies introduced to us, I have been looking at my life and myself on a deeper level" (p. 187).

CONCLUSION

T his chapter discussed the importance of background knowledge in terms of your students' reading and learning. As their teacher, you can help your students reap the benefits of the good part of the *Matthew Effect* equation, growing exponentially richer in knowledge and competence. You can devise anticipation guides that tap into the prior knowledge they have on curricular topics and help them to connect that background to new texts. You'll also provide information and many classroom texts, materials, and resources that can increase their background knowledge of other areas that they will pursue. Your stories, your enthusiasm, your guidance ensure that your students become richer in understanding and intellectual curiosity. You'll be part of the joy of learning. You won't have to worry about "mere facts versus in-depth exploration" because you will find ways to navigate that terrain so that neither breadth nor depth suffers as your students explore the riches of your curriculum.

This chapter also started you thinking about crucial aspects of comprehension, particularly ways in which you can help your students understand the patterns of organization authors use to make texts coherent. Specific instruction can improve students' understanding of the texts they read in order to learn the concepts they need to achieve in your subject. Using pre-reading strategies, story structures, and graphic organizers will support readers at all levels in your classroom. Sweet and Snow (2002) assure us that, as we connect thinking strategies to our content lessons, "If students learn that strategies are tools for understanding conceptual content of text, then the strategies become purposeful and integral to reading activities" (p. 40).

As you embed strategy instruction in content lessons, your students will learn to connect the thinking strategies to their learning of material. The following chapter will continue to deal with comprehension and thinking skills.

| **WEBSITES** | CHAPTER 4 | Access these links using the Kane Resource Site. |

American Association of Family and Consumer Sciences
www.aafcs.org/

American Council on the Teaching of Foreign Languages
www.actfl.org

Council for Exceptional Children
www.cec.sped.org

Diane Stanley
www.dianestanley.com

Han Nolan
http://hannolan.com

International Reading Association
www.reading.org

Jean Craighead George
www.jeancraigheadgeorge.com

Ken Mochizuki
http://kenmochizuki.com

***The Magic School Bus* series**
www.scholastic.com/magicschoolbus

National Art Education Association
www.naea-reston.org/

The National Association for Music Education
www.menc.org

National Council for the Social Studies
www.socialstudies.org/

National Council of Teachers of English
www.ncte.org/

National Council of Teachers of Mathematics
www.nctm.org/

National Science Teachers Association
www.nsta.org/

Roald Dahl
www.roalddahl.com

Sharon Creech
www.sharoncreech.com

Stephen R. Swinburne
www.steveswinburne.com

APPLICATION ACTIVITIES

4.1 Choose a text in your curriculum area, whether it be a trade book, newspaper or magazine article, primary source document, or textbook chapter. Create an assignment using K–W–L–S brainstorming, webbing, or the "list–group–label" strategy that will activate and extend students' prior knowledge of the topic addressed in the text. If possible, try it out with a group of students or your own classmates.

4.2 Use Alvermann and Phelps' recommendations listed on page 108, as well as any ideas you want from the sample anticipation guides in Figures 4.11 and 4.12, to create an anticipation guide for a text in your subject area. Ask someone in your class or someone else you know to complete the guide and give you feedback, or share and receive feedback on the Kane Resource Site. The answers may tell you if you made any statements too passage dependent, or if any are ambiguous or unnecessary. They may also let you know which ones stimulated the kind of thinking and prior knowledge that could help readers better engage with the author's ideas.

4.3 You should provide your students with direct instruction and practice recognizing organization patterns in text. The following sentences are ones I've collected for that purpose. I adhered to the criteria that my examples had to be authentic (not made up for the purpose of creating a worksheet) and had to be interesting or thought-provoking. Determine which relationships, time order (TO), cause–effect (CE), compare–contrast (CC), problem–solution (PS), or description (D), are exemplified in each quote. There may be more than one, and you may find some disagreement when you compare answers with your peers. That's ok; listen to each other's reasoning. When you are done, begin a folder or computer file labeled "Patterns of Organization," where you can collect your own content-specific examples and encourage your students to add their discoveries from their wide reading. You might devote a part of your class website to this activity.

1. "Criticizing liberal education within academe is like criticizing motherhood in a maternity ward" (Noddings, 1992, p. 28).

2. "Curing cancer would do to the health care industry what the end of the Cold War did to the defense establishment" (Dreazen, 1998, p. A8).

3. "People ask me what I am going to do next. I feel I can hardly write a sequel to *A Brief History of Time*. What would I call it? *A Longer History of Time? Beyond the End of Time? Son of Time?*" (Hawking, 1993, p. 38).

4. "Chloe thought she would drown in her own sweat . . . Lot's wife was not as sweaty as she. Neither was the Atlantic or the Pacific. Between the sweat and the tears, she was being pickled in her very own brine" (Konigsburg, 1993, p. 27).

5. "I'm sorry to disappoint prospective galactic tourists, but . . . if you jump into a black hole, you will get torn apart and crushed out of existence. However, there is a sense in which the particles that make up your body will carry on into another universe. I don't know if it would be much consolation to someone being made into spaghetti in a black hole to know that his particles might survive" (Hawking, 1993, p. 116).

6. "The name *black hole* was introduced only in 1967 by the American physicist John Wheeler. It was a stroke of genius: The name ensured that black holes entered the mythology of science fiction. It also stimulated scientific research by providing a definite name for something that previously had not had a satisfactory title. The importance in science of a good name should not be underestimated" (Hawking, 1993, p. 116).

7. "[Linus] Pauling was a scientific giant, imaginative, bold, and unafraid of anyone and anything. He leaped over the boundaries of disciplines, from chemistry to physics to biology to medical research. He fizzed with ideas, which seemed to shoot off as fast as sparks from a pinwheel. He tied concepts and information together in ways no one had before and used his persuasive, outgoing personality to convince the world he was right. He was audacious, intuitive, stubborn, charming, irreverent, self-reliant, self-promoting—and, as it turned out, almost always correct" (Hager, 1998, p. 9).

8. "Don't try to make life a mathematical problem with yourself in the center and everything coming out equal" (Kingsolver, 1998, p. 309).

9. "Among the themes in [Elie] Weisel's writing are the conflicts between silence and speech, madness and sanity, indifference and empathy, hope and despair" (Bayer, 2000, p. 88).

10. "With ever more refined tools and techniques, the genetic engineer manipulates a DNA molecule

that would be almost a meter long if unwound from the nucleus of a human cell, yet is so infinitesimally thin that 5 million strands can fit through the eye of a needle" (Stix & Lacob, 1999, p. 2).

11. "When Albert Schweitzer walked into the jungle, bless his heart, he carried antibacterials and a potent, altogether new conviction that no one should die young. He meant to save every child, thinking Africa would then learn how to have fewer children. But when families have spent a million years making nine in the hope of saving one, they cannot stop making nine. Culture is a slingshot moved by the force of its past" (Kingsolver, 1998, p. 528).

12. "We must take seriously our own learning—from the first day one makes a commitment to become a teacher until the day that one decides to retire from the profession—and make it as high a priority as eliminating the achievement gap that robs so many students of the opportunity that, as Americans, they are entitled to" (Snow et al., 2005, p. 223).

4.4 Choose several pages of a text within your field to examine and analyze in terms of organization and relationships. It can be a story, a document, a section of a textbook chapter, or a newspaper or magazine article. Code it in the margins using the symbols TO (time order), CC (compare–contrast), CE (cause–effect), PS (problem–solution), or D/E (description/enumeration), and underline clue words in the text. Determine whether there is an overarching pattern of organization used by the author. Then, decide how you could best help your students cue into the relationships within the text in order to deepen their comprehension. Create a set of directions or a guide to enhance their reading.

chapter 5

Metacognition and Critical Thinking

"Wisdom begins in wonder."

SOCRATES

"Understanding is a kind of ecstasy."

CARL SAGAN

Literacy educators attend to many, many aspects of thinking. The previous chapter dealt with teachers and students acquiring the knowledge of and beginning to think like members of the disciplines you are preparing to teach. The latter section of this chapter focuses on critical thinking, although we've already started on that topic, for thinking like a scientist, or a writer, or an artist, or a mathematician does of course involve thinking critically. In this first section, however, I'd like you to concentrate on the concept of *thinking about thinking* (or *knowing about knowing*) and more specifically, thinking about your own reading and learning processes.

METACOGNITION

> Metacognitive strategies are mechanisms that emanate from the reader's awareness of the cognitive demands of the text, the goals and purposes that will be accomplished in reading given texts, and the need to generate a variety of cognitive strategies in accomplishing these objectives. Metacognitive strategies include accepting responsibility for and analyzing one's own learning, monitoring comprehension to ensure understanding, actively generating learning strategies such as notetaking, reading, reciting, and rereading to facilitate memory for concepts that are difficult to remember, shifting strategies in accord with the difficulty level of the text, and like mechanisms. (Vellutino, 2003, p. 66)

Think about how you went about tackling this quote, taking that print on the page and transforming it into something meaningful in your mind. How did you extract and construct meaning, making sense of the author's words? If the term *cognitive* is unclear to you, you might have to look somewhere to refresh your memory. You might have noticed that the last sentence was long, but consisted of a list of examples of learning strategies, and this recognition of the structure might have helped. You might be aware that you have asked the author, or yourself, a question, such as "Is there another word for *mechanisms* that would work better for me?" Perhaps you recognized rereading as a strategy you use when your comprehension of other texts begins to break down. Or you might have actually visualized notetaking, creating a picture in your mind to help you remember this concrete, specific activity. All of these are examples of your own monitoring of your reading—in other words, metacognition.

Metacognition is the process of being aware of one's thinking and reading (Flavell, 1976). It's knowing about how you come to know; it's about being able to step back and use language to describe cognitive processes. And it involves monitoring the process of reading, controlling the cognitive process, and self-control (Paris & Winograd, 1989). If you ask children, adolescents, or adults *how* they read, they'll likely be able to answer you, and some answers may surprise you. Rosenthal did just that and then compiled the book *Speaking of Reading* (1995). Here is a sample quote she obtained during an interview that is rich with metacognitive reflection:

> I'll read about a hundred pages of a book to get the big picture, then go back to read it a second time for details, for examples. . . . I get very involved reading technical material. . . . An hour session gives me a lot to digest, and it can really inspire me. After that hour, I play with the thoughts I've gained and synthesize them into other ideas I may be working on.
>
> —*Gerald Eisman* (p. 164)

As a content area teacher, you can help your students become better comprehenders, and more efficient and productive readers of content area materials, if you teach them to be aware of how they read, and especially to think consciously about what they do when reading breaks down. We've all had the experience of suddenly stopping while reading and saying to ourselves, "Wait a minute! I just read two pages and nothing has sunk in!" Good readers monitor their reading automatically and change their pace when needed. Proficient readers choose from appropriate fix-up strategies to solve problems that occur while reading challenging text (Keene, 2003). But readers who struggle may not recognize when they don't understand the material, or may not know what to do if they do come to that stopping point (Smith, 1991). They are likely, for instance, just to keep reading. Good readers at times decide to do this, but they also may realize that they're tired and should take a five-minute walk, or that there is some background they're missing that they should look up before reading on, or that they're becoming cognitively blocked by the emotion of failure anxiety and must deal with that first.

You can help your students realize that they have an executive control center that they can activate to help monitor their progress toward goals and make wise decisions, including regulating, monitoring, and taking corrective action when necessary while reading, as well as knowing themselves as learners.

Instructional Strategies for Enhancing Metacognition

Students must understand what metacognition is and how it can help them comprehend text, and should be taught how to monitor their reading (Alvermann, 2002; Mason, 2004; Swinehart, 2009). Metacognitive strategies concentrating on process and reflection can be used across the curriculum, in science (Conner & Gunstone, 2004; Lovrich, 2004), math (Pugalee, 2004), theatre (Davis, 2005), history (Spector & Jones, 2007), and other areas. Most of the reading strategies modeled in this text can be considered metacognitive strategies. When students independently apply the K-W-L-S strategy explained in Chapter 4, for example, they are using the structure to help themselves think about their reading process and comprehension. This section discusses several other ways you can teach and encourage your students to use metacognitive strategies.

Direct instruction of self-corrective strategies

A statement that you may think goes without saying, but that struggling readers often must be reminded of, is that reading should always make sense. If it does not make sense, they should try metacognitive corrective strategies. Some students need to be taught corrective strategies that they can use to monitor their reading. Examples include:

- Put a confusing passage into your own words.
- Use visual aids.
- Reread.
- Read ahead for clarification.
- Slow down.
- Check a reference (e.g., a dictionary).

Swinehart (2009) describes how she teaches her eighth-grade students to employ metacognitive strategies in order to become proficient, flexible, and independent readers. She explains to them how they have "the right to have access not just to content but to thinking about that content" (p. 25). She does not shy away from using the vocabulary of thinking as she models her thinking for students. For example, she might say, "'Given that the author of this primary source text uses negative connotations when describing British royalty, I can infer it was written by a colonist'" (p. 32). She encourages and models visualization as a way to focus the students on their thinking as they read texts.

Swinehart considers metacognitive awareness as especially important for English learners. When given strategies for breaking apart a text and then building on their growing understandings, English learners will improve their ability to self-monitor and think independently, ultimately leading not only to language development but also to the skill of advocating for themselves as readers.

Various literacy researchers (e.g., Taylor & McAtee, 2003; Wilhelm, 2001) recommend teaching metacognitive strategies along with other literacy strategies. Winograd, Wixson, and Lipson (1989) devised steps for doing so, consisting of the following:

1. Describe the strategy.
2. Explain why it is important.
3. Demonstrate it.
4. Explain when and where to use it.
5. Explain how and why to evaluate it.
6. Provide guided practice and application.

Teaching in action: *Global Studies.* Let's listen in as Mr. Kilpatrick incorporates these steps into a lesson about putting a passage into one's own words in his global studies class. They're studying present-day Africa, and he's reading from an article in *Smithsonian* called "Born into Bondage" (Raffaele, 2005):

[Step 1] As I'm reading, sometimes I realize I'm not quite following, or I'm confused. When this happens, one of the things I do is try to put the passage into my own words.

[Step 2] This is important because if you can rephrase something, you probably understand it; you've made the knowledge your own.

[Step 3] I'll show you what I mean with a sentence from this article. (Reading) "Niger is a source, transit, and destination country for men, women and children trafficked for the purposes of sexual exploitation and forced domestic and commercial labor" (p. 66). Hmmm. . . . we don't use "trafficked" as a verb very much. Ok, I'll say, people are being taken *out of* and brought *into* the country of Niger as slaves. They'll be exploited sexually—I'm remembering the example we read on the previous page of the woman whose daughter, born as the result of rape by her master, was given away when she was six as a present to the master's brother, while her mother watched in silence for fear of being whipped. Anyway, back to rephrasing the sentence. They'll also be used for work within homes—I'm sure for cleaning and caring for children—and for commercial purposes—work on farms or in businesses, I guess.

[Step 4] Use this strategy of putting a passage in your own words as you're reading homework assignments and reviewing for tests. Maybe you can even use a family member as an audience for your reworded text. But even if you just say it to yourself, you can tell if you've captured the author's meaning.

[Step 5] Once you've tried the strategy, evaluate how it's working for you. Do you feel comfortable with your rewording, confident that you get the gist of what the text said? Do the concepts make sense now?

[Step 6] We'll stop every once in a while as we finish this article on present-day slavery to try out the metacognitive strategy of putting text into our own words. Use it frequently, and let me know if you want a turn sharing a time you've used it with your group members. We'll continue to use the strategy all year, so that it really becomes part of your reading toolkit.

Think-alouds

You can model a think-aloud for students that focuses on thinking about the actual process of reading and monitoring comprehension, and then you can encourage students to use the strategy.

Teaching in action: *Biology.* Imagine a biology student, Gabi, who has been assigned to read an article called "The Incredible Sponge" (Genthe, 1998) for homework. Listen in on her think-aloud as she applies the K-W-L-S strategy to the assignment:

(K) Ok, I've got to "activate my schema," as Ms. Cruz tells us. So, what do I already know about sponges? Not much! The first thing I think of is the sponges we use for cleaning, but I know they're artificial. Ok, sponges are living, and they live in the sea. They're probably different colors. They must feed off some little things floating around them. I don't think they move around; they're stationary. (Pause) Well, I guess it's on to Step Two. What do I *want* or *need* to know about sponges? I do want to find out what they eat. And I wonder how they reproduce? Are there really female and male sponges, mothers and babies? My mind is kind of chuckling at that. And how do we get them out of the sea? Do we take them dead or alive? And what are they used for?

As Gabi reads the article, she fills out the third category, either in writing or in her head, noting what she's learning and maybe where she's confused, or by talking aloud again. A few of her thoughts may go like this:

(L) I never knew sponges had poison in them! But I guess they have to defend themselves from other animals. And they can be used for medical purposes for humans, how about that? They have such complicated names, *Dysidea frondosa* and *Plakortis simplex.* I hope we don't have to remember those. No, Ms. Cruz told us just to read for the main ideas. Ok, I like this image of the sponge acting as a condominium for all sorts of tiny sea creatures needing a safe haven. I'll remember that. Oh, neat, a sponge acts as a filter, pumping water through and feasting on bacteria and plankton. I guess I was wrong about them never moving. At least the larvae creep about, it says, searching for a place to grow into adults. And now it says sponges can crawl over the seabed, "contrary to long-held popular and scientific opinion. . . ." (Pause) Ok, I'm done. I didn't understand every little scientific detail, but I sure know a lot more about sponges than when I started. Now, for the "Still Need to Know" stage of our strategy, where do I go from here? Well, I'd like to learn more about those pharmaceutical properties the article mentioned. I could ask Angel's mother; she's a nurse.

Notice that Gabi reflected on both content and her own reading process. She thinks about sponges, stating new knowledge as she gains it, and she shows metacognitive awareness as she consciously applies the K-W-L-S strategy her teacher taught her. She monitors her reading and learning. Note also the affective aspects involved—her interest, her chuckling at images.

For further study of the think-aloud process, I recommend Jeffrey D. Wilhelm's *Improving Comprehension with Think-aloud Strategies* (2001). To try a think-aloud for yourself, monitor your thoughts as you read a passage from a text of your choice. Either jot down your thoughts as you proceed or talk into a recorder and transcribe your words later. Then, reflect on what you discovered or learned from eavesdropping on your own thoughts. Notice that some of your thinking is about content, while some is monitoring the process of your reading and comprehension; the latter represents metacognition.

Eva-Wood (2008) encourages teachers to use what she terms *think-and-feel-aloud instruction* (p. 565). While recognizing the focus in the field on reading strategies, think-alouds, and metacognition, she laments that "both research and theory seem to neglect the messy discussion of the role of affect in metacognition. . . . Discussions of metacognition need to be extended to incorporate sensory and emotional responses more explicitly" (pp. 574–575). She models this by including her words and those of a fellow teacher as they encountered and constructed meaning from an Emily Dickinson poem. The students who were watching and listening to them were able to get a look into their minds and hearts as they verbally expressed their initial understandings, further grappling, and emotions as they read.

I use a personal experience to demonstrate the think-and-feel-aloud strategy to my students. I had a strong emotional response to a journal article I read about a strategy that was purported to increase adolescents' motivation to read and think critically. I felt uncomfortable, and ultimately angry, as I read about the "Imposter Strategy" (Curran & Smith, 2005), which involved embedding false information into reading passages relating to art, math, science, and English literature, then asking students to find the mistakes. I had to confront my negative emotions and ask what caused them and what they meant. I realized that the recommended strategy was contrary to my philosophy of always teaching with authentic texts. Furthermore, as a veteran teacher and reader, I knew that there were innumerable examples of mistakes, inaccurate information, logic fallacies, and ethical dilemmas within existing texts, so it bothered me to think about deliberately infusing more mistakes into reading passages when we have so many at our fingertips. I decided to talk back to this text, which resulted in another article (Kane, 2007) offering a more authentic way to reach the goals that the original authors and I shared. If I had not employed metacognitive analysis of my reading and reactions, my thinking would have gone nowhere. I have learned to pay attention when I find myself, while reading, writing NO! in the margins.

Embedded questions

Readers who have poor comprehension use metacognitive strategies much less frequently than do skilled comprehenders (Duffy, Roehler, & Hermann, 1988). But they can improve their comprehension when taught metacognitive strategies (Hoffer, 2009; Nolan, 1991). A teacher gives metacognitive instruction when he embeds questions that simulate the metacognitive strategies that skilled readers use and that activate conscious thinking about reading processes while reading (Walczyk & Hall, 1989). Weir (1998) used *embedded questions* and much classroom discussion to help her middle school remedial readers increasingly use metacognitive strategies independently. Initially, she cut up short stories and required her students to stop at various points in their reading to answer such questions as,

- "What do you think will happen next?"
- "What are you wondering about at this point?"
- "What was the most confusing part of this story? How did you handle it?"

Later, she had the students analyze their work and identify the strategies they used. Finally, students had to read a short story independently and annotate it themselves with predictions and questions. By examining their annotations, Weir could understand the students' metacognitive processes. Test results showed gains in many of her students' reading competency levels, and in a video-recorded interview with her students, she received comments like the following from Annie:

> Now when I read, I try to go into it more, like what is he trying to tell us? Why is he writing this book? But before, I just read it. I didn't really care. Now I can go into it more deeper. I can ask myself questions and see if I understand the book. I can question myself and see how I understand it. (p. 466)

Figure 5.1 shows a reading guide that uses embedded questions to aid comprehension, monitoring, and reflective thinking while reading a nonfiction book.

APPLICATION ACTIVITY 5.1 (SEE PAGE 150)

Process checks

Moore, Moore, Cunningham, et al. (1994) recommend the use of *process checks,* giving students questions they can ask to monitor their strategies while reading. Before reading, you can ask, or teach the students to ask themselves,

- "How will you remember this?"

- "What are some things you might do to learn this information?" (p. 98).

After reading, simple questions can be asked:

- "What led you to that conclusion?"
- "Why do you say that?"
- "How did you figure that out?"
- "How did you approach this?"

Similarly, Niles (1985) suggests that teachers first ask questions about the reading process, thus making it visible. Questions can focus on

- making predictions,
- confirming or disputing the predictions,
- noticing certain text structures such as headings or the organization of paragraphs.

Gradually, over time and with practice, students can internalize these questions and learn to use them strategically during their independent reading. It's important that you help the students realize the purpose of these questions in terms of monitoring and enhancing their comprehension; many of them have been inundated for years with questions that seemed purposeless to them, or that they needed to answer to show that they understood content material they had read.

Questioning strategies are important and beneficial before, during, and after reading. Subsequent

FIGURE 5.1 A reading guide using embedded questions.

INTRODUCTION: You've learned through our textbook chapter and my lecture that Denmark holds the unique position of being the only country in Europe that saved the majority of its Jewish population during the Holocaust. We've hypothesized some reasons for this. For homework, you're going to read the chapter "Resistance Begins" in Ellen Levine's *Darkness Over Denmark: The Danish Resistance and the Rescue of the Jews* (2000). You'll find out some fascinating details and meet some heroic rescuers. This reading guide will help you comprehend the text and think about the topic and your reading process as you read.

DIRECTIONS: Stop at the end of each section (indicated in parentheses) and answer the questions before reading on.

AFTER SECTION ONE: Those conquered Danes who favored resistance felt that the policy of *negotiation* with the Nazis was the equivalent of *collaboration*. Do you see their point? Do you agree? Can you see how the gradual increase of concessions they had to make was making the Danish gov-

ernment "Danish in name only" (p. 30)? What questions do you have at this point? If you're confused, reread this section before proceeding.

AFTER SECTION TWO: Why did medical student Jorgen Kielor join the student protest on November 21, 1941? What were the demonstrators protesting? What resulted from the newspaper pictures that showed the police beating and arresting fellow Danes? How are you feeling at this point? Can you imagine yourself there? Do you think you would have joined the protestors?

AFTER SECTION THREE: Why couldn't the Danes trust official news reports in Danish papers? What other sources of information did they find? What were some examples of passive resistance the Danes used on an everyday basis? Do you think you would have printed or distributed the underground pamphlets urging resistance of your Nazi occupiers? How do you like this chapter so far? Think of a couple of questions you'd like answered in the next chapter, "Resistance Grows."

chapters provide further instruction on creating good questions to enhance discipline-based literacy.

Guest speakers

An authentic way of helping students understand how people in various fields gain and create knowledge, and how they think about their own learning, is to invite practitioners in to talk with them about how they go about working and learning. Think of your friends and acquaintances who might be willing to share what they do and how they think while doing it. I've invited my neighbor to talk to my classes about his experiences and reflections as an army chaplain in Vietnam. He had to learn many new things and make crucial decisions during his tours of duty. The parents and guardians of your students are a rich resource for you to tap. There are most likely parents who have jobs related in some way to math, science, technology, government, literature, education, the arts, business, child development, history, law, social work, and psychology. Some will be delighted to share their learning processes, reading materials, stories, and advice with the next generation. For those who can't come in, you might invite them to share thoughts with the class through a letter, blog, self-made video, or podcast. Your students can compose an initial letter to take home to their parents, asking them to visit or write. You can customize the invitation according to your specific needs.

During the talks, you and your students can interact with the speakers, asking specific questions that get at metacognitive issues. For example, a class might ask a visiting artist, "Do you see in your mind before you start exactly what you want your faces to look like, or do you just paint and see what kind of a face develops?" or a visiting scientist, "What do you do when you're analyzing the data you've collected from your experiment and some numbers don't add up, or the conclusion just doesn't seem logical?" Later, your class can analyze the speakers' messages to see whether you can get at how they think about the processes involved in their learning in authentic contexts, how they think on the job to accomplish tasks, solve problems, and originate new ideas. Some speakers are willing to answer follow-up questions via letters, e-mail, phone calls, or interaction via the teacher's web page.

The SQ3R study strategy

The term *SQ3R* might sound familiar to you—it's been around since 1946 (Robinson). Perhaps it was a strategy that really worked for you and you still employ it independently in your own reading. A few students in my classes extol its usefulness when I survey them, though most say it was an isolated activity they learned in some class and then forgot when they went on to another teacher; they never recognized it as a useful strategy for other types of reading.

The steps in SQ3R include:

1. **Survey:** students read the title, introductory paragraph, main headings, and chapter summary and examine any illustrations.

2. **Question:** students rephrase the main headings into questions to be answered during reading or generate their own questions.

3. **Read:** students read the material to answer the questions as well as for other purposes set before reading.

4. **Recite:** students recite the answers to the questions they developed.

5. **Review:** students recall the answers to the questions and the general structure of the material.

Readers can apply this study system in any content area, thus monitoring and assisting their comprehension. Other study systems include:

PORPE: **P**redict, **O**rganize, **R**ehearse, **P**ractice, **E**valuate (Simpson, 1986)

REAP: **R**ead, **E**ncode, **A**nnotate, **P**onder (Eanet & Manzo, 1976) (see p. 159)

STAR: **S**kim and Set purpose, **T**hink, **A**nticipate and Adjust, **R**eview and Retell (Stephens & Brown, 2000).

Students might benefit from trying several systems and finding the one most beneficial to them. The Study System Tryout activity in Figure 5.2 encourages students to select or create their own system.

APPLICATION ACTIVITY **5.2** (SEE PAGE 150)

Metacognition Overload?

Of course, there may be such a thing as too much metacognition. Practitioners, whether they be musicians, athletes, artists, writers, actors, or readers, often do best when they are not consciously thinking about discrete parts of their performance. Madeleine L'Engle (1972) tells of Dmitri Mitropoulos, who, when asked to explain the effect his conducting had on orchestra and audience, replied that he wouldn't try for fear of becoming like the centipede who was asked by another bug which of his hundred legs he moved first when he walked. The centipede began analyzing the question and in the process lost the ability to walk. L'Engle concludes, "Bug or centipede,

FIGURE 5.2

Study system tryout.

The steps in this activity are as follows:

1. Model the use of several study systems.
2. Discuss with students what they seem to have in common, and invite students to use these strategies when reading informational texts.
3. After students have tried various strategies, discuss which ones seemed most helpful.
4. Encourage students to create their own combinations of study systems that seem most helpful to them. Some systems created by students might look like these (Stephens and Brown, 2000, p. 113):

    GOAL: Glance through, Order information, Adjust, Learn by retelling

    LAFF: Look over, Ask questions, Find answers, Follow through by reviewing and retelling

Source: N. L. Cecil and J. P. Gipe, *Literacy in the Intermediate Grades: Best Practices for a Comprehensive Program.* Copyright © 2003 by Holcomb Hathaway. Used with permission.

BookTalk 5.1

In the Preface of *Conned Again, Watson: Cautionary Tales of Logic, Math, and Probability* by Colin Bruce (2001), the author shares his purpose for writing the book. "There are math books and business books that between them cover the topics described here, but for many people they are rather dry reading. I have always enjoyed the ancient tradition of teaching with stories that contain a dire warning. . . . Tell a tale of someone whose mistake has really awful consequences, and the moral becomes easy to remember" (p. viii). And so he uses classic Sherlock Holmes stories to teach about fallacies of logic and tricks of statistics. He also gives his readers advice as to how to tackle his stories. "Please read them just for fun. If in the process you soak up a little knowledge about . . . how not to be deceived by statistics and the modern-day con games all about us, I will be delighted" (p. viii). Colin Bruce sounds like a good teacher to me. I think I'll go on to read *The Einstein Paradox: And Other Science Mysteries Solved by Sherlock Holmes* (1998) and *Schrödinger's Rabbits: The Many Worlds of the Quantum* (2006).

BookTalk 5.2

Throughout our busy daily lives, and perhaps especially as teachers, we're called on to make quick decisions—sometimes seemingly instantaneous, and often crucial. Does critical thinking play a part in these? Malcolm Gladwell helps us understand snap decisions in *Blink: The Power of Thinking Without Thinking* (2007). He tells stories involving art critics' hunches, gamblers' sweaty hands, and psychologists' predictions as he gives suggestions and insights about intuition. What would we call our thinking about "the power of thinking without thinking"—meta-metacognition? Ultra-metacognition? Counter-metacognition? Or should we stop trying to think so hard and just enjoy the two-second journeys he takes us on?

we're apt to get tangled up in legs when we begin to analyze the creative process: what is it? why do people write—or paint—or sing?" (p. 172). Santiago Ramon y Cajal, a Nobel laureate in physiology, considered the field of neuroanatomy an extension of himself, and advised his students, "'Lose yourself in the observation and become the thing you're studying.' For him, this meant becoming a cell neuron and imagining the world of neurons by living among them" (Siler, 1996, p. 5).

Scientist Barbara McClintock has a way of talking about her work process at the point when she is on the brink of a discovery, which represents a marvelous blend of losing oneself in thought, while on some level remaining highly aware:

> You let the material tell you where to go, and it tells you at every step what the next has to be because you're integrating with an overall brand new pattern in mind. You're not following an old one; you are convinced of a new one. And you let everything focus on that. (Keller, 1983, p. 125)

BookTalk Online 5.3

How to Catch a Shark: And Other Stories About Teaching and Learning (1998) by Donald Graves, *A Life in School: What the Teacher Learned* (1996) by Jane Tompkins, *The Girl with the Brown Crayon* (1997) by Vivian Paley, and *Composing a Teaching Life* (1996) by Ruth Vinz are all books written by teachers about their thinking, their learning, and their advice. Hear more at the Kane Resource Site.

Part of the art of teaching reading is to know when to let your students continue on automatic pilot, and when to help them analyze the steps they're taking toward comprehension. You'll find that some students do fine without obvious metacognitive activity, while other students are helped when you provide them with a structure to monitor their reading and thinking processes. Sometimes, as students talk to each other while they are immersed in a learning activity, they naturally analyze the meanings they constructed, as well as how they got there. One teacher watched and listened as groups of a colleague's art students shared projects, and told him, "This artwork is as sweet a piece of metacognition as you can imagine. The kids are seeing how they think and seeing how other kids' minds work. They can actually be let into their heads and see what others see when they read!" (Wilhelm, 1997, p. 142).

All of the strategies presented and modeled in this text are here for you to use as appropriate for your particular context and your students' varying needs. Occasionally, you may introduce and teach a strategy, support your students' attempts to apply and practice it, and then allow them to decide whether the procedure is helpful. Peters (1996) provided questions in the form of a metacognitive reflective guide that may help students determine how certain reading guides work as comprehension tools. You might try applying these questions to one of the guides you completed: "How well did the reading guide work?" "How did it help you understand what you were asked to read?" "What changes would you make to improve the guide?" "How might you use the guide with other types of reading assignments you have?" (p. 206)

Block and Johnson (2002) advocate teaching comprehension, including metacognitive strategies, to students in authentic settings; that is, while reading for content:

> We must no longer teach comprehension as a set of separate, segmented strategies. We must demonstrate it as a set of ever-changing interactions of thinking processes at specific points in a text. We must demonstrate the ebb and flow that occurs when the reader adds new thought processes to create complete, rich meanings. Many students can memorize strategies that they are shown, but they cannot transfer the strategic thinking independently. (p. 55)

As you teach metacognitive strategies, keep these words of Davis (2005) in mind: "Process and reflection in any domain are sustained by and enrich the ability to think—and to think about thinking—that distinguishes us as human beings" (p. 17).

HELPING STUDENTS TO THINK AND READ CRITICALLY

ACTIVATING PRIOR KNOWLEDGE   5.1

I'm sure you've heard the phrase *critical thinking* as a goal for our students and for everyone else, because we're living in times that demand it more than ever. But what is it? How is critical thinking different from just plain thinking? Take a moment to define the term for yourself. Free associate, make a semantic web, jot down examples, anything to help you operationalize the concept and become aware of what you already know about it. Compare your ideas with others'. Then reflect on these two examples of advice from chemist Linus Pauling. As he accepted the Nobel Prize for Chemistry, he said to his audience:

> When an old and distinguished person speaks to you, listen to him carefully and with respect—*but do not believe him.* Never put your trust in anything but your own intellect. Your elder, no matter whether he has gray hair or has lost his hair, no matter whether he is a Nobel laureate, may be wrong. . . . So you must always be skeptical—*always think for yourself.* (Hager, 1995, p. 108)

Another time he exhorted a group of college students:

> You must always search for truth. . . . Truth does not depend upon the point of view. If your neighbor does not see things as you do, then you must search for the truth. If a statement is made in one country and not another, then you must search for the truth. (p. 103)

Defining Critical Thinking

Let's examine a few definitions of critical thinking set forth by educators. You'll see some similarities and some differing points of emphasis. Using them together, you should begin to have a richer understanding of the concept.

- *Critical thinking* The thought processes characteristic of creativity, criticism, and logic in literature, the arts, science, and other disciplines; divergent thinking. (NCTE & IRA, 1996, p. 71, Glossary)

- When we add the adjective *critical* to the noun *thinking*, we . . . are talking about searching for hidden assumptions, noticing various facets, unraveling different strands, and evaluating what is most significant. (Barnet & Bedau, 2005)

- Three types of skills—interpretive skills, verification skills, and reasoning skills—constitute what are usually referred to as critical thinking skills. . . . Mastering critical thinking skills is . . . a matter of intellectual self-respect. We all have the capacity to learn how to distinguish good arguments from bad ones and to work out for ourselves what we ought and ought not to believe, and it diminishes us as persons if we let others do our thinking for us. (Hughes, 2000, p. 23)

■ . . . critical thinking consists of seeing both sides of an issue, being open to new evidence that disconfirms your ideas, reasoning dispassionately, demanding that claims be backed by evidence, deducing and inferring conclusions from available facts, solving problems, and so forth. (Willingham, 2007, p. 8)

■ When students think critically, they interact with the text by skillfully analyzing the message, comparing that message with their previous knowledge, considering alternate positions, and synthesizing the information gained into a richer knowledge base. (Pescatore, 2007/2008, p. 326)

■ . . . there are specific types of critical thinking that are characteristic of different subject matter: That's what we mean when we refer to "thinking like a scientist" or "thinking like a historian." (Willingham, 2007, p. 8)

Can Critical Thinking Be Taught?

Of course, we want our students to become independent thinkers, critical thinkers. And as content area teachers, we are responsible for helping them reach this goal. But how? Can higher-level thinking actually be *taught*? This question has generated much debate and research, and experts sometimes disagree on how teachers should handle teaching in this area. Csikszentmihalyi (1996) believes, "It is easier to enhance creativity by changing conditions in the environment than by trying to make people think more creatively" (p. 1). The same can be said for critical thinking.

Johnson (2000) has labeled three types of thinking instruction. The first is the *stand-alone approach*, where teachers teach thinking skills separately from any subject-matter content, and then teach how to transfer those skills to situations and content areas. Second, the *immersion approach* rejects the direct instruction of thinking skills in favor of allowing thinking to develop naturally as a result of being engaged in content-related activities calling for high levels of thinking. Finally, Johnson recommends the *embedded approach*, using the meaningful context of content area instruction to teach thinking skills that students can immediately apply and that will help them learn the subject matter more deeply. The curriculum is enhanced, and mastery is realized over time with repeated exposure, instruction, and practice.

There will be opportunities every day for you to use such an embedded approach in your subject area, for your content will supply you with authentic examples of problems that call for much thought. Brown (1993) exhorts us:

> If you want young people to think, you ask them hard questions and let them wrestle with the answers. If you want them to analyze something or interpret it or evaluate it, you ask them to do so and show them how to do it with increasing skill. If you want them to know how to approach interesting or difficult problems, you give them interesting or difficult problems and help them develop a conscious repertoire of problem-solving strategies. If you want them to think the way scientists and historians and mathematicians do, you show them how scientists and historians and mathematicians think, and you provide opportunities for them to practice and compare those ways of thinking. (p. 232)

I hope that these ideas sound familiar to you at this point because I have tried from the very beginning to have you think critically using real texts. You were required to do some hard thinking about societies, rules, freedom, and pain after reading *The Giver*. In Chapter 3, you had to really think about what teaching might be like in a school that had thrown out the textbooks. The excerpts from literature and primary sources in each chapter are meant to challenge and enhance your thinking about literacy and pedagogy. The rest of this chapter introduces ways that you can enhance the development of critical thinking as your students become literate and knowledgeable in your subject area. Actually, the chapter's first section gave you a start; the metacognition strategies introduced there and the critical-thinking strategies coming up are not mutually exclusive; the former often call for higher-level thinking.

Strategies for Fostering Critical Thinking and High-Level Comprehension

Research shows that readers must be strategically engaged in the construction of meaning (American Psychological Association Presidential Task Force on Psychology in Education, 1993; Guthrie & Anderson, 1999; Learner-Centered Principles Revision Work Group, 1995).

Jones (2009) shares the perspective of a literacy coach who collaborates with teachers who promote a culture of thinking in their eighth-grade classroom, in which more than half the students are English learners. She describes the sense of belonging, a dedication to rigor and cognitive growth, and the teachers' ability and willingness to connect to students' interests and academic strengths. They frame the reading tasks in the classroom around the question, "What do good readers do when they encounter chal-

BookTalk 5.4

According to Lesesne (2007), mystery is the favorite genre of middle school students. And mysteries involve critical thinking and problem solving. Math teachers can take advantage of these two premises by booktalking some math-related mysteries. The eighth-grade protagonist of *Do the Math: Secrets, Lies, and Algebra,* by Wendy Lichtman (2007), is good in math; loves math; and uses equations, graphs, numerical rankings, formulas, and Venn diagrams in her daily life. That life happens to include two mysteries, one involving a cheating classmate, the other involving a possible murder. In the sequel, *Do the Math #2: The Writing on the Wall* (2008), Tess again uses math skills and concepts to analyze clues as well as decode and encode messages.

Blue Balliett's *Chasing Vermeer* (2004) features two sixth-grade friends; both like mysteries, art, learning, and problem solving. Teachers who introduce this book will want to have a set of pentominoes available, along with websites featuring games and puzzles involving the mathematical manipulatives. The following two books in the series, *The Wright 3* (2006) and *The Calder Game* (2008) supply both mysteries for the characters (and readers) to solve and information about art forms that offer a very cool way into the study of geometry.

lenging texts?" and they offer unwavering support as students practice the strategies their teachers have instructed and modeled, using authentic texts, so that students can communicate their understanding and their thinking effectively. Jones notes:

> My role as instructional coach has taken many forms: cheerleader, flame-keeper, and teammate. Mostly I have been a witness—of great growth and extraordinary teaching that has led students (whom many might view as on or over the edge due to socioeconomic and cultural differences) to engage in and take responsibility for their learning. (p. 128)

This section presents some strategies you and your students may find useful for developing critical thinking. But first, I want to emphasize our recurring theme of authenticity. There are many exercises and published instructional materials including electronic ones ready to assist you with the task of teaching critical-thinking skills. Most don't supply any data showing that students ever transfer these skills and apply them to actual situations in their lives. Research demonstrates that any gains shown after the use of special programs is modest and limited, and thus not educationally effective in light of their costs (Willingham, 2007). Critical

thinking should be taught not in isolation, but within the context of subject matter. If you're ever tempted or if someone else tries to persuade you to buy some critical-thinking kit, keep in mind what cognitive scientist Daniel Willingham reminds us, "Every hour students spend on the program is an hour they won't be learning something else" (p. 18). So, seek to become proficient in using the strategies that truly make sense in the context of your subject. Different curricular topics, educational goals, and student needs will help you determine which approaches fit best at any given time.

Showing how practitioners in the disciplines use critical thinking

Recall that in Chapter 4 you were given suggestions for helping students develop procedural knowledge through learning about practitioners in various academic fields. This is a very broad strategy, a heuristic. Before you give students any specific strategies to use for enhancing their own critical thinking, you can give them lots of scenarios showing the real critical thinking of actual people in specific contexts.

Teaching in action: *Multidisciplinary.* Here's one example. Scientists met in small groups after World War II to discuss what they learned from the experience of two atom bombs being dropped on cities in Japan. Much of their thinking and discussion involved new scientific knowledge, but they also pondered the future and the ethics of weapons and war. Much critical thinking was occurring as they questioned whether it was immoral to have developed the atomic bomb. Chemist Linus Pauling, recognizing that the bomb meant a changed role for scientists, wrote, "The problem presented to the world by the destructive power of atomic energy overshadows, of course, any other problem. . . . I feel that, in addition to our professional activities in the nuclear field, we should make our voices known with respect to the political significance of science" (Hager, 1998, p. 80). Pauling acted on this belief; he sent a petition to American scientists asking them to support a ban on all nuclear testing, and received more than 2,000 signatures, including some from Nobel Prize winners. He gathered 9,000 more from the world's scientific community and presented the petition to the United Nations (p. 111).

What a story for our students to think about! All those professionals critically thinking about the situation and coming to a decision, one way or another. How would our science students respond?

We could continue Pauling's story for our math, science, and social studies students; you'll find interdisciplinary connections as you read. In 1951, during the anticommunist repression in the United States, a military review board demanded that Pauling explain his political views:

Pauling replied with a long statement in which he made a scientific statement for free speech. The way he saw it, American politics could be thought of as a matter of statistics: "The principle upon which a true democratic system operates is that no single man is wise enough to make the correct decisions about the very complex problems that arise, and that the correct decisions are to be made by the process of averaging the opinions of all the citizens in a democracy. These opinions will correspond to a probability distribution curve extending from far on the left to far on the right. If, now, we say that all of the opinions that extend too far to the right . . . are abnormal, and are to be excluded in taking the average, then the average that we obtain will be the wrong one. And an understanding of the laws of probability would accordingly make it evident to the citizen that the operation of the democratic system requires that everyone have the right to express his [sic] opinions about political questions, no matter what that opinion might be."

Pauling was pointing out that no good scientist would lop off just one end of a set of findings, because the resulting average would be thrown off. In America, the attempt to lop off the views of those on the left wing of the political spectrum would have the same skewing effect—and so he concluded that the best system, the most scientific, democratic system, should be to allow free speech for all. (Hager, 1998, p. 105)

Think about how you might use this text with your students. Might it help them to think critically, and to realize that our everyday lives constantly call for critical thinking?

Teaching in action: *Physics.* Through books and articles, other scientists can also serve as co-teachers in our classrooms. Richard Feynman (1988), a Nobel prize–winning physicist, describes the thinking processes he used while on a commission investigating the Challenger explosion. He read earlier documents from engineers and seals experts, and found disturbing contradictions and data in some "flight readiness reviews," so he asked an expert to explain the logic within them. He discovered, "The analysis concluded that a little unpredictable leakage here and there could be tolerated, even though it wasn't part of the original design" (p. 138). Feynman gives his evaluation of *this* thinking:

> If *all* the seals had leaked, it would have been obvious even to NASA that the problem was serious. But only a few of the seals leaked on only some of the flights. So NASA had developed a peculiar kind of attitude: if one of the seals leaks a little and the flight is successful, the problem isn't so serious. Try playing Russian roulette that way: you pull the trigger and the gun doesn't go off, so it must be safe to pull the trigger again. (p. 138)

Think of ways you could have your students use this information to stimulate and propel their own thinking. It could lead to some powerful classroom discussion and increased awareness as they follow current events and debates among politicians, business representatives, scientists, religious groups, military leaders, and medical workers.

Discipline-based inquiry

As shown in the examples above, teachers can foster critical thinking and reading by taking a real problem or issue being discussed and debated within the discipline or in current events, and providing students with differing opinions from experts and/or thoughtful laypeople. Newspaper editorials and letters to the editor can provoke thought and invite students to join the conversation.

Teaching in action: *Social Studies.* For example, an issue that social studies teachers could raise involves the question of cultural authenticity in children's literature. Is it all right for authors to write about cultures outside their own, assuming they research the topic well? Should Caucasian authors write about people of color? What are the boundaries that determine whether one is an insider or an outsider relative to cultural groups? Fox and Short (2003) edited a volume around these complex issues, inviting essays from authors, scholars, librarians, illustrators, educators, and publishers. Teachers might ask students to reflect on the issue and form an opinion, then supply several essays from *Stories Matter: The Complexity of Cultural Authenticity in Children's Literature* (2003) as the impetus for further critical thinking, mediated and guided by the teacher.

The teacher's role is crucial, as Mandel (2003), discussing his previous research, explains:

> In *every* instance throughout the year, in *every* cooperative learning situation, the students worked at the level of the teacher's final questions or statements to the students. In other words, the last teacher statement or question to the group determined the subsequent critical thinking level of the students. This occurred whether the teacher was talking to the entire class, to one particular group, or to an individual student. . . . Teachers conducting cooperative work group experiences are not simply facilitators. Rather, they are directly responsible for the level of a student's critical thinking. (p. 30)

In order to promote critical thinking, teachers can collaborate to help students consider problems from different stances, as is customary in good critical thinking outside of schools.

Teaching in action: *Multidisciplinary.* For example, in Tracy Kidder's (www.tracykidder.com) *Mountains Beyond Mountains* (2003), the author tells of many dilemmas faced by the biography's subject, Dr. Paul Farmer, as he battles disease and poverty in Haiti. In one case, a mother brought her young son to Farmer's clinic. It was determined that he had a rare form of cancer, and he had virtually no chance of survival if he remained in Haiti, where there were not the diagnostic or therapeutic tools to treat him. Farmer got permission to have him transported to Boston, but it would cost at least $18,000 just to get him there. Ethical questions had to be asked, and there were no easy answers. Students could work with their biology teachers, economics teachers, social studies teachers, and librarians to replicate the kinds of thinking the people in this real case had to go through. They can consider and debate such questions as:

- What were his chances of survival *with* treatment?
- Who would, or might, lose services if that much money was spent on one person? Would it set a precedent?
- What else could that amount of money be spent on and how many people would benefit?

After students research, ask others' opinions, and write a persuasive essay relating their own conclusion, they can read further to see how the questions were answered and what the results were in this case. They'll encounter many other moral, political, scientific, and economic questions as they travel along with Dr. Farmer, as did ethnographer Tracy Kidder in preparation for writing this book.

You hold a potential solution to the problem that Hawking describes and that you may have personally experienced. By bringing in books, stories, and current newspaper and magazine articles illustrating the thinking processes of people in your field, and having the students respond to them and join the conversations, you encourage and facilitate critical thinking by your students. This can work for every discipline.

Teaching in action: *History.* For example, students in a history class could listen to recordings of Abraham Lincoln's major speeches throughout his career; it would be fascinating for them to hear him grapple with the issues facing him and the nation, sometimes changing his mind as his wisdom grew. For years, he agonized over the discrepancy between his personal opinion that slavery was immoral and his belief that it was not within his rights to force others to stop the practice in places where the law allowed it. (Recall from Chapter 3 that his contemporary, John Brown, thought very differently about the slavery dilemma.)

Others' thinking, from both the far and recent past, can help our students' thinking about the difficult issue of what to do when personal conviction and the law clash. We can bring in Thoreau's essay on *Civil Disobedience,* Sophocles' play *Antigone,* and texts by and about conscientious objectors during every war America has fought to provide further contexts within which to think critically about the topic.

ACTIVATING PRIOR KNOWLEDGE 5.2

Did your experiences in middle school and high school enable you to think critically about what you were learning and apply your thinking to real situations outside school? Try to think of some examples of when that happened. Or, if you have no examples, try to understand what went wrong. Write for a few moments in your learning log.

Now, read what physicist Stephen Hawking (1993) says on this topic:

What can be done to . . . give the public the scientific background it needs to make informed decisions on subjects like acid rain, the greenhouse effect, nuclear weapons, and genetic engineering? Clearly, the basis must lie in what is taught in schools. But in schools science is often presented in a dry and uninteresting manner. Children learn it by rote to pass examinations, and they don't see its relevance to the world around them. (pp. 28–29)

Do you agree?

ACTIVATING PRIOR KNOWLEDGE 5.3

Speaking of civil disobedience, can you think of a time when educators have been or might find themselves in a situation where their convictions about what is good, or not good, for children might be opposed to the law or to school policy? In such a case, what action might be called for? Is it ever right for a teacher to disobey a law? Write in your learning log for a few minutes, and share your examples and opinions with others on the Kane Resource Site.

Now reflect on these words of John Scopes at the end of his trial regarding his teaching about evolution; he was permitted to speak after the guilty verdict:

Your Honor, I feel that I have been convicted of violating an unjust statute. I will continue in the future, as I have in the past, to oppose the law in any way I can. Any other action would be in violation of my ideal of academic freedom—that is, to teach the truth as guaranteed in our Constitution, of personal and religious freedom. I think the fine is unjust. (Bryant, 2008, pp. 195–196)

Many teachers are grappling with what they consider to be harmful assessment practices imposed by their states. A 2001 issue of the *Phi Delta Kappan* included articles with telling titles: "Fighting the Tests: A Practical Guide to Rescuing Our Schools" by the well-known critic Alfie Kohn and "News from the Test Resistance Trail" by Susan Ohanian, which included a chart called "The Honor Roll of Resistance," citing teachers who refused to give standardized tests, sometimes at the cost of their jobs, sometimes resulting in arrest. The topic of assessment is explored in Chapter 10. For now, I present this example to show you that, as a professional, you will be faced with any number of opportunities to exercise critical thinking, to try to understand those whose convictions may differ radically from yours, and to act on your convictions.

You can find numerous examples in educational journals showing how teachers engage their students in thinking like members of a disciplinary field. The following descriptions give you a glimpse into a few such classrooms.

Teaching in action: *History.* Stoskopf (2001) lists historical-thinking skills that can be employed beneficially in classrooms. He recommends using primary source documents and having students examine them for the following:

- **Point of view.** How does the author's personal background and status influence what is being written?
- **Credibility of evidence.** How reliable is the source? Where did it originate, and for what purpose was it used at the time?
- **Historical context.** How does one see the past on its own terms? While this is never totally possible, historians are vigilant about not allowing present-day values to obscure the sensibilities of a past age.
- **Causality.** How does one avoid seeing past events as caused by just one factor?
- **Multiple perspectives.** How does one weigh different interpretations of the same event? (p. 469)

Stoskopf has seen that elementary, middle, and secondary teachers can get students engaged in such historical thinking. He provides an example of a fourth-grade classroom studying the era of the Pilgrims, using primary documents and secondary sources. He describes a seventh-grade unit on immigration, where students studied historical data, formed historical hypotheses, and compared these with other accounts of the demographics of Irish immigration. They wrote narratives about families they chose from actual records, and practiced literacy skills—they sometimes had to read information four or five times, with the teacher's assistance, to understand it. Stoskopf concludes:

> No, the students did not become historians after this eight-week unit. But they did develop self-confidence in their ability to stay with something that did not come to them automatically. They learned "facts" about history, but they did not rush through the curriculum simply to cover more and more. They learned how to think in a different and deeper way, and they were better able to remember the details of the period because the information was embedded in a meaningful context. (p. 470)

Discipline-based inquiry can be taught in any and every subject area.

Teaching in action: *Science.* Haugen (2001) explains how lessons using leeches taught students to think like scientists. An inquiry-based program (see the next section) involving the steps of engaging, exploring, explaining, evaluating, and extending or elaborating combined the hands-on experiences of laboratory activities with the use of reference books, journal articles, and the Internet that resulted in the students publishing a report on leeches. The students selected a question and then designed an investigation and researched possible answers. They sent their teams' unanswered questions to experts in the field who had agreed to be their online science partners. Haugen noted that the process was really an extended example of Ogle's K-W-L strategy, which was discussed earlier in our text.

Through their authentic research and their extensive reading, students learn that real scientists do not follow just one formulaic approach known as the scientific method. Problems differ; personal styles differ; there are many avenues of inquiry.

ACTION RESEARCH   **5.A**

Find an article about a classroom where the teacher and the students use an inquiry approach or use the kinds of thinking people in the disciplines use. Figure 5.3 lists possible sources, but you'll find many more as you check current educational literature. Or, visit a classroom, in person or via the Internet, that exemplifies disciplinary exploration and thinking about real problems. Write a reflection about what you learn.

Creating an inquiry-based classroom

Inquiry-based or question-based teaching calls for students to think critically and to be able to analyze and evaluate texts and topics. However, using questions in isolation or irregular junctures in

FIGURE 5.3

Selected examples of articles and books about discipline-based inquiry.

See more suggested titles in Appendix Figure 5.3

Aichele, D. B., & Wolfe, J. (2008). *Geometric Structures: An Inquiry-Based Approach for Prospective Elementary and Middle School Teachers.* Upper Saddle River, NJ: Pearson/Prentice Hall.

Meadows, L. (2009). *The Missing Link: An Inquiry-Based Approach for Teaching All Students About Evolution.* Portsmouth, NH: Heinemann.

Patterson, M., Crews, T. B., Bodenhamer, I., Carmichael, A., & Stewart, T. (2009). Inquiry-Based Learning in the Business Education Classroom. *Business Education Forum, 63*(3), 43–50.

Schultz, B., Yates, C., & Schultz, J. M. (2008). Digging into Inquiry-Based Earth Science Research. *Science Scope, 32*(4), 26–31.

Stone, C. K. (2008). Discipline-Based Art Education at Its Best . . . Miniature Chair Maquettes. *Arts & Activities, 142*(5), 26–27.

your curriculum does not constitute inquiry-based teaching. Rather this method becomes inquiry-based teaching when entire units of instruction are based on questioning strategies and questions are used to guide student learning. Students are asked questions for the purpose of getting them to think for themselves or together with their peers. Critical inquiry must be an actual stance you and your students adopt and live by throughout your course. Following are steps you can use to create an inquiry-based classroom.

1. Identify problem or issue for the inquiry yourself or brainstorm a topic with your students that is of interest to them.

2. Formulate one or more focused questions about the topic.

3. Guide the students in the exploration of the problem. Observe the students as they attempt to answer the question/solve the problem, providing them with feedback and facilitative questions.

4. Have them identify and refine a workable solution.

5. Have them demonstrate the results of their analysis and assertions of their solutions either orally or in writing.

Whitin and Cox, in *A Mathematical Passage* (2003), provide guidance for teachers who want to pro-mote inquiry in intermediate math classrooms. Many of the chapter sections offer credibility in terms of the activities investigated: "Mathematicians Keep Records and Pose Their Own Problems," "Mathematicians Are Skeptics Who Go Beyond the Data," "Mathematicians Create Their Own Language," "Mathematicians Discover Patterns and Relationships," and so on. The authors show how to develop a math workshop and how to nurture students as they articulate and investigate authentic problems. Inquiry becomes a way of "living a mathematical life" (p. 136).

Teaching in action: *English/Social Studies.* Pescatore (2007/2008) uses texts relating to current events to foster critical thinking in English and social studies. She gave her students an article from the *New York Times* on the (then) U. S. administration's policy on global warming, with guiding questions she prepared including:

- What does the writer want us to believe?
- How "balanced" is he in his presentation?
- Does he have an agenda?
- What other points of view are needed?
- How would you find them?

She found that her students engaged with the text and went beyond literal comprehension. She found one student's unsolicited response particularly rewarding:

> When I was reading and analyzing this article, I felt like at first I was confused to a point, but after reading over and over again, I started to drift away from "surface meaning" and started to go beyond the words. Asking about tone, point of view, and missing opinions really helped me to understand

BookTalk 5.5

Charles Wilson Peale was a portrait artist who had no formal scientific training, but whose lifelong interest in science, combined with excellent thinking, led him to the solution of *The Mystery of the Mammoth Bones* (1999). Author James Cross Giblin uses Peale's diaries and journals to tell how he went about the quest that resulted in much scientific knowledge about extinct animals and the age of the earth. You'll be inspired as you read this detailed account of a man so passionate about his two fields of study that he even named his children after artists (Rembrandt, Rubens, Raphael) and scientists (Charles Linnaeus and Benjamin Franklin). Readers get inside the mind of a practitioner to see real thinking working on real issues.

the writing.... Also what actually took me by surprise was the fact that while I was reading, writing, and analyzing, I paused for a minute and actually realized that I was enjoying my work! I felt as if it wasn't school work at all. I felt as if it was play, something I would have chosen to do on my own time. If I could do these every day I would. (p. 326)

The good news for the student is that the *New York Times* is indeed published every day and is available online. The good news for the teacher is that she found that helping her students employ strategies of researching, reflecting, and reacting led to "a critical literacy that is ultimately empowering. It goes beyond thinking critically to internalizing the lessons in individual ways and becoming a catalyst for action when one sees injustice or oppression" (p. 335).

Hoffer (2009) recommends providing students with authentic tasks that promote understanding of big ideas, then having both teacher and students listen as learners verbalize their thinking processes aloud.

Teaching in action: *Math.* Hoffer gives the example of an algebra teacher whose goal is that her students will understand the role of variables in linear equations. She instructs students to work in pairs to find the equations of two lines that are involved in a story problem. Seven different answers emerge as the class works toward the complex solution. Rather than merely tell the class which answer is correct, she has individuals come to the board and explain their thinking; class members are allowed to ask questions as they listen. Eventually, the class comes to consensus on the answer. The teacher asks the students to write the answer to the question, "What do I understand now about the nature of linear equations?" (p. 148). All along, the teacher's stance has been one of drawing learners' thinking out. Hoffer offers other guiding questions teachers can use as they aim for enhancing metacognition:

- What are you thinking?
- Are you sure? Why?
- Could you explain it another way?
- What might you need to double-check?
- What questions do you have? (p. 150)

BookTalk Online 5.6

Immigration Policy by Allan Allport, a *Point/Counterpoint* book that tackles the complex issue of immigration, can help students practice the dialogical thinking strategy. Read more at the Kane Resource Site.

Dialogical thinking strategy

One of the characteristics of real-life problems is that they are complicated, and decisions have both costs and benefits. Patients with life-threatening illnesses often must weigh and then choose between options that involve medical risks, financial considerations, effects on families, and quality-of-life issues. Business and political challenges involve finances, ethics, long- and short-term goals, and obstacles. There are winners and losers in most situations that call for critical thinking. *Dialogical thinking*, going back and forth between opposing opinions, truly trying to see both sides of an argument or understanding multiple perspectives, is a valuable critical-thinking skill. Teachers can promote dialogical thinking by playing devil's advocate (make the students aware that this is what you are doing) during discussions of problematic issues.

One approach you can teach your students is to draw up a visual representation of the pros and cons of potential actions to help them think before they draw conclusions. Sometimes, they can contribute ideas to such a chart from their own background knowledge. At other times, they can use information from a text you supply, or they can do research to learn the advantages and disadvantages relative to a topic they're studying. Figure 5.4 provides a guide for applying dialogical thinking to the issue of pet cloning. Students can use it as a model as they explore various viewpoints on other issues. They might use a similar strategy as they give an oral presentation on censorship, immigration policies, or technology in schools.

The REAP strategy

Read–Encode–Annotate–Ponder (Eanet & Manzo, 1976; Manzo & Manzo, 1997) is a structured approach to critical thinking about a text. It consists of the following steps:

1. **R:** Read to discern the writer's message.
2. **E:** Encode the message by translating it into your own words.
3. **A:** Annotate by cogently writing the message in notes for yourself or in a thought book or on an electronic response system.
4. **P:** Ponder, or further reflect on, what you have read or written, through discussion and by reviewing others' responses to the same materials and/or your own annotation. (Manzo & Manzo, 1997, p. 170)

As with other strategies, the REAP steps represent what skilled readers often do. As they read, they might jot in a margin a personal reaction (positive or

FIGURE	5.4	An example guide for applying dialogical thinking to the issue of pet cloning.

DIRECTIONS: Before writing anything down, think of what comes to mind when you hear the word *cloning*. Then take a few minutes to brainstorm about the pros and cons of pet cloning. Fill in the chart provided below. If you need help getting started, here are some things to think about:

- the 55 million pet dogs in America
- the little girl whose cat just got hit by a car
- the numerous animals in shelters waiting to be adopted

- the boy whose favorite dog has become old and feeble
- the high costs of the cloning procedure
- the likelihood (or lack thereof) of successful cloning

PROS

_____

_____

_____

_____

CONS

_____

_____

_____

_____

Meet with a partner to share your lists. If one side is longer than the other, take on the perspective of someone who is in favor of or opposed to pet cloning, and imagine what arguments each would use. Also, try to categorize the specifics you have in the columns. Which are economic arguments? social? ethical? practical?

Now, read the article "CLONING—Copy Cat—The First Cloned Pet Sure Looks Harmless. Would a Cloned Human?" (*Time*, February 25, 2002, pp. 58–59). Add to your chart any new information you have obtained. Then, answer the following questions:

1. How might cloning eventually affect our society?

   _____

   _____

2. Would you be willing to spend $1,000 for a chance to get your pet cloned?

   _____

3. Assuming you or a friend answered yes to Question 2, how might you earn and budget the money for the procedure?

   _____

   _____

4. Think of other ways that cloning could relate to math. Make a list. You can collaborate with your partner on this.

   _____

   _____

5. List other procedures or policies where cost is a factor that sometimes affects decisions involving ethical or controversial issues.

   _____

   _____

6. Look for articles or Internet sites that tell you where pet cloning has gone since the time this article came out. How many pets have been cloned? What benefits or drawbacks have resulted? What's the going rate to have a pet cloned?

   _____

   _____

—Erika Moshier

BookTalk Online 5.7

The series *Taking Sides* exemplifies dialogical thinking as each volume asks questions relating to a broad topic, then provides a "Yes" essay and a "No" essay by experts in the field. Read more at the Kane Resource Site.

negative), a critique, a connection to a current event or another text, a question about the author's intent or use of a literary device. As you model the strategy, show your students the different types and levels of thinking that can occur during annotation. Manzo and Manzo categorize REAP responses into two categories: *reconstructive responses*, which include summarizing and questioning, and *constructive responses*, which include personal views, critical responses, contrary responses, creative responses, and discovery responses. This last type consists of practical questions that must be answered before the text can be judged for accuracy or merit, thus leading to more reading, research, and rethinking.

As students apply and practice the strategy and become increasingly independent, you can help them self-monitor and evaluate how well the strategy is working for them.

ACTION RESEARCH 5.B

The best way for you to make the REAP strategy your own is to try it out. Follow the four steps as you read the text in Figures 5.5 and 5.6 on pages 142 and 143. Then, write a reaction synthesizing the two articles, as well as bringing in your own thoughts and information from other sources on the subject of genetic engineering in light of this new discovery of unforeseen consequences. As you ponder, evaluate how well these writers made their points. Do you disagree with anything either has said? Where would you place yourself regarding this issue if one end of a continuum said "Halt all production now!" and the other was labeled "Full speed ahead!"? How well did the REAP strategy work for you, and for those with whom you discussed your responses and your thinking?

If you find the REAP strategy beneficial, and if you have students for whom you think it might be helpful, model the strategy, using these articles and your own step-by-step notes. Or you can teach them using texts relevant to the curriculum you teach. You might ask students to bring in newspa-

per, Internet, or magazine articles to see whether the strategy works for different types of text. Give students guided practice, and encourage them to use the strategy on their own, with texts from their other classes and with self-selected reading. They could keep a REAP section of their learning logs or a REAP file on their laptops.

Directed reading–thinking activity

The *directed reading–thinking activity* (Haggard, 1985; Stauffer, 1980) is a structured yet flexible strategy that can help you guide your students through reading a particular text; eventually, the "directed" part is eliminated as students learn to apply the strategy's steps to enhance and monitor their own comprehension and use their thinking skills as they make predictions. There are pre-reading, during reading, and post-reading stages.

Pre-reading. Before reading, the teacher:

- Assesses the students' prior knowledge about the topic.
- Provides any necessary background knowledge.
- Teaches any necessary vocabulary, or encourages students to use the surrounding context to figure out what certain words mean.
- Helps the students set a purpose for reading and predict what the text might be about or what points might be raised or covered.
- Asks the students to write down hypotheses and then share them. This can be done with partners or in small groups.

Teaching in action: *Math.* For example, Mr. Yang is a math teacher whose class will be learning about probability. He's chosen to use the chapter "The Mathematics of Kindness: Math Proves the Golden Rule" from the book *The Universe and the Teacup: The Mathematics of Truth and Beauty* by K. C. Cole (www.kccole.net) (1998). He asks his students to free associate and make a class chart based on the terms *probability* and *game theory*. He also asks whether they know what the Golden Rule is. Most do, and he posts a chart with "Do Unto Others as You Would Have Them Do Unto You" on the wall. After that, Mr. Yang teaches four vocabulary words that he determined are crucial to his students' understanding of the text: *paradox, dilemma, altruism,* and *symbiosis.* He tells them that they may encounter a few other unfamiliar words, but they should be able to figure them out by the way they are used in the essay's context. Next, he asks them what they think they might learn from this text and accepts any predictions as valid.

FIGURE **5.5** REAP strategy sample text 1.

Cornell bioengineering study: Canary in the mine shaft

A century ago, coal miners would take a canary down into the shaft with them to test whether the air was breathable. If the bird keeled over, they knew they had better get out fast.

Scientists should be paying the same brand of heed to the monarch butterfly. It may be warning us about impending ecological disaster.

Researchers at Cornell University have concluded that the pollen from a genetically engineered insect-resistant corn may be killing the butterfly's larvae. Until the discovery was revealed last week, the corn had been thought to be safe for "friendly" insects, as well as humans and other mammals. The research raises concerns that bioengineering may lead to unintended consequences for other species.

Development of the hybrid corn has been hailed as a major breakthrough in agriculture. It produces a natural toxin that kills an insect, the European corn borer, responsible for $1.2 billion in crop losses a year. The new product eliminated the need to treat corn with insecticides, which were only marginally effective against the corn borer and are toxic for other species. The bioengineered strain of corn will be planted on about 16 million acres this year.

Pollen from the "Bt" corn is carried by the wind and comes to rest on other plants such as milkweed, the only thing that monarch caterpillars eat. Research conducted before the hybrid corn was approved for commercial use did not study the possible effects of windblown pollen, the Cornell scientists said. Researchers "weren't really thinking about the toxin flying around and how it affects feeding on their own host plants," said Linda S. Rayor, a Cornell entomologist and co-author of the study.

In the laboratory, monarch larvae that ate milkweed that had been dusted with the pollen of Bt corn ate less, grew at a slower rate and died faster than larvae that were fed milkweed that hadn't been dusted. The Cornell scientists plan to study the effect of the pollen on other species of insects.

Predictably, the report was not welcomed by the corn industry, where the bioengineered corn has increased in popularity every year since it was introduced in 1995. Corn growers cited the environmental advantages of bioengineered crops—reduced use of pesticides and herbicides, as well as more abundant food. They called for more research before any conclusions are reached about the safety of the hybrid varieties.

On the other side of the question is the Union of Concerned Scientists, an independent alliance based in Cambridge, Mass. "This should help people understand that genetically engineered crops bring with them risks that have not yet been properly raised or studied," said Jane Rissler, a UCS plant pathologist. She said the UCS plans to ask the federal Environmental Protection Agency to halt approval of all engineered corn varieties.

It would seem prudent to err on the side of safety. The risks of delaying approval of bioengineered crops would seem to hold far less potential for harm than the possibility of a genetic genie being inadvertently released to create biological havoc.

This is not a call to halt bioengineering. The practice holds great promise for feeding an increasingly crowded planet. Nonetheless, genetic research and development must include complete research on its effects on species not targeted by the new strains. The Cornell researchers—and their monarch subjects—may have alerted us to a real peril in time to head it off.

During reading. During reading, the teacher guides the students through the reading process and monitors them to determine any difficulties. The teacher:

1. Has students read silently, checking periodically to verify their predictions throughout the text.
2. Uses questions such as "What do you think about X?" "Why do you think that?" "Was your prediction confirmed?" "What evidence shows it was or was not confirmed?" and "Does anyone want to change a prediction based on what we've read so far?"
3. Asks them to extend their thinking by summarizing what they read and predicting what may happen next.

Mr. Yang directs his students to read silently to a certain place in the text, at which point they discuss which, if any, of the class's predictions were confirmed. He conveys that this is not a contest, that the "right" predictions were not necessarily any more clever than the ones that were disconfirmed. He says, "Think of what you do when you read a mystery; you're making guesses as to who committed a crime, or why, or how; and there will always be a few surprises in a good story."

The students then make further predictions based on the line where the reading begins again—"Axelrod invited experts in game theory to a tournament of repeated games of prisoner's dilemma" (p. 118). What do the students think will be the outcome of this tournament? On the next page, they predict again, at the point in the text when Axelrod holds a follow-up tournament in which not only game theorists, but also researchers in biology, physics, and sociology participate. And they predict yet again when, "In a final round, Axelrod wanted to see what would happen if he pitted all the programs against each other in a kind of Darwinian evolution" (p. 119). Mr. Yang predicts

FIGURE **5.6** **REAP strategy sample text 2.**

Unintended consequences: Genetic engineering worth some risks

The short story, as I recollect it, was set in a future where time travel had become possible. A fellow signed up to tour the primeval past and, like others, was cautioned to remain on the floating path and to touch nothing, because even the smallest alteration in the past could have huge consequences. He made the trip and marveled at the exotic plants and creatures of an era beyond reckoning. He scrupulously stayed on the path, but returned to his own time to find everything changed grotesquely, and in no way for the better. Puzzled, he sat down, only to discover, from the evidence on his shoe sole, that in the ancient past he had stepped on a butterfly.

The tale came back recently with the news that a study has found that a popular new corn, genetically altered to ward off insect pests but believed harmless to other insects, produces a pollen that kills monarch butterflies.

No one seems to know quite what to make of this, so far. The pollen is quite toxic to monarchs exposed to it in the laboratory, but it is not clear whether many of the butterflies encounter it in the fields.

The real danger may be quite small, or not quite small. No one knows. But everyone does know this: monarch butterflies are lovely, one of those occasions of grace that the same nature which produces droughts and volcanoes and other tumults tosses off casually, as if to make up in small things for its larger lapses.

The science of genetics is beyond me. . . . And I am not among the instinctive naysayers who, like the Luddites, would smash every novelty out of fear it surely will bring more ill than good. The status quo, by definition, won't get us anywhere.

There are risks in any change and we are reaching a point, as I understand it, where our cleverness may offer us huge changes from this still new science and bring them ever faster. Genetic engineering holds the promise, among other benefits, of more food, more safely produced. This corn, for instance, lets farmers forgo pesticides. That's good.

But such is our vanity, forever triumphing over experience, that we believe in our ability to extrapolate all the consequences of our innovations, and to judge each good or not good and weigh the balance soundly.

There are those who would so straiten genetic engineering that it could barely move. Never mind that it might—just might—be the technology that ends illness and hunger and the human strifes, from bellyache to war, that come of those.

The same science that is improving corn harvests has been approved for growing potatoes and cotton, too. I suppose we must now wonder whether there will be side effects we regret. Even the canniest science cannot repeal the law of unintended consequences, but mere alarmism does more to stymie than to guide. We have to try. It is in us to try.

We must be careful, though, not to step on the butterflies.

Tom Teepen is national correspondent for Cox Newspapers. *He is based in Atlanta.*

From "Unintended Consequences: Genetic Engineering Worth Some Risks," by Tom Teepen, 5/26/99. Copyright © 2002, Cox News Service. Reprinted with permission.

---

that motivation will be high as students read to have their hunches verified or to find out what happened instead, and why. His prediction is confirmed.

Post-reading. After reading, the teacher debriefs the event with the students. The teacher:

1. Guides the students to determine whether their purposes for reading were met.
2. Asks them to summarize what they learned from reading.
3. Discusses the material and the accuracy of their predictions.
4. Asks students to point out sections that support or refute their predictions.
5. Directly instructs students in skills and/or provides follow-up enrichment activities.

In the post-reading phase of the activity, Mr. Yang guides the students in a debriefing as they discuss whether their purposes for reading were met and whether they had to revise their predictions and thinking as new information and explanations were given in the text. At this point, the students can state the main ideas and subordinate details, and ask any remaining or newly generated questions.

In Mr. Yang's role as math teacher, he might ask students to state what they learned from the text about game theory and probability. He'd ask if there were any surprises, and he might get answers such as, "Yeah, I would have thought 'survival of the fittest' meant being competitive instead of cooperative, but now I know that's not always true," or "I can't believe that 14 robots learned to cooperate to retrieve a puck even though they weren't programmed to. Maybe people should learn from them!" He'll encourage conversation, inquisitiveness, student theory-building, and then say, "Now you're ready to begin our textbook chapter on probability. Before opening to page 234, any predictions about what you'll learn?"

Strategies involving questioning

Teacher-generated questions. The questions teachers pose to students are highly influential in guiding learning (Alexander, Jetton, Kulikowich, et al., 1994; Atwell,

2007; Konold, Miller, & Konold, 2004; Schellings & van Hout-Wolters, 1995). Look back at the Traditional Worksheet for *The Giver* (p. 5) and then the Literature Circle Guide (p. 6) in the Introduction of this book. Recall that the first set of questions about *The Giver* was very different from the second. I started you thinking back then about the value and importance of questions. Many readers of the novel, of course, do better with no questions than with chapter-by-chapter checks that slow down the reading and make it less enjoyable. Yet, other readers might require teacher direction, and could find questions helpful as they construct meaning from this unusual and sometimes ambiguous dystopian work. As a content area teacher, it's important that you know *when* and *how* to use questions, and how to ask the kinds of questions that evoke the best thinking from your students. Once you know this, you can evaluate the questions in your students' textbooks or on supplementary instructional materials such as worksheets or publisher-provided tests.

One classification of questions divides them into levels.

- *Literal-level questions* can be answered directly from the text because the information is explicitly stated.

- *Interpretive* or *inferential-level questions* can be answered by piecing textual information together or by figuring out what is implied by the words of the text. Here readers perceive connections among the ideas presented and conceptualize the ideas created by those connections (Herber, 1978).

- *Applied* or *evaluative-level questions* require students to go beyond the text and answer from their background knowledge, or to give opinions or bring their feelings into their answer. They may require readers to make critical judgments about the ideas or the reasoning presented in the text.

Again, looking at the questions on pages 5 and 6, you can see that all levels are covered in the first set of questions. Yet, the questions in the second set are likely to lead to more interesting and critical thought and discussion. They are more challenging, and they offer students some choice in the direction they want their thinking to go. The novel is rich and complex enough to allow for these avenues and many more. Perhaps students can construct their own questions that are even better for them to pursue.

Because you will be very familiar with the texts you use and with the students you teach, you will be in a position to determine what kinds of questions you should use. As students answer questions and discuss a text, you can learn to ask probing, clarifying, or follow-up questions to foster higher-level thinking such as

analysis, synthesis, and evaluation. Your questions can also encourage creativity and inquisitiveness on the part of your students. You'll find that questions don't always fit neatly into the three categories, and that's all right.

ACTION RESEARCH   **5.C**

Read the following questions relating to the editorial in Action Research 4.B on page 96, "How Cruel Can Teachers Get?" Classify the questions according to their level: *literal, interpretive,* or *applied.* Decide which of the questions you think readers, or at least particular readers, might find helpful, and add any questions you think might also aid comprehension and further thinking about the topic.

L I A   What is the summer requirement for students in North Syracuse High School?

L I A   What is the editorial writer's opinion of the requirement?

L I A   What is the writer's opinion of the reaction of some of the students?

L I A   Do you think schools should mandate summer reading? Give pros or cons, then the rationale for your decision.

L I A   What was your reaction to the editorial? Was it an effective spoof? Evaluate the techniques the author used to craft the text.

Next, select a text in your content area and create a *three-level guide* (Herber, 1978) using literal, interpretive, and applied-level questions that could help students create meaning and think critically about the topic. Figure 5.7 shows an example of a three-level guide created by a preservice math teacher.

Question–answer relationships. Becoming familiar with the three question levels described previously and learning about *question–answer relationships* (QARs) may help students to understand the kinds of questions they're asked to answer. Raphael (1984) suggested the following categories for questions:

1. *Right there.* Words used to create the question and words used for the answer are in the same sentence.

2. *Think and search.* The answer is in the text, but words used to create the question and those used for an appropriate answer would not be in the same sentence.

3. *On my own.* The answer is not found in the text. (pp. 304–305)

FIGURE **5.7** A three-level guide.

DIRECTIONS: After reading the book *The History of Counting,* by Denise Schmandt-Besserat and Michael Hays (2000), answer the following questions. For the first part, you can find answers to the questions directly stated in the text. For the second part, you have to think about the question and search the text to support your answer; you have to make inferences and/or connect pieces of information. For the third part, use the knowledge gained from reading this text and your own previous knowledge to answer the questions.

LITERAL LEVEL:

1. In Papua New Guinea, what method of counting did the Paiela people use?

   _____

2. The most universal way of counting, the one the majority of people use today, is known as what?

   _____

3. What is the term for the largest number known today?

   _____

4. To what group of people do we owe the invention of abstract numbers?

   _____

INTERPRETIVE LEVEL:

1. Why are the digits of our counting system called Arabic numerals? Use the text to support your answer.

   _____

   _____

2. What are some of the advantages of using the Arabic numerals?

   _____

   _____

3. Who is believed to have invented the first counting system, and for what purpose was it invented?

   _____

APPLIED LEVEL:

1. Why do you think that numerals were first invented?

   _____

   _____

2. Which of these systems, Arabic, Roman, Hindu, Egyptian, or Greek, would you prefer to count with? Why?

   _____

   _____

3. Do you believe that zero has a numerical value, or is it an example of an abstract concept of a number? Explain your answer.

   _____

   _____

—Jayson St. Croix

BookTalk 5.8

Characters in quality literature for adolescents must face the same kinds of situations as real people do, and must exercise careful thinking when they encounter complex problems. In *Silent to the Bone,* by E. L. Konigsburg (2000), Connor is faced with a double-layered problem. He must prove to the authorities that his best friend did not drop his baby sister, as he has been accused. But in order to do that, he must figure out how to communicate with Branwell, who is in a juvenile detention facility and has not uttered a word since the 911 call was made back when the baby was severely (perhaps critically) injured. You can follow along as Connor analyzes data, tries solutions, forms hypotheses, and grapples with aspects of the dilemma.

Variations on these terms exist. You may prefer to think of text-based questions as either *right-there* or *putting-it-together,* while questions requiring information from both the text and the reader can be called *author-and-you* QARs. Attending to the type of question and thinking about the reader's role in answering it is a metacognitive process that can help students as they think about ideas in text.

You could look through this textbook for examples of questions that represent each type. For example, think once more about *The Giver*. A question such as, "What color eyes does Jonas have?" is a *right-there* question, for the text supplies the answer. The question, "What, besides eye color, do the characters who have light-colored eyes have in common?" is a *think-and-search* question. By putting together information the text provides in different places about the several characters with light eyes, readers can construct an answer. The questions "What might be the significance of the light-colored eyes?" and "Why do you think the author chose to point out the eye color of the characters?" are *on-my-own* questions. No amount of looking through the book will uncover the answers. Thinking, discussing, and relating the text to other stories with color symbolism can lead to plausible answers, though students will not come up with exactly the same conclusions, and that's fine. When you ask questions that go beyond the text, an extended investigation and stimulating project can result. For example, you might ask a class, after they have finished *The Giver*, if they think the story could be prophetic, warning about what our society could become. They could then list ways that our society has become either more or less like that of the novel's dystopian society since 1993, when the book was published. Students might look up data about infanticide and euthanasia, debate recent laws (such as those having to do with wearing bike helmets or cell phone use while driving) that might make life safer but take away some freedoms, or interview parents about mandatory preschool. Figure 5.8 provides an example discussion guide that uses *think-and-search* and *on-my-own* questions.

APPLICATION ACTIVITY 5.3 (SEE PAGE 150)

Student-generated questions. As important as good questioning is as a teaching strategy, you'll also want to foster good questioning from your students at every phase of the reading process. You can teach them to survey a text before they start reading and formulate questions based on titles and subtitles. This strategy helps them focus and read actively.

Questioning the author (QtA). A strategic reader continues to question the author during the actual reading of the text. You can teach your students to use a procedure called, appropriately, *Questioning the Author* or QtA (Beck, McKeown, Hamilton, et al., 1997). The process involves the whole class as they read a text for the first time so that they can actively and collaboratively grapple with concepts and construct meaning from the material. The teacher asks queries such as "What is the author trying to say here?" "Did the author explain that clearly?" "Does that make sense when compared with what the author has told us before?" (Beck et al., 1997). An essential feature of QtA is the recognition that texts can be fallible, since they are written by one or more fallible authors. Helping students understand this will require teachers to select texts and model the strategy of generating and then answering queries about the texts. After some practice and teacher–student collaboration, students can lead the discussion and/or use the strategy independently (Liang & Dole, 2006).

Here's an example of QtA in action. One of my students, Mariabeth, responded to the novel *Al Capone Does My Shirts* (2004) by asking the author, Gennifer Choldenko, questions about what happened after the story ends:

- Will Natalie enjoy school at Esther P. Marinoff? Will it be a success or will she be shipped back to Alcatraz Island?

- How will Moose react to his sister being away? Will he feel a bittersweet sorrow grow in his heart? Will he be bored with all the free time he now has in Natalie's absence? Will he occupy his time playing ball with his friends from school or by getting into trouble with the infamously bossy and mischievous

FIGURE **5.8**   A preservice teacher's guide to discussion using *think-and-search* and *on-my-own* questions.

DIRECTIONS: We have read *Bridge to Terabithia*, by Katherine Paterson (1977), and *Mick Harte Was Here*, by Barbara Park (1995). We have also read some excerpts from articles and nonfiction books from the school library on the topic of families grieving a child's death. Now, it's time for you to put it all together and talk with each other about what you've learned and how you're feeling. Start by sharing your journal responses and asking each other any questions that are on your mind. Then, use any of the following questions to continue the discussion.

1. How does the type of relationship between the main character and the character who dies in each book affect the main character's relationship with his or her family?

2. How does the way Phoebe's parents cope with Mick's death differ from the way Leslie's parents cope with her death? What do you think might be reasons for the differences?

3. Both Jess and Phoebe go through a period of disbelief after being told of the deaths. What are some examples of their denial? How does this phenomenon connect to what we've learned about what the experts say about the grieving process?

4. Even though the deaths were accidental, both Jess and Phoebe blame themselves for the tragedies. How does each character resolve the feeling of guilt? Do you think they would have acted differently if the deaths were anticipated (if, for example, someone had died of cancer)?

5. Which book did you like better? Why? What will you take away from each story? What would you say to Phoebe or Jess?

Piper? Will the Flanagans' marriage undergo some dramatic changes?

Mariabeth showed active engagement through her initiation of these questions. She ended up requesting a sequel from the author to end her insatiable wondering about how things would evolve. (Happily, Choldenko did come out with a sequel, *Al Capone Shines My Shoes*, in 2009.)

Reciprocal teaching. *Reciprocal teaching* (Palincsar & Brown, 1984), gets students actively involved in

- predicting
- clarifying
- generating questions, and
- summarizing.

After you teach and model each of these four stages, students form dyads or triads, and one person at a time plays the role of the teacher and leads a discussion of the text using the stages. The student asks questions that call for thinking beyond the literal level.

Research shows that reciprocal teaching helped elementary students who were taught reading strategies and then allowed to practice them using reciprocal teaching (Spörer et al., 2009); low-performing students in urban settings (Carter, 1997); and students who were struggling with literacy tasks (Cooper et al., 2000). It's recommended for readers using multiple forms of texts, including electronic sources (Lubliner, 2001). Oczkus's professional book *Reciprocal Teaching at Work: Strategies for Improving Reading Comprehension* (2003) gives ideas for applying the strategy in whole class sessions, guided reading groups, and literature circles. She provides a rubric showing what to look for as teachers observe and assess students at work, and provides a way for students to self-assess as they apply the strategy. For example, one form begins with "How am I predicting?" followed by a checklist of behaviors before, during, and after reading (e.g., "I stop and use clues from the reading to make more predictions or to change my predictions." "I check my predictions to see if they came about in the text." [p. 202]), indicating that predicting is indeed being done.

Teaching in action: *Math.* The following scenario will exemplify the reciprocal teaching strategy at work. In a high school math class, students are divided into groups of four and assigned five pages from the book *Real-Life Math: Everyday Use of Mathematical Concepts* (Glazer & McConnell, 2002). The four stages of reciprocal teaching were modeled by the teacher and practiced by the students several times during the semester. Now the teacher is circulating among the groups, facilitating as needed.

> **Elbia:** I'm the summarizer, so I'll start, ok? Ms. Okumu says it doesn't matter what order we go in. We read the section called "Exponential Growth" on pages 30–34. I think the main point is that exponential growth is based on repeated multiplication, and that there are examples of it all around us. One example is the population explosion that occurred when rabbits were introduced into Australia, where they had no natural enemies. There are also situations involving money that show exponential growth, like earning compound interest. It's important to understand exponential growth, and to recognize that it's the basis of scams, like chain letters. Don't believe those empty promises of getting rich just by passing along a letter to some friends and sending your hard-earned money to the first person on the list!

> **Giulia:** Thanks, Elbia. Since I've been assigned the role of questioner, I'll ask you three a few questions to see if you understood the passage. Ok, here

goes. Number One: The text says some scientists say that carbon dioxide is increasing in the upper atmosphere exponentially. Why is that a problem?

> **Rudolph:** It's not bad in the early stages, just like a few rabbits were no big deal in Australia. But as the carbon dioxide increases exponentially, global warming can be a result. No good!

> **Giulia:** Exactly. Good connection of examples, Rude. Ok, how about this? Who runs a bigger risk, people who buy into franchises at an early stage or a late stage?

> **Olivia:** If it's a fraud, where franchises sell further franchises, the originators can make millions and the latecomers lose their money. So I'll buy in early, please!

> **Giulia:** Very funny, Liv. But you made your point. Let's hear more from you now, our esteemed "clarifier."

> **Olivia:** Well, I'm in charge of pointing out difficult or potentially troublesome parts, and figuring out how we can go about, well, *clarifying* those confusing parts. I thought I was following the examples of the concept of exponential growth pretty well, and I found the graphs helpful. But then I came to the sentence "When the growth factor is less than one, the curve will decrease" (p. 31). And I went, "Huh?" Luckily, the authors gave a hint right after that, so I followed their advice and looked back at the section called "Exponential Decay," and I saw graphs with curves going the opposite direction, and saw the example of the exponential decay of a radioactive substance. We learned about that in chemistry. So, does everyone get it?

> **Rudolph:** Yeah. We're running out of time, so I'd better play the role of predictor, and if we have time we'll come back for more clarifying and questioning. Ok, the next part gives online sources for learning more about exponential growth. What do I see in my crystal ball? I think we'll get more examples of both legitimate uses of the concept, and more schemes that we'd better beware of. The headings tell us what to expect. I'm going to check out the one for pricing diamond rings. One of you can go to the one on the U. S. national debt. I predict I'll have more fun than you!

BookTalk Online 🎙️ 5.9

Michele Lemieux's *Stormy Night* (1999) gives voice to some of the hopes and fears that students may have. Hear more at the Kane Resource Site.

BookTalk Online   5.10

Freakonomics: A Rogue Economist Explores the Hidden Side of Everything (2005) by Steven D. Levitt (pricetheory. uchicago.edu/levitt) and Stephen J. Dubner (stephenj dubner.com) can spur critical thinking as an economist offers anecdotes and figures to explain how the world works. Read more at the Kane Resource Site.

CONCLUSION

Please listen in on the reflection shown in Figure 5.9 by a middle school math teacher about a book, about her own reading, about her students' reading. It represents active reading and critical thinking, and so can serve as a model for you.

This chapter provided suggestions for helping students comprehend texts; think critically about ideas, concepts, and positions in texts; and become intellectually engaged and eager to learn more about topics. It's important to remember that these strategies are not there just for our convenience in planning and teaching. We must model the strategies and provide practice using authentic materials and the real contexts of our disciplines and our classrooms so that students can internalize them. Our goal is also to help our students to become strategic learners, knowing when to apply the strategies that work best for them. Some students do better with certain strategies than with others. So, encourage self-selection, adaptation to personal needs, and self-assessment whenever possible. Recent research has indicated that what makes a difference in students' comprehension has to do not so much with a particular strategy as with the cognitive and metacognitive

---

FIGURE   **5.9**   **A teacher's reflection after reading *The Phantom Tollbooth*.**

Reading Phantom Math

Jennifer St. Onge

I have attempted to teach my students to read their textbooks, and I devote several lessons to this each year. However, I am always disappointed with my results; my students seem to read their textbooks as they would a novel, but with much less comprehension. A technical text requires slow, repetitive reading that is frequently interrupted for the sake of self-monitoring. Perhaps, by asking them to immediately jump from the narrative or expository text they are accustomed to, and into technical text, I am asking them to do the impossible. By first starting with a novel that requires slow and careful reading, and later, through activities involving several types of technical genre, possibly my students can grow accustomed and even skilled in the area of technical reading.

The Phantom Tollbooth requires reading strategies similar to those required to read a math textbook. This novel contains so many clever puns, riddles, twists, and turns, that a "quick read" would [enable students to] glean little understanding of the full meaning of the book. For example, as Milo travels through The Lands Beyond, the first character he meets is the Whether man. In response to Milo's question regarding the road to Dictionopolis, he replies:

> "Well now, well now, well now, . . . I don't know of any wrong road to Dictionopolis, so if this road goes to Dictionopolis, it must be the right road, and if it doesn't it must be the right road to somewhere else, because there are no wrong roads to anywhere. Do you think it will rain?"

Actually, this strange little man has a very good point, but it would probably be lost on a reader who does not stop to reexamine the Whether Man's words.

Not only is *The Phantom Tollbooth* an excellent exercise in detailed reading, but hopefully, it imparts to the students the value of math and its unique nature. When Milo questions the importance of numbers and problems, as do many of my students, the Dodecahedron replies:

> "If you had high hopes, how would you know how high they were? And did you know that narrow escapes come in all different widths? Would you travel the whole wide world without knowing how wide it was? And how could you do anything at long last . . . without knowing how long the last was? Why, numbers are the most beautiful and valuable things in the world."

In Digitopolis, the reader is challenged to comprehend the concept of averages, infinity, and fractions through physical descriptions and through careful reading.

The realization that there are different modes of reading only struck me in college; I wasted hours before that epiphany, reading things I did not understand. Through guidance, repeated modeling, and practice on increasingly technical texts, students can learn to be effective readers, and to employ appropriate reading strategies to any genre—even to math textbooks. The goal of Milo's journey was to return Rhyme and Reason to the Kingdom of Knowledge. As teachers, it is our job to ensure that these two never depart from the knowledge that we try to impart to our students.

processes students use as they read, set goals, and proceed appropriately with their reading (Pressley, 1995).

You've now begun to explore metacognitive processes—both your own and your students'. Thinking about thinking, learning, reading, and monitoring the processes you use to be more efficient and successful can make a positive difference in academic growth. You can teach your students strategies that tap into metacognitive thinking, and model them yourself. It's a fascinating realm to explore, as is the area of discipline-based inquiry. Learning about how practitioners think and act in authentic situations can make your subject come alive for your students. No longer will math, chemistry, English, geography, health, Spanish, and art be topics confined by school walls and academic calendars. You can be a leader in a discipline-based community of inquisitive minds. The remaining chapters build on the ideas presented thus far; more and more you'll see how the topics connect and allow you to grow as a knowledgeable, metacognitive, discipline-based teacher.

WEBSITES   C H A P T E R 5   Access these links using the Kane Resource Site.

K. C. Cole
www.kccole.net

Stephen J. Dubner
stephenjdubner.com

Steven D. Levitt
pricetheory.uchicago.edu/levitt

Tracy Kidder
www.tracykidder.com

APPLICATION ACTIVITIES

5.1 Choose a text in your curricular area that might be difficult for readers who struggle at your chosen grade level. Make a copy of it, and cut and paste to embed questions at certain points to help students make predictions, attend to relevant details, pose questions, think about significant vocabulary, recognize mood or tone, or reflect on points that are implied instead of directly stated. Remember that the purpose of your questions is to guide and help, rather than test, your students' comprehension. Weir (1998) gives these examples of typical embedded questions you might use or adapt:

- What do you think will happen next? Make a prediction.
- What are you wondering about at this point? Write a question.
- Underline the quality about character X that the author emphasized.
- Stop and visualize X. Draw a sketch of your visualization.
- What was the most confusing part of this story? How did you handle it? (p. 461)

5.2 Always try out a strategy yourself before recommending or teaching it to your students. Choose a chapter from a textbook at any level, or another piece of expository text, and apply SQ3R:

- SURVEY the piece. Notice headings, topic sentences, accompanying graphs or pictures; read the first and last paragraphs.

- Turn the subheadings into QUESTIONS.
- READ to find the answers to the questions you composed.
- RECITE your answers.
- Actively REVIEW the material.

Here's an example of the Questioning step. A heading in this chapter is "Metacognition Overload?" As a reader, you might ask, "What will this section tell me about what that term means? Why does it have a question mark after it?" You'll then read to obtain answers to your questions.

Now reflect on the process you went through. Was the strategy helpful? Are you able to transfer it to other situations? Do you think you'll retain the information longer than if you had simply read the text without applying SQ3R? Do you think SQ3R might be beneficial for the students in your content area classes?

5.3 Create at least one question at each of the literal, inferential, and evaluative levels for each of the texts on genetic engineering in Figures 5.5 and 5.6. Aim for questions that you think would really help students comprehend the passages, think about the implications of the ideas presented, and form judgments based on the information given. Then, label your six or more questions in terms of what kind of QAR is represented. Compare your questions with others, and discuss which are the most helpful or stimulating questions and why that might be. Next, follow the same procedure for a text you select related to your discipline. Share your questions with the Kane Resource Site community.

chapter 6

Vocabulary Development and Language Study

In Norton Juster's children's classic *The Phantom Tollbooth* (1961), the king of Dictionopolis sends the young protagonist Milo on a journey, giving him a small box that he claims promises protection:

> "In this box are all the words I know," he said. "Most of them you will never need, some you will use constantly, but with them you may ask all the questions which have never been answered and answer all the questions which have never been asked. All the great books of the past and all the ones yet to come are made with these words. With them there is no obstacle you cannot overcome. All you must do is use them well and in the right places." (pp. 98–99)

This chapter explores various aspects of vocabulary and language development, both for yourself and for the students in your content area classes. We'll notice how authors and textbooks use words "well and in the right places" and find ways we can do that also. Keep in mind that, although I'm separating vocabulary from comprehension in order to talk about it, the two are intimately connected. Think about these words of Cox and Zarillo (1993): "We comprehend because we know the meanings of enough of the words in a story to make sense out of what we have read. The converse is also true: We grasp the meanings of the words because we know what the story or the article is about" (p. 13).

"If you believe in the power of words, you can bring about physical changes in the universe."

N. SCOTT MOMADAY

ACTIVATING PRIOR KNOWLEDGE   6.1

Before you read on, please take a few minutes to answer the following questions in your learning log. Your answers will help you connect your own experiences with much of the information in this chapter.

1. How many words do you know? (You're not allowed to say "A lot." Take a guess and put down a number.) Are you happy with the level of your vocabulary knowledge? How's your "vocabulary self-esteem"?

2. How did you learn the words that are now in your vocabulary? List as many ways as you can.

(continued)

3. How many words do you think a typical child entering kindergarten knows?

4. Try to think of some words you know today that you didn't know a couple of years ago. List them. (Hint: Think of courses recently taken, new developments in your field, new hobbies, words from movies or television or the Internet.)

5. Have you ever been unable to follow or participate in a conversation because you lacked the vocabulary? (A group may have been talking about computers, sports, accounting, etc.) Do you remember any of the words that were tossed around?

6. Define the word *regicide*.

7. Define the word *lexiphile*. I'll even give you some context to help you with this one. "The goal of instruction should be to develop what one lexiphile has termed *word consciousness*. Encounters with words should be playful, so as to provoke curiosity and an interest in word study" (Anderson & Nagy, 1992, p. 46).

8. List at least five of your favorite words.

9. List at least five words little kids think are neat.

10. Write a definition of the word *culture;* imagine you're trying to explain the concept to someone who doesn't know the word. Then, free associate to come up with as many phrases using the word as you can (which may in turn help your explanation).

In their review of research on vocabulary instruction, Baumann and Kame'enui (1991) begin by quoting Voltaire as saying, "Language is very difficult to put into words" (p. 604) and conclude that the reciprocal, "Words are indeed very difficult to put into language (instruction)" (p. 627), is even more challenging for educators. I concur. I've divided this chapter into four sections, all of which overlap to some extent. First, I address several aspects of words and vocabulary growth in general. Next, I discuss some of the ways we as teachers can revel in language ourselves and build enthusiasm for language study along with vocabulary growth in our classrooms. Then, I present some specific strategies for teaching vocabulary in relation to literacy in the content areas, and last I address language issues connected to English learners.

HOW MANY WORDS DO WE KNOW? AND WHAT EXACTLY *IS* A WORD?

Chances are your answer to the first question from the Activating Prior Knowledge (APK) 6.1 exercise differs from your classmates' or friends' estimations of their accumulated word knowledge.

The variance might have to do with the fact that some of us really do know many more words than others. It also might be due in part to the fact that our concept of large numbers is often far from accurate. I've had students guess they know 1,000 words and others say a billion. Both guesses are way off. Another possible reason for the varied answers has to do with how individuals interpret the question. What do I mean by a *word?* Is *bear,* for instance, one word or many, depending on whether it's used in the phrase grizzly bear, the right to bear arms, bear a child, bear malice, bear a resemblance, can't bear to look, a bear of a man, a bear market, bear with me, and so on? We call such words *multimeaning* or polysemic words, and they abound. *The Oxford English Dictionary* lists 464 meanings for the word *set* alone (Ash, 1999).

If you know a word fairly well when you encounter it in a text but can't spout its definition out of the blue, can you count it as a word you know? The former is considered *receptive vocabulary,* relating to listening and reading; the words we can actually produce in our own talk are part of our *expressive vocabulary,* that related to speaking and writing.

Experts disagree on the size of people's vocabularies—of course, it depends on how vocabulary is defined. Crystal (1995), for example, found that adult subjects reported knowing about 25 percent more words than they actually used, reflecting a difference between receptive and expressive vocabulary. Nagy and Anderson (1984), after an analysis of a thousand items of published materials in use in schools, concluded that there are about 88,500 distinct words in printed school English, and that "the average high school senior may well know about 40,000 words and that the average child in elementary school or high school probably learns 2,000 to 3,000 new words each year" (p. 305). They go on to point out the futility of trying to teach the 20 words a day necessary to reach this goal; obviously, most of us must have learned most of the words we know in some way other than vocabulary-building workbooks in school. I'm sure you answered Question 2 (APK 6.1) with other routes to vocabulary acquisition, perhaps including recreational reading; listening to parents, siblings, teachers, television, and friends; independent study at times when you were self-motivated and set a goal for yourself, perhaps for the purpose of raising your score on the verbal section of a standardized test used by colleges. Experts, however, do agree that the single most effective way to increase vocabulary is by wide and regular reading (Allen, 2006; Cunningham & Stanovitch, 1998; Johnson, 2001; Krashen, 1989; Nagy, 1989). Sarah, an avid ninth-grade reader, reported: "My language is changing. I don't understand it. I read all those books

How Early (and How) Does Vocabulary Development Occur?

Let's go back to Question 3 in Activating Prior Knowledge 6.1, where you guessed the size of a young child's vocabulary. Research shows that from ages two to six children learn around 10 words a day, so by age six they may know 14,000 words (Clark, 1993). Any parent can actually observe children experimenting with words. For example, my three-year-old Christopher was frustrated with me and knew he was not allowed to use the word *hate*. But he needed a word equally powerful and finally blurted out, "I don't like you one *smithereen!*" A couple of years later he led me to a snow fort he and a friend had made, with an entrance he announced was "virtually invisible." Surprised, I asked him what *virtually* meant, and he replied, "I don't know; I just know how to use it." Author Madeleine L'Engle, perhaps best known for her children's classic *A Wrinkle in Time* (1962), recalls how she learned vocabulary by encountering new words in her reading for fun. "I didn't stop to look up the new words; I was far too interested in what I was reading. By the time I'd come across the word in two or three books, the shades of its meaning would automatically become clear, and the word would be added to my vocabulary" (1972, p. 148).

and then I find these words just coming out of my mouth. I don't even know where they come from. Sometimes I feel like I'm in *The Exorcist* and have words spewing out!" (Allen, 2007, p. 95).

THE RICHNESS OF WORDS: DENOTATION, CONNOTATION, SHADES OF MEANING, AND SPECIAL MEANINGS

Students should become aware that many words have *connotations*, various associated and evaluative meanings, as well as *denotations*, the explicit, literal, or direct meanings. You can give your students the dictionary definitions of those terms, but examples from real contexts often help more. So, whenever you encounter words with special connotations in authentic contexts, take advantage of the opportunity to share examples with your students. Sometimes, an exaggerated example works best when you are first explaining a concept such as *connotation*. In a "Peanuts" cartoon by Charles Schulz (1980), Sally tells Linus to get off her porch. Linus replies, "This isn't a porch. This is a stoop. A porch has a railing all around it, and a roof over it, and it's all white, and it has a swing and some rocking chairs . . . and a little table with lemonade glasses and warm nights, and fireflies, and crickets, and soft music, and a moon in the sky. . . ." Linus is referring to the things that resonate in the minds of listeners when they hear the word *porch*.

Here's another example. In literature, the genre that was formerly known as *adolescent literature* is now more commonly referred to as *young adult literature*. Teenagers were avoiding the books targeted for them because the term "adolescent" has developed a negative connotation. Various groups of people changed their preferred names because of connotations associated with certain terms, which may have started out as purely descriptive.

Some multimeaning words can have either a positive or negative connotation depending on the context in which they're used. A *bond* can be a negative thing, chaining a prisoner or limiting a person emotionally in some way. But a *bond* between friends, teammates, or family members is usually seen as a good thing. Help your students ponder the complexity and richness of our language by sharing your own fascination with words, by using rich vocabulary in your lessons and conversations, by pointing out interesting language issues in the readings you assign.

Remember how *The Giver* began with Jonas searching for just the right word to describe how he was feeling? After rejecting several, he settled on *apprehensive*; he had struggled for precision and achieved it. It's really important for students to play around with, to manipulate, the essential words of the disciplines and to aim for exactness and thoroughness. Take the word *culture*, for instance, a word crucial to social studies, which I asked you to play with in Question 10 of APK 6.1. The dictionary definitions, including "the quality in a person or society that arises from a concern for what is regarded as excellence in arts, letters, manners, scholarly pursuits," as well as 11 others (*Merriam-Webster*, 1996), might help or they might confuse further. We must realize that many students have difficulty deciding which dictionary definition fits their needs. A textbook glossary may also define the word, or the word might be explained in a passage. When students pay attention to all of the various contexts in which they hear and see the word, they gain a deeper understanding, complete with nuances and connotations.

A Content Area Application

Imagining I was a high school math teacher about to embark on teaching a course in statistics to advanced upperclassmen, I looked through the textbook *Statistics by Example* (Sincich, 1990). I found few words that could be considered in the *general vocabulary* category with which I thought students would have difficulty. There were, however, many words that the students might know in their general sense, but that take on a special meaning in the field of statistics—*specialized vocabulary* words, including *frequency, population, sample, reliability, distribution, center, mean, median, mode, uncertainty, event, parameter,* and *frame.* I want to teach these words directly and carefully, helping the students to relate them to their more typical meanings while alerting them to the precise meanings they take on in the context of our course. Finally, I found many words and phrases in the *technical vocabulary* category: those unlikely to be found anywhere outside a statistics setting, but crucial to an understanding of the principles of the course. It is my job to teach the terms *standard deviation, empirical rule, interquartile range, z-score, discrete random variable,* and *confidence coefficient* so that students can comprehend the text and the subject matter.

I've asked my students to brainstorm phrases using the term *culture* and its derivatives. In addition to many social studies–related definitions, some students note that in a biology or health setting, the word is used with a quite different, specialized meaning—they supply *throat culture* and scientists growing *cultures* in dishes. Depending on a teacher's purpose, a next step could be arranging those terms into categories, perhaps creating a *graphic organizer,* a visual representation of these associations. Then, student "word detectives" can be on the lookout in their future reading for further examples to add to the list; they can explore websites or library catalogs to find titles incorporating the word. Having consciously played with the word (and hence the concept) and found it exemplified in outside sources, students have a better understanding of their textbook passages dealing with culture. And they can use the concept when they discuss issues themselves—they can apply their concept knowledge as they talk about the culture of the utopian/dystopian society represented in *The Giver,* for example.

We now certainly have a much deeper understanding of the concept *culture* than any dictionary could give us; we've listened to real people, ourselves and experts, grapple with this important word's meaning. You and your students can do the same with many terms in your specific curricular areas.

TYPES OF VOCABULARY WORDS IN CONTENT AREA TEXTS

It is helpful for teachers to recognize that their students will come across different categories of vocabulary words in their reading and study. *General vocabulary* words are those used in everyday language, although they certainly might be unfamiliar to us or to our students. Examples include *ambivalent, miser, serendipity, confirm.*

Content-specific words, or *special vocabulary,* include words that may be part of our students' regular vocabulary, but that take on a specific meaning in a particular content area, such as *culture* in biology, *latitude* in geography, *congestion* in medicine, or *confirm* in religion. *Evolution* takes on a certain meaning in science. Students encountering the word *revolution* in astronomy class and then later in history class must recognize that the word does not refer to the same thing in both classes. Zwiers (2008) lists several dozen common terms that take on specialized meanings in math, including *balance, coordinate, plane, irrational, round, axis, radical, function, tangent, mixed, field,* and *product* (p. 94). He recommends showing students how to interpret and remember some of these dual-meaning expressions by making concrete connections to the more normal meanings. "For *slope* they can think of a hillside, for *balance* they think of a scale, for *factor* they think of parts in a factory, for *odd* they think of strange" (p. 95). Even verbs instructing students what to do in math can be confusing: "plot, graph, interpret, calculate, estimate, construct, convert, . . . isolate" (p. 95).

Finally, *technical vocabulary* refers to words that are used only in particular disciplines, such as *fractal, isotherm, pointilism, iambic pentameter.* Much of what people outside a discipline might consider jargon is actually technical vocabulary. Think of words and phrases you've had to learn in your education classes: *metacognition, morpheme, dyslexia, zone of proximal development.* Some of the words you listed for Questions 4 and 5 in the APK 6.1 exercise are probably examples of technical vocabulary.

ACTION RESEARCH 6.A

Johnson (2001) lists words within several discipline categories, giving the following directions to readers, which I pass on to you: "As you read these lists, consider the first meaning that comes to your mind for each word and then think of the meaning that usually is associated with the word in the named discipline" (pp. 97–98).

MATH

foot	solid	root	peck
square	power	product	yard
mean	curve		

SCIENCE

motion	force	fault	degree
wave	current	resistance	host
matter	charge		

SOCIAL STUDIES

key	bill	race	legend
product	plain	ruler	crop
run	cabinet		

ENGLISH

case	mood	tense	article
subject	tone	romance	dash
voice	stress		

From Dale D. Johnson, *Vocabulary in the Elementary and Middle School.* Copyright © 2001. Published by Allyn & Bacon, Boston, MA. Copyright © 2001 by Pearson Education. Reprinted by permission of the publisher.

You might use these words in a game to demonstrate to your students that words take on specialized meanings within subject areas. Present the ones appropriate to your discipline, have the students look at them and think about their usual meanings, then ask them to talk about the special meaning each has in the subject you teach. Lively discussion will ensue as students work together and think of definitions and examples to complete the exercise. You and they may be able to add other words to the list.

In content area instruction, the specific meanings for concepts and words, along with all they imply, are central and must be understood and remembered—the terms are often necessary building blocks for subsequent lessons (Blachowicz & Fisher, 2000). So, as wonderful as the incidental and independent learning of words is in general, you must provide direct vocabulary instruction and teach and model vocabulary-building strategies in many subject-specific lessons.

Furthermore, Moore et al. (1994) point out that as content area teachers we had better think broadly about what constitutes a word. "Phrases, symbols, abbreviations, initials, and acronyms all occur in the material students read in content areas. While these terms are not technically 'words,' they are entities for which meanings must be built" (p. 198). So, you can have students create a chart: "Initializations and Acronyms We Know and Love." Challenge the other subject area teachers to see which discipline can claim the most acronyms and initializations. (An acronym is pronounced as a word, while an initialization is pronounced as the letters that form it.) I'll get you started:

> Science: DNA, LASER, AIDS, RADAR, NASA, SCUBA, SONAR, TEFLON, EKG, HIV
>
> Math and Technology: CD-ROM, LCD, ANOVA, CPA
>
> Social Studies: IRA, AFL-CIO, NAACP, AWOL, NATO, SWAT, ZIP, CEO, GNP
>
> Education: LD, ESL, LEP, IEP, TESOL, ADA, GPA, IQ, PTA

For further help, you can check out the *Acronyms, Initialisms, and Abbreviations Dictionary*, published irregularly and complete with periodic supplements by Gale Research of Detroit. Also, ask your students for some of the shortcut words they use while talking to their friends via e-mail and text messaging. They might offer TPTB (the powers that be), WYSIWYG (what you see is what you get), EOL (end of lecture), IMO (in my opinion), RSN (real soon now), PMFJI (pardon me for jumping in), MHOTY (my hat's off to you), and TYVM (thank you very much). Students can recognize that language is changing; they're helping to change it!

APPLICATION ACTIVITY 6.1 (SEE PAGE 187)

CONTROLLED VOCABULARY: GOOD IDEA OR BAD?

Core programs or *basal readers* (traditional published reading programs) and textbooks often control the vocabulary used so that students are not confronted with too many difficult words at once. Formulas for determining appropriate grade levels of reading materials, discussed in Chapter 3, usually use the length of words or number of syllables as a criterion. Instructional materials are often created to conform to established reading levels. But many reading experts, as well as authors, disagree vehemently with this practice. Thompson (1996b) provides lists of words found in children's classics that are quite a contrast to the types of words typically found in school reading. Examples include "diffidence, placid, adhere, quietus, miscreant, quixotic, reproof, condescend, somber, enigma, phlegmatic, undulate, sublime, resolute, strident, din, amicable, amorous . . . ," all from Barrie's *Peter Pan* (p. 63). He concludes:

> Educational practice has tricked us all into thinking that such vocabulary is not for children, that it is developmentally inappropriate, or that it should be postponed until some imaginary later appropriate time. Well, I think that any little child who can handle a big term such as *Sanfranciscofortyniner* or *teenagemutantninjaturtle* can handle *fastidious*, and that we are committing national intellectual suicide with our age-graded pistol. (Thompson, 1996b, p. 64)

Madeleine L'Engle, speaking as an author who respects children, concurs:

> The more limited our language is, the more limited we are; the more limited the literature we give to our children, the more limited their capacity to respond, and therefore, in their turn, to create. The more our vocabulary is controlled, the less we will be able to think for ourselves. We do think in words, and the fewer words we know, the more restricted our thoughts. As our vocabulary expands, so does our power to think. (1972, p. 149)

PROMOTING LANGUAGE STUDY

Harmon (2000) listened to seventh-grade students of varying reading abilities as they described how they figured out word meanings. She reports that, not surprisingly, the capable, avid reader used the most strategies the most efficiently and flexibly: Lyn attended to syntax and to parts of words, considered context within sentences and beyond sentences, and considered story plot and authors' styles. A much less able and avid reader, Angela, used a narrow range of strategies, focusing only upon the sentence containing the targeted word; she did not consider using a dictionary, preferring to skip words or ask for help. (Skipping words and asking for help are both fine avenues for you and your students to use at certain times, but must not be the only or necessarily the first means you employ.) Harmon uses her data to conclude that some students require support, encouragement, and access to challenging materials and opportunities to read widely. Others need more explicit instruction to develop more efficient and effective independent word learning strategies, as well as the knowledge and confidence that they can become strategic learners and make good decisions about unfamiliar words they encounter.

Your students can learn more of what they have to in your subject area if you help them to be aware of vocabulary issues, and teach them a variety of strategies to deal with new words they encounter. The following sections detail some ways to expand the vocabulary necessary for your students' understanding of texts in your field, and ways that you can encourage students to explore language and increase their vocabulary independently. The resources provided also help *you* increase your store of words and concepts and become an enthusiastic model and resource for your students. Perhaps the most important thing to keep in mind, in the words of vocabulary expert Janet Allen (2006): "Learners need vocabulary instruction that is generative so they are learning *how to* learn new words they encounter during independent literacy experiences" (p. 17).

Teaching Students to Use Structural Analysis

Were you able to define *regicide* (APK 6.1, Question 6) in the opening exercise? If so, do you know *why* or *how* you know that word? If not, can you come close, or can you at least guess what it might have to do with? Can you identify its part of speech? Think of other words you know that end in *-cide. Suicide,* you say? *Homicide, herbicide, pesticide, genocide, infanticide?* If you've taken Latin, you'll probably add *fratricide, patricide, matricide.* (I've had some kids guess that this last word means the killing of a mattress, which is okay; word play is good.) To help students understand the word *regicide*, have them think of the word *regal* and use the target word in context: "*Hamlet* is a play about regicide." Through induction, the students can now conclude that *regicide* refers to the killing of a king. Interestingly, a new word, *medicide,* has recently entered our language to refer to doctor-assisted suicide. *Bullycide* refers to suicide that is at least partially the result of being bullied. And there's a book titled *Readicide: How Schools Are Killing Reading and What You Can Do About It* (Gallagher, 2009).

Question 7 of the APK 6.1 exercise was included to help you realize how we learn language and generalize and hypothesize about new words based on what we already know. You may have tackled the unfamiliar word *lexiphile* by comparing it to similar words you do know. *Lexicon* and *lexicographer* may have helped, combined perhaps with *bibliophile, pedophile, technophile, Anglophile,* or *Francophile.* "A person who loves words, who studies language" is a very good guess, but a "wrong" one—Anderson and Nagy (1992) tell us that looking up the word *lexiphile* in the dictionary will not help because "it is a word we made up" (p. 47).

BookTalk 6.1

A very busy book invites readers to solve riddles and find keys to decipher vocabulary based on Greek and Latin roots. Readers who interact with *Cryptomania: Teleporting into Greek and Latin with the Kryptokids,* by Edith Hope Fine (www.edithfine.com) (2004), will visit Mathopolis, where cartoon figures using speech bubbles teach words such as *radius, obtuse, acute, plane,* and *parallelogram,* along with prefixes and roots including *dia-, sesqui-, ped-, centi-, hex-, -gon, poly-, -polis,* and *octo-.* Dialogue between a squirrel and a bird goes like this: "Eschew sesquipedalianism!" "Right! I'll avoid using words that are a foot-and-a-half long!" (p. 27). The visual story also takes readers to the classical world, the world of the skies and seas, terra firma, and back to Alphasaurus Academy. It ends with a Greek and Latin glossary and index as well as an English glossary and index. Some students will want to go on the whole journey with the Kryptokids, figuring out clues with them, while others will prefer to skip right to the back and use the book as a reference tool or an efficient way to reach their goal of increasing their vocabulary.

Breaking words into meaningful parts

Teaching your students the strategy of breaking words into meaningful parts, or *morphemes,* is a tremendous way to help them understand terms and concepts they must know and discover the meaning of new words. Morphemes include *root* (or base) *words,* as well as *affixes* (*prefixes,* which come before roots, and *suffixes,* which follow them). Research shows that a morphological awareness on the part of students makes a significant contribution to reading ability (Carlisle, 1995; Carlisle & Nomanbhoy, 1993; Rasinski & Padak, 2008). This makes sense, since Padak et al. (2008) tell us that up to 75 percent of English words are derived from Latin or Greek roots.

Winters (2009) shares strategies such as:

- engaging in interactive morpheme discussions;

- using graphic frames such as morpheme triangles (putting the target word in the middle and various morphemes in the corners) to help students analyze the structure of words;

- choosing words students will encounter in upcoming content reading selections;

- creating personal and group morpheme dictionaries; and

- conducting web searches for Greek and Latin morphemes.

Guidelines for teaching about morphemes include giving explicit instruction in disassembling words into roots, prefixes, and suffixes; and teaching students about word families, consisting of root words and their derived forms (e.g., *marine, submarine, aquamarine, mariner*).

Teaching in action: *Health.* For example, a health class learning about autism would benefit from a mini-lesson on the term's derivation, since it is built on the root *aut-,* a variation of *auto-,* referring to self, and the suffix *-ism,* meaning condition of. Students might brainstorm other words they know that use these morphemes: *autobiography, automobile, autocrat, automatic, automaton,* and a term they might have actually learned in health class, *autoimmune illness*; and *baptism, charism, organism, racism.* The teacher could ask what characteristics of people with autism would have led medical experts to create this label for the condition. Students could be challenged and shown how to research when and how the term came into use. See Figure 6.1 for common suffixes and prefixes relating to content areas.

Etymology

An expedient way to enlarge your own vocabulary and that of your students is to learn a bit about *etymology,* which involves the history and derivation of words. You might be pleasantly surprised at how much enthusiasm young people can show about the so-called *dead* languages, Greek and Latin. Boyce (1996) tells the story of a verbally gifted child whose life was changed by Latin:

> Not until she took Latin in high school did Nadine find the intellectual substance about words that matched her voracious appetite. Nadine says, "In Latin, I enjoyed memorizing vocabulary; I could memorize it instantly. My favorite Latin root is sesqu—consequence, sequel, consecutive, sequence—a cool word!" Nadine's only memory of vocabulary study throughout her school career is of her Latin classes. Her own voracious reading and her constant compiling of word lists nurtured the ability that school neglected. (p. 262)

Boyce highly recommends that vocabulary study include learning Greek and Latin etymology, "with special attention to the aesthetic and intellectual surprises that are not apparent from dictionary definitions" (p. 173). This kind of delight happened to me with the morpheme *nano-.* I recently noticed how often I come across words beginning with this word part—*nanoseconds* and *nanobes* (organisms ranging from 20 to 150 *nanometers* in length). I looked up

| FIGURE | 6.1 | Prefixes and suffixes relating to content areas. |

Find print-ready versions of the lists below, separated by content area, on the Kane Resource Site.

PREFIXES

Science

Prefix	Meaning	Word
bio-	life, living organism	biology, biopsy, biome
de-	opposite of/reverse	deactivate, defrost
post-	after	postnasal, postpartum
pre-	before, prior to	Precambrian, prevent
non-	not: absence of	nontoxic, nonconductive
micro-	small	microscope, microcosm
sub-	under/below	submarine
iso-	equal, alike	isobar
therm-	heat	thermometer

Math

Prefix	Meaning	Word
bi-	two	bicycle
dia-	across	diameter
semi-	half	semicircle
poly-	many	polygon
tri-	three	triangle
kilo-	1,000	kilometer, kilogram
deka-	10	dekameter, dekagram
deci-	1/10th	decimeter
centi-	1/100th	centimeter, centigram
milli-	1/1000th	millimeter

English

Prefix	Meaning	Word
bio-	life	biography
co-	together	coeditor
auto-	self, same	autobiography
de-	reverse, do opposite	debate
pro-	before, preceding	prologue
post-	after	posthumous, postclassical
intro-	within	introspection
re-	back again	recall, remake
extra-	beyond, above	extraordinary
in-	opposite of	incorrect

Social Studies

Prefix	Meaning	Word
dem-	people	democracy, demography
bio-	living organism	biological warfare
co-	together	coexist
dys-	defective, bad	dysfunction
post-	after	postwar, postcolonialism
pre-	before, prior to	predominant, prehistoric
non-	not	nonconstitutional
hemi-	half	hemisphere
inter-	between	interstate, international
trans-	over, through	transcontinental

SUFFIXES

Science

Suffix	Meaning	Word
-ia	names, diseases	phobia
-iatry	art of healing	podiatry
-logy	theory, study of	biology, geology
-ify	to make, or cause to become	purify, acidify, humidify
-cle/-cule	little or small	molecule

Math

Suffix	Meaning	Word
-ic, ics	arts, sciences	arithmetic
-ible	can be, able to be	divisible
-ation	act or process of	computation

English

Suffix	Meaning	Word
-ism	theory or state of	criticism
-logue	speech, discourse	monologue, prologue, dialogue
-phone	sound, instrument that creates sound	homophone, telephone
-an/, -ean/-ian	having to do with	American/ Shakespearian
-ence, ance	action, state of, process	reference, performance

Social Studies

Suffix	Meaning	Word
-acy/-cy	state of being	democracy
-ation	forms (n.), from (v.)	civilization/ information
-ical/-ial	of the nature of	critical, political, territorial
-ite	native of or descendant	Israelite
-an/-ean	having to do	Shakespearian
-ize	to become like	Americanize
-dom	state of or condition of	kingdom, freedom

Source: Created by Renée Warren. Used by permission.

nano- in an old dictionary and found it there with the definition of one-billionth, or 10 to the –9 power. Then, I looked it up in a newer dictionary, where I found the previous definition, plus "a combining form with the meaning 'very small, minute' used in the formation of compound words" (*Merriam-Webster*, 1996). Scanning the page, I found the words *nanogram, nanoid, nanomole, nanoplankton*, and *nanotechnology*. An added treat was reading that *nano-* came from the Greek word meaning *dwarfish*. Now I can update online and have found these additional compounds: *nanometer, nanocrystal, nanosecond, nanotube, nanoparticle*, and more.

Finding out where words originated can be fascinating, as well as helpful in terms of understanding their meanings. Some words, including terms students must know for the disciplines they study, have interesting beginnings. For example, the math term *integer* comes from the Latin for "untouched"—a good word for something that is intact, whole. Students could connect *integer* to a related word, *integrity*.

Hennings (2000) recommends several instructional principles for content area teachers to use when adolescents are "analyzing and sorting words into groups based on shared elements, searching for structurally and etymologically related words, and discovering generalizations about word connections—all at the point of use, when study is most relevant and meaningful" (p. 269). You can:

- Highlight Latin and Greek roots across the curriculum.
- Associate and visually highlight new terms derived from a root with words the students know that share the root. (For example, students in middle school might know that the root *-phobia* means fear, and they might know the meanings of some combinations, such as *claustrophobia* and *agoraphobia*. Science teachers can then add *astrophobia, arachnophobia, aquaphobia, vaccinophobia, zoophobia, photophobia, ornithophobia*, and *metereophobia* to their vocabularies.)
- Give attention to prefixes that carry a negative message (such as *anti-, dys-, counter-/contra-*, and *in-/im-/ig-*).
- Encourage students to explore meanings and etymologies using dictionaries and online sources such as the *Merriam-Webster* website (www.m-w.com) or www.word-detective.com.

Hennings concludes:

> Some content area specialists may be fearful of "wasting" instructional time allocated to their discipline on word study investigations. Just the opposite is likely; time spent in meaningful, contextually relevant word study facilitates students' understanding of the subject discipline. . . . To this end, content area specialists must keep alert for "teachable moments" when they can integrate word study into ongoing content area lectures and discussions. To do this successfully, they must become knowledgeable about word relationships, especially connections based on Greek and Latin roots, prefixes, suffixes, and suffixlike elements. (p. 278)

Padak et al. (2008) offer two compelling reasons to teach etymology. Students will be able to "coordinate sound and sense when they encounter new words" (p. 7). In addition, "The study of word origins and derivatives helps students grasp an essential linguistic principle: English words have a discernable logic because their meanings are historically grounded. This knowledge, used in conjunction with word analysis skills, empowers them as learners" (p. 7).

Structural analysis does not help us figure out vocabulary words 100 percent of the time. Occasionally, something a student might think is a prefix, root, or suffix isn't (e.g., *decide* does not belong with the other *-cide* words we brainstormed previously; *silver* ends in *-er*, which functions as a suffix in many words, but not in this case; *lens* ends in *-s* but is not a plural). And a morpheme may have multiple meanings: *homo-* from Latin means *man*, while *homo-* from Greek means *same*). Help your students realize that paying attention to word structure is very beneficial, but is only one of many strategies they'll use to figure out word meanings.

Teaching Students to Use Context Clues

Authors want their readers to understand the terms they use so they often define words as they go along; that is, in the *context* of their piece. Students might panic when they see words unfamiliar to them, but if they just keep reading, they'll often find that the meaning has been supplied. As they read their textbooks, primary sources, standardized tests, Internet sites, literature, and other texts, the skill of making inferences about the meanings of words based on what makes sense given the surrounding words will serve them well.

Teachers who model figuring out words in real texts through the surrounding words and sentences give students the tools to develop ways to figure out unfamiliar words they encounter (Fisher, Frey, & Lapp, 2008). In addition, as noted by Bromley (2009),

> when students share with others the ways they use context clues, they promote the metacognitive modeling and social interactions that build independent strategies. When students explain how they use context and understand the multiple dimensions of a word, this process can be as rich as or richer than some teacher explanations. (p. 60)

Authors typically have a targeted audience—they address readers they assume know most of the words they use. But often, authors are trying to introduce new concepts, at least new to their targeted readers, so they define words at appropriate times. Biologist E. O. Wilson's *Consilience: The Unity of Knowledge* (1998) contains this example: "Scientific evidence is accretionary, built from blocks of evidence joined artfully by the blueprints and mortar of theory" (p. 59). Two sentences later the word that was just defined is used again: "Only very rarely, as in the theories of natural selection and relativity, does an idea change our conception of the world in one quantum leap. Even the revolution of molecular biology was accretionary, building upon but not fundamentally altering physics and chemistry" (p. 59). The repetition helps; this is *considerate text*.

If I as a reader had not known the word *accretionary,* I didn't have to stop and look up the word or use structural analysis (though I could have done either). The strategy of simply reading the sentence worked well. You as an adult, fluent reader use this strategy naturally all of the time without even realizing it; it has become automatic. It may, however, be necessary to directly teach your students the strategy of reading ahead to get more information or context; reinforce this strategy using real examples that they find in textbooks, trade books, and primary sources. "Think aloud" to show them how you use clues and put information together to figure out the meanings of terms as they are used in particular contexts.

Another device authors may use is supplying, not the definition, but an example that leads to the reader's knowing the meaning of the word. E. O. Wilson (1998) uses the word *paradox*: "Gene-culture co-evolution may seem to create a paradox: At the same time that culture arises from human action, human action arises from culture" (p. 166). He then further clarifies the word by using a synonym in the following sentence: "The contradiction evaporates, however, if . . ." (p. 166). Again, not necessarily easy reading, but considerate text.

Finally, there are times when the author gives neither the definition nor an explicit example, but readers can still take a pretty good guess at a word's meaning by its use in a sentence or a passage. They may only get an approximate meaning at any one time, but when they encounter a word repeatedly, the meaning is confirmed and refined. For example, take the word *formidable*. During one lesson on vocabulary development, my class read an article containing the following sentence: "If the average high school senior knows forty thousand words . . ., you would have to teach twenty words a day to cover them, a . . . formidable task" (Anderson & Nagy, 1992, p. 14). The very next article we read contained a list of words the author

selected from a children's classic, followed by "Impressive, don't you think? . . . These are formidable and advanced words—erudite even" (Thompson, 1996b, p. 63). The following week, these students were reading the young adult novel *Summer of My German Soldier* (Greene, 2000) when they came across the word again. As we hear or see a word in a variety of contexts, the word is added to our receptive vocabulary, and eventually to our expressive vocabulary. It's easy to see why so many experts recommend wide reading as the single best way to increase vocabulary.

Edwards, Font, Baumann, et al. (2004) point out the efficacy of teaching students morphemic analysis and the use of context clues together. If students apply the combined approach, they'll be able to figure out the meanings of many words they come across in their content-related texts. Blachowicz and Fisher (2004) also advocate using this approach: "Using morphology along with context is the most effective way to unravel the meanings of new words" (p. 222).

Readers must have a repertoire of strategies to choose from and the persistence to try another when one doesn't help. Graves (2008) asserts that evidence shows there is no single best approach to teaching individual words, and we shouldn't try to make one size fit all; a multifaceted, long-term approach is desirable. Several of his suggested strategies combine using context clues with other methods, for example:

■ The *context-dictionary-discussion procedure* involves the teacher using a targeted term in the context of a meaningful sentence, asking students to look up the word in a dictionary, and then discussing the definitions the students find, giving feedback on their interpretations.

■ The *context-relationship procedure* involves more preparation time but takes only about a minute of time in class. The teacher creates a paragraph or selections that use the target term several times, including one time that actually gives the meaning of the word. She then gives a multiple-choice item to check students' understanding, providing access to the paragraph on a screen. The teacher will confirm the correct answer, discuss the word further, and answer student questions.

BookTalk Online 6.2

Tooth and Nail: A Novel Approach to the New SAT by Charles Herrington Elster (members2.authorsguild.net/chelster) and Joseph Elliot (1994) goes beyond flashcards and weaves SAT vocabulary words into a mystery story. Hear more at the Kane Resource Site.

Teaching in action: *English.* Let's listen as Ms. Christopher uses the context-relationship procedure to help her students come to an understanding of a word:

> **Ms. Christopher:** You've indicated that you're unsure of the meaning of *didactic.* So let's see how some people use the term. I have a review here of Madonna's first children's book, *The English Roses* (2003). I'll project part of the review on the screen.
>
> > "A girl they do not like is Binah, who is too pretty and too perfect. Enter Nicole's mother, who in a little speech for which the word didactic was invented, tells them that poor, lonely Binah could use a friend" (Booklist, 2003).
>
> In a different review of the same book, we can read a similar opinion, which I will also project.
>
> > "The overly long narration is authoritarian . . . , the characters all sound alike . . . and the didacticism is relentless" (Horn Book Guide, 2004).
>
> Sounds like we're pretty much getting hit over the head with a lesson, doesn't it? Now let's look at a sentence from a review of the biography *Elie Wiesel: Witness for Humanity* (Koestler-Grack, 2009). This is from a reviewer commenting about the *Life Portrait* series:
>
> > "Many photos, images, and sidebars . . . contribute to well-done volumes that inform without being didactic and educate without preaching" (VOYA, 2009).
>
> Any thoughts at this point about the word *didactic?*
>
> **Elena:** I think if I write a book I don't want it to be called didactic!
>
> **Ms. Christopher:** It does often have a negative connotation. Let's see which meaning you would pick given three choices.
>
> She writes on the board:
> a. sarcastic or witty
> b. overly detailed and flowery
> c. tending to moralize
>
> **Class members:** C!

Students must be taught that they can use multiple strategies to figure out words. Also, a metacognitive component should be included. You'll recall from the last chapter that metacognition involves an awareness of and control over one's cognitive processes. Students exhibit *metalinguistic* ability when they reflect on and monitor their learning about words and language.

Teaching Students to Use Reference Materials

When the interdisciplinary discussion group I belong to met recently to discuss the book *Unto Others: The Evolution and Psychology of Unselfish Behavior* (Sober & Wilson, 1998), a biologist brought along a glossary of terms relating to genetics for those of us, like myself, who were not scientists. This colleague realized that we did not represent the author's target audience, and might need help with the vocabulary and concepts that the authors assumed readers would know. The glossary was a much appreciated tool.

Help your students learn that references, such as dictionaries, atlases, and compilations of facts and terms, can greatly aid their reading and understanding. Too many students consider dictionaries boring and deadly because they have been subjected to seemingly endless assignments such as "Look up these 10 words in the dictionary and copy the definitions. Use each word in an original sentence." Moore et al. (1994) state:

> The most common vocabulary activity in classrooms at all levels is to assign students to look up words and write their definitions. This frustrating practice is like expecting that you could get to know some new people by looking them up in *Who's Who* and writing down their distinguishing characteristics. Such an activity is helpful only if you already know something about the people and want to find out more. In the same way, dictionaries are wonderful resources for adding to or clarifying a word's meaning. (p. 224)

Out of context, few of us learn words by looking them up and memorizing someone else's definition. In fact, this practice can lead to misunderstandings.

Mountain (2007/2008) immersed her ninth graders in the use of the thesaurus. They discussed synonyms in groups to decide which ones worked best in certain contexts, designed and solved cross-synonym puzzles, arranged words on a Synonym/Antonym Continuum (Bear et al., 2004), found synonyms in riddles, participated in synonym bees, and applied thesaurus skills to improve their writing. They laughed together at the picture book *Thesaurus Rex* (Steinberg, 2003) and used it as a model to create their own rhymes and patterns. The class truly acquired word consciousness (Blachowicz & Fisher, 2004). Mountain exults, "The thesaurus became a favorite with my students when we started using it for synonym games and puzzles. These activities led to vocabulary growth for the students and improvement in their choices of words in oral and written work. . . ." (p. 318).

I suggest that you keep lots of reference materials on hand as part of your classroom library for your students' perusal. When they *choose* to leaf through

BookTalk 6.3

How do dictionaries get written? Who does the work so that we can open to a page and find the meaning we're looking for? There are fascinating stories that answer these questions. *Dictionaries—The Art and Craft of Lexicography,* by Sidney Landau (2001), explains the principles underlying the making of "wordy" reference books. *Caught in the Web of Words,* by K. M. Elizabeth Murray (2001), is a biography of the author's grandfather, James Murray, the man most responsible for the creation of the *Oxford English Dictionary,* the definitive source for word lovers. Then, there's *The Professor and the Madman* by Simon Winchester (1998). This bestseller's subtitle is enticing: *A Tale of Murder, Insanity, and the Making of the Oxford English Dictionary.* Enjoy!

FIGURE 6.2

A sampling of books on language.

See more suggested titles in Appendix Figure 6.2.

Abley, M. (2009). *Camp Fossil Eyes: Digging for the Origin of Words.* Toronto, ON: Annick Press.

Good, C. E. (2002). *A Grammar Book for You and I . . . Oops, Me!* Sterling, VA: Capital Books.

Gorrell, G. K. (2009). *Say What?: The Weird and Mysterious Journey of the English Language.* Toronto, ON: Tundra.

Kipfer, B. A., & Chapman, R. L. (2008). *American Slang* (4th ed.). New York: Collins Reference.

O'Connor, P. T. (2009). *Origin of the Specious: Myths and Misconceptions of the English Language.* New York: Random House.

---

a dictionary, or explore an atlas, even though the terms and information they read are not within the wider context of a passage or book, learning can take place. Some people really do choose reference books for pleasure reading, and certain of your students might prefer reading from a book of phrases to reading a few paragraphs from a novel or a textbook assignment if they only have a few minutes before the bell rings. Encourage this independent pastime, and listen actively should your students choose to share their discoveries with you. I have included a bibliography of reference books pertaining to language in Figure 6.2. Peruse them, enjoy them, and add excerpts that relate to topics in your curricular area to your repertoire of stories. You can also give booktalks to entice your students to read about the living, lively language they use.

Exploring and Playing with Language

Question 1 of the APK 6.1 exercise, designed in part to help you bring to a conscious level how you feel about your personal vocabulary achievement at present, has resulted in my students, future teachers, admitting to being discouraged about their own vocabulary level and growth. They complain of having forgotten the words they learned in high school for the SATs and final course exams and find learning the vocabulary associated with all of their college courses a daunting task. Some have even developed a fear of words: *logophobia!* Yet, their answers to Questions 8 and 9 (APK 6.1) show them that they have not entirely lost the ability to appreciate the beauty and interest of words or the ability to play with language. Take a moment to listen to the words

your classmates picked as favorites, and share your own. You'll be able to categorize them according to why they were picked. My students always come up with words they like because of the way they sound: *happenstance, cornucopia, passé, incorrigible, sophisticated, exquisite, onomatopoeia, Mississippi.* Others are favorites because of their meanings or associations: *love, payday, peace, chocolate, family.* Once in a while someone offers a word, such as *serendipity, lullaby,* or *bubble bath,* that fits in both the sound and association categories. I look around at this point in our sharing and notice that my students are smiling and nodding as they hear and savor the words being mentioned. This increases as we share words that young children tend to love: *mine, why, candy, Mommy, Tyrannosaurus Rex, NO, Dad, Tigger, awesome, supercalifragilisticexpialidocious.*

> *"For students who have learned to play with words, literature and all language become the playground."*
> **BOYCE, 1996, P. 269**

Children pick up words easily and are very curious. One day I had some neighborhood children in my house; they like to play library with my hundreds of books and thus, help me keep them in some order. I said to 11-year-old Jeff, "Here's a book on the Industrial Revolution I think you might like." Alex, my six-year-old niece, piped up, "I already know what that is. Animals turned into people." I replied, "I said *revolution.* Where did you learn about *evolution?*" She responded casually, "I

Books with Characters Who Love Words

We don't see many characters in children's and young adult books learning new words by studying lists for midterm exams—perhaps because that is not the stuff adventures are made of. But readers who pay attention, as we can help our students do, can see vocabulary acquisition at work as they read literature. For example, in Antoine de Saint-Exupéry's classic fantasy, *The Little Prince* (1943), a geographer, while recording everything from mountains to seas, explains to the little prince that he does not record flowers because they are ephemeral. Our protagonist asks:

> "But what does that mean—'ephemeral'?" . . . "It means, 'which is in danger of speedy disappearance,'" replies the geographer. "My flower is 'ephemeral,'" the little prince said to himself, "and she has only four thorns to defend herself against the world. And I have left her on my planet, all alone!" (pp. 65–66)

He has his first moment of regret; both the character and the reader are emotionally involved with the flower at this point. Thus, *ephemeral* is likely to be remembered, especially if the teacher or student uses it in other applications soon after.

Kevin, one half of the inseparable duo known as *Freak the Mighty* (Philbrick, 1993), is a boy who has known since he was seven, when he looked up the name of his disorder in a medical dictionary, that he wasn't going to have a very long life—his bones won't grow, but his internal organs continue to enlarge. His heart will grow too big, literally, for his body. What *does* grow at a rapid rate is Kevin's knowledge, particularly his vocabulary. He carries a dictionary with him and uses it when his overgrown friend Max becomes confused when he talks about such things as *archetypes, relativity,* and *ichthyology.* "Freak's Dictionary" is included at the end of the book. Students will laugh at Kevin's spin on some of the definitions.

The ambitious 12-year-old narrator of Bette Greene's *Summer of My German Soldier* (2000) is working her way through *Webster's Collegiate Dictionary* in order to meet her goal of someday knowing the meaning of every word in the English language. She knows all kinds of words,

"thin ones like ego and ode. Fat ones like harmonic and palatable . . . beautiful ones like rendezvous and dementia praecox . . . ugly ones like grief and degrade" (p. 72). Like our friend Jonas in *The Giver,* she's concerned with the precision of language. She explains to a reporter, "Like a moment ago you used the word aptitude, and because you didn't think I understood, you substituted the word ability. But you didn't actually mean ability. We both know that I don't have the ability to be a reporter today, but I just might have the aptitude" (pp. 92–93). Readers of this historical novel will see how Patty's knowledge of words and concepts becomes armor and solace when her family and town turn against her for harboring an enemy prisoner of war.

You may come across many other books in your own reading that have characters who love language and use words carefully, purposely, or playfully. Share them, and encourage your students to do the same. You might have a poster on your classroom wall devoted to titles and examples related to the topic of language use by characters, fictional and real. To get started, check out *Multiple Choice* by Janet Tashjian (2001), *The Mozart Season* (2000) by Virginia Euwer Wolff, *Silent to the Bone* (2000) by E. L. Konigsburg, and *Word Nerd* (2008) by S. Nielsen.

BookTalk 6.4

The Music of Dolphins (1996), by Newbery Medal winner Karen Hesse, doesn't exactly fit the category "Characters Who Love Words," because language is an uncomfortable fit for Mila, a feral child who spent most of her life with dolphins before coming to the Language Institute. But you'll certainly be stimulated to ponder the relationship between thought and language, as well as what it means to be human, as you experience Mila's struggle to become vocal and literate, and to acquire the culture of her new environment. You'll witness the frustration of her teachers, and, with the characters, you'll face some ethical dilemmas regarding freedom and control.

read it in a book." My attention went back to Jeff, and I forgot about the incident until Alex's mother told me that when she got home from work that night, Alex greeted her with, "Mom, what's *revolution?*" and then went around the house that night singing "evolution–revolution" under her breath. She was playing and learning.

Somehow, we have to keep that level of curiosity high in our students, and of course in ourselves, too.

Johnson, Johnson, and Schlichting (2004) contend that word play should not be considered an extra or add-on to subjects taught in school. They give examples of newspaper headlines that rely on readers' ability to recognize allusions, plays on words, idioms, proverbs, slang, and ambiguities. Comprehension is compromised when readers take figures of speech and euphemisms literally. Teachers can teach and provide opportunities for manipulating language through logology—in other words, word play. "Such instruction will pay off in two ways: by generating and enhancing students' interest in language and by helping students deal with the many facets of oral and written language as listeners, speakers, readers, and writers" (p. 198).

Blachowicz and Fisher (2004) make the following research-based statements regarding word play:

- Word play is motivating and an important component of the word-rich classroom.
- Word play calls on students to reflect metacognitively on words, word parts, and context.
- Word play requires students to be active learners and capitalizes on possibilities for the social construction of meaning.
- Word play develops domains of word meaning and relatedness as it engages students in practice and rehearsal of words. (p. 219)

In addition to wide reading, they recommend providing a "flood of words" (p. 221) by reading to students often in order to expose them to terms they would not encounter otherwise. They show how word play and manipulation can draw on and enhance syntactic, morphological, and metacognitive awareness. Teachers can employ category and memory games, coded messages, jokes and puns, and computer exploration to increase vocabulary development in subject areas.

Word games and alphabet books are two ways teachers can incorporate word play in their content area classrooms.

Word games

Word games have always been popular, in every age and at every age. Children love to rhyme, to try out new words, to invent new languages with their friends. Every generation coins terms and uses words in ways their parents didn't. But some word games can bring family members of various ages together and prove that everyone can learn new words. SCRABBLE®, for instance, has been popular for decades and is still going strong (now also in electronic format). New players can watch veterans take a word that was created on the board and make it a compound word, or add an affix. Picture three of your students engaged in a game at lunchtime. Evan puts down the word *decide*. Elbia adds a *d* at the end, making the verb past tense or turning the word into an adjective. Luke applies the prefix *un-*, then Evan adds the suffix *-ly*, changing the word to an adverb. Elbia looks over her letters and asks if someone can do something "semi-undecidedly."

They decide to look in a reference book to see. These students are having fun, thinking creatively, and learning about language issues.

Supplying your classroom with games and books that employ and play with words can only help your students. These materials might not relate directly to the topics you're teaching, but they can make your students eager learners and sharper thinkers; perhaps yours will be the classroom that students love to visit after school to have competitions with students from other class periods. You'll have the opportunity to talk informally with students, to chat and laugh while you observe them play language games or play along with them. In addition, you can use the formats of these games or books to create, or encourage the students to create, similar challenges using subject-related words. Figure 6.3 offers some language-based games, books, and websites.

Bromley (2009) has created a word game strategy, "interview a word," which involves choosing key words or concepts from something students have read, having teams "become" their target word by answering questions while taking on its perspective, and having other teams guess the word being explicated. Figure 6.4 shows an example of the strategy, using an assessment concept you will become more familiar with in Chapter 10. After reading it, you might want to try the strategy yourself, perhaps using a term or concept such as *metacognition,* or *word consciousness,* or another that relates to the discipline you will teach.

Maybe you're thinking that, as a content area teacher, you really don't have time for playing with words in general. In that case, I encourage you to make up activities and games that promote word

FIGURE 6.3

Language-based games, books, and websites.

See more suggested titles in Appendix Figure 6.3.

Casagrande, J. (2006). *Grammar Snobs Are Great Big Meanies: A Guide to Language for Fun and Spite.* New York: Penguin Books.

Harvey, A. (2009). *African Acrostics: A Word in Edgeways.* Somerville, MA: Candlewick Press.

L Is for Lollygag: Quirky Words for a Clever Tongue. (2008). San Francisco: Chronicle Books.

MacLeod, E. (2009). *Why Do Horses Have Manes?* Toronto, ON: Kids Can Press.

Salinger, M. (2009). *Well Defined: Vocabulary in Rhyme.* (S. Henderson, Illus.). Honesdale, PA: Wordsong.

FIGURE 6.4 An example of the "interview a word" strategy.

Questions adapted from Bromley, 2009, p. 67

Target Concept I Interviewed: AUTHENTIC ASSESSMENT

Q: Nice to meet you, A. A. Can you tell me who your relatives are?

A: Hmm, let's see. Kidwatching, formative assessment, and standardized assessment (a distant relative).

Q: Would you ever hurt anyone? Who? And why?

A: No, I'm the good guy, at least in the eyes of the author of this textbook. I'm here to help teachers and kids.

Q: Are you useful? What is your purpose?

A: Very useful! When teachers use me, they can tell how their students are understanding their content; what strategies they use as they read real, meaningful, and relevant texts in their disciplines; and what kinds of instruction, modeling, and scaffolding teachers might provide to enhance their curricular knowledge and skills.

Q: What or whom don't you like? And why?

A: I don't like isolated drills that don't connect to real situations or literature; I don't like kids being subjected to test-prep kits and scripted programs; I don't like anything that's fake; I don't like frauds.

Q: What or whom do you love? Why?

A: I love authenticity in lessons and life as well as in testing. I love the happy faces on teachers and kids when they're engaged in meaningful tasks, such as reading a trade book relating to a concept necessary for the understanding of a discipline.

Q: What are your dreams?

A: I have a dream that one day there will be no more time wasted, time taken from instruction, to prepare for high-stakes tests that ultimately tell very little about what students need to excel in the learning of the subjects we love so passionately.

study (and simultaneously play) to help your students remember the concepts in your subject, for example:

1. Make cards with definitions on the top and vocabulary terms (for different definitions) on the bottom. Make enough cards for each student to have at least one.

2. Read the first definition, and whoever has the card with the answer calls it out.

3. Then, that person reads the definition on her card, and another person answers.

4. Continue this routine until all terms are matched with definitions. (The last answer should be on your card.)

You can also play the game by saying the term first, with the answer being the definition. It works well as a review at the end of a unit. Figure 6.5 gives examples of these cards.

FIGURE 6.5 Examples of vocabulary game cards for an algebra class.

Definition: The sum formed by changing the sign of the subtrahend in a subtraction problem and then adding.

[Another card has "algebraic subtraction" on the bottom.]

Term: Conditional equation

[Another card will have the definition to match this.]

Definition: A number or quantity placed before and multiplying another quantity.

[Another card has "coefficient" on the bottom.]

Term: Variable

[Another card will have the definition to match this.]

Alphabet books

Another way to play with words and enhance vocabulary is through the use of alphabet books. "Alphabet books?" you say. "Aren't they just for little kids?" Absolutely not. You'll be amazed at the sophistication and the instructional potential of many alphabet books once you start exploring them through your new lens as a content area literacy teacher. They can help your students grasp concepts, encounter new terms, and appreciate the creativity and artistry of the authors and illustrators within the genre. For example, readers may pore over the detailed artwork in Graeme Base's (www.graemebase.com) *Animalia* (1986) from the science teacher's classroom library while having the concept of alliteration reinforced; and as they explore the "I" page and read "Ingenious Iguanas Improvising an Intricate Impromptu on Impossibly Impractical Instruments," they may note parts of speech, prefixes, and suffixes.

Science teachers can tap into the affective realm when teaching about the destruction of habitat and extinction of species by using books such as *V for Vanishing, The Extinct Alphabet Book,* and *Aardvarks, Disembark!* Figure 6.6 provides a sampling of alphabet books you could choose from as you create a classroom library that matches your curricular topics and goes beyond them. You might also choose some alphabet books just for their beauty, innovation, cleverness, and aesthetic appeal.

My preservice teachers enjoy creating alphabet books to teach vocabulary terms related to their curriculum. Figures 6.7 and 6.8 show examples of their products.

APPLICATION ACTIVITY   6.2   (SEE PAGE 187)

FIGURE   6.6   Content-relevant alphabet books appropriate for middle and high school students.

See more suggested titles in Appendix Figure 6.6.

MATH, SCIENCE, AND TECHNOLOGY

Dolphin, C. (2009). *Angles to Zeros: Mathematics from A to Z.* Edina, MN: ABDO Publishing.

Farrell, J. (2007). *Stargazer's Alphabet: Night-Sky Wonders from A–Z.* Honesdale, PA: Boyds Mills Press.

Gagliano, E. (2009). *V Is for Venus Fly Trap: A Plant Alphabet.* (E. Traynor, Illus.). Chelsea, MI: Sleeping Bear Press.

Schwartz, D. M. (1998). *G Is for Googol: A Math Alphabet Book.* Berkeley, CA: Tricycle Press.

Smith, M., & Smith, K. (2008). *W Is for Wave: An Ocean Alphabet.* Chelsea, MI: Sleeping Bear Press.

ENGLISH AND FOREIGN LANGUAGES

Cooling, W. (2005). *D Is for Dahl: A Gloriumphious A–Z Guide to the World of Roald Dahl.* New York: Viking.

Hershenhorn, E. (2009). *S Is for Story: A Writer's Alphabet.* (Z. Pullen, Illus.). Chelsea, MI: Sleeping Bear Press.

McCurdy, M. (2010). *Walden Then and Now: An Alphabet Tour of Henry Thoreau's Pond.* Watertown, MA: Charlesbridge.

Morales, Y. (2008). *Just in Case: A Trickster Tale and Spanish Alphabet Book.* New York: Roaring Book Press.

Wilber, H. L. (2008). *Z is for Zeus: A Greek Mythology Alphabet.* (V. Juhasz, Illus.). Chelsea, MI: Sleeping Bear Press.

FINE ARTS

Domeniconi, D. (2006). *M Is for Masterpiece: An Art Alphabet.* (W. Bullas, Illus.). Chelsea, MI: Sleeping Bear Press.

Johnson, S. (2008). *A Is for Art: An Abstract Alphabet.* New York: Simon & Schuster Books for Young Children.

Krull, K. (2003). *M Is for Music.* Orlando, FL: Harcourt.

Marsalis, W. (2005). *Jazz A-B-C: An A to Z Collection of Jazz Portraits.* Cambridge, MA: Candlewick Press.

Raczka, B. (2007). *3-D ABC: A Sculptural Alphabet.* Brookfield, CT: Millbrook Press.

SOCIAL STUDIES

Cheney, L. (2003). *A Is for Abigail: An Almanac of Amazing American Women.* New York: Simon & Schuster.

Demarest, C. L. (2005). *Alpha, Bravo, Charlie: The Military Alphabet.* New York: Margaret K. McElderry Books.

Osornio, C. L. (2010). *The Declaration of Independence from A to Z.* (L. Johnson, Illus.). Gretna, LA: Pelican Publishing.

Paulson, T. (2000). *Rainforest ABC.* New York: Winslow Press.

Shoulders, D., & Shoulders, M. (2010). *G Is for Gladiator: An Ancient Rome Alphabet.* (V. Juhasz, Illus.). Chelsea, MI: Sleeping Bear Press.

INTERDISCIPLINARY AND MISCELLANEOUS

Chester, J. (2005). *The Young Adventurer's Guide to Everest: From Avalanche to Zopkio.* Berkeley, CA: Tricycle Press.

Fredericks, A. D. (2009). *A Is for Anaconda: A Rainforest Alphabet.* (L. Regan, Illus.). Chelsea, MI: Sleeping Bear Press.

Gaimon, N. (2008). *The Dangerous Alphabet.* (G. Grimly, Illus.). New York: HarperCollins.

Herzog, B. (2007). *E Is for Extreme: An Extreme Sports Alphabet.* (M. Rose, Illus.). Chelsea, MI: Sleeping Bear Press.

Salas, L. P. (2010). *S Is for Score!: A Sports Alphabet.* Mankato, MN: Capstone Press.

FIGURE **6.7** **Pages from an alphabet book for high school mathematics.**

Letters in Math?!

A is for Algebra, the study of.

B is for Base angles, the bottom angles of a triangle.

C is for Congruent, a term meaning equal.

D is for Dilation, the size of a shape.

E is for Ellipse, a circle squashed in the center.

F is for Function, sometimes seen as a machine.

G is for Geometry, the study of shapes.

H is for Hyperbola, the set of all points that looks like this:

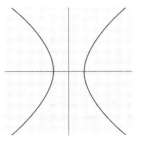

I is for Imaginary number, a number that does not exist— but does in an imaginary context!

J is for Joining line segments, two or more nonparallel line segments.

K is for Kite, a geometric figure with two congruent sides.

L is for Logarithm, another way to write an exponential equation.

M is for Monomial, an expression with one term.

N is for Negation, meaning the negative of a statement.

O is for Octagon, an eight-sided figure.

P is for Parallel lines, two lines that never meet.

Q is for the Quartic function, a function of degree 4.

R is for the Radical numbers, numbers that have decimals.

S is for Slope, the elevation of a straight line.

T is for Trinomial, an expression with three terms.

U is for Undefined, occurs when dividing any number by 0.

V is for Vector, a quantity with both direction and magnitude.

W is for Width, the thickness of an object.

X is for the X-axis, the horizontal axis in a plane.

Y is for the Y-axis, the vertical axis in a plane.

Z is for the Z-axis, which makes a plane three dimensional.

—*Alisha James*

FIGURE **6.8** **An alphabet book for American history.**

An Alphabet of Indians*

A is for Apache, who know the desert well.

B is for the Blackfeet. In the northern plains they dwell.

C is for Cheyenne. They are always counting coup.

D is for Dakota, sometimes called the Sioux.

E is for the Erie, a people near the lake.

F is for the Flathead; strong cradles do they make.

Gabrielino starts with G. They live along the Bay.

H is for the Hopi. They make things out of clay.

I is for the Iroquois, 6 tribes or 5 at least.

J is for Jicarilla, Apaches in the East.

K is for the Kickapoo. They live in many places.

L is for Laguna. Kosharis† paint their faces.

M is for the Mohawk. They protect the northern door.

N is for the Navajo, "code talkers" in the war.

O is for the Osage, out on the southern plains.

P is for the Pima; remember Ira Hayes[+].

Q is found in Quapaw. They're related to the Sioux.

R is for the rivers that provide for me and you.

S is for the Seneca. They live in New York State.

T is for Tuscarora. They arrived a little late.

U is for the Ute, surviving on the basin.

V is for the vision quest, known to many nations.

Wompanoag starts with W; so does where, and when, and why.

Nothing starts with X; I'm not even going to try.

Y is found in Yaqui, way down in Mexico.

Z is for the Zuni, a good Pueblo tribe to know.

* The author, who is a member of the Mescalero Apache Nation of New Mexico, prefers the term "Indians" to "Native Americans."

† Kosharis—ceremonial clowns among the Pueblo nations.

[+] Ira Hayes—a member of the Pima Nation; he was photographed holding up the flag at Iwo Jima (the man in the back).

—*Stephen Crawford*

Celebrating the Birth of New Words

People coin new words as needed, sometimes by combining two existing words or morphemes, as in *cognitive science, bioethics, sociobiology, neuroscientist, pseudoscientist, psycholinguist, biochemical, computer science, psychophysiological, neurobiologist, Social Darwinism.* In Chris Crutcher's young adult novel *Stotan!* (1986), we learn that a *Stotan* is a very special kind of athlete, combining the characteristics of a *Stoic* and a *Spartan* (p. 27). Wilson, in *Consilience,* uses a Scottish term, *satisficing,* joining the meanings of *satisfying* and *suffice,* to discuss how humans make choices (p. 136).

I read on the Oxford University Press blog (OUP blog) that the compilers of the *New Oxford American Dictionary* had chosen the verb "unfriend," meaning to remove a person as a friend on a social networking site, as the 2009 Word of the Year. The site also listed many new Twitter-related words, including Tweeps, Tweetup, Twitt, Twitterati, Tweepish, Twitterature, and Tweetaholic, as well as numerous Obamisms, such as Obanomics, Obamerama, Obamanos, Obamanation, Obamanator, and Obamalicious (http://blog.oup.com/2009/11/unfriend, retrieved January 6, 2010).

Sometimes authors include word origins as part of a more extended explanation of new or difficult concepts. Note the following example:

> The term "meme" was introduced about twenty years ago by the British biologist Richard Dawkins, who used it to describe a unit of cultural information comparable in its effects on society to those of the chemically coded instructions contained in the gene on the human organism. The name harks back to the Greek word *mimesis,* or imitation, for as Dawkins pointed out, cultural instructions are passed on from one generation to the next by example and imitation, rather than by the shuffling of genes that occurs between sperm and ova. Perhaps the best definition of a meme is "any permanent pattern of matter or information produced by an act of human intentionality." (Csikszentmihalyi, 1993, p. 120)

If students are taught to be aware of strategies like this that authors use, they can apply good reading strategies to learn the word, connecting it to its origin if that's helpful. Comprehension, as well as vocabulary development, may be increased.

Using Language Exploration Centers

Some teachers set aside a corner of the classroom or some other space and fill it with resources, including those mentioned previously. In a class where several kinds of activities are going on (e.g., a reading–writing workshop), a learning center like this could offer opportunities for individuals or small groups. You might have project suggestions, or students could simply set their own goals and use the learning center to meet them. The results of their explorations can be posted on your word walls, or students can present their findings to the class. For example, in a high school science class, a study group might explore the use of metaphoric language and similes in the nonfiction of biologist Barbara Kingsolver and post the findings as shown in Figure 6.9.

Highlighting Language Connections in Your Discipline

You may get the occasional student who tries to tell you that talk about language should be left in the English classroom. You can assure him that is not the case, nor should it be. People in every field take words seriously. Language issues are central to every subject area; it's up to you to show the students how to capitalize on the benefits language study can provide them as they learn the discipline you teach.

FIGURE 6.9 Group language exploration.

Similes We Found in Barbara Kingsolver's *High Tide in Tucson: Essays from Now or Never*

"A magazine piece is meant to bloom like an ephemeral flower on the page, here today and recycled tomorrow . . ." (p. ix).

"*Want* is a thing that unfurls unbidden like a fungus, opening large upon itself, stopless, filling the sky. But needs, from one day to the next, are few enough to fit in a bucket, with room enough left to rattle like brittlebush in a dry wind" (p. 13).

"The schoolhouse's plaster ceilings are charted with craters like maps of the moon and likely to crash down without warning" (p. 35).

"The part of my soul that is driven to make stories is a fierce thing, like a ferret—long, sleek, incapable of sleep, it digs and bites through all I know of the world" (p. 43).

BookTalk 6.5

Have you ever felt insecure because you know a word from seeing it in print, but you're not really sure how to say it? *The Big Book of Beastly Mispronunciations: The Complete Opinionated Guide for the Careful Speaker,* by Charles Harrington Elster (1999), can come to your rescue! In his introduction, the author sort of gives his own booktalk, promising:

> *The Big Book of Beastly Mispronunciations* is much more than a dry list of acceptable and unacceptable pronunciations. It provides historical background. It reports the opinions of numerous authorities. It offers pithy explanations and passionate opinion . . . a concise and accessible discussion of past and present usage, alternative pronunciations, levels of acceptability, analogies and tendencies, the vicissitudes of human nature, the terrible swift sword of phonetic justice. (p. xi)

I've read lots of entries and received confirmation on pronunciation, as well as entertaining commentary on words such as *gondola, awry, en route, entrepreneur, remuneration, albeit, schism, eschew, assuage,* and *diaspora.* I chuckled throughout as I learned. And I'm much more secure about speaking in public! So, I recommend this book to you.

BookTalk 6.6

Want to learn more than 100 math terms and have fun in the process? Check out David M. Schwartz's (www.davidschwartz.com) *G is for Googol: A Math Alphabet Book* (1998). For each letter of the alphabet, Schwartz explains a mathematical concept, mathematician, or application. He includes stories, history lessons, problem-solving techniques, and problems for readers to try. Hilarious pictures by Marissa Moss accompany his mini-lessons on topics ranging from the abacus to the concept of a zillion. In addition to the targeted word, he adds lists of other mathematical words beginning with each letter, which are later defined in a glossary.

One of my favorite chapters is "M Is for Möbius Strip." Schwartz teaches the meaning of the term inductively by instructing readers to make a loop from a strip of paper, give it a twist, and tape the ends together. In the course of his explanation, Schwartz defines *topologists* as "mathematicians who study what happens to various shapes and solids when they are pushed and pulled and twisted and cut and contorted in different ways" (p. 26) and states that a topologist would say that a Möbius strip has only one side. He gives an example of a kind of conveyor belt being an industrial application of the principle, and he gives suggestions for experiments that readers can do to examine the properties of the concept.

If you teach a subject other than math, you could use this book, along with its companion, *Q Is for Quark: A Science Alphabet Book* (2001), as a model and encourage your students to make an alphabet book using words from history, science, art, physical education, and so on.

There is a vital connection between math and literacy. The greater the students' ability to read and write, the greater their comprehension of math is likely to be (Maida, 1995). Students sometimes fail at math because of a difficulty understanding the word problems used to show the application of math skills. Students need to understand that math is a language and that language is used to teach math. Vocabulary is essential to math; certain concepts and terms are prerequisite for understanding many math principles.

Some textbook authors recognize the need to help students understand math through the use of language. They may highlight or box definitions and key words, or explain terms further in marginal notes. Teachers, of course, must make sure their students take advantage of and use the language aids the textbooks supply. Math textbooks might also help students see and make connections beyond numbers and math theories by using language to present cases and real-world applications. For example, *A Survey of Mathematics with Applications* (Angel, Abbott, & Runde, 2005) has sidebars titled "Mathematics Everywhere," "Did You Know," and "Profile in Mathematics," containing fascinating stories, con-

cept applications, and explanations of mathematical terms, including *Fibonacci sequence, compound interest, tree graph, scientific notation, inverse variation, linear functions, matrix, symmetry, topological equivalence, fractal geometry, chaos theory, identity element, the law of large numbers, conditional probability, permutation,* and many more.

You'll be well prepared to begin a discussion of transdisciplinary math projects if you read books on math topics yourself. For example, I found the table of contents of *The Universe and the Teacup: The Mathematics of Truth and Beauty,* by K. C. Cole (1998), to be quite inviting. I wasn't intimidated by chapters with names such as "The Signal in the Haystack," "Fair Division: The Wisdom of Solomon," and "Emmy and Albert: The Unvarying Nature of Truth." Math and language work beautifully together.

Exploring Vocabulary Within Literature Circles

When small groups of students are discussing texts and learning from each others' responses in literature circles, vocabulary enhancement can be quite naturally worked in. Harmon (1998) conducted a case study of vocabulary teaching and learning in a seventh-grade literature-based classroom. She reported rich examples of students choosing words from texts to discuss and employing a variety of tactics, including

- defining words they looked up before the literature circles met,
- asking group members for definitions and ideas,
- reading aloud from passages containing targeted words,
- modeling their behavior on their teacher's actions, such as using synonyms, constructing word meanings, asking for comments.

Harmon notes, "These reflections about new words were springboards for critical discussions about important new concepts and literary elements in the readings" (p. 522). Figure 6.10 shows a poster created by literature groups in a history class that read books about World War II and, among other things, kept a record of words from the books that they added to their vocabulary.

Modeling and Encouraging Voluminous Self-Selected Reading

Have I mentioned that I'm a proponent of wide reading? The importance of pleasure reading can't be overemphasized. Research shows that vocabulary knowledge is an important predictor of reading comprehension, and that from 25 to 50 percent of the estimated growth of students' vocabulary can be attributed to incidental learning from context while reading (Baumann & Kameenui, 1991; Nagy et al., 1987; Nagy, Herman, & Anderson, 1985). Cunningham and Stanovitch (1998) explain:

> If most vocabulary is acquired outside of formal teaching, then the only opportunities to acquire new words occur when an individual is exposed to a word in written or oral language that is outside his current vocabulary. . . . this will happen vastly more often while reading than while talking or watching television. (p. 10)

Their research demonstrated that "reading yields significant dividends for everyone—not just for the 'smart kids' or the more able readers. Even the child with limited reading and comprehension skills will build vocabulary and cognitive structures through reading" (p. 14).

Encourage your students to read independently. Share with them the benefits to their vocabulary and comprehension. Perhaps more important, model the

---

FIGURE   6.10   A literature group vocabulary project.

New and Interesting Words Our Literature Groups Found in Books About World War II

Number the Stars

Resistance, rationed, insolently, synagogue, exasperated, congregation, haughtily, implored, appliquéd, dubiously, protruding

Darkness Over Denmark: The Danish Resistance and the Rescue of the Jews

tribunal, covert, sabotage, cryptic, Torah, Aryan, martial law, haven

The Devil's Arithmetic

Seder, prophet, Yiddish, portents, cauldron, tremulous, discernible, rabbi

The Hiding Place

Gestapo, barracks, Gentile, imperceptibly, yearning, deportation, threadbare, interminable, recurrent

The Good Fight: How World War II Was Won

infamy, isolationists, relocation center, blitzkrieg, bunkers, pillboxes, authoritarian, ex post facto, embargo, kamikaze

I Have Lived a Thousand Years

intolerable, desperation, straggle, liquidated, infirmary, stamina, interrogation, internment, inexplicably, confiscate, pandemonium, deportation, liberate practice yourself and share information about what you are reading with them. Give regular booktalks, build a classroom library, provide time for reading, and listen to students as they talk about what they're reading and show that they are indeed reaching your goal of having them become more conscious of the language and concepts in your subject.

Developing Word Consciousness

You are given ways in this section to improve your own vocabulary, as well as those of the students in your content area classes. You'll become attuned to noticing the language in the texts you read (called developing *word consciousness*), and you'll find new ways to play with and have fun with words.

Scott and Nagy (2004) define word consciousness as "the knowledge and dispositions necessary for students to learn, appreciate, and effectively use words. Word consciousness involves several types of metalinguistic awareness, including sensitivity to word parts and word order" (p. 201). They believe that "teachers need to take word consciousness into account throughout each and every day" (p. 202). They give suggestions as to how to go about this, including

- talking about the language choices of good published writers,
- guiding student experimentation with language as they author texts, and
- teaching specific words.

SPECIFIC STRATEGIES FOR TEACHING VOCABULARY IN CONTENT AREA LESSONS

The previous section dealt with various ways you can help your students become language enthusiasts and independent word explorers. This section focuses on ways you can help your students learn the vocabulary necessary for particular lessons, curricular topics, and reading materials in your discipline. As usual, my categories are not entirely discrete; you'll find them overlapping.

Direct Teaching of Definitions

Although a great deal of vocabulary knowledge can be and is gained incidentally from context (e.g., Adams, 1990; Marzano, 2004; Schatz & Baldwin, 1986), research shows that "if you want a student to know what a particular word means, explaining it is unquestionably more effective than waiting for the student to encounter it numerous times in context" (Nagy & Scott, 2000, p. 277). There will be

many times when you'll point out to students that, in order to comprehend a certain reading, whether it be a textbook section, a primary document, a literary selection, or an article, they'll have to know the meaning of certain words, possibly vocabulary they have not previously encountered. Specialized and technical words, explained earlier, usually require direct instruction. Often you'll do this before students begin reading an assigned text. Similar to the preview strategy modeled in Chapter 4, the teacher can script an introduction calling attention to key terms. Or she can hand out a list of words and definitions the students can keep handy as they read.

Teaching in action: *History.* The following scenario illustrates what direct teaching of a vocabulary term for an American history lesson might sound like:

> For the next few weeks, we'll be reading and writing oral histories, so I want to begin by making sure you understand the term itself. I know you know what *history* is, since we've been studying it all year; and I assume you know what oral means in several contexts: you go to your dentist to take care of your oral health, and you've had oral exams and oral reports in this class and English class. Oral has to do with the mouth, or spoken word, so when I tell you the meaning of *oral history*, it should make sense to you. An oral history is compiled by collecting testimony from one or more persons who have lived through an experience. An interviewer asks questions, listens, and writes down or tapes the words she hears. Later, the data can be transcribed and organized in written form, so it's possible for us to read some oral histories.
>
> Reading oral histories is a great way to learn American history, because we're so aware that the words we're reading were voiced by an eyewitness, someone who felt what the event was like and whose life was impacted by the events. We're going to explore some oral histories in books and on the Internet regarding immigration, the Great Depression, the Vietnam War, and the Civil Rights movement. After we read several oral histories, you'll have a richer understanding of the term. But now, rather than my just continuing to talk about oral histories, I'm going to read you one. *Osceola, Memories of a Sharecropper's Daughter* (2000) contains the thoughts and words of an old woman recalling her childhood. The author, Alan Govenar, interviewed Osceola over a period of 15 years before he wrote this book. Let's begin this fascinating oral history. Oh, first, let's make sure we all know the meaning of the word *sharecropper* in the title. . . .

Figure 6.11 shows how a math teacher plans to provide and teach vocabulary in preparation for her students reading *The Phantom Tollbooth*.

FIGURE **6.11** A graphic organizer and word list for *The Phantom Tollbooth.*

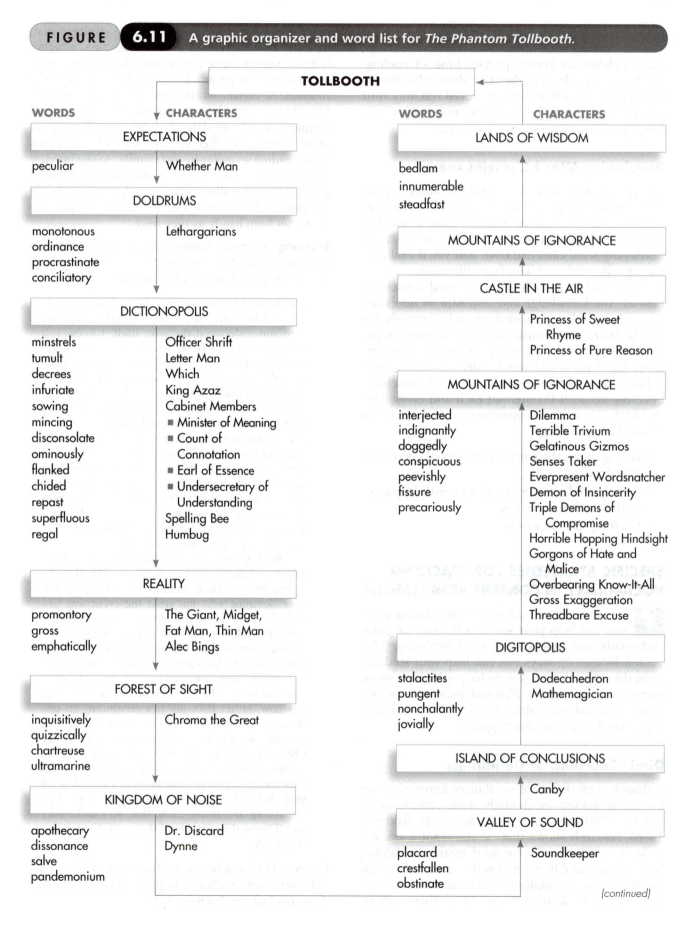

TOLLBOOTH

WORDS | **CHARACTERS**

EXPECTATIONS

peculiar | Whether Man

DOLDRUMS

monotonous | Lethargarians
ordinance
procrastinate
conciliatory

DICTIONOPOLIS

minstrels | Officer Shrift
tumult | Letter Man
decrees | Which
infuriate | King Azaz
sowing | Cabinet Members
mincing | ■ Minister of Meaning
disconsolate | ■ Count of
ominously | Connotation
flanked | ■ Earl of Essence
chided | ■ Undersecretary of
repast | Understanding
superfluous | Spelling Bee
regal | Humbug

REALITY

promontory | The Giant, Midget,
gross | Fat Man, Thin Man
emphatically | Alec Bings

FOREST OF SIGHT

inquisitively | Chroma the Great
quizzically
chartreuse
ultramarine

KINGDOM OF NOISE

apothecary | Dr. Discard
dissonance | Dynne
salve
pandemonium

WORDS | **CHARACTERS**

LANDS OF WISDOM

bedlam
innumerable
steadfast

MOUNTAINS OF IGNORANCE

CASTLE IN THE AIR

Princess of Sweet
   Rhyme
Princess of Pure Reason

MOUNTAINS OF IGNORANCE

interjected | Dilemma
indignantly | Terrible Trivium
doggedly | Gelatinous Gizmos
conspicuous | Senses Taker
peevishly | Everpresent Wordsnatcher
fissure | Demon of Insincerity
precariously | Triple Demons of
   | Compromise
   | Horrible Hopping Hindsight
   | Gorgons of Hate and
   | Malice
   | Overbearing Know-It-All
   | Gross Exaggeration
   | Threadbare Excuse

DIGITOPOLIS

stalactites | Dodecahedron
pungent | Mathemagician
nonchalantly
jovially

ISLAND OF CONCLUSIONS

Canby

VALLEY OF SOUND

placard | Soundkeeper
crestfallen
obstinate

(continued)

FIGURE 6.11 Continued.

Structured Overview (Graphic Organizer)

For *The Phantom Tollbooth* by Norton Juster

Included here are a structured overview on the entire book and a word list. The overview is to be presented before the students read the book. The word list will be handed out after the following discussion. The word list was put together to assist the students while they read.

When the structured overview is presented I will **ask the students to observe** the different areas that the main character travels to, the characters he encounters in each area, and the vocabulary that is present in each section of the book. I will then start with the vocabulary listed for Expectations on the overview. I will **ask for definitions** in the students' own words. If students do not come up with a definition for a certain term, I will try to give clues. If students are still puzzled about a certain term or terms, I will skip over them because the students will become familiar with all the meanings when they receive the accompanying guide. Then I will **ask if anyone can try to describe an area based upon the name of the area** and the characters listed for each area.

Some examples of questions that I can ask to stimulate background knowledge and increase the classes' interest and curiosity in reading the story:

What is the purpose of a tollbooth?

What is a Witch? What do you think a Which is? The two names sound the same; how do they differ in meaning? Describe what you believe the behavior and appearance of a Which would be.

Word List

For *The Phantom Tollbooth* by Norton Juster

peculiar (1) exclusively individual; distinctive. (2) odd; strange.

monotonous (1) continued in the same unvarying tone. (2) unvarying. (3) wearisome because of this.

ordinance (1) an established rule, rite, or law. (2) a statute or regulation, especially one of a local government.

procrastinate to put off to a future time; defer.

conciliate (1) to win or gain the affections of. (2) to reconcile.

minstrels (1) in medieval times, any one of a class of men who traveled about singing their compositions to the accompaniment of a harp or a lute. (2) a performer in a minstrel show (a variety show).

tumult (1) the noisy commotion of a number of people; uproar. (2) great confusion or disturbance of the mind or emotions.

decree (1) an ordinance, law, or edict. (2) a judicial decision: to determine, settle, command, or establish by decree; ordain: to make or publish a decree.

infuriate to enrage; madden.

sow (1) to scatter or plant in or on. (2) to instill as an idea, or disseminate, as propaganda.

mincing affectedly elegant.

disconsolate (1) sad; inconsolable. (2) cheerless.

ominous foreboding evil; inauspicious.

superfluous more than enough or necessary; excessive.

flank (1) a side of anything. (2) the right or left side of a formation, army, etc.: to be located at the side of.

chide to reprove, usually mildly.

repast a meal; food and drink.

regal of or pertaining to a king; royal.

promontory a headland; high peak jutting into the sea.

gross flagrant, bad, unrefined.

emphatic (1) uttered with emphasis. (2) forcible; significant.

Vocabulary Guides to Accompany Texts

If you identify the vocabulary that students will need or that you anticipate they may have trouble with, you can help them to prepare for their reading by completing a guide you create, or let them complete the guide as they progress through the text. Having your reading guide as a tool will in some way be like having you with them, even if they're reading outside class.

Teaching in action: *Social Studies.* Here's a scenario of what might go through a social studies teacher's head as she's planning a lesson based on the text *Into the Land of Freedom: African Americans in Reconstruction* by Meg Greene (2004):

> I think most of my students will be able to understand this story, but I'll need to teach a lesson (direct instruction) on Black dialect so they won't be confused when they come across sentences like, "I know whut de trouble," she explained. "Dey s'pose we all wants ter be free." (p. 7)

Also, there are key words that are essential for their comprehension. I want to find out, and I want my students to become aware of, their knowledge of crucial terms and concepts. I've looked through the first few chapters, and selected the following vocabulary to focus on: strife, abolition, "Day of Jubilee," "Emancipation Proclamation," reconstruct, citizenship, constitutional amendment, and sharecropper.

I think I'll use the "Knowledge Rating Strategy" (Blachowicz, 1986). I'll list the words and ask them to check off how well they know the word. Can they define the word? Use it? Have they at least seen it? Or is it totally new to them, so that they can't even guess what it means? That will be a starting point for our vocabulary discussion that will help make the reading go smoothly for them.

Figures 6.12 through 6.14 are examples of vocabulary guides created by preservice education students for discipline-specific texts. Find another guide online at the Kane Resource Site. Critique them and think of ways to modify them for the texts your students use.

FIGURE 6.12 A vocabulary guide for science.

Name _____   Date _____   Biology   Mitosis

Envision it. A sphere, and inside it lies a structure that looks like a small X. You notice that the X now duplicates itself to form a mirror image (XX). They move to the **middle** of the sphere and then each X moves **back** (X X) from the other. The sphere isn't large enough for the two of them, so it begins to split. Eventually, the cell pinches in two, and there is a **distance** between them now. You have just witnessed *mitosis*.

Not impressed? How about this? Mitosis is occurring thousands of times every minute in your body. In fact, by this time tomorrow, your body will have made more cells than there are hairs on your head. This process is what makes us grow, heals our wounds, and keeps us healthy.

Fortunately, such a complicated process as this can be broken down into five easy steps. It's easier to understand if you know what the names of the steps mean.

Before you read the section from your textbook on mitosis, I want you to consider these definitions.

WORD PART	DEFINITION
phase-	stage
inter-	between
pro-	before
meta-	change/middle
ana-	back
telo-	distant

You may have heard other words that contain these word parts. Jot down examples as you think of them. Now, reread the opening paragraph of this guide, and then read the textbook section on mitosis, noting especially the explanations for the words listed. Write the definitions, using the words in the text or your own words to explain the term.

Interphase: _____
_____
_____

Prophase: _____
_____
_____

Metaphase: _____
_____
_____

Anaphase: _____
_____
_____

Telophase: _____
_____
_____

—*Dan Mainville*

FIGURE **6.13** **A vocabulary guide for literature.**

On Monday, we will start reading *A Separate Peace* by John Knowles (1960). This reading guide is to help you understand words that you will encounter and may not be familiar with. This exercise offers you another way to learn and grasp new words. For Monday, fill out the rest of the columns for each word listed. I have given you an example to get you started.

I will collect the guides to see how well they work for you, and then you will enter this into your learning log. Have fun!

Helpful Hint: It is okay to talk with parents or friends for ideas. It is actually encouraged and will most likely heighten your understanding of the new vocabulary.

NEW VOCABULARY	WHAT IS IT?	WHAT IS IT LIKE?	WHAT ARE EXAMPLES?	WHAT OTHER CONCEPTS FIT IN THIS CATEGORY?
contemplate	*Verb: to view or consider with continued attention*	*talking to yourself, in your head, about something*	*staring into your closet, trying to decide what to wear*	*thinking, rationalizing, figuring out*
interval				
convalescence				
prodigious				
reverberant				
inanimate				
primitive				

—*Donna Johnson*

FIGURE 6.14 Reading guide for lessons in math, English, or health/wellness using *An Abundance of Katherines.*

BEFORE READING

Having a relationship can be really tough, especially for high school students. There are the stresses of knowing whether or not a relationship will last, doubts of feelings, and of course the heartbreaking effect of being "dumped." In *An Abundance of Katherines* (2006), by John Green, we are invited into the life of Colin Singleton, a recent high school graduate who sets off on a road trip with his best friend to "find his missing piece."

Step 1: Look up each of the following words in an online dictionary; knowing these terms will help you with your reading of the novel:

prodigy _____

_____

genius _____

_____

anagram _____

_____

theorum _____

_____

Step 2: You will soon find out the history of who Colin Singleton is, and why he is passionate in his quest to find a mathematical formula that can predict the result of any relationship. Answer the following questions to arouse your intellectual curiosity:

- Do you think it's possible to develop a mathematical equation that could tell you how long a relationship will last, who will break up with whom, and if the relationship will be worth it? Why, or why not?

_____

_____

_____

- Consider the possibility that you are trying to develop such an equation. What types of variables would you want to include (e.g., age, personality type, popularity, etc.)? Try to list at least 4 things.

_____

_____

_____

Now you will read *An Abundance of Katherines,* and experience the wonders of a prodigious mind.

AFTER READING

Now that you've read the story, complete the following:

1. Write down your full name, and come up with as many anagrams as you can that make grammatical sense.
2. What did you learn from this story about history? science? math? English?
3. We learned that Colin is extremely passionate about learning and wanting to be "known" for something. What is something that you are passionate about, and how could you become "known" through it?

—Ashley Wheeler

ACTION RESEARCH   6.B

The vocabulary guide below, based on the "Knowledge Rating Strategy" (Blachowicz, 1986), is accompanied by a newspaper article middle school math students may find interesting. Complete the chart, then answer the questions based on your reading. Think about whether students could be helped by having this vocabulary strategy accompany their reading of the text.

Directions: The chart lists several words that you'll encounter in the article "Student Shows Big Interest in Math." For each word, check the column that indicates your level of knowledge about it.

Word	I can define	I can use	I've seen it	Clueless
nought	○	○	○	○
centrillion	○	○	○	○
mere	○	○	○	○
googol	○	○	○	○
centrillionth	○	○	○	○
Timillion	○	○	○	○
cryptography	○	○	○	○
googolplex	○	○	○	○

As you read the article, see how many of the unfamiliar words you can determine the meaning of. Which ones are defined in the text? Which can you figure out by using the context? Do you need to know every word in order to comprehend the passage? Write down a brief definition or synonym for the listed words. There's at least one word you may have to look up in the dictionary or ask someone the meaning of. Can you think of other words named after their discoverers or inventors?

STUDENT SHOWS BIG INTEREST IN MATH

By Larry Richardson

CAZENOVIA—Tim Gioncchetti's effort was all for nought. Nearly 92,000 noughts, in fact.

Inspired by a discussion of large numbers in his seventh-grade math class, Tim spent a month printing and taping together a number that's 735 feet long.

That's longer than the Washington Monument (555 feet) is tall. It's longer than 2 1/3 football fields (at 100 yards apiece). And it's nearly as long as Tim's favorite ill-fated ocean liner, the Titanic (882 feet).

His number, which doesn't have a name, is a 1 followed by 91,809 zeroes. The largest named number, according to one dictionary, is a centrillion, which has a mere 303 zeroes.

Tim recently showed up in math class with his number wrapped around a spool. Barry Parker, his math teacher at Cazenovia Middle School, said the project started innocently enough.

"We were discussing large numbers, and we were talking about a googol, which is a one followed by 100 zeroes," Parker said. "I stated it would be impossible to write a googol to the googol power, or a centrillion to the centrillionth power.

"Tim took that as a challenge to create a huge number, larger than he had ever seen before or that we had ever talked about."

Tim said he took a centrillion and raised it to the 303rd power. Then he calculated that he needed to print 26 pages—with 54 rows of zeroes on each page—on his home computer to tape the number together. He cut each horizontal row of zeroes into separate strips and attached them with cellophane tape—six rolls of it.

He said he spent up to an hour a day for a month cutting out the zeroes and taping them together.

Tim said he will call his number a Timillion until someone gives the number an official name.

"That could take a long time," said Andrew Odlyzko, who heads the mathematics and cryptography research department at AT&T Labs in Slorham Park, NJ. "There is no official organization in charge of naming numbers," he said.

"While the dictionary stops at a centrillion, some huge numbers have been named," said Odlyzko. "A googolplex, for example, is a one followed by googol zeroes," Odlyzko said.

"That is a lot larger than your chap's number," he said.

Odlyzko said Tim's project is good for someone that age to do. "It's nice to encourage people to play around with numbers," he said.

Parker displayed the spool holding the Timillion in his classroom.

"We will take Tim's word for it that there are 91,809 zeroes," he said. "We didn't count them."

The Herald Co., Syracuse, NY © 1998/1999 *Herald-Journal/The Post-Standard*. All rights reserved. Reprinted with permission

This reading exercise serves several purposes. It can help students acquire technical vocabulary and concepts in the field of math. It provides practice reading the newspaper genre. It can help students gain confidence in the strategies they can use to figure out new words in math and other areas, and it may serve as motivation to spark their own mathematical reasoning and curiosity. You might connect it to the search that is currently being conducted by mathematicians to identify the largest prime number. You could give booktalks for *How Much Is a Million?* by D. Schwartz (1985) and *Anno's Mysterious Multiplying Jar* by M. Anno (1983a). You could ask a couple of actual math questions based on the text.

Word Walls

No matter what your subject area, have your students post new words they acquire in visible places around the classroom—alone or with definitions, examples, or sample sentences. They can be in list form, in semantic webs, or arranged in categories; they can be accompanied by pictures or placed within student artwork. The words can be selected by the students from their textbooks, or they can represent new words found in outside reading. The word walls serve to reinforce terms and concepts you have taught, as well as introductions to new words. Students may use them in their writing, to ask questions, to share proudly with others their knowledge and discoveries of new words, to discuss relations between words or shades of meanings. Word walls don't have to use any of your precious teaching time; they are simply there adorning your walls and adding interest to the surroundings.

Harmon et al. (2009) promote the use of interactive word walls (ones involving the active engagement of students; for example, they add words in which they are interested) in middle and high school content classrooms to enhance vocabulary learning. Through interviewing students, they found that students considered word walls to be important classroom tools and actively used them to complete assignments, study, remember, and write. The authors designed instruction that directed students to create associations for new words through the use of symbols and color, and modeled how to apply words to real situa-tions. They allowed students to choose words to put on the word wall for the class to explore. They found that students valued the active engagement, working collaboratively, and playing the role of the teacher while presenting words. Students using word walls showed better achievement than a control group.

Allen (2007) also advocates using word walls in secondary content classrooms, where students encounter so many academic and specialized terms, though she cautions that when she put the words on the wall randomly, her struggling readers and English learners found it too chaotic and overwhelming to be helpful. She advises, "Words need to be organized alphabetically or topically for most students to access them when needed" (p. 96).

Figures 6.15, 6.16, and 6.17 illustrate various types of word walls. The possible variations for you and your students, however, are endless!

Vocabulary Notebooks

Marzano (2004) advocates the use of vocabulary notebooks in content classes. He offers the following guidelines for incorporating the notebooks in middle schools:

- Set a time each day when all students, teachers, and administrators read from a self-selected book.
- Have students identify words that interest them from their reading and ask them to attempt to determine their meanings from the context.

FIGURE 6.15 Example word wall: words we found that connect to the concept of thinking.

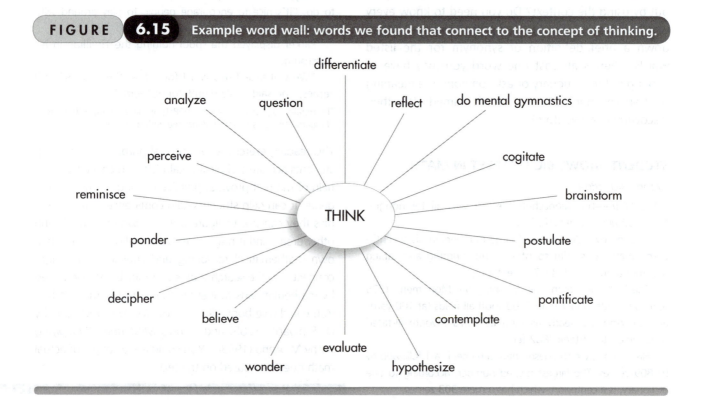

FIGURE 6.16

Example word wall: Math words we know and love.

dodecahedron
game theory
exponential
parabola
fractal
calculus
geometric
histogram
coefficient
complementary

triskaidekaphobia
topology
googol
tangram
pi
factorial
quadratic
symmetry
Fibonacci
polynomial

FIGURE 6.17

Example word wall: Ms. Morley's morpheme magicians.

MORPHEMES

A *morpheme* is the smallest meaningful linguistic unit. We've found these words that combine morphemes. Can you figure out their meanings?

pseudoscience
postmodern
prenatal
neoclassic
hydroelectric
megabyte
postnasal
socioeconomic
subterranean
chronology
antiestablishment
parisitophobia

- Have them record the words and their speculations about the meanings in a dedicated vocabulary notebook.
- On occasion, have students share their vocabulary words with each other.
- Provide time for students to verify the guesses about their words' meanings by checking a dictionary.

The students in Marzano's exemplar are not passive recipients of this knowledge. They put their speculations about the word meanings into their own words and talk with each other about their self-selected vocabulary. Students can also be encouraged to include visual representations and applications of their words in their vocabulary notebooks.

APPLICATION ACTIVITY 6.3 (SEE PAGE 187)

Use of Analogies

Creating analogies and constructing images can be effective tools to forge lasting links between words and

their meanings. Do you recognize when you, your students, people you talk with, or authors utilize analogy, connecting ideas and images by way of comparison?

You're familiar with the first sentence of Lincoln's Gettysburg Address: "Fourscore and seven years ago, our forefathers brought forth, upon this continent, a new nation, conceived in liberty, and dedicated to the proposition that all men are created equal." Try saying it out loud, really listening to the sounds and cadence of the sentence. Here's how Thompson (1996a) describes what he hears:

> Lincoln was using the music of the voice to enhance and support his meaning, and only by hearing the music can we understand the grammar. For the first 14 words, Lincoln is playing the bass notes, the *os* and the *us* enriched by the *rs*. Hear the sounds: *four score, year, ago, our, forefather, brought, forth, upon, continent.* Lincoln is playing an oboe or a bassoon. And then suddenly, rising above the low tones, we have sounds, alliterated with *ns*, that are higher and lighter—a flute: *new, nation.* And all of this leads to the finale: the most important word, uttered last so that it echoes in the silence at the end of the sentence: *equal.* Equal. (p. 166)

Thompson goes on to interpret the language of the speech in terms of assonance, consonance, and alliteration, but he began with a comparison, utilizing an analogy to music made by instruments that helps readers understand what he means by those words.

Sometimes, we can begin to comprehend a new concept by comparing it to something we already know. When we use relationships, and point out how an unfamiliar concept is like and unlike a familiar one, we can help students learn and remember new information and terms. We can also listen carefully for the images our students create naturally and encourage them to strive consciously to create metaphors that help them understand and remember concepts. For example, Whitin and Whitin (1996), after teaching the concept of geometric progressions in an intermediate grade math class and having students experiment with some on their calculators, asked, "What do these numbers remind you of? What pictures do you have in your mind as you see numbers like these getting larger and larger?" (p. 62). One

child, Andrew, wrote, "It reminds me of an avalanche because the numbers are snow fall[ing] down a mountain" (p. 62). Other children went on to interpret the meaning of his analogy. Danielle said, "An avalanche starts off . . . it pours down. The avalanche starts kind of small, and then starts getting bigger and bigger and bigger" (p. 63). Language play helped the students comprehend a mathematical concept.

Use of Visuals

A similar instructional strategy involving verbal–visual associations has been used successfully by high school teacher Gary Hopkins (Hopkins & Bean, 1998/1999) in the Native American community where he teaches. The steps are as follows:

1. The student draws a "Vocabulary Square," divided into four boxes.
2. In the upper-left, the student writes a content term or a root, prefix, or suffix.
3. Next to it the student writes the definition.
4. In the third box, the student puts an example of the concept.
5. In the final box, the student draws a picture of the example.

Students showed engagement with this type of word study, which led to lively class discussions, use of independent problem-solving skills, and good performance on tests (see Figure 6.18).

FIGURE   6.18   Vocabulary square for science.

WORD:	DEFINITION:
marsupial	*a mammal whose young stay in a pouch on their mother's body for months after birth*
EXAMPLES:	ILLUSTRATION:
opossum	
kangaroo	

FIGURE 6.19

Samples of visual dictionaries available for content area learning.

See more suggested titles in Appendix Figure 6.19.

Arabic-English Visual Bilingual Dictionary. (2009). London: Dorling Kindersley.

Balka, D. S., Bana, J., Hoover, C. M., et al. (2007). *Visual Math Dictionary.* Rowly, MA: Didax Educational Resources.

Chinese-English Bilingual Visual Dictionary. (2008). London: Dorling Kindersley.

Kalman, B. (2008). *A Visual Dictionary of a Colonial Community.* New York: Crabtree Publishing.

Wilgan, M. (2009). *The Visual Dictionary of Illustration.* Lausanne, Switzerland: AVA Publishing.

Pictures and illustrated texts can be most helpful to students learning new terms. Labeled pictures and diagrams make concepts clearer and help students retain the information. Many illustrated informational books are full of vocabulary. Figure 6.19 lists some *visual dictionaries* and related material. As with alphabet books, you and your students can use these as models and create visual dictionaries for your own classroom library. We'll explore visual literacy and visual texts more thoroughly in Chapter 9.

Semantic Feature Analysis

Semantic feature analysis, developed by Johnson (Johnson & Pearson, 1984), can be used to clarify and enrich the meanings of known words, as well as to pre-teach words that are important to the comprehension of an assigned reading. It uses a grid that relates words in a category based on identifying characteristics; it invites comparison and contrast.

Following is an outline of steps for creating a semantic feature analysis (Nagy, 1998):

1. Select words that form a semantically close group. At least some of the distinctions should be immediately understandable to students.

2. On a chart, use the selected words as labels for the horizontal rows.

3. For the column heads, decide on a number of words or phrases describing components of meaning shared by some of the words or phrases that distinguish some words from others.

4. One square will represent the intersection of a given word and a semantic feature. Ask students if the feature is shared by each given word. Discuss why or why not.

5. Record in the square whether or not, or to what extent, the feature applies to the word.

Figure 6.20 shows a student's semantic feature analysis strategy used during a chapter on the Middle Ages.

Vocabulary Think-Alouds

Recall the discussion of think-alouds in Chapter 5, a strategy that can help students verbalize the mental strategies they use as they read. Think-alouds can be helpful in terms of understanding and improving the strategies that students use as they tackle unfamiliar words in their reading. The use of vocabulary think-alouds has multiple benefits.

FIGURE 6.20 **Example of semantic feature analysis for social studies.**

Category: Males in the Feudal System

	OWN LAND	WORK LAND	DEFEND LAND	ARE LIKE SLAVES
King	+	−	−	−
Lords	+	−	+	−
Lesser Lords	+	−	+	−
Knights	+	−	+	−
Serfs	−	+	+	+

—Matt Wieczorek

Listening to the students helps you to know which strategies they use, how well the strategies are working for them, and what instruction or further guidance you can provide. They also help students reflect on their thinking, bringing their processes to a conscious level that makes them more aware of their skills, their problem areas, their active participation in bringing meaning to text. This, in turn, may make them more likely to employ the strategies you've taught them, including using structural clues, context, and reference materials, as they continue to read materials that are assigned or that they pursue independently.

School and Community-Wide Vocabulary Focus

The growth of vocabulary is a noble goal for individuals and groups. Most people, as you learned from Question 1 in the APK 6.1 exercise, would like their vocabularies to be larger than they are presently. Some schools have made this goal a focus for the school year or at least some part of it.

Teaching in action: *Interdisciplinary.* Several sixth-grade students I teach in a weekly religion class told me of the "Vocabulary Celebration Week" their middle school was promoting. Every teacher had thought of some way to bring words and language to the fore. Students all carried new words in their pockets throughout each day. They could be stopped in the hall by upperclassmen and teachers who were part of the "Vocabulary Patrol," ready to reward with small prizes those students who could pull out a word from their pockets and give its definition. There were word walls and posters in stairwells, there were challenges from the principal over the loudspeaker each morning, teachers made banners proclaiming great new words. The students were excited, and when I questioned them several months later about the words they had learned, their recall proved strong. Although extrinsic rewards and designated "weeks" or "celebrations" like this one are certainly not the entire answer to enhancing the student body's collective vocabulary, they can raise the students' consciousness about words and language and may help them see their elders learning as well. As one of many ways to encourage language growth, school-wide efforts can be fun and productive. As an individual teacher, you can continue the celebration throughout the year.

"Read a Million Minutes" is a month-long program that has fostered and encouraged wide reading in several states for two decades. Students set individual goals and read independently from a variety of genres, sometimes connected to a theme, to contribute toward the statewide goal of reading a total of 60 million minutes. Special community activities add to the enthusiasm, and teachers report an increased interest in reading among students. Johnson (2001) connects this to vocabulary development. "Imagine the number of new words learned by the students of a state who read a combined total of sixty million minutes in a month" (p. 42).

APPLICATION ACTIVITY 6.4 (SEE PAGE 187)

Adapting Strategies for Striving Readers and Students with Reading Disabilities

Strategies for figuring out new words and building vocabulary do not work equally well for all students. And the adaptations you make for the readers who struggle in your classes will depend on individuals' strengths and specific disabilities. I'll give several examples of different strategies to use. A study conducted by Keehn, Harmon, and Shoho (2008) showed that eighth graders who were reading below grade level increased vocabulary acquisition after participating in readers theatre during a six-week short story unit. The researcher and teachers had selected words to introduce, teach, and use in readers theatre scripts; students thus received multiple exposures to targeted vocabulary as they read their scripts over and over.

Harmon et al. (2008) found that having eighth-grade students self-select vocabulary to learn during a unit on the Holocaust met the needs of struggling readers particularly well; they were able to target some of the crucial words for understanding expository texts. The authors explain the benefits of the approach. "The actual process of selecting, thinking about, and evaluating the importance of a word used in a passage requires students to think metacognitively as they make their word selections" (p. 51).

Ebbers and Denton (2008) recommend using a variety of research-based instructional strategies with older struggling readers, who often tend to avoid reading and frequently have trouble inferring meanings of words from context. These include the direct teaching of suffixes, roots, and prefixes, as well as the promotion of word consciousness in a learning environment that encourages active engagement with and discussion about words. They suggest explicit teaching of academic words that students will encounter across the curriculum and words necessary for understanding particular texts. They stress the importance of giving students a rationale for learning vocabulary and demonstrating its potential benefits. The authors advocate for a school-wide, cross-content, collaborative approach in order to help students "habitualize the use of effective strategies for learning and remembering words" (p. 100).

So, be ready to teach your students with reading disabilities a repertoire of vocabulary strategies that fit their particular strengths and needs. Don't overwhelm them with too many new words at a time, and give encouragement, opportunities for practice, and instructional support.

LANGUAGE ISSUES RELATING TO ENGLISH LEARNERS

You've learned that all of your students require varying degrees and types of help from you as they learn the general, special, and technical vocabulary that allows them to progress in their understanding of and exploration in the subject you teach. In Chapter 4, you were asked to think about how issues relating to prior knowledge might affect how your students with limited English proficiency would learn, and how scaffolding your instruction would be different as you helped them acquire the background knowledge the English speakers would likely already have. Now, I'd like you to think about vocabulary and grammar in relation to those students who are learning English. At first, it might seem that they (and you) are faced with an insurmountable task. How can you teach them all of the English words the other students have acquired over 12 or 16 years? And if they don't speak English fluently, how will you ever get them to comprehend the sophisticated concepts and specialized vocabulary of your curriculum? How will they be able to read the textbook, and write reports and journals and test answers?

Teaching in action: *English.* To begin to answer these questions, let's listen in as co-teachers Jennifer and Jill facilitate students' use of multiple strategies to grapple with a word while reading Ray Bradbury's *Fahrenheit 451:*

> "One place that I really struggled today was when I got to the word *mausoleum,*" shares an ELL student, Allyson. . . .
>
> I [Jennifer] ask, "Who would like to share what their group thought it meant? Right now don't worry if you are right or wrong, just share what you discussed and your thinking behind your answer." . . .
>
> "We thought it was like a museum because *mausoleum* kind of sounds like *museum* and we were visualizing a big marble room like in a museum we've visited," Katie, an ELL student, says. One reason Jill and I explicitly teach visualization as a metacognitive strategy is that we have found it

especially beneficial for many ELL students, since it scaffolds other strategy usages.

> "Great job!" praises Jill. "It was smart thinking to picture the word based on other descriptions Ray Bradbury shares with us. You also visualized and connected your schema to the word to help you figure out what you thought it meant. Who else would like to share?"
>
> Another student adds, "Antonio and I thought of a place where people died because we saw the word *tomb* later in the paragraph. But we still don't know—is it like a cemetery or a hospital?"
>
> "I think a cemetery because it makes more sense," Larry replies.
>
> "Tell us more—what do you mean 'it makes more sense'?" I probe.
>
> "Well, the next part of the story is about how Montag's wife has overdosed on sleeping pills . . . it sounds more like she is in a place full of death. I think Ray Bradbury says she is in the bedroom later, and that made me think it just sounded like a cemetery with this dead body in it." (Swinehart, 2009, pp. 28–29)

Here's another scenario provided by Scott, Nagy, and Flinspach (2008), who recommend keeping in mind the importance of identity and the social nature of learning academic language as well as the cognitive and metalinguistic skills needed:

> Huron, a sixth grader, takes out his writing assignment. As he begins to write a narrative about his cousin arriving from Mexico, he pulls out his word catcher booklet, where he has stored words and phrases that help him express his ideas. When he finishes his first draft, he goes with a friend to a "shades of meaning" tree on a bulletin board to look for more powerful language for their stories. Together they find the word monstrous on a leaf with other words for BIG and they find gloomy for SAD. They discuss whether or not these words would fit into the narrative and whether monstrous is related to el monstruo in Spanish. When he completes his narrative, Huron reads it aloud to the class, and his classmates ask questions about both his cousin and his writing. (p. 198)

The authors explain why and how a blended approach to teaching academic language, exemplified in the scenario, is so helpful to an English learner:

> Huron sees himself as a writer . . . he has confidence that other classmates will help him prepare his piece and will want to hear what he has to say. The assignment has personal meaning for him. . . . He is word conscious and understands that word choice is a tool to communicate ideas. (p. 199)

They further emphasize, "Knowledge about academic vocabulary is likely to remain inert unless a student adopts a literate identity in which academic vocabulary is an essential aspect of the community of practice in the classroom" (p. 200).

Since it is impossible to teach all the words of a language, it's extremely important to select words with high utility, those that are used often. A *New Academic Word List* (Coxhead, 2000) was developed for the English language, which is helpful for teachers responsible for the literacy of English learners. Cobb and Horst (2004) ask whether similar lists could be identified for other languages, pointing out that the 2,000 most frequently used word families in French serve academic and everyday purposes very well. They recommend combining naturalistic learning with using resources and technologies that can enhance vocabulary.

Jesness (2004) suggests focusing on key prefixes and suffixes and teaching English learners to apply them to root words as a way of rapidly increasing the number of words and concepts known. He also advocates using multiple modes of instruction for what he calls layered vocabulary learning:

> It is important to remember that we do not learn all of the aspects, definitions, and nuances of a word at once. From the sentence, "There was a lovely gardenia in the bouquet that Johnny gave to his mother," one can conclude that a gardenia is a flower. When learners see a picture of a gardenia, their knowledge of that flower increases. If they see, touch, and smell a real gardenia, that knowledge increases again. If they study the life cycle of the gardenia in biology class, they will know even more. (p. 36)

As I've said before, you are not alone as you face this task, and no one expects you to be the expert on ESL issues. Don't be hesitant to ask for assistance from your district's ESL teachers and literacy coaches. The more you can specify your needs and those of your students, the better they can provide support and resources. Get to know your students, help them feel comfortable, find out what they know in terms of English and in terms of your subject area. They may come with a lot of content knowledge in their native language, even more than your English-speaking students. Depending on their first language, there might be words that are similar to the English words you'll be using as you teach. So, keep in mind that a deficit model must be avoided. English learners do not have a *problem*, or something *wrong* with them, just different needs because of their unique circumstances. Help them to rejoice in the wonderful words they bring with them, even as you teach them wonderful new words in English. Learn some of *their* words, and have some content materials and recreational reading materials in the students' first language. The Internet can supply you with many texts in virtually any language. Check out the International Children's Digital Library at www.childrens library.org. It's appropriate to have reference books such as *NTC's American English Learner's Dictionary: The Essential Vocabulary of American Language and Culture* (Spears, 1998) and *The Concise Oxford Dictionary of English Etymology* (Hoad, 2003), and to teach the students how to use them along with other reference books in the library. Students learning English recognize and say that vocabulary is an issue for them. Gunderson (2000) found, "A large majority of students suggested that their learning of academic content in English would have been improved if they were allowed to consult their bilingual dictionaries or bilingual classmates who could explain difficult vocabulary" (p. 702). As one 16-year-old boy plainly put it, "We know hard words, chemistry and physics words, in Polish, but not English" (p. 702). So, do whatever makes sense to bring the two languages together as English learners grapple with concepts and content in your classes.

In addition, have books at hand, such as some of the alphabet books discussed earlier, that celebrate the beauty of language and will intrigue all students to learn at least a bit about a variety of languages. Encourage students to share words from various languages with each other. Convey the message and attitude that bilingualism is an asset; we do not want students who are learning English to lose their first language—developing and growing in both can go hand in hand.

BookTalk 6.8

I can't think of a better description of Dorling Kindersley's *One Million Things: A Visual Encyclopedia* (Chrisp, 2008) than the one on the back cover: "It's like a museum, a search engine, and the world's biggest garage sale rolled into one." The photographs are stunning, and sometimes enlarged, such as the one on a double page spread (pp. 26–27) showing an insect that has been magnified to about a foot and a half so that details of its anatomy (antennae, thorax, abdomen, eyes, wings, etc.) can be seen clearly. Subjects are organized into categories, including People and Places, Art and Culture, Science and Technology, Nature, and Space. Facts abound, as do vocabulary terms, but readers can study the clear photos as they read information using the specialized and technical terms in a context that explains them. Students might ask you, "Are there really one million things depicted in this book?" and you can help them apply the estimating strategies they've learned in math class to answer their own question.

You may easily add books such as *Cool Salsa: Bilingual Poems About Growing Up Latino in the United States* (Carlson, 1995) to your classroom library. A series of visual bilingual dictionaries published by Milet includes English–Chinese, English–Vietnamese, English–Arabic, English–Turkish, and English–Spanish. *The Oxford Picture Dictionary* can be very helpful. Have the audio versions of some of your texts available, too, so that students can look at the print as they listen to the English. Your students might be eager to contribute books or ideas to further enhance your selection of texts in languages other than English. There are electronic dictionaries and talking dictionaries that can benefit students who are learning content and learning the language simultaneously. Encourage them to use any and all materials that will enhance their vocabulary and grammar.

Reid (2002) explains the advantages of using children's and young adult literature with English learners in math, science, and social studies classes. She recommends picture books, and especially picture dictionaries, for students at a basic level. She advocates the use of popular historical fiction series books, such as Scholastic's *Dear America, My Name Is America,* and *Royal Diaries* series, because

> When students become involved in reading a series of similar books, they absorb the language patterns and the conventions of plot, character, and sequence of the genre, and improve their reading fluency. Often series become popular with a group of readers, inspiring discussion about the characters and events; collecting and reading the books in the series becomes a socializing force as well as a way of learning about history. The language in these series often represents a modern version of the historical dialect. (p. 63)

Helman (2008) lists key ideas found in research studies analyzing successful vocabulary interventions with English learners:

- Presenting words in meaningful contexts, such as interesting texts.
- Planning lessons that motivate students and encourage participation.
- Conducting in-depth interventions that take place over time with repetition and review.
- Including discourse around text in lessons.
- Building students' background language vocabulary study.
- Teaching students to apply strategies for word learning, such as morphemic analysis.
- Including scaffolding in lessons, such as with simplified syntax, visual materials, or oral language practice activities. (p. 215)

Keep several things in mind as you teach vocabulary to students with diverse language backgrounds. Because most textbooks are written for native speakers of English, they may use figures of speech, idioms, and words with multiple meanings that can cause ESL students difficulty. As you plan your lessons, read the text with the purpose of spotting some of the things you think may require explanation or clarification. Also, encourage the students to tell you when a term confuses them—and then teach it gladly.

As much as possible, teach concept development before vocabulary. If students experience a concept through a demonstration, hands-on experiments, simulation, role-playing, games, or the use of visuals, if they first acquire an understanding of a principle or idea, it's easier to learn the word for it. For example, a science teacher can demonstrate the concept of *condensation* before or while teaching the term. Aim for knowledge and understanding of vocabulary rather than just memorization. Many of the activities described previously, such as the use of graphic organizers and semantic feature analysis, work well with ESL students. You'll note that many of the teaching strategies mentioned are examples of good teaching in general, benefiting all learners. So, choose meaningful activities that foster language growth and conceptual development simultaneously.

Of course, these students' vocabulary and knowledge of and ability to use grammatical structures of English are enhanced as they learn in authentic contexts with a lot of social interaction with their peers. A language-rich environment helps them flourish. But keep in mind that, although it only takes a couple of years for English learners to reach a level of proficiency in terms of conversational skills, it takes several years for many ESL students to reach a level of academic proficiency in English comparable to their native English-speaking classmates (Cummins, 1994). Teachers in content areas must be patient and persistent, and schools must make a long-term commitment to ensuring the academic progress of diverse learners. Vocabulary development is one aspect of this progress, and middle and high school teachers will do well to internalize these words of Cummins:

> The teaching of English as a second language should be integrated with the teaching of other academic content that is appropriate to students' cognitive level. By the same token, all content teachers must recognize themselves also as teachers of language. (1994, p. 56)

Figure 6.21 summarizes recommendations for teaching vocabulary to English learners.

As you find ways to help your English learners to be successful and to grow in both language pro-

FIGURE 6.21   Recommendations for teaching vocabulary to English learners.

- Get to know your students and help them feel comfortable.
- Find out what they know about English and your content area.
- Avoid thinking of them as having a problem.
- Learn some of their words.
- Have some content and recreational reading materials in the students' first language.
- Provide bilingual dictionaries.
- Allow them to consult with other bilingual classmates.

- Make available alphabet and other books that celebrate language.
- Convey the message and attitude that bilingualism is an asset.
- Read the textbook looking for figures of speech, idioms, and words with multiple meanings that can cause problems.
- When possible, teach concept development through hands-on activities before vocabulary.
- Provide authentic contexts for vocabulary use and a lot of social interaction with peers.

---

ficiency and disciplinary knowledge, I hope you'll also find ways to share your ideas with other teachers and contribute to the field of education. Gunderson (2008) decries the fact that we have known for more than 40 years that English learners are at great risk for failure in our present school systems, and that so little progress has been made to reverse this "national disgrace" (p. 187). He uses an analogy to challenge us:

> President Kennedy established the goal that the United States would visit the moon by the end of the 1960s, and it happened. It seems that the same awesome determination and purpose could be focused on discovering how science, math, social studies, and English teachers can teach successfully in classrooms that include increasing numbers of ESL students. And, after all, isn't this the explicit promise of inclusive education? Surely this cannot be more complex and difficult than putting a man on the moon! Can it be more difficult than rocket science? (p. 187)

CONCLUSION

Blachowicz and Fisher (2000) summarize the main principles that research suggests should guide vocabulary instruction as follows:

1. Students should be active in developing their understanding of words and ways to learn them.
2. Students should personalize word learning.
3. Students should be immersed in words.
4. Students should build on multiple sources of information to learn words through repeated exposure. (p. 504)

The ideas and suggestions in this chapter are consistent with these principles. After reading this chapter, you should have many vocabulary and language issues to think about. We talked about various types of vocabulary that enable your students to learn, read, and flourish in your content subjects. You've been given language issues to ponder and reflect on as you pursue your own studies and prepare to teach. I've provided examples of specific strategies that you can use to enhance your students' vocabulary and teach terms and concepts, and you now know of many resources that will help your classes explore language in general and within your field of study. You've had opportunities to apply instructional strategies to lessons and texts that contain crucial vocabulary or involve issues relating to language. The final section expanded your understanding of how you can help students with limited English proficiency, being a good teacher of language and content simultaneously.

I'm sure you realize now what an enormous and important part vocabulary will play in your students' learning. And there is no one best way to build the content-specific vocabulary your students must have to thrive in your courses. At times, you might employ direct instruction, connecting new words through examples, nonexamples, and definitions to concepts or other words already known; you'll respond to students' questions and needs, provide structure through vocabulary guides, and also encourage independent language play and exploration. Your methods will vary based on particular texts, classes, situations, individuals. Model inquisitiveness and provide opportunities for social interaction and collaboration focusing on language issues within your subject area. Show students how to be metacognitive as they employ strategies to learn technical vocabulary and figure out new words based on structure or context. Be a language lover yourself.

WEBSITES — CHAPTER 6 — Access these links using the Kane Resource Site.

A.Word.A.Day
http://wordsmith.org/awad/index.html

Charles Herrington Elster
members2.authorsguild.net/chelster

David M. Schwartz
www.davidschwartz.com

Edith Hope Fine
www.edithfine.com

Fritjof Capra
www.fritjofcapra.net

Graeme Base
www.graemebase.com

Immigration Vocabulary
http://memory.loc.gov/learn//features/immig/
vocabulary.html

International Children's Digital Library
www.childrenslibrary.org

Merriam-Webster Online Dictionary
www.m-w.com

Oxford University Press blog (OUPblog)
http://blog.oup.com/2009/11/unfriend

Read Write Think
ReadWriteThink.org/classroom-resources/
lesson-plans/

Spanish Language Games
www.donquijote.org/spanishlanguage/games

Spanish Vocabulary Games
www.gamequarium.com/spanishvocab.html

The Word Detective
www.word-detective.com

Vocabulary University
www.vocabulary.com

ZDaily.com Daily Vocabulary Quiz
www.zdaily.com/word.shtml

APPLICATION ACTIVITIES

6.1 Cartoons and comics have wonderful vocabulary representative of all three vocabulary categories that connects to content areas. My folder labeled "Vocabulary in Comics" holds many examples from "Peanuts," "Dilbert," "Calvin and Hobbes," and so forth. Begin your own file of cartoons that involve general, special, or technical vocabulary words for your subject area, as well as other areas. Your colleagues will thank you as you pass appropriate cartoons to them, and you'll show your students you can go beyond the boundaries of your subject. You can share these comics using a bulletin board, to which students can add any time they find an appropriate comic fitting the category.

6.2 Using the student-made examples in Figures 6.7 and 6.8, or any of the books from the bibliography of alphabet books, create an alphabet book that teaches or reinforces terms related to a topic in your subject area. You can illustrate it if you wish. Be sure to begin a file of alphabet books, so that as you and your students compose others, you'll have an organizational plan. Think of the wonderful display you can make when you have multiple teacher- and student-made alphabet books.

6.3 Our students, like the book characters mentioned earlier, can be taught and encouraged to pay attention to the words they hear and find through their life journeys. But we must start with ourselves. So, begin a vocabulary list or journal or notebook of your own. Collect words from your friends and family, from your reading, from lectures and conversations. Notice language-related issues and practices in your classes, work settings, and schools you visit. You might organize the words by categories, perhaps related to your content area topics. Be alert and ready to be surprised by words that are perfect to describe something you are thinking or feeling. Share your discoveries with others, and know that you'll be able to share your enthusiasm with your students, as your vocabulary and theirs are enhanced.

6.4 Choose a text, perhaps a chapter of a textbook or an article, and make a list of the key terms and concepts necessary for the comprehension of the material. Create a vocabulary guide using one of the strategies modeled in this chapter, or write a narrative (perhaps accompanied by a picture or graphic organizer) explaining how you would teach the vocabulary in preparation for or in conjunction with the reading material. Share your guide and respond to others on the Kane Resource Site.

7 chapter

Writing in the Content Areas

You've no doubt noticed that writing was addressed and activities and strategies incorporated in previous chapters of this book. Many of the Activating Prior Knowledge and Action Research activities and sample reading guides involved writing. It is an integral component of literacy—very much connected to the process of reading; it's not just an add-on. Although we should think of literacy as holistic, sometimes the interrelated components have to be separated in order to discuss and understand them; it's simply impossible to talk about everything simultaneously. Therefore, in this chapter, the focus is on writing in the content areas—but not in total isolation; you'll see that reading, talking, listening, viewing, and thinking are still involved.

ACTIVATING PRIOR KNOWLEDGE   7.1

Quickly answer the following questions:

1. Would you advise a friend to take guitar lessons from someone who doesn't play the guitar?

2. Would you take skiing lessons from someone who doesn't ski?

3. Would you send your child for writing lessons to someone who doesn't write?

"The Scripture rule, 'Unto him that hath shall be given,' is true of composition. The more you have thought and written on a given theme, the more you can still write. Thought breeds thought. It grows under your hands."

THOREAU, 13 FEB 1860

I'm sure the first two questions were simple for you. But the third may have caused you to pause because, in actuality, many students are given writing instruction in classrooms by teachers who do not practice the craft. You *will* be a teacher of writing, as well as a teacher of reading in your content area; it will be your responsibility to show your students how to think through writing, as well as how to use writing to demonstrate their knowledge and skills. I hope you'll take this quote by writing expert Donald Graves (1993) to heart:

Teachers are the most important learners in the classroom. It is the quality of our learning . . . that [is] the source of greatest influence, far transcending any elegant methodologies we may have acquired. We invite children to join us as we explore better ways of writing, to try new investigations in

189

science, to look for other ways to solve a mathematical problem. (p. 361)

Writer and teacher Tom Romano (2007) insists that "Those who teach a craft ought to do the craft. . . . Teachers who write demonstrate to students someone who loves to think, explore, and communicate through writing. Teachers who write know the challenges, failures, and triumphs of composing with words. They know the emotional territory students inhabit when they write" (p. 171).

So, consider writing a document-based essay to show your students, or a review of a musical performance you attended that you've submitted to your local paper, or a letter to an elected official. Romano promises your efforts will bear fruit. "[Teachers who write] not only have empathy for student writers but also gain credibility in students' eyes" (p. 171).

WRITING PROCESSES

Perhaps you recall your teachers providing formulas for writing essays or reports. These may have worked very well for you, or you might remember feeling resistant about organizing index cards, handing in an outline before you could start writing, or writing a thesis statement in a certain place in the introductory paragraph. Actually, researchers, teachers, and writers have discovered over the past several decades that there is no one correct way to write—people have unique styles and preferences that work best for them, and individuals follow different procedures depending on their purposes and targeted audiences (e.g., Calkins, 1986; Flower & Hayes, 1984; Moffett, 1968; Murray, 1985; Perl, 1979; Rief, 2007). Yet, most people do demonstrate that they go through processes that can be viewed as overlapping stages, which are not usually neat or discrete, or as linear as some textbooks would have you believe. The writing process is *recursive*; that is, writers tend to circle back to earlier stages because of things that happen at later stages.

Writing Stages

Let's look at some generally accepted categories of writing stages that researchers and authors of all types and ages have observed, including planning, drafting and revising, editing, and publishing.

ACTIVATING PRIOR KNOWLEDGE	7.2

Take a moment now to inventory your present writing. Make a list of the types of writing you do in your daily life. How much of it is academic? Is any of it creative writing (at least loosely defined)? Is any self-sponsored, writing that you *choose* to do as opposed to writing that was assigned? Do you practice the type of writing you expect your students to produce for you and for school or state assessments?

Now, take a few minutes to sketch a brief writing autobiography. When and how did you learn to write? What kinds of writing were required of you as a student? What other types of writing did you participate in, and for what purposes? For what audiences do you write? Did you ever, and do you now, think of yourself as "a writer"? In what ways has your writing changed over time?

Planning

This stage, also known as *rehearsal,* starts as soon as a person gets an idea or assignment or recognizes a need to produce a text of some sort. The wheels start turning, and the writer might experience fear, or dryness, or excitement. Sometimes, the ideas are tumbling around so fast they can't all be captured. This stage can be chaotic, and that's normal. Some writers organize their ideas and write an outline before they actually begin a draft of the piece. It's a good idea at this stage to think of what the writing's purpose is and who the intended audience is.

Here's an example of a writer at the planning stage. In the book *Anastasia Krupnik,* by Lois Lowry (1993), the title character is sitting in a class, having just been told by her teacher that they were going to write poetry to share during Poetry Week:

> Somewhere, off in a place beyond her own thoughts, Anastasia could hear Mrs. Westvessel's voice. She was reading some poems to the class; she was talking about poetry and how it was made. But Anastasia wasn't really listening. She was listening instead to the words that were appearing in her own head, floating there and arranging themselves into groups, into lines, into poems. (pp. 7–8)

The planning stage often includes data collection and other forms of research so that the writer has new information to ponder, analyze, synthesize, and write about. The teacher's role at this point can be to get the students brainstorming, freewriting, clustering and organizing ideas, asking thought-provoking questions, and forming a thesis statement. She can suggest resources to explore, writing formats to use, and outline or graphic organizer templates. She can remind students of the patterns of organization writers often choose to use, including sequence, cause–effect, problem–solution, and compare–contrast (see Chapter 4).

Drafting and revising

The drafting and revising stages involve the actual physical text composition. Drafts can be done on a computer, though some prefer doing early drafts by hand, and some writers dictate their drafts into a recorder or to a scribe. Students should understand that it's natural if their first drafts are sloppy or a bit chaotic, because drafts are subject to change. Some revision might happen as the writer is drafting, or a writer can complete a draft before thinking about how she will change it, perhaps allowing some incubating time between drafts. Revising often involves major changes in terms of subject matter, organization, and style. Here's what Betsy Byars (www.betsybyars.com), a noted author of children's books, says about this stage:

- I start on the word processor and write as much as I can. Then I print it.

- I take what I've printed, go sit somewhere else—like the porch—read it, say, "This is terrible," and start working on it.

- I go back to the word processor, put in the changes, and print it.

- I take what I've printed, go sit somewhere else, say, "Oh, this is still terrible," and rewrite it.

- I keep doing this until I say, "This is not as terrible as it used to be," then, "This is getting better," and finally (hopefully), "This is not bad at all." (p. 2)

Writers often revise based on comments from editors or peers they've entrusted with their drafts. Based on this, teachers often require or encourage *conferencing*, either with the teacher or with fellow students. The second section of this chapter offers suggestions as to how you can utilize conferencing time and teach skills to the students so that they can truly be a help to one another.

Editing

At this point, the writer is proofreading, checking grammar, spelling, and cohesiveness at the sentence and paragraph level. Again, this is not always a discrete stage. Some writers edit as they draft and can't continue pouring out ideas till they back up the cursor and fix that typo. There are also times while editing that we are struck with a new idea that requires us to head back to the drafting board for some major reorganization. Published writers have copy editors to go over their manuscripts at this crucial stage; students often choose proofreading buddies to exchange papers with—it's usually easier for us to see others' mistakes than to catch our own because we're so close to our own work and know what it's *supposed* to say. There's a rough draft of the Declaration of Independence housed in the Library of Congress that shows the messiness of the writing at the revising and editing stages. There are numerous cross-outs and substitutions, most made by Thomas Jefferson, but some contributed by John Adams, Benjamin Franklin, and others—the changes show both political compromise and an attention to word choice.

Publishing

At last, a piece is ready to be read by or presented to an audience. Publication can be informal, such as when a teacher displays student writing in the hallway, on a bulletin board, or on a class website. Some teachers have authors' teas, allowing student writers to read from their works in an atmosphere of celebration. Some have class magazines individually bound for students, with contributions from the members of a writing workshop or from student researchers involved in a group inquiry. You can laminate pieces and file them in attractive boxes for the students to peruse, or paper the classroom walls with poems, reports, position papers, drawings, and letters. Encourage your students to give their writing accomplishments as gifts to family and friends. They can let their voices be heard by sending letters to the editor of their local newspaper or creating a student column in the newsletter their school district shares with the community. Put the published letters into a class collection or post them prominently for others in the school, or the public library, to see. It's easier than ever to put student work on class or district websites to share with the community and beyond. Publication can take an oral form too. Students can record book and movie reviews, recite their poetry or opinion mini-essays over the loudspeaker during morning announcements, sing or read their work at a podium in your classroom or at a school assembly. Listen to suggestions and ideas from your students regarding original and innovative publication formats and places to post or perform works they've composed.

Seeing one's work go public can be a time of intense and changing emotions, as Barbara Kingsolver attests in her reflection on the publication of her first novel *The Bean Trees* (1988):

For many, many years I wrote my stories furtively in spiralbound notebooks, for no greater purpose than my own private salvation. . . . The pages that grew in a stack were somewhat incidental to the process. They contained my highest hopes and keenest pains, and I didn't think anyone but me would ever see them. . . . Now it was going to be laid smack out for my mother, my postal clerk, my high school English teacher. . . . To find oneself suddenly published is thrilling—that is a given. But how appalling it also felt I find hard to describe. (Kingsolver, 1995, pp. 36–37)

Is some sort of publication always necessary? Well, no, but it's nice and can be rewarding and motivating. A young girl who lives near me had a journal reflection she wrote during her childhood years about her parents' divorce selected by the editors of *Chicken Soup for the Soul* (Canfield & Hansen, 1993), and was quite excited. Figure 7.1 lists possible avenues to publish student writing.

6 + 1 Trait Writing

Many content area teachers are taking advantage of a model of process writing called 6 + 1 Trait Writing, developed at the Northwest Regional Educational Laboratory (NWREL, 1998/1999; www.nwrel.org). Assessment and instruction in this framework focus on the following attributes of good writing, commonly labeled traits:

1. *Ideas*. The purpose and message are clear and supported with good examples and details.
2. *Organization*. The order makes sense and clear transitions are provided.
3. *Voice*. The text has a mood, a personality, a specific tone—formal or informal—that expresses what the writer wants the reader to feel.
4. *Word choice*. The writer uses a variety of interesting words to aid understanding and create an aesthetic response.
5. *Sentence fluency*. The writer constructs the sentences to flow smoothly when they are read aloud.
6. *Conventions*. The grammar, spelling, punctuation, and so forth are appropriate for the text.
+1. *Presentation*. The final product is both informative and aesthetically pleasing.

LEARNING FROM THE PROS: THE WRITING PROCESSES OF PROFESSIONAL WRITERS

N o matter what our content area, we can provide a positive atmosphere, good modeling, and constant encouragement to our student writers. We can display inspirational quotes such as the following on our classroom walls and our Web pages:

> Writing is hard work. A clear sentence is no accident. Very few sentences come out right the first time, or even the third time. Remember this as a consolation in moments of despair. If you find that writing is hard, it's because it *is* hard. It's one of the hardest things that people do. (Zinsser, 1994, p. 488)

If you are a teacher who believes in having students read far beyond their textbooks, you should

---

FIGURE **7.1**

Possible places to send student manuscripts.

Blue Jean, P.O. Box 90856, Rochester, NY 14609

"My Turn" Essay Competition (Kaplan and Newsweek), www.kaptest.com or 1-800-KAP-TEST

National Gallery of Writing, www.galleryofwriting.org

Scholastic Art and Writing Awards, Alliance for Young Artists and Writers, Inc., 555 Broadway, New York, NY 10012

TeenInk, www.teenink.com

Upwords, www.upwordspoetry.com

Virtualology, www.virtualology.com/studentsubmission

Voices from the Middle, NCTE, 1111 Kenyon Road, Urbana, IL 61801

www.cyberteens.com/cr

---

build and continually increase your classroom library so that your students can read content-related material in many genres. They'll recognize many authors and will surely have some favorites—use this to your advantage when helping them to write. There are resources available that can let your students, and you, in on the secrets of the trade as described by the published writers themselves. Guide them as they ask questions about authors and then search for answers. Many popular authors of young adult literature have inviting and informative websites. The next sections answer questions related to writing process, using some relevant quotes from winners of the Newbery Medal for social studies–related books.

Where Do Writers Get Their Topics and Ideas?

Students sometimes lament that they have nothing to write about; they don't know how to generate ideas. Writers often give tips and stories that can help. Lois Lowry wrote *Number the Stars* (1989) based on information and details a close friend gave her about growing up in Europe during World War II. Mildred Taylor has written family stories her father told her of "great-grandparents and of slavery and of the days following slavery; of those who lived still not free, yet who would not let their spirits be enslaved" (1976, p. vii). One result was *Roll of Thunder, Hear My Cry* (1976). Russell Freedman, whose *Lincoln: A Photobiography* (1987) won the Newbery Medal, says he enjoys writing about "people whose lives have something to tell us, perhaps, about leading our own lives. . . . I was drawn to Eleanor Roosevelt because

BookTalk 7.1

Would you like to give your students a lovely example of a writer going through the stages of the writing craft? Introduce them to Randall Jarrell's *The Bat-Poet* (1996). The flying protagonist's response to nature and life takes a creative form, and his composing processes are detailed, even including an example of writer's block and advice from a "peer consultant":

> But it was no use; no matter how much the bat watched, he never got an idea. Finally he went to the chipmunk and said in a perplexed voice, "I can't make up a poem about the cardinal."
>
> The chipmunk said, "Why, just say what he's like, the way you did with the owl and me."
>
> "I would if I could," the bat said, "but I can't. I watch him and he's beautiful, he'd make a beautiful poem; but I can't think of anything." (p. 25)

The Muses have not abandoned the bat forever. Later, he's listening to and thinking about a mockingbird:

> And at that instant he had an idea for a poem. . . . He flapped slowly and thoughtfully back to his rafter and began to work on the poem.
>
> When he finally finished it—he'd worked on it on and off for two nights—he flew off to find the chipmunk. (p. 27)

Students will appreciate, after reading this account of the bat's struggles, that finishing a piece of writing requires hard work, inspiration, careful observation, and time. They might be inspired by this little artistic creature to write in response to their environment or to issues raised in your class. They might even take on the voice of a bat or another creature, as Jarrell did in this delightful tale of beauty. This book is ideal for reading aloud to a class and has appeal for a wide age range.

of the quality of her heart; to Crazy Horse because of his courage and his uncompromising integrity; to Abraham Lincoln because of his spirit of forgiveness" (Freedman, 1988, p. 451). Walter Dean Myers, with over 80 books to his credit, explains:

> Every piece of nonfiction that I do begins with a question. I work very hard to come up with the right question, one that will allow me to explore the subject in depth and make it come alive for my readers. The question format also gives me direction. (Robb, 2004, p. 73)

Karen Hesse, winner of the 1998 Newbery Medal for her historical novel in free verse *Out of the Dust* (1997), says she loves research, dipping into another time and place and asking tough questions. She immersed herself in documents that allowed her to understand life in the heart of the Dust Bowl during the Depression, and saturated herself "with those dusty, dirty desperate times, and what I discovered thrilled me" (Hesse, 1998, pp. 424–425). She based the book partly on articles in the 1934 *Boise News* that told of a mother who accidentally poured kerosene on a lit stove. She explains, "I never make up any of the bad things that happen to my characters. I love my characters too much to hurt them deliberately. . . . It just so happens that in life, there's pain; sorrow lives in the shadow of joy, joy in the shadow of sorrow" (p. 423).

Learning about the authors' excitement while researching may help our students as they explore and gather information for their writing. Elizabeth George Speare, author of *The Witch of Blackbird Pond* (1958), a historical novel set in Puritan times, challenges young people, "Follow my own process. Take some little incident that you read about in a history book. Try to imagine that you are actually there. . . . What would conversations around you be about? What would the place look like? Write about it" (Kovacs & Preller, 1991, p. 131).

Many writers keep some kind of ongoing journal or notebook and recommend that other writers (including teachers) do the same. Elliott (2008) defines a writer's notebook as "some form of a notebook that writers use to collect ideas, observe, try out craft, plan, vent, reflect, sketch, and remember" (p. 68). She gives ideas for using writers' notebooks across the curriculum, including science, social studies, and the arts. Members of a school community can reflect on field trips, interviews with guests, political events; describe personal responses to works of visual art and music; plan for sports and academic competitions; jot down ideas for fanfiction or a letter to the editor; record stages of problem solving (or creation of a puzzle) in math.

Do Writers Really Revise Their Drafts?

The short answer is yes, which might surprise students who see revision as a school-imposed rule or as busywork. Author David Quammen tells why, explaining that he rereads and revises the essays he writes keeping the reader in mind:

> With every sentence, every paragraph I write, I'm thinking about the reader, trying to imagine his or her responses, expectations, desires, possible confusions. What does the reader want? Is the reader bored at this point? Does the reader need a surprise, an informal remark, a joke to refresh interest? Clarity is part of this. It's important

for a writer to imagine, foresee, and then bypass any possible confusions. . . . Misinterpretations are generally the writer's responsibility more than the reader's. (Robb, 2004, p. 255)

Karen Hesse gave the manuscript of *Out of the Dust* first to her daughters and revised it based on their comments; then she gave it to friends, revised it based on their comments, and continued this process, listening very closely to her readers' remaining questions. However, authors don't always act on the advice they are given. For example, Lois Lowry's editor felt she had too many references to the high, shiny boots of the Nazi soldiers in *Number the Stars*. But Lowry had met a woman who, as a toddler, hid under floorboards and watched her Jewish mother being taken away by soldiers. When the woman was asked what she recalled, she answered that she remembered the high, shiny boots. So, Lowry kept all of the references to the boots in her book, deciding, "If any reviewers should call attention to the overuse of that image . . . I would simply tell them that those high shiny boots had trampled on several million childhoods, and I was sorry I hadn't several million more pages on which to mention that" (Lowry, 1990, p. 420). Our students can learn from these mentors that conferences and feedback are good, but they own their writing and are responsible for final decisions.

Other questions students might choose to ask published writers include how they first got published, how much money they make from their writing, what they do when they're not writing, what they like to read, when they first started writing, and what they do when someone doesn't like their work. Teachers can facilitate the process of finding sources that answer these and other student questions. Figures 7.2 and 7.3 list resources that provide students, and you, with a good start.

There are also visiting authors' programs that your school could become involved with—the students can receive answers to their questions firsthand. Students might be motivated to read the author's works prior to the visit, and funding can be raised through such organizations as a parent–teacher association or a community or business–school partnership. You can also check the Skype an Author Network (www.skypean

author.wetpaint.com) for information about virtual classroom visits and a list of authors eager to connect in this way. After an author visit, more opportunities for writing may arise as students reflect on what they learned and write follow-up messages, perhaps to the author's website. Refer to the books *Dear Author* (*Read Magazine*, 1995) and *Dear Author: Letters of Hope* by Joan Kaywell (2007) for examples of letters readers wrote about books that affected them deeply.

Another way students can learn from the pros is to read examples of authentic writing in the disciplines. *Galileo's Commandment: An Anthology of*

FIGURE 7.2

Resources for exploring the processes of writers.

See more suggested titles in Appendix Figure 7.2.

Bidini, D. (2007). *For Those About to Write: How I Learned to Love Books and Why I Had to Write Them.* Toronto, ON: Tundra Books.

Kaywell, J. (2007). *Dear Author: Letters of Hope.* New York: Philomel.

King, S. (2000). *On Writing: A Memoir of the Craft.* New York: Scribner's.

Lamott, A. (1994). *Bird by Bird: Some Instructions on Writing and Life.* New York: Anchor Books.

Robb, L. (2004). *Nonfiction Writing from the Inside Out: Writing Lessons Inspired by Conversations with Leading Authors.* New York: Scholastic.

FIGURE 7.3

"How-to" resources on writing and teaching writing in various genres.

See more suggested titles in Appendix Figure 7.3.

Borrowman, S. (2005). *Trauma and the Teaching of Writing.* Albany: State University of New York Press.

Fletcher, R. (2007). *How to Write Your Life Story.* New York: Collins.

Hanley, V. (2008). *Seize the Story: A Handbook for Teens Who Like to Write.* Ft. Collins, CO: Cottonwood Press.

Kamberg, M., & Riddle, J. (2008). *The I Love to Write Book: Ideas and Tips for Young Writers.* Milwaukee, WI: Crickhollow Books.

Robb, L. (2010). *Teaching Middle School Writers.* Portsmouth, NH: Heinemann.

BookTalk Online 7.2

Lives of the Writers: Comedies, Tragedies (and What the Neighbors Thought) by Kathleen Krull (1994) (www.kathleenkrull.com) delves into the eccentricities and writing processes of 20 famous writers. Hear more at the Kane Resource Site.

Great Science Writing, edited by Edmund Blair Bolles (1997), is a wonderful place to start. You and your students can read excerpts of pieces by Isaac Asimov, Stephen Jay Gould, Leonardo da Vinci, Charles Darwin, Pavlov, Marie Curie, Carl Sagan, Voltaire, Albert Einstein, Primo Levi, and many more great people who composed expository masterpieces. Students will no longer be able to think of writing as simply an academic exercise. These writings went places! More recent anthologies include *The Oxford Book of Modern Science Writing*, edited by Richard Dawkins (2008); *The Best Science Writing of 2008*, edited by Sylvia Nasar and Jesse Cohen; and *The Best American Science and Nature Writing of 2008*, edited by J. E. Groopman and T. Folger.

ACTIVATING PRIOR KNOWLEDGE 7.3

I've briefly outlined and explained current thought on the writing process, and you've been given a few quotes and examples showing bits of what some writers have to say about their writing processes. Now, on a sheet of paper, reflect through writing on how *you* write. Can you identify the typical stages in your own work? How do you get your ideas? What do your prewriting and drafting stages look like? How would you describe your revision stage? How much time do you spend at the different stages? Do you ever get "writer's block"? Do you have any rituals you follow as you write, or are there any special tools that you use? (Some writers use a special pencil; I need several flavors of ice cream to keep me going.) Where do you write best? When? Under what circumstances? Are you a solitary writer, or do you involve others, asking for help or feedback? In what ways, if any, do you post your writing on the Internet?

As you think, you'll probably realize that the answer to each question is "It depends." It depends on the assignment, or the purpose for your writing. It depends on the audience; will it be a teacher who reads the finished product, or a newspaper editor and possibly the subscribers, or your friends and colleagues? Now, think of at least two specific cases in your recent past. Choose one self-initiated piece of writing and one school paper or other assigned topic, and reflect on the stages again. Understanding your own writing, the cognitive, affective, and physical aspects of it, will help you to understand your students' needs as they write in your content area and will help you talk with them about their writing and encourage them to write to learn and to express themselves.

ACTION RESEARCH 7.A

We're off on a collaborative writing adventure to give you a feel for going through the writing process stages. It will result in a new text about teaching and learning. You are responsible for a short essay that may become part of a compilation, perhaps in hard copy, perhaps on a class Web page. The book must have a theme relevant to a content area literacy course for teachers, so you have two broad options:

1. Write a memoir of some learning experience you have had.
2. Write a description of a teacher you have known.

As you write, be aware of the recursive stages you go through, and keep a record of the piece in progress; save drafts and journal entries. The following paragraphs will help you reflect on your composing process.

PLANNING. How do you think of ideas and identify a topic for your essay? You might read several samples to get your thinking started and your memory jogged; suggestions are listed in Figure 7.4. One sample, Bailey White's "One-Eared Intellectual," is in Figure 7.5. Notice the crafting of the essays or sections of the books that relate to describing teachers. Experiment with ways to tell your story.

DRAFTING. Do you write right at the computer? Are you following an outline? Are ideas changing or new ideas coming to you as you write?

PEER REVIEW/CONFERENCING. In class or out of class, meet with two or three people in a writing conference. Each of you should read your piece aloud, and invite the listeners' responses and suggestions. As you listen to others' texts, think of how they affect you. Be as specific as possible in your response to others' drafts. When my students say to their group members, "Oh, that's good. Don't change a thing," the writer hasn't learned much. But if a listener explains what made her laugh, what part wasn't clear, or how the ending might be stronger, or when she gives a specific suggestion, such as "I think a bit of dialogue would make this confrontation between you and the principal come alive," the writer has something new to think about.

REVISION. Consider your peers' reactions and decide where you want to go with future drafts. You might reject some of their ideas; you might surprise yourself with a whole new direction or a different slant or point of view. Play around some more with the crafting of your essay.

(continued)

EDITING. Proofread your work. Read it out loud so you can hear how the sentences sound. Use a spell check and grammar check. Many people do not pick up their own sentence level errors, so giving your text to someone else—a parent, sibling, or buddy editor—to go over is a good idea. Offer to reciprocate.

PUBLISHING. Prepare copies of your text for your classmates. Be sure you have a title, and your name and e-mail address. A few people in my classes always volunteer to work on a cover, creating titles such as *Looking Ahead by First Looking Back* and *Yesterday's Lessons: A Compilation of Memoirs by Tomorrow's Teachers;* they use original artwork or graphics found on the Internet. Collect all of the essays and combine them with your own, or post your essays on a class website or on the Kane Resource Site. Your final step is to read the book and enjoy! My students are invariably amazed at the variety of topics and styles of writing represented in the finished product. There will be a lot to respond to—that's what the e-mail addresses and the Kane Resource Site discussion forum are for. Send a note to someone whose essay made you understand a particular point of view, or concept about pedagogy, or teacher behavior. Let someone know if you had a similar experience to the one she wrote about, or if you respectfully disagree on some point. In short, let your fellow writers hear from their fans.

FIGURE 7.4

Examples of descriptions of teachers or learning experiences.

See more suggested titles in Appendix Figure 7.5.

Codell, E. R., & Pham, L. (2006). *Sing a Song of Tuna Fish: A Memoir of My Fifth-Grade Year.* New York: Hyperion Books for Children.

Esquith, R. (2003). *There Are No Shortcuts.* New York: Anchor Books.

Kidder, T. (2001). *Among Schoolchildren.* New York: Perennial.

Miller, D. (2009). *The Book Whisperer.* San Francisco: Jossey-Bass.

Romano, T. (2008). *Zigzag: A Life of Reading and Writing, Teaching and Learning.* Portsmouth, NH: Heinemann.

FIGURE 7.5   Excerpt: A description of a teacher as "One-Eared Intellectual."

In my town there lives a man with an enormous intellect and only one ear. When I was a little girl, I thought that the two things were connected, that giving up one ear was simply the price you had to pay to be that smart. Later I learned that he had lost the ear in an automobile accident and had gotten his education in the usual way at Duke University.

Mr. Harris has a pair of glasses with an artificial ear attached to the temple. It matches his real ear perfectly; and as long as he keeps his glasses on, everything is fine. . . .

Mr. Harris is not stingy with his knowledge. He loves to teach people things. His hobby is substitute teaching. So about once a month he calls me on the phone. "Any teachers sick or pregnant at your school?" he asks.

"No," I say, "we're all fine."

Mr. Harris's dream is that a teacher will take a maternity leave. That would give him six weeks in the classroom, maybe more, if there are complications.

Mr. Harris could teach anything, but he always teaches physics. It doesn't matter if the class is supposed to be English, political science, history, kindergarten, or second grade—Mr. Harris just walks in, sweeps the teacher's lesson plans off the desk, and teaches physics.

Mr. Harris has been teaching physics as a substitute teacher for many years now, and the people in our town are remarkably knowledgeable in the subject. You can walk up to almost anybody on the street and ask, "Do you know any physics?" That person will get a wild look in his eye, gasp, and recite, "Yes, momentum is the product of the mass and the velocity of a particle." Or, "Hard radiation is ionizing radiation with a high degree of penetration." Or, "A watt is the power resulting from the dissipation of one joule of energy in one second."

You see, Mr. Harris is a vigorous teacher. He doesn't just wander around the classroom with a piece of chalk in his hand and mumble. He gets excited about physics. He yells. He bangs on the desk. He scribbles wildly on the chalkboard. And invariably, in his pedagogical heat, he will forget himself for an instant and whip off his glasses. The ear comes off too. It is an unforgettable moment. Whatever Mr. Harris is saying when that ear comes off is seared into memory forever. It's the ultimate audiovisual aid. (White, 1993, pp. 197–199)

Another project you might do with your own students is set up a center with biographies and autobiographies representing various levels of difficulty that explore the lives of practitioners of diverse backgrounds and both genders. The resulting class book is a way of celebrating students' research, thinking about, and writing about important people in the discipline when they were at the ages of the students themselves.

LITERARY CHARACTERS WHO WRITE: MODELS AND MOTIVATORS

In previous chapters you learned about using literature involving characters who care about vocabulary and language, and characters who are readers and problem solvers. There are also many books featuring characters who write in a variety of settings and genres. No matter what your subject area, there are literary models you can use to make points in your content lessons and help students reflect on the purposes and processes of writing. There are examples of characters who keep journals, such as Anastasia Krupnik keeping track of her rapidly growing gerbil population using her science notebook (Lowry, 1984).

A science teacher could use these humorous entries to make serious points about the way scientists observe carefully and systematically, recording data meticulously as they observe changes in whatever they are tracking. Students can follow suit, keeping their own science notebooks to record their daily observations about the weather, the night sky, baby chicks, mold on bread, or the changing colors of the leaves surrounding the school during the fall. They can write hypotheses, and later write how those educated guesses were confirmed, or how data analysis led to a revision of the hypotheses. Klentschy and Molina-De La Torre (2004) point out that students writing in science notebooks can make notes about how substances react as conditions change, make predictions, connect causes and effects, use experiences to develop operational definitions of concepts, combine data from a variety of sources, and support claims using data. They contend:

> Writing enables students to express their current ideas about science content in a form that they can examine and think about. . . . The first goal of writing is to understand. Writing is an instrument to think with. (p. 345)

Anastasia used her science notebook for these purposes. She's a good literary model.

Letters from Rifka, by Karen Hesse (1992), consists of a series of letters composed by a 12-year-old Jewish girl as she flees Russia for America in 1919. She uses the blank pages and margins of her poetry book, a gift from her cousin, to write letters telling of the trials that so many immigrants had to endure. She writes her last letter from Ellis Island, before sending her cousin the book, in hopes that its words will offer comfort: "At last I send you my love from America. Shalom" (p. 145). You can see how this book could tap into the affective realm of your students' learning, while building content knowledge and expressing the value of writing.

Some books for adolescents have characters completing writing assignments for school. For example, in Edward Bloor's *Tangerine* (1997), Paul is part of a group working on a science project related to tangerine growing. Readers are let in on aspects of their collaborative exploration. Also, the entire stories of *The Outsiders* (Hinton, 1967), *Rats Saw God* (Thomas, 1996), and *My Most Excellent Year: A Story of Love, Mary Poppins, and Fenway Park* (Kluger, 2008) are framed as school assignments.

Your students should think about and monitor their own composing processes, and literature again provides examples of metacognition. In Madeleine L'Engle's Newbery Honor Book *A Ring of Endless Light* (1980), the narrator writes a sonnet for a dead baby dolphin and concludes, "I had not, as it were, dictated the words, I had simply followed them where they wanted to lead. . . . I felt the good kind of emptiness that comes when I've finished writing something" (p. 172). When a friend asks her where she is when she's in the middle of a poem, she replies, "I'm not sure. I'm more in the poem than I am in me. I'm using my mind,

BookTalk 7.3

We know writers can write memoirs of their lives, which of course would include anecdotes showing learning experiences. Is it possible to write a memoir of the writing process? The title of Stephen King's (www.stephenking.com) *On Writing: A Memoir of the Craft* (2000) suggests an affirmative answer. He combines writerly advice, lots of examples from the works of his favorite authors, descriptions of his teachers (imagine having a young Stephen King in your class), and memories of adolescent experiences that he learned from, so it's a perfect book to stimulate your own memoir writing. In addition, after introducing a scenario and suggesting a creative exercise to tackle, King invites readers to drop him a line at www.stephenking.com to let him know how it worked, in other words what the writing process was like. So, if you want a famous audience for your writing, read this book and accept your invitation to join Stephen King's writing community.

BookTalk   7.4

Epistolary novels are narrated through letters; *The Guernsey Literary and Potato Peel Pie Society,* by Mary Ann Shaffer and Annie Barrows (2008), is a work of historical fiction that uses this device quite successfully. When I began reading the letters between a writer and her editor, the writer and her best friend (the editor's sister), and the writer and many new friends she meets through her correspondence, I knew next to nothing about the Channel Islands and their role in World War II. I can now visualize parts of Guernsey Island, thanks to descriptions characters have supplied. I know something of the deprivations and humiliations experienced by the islanders during their years of Nazi Occupation. In short, I learned history while thoroughly enjoying this book filled with characters who love books—people after my own heart. Writing on many levels, for many purposes and audiences, and in a variety of forms, is highlighted in delightful ways.

really using it, and yet I'm not directing the poem or telling it where to go. It's telling me" (pp. 162–163). Students can use this passage as a springboard to discuss how they feel when writing; for example, troubled at the beginning, euphoric in the middle, frustrated at the revision stage, or satisfied at the end. For some, this quote will resonate; others will contrast the character's writing process with their own.

Figure 7.6 provides a sample of books containing literary characters who write. There are many more. Some may be appropriate for your classroom library; you might choose others to read aloud or assign as a supplement to other curricular materials.

FIGURE   7.6

Books featuring characters who write.

See more suggested titles in Appendix Figure 7.6.

Feinstein, J. (2005). *Last Shot: A Final Four Mystery*. New York: Knopf/Random House.

Greenwald, S. (2006). *Rosy Cole's Memoir Explosion*. New York: Farrar, Straus & Giroux.

Howe, J. (2005). *Totally Joe*. New York: Atheneum Books for Young Readers.

Lubar, D. (2005). *Sleeping Freshmen Never Lie*. New York: Penguin.

Spinelli, J. (2007). *Love, Stargirl*. New York: Alfred A. Knopf.

TEACHING WRITING IN THE DISCIPLINES

Imagine being interviewed for your first teaching job and being asked the question, "How will you teach writing to your middle school or high school students?" Your initial reaction might be, "Excuse me, I'm the one here about a math position," or "I'm going to teach chemistry; the English teacher down the hall will handle writing," or "Of course, I'll *use* writing in my history class, but I expect the students to come to me knowing *how* to write." But then you'd remember what you've learned about every teacher being a literacy teacher and know that you will need to integrate teaching students about writing into your class.

ACTIVATING PRIOR KNOWLEDGE   7.4

Your own experience as a student can inform your present thinking about where and how writing will fit into your courses. So, follow these steps to tap into your prior knowledge.

STEP 1. Make a chart of the different subjects you took in high school. Think back to the types of writing you did in these subjects. Was writing considered important? Was it used as a tool for learning or only to show what you had learned? Are there memorable products you wrote, papers or projects you were proud of? Were you a confident writer in the various courses you took?

STEP 2. Think of yourself as a teacher of whatever discipline you are pursuing. How will you use writing in your course? What place will it have? What types of writing should your students have ability or proficiency in?

STEP 3. Think again of your preferred discipline, the one you hope to teach and encourage young people to understand and perhaps pursue for a future career. What kinds of writing skills are required of people who actually work in the field? What genres and types of writing are important and useful to them? What are some specific examples of texts you have read that were written by scientists, mathematicians, doctors, historians, musicians, artists, or business or government leaders?

A major reason for teaching writing in the disciplines is that it's an authentic place to do so. Zywica and Gomez (2008) explain:

Students often assume that scientists do exciting experiments and field work but rarely read or write. In fact, scientists read prior research related to their experiments, write laboratory reports, develop content for popular and scholarly journals,

How Early Does Writing About Content Begin?

Children who are at the emergent stage of literacy already have important thoughts that are connected to learning in content areas. Notice the invented spelling in these two war stories written by first graders:

> I was in worldwar 2. I was on the U.S.A team. the other team was British Colambia. I was trying to out run a bomber with an army plane. The other plane was shooting at me but I knocked him out of the sky. Another plane was in the sky but I knocked him out of the sky too. I was captured by the other team but I got out and got away.

> The War Chapter 1
>
> It was the day of the Sevle War. It was South Amareca against North Amarica. North Amar was winning.

South Amarica had lost five men alredredy. The Tank is here! Chapter 2.

> The solgers came marching ahed of the tank. The soljers shouted with joy. The tank is here! The captain of South Amarica looked afraid. He said to his men we have to hurry or we will lose. In the House Chapter 3. The men ran to the house. They wanted to get thary lunch frist. but when they got to the house it was emtey! Then theye new what happend The war was over nobody had won.

Teachers can celebrate the imagination and willingness to experiment with narrative writing shown by children. And we can encourage continued exploration and invention through composing as they progress through their school careers.

and must be able to share their experiences with other colleagues. While reading, scientists, like other expert readers, often make jottings and other marginalia in books and articles. (p. 157)

We can help our students, as apprentices, to participate at some level in the literacy experiences of the practitioners of our fields.

Kinds of Academic Writing

The past few decades have seen the flourishing of research, theory, and practice related to the more specific topics of writing in the disciplines and writing across the curriculum. Applebee, Auten, and Lehr (1981) researched the kinds of writing high school students were asked to do in six subject areas. They found that writing activities, though numerous and consuming an average of 44 percent of classroom time, consisted of *mechanical* writing (e.g., worksheets, fill-in-the-blank exercises, math calculations) and *informational* writing (e.g., summaries, notetaking, essays). Students were rarely given the opportunity for personal writing or writing for intellectual exploration. In 1994, Applebee found students spending an average of only two hours a week on writing, and their writing performance showed that many students at each grade level continue to have serious difficulties producing effective persuasive, informative, or narrative writing. Yet, evidence from classrooms (e.g., Atwell, 1998; Bennett, 2009; Rief, 1992) indicates that it doesn't have to be this way. Researchers have found many benefits to a variety of writing, including that reading and writing can work together to promote critical thinking (McGinley, 1992; Shana-

han & Tierney, 1991; Tierney, Soter, O'Flahavan, et al., 1989), and that writing essays enabled students to gain knowledge, as well as improve their thinking about the actual content (Graham & Perrin, 2007; Hillocks, 2006; Nagin, 2006).

Yet, in far too many secondary level content area classes, writing plays but a small part (Graham & Perin, 2007; College Entrance Examination Board, 2003). Irvin et al. (2009) believe this can change:

> It stands to reason that good writing instruction, interesting writing assignments, and ample opportunities to write add up to improved student achievement, improved readiness for college and the workplace, and improved likelihood that students will participate actively as citizens. . . .
>
> Make no mistake—the expectation that all teachers will embed writing instruction in content teaching and learning is a lofty goal. Achieving this goal will require the buy-in and concerted efforts of teachers and administrators across the school. (p. 90)

Ways of Using Writing in Content Area Classes

This section explains a number of ways that students in your content areas can write in order to learn, to better understand material they read, to think critically and reflectively about content, to improve their writing skills, and to show what they have learned.

Writing in preparation for reading

If students are asked to reflect in writing and perhaps commit themselves to a stance on an issue before reading a text on a particular topic, their minds will be activated so that they will be motivated to read and actively engage with the information. They will also be cognizant of the background knowledge they can bring to the text, especially if students share and discuss their pre-reading writing.

Teaching in action: *Science.* Here is an example of an in-class writing assignment that students can be given before reading Peter Dickinson's science fiction novel *Eva* (1988) and related articles on ways scientists are using animals to advance medical treatment for humans:

> Drivers in many states are given the opportunity to sign a donor card at the time they get or renew their drivers' licenses, letting it be known that in case of an accident that takes their life, they wish their organs to be donated for transplant. Imagine that sometime in your driving future you can also indicate one or both of the following:
>
> - In case of impending death, if my body cannot be saved, I wish my mind and memory to be implanted in the body of an animal or another human whose mind has gone.
> - In case of impending death, if my mind cannot survive, I wish to donate my body to be the host of someone else's mind.
>
> Write for about 10 minutes on whether you would agree to either of these wishes, or if you would honor similar wishes of a loved one if a doctor left the decision up to you. You can react in terms of practical or ethical considerations. (Based on an anticipation guide by student Erica Lyon.)

The "What If?" strategy can also be used to activate students' thinking and emotions in preparation for their reading assignment. This strategy involves activating one's mind to possibilities and repercussions by asking what would follow from a certain premise. What if a cure for adult autism is found? What if a hurricane is strong enough to cause a levee to break? What if a journalist is coerced by a government to reveal her sources? Engineers and architects ask themselves "What if?" as they study problems and seek solutions. Novelists get new stories this way; marketers get new customers. Figure 7.7 shows a preservice social studies teacher's use of the strategy in a pre-reading guide.

Writing to imitate a writer's style or structure

A valuable strategy students can use involves writing their own stories or information pieces based on formats of model books you provide. They can pay attention to published authors' dialogue, techniques, and story development and then experiment them-

BookTalk 7.5

In the event this exercise makes you curious about the book, allow me to insert a booktalk. As you know, medical knowledge and technology have advanced to the point where doctors can do things now that raise questions regarding morality and ethics. Readers are confronted with some hard choices in the futuristic novel *Eva* by Peter Dickinson (www.peterdickinson.com) (1988). After an accident, Eva awakes in a hospital to find that her mind has been implanted in the body of a chimpanzee, while her old body is dead. Her parents chose this bold and risky course of action over losing her altogether. Think what science can learn through this great experiment! And think of future possibilities if the experiment succeeds! This book is guaranteed to generate lively discussion among animal lovers, future sociologists and medical workers, science fiction fans, and imaginative students in your social studies, health, science, or English classes. Its multiple themes make it a good choice for interdisciplinary study.

You may also offer your students more recent fiction to see where authors have taken this topic. *The Adoration of Jenna Fox* by Mary E. Pearson (2008) features a protagonist who wakes up after an accident and eventually discovers that 10 percent of her brain was all that could be saved, and that she is now in a synthetic body, filled with biogel. In Meg Cabot's *Airhead* (2008), the main character, again after an accident, has experienced a whole-body transplant, and now has the body of a supermodel whom she formerly despised.

BookTalk 7.6

What if Franklin D. Roosevelt had not won a third term in 1940? What if, instead, Charles Lindbergh, of aviation fame (and with an anti-Jewish and an isolationist ideology), had been elected president? How would subsequent events unfold differently than we've learned in our history books? Philip Roth uses the "What If?" strategy to create an alternative history of the World War II years in *The Plot Against America* (2004). Students can read the book or listen to the story read by Ron Silver (2004). The experience might inspire them to map out their own alternative versions of recent history or that of the distant past, starting with that all-important imagination starter, "What if . . . ?"

FIGURE **7.7** **An anticipation guide involving student writing.**

DIRECTIONS: React in writing to the following "WHAT IF?" prompts.

1. WHAT IF you lived in a climate that was desperately hot and dry, where temperatures can reach 130 degrees F? In this heat, WHAT IF you were forced to dress every day in heavy cloth covering you from head to toe?

2. WHAT IF you were forced into marriage for reasons other than love that you would never have the opportunity to understand? WHAT IF your family forced this marriage? WHAT IF you were still a teenager? (Picture yourself married now.)

3. WHAT IF your happiness depended on the kindness of others? WHAT IF the one to determine whether you shall live, die, smile, or cry was not you? WHAT IF every aspect of your life was under surveillance and out of your control?

4. WHAT IF you were born into a country where the birth of one gender was considered a blessing and the other a curse? WHAT IF you were born of the cursed gender?

5. WHAT IF you lived in a land where polygamy is condoned? WHAT IF your father had several wives?

A certain woman who lived this life didn't need to ask these WHAT IF questions. While reading the book *Princess: A True Story of Life Behind the Veil in Saudi Arabia*, by Jean Sasson (2001), keep these questions and your answers in mind. This is an attempt to further your understanding of the diversity of cultures in this world. What is acceptable in one culture can be punishable in another. Write a brief reaction to the book and reflect on how the WHAT IF questions affected your reading.

Note: This book tells the story of one Saudi princess. You cannot judge the country or the culture just by this book. We will be doing more research, and we'll be talking about whether there is such a thing as universal human rights and how we might react to situations where these rights are violated.

—Judith Miller

selves. For example, students may be familiar with the McKissacks' *Christmas in the Big House, Christmas in the Quarters* (1994). They could use that same contrasting pattern to write about life today in suburbs, urban areas, and rural places.

Introduce your classes to the concept of *intertextuality,* "one writer (or film-maker or artist) elaborating upon or consciously paying homage to the works of another" (Abair & Cross, 1999, p. 85). Intertextuality was at work in Jean Little's poem "After English Class," which you read in Chapter 3. When it is done with humor as a spoof, it's known as parody. Students may be familiar with examples that abound in the television show *The Simpsons.* They might have fun writing poems copying the rhythm of a famous poem but substituting their own topics. John Scieszka and Lane Smith's *Science Verse* (2004) does exactly that.

Modeling their writing on published texts serves multiple purposes because the strategy forces students to pay attention to writing styles, structures, tones, and conventions, and it provides an avenue for them to express their own emotions or convey their knowledge of a topic. They might produce classroom books for future classes, or they could "publish" texts for younger students in the school, explaining content area principles. For example, after reading Thomas Locker's *Water Dance* (1997), a picture book with beautiful oil paintings and a poetic text that explains the water cycle, students could create companion texts illustrating and detailing other aspects of science.

Teaching in action: *Math.* Math students could read *Sir Cumference and the First Round Table: A Math Adventure* by Cindy Neuschwander (1997) and, after learning about the parts and properties of a circle from characters such as Lady Di of Ameter and her son Radius, could create their own stories explaining other mathematical principles. Math teacher Genevieve F. Wahlgren (1997) reports exciting results when her students created mathematical storybooks about topics such as negative exponents after examining examples of professional mathematics writing. They held peer conferences over drafts and interacted with the school's computer specialist and media specialist as they used word processing and graphics to complete their books.

Freewriting and responding to prompts in journals

Another way to incorporate writing is to encourage students to respond freely after reading literature purely for pleasure or as part of their course work.

Teaching in action: *Social Studies.* Here are some suggestions a social studies teacher might give her students taking a "Participation in Government" course:

During this course you'll be reading a lot, and from different types of texts, including newspapers, magazines, novels, biographies, and government reports. In your dialogue journals, you have the opportunity to respond in any way you want to the selections you read. At times you'll post your responses on our class wiki, and you will have the opportunity to give and receive feedback from me as well as your classmates. The best way is to let the text speak to you and respond accordingly. Don't decide beforehand what kind of a response you will make.

Aim for depth of understanding, insight, and application to real life (especially in relation to your participation in government, your active role as an informed citizen). Possible ways to respond include:

- Discuss the emotional impact the text had on you.
- Discuss the writer's craft. Analyze the structure or write some favorite sentences.
- Connect this work to other texts you've read.
- Imagine how someone with a different philosophy, or belonging to a different political party from that of the author, would react.
- Write to the author or to a character.
- List things you learned from this text or points you disagreed with.
- Write a review of the text for a newspaper or magazine.
- Write a letter to a friend, telling her why she absolutely must read this text.
- Create a visual representation of this work—a poster, a graphic organizer, or concept map—showing relationships, a work of art demonstrating your response.
- Connect the text to issues we've discussed in class (responsibilities of elected officials, lobbying, social justice, responsibilities of citizens, balance of power, power and corruption, branches of government, special interest groups, etc.).
- Write a poem as your response.
- Write to a historical figure of the past, asking his or her opinion of the issues raised in the text you read.
- Write a letter to the editor of your local newspaper or to an elected official.

Teaching in action: *Math.* Whitin and Cox (2003) explain how journals can be used in a math classroom. Fifth-grade teacher Robin Cox taught her students to record their thoughts and wonderings, draw pictures and create charts, show their understanding of concepts. She found that, "Their writing gave me a window into their thinking. . . . Their writing helped me plan what to do next" (p. 16). There was also a class journal that students could bring home, to connect math with their out-of-school lives, thus fostering "a mathematical view of the world" (p. 12). Sample entries sounded like this:

> Aaron: I was shooting the basketball and I thought if I scored 12 points and 1 free throw in one game, and in the next game I scored 2 points and 2 free throws, how many points do I average a game? (p. 11)

> Hedda: Now we are jumping from bed to bed like monkeys. I wonder how high the average person jumps. Now Hedda is talking on the phone with Leslie. I wonder if they talk three hours a day, how much they will talk in one year. (p. 12)

Teaching in action: *History*. Hurst (2005) studied the results of using learning logs in middle school and high school history classes. Students were asked to read assignments and keep a two-sided learning log, recording on one side points they found interesting in the text, and writing comments and reactions on the other. Students shared log responses during a subsequent class discussion. Hurst later analyzed surveys completed by the students, and found that 98 percent of the students reported that they had indeed read at least part of the assignment, and that 72 percent indicated that reading for interest, instead of the usual purpose of reading for what would be on a test, had helped them remember material better.

Teaching in action: *Science*. Hargrove and Nesbit (2003) note the authenticity of using science notebooks, since students can be shown that actual scientists use notebooks as they investigate problems and explore the world. A teacher, who of course would keep her own notebook, could model and teach how to frame a question, create hypotheses, describe actions taken, and note what was learned. Science notebooks can contain narratives, diagrams, graphs, and drawings. They can document revisions in thought as students learn more and come back to problems.

In *Using Journals with Reluctant Writers: Building Portfolios for Middle and High School Students*, Abrams (2000) shares journal-related activities he developed for "'alternative education' students, . . . the teenagers who don't fit into traditional settings, such as the chronic non-attenders, students who have trouble with the law, girls who are pregnant, students with learning difficulties, youth who question every authority figure, students who have trouble with drugs, teenagers who are having difficulty growing into adults" (p. 1). He has found that the activities work well with students who are at risk of failure because our educational system has failed to meet their needs. You will at some point have students in your class fitting every one of these descriptions, so learning about these activities and then creating oth-

ers to fit your curriculum can be helpful. For each of 45 topics, Abrams provides prompts to stimulate students' thinking as they write in their journals, then an essay prompt, an extension activity, and a suggested video to watch and react to. Often, he includes a suggested reading. For example, for the topic "Occupations," he provides prompts for journal writing, including the following:

- Some people believe that you should be paid according to how difficult your job is. What jobs should be paid the most in our society? Why? What jobs are the most overpaid in our society? Why do you think so?

- What characteristics are important to you when you think of a future occupation? Would you rather work inside or outside? Alone or with others? Do physical labor or work with your mind? (p. 76)

Writing book reviews

We often hear jokes, as well as moans, when the topic of the dreaded *book report* is raised. Most of us remember having to prove we read a book by writing a report, sometimes monthly or weekly, usually following a prescribed formula. Ask your peers about book reports and you'll elicit confessions of copying from book jackets, reporting on imaginary books, and so forth. But think about it—virtually no one outside a classroom has to write a book report! On the other hand, *book reviews* are a wonderful genre, and we can give our students many examples of this evaluative form of writing from real sources as we encourage them to try their hand at crafting reviews of content area–related books they've read.

I keep a "Book Review File," where I collect published reviews, as well as student-written ones. For example, in an issue of the *Journal of Adolescent and Adult Literacy,* there are several reviews of Gary Paulsen's Civil War novel *Soldier's Heart* (Davenport, 1999)—three written by college secondary education students and one by their professor. These are great models to share with my social studies preservice teachers. Encourage your students to send their reviews in to journals, or to websites that invite reviews, and to post reviews around the classroom and respond to those written by others. The opportunities are endless. The following is a letter I received from an eighth grader, Natasha, whom I met just once and subsequently sent a copy of Hans Nolan's book *Dancing on the Edge*. Here's her unsolicited review:

> Dear Sharon,

> I finished *Dancing on the Edge!* Thanks for giving it to me!! Here's my honest opinion . . .

> I started out thinking I was going to love it. I thought all the aura and séance stuff was really

cool & spiritual. I liked it up until the point where she was sent to the hospital for her burns. I was really inside her mind, but it went downhill from there. I didn't like when she went into therapy at the hospital, and I didn't like the psychiatrist at all. At that point, it started getting away from the spiritual stuff and turning into a "problem novel." I hated all the scenes with the psychiatrist. I thought it was getting whiny but the low point was when the author portrayed Gigi as a bad phony person. (And the Aunt as a good person changed through psychology.) In the end it turned out happily, all due to the wonders of therapy. Really, I don't like books with therapists solving everything, because that stuff is phony to me. It was well written, though. I just wish it had stuck with the spiritual stuff.

The "problem novel" category is hard to fill with good books, and *Dancing on the Edge* is pretty good. I have two suggestions of "problem novel" books I liked a lot. *The Tulip Touch* + *Speak*. They are both really well written & not whiny at all. Also, both heroines solve their own problems themselves without therapy! That I like. *Speak* is about a girl getting raped, but it's very subtle and not superficial or scary. *Tulip Touch* is about being friends with a troubled girl, and is very powerful.

Both of the books Natasha mentions are related to issues of mental health and mental illness; they could lead to discussion, debate, and further research in psychology, health, or science classes.

Figure 7.8 is an example of a reading guide containing a book review guide for a middle school or high school Spanish classroom.

Writing to reflect on thinking processes

Recall that Chapter 5 dealt extensively with metacognition, especially in terms of students' monitoring their reading and thinking processes. In various exercises earlier in this chapter, I asked you to reflect on your writing processes. Although you have participated in these various stages of composing for years, you may not have been consciously aware of the fact that you were prewriting or revising as you were drafting. Now, as a result of completing the exercises' prompts, you have thought about your writing metacognitively. When students write about the thinking process they go through to write a piece or solve a problem, they learn something that may transfer to other situations and might also help us as we guide them. Recall in Chapter 5 when I demonstrated how you could model a "think-aloud" for your class as you read a text. Similarly, your students can benefit by watching you write a piece in front of them:

FIGURE   7.8   Reading guide for *Becoming Naomi León* by Pam Muñoz Ryan (2004).

DIRECTIONS: You are about to embark on a journey with Naomi, the narrator and main character of *Becoming Naomi León*. Completing this guide at various stages of your literary journey will help you be an engaged, active traveler.

BEFORE READING: Your journey is going to take you from Lemon Tree, California (in San Diego County), to Oaxaca City, Mexico. On our world map, locate both places, figure out from the legend about how far away they are from each other, and approximate how long it would take to drive from one city to the other. Or, go to a website such as MapQuest and ask for driving directions from Lemon Tree to Oaxaca City. Note the total time you're told it should take.

DURING READING: A. Naomi keeps a notebook where she makes lists of various ideas, names, discoveries, and worries. In your Spanish Learning Log, keep a list of things you learn on your journey that are related to Spanish culture.

B. Naomi keeps a "Splendid Words List." Keep a list of new Spanish words you encounter during your reading. If you can figure out or guess what they mean from how

they're used, write the meanings, also. If you need to, consult your Spanish–English dictionary.

C. Keep a list of sentences or images that strike you as original or clever. For example, I liked the very first sentence in the book, "I always thought the biggest problem in my life was my name, Naomi Soledad León Outlaw, but little did I know that it was the least of my troubles, or that someday I would live up to it" (p. 1). Also note things about the plot, characterization, setting, or theme that you either liked or are bothered by.

AFTER READING: A. Write a short book review (up to one page) telling potential readers what you thought was good, or not so good, about this book. Keep in mind the book reviews we've read in our library and on book stores' websites. Would you give this book a starred review?

B. When you've finished your review, find out how others reviewed the book. You can search the Internet for official reviews found in *The Horn Book Magazine, KLIATT,* the *New York Times Book Review,* and other such sources; or you can go to Amazon.com and discover what other readers like you have written. How do they compare with your critique of the book?

Sharing and demonstrating [your] craft with students, metacognitively thinking aloud during different types of text composition. Thus, student writers observe firsthand the realistic joys and frustrations of refining a thesis statement, reorganizing ideas, omitting unnecessary details, deciding on vivid words to describe a setting or characters in a short story, creating imagery in a poem, or engaging in other contextual aspects of writing. (Sanacore, 1998, p. 394)

National and state standards for most of the disciplines require student reflection on process, and some assessments in math now require students not only to solve multistep problems, but also to explain in writing how they arrived at their solution. This is an example of metacognitive thinking, and a good rationale for incorporating writing into math class.

Teaching in action: *Math.* The following is an example of a fifth-grade student's written explanation of thinking through a problem. Lauren's words (which the authors kept intact in terms of grammar) were accompanied by three labeled pictures of the steps she followed:

> I worked in the water group. My potato shape was 154 drops and my squash shape 157 drops. When I was in my group, I worked out my problem, then I made up + solved another. How many drops of water in a spoonful? Without actually doing it yet I calculate it. I found out that there are 70 drops in one spoon. I figured out there are 3 spoons in the potato and about 2 or 3 in the squash when I calculated. When I actually tried it out, my calculations were right on the nose. (Whitin & Cox, 2003, p. 70)

Calculus teachers Joanna O. Masingila and Ewa Prus-Wisniowska (1996) use writing to both develop and assess their students' understanding of concepts. Sometimes, they require writing from carefully constructed prompts, encouraging students to connect new ideas with prior knowledge. One example they give is:

> Explain the similarity in, and difference between, using a vertical line to test whether a rule is a function and using a horizontal line to test whether a function is a one-to-one function. (p. 96)

The authors found that writing from a prompt

> allows students to express and teachers to see the personal nature of making sense of a new idea. A new idea makes sense for a student if he or she is able to link it with a network of mental representations. Writing from a prompt encourages students to forge new links and think reflectively about the links they have already made. (p. 97)

These same teachers involve their students in writing performance tasks to demonstrate and communicate their understanding. The students first complete a task or conduct a mathematical investigation and then write out the process they went through. Masingila and Prus-Wisniowska found the use of group performance tasks to be especially valuable, as students collaborate and assess and build on one another's ideas. Through writing, their critical thinking is put into words.

Consider having your students write instructions related to some topic in your field, whether that might translate to specifying directions along the Oregon Trail, writing recipes, creating a computer program, or instructing readers how to compose a business letter, draw manga characters, or play a video game.

The RAFT strategy

Students' thinking, as well as their writing skills, may be enhanced by understanding and then arguing from a point of view other than their own. The RAFT strategy (Santa & Havens, 1995) provides a way to do that. The acronym RAFT stands for Role, Audience, Format, and Topic—all aspects students must pay attention to as they write. The teacher creates content area–based writing prompts, assigning each of these parts to students based on material they have read and topics they have covered; or students may make their own decisions. Following is a procedure for a RAFT assignment.

1. Create a content area–based writing assignment.
2. Assign a **Role** to students based on material they have read and topics they have covered, or have students make their own decisions.
3. Have students choose an **Audience** to whom to write.
4. Ask them to select an appropriate **Format** for their writing assignment (a letter, poem, etc.).
5. Have students write their piece based on one of the **Topics** relevant to the writing assignment.

For example, in terms of *role*, students could be asked to think as a political leader, a fictional character, a slave at the time the Civil War was imminent, or even a virus or a river. The narrator of *The Book Thief* (Zusak, 2006), set in Nazi Germany, is Death! Audiences can vary similarly, as can formats. The students' aim in RAFT writing pieces is to use an authentic voice for a particular purpose, such as explaining or persuading. I'm in favor of giving the students as much control and choice within the guidelines of this activity as possible. That way, you'll enjoy reading the different creative products, and the students, through sharing, will be exposed to a larger number of possible ways of reasoning.

As Alvermann and Phelps (1998) remind us, personal motivation is crucial in writing, and "a role or topic that may seem 'creative' to one person may hold little attraction to another. Not every student will be eager to write from the point of view of a rain forest animal, Captain Ahab's second mate, the unknown variable in a two-step equation, or a red blood cell traveling through the circulatory system" (p. 282). Interestingly, since this quote came out, *Ahab's Wife, or The Star Gazer: A Novel* (Naslund, 1999) has become a best seller—a good example of the RAFT strategy because the novelist takes on an unusual point of view—that of Ahab's wife—to spin a story off a classic!

Show examples of published writing that model the RAFT strategy. Letters to the editor in a newspaper often identify the writers' role or identity, address particular people or communities, or explain their reasons for expressing their opinions on a particular topic of concern. Certain novels exemplify characters who come at an issue from varying, sometime opposing, perspectives. *Bull Run,* a novel of the Civil War by Paul Fleischman (1993), has 16 narrators, equally divided between the South and the North, each telling his or her version of what happened during the war. Diane Siebert has a series of geography-related poems, *Mojave* (1988), *Heartland* (1989), and *Sierra* (1991), with a desert, heartland, and mountain (respectively) narrating about themselves and their characteristics. A social studies, earth science, or English teacher can ask her students to listen as the voice from *Sierra* begins:

> I am the mountain,
> Tall and grand.
> And like a sentinel I stand.
>
> . . . I am the mountain.
> Come and know
> Of how, ten million years ago,
> Great forces, moving plates of earth,
> Brought, to an ancient land rebirth;
> Of how this planet's faulted crust
> Was shifted, lifted, tilted, thrust
> Toward the sky in waves of change
> To form a newborn mountain range. (unpaged)

From *Sierra* by Diane Siebert. Text copyright © 1991 by Diane Siebert. Used by permission of HarperCollins Publishers.

In class, students could do some expressive writing, creating similar poems using the voice of the Mississippi River or a glacier or an ocean. Or they might choose a different format, such as a letter or a travel brochure or an obituary.

Teaching in action: *Science.* Here's a sample RAFT assignment a science teacher might give after students have read Peter Dickinson's *Eva*, the novel discussed earlier in this chapter. "Choose a character (ROLE) from the novel and write a piece explaining his or her position on one of the TOPICS relevant to

the story. Choose a logical AUDIENCE and an appropriate FORMAT and tone."

One student might write an impassioned plea from Eva's mother begging the medical community to halt the procedure of implanting human minds into the bodies of chimpanzees, citing the difficulties she now has relating to her daughter. Another could write a report in the voice of Eva's researcher father arguing the importance of *continuing* the procedure and the subsequent research. A particular student who is a proponent of animal rights might choose to take on the role of the ghost of Kelly, the chimp that was killed so that its body could host Eva's mind. Someone interested in animal cognition could play around with the thoughts that might be going on in the chimpanzees who interact with Eva/Kelly, wondering about her differences as they try to learn the knot-tying skills she teaches them. The format chosen for this might be a personal reflection with self as audience.

The benefits of the RAFT strategy can be far-reaching because in actuality, almost all writing done in the disciplines, whether research reports, government documents, funding proposals, or interoffice memos, requires the writers to identify their role, know their intended audience, adhere to sometimes narrowly prescribed and rigid formats, and stick to the topic at hand. Tell your students that RAFT can be with them forever as a valuable tool (or even a life-saving device) through their writing lives!

APPLICATION ACTIVITY **7.1** (SEE PAGE 221)

Quick writes

Sometimes, you may find you have students who are so used to regurgitating information that that's what they think you mean when you ask them for a response to a lesson or a reading. Or they're so familiar with fill-in-the-blank comprehension exercises that they're reluctant or afraid to write anything at all unless given a strict framework. Encouraging them to think actively about what they're hearing or reading, to be aware of their reactions, and to write succinctly can work wonders. Quick writes (Ruddell, 1993) are brief, open-ended opportunities for students to reflect on their immediate learning experiences. They can be used to focus a class discussion, emphasize the key points of a lecture, or require students to synthesize information. I know a teacher who asks students in her social studies education class to fill out an "exit slip" every day before they leave, stating a key point they understood from the class and responding to it. Here's what one looks like:

KEY POINT: I heard you say over and over again today that all of us exhibit some racist characteristics without even realizing it.

MY RESPONSE: Oh, boy, I'm feeling angry and frustrated, and, yes, guilty. You know what? I feel like you tried to MAKE us feel guilty. Well, I haven't done anything wrong. It's not my fault there was slavery, or Jim Crow laws, or riots, or that there are neo-Nazi groups today. I am not a racist! Please stop telling me that I am.

The teacher uses the cards to reflect on the students' understanding of the lesson; she can post the index cards in the room so the students learn from each other, and can use them as a transition to future lessons.

Similarly, teachers can use entrance slips at the beginning of a class to focus attention on the day's topic, or during a lesson to see how well students are understanding it and to help students reflect on ideas and information. Unrau (2008), in order to find out about his students' understanding of a topic or get their minds reengaged, asks them to "play DEAD," or drop everything and draft, for a couple of minutes. It's a time for them to reflect on their learning and to ask questions that will help the teacher determine where to go next in instruction. Altieri (2009) shows how the use of admit and exit slips can reinforce students' mathematical ability.

Summary writing

A summary is a statement of the main points of a reading without commentary. It is a good way for students to separate main ideas and essential supporting details from less crucial details and to show they comprehend a text. The process of condensing a longer text into a shorter one stimulates students to think actively about and synthesize main ideas, making it a valuable study strategy. Because students use their own words to restate the important points, they will likely understand and remember the information (Hill, 1991). Students can be taught to attend to good topic sentences, combine related ideas, and delete redundant material. Encourage students to summarize reading assignments in their notebooks. Following are guidelines a teacher can use to teach students how to summarize a reading passage (Cecil & Gipe, 2003).

1. Have students preview, think, and read. Ask students to preview the entire passage and think about what they expect to learn. Then have them read the passage.

2. Have students ask themselves, "What does the author keep talking about? What is the author trying to say about this topic?" This will be the main idea, or the thesis, of the material.

3. Have students ask the same two questions in step 2 about each paragraph, or group of paragraphs. Ask them to write that idea in their own words in one sentence but leave out details, examples, or stories, giving only the important idea.

4. Have students continue this process for the entire reading selection.

5. Have students check their sentences against the passage, ensuring that they tell the most important ideas, not the details. Have them make sure that nothing is repeated; that the sentences are their own words; and that their first sentence gives the overall main idea, or thesis, of the entire selection, with the following sentences supporting the meaning of the first sentence.

Guided writing

There are times when providing a structure for student writing is appropriate and beneficial, and there are any number of ways to guide the students. Creating writing guides that help students respond to texts and explain their thinking and learning is one of the most important ways you teach and support them as they strive to grow in content area knowledge. The *Guided Writing Procedure* (Konopak, Martin, & Martin, 1987; Smith & Bean, 1980) provides sequential steps, including:

1. Brainstorming prior knowledge
2. Organizing and labeling the ideas generated in small groups or as a whole class (perhaps creating a semantic web)
3. Writing individually on the topic using the information dealt with thus far
4. Reading an assigned relevant text
5. Revising their first piece of writing based on their comprehension of the text

Some form of assessment completes the procedure. Research has shown that this procedure results in higher-level thinking and better synthesized information on assessments (Konopak, Martin, & Martin, 1990).

Teachers can adapt the *Guided Writing Procedure* to suit their purposes, or start from scratch to create writing guides that generate the kind of product they want. For example, a science teacher might ask students to create a FAQ sheet on topics relating to weather—students can decide together what might qualify as "Frequently Asked Questions," and then answer them to show they know the information and to share it with others who may not. A tighter structure, maybe even a template, can be offered to students as they write up lab reports.

Teaching in action: *Health.* For example, a seventh-grade health teacher provides the following guidance to his students who are writing reports for his class. He requires each student to choose a disease or disorder, research a number of reference sources, and write an essay (perhaps for inclusion in a class book or Web page) consisting of paragraphs that detail information in the following order: *causes, symptoms,* and *treatments.* Students can learn a lot as they read their classmates' pieces, and the structure provided can help them in terms of comprehending and remembering. The teacher allows individual writers to adapt his guidelines to fit *their* needs and writing styles. Figure 7.9 is an essay written by a seventh-grade boy

in response to this assignment. Notice how he weaves the academic information into his personal narrative.

APPLICATION ACTIVITY   7.2   (SEE PAGE 221)

Fisher and Frey (2003) recommend using the gradual release of responsibility model (Pearson & Gallagher, 1983) with struggling adolescent readers and writers. The model consists of four stages and may look like the following in writing instruction:

1. *Demonstration stage:* the teacher models writing with the students, for example, using a think-aloud.
2. *Shared demonstration:* teachers and students participate in shared writing where the students help plan the text and tell the teacher what to write.
3. *Guided practice:* the students do the writing while the teacher suggests strategies they may use and provides instruction on those strategies.

FIGURE   7.9   An essay written for a seventh-grade health class.

My mother had just gotten off the phone and she was crying.

"What's wrong?" I asked.

"The new baby's gonna have Down syndrome."

This came as a shock to me. My aunt had already had six perfect kids; why should this one be any different? Also, some kids make fun of retarded kids. Was he going to be made fun of?

Three months into her pregnancy, my aunt went to get a test. This was to assure her, since she was 41, that there would be nothing wrong with Mario (his name had already been picked out). One month later, the results came in; Mario Mazza was going to have Down syndrome.

For the next five months, my mother kept bringing books home from the library about Down syndrome. People with the condition have 47 chromosomes instead of the 46 that other people have. It's amazing that one chromosome, one tiny, microscopic chromosome, could mean the difference between a [genetically] normal person and one with Down's. The more I read, the more surprised I was with the disorder. Only one out of every 1,000 babies gets it and it is caused by an abnormality with the genes in one parent. I still can't figure out why it happened to my aunt's seventh baby and not her first.

Down syndrome was named after a British physician by the name of John Langdon Hayden Down, who first explained the disorder in 1866. The condition was called

Mongolism, but that term is not used much today because it's very offensive. . . .

Physical therapy is used to develop the poor muscles that most Down's babies have. (Mario's brothers and sisters have to fly him around like an airplane.) The most serious threat to Mario, however, was possible heart problems. This, along with respiratory disorders, is somewhat common among Down's babies.

As the months went on, we prayed for Mario's case to be mild. Some babies with the disorder are more severely retarded and have to be institutionalized. At these homes the babies do not develop to their full potential. But for some babies, the potential is very high. Christopher Burke, star of the TV show *Life Goes On,* makes more money than most people. Another child with Down syndrome I read about could do fifth-grade math when only in fourth grade. In these cases, Down syndrome could easily be called Up syndrome!

It was October 2, and Mario was a week overdue. Finally, the call came. Mario was born. Tests had been done to see if he had any heart disorders and there were none. He was healthy as could be.

Mario is now three months old and doing great. He smiles all the time and hardly ever cries. Everything about him is beautiful. He has a lot of hair that his mother spikes sometimes. Although he got tons of toys for Christmas, the most important thing he has is our love.

—Pat Kane

4. *Independent practice:* the students write by themselves, using the skills and strategies they have learned, or with a peer.

As a teacher and her students move through the phases, the level of teacher support decreases as learner control increases. The teacher provides much instruction, demonstration, modeling, and guidance before expecting students to handle writing assignments on their own. Fisher and Frey conclude:

> Too often instruction minutes are wasted when students are given independent writing prompts for which they are unprepared. . . . The gradual release model provided a way for the teacher to scaffold instruction to the point that students were more successful independent writers. (p. 404)

Writing letters in the content areas

Chapter 3 introduced *Letters of a Nation: A Collection of Extraordinary American Letters,* edited by Andrew Carroll (1997), and explained how letters can be used to help students analyze and think critically about issues. Now, I'd like you to think about such a source in terms of encouraging your students to write. Students can use the real letters as models for their own writing. They can experiment with taking on the roles of famous people and writing creative letters to each other based on the examples provided in books such as Carroll's or *Famous Letters: Messages and Thoughts That Shaped Our World* edited by Frank McLynn (1993).

Secondary students should also know how to write business letters for various purposes. You might ask them to bring in copies of real business letters their family members have written, either for their jobs or from home. Provide some of your own and keep a file for future reference. You can also help your students write business letters for authentic purposes—to express opinions, complaints, or praise or to request information. One sixth-grade team I visited was planning a class trip to Cape Cod at the end of the school year. For months preceding the expedition, students wrote to chambers of commerce and other offices in places they would be visiting, asking those questions they really wanted answered. The replies they received further validated their teachers' assertions that business letter writing is an authentic task that takes place outside, as well as within, classroom walls.

High school students often have an urgent need to learn how to write a cover letter for employment or for college applications. Writing about their strengths and interests may seem daunting to students, thus providing an authentic opportunity for teaching and learning. You can let students know that such letters have been necessary for centuries, and provide the following example from Leonardo da Vinci's 1482 letter to the Duke of Milan seeking employment as a military engineer:

> I am emboldened . . . to seek an appointment for showing your Excellency certain of my secrets.
>
> 1. I can construct bridges which are very light and strong and portable, with which to pursue and defeat the enemy; and others more solid, which resist fire or assault yet are easily removed and placed in position. . . .
>
> 3. I can also make a cannon which is light and easy to transport, with which to hurl small stones like hail, and whose smoke causes great terror to the enemy so that they suffer heavy losses and confusion. . . .
>
> 8. In times of peace, I believe that I can give you as complete satisfaction as anyone in the construction of buildings both public and private, and in transporting water from one place to another.
>
> I can further execute sculpture in marble, bronze and clay, also in painting I can do as much as anyone else, whoever he may be. (McLynn, 1993, p. 57)

He got the job.

There are innumerable authentic ways to use letter writing and letter reading in your subject areas. For example, ninth-grade teacher Sharon Morley involved her class in a project based on Jim Burke's (www.englishcompanion.com) *I Hear America Reading: Why We Read What We Read* (1999). She composed a letter that she sent to newspapers around the country, inviting readers to write to her class about how reading has affected their lives. They received dozens of responses to the pilot phase of the project. Her students read and discussed them, found patterns, learned about the geographic areas the respondents lived in from the descriptions in their letters, and used the recommendations in the letters as they selected new books to read for a reading workshop and for pleasure reading at home. The students composed new letters to send to other newspapers.

APPLICATION ACTIVITY **7.3** (SEE PAGE 221)

APPLICATION ACTIVITY **7.4** (SEE PAGE 221)

Writing research papers

Are research papers in high school worth the time and effort on the part of teachers and students? You may recall dreading a research assignment, only to find that you really got into the topic once you started. Or you might have experienced having your initial excitement about exploring a topic squelched when a teacher seemed to care more about the correctness of your footnotes than about your discoveries and analysis of data. Research projects have the potential to enhance content learning, while combining exploratory and explanatory writing. In the early stages and early drafts, students can be writing to learn about their selected topic and about how they think about it and what they wish to say about it. As they revise, they can concern themselves with how they should present their information and write to show what they learned. Teachers can instruct about such things as proper formatting, use of the Internet, and the use of citations within the context of the students' inquiry and writing processes.

White (1999) warns teachers about the research paper: "The basic problem in teaching the research paper is to reverse students' preconception that research means collecting other people's opinions and patching them together with a bit of rhetorical glue" (p. 20). I think we can help students realize that research is done outside classroom walls all the time by people in various work fields, as well as by consumers. Perhaps the most important step is to formulate an important question or to recognize a need to know about something. Virtually anyone who has had a loved one diagnosed with an illness knows the value of research; we search for books, articles, Internet sites, and people who can give us information about colon cancer, drug addiction, clinical depression, whatever. Students can brainstorm together to list reasons why product marketers, doctors, English teachers, and other professionals might do research, as well as how they might go about finding answers to their questions.

Teaching in action: *History and English.* Let's say you're an American history teacher who will collaborate with an English teacher on a joint research paper assignment for your students. You want your students to formulate a question they really care about and want to spend time investigating. You might show your class an example of a historian who went through essentially the same process you expect of them. Peter Burchard comes to your aid. In the Introduction to *Lincoln and Slavery* (1999), he tells his readers what prompted his research:

> In my youth, I happily embraced what had become the Lincoln myth. Later, when I learned about his early compromises over slavery, I found excuses for him. When I heard what he said about the possibility of segregation of the races, I was . . . uncomfortable. . . . It saddened me to learn that, until two years or so before his death, he promoted the almost universal belief that black people were inherently inferior to those of other races. . . .
>
> I have always wished that I could talk to Lincoln, ask him questions, listen to him, wished that

I could get acquainted with the flawed and complicated man behind the myth. (p. x)

In a bibliographical essay at the end of the book, Burchard shares his process of seeking answers to his questions about Lincoln and slavery. He used some primary sources, such as *The Black Abolitionist Papers* (Ripley, 1992) and Lincoln's recorded speeches, proclamations, and letters, as well as secondary sources by several well-respected Lincoln biographers. One interesting path he took was to analyze what Lincoln's contemporary, ex-slave Frederick Douglass, had to say about Lincoln's words and actions. The results of Burchard's authentic search to understand the president and the issue are recorded in *Lincoln and Slavery*, a book I would certainly want in my classroom library.

A popular alternative to the traditional research paper format is the multigenre research project, where students are given the opportunity and guidance to more creatively compose and present the results of their inquiry (e.g., Allen, 2001; Romano, 2000). Hughes (2009) offers a picture of sixth graders presenting their research in the form of monologues, letter writing, murals, and dozens of other genres. She includes a rubric teachers can use while judging the quality of student work in categories such as genres selected, table of contents, reflective letters, bibliographies, and overall presentation.

Students as social action researchers. Students benefit from the reading, writing, thinking, and constructive social action involved in the following research project.

Teaching in action: *English.* Elaine Murphy (2001) encouraged her eighth-grade students to use several kinds of writing as they researched a topic that would actually make a difference in their curriculum and other students' lives. The district was asking questions related to what literature should be taught in the twenty-first century, and had formulated a checklist of criteria related to dismantling of stereotypes, providing opportunities for discussion that could foster community relations and respect for diversity, and promoting higher-level critical-thinking skills. Murphy's students read books of their choice and contributed to an annotated bibliography organized by topic. As they read, they kept journals relating the books to the topic question, their personal experiences, and the problems and values of their community. Students shared their journals through the process of serial collaboration:

> Each student read the journal of another student, wrote questions, or offered new perspectives in the space below the writing of the journal's owner and passed the journal to still another student, who

repeated the same process. The passing process continued until five students had the opportunity to respond to the journal. In this way students received exposure to five different novels being read by other students, and each journal owner received five new perspectives on the novel he/she was reading and writing about. The last person in the journal-passing chain also selected a single insight . . . for sharing with the large group. . . . I also read each journal, offering my own questions and encouragement and clarifying points of confusion. (p. 112)

These eighth-grade researchers wrote paragraph-length book blurbs or reviews on the books they read (some submitted theirs to the NCTE journal *Voices from the Middle* for publication consideration). They then conducted library research on topics presented in their books, such as cerebral palsy, restorative justice, obsessive–compulsive disorder, and peer pressure. The next phase of the project involved students reading a variety of real-world persuasive texts, such as a Nike T-shirt advocating volunteerism, a letter to the editor, brochures from other schools, a public service ad, and movie reviews. Students were required to analyze the writing and identify the thesis and intended audience, as well as judge the effectiveness of visual and rhetorical elements. Finally, students submitted their own persuasive pieces, using a variety of formats, aimed at a number of different, real audiences.

Teenagers as reader response researchers. An effective way to combine reading and writing, as well as develop higher-level thinking skills, is to have students analyze their classmates' responses to a text and write a report synthesizing the data and reporting their findings. I model this strategy by passing out index cards to my students and asking them to write a free response to a poem I read. I collect the cards, and the next day read an analysis I've written of the data they gave me. Based on responses to the poem "First Writing Since" by Suheir Hammad in the book *Shattering the Stereotypes: Muslim Women Speak Out* (Afzal-Khan, 2005, pp. 90–94), I might say:

I found that your responses fell into two main categories, which I labeled text-based responses and reader-based responses. Text-based responses included the following: Several of you talked about the way the poem sounded: the effect of the initial consonant sound in the phrase "driving debris and dna" (p. 90), the repetition of words and phrases, the use of first person. One person mentioned the structure of the numbered stanzas. One mentioned the symbolism inherent in the word "ashes" (p. 90) and the phrase "the phoenix has risen" (p. 91). Many of you were striving for meaning as the narrator gave lines that described her fears and her politi-

cal stance and made comparisons to other things you've learned in social studies (e.g., the KKK, the CIA, the Oklahoma bombing).

On the other hand, many of you responded with emotions and memories of your own. Three people wrote about where they were on September 11, 2001. One person tried to step into the shoes of the Arab narrator, imagining what it had to feel like for her. Another said this poem made her feel guilty as well as incredibly sad. Someone offered a hope that we can learn something from this poem, so that we can all work together for social justice. The responses were varied, though many of you indicated in some way that you liked the poem or found it powerful and moving.

After I read my report of primary research and we discuss how I organized and thought about and interpreted the data, someone invariably asks, "What were you looking for?" The old "What do you want? What's the correct answer?" questions surface. I assure them that I'm interested in whatever happens when a reader comes together with a text. From then on, we begin every class with a student reading a short text she's selected. She can request a free response, or she can ask specific questions of her respondents. She then becomes responsible for writing a paper analyzing the data she collects, drawing tentative conclusions about texts or readers, and discussing the significance of her findings. In short, she must conduct herself as a researcher. I'm always amazed at the range of topics students write about, and the depth of their theorizing based on the data they obtain from classmates.

Model and use this strategy in your content area classes with any number of types of text. For example, social studies teachers could ask students to bring in newspaper and magazine articles on political situations or other current events; science teachers can help students find texts dealing with ethical dimensions of scientific breakthroughs. This "Student Turns Reader Response Researcher" project has multiple benefits. First, it enables the class to function as a community. The rest of the class knows that the reader for the day is depending on them for thoughtful responses so that he'll be able to write a good paper. That gives them a meaningful reason for writing, and they usually do their best. Equally important is the fact that the daily writing activity is enjoyable. Students are eager to listen to the texts their classmates have selected, and often want to pursue a discussion of interpretations after writing their responses. Finally, the research focus and multiple avenues of exploration get the students to go far beyond the traditional questions they associate with texts: "What is the main idea? What do the symbols mean? What is the theme of the work?" Instead, students formulate the questions they want answers to, and go about gathering and analyzing data that either produces knowledge related to their questions or raises further important questions about readers and texts. They share what they create and learn from each other's contributions to the community research.

Creative writing for deep understanding

Writing can help students explore concepts in your content area classes in new and playful ways. We know, though our students might not, that many mathematicians, scientists, journalists, artists, politicians, musicians, architects, economists, environmental engineers, and historians learn and think new thoughts as they scribble, write notes to themselves or to colleagues, draft versions of new ideas they're trying to pin down, or apply new ideas to old contexts.

Teaching in action: *Math.* Mathematician and teacher Peggy House considers the most significant outcome of using writing activities to be her students' recognition that "mathematics has a playful dimension, a recreational fascination as well as a serious purpose, creativity as well as precision" (1996, p. 94). She recalls her own use of imagination when, in eighth grade, she received the assignment to write an autobiography of a nickel, and she "played with ideas of multiples and factors, decimals and fractions, shape, and size, and more" (p. 89). Following are two of her students' responses to her request to think about what number they would choose to be:

> My reason for wanting to be Zero is that nothing would be expected of me.
> If I was Zero, transportation would never be a problem because I could just roll to my destination. Also . . . I could easily visit my best friend, one, and we could make a perfect ten.
> Another advantage of being Zero is that, no matter how many other zeros are around, the crowd never increases. Also, no matter how big a number is, all I have to do to bring it down to my size is to multiply with it. . . . (Mike, p. 90)

> I would be pi, because pi is one of the most distinguished numbers around. Not only that, but pi goes on forever. And I would be of untold importance to geometry. . . .
> As the number pi, I would have many friends. I would be inseparable from the circles, and, since I would contain many digits who appear in a most unpredictable fashion, I would never become stale or uninteresting. (Don, p. 90)

House's students also create mathematical newspapers with math-based puzzles, cartoons, features, advertisements, and editorials. They show their understanding of topics by constructing limericks and prob-

lem stories for peers to solve; they write parodies, sequels, and spin-offs of other literary works with such titles as *The Wizard of Odds, Equilaterella, Alice in Cartesian Land,* and *Star Tech: The Next Iteration.* Here are two verses of a long song her students composed:

My Favorite Things

Arc sines and cosines, a heavenly vision;
Cubic equations, synthetic division;
Functions with zeroes that make my heart sing:
These are a few of my favorite things. . . .

Inverse relations, continuous functions;
Logical thinking, the rules of disjunctions;
Infinite series with limit and bound:
These are the things that will make my heart pound.
(pp. 93–94)

From "Try a Little of the Write Stuff," by Peggy House. Reprinted with permission from *Communication in Mathematics, K–12 and Beyond: 1996 Yearbook,* copyright © 1996 by the National Council of Teachers of Mathematics. All rights reserved.

You can see that they used specialized vocabulary and complex concepts that show a comfort and familiarity with their subject. These students are not merely having fun; they're learning.

Teaching in action: *Science.* Seventh-grade teacher Leslie Franks, inspired by Leggo and Sakai's (1997) query, "What would happen if science and writing were presented as interrelated ways of knowing the world?" (p. 20), asked her students to write about weather using a variety of genres. For three weeks they recorded information and observations, and responded daily to one of five prompts. Franks added an art component, having students draw pictures of cloud formations and of summer and winter solstice. After writing solstice poems, about 80 percent of the students could explain the reason for the seasons, far more than could do so after being taught the concept in both geography and science classes. Even more were able to articulate a quality definition for winter and summer solstice. Students told their teacher in written reflections that keeping a science journal and painting and drawing "helped them learn more and more about themselves as learners, both in science and in writing" (Franks, 2001, p. 324).

Document-based questions and essays

A prevalent type of writing required in social studies classrooms and on some standardized tests uses *document-based* or *data-based questions* (DBQs). As the name suggests, the questions call for students to comprehend, interpret, and analyze documents or other data the teacher or test provides. Then, the students synthesize information from two or more sources related to a theme, an issue, or a problem in order to craft an essay noting patterns or contrasting information found in the various data. This type of reading and writing calls for higher-level thinking skills, going beyond literal comprehension. DBQs have been used on advanced placement exams for many years, and provide an authentic form of assessment because, as high school social studies supervisor Alice Grant points out, "They measure not only what students have learned, . . . but also the intellectual habits they've developed in the process and whether they can apply those skills to completely new information they haven't seen before" (Strachan, 2000, p. 24). When answering DBQs, students perform tasks similar to what historians and social scientists actually do with data sources: generalize and think critically, forming conclusions, hypotheses, and opinions.

What kind of data are used for these DBQs? All genres can be represented. Teachers have brought together poetry, excerpts from political documents in archives, quotations from philosophers, eyewitness accounts, letters, memoirs, political cartoons, maps, charts, tables, paintings, diary entries, and official memos. For younger, inexperienced, or struggling readers or writers, you can start teaching and modeling the synthesis that DBQs require using just two sources. Some high school teachers challenge advanced students with as many as eight pieces of data to work with. With DBQs, students have the opportunity to take positions on issues, support their conclusions, draw analogies, and see issues from multiple perspectives.

How can you teach this kind of thinking and writing within the context of your curriculum? Have your students watch, allowing for comments and questions, as you model the process using an interactive whiteboard, overhead projector, or computer and LCD projector.

Teaching in action: *History.* A history lesson might begin like this:

> **Teacher:** We've been studying events leading up to the American Revolution. Let's look at several pieces of data I found in the book *Countdown to Independence: A Revolution of Ideas in England and Her American Colonies: 1760–1776* (Bober, 2001). I'll show them one by one on the overhead:
>
> 1. Here's a quote from the pamphlet "Letters from a Farmer in Pennsylvania, to the Inhabitants of the British Colonies," by John Dickinson, which was influential in arousing opposition to the Townshend Acts, which, you'll recall, allowed arbitrary taxation of the colonists by Parliament:
>
>> Let these truths be indelibly impressed on our minds—that we cannot be happy

>> without being free—that we cannot be free without being secure in our property—that we cannot be secure in our property if without our consent others may as by right take it away. (p. 123)
>
> 2. Now here's a picture of the cover of an English publication by the great writer Samuel Johnson. The title is *Taxation No Tyranny; An Answer to the Resolutions and Address of the American Congress.* The caption underneath gives a quote from it, where Johnson wonders how it is "that we hear the loudest yelps for liberty among the drivers of slaves?" (p. 265).
>
> 3. Here's a photograph of an American teapot with a political slogan inside a decorative border: No Stamp Act.
>
> 4. Here we have a map of the 13 colonies.
>
> 5. Now this is a political cartoon created by Benjamin Franklin. It shows a rattlesnake, in pieces, all labeled with the initials of individual colonies. Underneath the picture are the words, "JOIN, or DIE" (p. 36).

The teacher allows a discussion about these data, and clarifies or expands information based on the students' responses and questions. Then, she introduces a question leading to a DBQ essay:

> The last sentences in this great book were written by John Adams to his wife Abigail. The "accomplishment of [the Revolution] . . . was perhaps a singular example in the history of mankind. . . . Thirteen clocks were made to strike as one" (p. 321). Now, use the data supplied from the book and your knowledge of the decades leading to the American Revolution to write an essay about how the war came about, leading to Adams' reflection.

The teacher facilitates student discussion of how they might organize their ideas, connect the pieces of data, and use the data to support their points. He or a student can outline and draft the essay as the rest watch and take notes. Students can flesh out the essay for homework or follow the modeled process to write a different DBQ essay.

Data-based writing is not limited to the social studies. Think of the various sources I mentioned about teaching the subject of robotics. Articles, books, pictures, cartoons, firsthand accounts by inventors, critiques by fellow scientists, statements by patients who have artificial hearts or other robotic devices implanted, and poems can be sources the students can use to analyze and synthesize information. English teachers can use a combination of works by certain authors, works about those authors, or interpretive studies of the authors' works. Figure 7.10 lists some resources that can help teachers find documents and other data

FIGURE 7.10

Resources for obtaining documents and data related to curriculum.

See more suggested titles in Appendix Figure 7.10.

Downey, G. (2007). *The 10 Most Important Documents in History*. Oakville, ON: Rubicon Publishing.

Hudson, W. (2004). *Powerful Words: More Than 200 Years of Extraordinary Writing by African Americans*. New York: Scholastic Nonfiction.

Ideals Publications. (2007). *America's Words of Freedom: Speeches, Documents, and Writings That Moved Our Country*. Nashville, TN: Author.

Panchyk, R. (2009). *The Keys to American History: Understanding Our Most Important Documents*. Chicago: Chicago Review Press.

Saari, P., & Carnagie, J. (2009). *Colonial America: Primary Sources*. Detroit, MI: UXL.

that make curricular inquiry exciting and fruitful, and can be used as data for the students' writing.

Writers often really do the type of thinking and constructing that DBQs require of students; knowing this may help your students understand the purpose of the exercises you ask them to do to practice the method. In his acceptance speech when he was awarded the Laura Ingalls Wilder Medal by the American Library Association in 2001, Milton Meltzer discussed his research and writing method. For his first book, he decided to write about something he knew little about, but wanted to know a lot about, which was African American history. He had grown up in Worcester, Massachusetts, which had been a station on the Underground Railroad. He had read the antislavery poets in school, including Walt Whitman, who used the first person to narrate the perspective of a slave; James Russell Lowell, whose "lines hurt, for he indicted whites of his time who failed to protest slavery" (Meltzer, 2001, p. 426); and John Greenleaf Whittier, whose poems and life story proved to Meltzer that words had consequences. Meltzer began his research for his book on black history in the 1950s, discovering that the subject was almost entirely omitted from school books, and that university scholars' published work "served to harden racism and entrench inequality" (p. 427).

Meltzer decided to combine narrative text with paintings, drawings, photographs, and facsimiles of documents, posters, and cartoons, a structure he has used ever since. So, you could use Meltzer's books themselves as sources of multiple pieces of data that students can interpret and synthesize. Figure 7.11

BookTalk 7.7

Want to take students on a literary field trip through American history? One way to do that is by using documents that shaped thinking and led to action. Using *Words That Built a Nation: A Young Person's Collection of Historic American Documents* by Marilyn Miller (1999), your students can focus on the writing and the content of the Declaration of Sentiments presented at the Seneca Falls Convention, or excerpts from Harriet Beecher Stowe's *Uncle Tom's Cabin,* Woodrow Wilson's "Fourteen Points," Martin Luther King Jr.'s "March on Washington Address," Richard Nixon's letter of resignation, John F. Kennedy's speech at the Berlin Wall, Rachel Carson's *Silent Spring,* Cesar Chavez's speech to striking grape workers, and more. Readers can savor quotes like "The Eagle has landed," "Remember the Ladies," and "December 7, 1941—a date which will live in infamy" in their contexts, and with background information about the authors and responses to the documents, as well as photographs to aid comprehension. Instead of just learning about *Brown v. Board of Education of Topeka,* students can read the Supreme Court's decision that Earl Warren authored. The words and the presentation of the documents in this book are powerful. History is not forgettable when your students experience it through this medium.

lists some of his works, which have to do with social change: "How it comes about, the forces that advance it, and the forces that resist it, the moral issues that beset men and women seeking to realize their humanity" (p. 427). Students can study his style and the structure of his books, and use them as models when they put together a story based on data they discover through research.

As with other literacy strategies, you can't just give the students the DBQs and the data and expect them to be able to write an essay. You must *teach* them how to

BookTalk Online 7.8

A Primary Source History of the Colony of New York (Kupperberg, 2006) and *A Primary Source History of the Colony of Virginia* (Whiteknact, 2006) are part of a series by the Rosen Publishing Group on the 13 original colonies and have a focus on authentic documents. Read more at the Kane Resource Site.

FIGURE **7.11**

A sampling of Milton Meltzer's books containing multiple forms of data.

See more suggested titles in Appendix Figure 7.11.

Albert Einstein (2007). New York: Holiday House.

Henry David Thoreau: A Biography (2007). Minneapolis: Twenty-First Century Books.

Tough Times (2007). New York: Clarion Books.

Willa Cather: A Biography (2008). Minneapolis: Twenty-First Century Books.

John Steinbeck: A Biography (2008). New York: Viking.

BookTalk Online 7.9

Galileo's Commandment: An Anthology of Great Science Writing, edited by Edmund Blair Bolles (1997), is full of examples of beautiful writing by scientists. Hear more at the Kane Resource site.

analyze, interpret, compare and contrast, apply background knowledge, and synthesize. Scaffold instruction so that they aren't overwhelmed with the task. The think-aloud procedure discussed in Chapter 5 allows you to model your own thinking as you read documents and write about them. Start simply—every day in city newspapers there are political cartoons. Paper your walls with them as the year goes on, and spend just a moment letting the students hear your thoughts as you interpret a cartoon in light of current events, or inviting students to do the same for their classmates. Then, comment on a newspaper article and an editorial on the same topic, working your way up to using multiple data sources addressing an issue from different or opposing viewpoints. Write an essay on chart paper and share your thoughts as you draw from your available sources; weigh the reliability, validity, and importance of the evidence; analyze conflicting perspectives, cross out lines you decide to change; create a thesis statement, introduction, and conclusion; use supporting evidence in middle paragraphs, and so on.

You can also guide students and give them a process to follow as they tackle a DBQ. For example, you can instruct them to:

- Read the question carefully to determine the required task, underlining key words, names, places, and issues.
- Write down what they already know about the topic and period.
- Identify each document's type, author, time written, point of view.
- Group documents according to relationships (e.g., data that support a position, data that do not).
- Outline their essay.
- Construct an introduction, a thesis statement, body paragraphs, and a concluding paragraph explaining evidence from the data.

Students who have delved into curricular topics, argued and critiqued positions, found primary sources, formed hypotheses, and expressed opinions in your classroom throughout the year should not find these data-based essays foreign or threatening. For those you see struggling, examine their work-in-progress and talk to them to find out where the difficulty lies. Then, decide whether to try easier DBQs (perhaps with fewer data sources or a simpler task), to reteach parts of the process, or to model the procedure again. Encourage students to deal with this as a powerful way to think and write, and help them as they practice the craft. And, of course, have many books in your classroom library that include multiple perspectives and varied data. Chapters 8 and 9 provide many titles of books that contain interviews and visual texts that have potential as stimuli for data-based writing.

Writing for Critical Thinking and Social Action

In Chapter 5, you were encouraged to learn and construct ways to help your students use higher-level thinking skills in a variety of ways. Writing is one excellent way to promote such thinking. As your students write their thoughts about what is going on around them, current events, controversial issues in your discipline, and literature, they clarify their thinking and discover new ideas and potential solutions. Of course, reading is often an integral part of this process too. The following examples show teachers using writing for the purposes of fostering critical thinking and promoting positive action for social change within the classroom and beyond.

White (2007) began an online discussion group so that middle school students could converse about literature and other topics with some preservice teachers at a university. The TalkBack Project blog was a success, even involving one of the students' fathers who was serving in Iraq and wanting to be part of the literature circle. When administrators decided the project should end due to fears about outsiders' possible access to the blog, students were upset. White suggested the students write to administrators, which they did, with results:

The power of the written word was evident in the reaction of all of the parties involved . . . the administrators were able to see how the collaboration on the TalkBack Project blog had become an important part of my students' lives. One student wrote, "By taking away our access to the TalkBack Project blog, you have taken away my voice." . . . The passionate testimonials from the TalkBack Project participants prompted officials to look into the possibility of hosting a blog discussion on our existing school network. (p. 95)

Zenkov and Harmon (2009), through a project called "Through Students' Eyes" (TSE), helped urban youth to engage in authentic writing activities that could make a difference in theirs and others' lives. The diverse group of students, who were living in poverty, used photographs and accompanying reflections to document "what they believe are the purposes of school, the supports for their school success, and the barriers to their school achievement" (p. 575). The project involved public exhibition of artwork and writing in gallery spaces. The students' work caused change in their teachers: In response to this project and these youths' perspectives we now more often integrate issues of schooling and social justice— including analyses of our communities' tenuous relationships to schools—into our curricula (p. 583).

Teaching in action: *Literature.* High school teacher Linda M. Christenson (2000) consciously tries to teach writing and reading in a predominantly African American, working-class neighborhood, as "a sustained argument against inequality and injustice" (p. 54). Her senior-level Contemporary Literature and Society course carries both history and English credit, and is centered on the question: "Is language political?" Her students write poetry and critical essays in response to texts about culture and language written from diverse perspectives; they explore their linguistic heritage, and they "write the world." Christenson explains what this means in terms of the teacher's role:

> Creating a critical-literacy classroom still means teaching students to read and write. But instead of only asking students to write essays that demonstrate a close reading of a novel or engaging in a literary evaluation of the text, critical literacy creates spaces for students to tackle larger social issues that have urgent meaning in their lives. . . . When students are "steeped" in evidence from one of the units, they begin to write. I want them to turn their anger, their hurt, their rage into words that might affect other people. We talk about [potential] audiences and outlets—from parents, to teens, to corporations. (pp. 62–63)

Christenson helps her students write a test using the format of the SATs but the content, culture, and vocabulary of their school. They travel to nearby colleges, where they give their test to preservice teachers and discuss the results and implications. "My

students have a real audience whose future teaching practice will hopefully be enlightened by their work. They see that what they learn in school can make a difference in the world, and so can they" (p. 64).

These descriptions were intended to help you visualize some of the many ways teachers model, instruct, and create or seize opportunities for writing to think critically about content and issues. Now, I'd like you to take this opportunity to think through writing. How might you apply these lessons to your own teaching in your content area? What kinds of writing to think could you teach your students to do so that, in Christenson's words, "They see that what they learn in school can make a difference in the world, and so can they" (p. 64)?

Writing on Demand

Writers vary in terms of the amount of freedom they have to choose topics and set their own schedules. A well-established novelist might be able to choose any topic and determine a timetable for completion after consulting with his editor. In contrast, a beginning journalist will most likely be given an assignment, be told where to go, and be given a firm deadline. Similarly, in schools, some teachers and student writers could have a great deal of flexibility and ownership for some written projects, but it's likely that there will be times when your students' knowledge and skills will be assessed by exams that involve writing to a prompt. Students in a senior high English class could be asked on a state exam that must be passed in order to graduate to read a poem and an essay on seafaring and then synthesize ideas from the two texts in an essay. History students could be given several texts and visuals having to do with oil distribution and consumption in several countries, and be asked to answer a DBQ using those sources. Science students might have to interpret evidence from an experiment to form a conclusion, and then write about the process they used to reach their answer. So it's essential that you know how to help students write well about a topic someone else has chosen. Angelillo (2005) goes further in advocating an attitudinal stance with regard to writing on demand:

> Teach students to glory in engaging with someone else's ideas or new ideas. There is also the grand satisfaction that comes from wrestling with an idea, from sweating and struggling to figure it out until the light of perception shines. The power and empathy that come from engaging with another's ideas reveal shades of understanding that might remain unknown had someone not offered something else to think about. Teachers rob students of this experience if they do not teach them how to

struggle to understand and then to write about that new understanding. (p. 74)

So how do we go about teaching our students to produce quality writing that demonstrates learning, especially when the writing on demand might be part of a high-stakes, and therefore high-anxiety producing, assessment? Actually, students can be reassured that writing on demand is nothing new; they've had to do it throughout their academic careers, probably as part of their daily environment. Several of the writing forms discussed previously, such as quick writes and summaries, could involve teacher-given prompts, and they often have the purpose of stimulating new thought and getting students ready for deeper learning. The activities contained in the Activating Prior Knowledge boxes in this book involve you responding to prompts I give you.

Angelillo (2005) recommends teachers use the *fishbowl* strategy so students can see modeling on how to make another's topic your own. For this strategy, two or more teachers sit in the room's center, and assign topics somewhat unfamiliar to the other; students watch while each in turn makes the topic her own, maybe having an internal dialogue about what knowledge or experience it connects to, how to bring some emotion to the topic, how to ask questions. Students observe the participants closely, and later can give comments, ask questions, or try it themselves. Although this step involves conversation based on prompts, it can lead to similar situations where the respondent writes an answer rather than talks it out.

Teaching in action: *English and Science.* Picture Magdalena, an English teacher, in a fishbowl setting with Erik, a science teacher.

> **Erik:** Okay, here's my prompt. Imagine you are on our district curriculum committee. The members are meeting because some parents have objected to the way we teach the topic of evolution. What would you say to these community members?
>
> **Magdalena:** I would tell parents that I would encourage students to go beyond their textbooks, to research what scientists are saying—especially scientists who are willing to talk about their own religious beliefs or spiritual lives, so students can see that evolution and religion are not mutually exclusive. I remember a couple of good articles in the *Smithsonian Magazine* . . . (Timer goes off.)
>
> **Erik:** Good initial thinking. I could help you write about your ideas and tell you some good articles to read. But now it's your turn to give me a prompt.
>
> **Magdalena:** Yeah, I like this part. As you know, we English teachers have a love for metaphor. So talk to me about the value of a speaker or writer using metaphor.

> **Erik:** Yikes! It's not like I read a poem with my coffee this morning. But, okay, I can do this, because actually, scientists use metaphor all the time when they're trying to explain difficult topics. They compare one thing to another . . . (Conversation continues.)

Teaching in action: *Social Studies.* Teachers can use writing on demand as part of lessons, to engage students emotionally while activating their knowledge on a topic. A social studies teacher might give the following prompt at the beginning of a class:

> We've been studying current events relating to national policy all semester. I'd like you to spend 10 minutes answering the following prompt in your learning log:
>
> "You were recently appointed as a presidential advisor. Write a memo to the president, giving advice on one of the following issues: war, the economy, energy use, immigration. Be as specific as possible."

After students have written, they can share their ideas, and the teacher can point out how they were able to quickly assess the question and access information they acquired from earlier lessons and outside reading to formulate an answer.

Teachers can prepare students for writing on demand by teaching them to analyze the prompts given. Gere, Christenbury, and Sassi (2005) offer five prompt analysis questions students can ask when facing an assignment:

1. What is the central claim or *topic* called for?
2. Who is the intended *audience*?
3. What is the *purpose* or *mode* for the writing task?
4. What *strategies* will be the most effective?
5. What is my *role* as a writer in achieving the purpose? (p. 67)

Students' self-efficacy with regard to writing on demand should increase as they practice the skill and learn strategies from their content area teachers.

Adaptations for Students with Writing Disabilities

The writing process will be extremely difficult for some of the students you teach, and accommodations or different forms of instruction will be necessary for them to be successful at completing the writing tasks you require. Singer and Bashir (2006) point out that the demands of writing are staggering; for people with language learning disabilities, writing can break down at a number of levels, since writing involves managing multiple processes at the same time. Students can have problems planning, organizing, generating, and/or revising. They can exhibit difficulty due to poor working memory, linguistic knowledge, processing speed, metacognitive processing, reading skills, ability to retrieve words and ideas, ability to attend to a task, and any number of other cognitive and affective factors.

Students with identified writing disabilities may have IEPs calling for resources such as the use of a scribe or a note taker. These students dictate what they want to say and another person does the handwriting for them. Other students might benefit from being able to use a laptop at their desks, or might need to speak their reflections into a voice recorder. Talk with your students to determine what difficulties they're having, and seek assistive technology and human resources to support them.

As you instruct students in writing the particular kinds of reports or genres required for your subject, struggling writers might need more examples, more direct instruction and modeling, more opportunities to revise drafts, or more time to complete the writing tasks. Work with the students and other professionals in your school to enhance their writing experiences and growth.

At times, you might give alternative assignments to certain students who have a writing disability. They can give an oral presentation, for example, applying and synthesizing information that the other students are writing about. Instead of taking a paper-and-pencil test, they might demonstrate their learning better on an oral exam.

Some students may come to you already feeling defeated in the area of writing due to repeated failures throughout their years of schooling. If they lack confidence, they may not like to write and may resist or act as though they don't care.

Singer and Bashir (2006) note the potentially devastating effect of chronic failure with writing on students with language learning disabilities:

> It creates a repeating, self-defeating cycle, wherein unsuccessful output causes the student to attribute failure to poor innate ability, which reduces self-efficacy and results in task avoidance. This can result in a reduced opportunity to acquire a broad repertoire of writing skills and strategies, leading to further failure, reduced self-efficacy, task avoidance, and so on. (p. 578)

So, when you have students who do not complete writing assignments, discover the reasons why and work to reverse some of the damage that earlier experiences may have caused.

HELPING ENGLISH LEARNERS WRITE IN CONTENT AREAS

Consider this explanation given by a non-native English speaker about his writing process:

While choosing Chinese words is second nature to me, extracting the proper English word is much more difficult. In casual communication, my inner thoughts are like free river flowing down directly from my mind to the paper. I can write whatever appears in my mind. When I write compositions, I come into trouble. There are many good sources I could get from the Chinese culture while I write in Chinese; such as literary quotations, famous old stories, and ancient word of wisdom. These rich sources definitely influence my paper quality in Chinese. Unfortunately examples like this are very hard to translate into English. Sometimes I try to make a joke, but it loses its impact in translation. (Connor, 1997, p. 198)

As a content area teacher who uses writing as an integral part of the learning process, you must become aware of how you can help English learners with their writing. Although you are expected to be neither a writing nor an ESL expert, you can encourage English learners and help them realize that "their writing in English is not bad just because it exhibits some rhetorical features of their first language" (Connor, 1997, p. 208). If you understand that there are differences in the written products of native English speakers and ESL students, and have a great respect for the language they come to you with, even as you help them acquire the language of their new school community, you'll look on these differences not as "errors" that imply deficiencies, but simply as differences. Connor concludes:

> Teachers need to be aware of cultural differences in their students' writing and understand their students' composing and revising behaviors. In addition, they need to be sensitive to differing interactional patterns across cultures and adjust collaborative writing groups and other classroom activities accordingly. (p. 208)

So, learn all you can about the cultures and backgrounds of the students in your classroom. Celebrate all the knowledge about language and writing they bring with them, even though it may be different from what you're used to and from your expectations for native English speakers. Quinn (2001) encourages teachers:

> Finding information on immigrant cultures is as easy as asking pertinent questions and observing children's actions in the school. Talking with students and bringing the literature of all cultures into a classroom will provide the wisdom and food for thought that a teacher needs to teach immigrant children. Creating an environment in which all students are welcome moves marginalized students within the lines of a classroom community and gives them the courage and time to experiment with American ways of life. (p. 49)

How does this advice translate into practice? Educational journals are full of teachers' stories of their own learning in terms of how to teach literacy to students from different cultures. For example, Shafer (2001) shares his own and his students' growth during the two years he taught in a rural, Spanish-speaking community of migrant families outside Miami. He recognized two goals common to teachers working with non-native speakers of English:

> There is an urgent need to move judiciously, to teach English with a clear understanding of the fealty these students have for their parents and the heritage they personify. At the same time, there is the concomitant desire to introduce them to an English-speaking world that will offer them increased opportunities both economically and socially. (p. 37)

Shafer crafted his writing instruction and assignments around a series of problems that related to his students. He taught them the importance of using Standard American English, for example, as they wrote formal letters to potential employers. "Instead of mechanically adhering to rules from a book simply as a way to complete an exercise, they were applying them to a literacy experience that made sense. Suddenly correctness was seen in an authentic context" (p. 41). Grammar became part of a problem-solving strategy. Shafer showed his respect for the sophisticated use of *code-switching* (the alternating use of two languages for a purpose) when his students were using other genres such as letter writing.

McDonough and Shaw (2003a) also provide ways to offer English learners opportunities for writing to a variety of audiences for authentic purposes. Their ideas include having students write

- Instructions and invitations to other students
- Information about the school for new students
- Lists, diaries, and notes for themselves
- Letters to pen pals
- Notes to their teachers and to other people in the school asking them about hobbies and interests
- Letters to organizations answering ads and requesting information. (p. 161)

Houk (2005) also advocates having English learners write in meaningful contexts, whether it be shared writing, where the teacher listens to what they say and writes it down; interactive writing, where students take some of the responsibility for the actual writing of what they are verbalizing; guided writing, where the teacher gives some direct instruction and then students apply the lesson to their composition; or independent writing. Jesness (2004) reminds teachers that the language errors of English learners "should be seen in the same light as errors in speech, an unavoidable part of learning a new language" (p. 68). Content area teachers should offer many opportunities for students to practice their writing without being penalized for spelling or grammar inconsistencies.

Content area teachers can help English learners by using reading as preparation for writing and writing as preparation for reading. If students read about a topic from multiple resources representing a range of difficulty levels both before and during writing, they build a sufficient repertoire of vocabulary and concepts (Farnan, Flood, & Lapp, 1994; Krashen, 1981). Students also can organize their thoughts about content topics through writing before reading assigned texts. These strategies may also be appropriate for other students in your classes, including those struggling with literacy for any number of reasons. You can find many resources in books and articles and online that give practical suggestions and share activities that have worked for middle and secondary content area teachers. Teacher Beti Leone (Short, 1999) recommends the use of daily math journals, where students answer the questions: "What did I learn about math today?" and "How can I use what I learned outside of math class (e.g., at home, on the job, in recreation, in other classes)?" (p. 187).

Writing can help English learners, as well as other students, to deal with and share issues of identity. Shagoury (2007) shares her experience with a student from Bosnia who resisted conversation and collaboration, but who was able to communicate some of her anguish resulting from her memories of war and loss. "Telling the stories of these vivid experiences etched in her mind helped Zernia begin to come to terms with her past and take more control of her present. She needed a genuine audience, and she found that in her reading and writing workshop community" (p. 40). Fernsten (2008) discusses the writer identities that ESL learners take on. "Too often ESL speakers and writers accept the judgments [of incompetence] of teachers as truth, unaware of the social and political realities that reinforce the labeling" (p. 44). The author shares a case study of one writer, and gives implications for teaching, including ways we might empower students to ask teachers for the opportunity to rewrite papers and for models of what the teachers consider good papers. She advises, "Discussing writing as a thinking process and not simply as a matter of language accuracy can help students whose language varies from dominant forms and who are contending with a variety of linguistic issues" (p. 51). She believes that teachers can help students change writer identity from negative to more positive.

In an aptly named article, "What's a (White) Teacher to Do About Black English?" (2001), Jonsberg shares how she both shows and teaches respect for her bilingual students who speak Black English, or Ebonics. She refuses to accept adjectives such as "corrupt," "broken," or "defective" to describe dialects. She helps her students, Black English speakers included, learn not to talk about "bad English" and "good English," but instead to recognize the rule structures of different dialects and "different forms of a living and continually changing English" (p. 52). She recognizes the obligation of teachers to help students be facile and fluent in Standard American English, to open up the "Language of Wider Communication" (Smitherman, 1997), but is convinced that we and our students can together "find some ways to play with language that will bring all these ideas to the surface without pedantry and prescription, without alienation from either (or any) kind of speaking" (p. 53). A noble goal for all of us.

Hollie (2001), while expressing a philosophy similar to Jonsberg's, laments:

> Still, many African American students will walk into classrooms and be discreetly taught in most cases, and explicitly told in others, that the language of their forefathers, their families, and their communities is bad language, street language, the speech of the ignorant and/or uneducated. (p. 54)

Hollie shares instructional strategies that can "facilitate the acquisition of Standard American English in its oral and written forms without devaluing the home language and culture of the students" (p. 54). The author's research-based recommendations include designing instruction around the strengths and learning styles of English learners and infusing their history and culture into the curriculum. You can apply these principles in ways that make sense in your specific curricular area as you help all your students write well in your discipline. Figure 7.12 provides a summary of recommendations for helping English learners write in the content areas.

Helpful suggestions for teachers who would like to learn more about linguistic diversity, and how teachers can respect and honor students' language variations while still empowering them with knowledge of standard English, can be found in *In Other Words: Lessons on Grammar, Code-Switching, and Academic Writing* by David West Brown (2009).

CONCLUSION

There are many ways you can use writing to your students' benefit, inspiring them to grapple with the challenges of your discipline, while reinforcing knowledge and thinking skills. In addition, the sharing of your writing and your enthusiasm, commitment, and encouragement can promote a lifelong love of learning. Sanacore (1998) urges teachers and administrators to foster the writing habit among students by building a positive professional attitude toward writing in school, creating a learning environment that nurtures writing growth, providing extended blocks of time for writing across the curriculum, guiding writers in a variety of experiences (including expository, narrative, poetic, and descriptive), helping writers to go public, supporting a visiting authors program, and inviting parents to be partners in promoting the lifetime writing habit. I think he gives very sound advice.

Stephen King concludes his book *On Writing* (2000) not so much with advice as with encouragement, which I'd like to pass along to you and your students now:

> Some of this book—perhaps too much—has been about how I learned to do it. Much of it has been about how you can do it better. The rest of it—and perhaps the best of it—is a permission slip: you can, you should, and if you're brave enough to start, *you will*. Writing is magic, as much the water of life as any other creative art. The water is free. So drink.
> Drink and be filled up. (p. 270)

I'd like to end this chapter with two of my favorite sentences from E. B. White. They close *Charlotte's Web* (1952) and deliver one of the best compliments I've ever heard: "It is not often that someone comes along who is a true friend and a good writer. Charlotte was both" (p. 184). May the same be said of you and your students.

FIGURE 7.12 Recommendations for helping English learners write in the content areas.

- Show respect for all languages in your classroom.
- Learn about the cultures and backgrounds of your students.
- Bring the literature of different cultures into your classroom.
- Create writing assignments that are meaningful to your students, including ones that ask them to use Standard American English for authentic purposes.
- Use reading as a preparation for writing and writing as a preparation for reading.
- Assign daily or regular journal writing.
- Design instruction around the strengths and learning styles of your students.

WEBSITES **C H A P T E R 7** **Access these links using the Kane Resource Site.**

Betsy Byars
www.betsybyars.com

CNN
www.cnn.com

Cyberteens
www.cyberteens.com/cr

Historical Documents
http://teachers.sduhsd.k12.ca.us/tpsocialsciences/
documents.htm

Jim Burke
www.englishcompanion.com

Kaplan and Newsweek
www.kaptest.com

Kathleen Krull
www.kathleenkrull.com

National Gallery of Writing
www.galleryofwriting.org

National Geographic Online
www.nationalgeographic.com

Peter Dickinson
www.peterdickinson.com

Skype an Author Network
www.skypeanauthor.wetpaint.com

Stephen King
www.stephenking.com

TeenInk
www.teenink.com

Upwords
www.upwordspoetry.com

APPLICATION ACTIVITIES

7.1 Create a RAFT assignment based on a relevant text in your content area. Give students suggestions and guidance for writing. Be sure to take on the role of a student as you try out your own assignment. The following examples might spark some ideas:

1. Take on the role of Thomas Jefferson at the First Continental Congress. With your fellow delegates, argue your position of wanting to break away from England.

2. Write a memo from the point of view of your principal regarding proper behavior in the school hallways and stairways. Do not at this point try to give any other position. Be as convincing and rational as possible.

3. Write a letter to your Board of Education, which is considering changing the name of your school from Mulberry Street School to Elizabeth Blackwell Middle School. Let your voice, whether pro or con, be heard in the debate.

7.2 Choose a text appropriate for middle or secondary students in your subject area. Create a writing assignment based on one or more of the types of academic writing and instructional strategies described in the section "Ways of Using Writing in Content Area Classes" (e.g., imitation, freewriting, quick writes, summaries, etc.). Write clear directions for your students, and reflect on how it might benefit them, what you expect to get from them, and what you might discover from their writing. Share and receive feedback for this writing assignment on the Kane Resource Site.

7.3 It's time for you to try your hand at writing a letter. Choose from the following options or create one that serves a need or interest of yours:

1. Select a topic currently being debated in the news, and write a letter to the editor of your local paper expressing your opinion. Be sure to send it; don't view it just as an academic exercise. Save it in a "Letters to the Editor" file to share with your own students.

2. Write a letter to a person actually working in the field you are preparing to teach. It might be a local scientist, artist, historian, actor, accountant, or politician; or write to a scholar at a university or research center regarding a study or an article you read, giving your opinions or asking any questions the text elicited. Again, send it. You may get a response that you can share with your students.

3. Write a letter using a primary source letter from a noted person in the field you teach as a model for style or formality, or write a letter responding to the position expressed in that letter.

7.4 Design an assignment for students that provides opportunities for them to use letter writing to express their opinions about issues relevant to your course or to seek information from people in your field. Be sure to supply names and addresses for them or sources where they can access these themselves. The Internet is a good source of addresses.

8

Speaking and Listening: Vital Components of Literacy

A s you know from your own experience and from Chapter 6, language is alive and dynamic, and thus the meanings, or at least the nuances and connotations, of words change over time. The glossary entry for *literacy* in the *Standards for the English Language Arts* (NCTE & IRA, 1996) reflects this:

> The standards outlined in this document reflect a contemporary view of literacy that is both broader and more demanding than traditional definitions. Until quite recently, literacy was generally defined, in a very limited way, as the ability to read or write one's own name. A much more ambitious definition of literacy today includes the capacity to accomplish a wide variety of reading, writing, speaking, and other language tasks associated with everyday life. (p. 73)

Manuel (1998) claims, "To be able to understand, critique and learn from spoken information is as necessary as the ability to read and write with precision and clarity" (p. 265). She points out instances where students are, on a daily basis, required to use spoken language:

> to negotiate with colleagues; interact with peers; nurture youngsters; empathize; decipher, decode and interpret complex audio-visual messages; speculate about the future and reminisce about the past; greet and converse with familiar people and strangers; and grapple with an array of challenges in their public and private worlds. (p. 266)

The NCTE/IRA (1996) *Standards for the English Language Arts* include attention to oral literacy and communication skills. Standard 4 states, "Students adjust their use of spoken, written and visual language (e.g., conventions, style, vocabulary) to communicate effectively with a variety of audiences and for different purposes" (p. 33). But no longer can we consider oral literacy to be the sole responsibility of English teachers. Integrating oral language activities with other disciplines' curricular material "ensures that students learn the material more thoroughly and practice speaking and listening skills in a focused but varied environment" (Maxwell & Meiser, 1997, p.

"How do we enable students to become more like the members of a jazz quartet, whose interplay good conversation sometimes seems to emulate? Conversation is akin to deliberation, a process that searches for possible answers and explores blind alleys as well as open freeways."

ELLIOT EISNER, 2002, P. 582

117). The National Council for Teachers of Mathematics' (1990) Standard 2 addresses "Mathematics as Communication," positing that students should "be able to reflect upon and clarify their thinking about mathematical ideas and relationships, express mathematical ideas orally and in writing, and ask clarifying and extended questions related to mathematics they have read or heard about" (p. 140). National and state standards for other disciplines make similar claims. Helping our students become skilled listeners and speakers is everyone's job. Welcome the challenge enthusiastically, because increased oral literacy can serve to help students reflect on, learn about, and grapple with issues related to all content areas.

Although the ideal would be to consider all of the aspects of literacy together because they are interrelated, in this chapter I focus on speaking and listening, as I did with writing in Chapter 7. In the examples, however, you'll often see evidence of listening and speaking working together with viewing, reading, and writing as students' literacy and content knowledge grow.

SPEAKING

ACTIVATING PRIOR KNOWLEDGE 8.1

Think of a time when you talked something (e.g., a problem, an issue, a text, a new idea) through with one or more people. Did new knowledge or understanding result? How did that happen?

Now, recall a class you were a part of at some level (middle school, high school, or college) where you think good discussions occurred. How did that happen? What was the teacher's method? Her role? How was student behavior in that class? What were the discussions about? Was the whole class involved or were students in small groups? Did leaders emerge?

Most of us like to talk. We may not all like to talk in a large group, but we can think of circumstances where talk is enjoyable and fulfilling, and sometimes leads to new insights or plans. We can demonstrate this to students by mentioning the historic July 9, 1848, discussion at the Hunt House near Seneca Falls, New York, where Elizabeth Cady Stanton and four other women expressed dismay over the voteless, propertyless status of women and decided to hold a convention. The Women's Rights Movement was conceived. Ten days later that convention was held, 300 joined the conversation, and the Declaration of Sentiments was adopted. Talk led to action and change. Albert Einstein and friends met regularly for years in a discussion group they called the Olympia Academy. They ate cheese, sausages, fruit, and tea, and they talked in order to learn, sometimes becoming so raucous that neighbors complained. The discussions had a large influence on Einstein's work (Severance, 2001, pp. 35–36).

The same is happening in some classrooms today. I recently visited a sixth-grade class that was holding fund-raising projects in order to send money to children in developing countries so that they would not have to work long hours in factories. The initiative came from the students themselves after they read about the problem, talked about their thoughts and feelings, and conducted research looking for solutions. Social justice was not just presented as an ideal here; action followed the productive discussion.

It's well documented, and personal experience probably tells you anyway, that most teenagers love to talk—on the phone, on the Internet, in class. Talk has been used as a means of learning since at least the days of Socrates, who used his questioning techniques to elicit talk from his pupils, leading to new knowledge and understanding. Research confirms that discussions help children clarify their thinking and increase their understanding of what they read. Some contemporary students have been fortunate enough to have attended elementary schools, and maybe also middle schools, where talk is valued as a productive way of learning and meaning-making; it is sanctioned and even encouraged. Yet, Bean (1998) notes that, unfortunately, as students move into the upper grades, "classrooms isolate students from each other at a time when they value conversation" (p. 158). In upper middle grades and in many high schools, talk is discouraged; it may be seen as too hard to control. Quiet and orderliness are valued. Student verbalization during teacher-led reading lessons is often limited to brief, literal-level, text-based responses (Carlsen, 1991; Gambrell, 1987) despite research that demonstrates an increase in inferential, higher-level comprehension when students discuss what they read (Gambrell, Pfeiffer, & Wilson, 1985; Kapinus, Gambrell, & Koskinen, 1991).

Bean (1998) heard from teenagers that there is a notable absence of classroom discussion in their schools, but there are plenty of worksheets to be completed silently and alone. He believes some teachers buy into what he calls a "myth of adolescence—that it is a hiatus or plateau period during which we really should expect very little from students beyond trying to keep them at bay through seatwork" (p. 156). Assumptions such as this too often result in "curriculum planning and delivery that optimizes teacher control and limits students' expression" (p. 156). Wells (1996) studied students in a ninth-grade setting who were not allowed to talk while learning. Students created an underground literacy consisting of elaborate secret notes and letters to each other, providing an authentic audience and context for writing that was missing in the classroom.

Fortunately, many teachers have discovered that talk is healthy and productive in middle school and high school subject area classes and have published accounts of their success and suggestions for others. For example, Nancie Atwell (1998) uses an image to convey the kind of talk that occurred in her classroom when she switched to a reading workshop approach. "My students taught me that the context of books they choose is ripe for rich, dining room table talk about literature" (p. 34). Her students surprised her by reading an average of 35 books per year, but she warns that reading alone is not enough. "Opportunities for social interaction around literature are another component of a reading workshop. Literary talk with a teacher and peers is crucial to kids' development as readers" (p. 40). Figure 8.1 lists resources that allow you to listen in on some interesting and stimulating classroom and out-of-school conversations and student voices.

All talk is not equal. The following sections deal with a variety of types of school talk and give examples and ideas for you to think about as you prepare to teach your subject. Keep in mind that one type of discussion is not inherently better than another; you should vary your formats and procedures depending on your objectives and the particular students you teach.

FIGURE 8.1

Resources that allow you to listen to young people.

See more suggested titles in Appendix Figure 8.1.

Carlson, L. M. (Ed.). (2008). *Voices in First Person: Reflection on Latino Identity.* (F. Morais, Illus., with photos by M. Rivera-Ortiz). New York: Atheneum.

Ellis, D. (2008). *Off to War: Voices of Soldiers' Children.* Toronto, ON: Groundwood.

Garden, N. (2007). *Hear Us Out! Lesbian and Gay Stories of Struggle, Progress, and Hope, 1950 to the Present.* New York: Farrar Straus and Giroux.

O'Brien, T., & Sullivan, M. (2008). *Afghan Dreams: Young Voices of Afghanistan.* New York: Walker.

Sallis, Z. (Compiler). (2009). *Our Stories, Our Visions: 40 of the World's Most Influential Women, 40 of Their Most Intimate Interviews, Powerful Voices Fighting for Change.* New York: Sterling Publishing.

Whole Class Discussion

ACTION RESEARCH   8.A

Before reading the next section, have a discussion about discussions with a few other people who are preparing to be teachers. A forum has been set up for this purpose on the Kane Resource Site. Some of the questions you might consider include:

- What should classroom discussions look like and sound like?
- When are whole classroom discussions appropriate?
- What is the teacher's role in a classroom discussion?
- How can a teacher encourage high-level thinking and critique during a discussion about a text or a curricular or current issue?
- What might some ground rules be for discussion that provide the proper balance between too much control and not enough?
- How should seating be arranged?
- What are some realistic expectations for teachers new to class discussions?

As you might expect, there are no simple answers to any of the questions in Action Research 8.A; rather, I advise you to listen carefully to talk in those classes you observe or participate in, and revise and refine your own thoughts according to what you learn. You can also reap the benefits of other observers' findings, interpretations, and reflections by reading books and articles focusing on classroom talk.

What should classroom discussions look and sound like?

Pace and Townsend (1999) noticed very different conversational styles and results in two classrooms where *Hamlet* was being read. In the first, discussion was teacher-controlled. The following is the researchers' interpretation of a particular exchange:

- First the instructor demonstrated that he was searching for a specific answer to his question . . . , a question he finally answered himself.
- Second, he dismissed the efforts of Roxanne as she consulted the text to answer the question. His reply to Roxanne—stating a line then restating the question—was nonresponsive and emphasized his textual knowledge and his desire for a specific answer.
- Third, he answered the question, which is an interpretive one, as though it had a fixed, correct answer.

- Finally, he suggested he knew Hamlet's perspective. . . . The instructor's responses and nonresponses suggest he is the sole source of knowledge in this setting. (p. 44)

In contrast, in the second classroom, described by the researchers as a dialogic class, multiple perspectives were examined and considered. After presenting an excerpt from a verbatim transcript of an initial discussion, Pace and Townsend again list several points of interpretation:

- First, though the teacher was the major contributor, she did not initiate this line of exploration or assume that she knew Hamlet's thoughts. Rather she entered a process of discovery with her students.

- Second, her language was laced with uncertainty markers ("I think," "sort of," "I'm not sure") that signaled the pliable nature of her thinking about Hamlet and suggested that she was not looking for "right" answers.

- Third, she modeled text referencing as a way of investigating literary meaning, thereby demonstrating a strategy that students might use in her absence to construct their own understandings. As is typical in a dialogic classroom, this teacher encouraged students to try out their ideas. She reminded them that "you have to make up your mind as you go along," an instruction that supported the ambiguous nature not only of this play but of the study of literature in general. (pp. 45–46)

These two examples of discussion types can be applied to texts beyond literature. For instance, if you are a science or social studies teacher, you might bring in newspaper articles and editorials about an environmental controversy involving the school neighborhood and encourage the kind of thoughtful discussion evident in the second teacher's methods. No matter what your subject area, you can encourage students to think through talking, to learn through listening to others, and to engage in discussion that could lead to a desire to learn more and to act.

Unfortunately, the most typical form of classroom discussion is recitation (Alvermann, 1986; Alvermann, O'Brien, & Dillon, 1990; Hoetker & Ahlbrand, 1968). I'm sure you recognize the format: the teacher asks a question and calls on a student, the student responds, the teacher gives feedback. Then, the cycle is repeated. Here's what recitation might sound like:

Teacher: Why did the Giver show Jonas the tape of his father releasing the baby? Moreka?

Moreka: Well, I think he respected Jonas and they sort of had a pact to be truthful. He wanted him to know the truth.

Teacher: Good answer! Any other ideas? Jacob?

Jacob: The Giver knows how whacko the society has gotten. The only way he'll get Jonas to take action with him is to rile him up and make him see the evils that are hidden from everyone else.

Teacher: Ah, and it worked, didn't it? So, what was this plan for action they came up with? Claudia?

If you observe a session like this, which some would not even call a true discussion, you may notice that it is quite likely that some students are not engaged. Also, it may seem like it is more a game of "Guess what's in the teacher's head," or more of a comprehension check than an open sharing of ideas and reactions. Too often, perhaps especially in math classes, what is called discussion is little more than going over problems and answers. You might be surprised at the number of students who agree with the child who concluded, "We have discussions so that kids who go to the bathroom can know what they missed" (Almasi, 1996, p. 3). There are ways to avoid this stilted quality and stifling atmosphere. Bean (1998) asserts, "A constructivist classroom is the antithesis of a place where the teacher controls learning with prepackaged answers to teacher-generated questions" (p. 160).

An authentic discussion adds new ideas and insight, not just a recapitulation of what a text or teacher has said. Conley (1995) points out that during whole group discussions, teachers can guide students through the writing process, teach vocabulary and concepts, play devil's advocate, or use some other form of generating controversy to further reasoning skills, provide transitions, generate new ideas, and form conclusions. The teacher can encourage students to ask real questions they want answers to, or to initiate discussion by reading aloud a journal response to a text. Teachers can ask questions that indicate an interest in the students' reactions and that raise more issues and possibilities, questions that actually invite participation instead of preordained answers about the text. In one classroom, the students and teacher brainstormed to come up with a list representing what might or should happen during a discussion; the resulting chart, posted in the classroom, included the verbs "question, clarify, refine, explain, justify, predict, speculate" (Gambrell & Almasi, 1996, p. 75).

When are whole class discussions appropriate?

Having a whole class discussion about a curricular topic or current interest is a common activity in classrooms, and it is appropriate at various times and for different purposes. According to Conley (2005), "Whole class discussion is most appropriate for uncovering misconceptions, demonstrating skills and procedures, and covering some fairly simple facts or concepts in a short amount of time" (p. 317).

Some educators favor teacher-oriented discussion at the beginning of a school year or unit, gradually moving toward student-centered discussions as the students develop their own strategies for understanding text and gain independence (Applebee, 1992; Gambrell & Almasi, 1994). It's perfectly fine for a teacher to ask questions early on in a unit to find out what students know about a topic or how they initially feel about a sensitive current issue in the school, the community, or the world. Or, if a complex topic, such as applications of statistical procedures, is being covered, the teacher may realize it is unwise to send students off in small groups until they are more comfortable and have more to contribute.

I like to hold a whole group discussion based on a common text early in any given semester. I tell my students that I could form smaller groups, and I will for future works that we read, but at this point, I can't be everywhere at once eavesdropping, and I can't bear to miss out on a single thing that's said! I want us to have a common bond and a common frame of reference for future lessons. But I also recognize that when I have a large circle we're losing something in terms of opportunities for more people to do more talking.

What is the teacher's role?

How involved, and how directive, should you be in class discussions? That depends on a number of factors. You might find that some of your classes need little structure or facilitation from you, while others flounder without your direct involvement. At times you might choose to say virtually nothing to avoid influencing the students' grappling with a text. Sometimes, I join my thoughts and responses to others. In some instances, I remind them that I'm just another reader, and my opinion isn't privileged; but in other circumstances, I might hold some knowledge that they don't have that makes my voice more one of authority.

In my classroom, when a student directs a comment to me, I may say, "Look to your classmates, not to me. Talk to each other." They're not used to doing this, so I must force myself to be the facilitator, modeling for them how to keep the conversation going in productive directions without taking over and acting like the ultimate authority.

That doesn't necessarily mean I can never give an opinion. Once, during a heated discussion on *The Giver* with preservice teachers, a student named Darryl said he didn't think this book should be read by middle school students because of the suicide in it. I looked around and no one seemed willing to take him on, so I said, "Let me join in as another reader, not the teacher. What suicide?" He referred to Rosemary's asking to be released and injecting herself. I replied, "I don't see that as suicide any more than Socrates drinking the hemlock, or St. Appolonia throwing herself into the flames

her persecutors had prepared for her to spare them the act of killing her." At that point others jumped in, allowing me to sit back and let it go on without me. Rapport had already been established, so Darryl did not think I was attacking him personally just because I offered an alternative to his interpretation. The students knew that I value different opinions, that I was not looking for the recitation-type talk most of them had experienced when they were secondary school students. It was fine with me if Darryl changed his mind and fine if he stuck by his original theory (which he did).

Another time, several in our whole class literature circle on *The Giver* thought that Lois Lowry would be in favor of euthanasia today, citing as evidence that the old people in the novel were released. I used this as a teaching opportunity, helping them to see the release of the old in the context of the whole story. It takes a lot of skill for a teacher to know when to do what during a discussion. We don't want to discourage thoughtful answers and tentative hypothesizing, but neither should we accept interpretations that are clearly outside those possible or plausible from the text. Think of other fields (e.g., music, the theatre, woodworking, chemistry), where a wiser or more experienced mentor guides beginners. Given the right atmosphere, rapport, and spirit, we can help our students rethink initial responses. And, luckily, the burden of giving or receiving a grade is totally absent during such discussions. Also, accept that if students stick to their original thinking, even if you consider it flawed, the sky will not fall; they will have many more opportunities to read material that will help them think deeply, grow in knowledge, and understand literary concepts and dimensions.

Young (1998), after analyzing interactions in several classrooms, concludes: "I also no longer think that teachers need to strive for a neutral position in class discussions. Teachers can voice their opinions in learning environments that encourage disagreement, debate, and respect for all voices. I no longer think that adolescents are uninterested in the opinions of teachers either" (p. 261).

How can a teacher facilitate discussions that encourage high-level thinking?

How does one achieve a classroom climate that is conducive to thoughtful, stimulating, and knowledge-building discussion? This is your responsibility as the teacher, whether the class is discussing a work of literature, a textbook selection, a newspaper editorial, a movie review, or a student-initiated, school-related concern.

You can facilitate discussion in a number of ways. The method selected depends on the topic, the particular mix of students involved, the time available, and so on. You might start off with a question that requires reasoning-level skills. Zwiers (2008) points out the difference between explicit, closed, or "display" questions (p. 103), the answers to which are generally known by the teacher already, and more open-ended questions that allow for longer and more personalized responses. Good open-ended questions, or elaboration questions, can enhance students' use of higher-order thinking skills, such as evaluation, synthesis, perspective, and application. Zwiers recommends having some "prompt posters" displayed containing some general open-ended prompts, such as,

- "Use hindsight to explain how this problem or event could have been avoided."
- "Do you have any more questions now than before reading?"
- "How does the author try to persuade you? Are you convinced? Why?" (p. 108, adapted from Robb, 2003)

Zwiers believes questions are overused in schools and recommends that we ask fewer questions in order to give more time for thoughtful answers, and that we implement assessments and learning tasks that are not dependent on questions. "Students have been bombarded by questions in all forms from their first day of school. They are tired of questions, especially other people's questions" (p. 110). He does believe we should help students learn to formulate their own questions that can lead to further learning. "Real-world people are asked to produce or perform, asking their own questions along the way, and are not being stopped every few minutes to answer less important questions" (p. 110).

One way to get students talking is to ask a good open-ended question, perhaps based on a text the class has just read, and call on one student, who then calls on another to continue. After that person gives an opinion or a problem-solving suggestion, she calls on yet another, perhaps from among those with hands raised, to continue the discussion. You might stay fairly quiet until the talk runs out of steam or a response requires correction, clarification, or expansion.

Another activity that can get students talking is "Take a Side" (Wilhelm, 2002; Zwiers, 2008). You can present an issue or have students read a text, then have them go to different spots in the classroom representing various positions. If they choose to remain in the middle of a continuum, they need to be able to give their rationale or evidence for being undecided or not at one of the poles. A science teacher might ask students if they remember how they felt when they first heard that Pluto was no longer considered a planet (or they could ask older siblings or parents), and to decide whether they think scientists should have left well enough alone and kept Pluto included in the classification of the solar system. After discussion from various perspectives, the teacher could give a booktalk for Neil de Grasse Tyson's *The Pluto Files: The Rise and Fall of America's Favorite Planet* (2009) (see BookTalk 8.1).

BookTalk   8.1

Do you predict your students would end up in opposite corners of the room if you posed the Pluto problem to them as in the exercise above? If so, you'll not be surprised that one of the chapters in Neil de Grasse Tyson's *The Pluto Files: The Rise and Fall of America's Favorite Planet* (2009, also available as a DVD, 2010, distributed by PBS) is titled "Pluto Divides the Nation." The book and DVD chronicle Pluto's fall from grace. Tyson refuses to take sole responsibility for the demotion of Pluto to "dwarf planet" status, despite the hate mail he has received; actually, the International Astronomical Union voted for the reclassification in 2006. If you want to hear this renowned and witty astrophysicist's personal recommendations for how teachers should now teach about Pluto, or get the lyrics to Pluto-related songs he includes, you'll have to read or watch *The Pluto Files!*

Susan Hynds, a university professor who spent a sabbatical coteaching in a middle school classroom, learned to transform the patterns of talk so that students could be more responsible for their own learning. Finders and Hynds (2003) offer this list of ways to facilitate class discussions:

- Ask no questions to which I already know (or think I know) the answer; in fact, ask no questions at all, if I can avoid it.
- Allow for "wait time" and rehearsal (in the form of freewriting, pair-shares, or just a brief "heads-down" time) before inviting all students into a large group discussion.
- Help students have something in their hands as well as their heads (a bit of writing, graphic organizer, drawing) before opening a discussion.
- Make abundant use of nonverbal prompts such as movies, songs, and photographs to stimulate discussion.
- Don't get obsessed with the amount of time that I hold the floor (teachers do often know more than students, after all), but try to bite my lip whenever a silence seems unbearable or sharing my own personal experience seems more tempting than waiting for students to share theirs.
- Find a way to recognize, but not spotlight, shy or reluctant students. (pp. 255–256)

Figure 8.2 provides a summary of recommendations for facilitating classroom discussions, and following are additional points to consider. Figure 8.3 shows a task sheet a math teacher uses as part of a concept lesson on arithmetic sequences, and a discussion he facilitates to encourage reasoning skills in his students.

FIGURE **8.2** **Recommendations for facilitating classroom discussions.**

FIGURE **8.2** **Recommendations for facilitating classroom discussions.**

- Encourage students to ask questions to which they *want* answers.
- Ask questions that raise issues and possibilities.
- Brainstorm a list of meaningful ways to participate (e.g., question, clarify, refine, explain, justify, predict, speculate).
- Direct students to speak to each other rather than to you.
- Model ways to keep the discussion productive.
- Give an opinion when appropriate.

FIGURE **8.3** **Task sheet used in a lesson on arithmetic sequences.**

EXAMPLES

3, 3.1, 3.2, 3.3, 3.4, 3.5, 3.6

–13, –2.9, . . ., 130, 141, 152

The amount of money each hour in a radio giveaway jackpot that begins with $100 and increases by $20 every hour until there is a winner.

15, 10, 5, 0, –5, –10, . . .

The amount of money in Betty's jar each Saturday if she starts with $60 and puts in exactly $7.50 each Friday night. (She never removes money or puts any in at any other time.)

22.6, 22.6, 22.6, 22.6, 22.6, 22.6

The number of bricks in the first, second, third, fourth, etc. row, arranged as follows:

NONEXAMPLES

7, 0.7, 0.07, 0.007, 0.0007, 0.00007

46, 6.78, 2.60, 1.61, . . . 1.02, 1.00, 1.00, 1.00

The monthly savings account balance of a person who puts in $750 the first month and leaves it there, allowing it to collect interest at the rate of 4% compounded monthly.

The ages of all the people in our class, listed in alphabetical order.

. . . 16, 9, 4, 1, 0, 1, 4, 9, 16, . . .

1, 2, 4, 8, 16, . . . , 1,048,576

1, 1, 2, 3, 5, 8, 13, 21, . . .

HOW ARE THE EXAMPLES ALIKE? HOW DO THEY DIFFER FROM THE NONEXAMPLES?

Write your first conjecture here:

_____
_____
_____

Write your second conjecture here:

_____
_____
_____

Write your third conjecture here:

_____
_____
_____

Write your fourth conjecture here:

_____
_____
_____

(continued)

FIGURE 8.3 Continued.

Mr. Citerelli: Bill, read your first conjecture.

Bill: The examples are alike because they're all in the same column. The nonexamples are in a different column.

Mr. Citerelli: That surely can't be contradicted. Now, let's hear an idea that might explain what I had in mind when I grouped the examples on the left and the nonexamples on the right. Okay, Mavis, you start: keep it going.

Mavis: The first thing I noticed is that both columns contain sequences. But those on the left have more of a pattern to them. Jeannie.

Jeannie: The ones on the right have patterns also. So, just having a pattern can't be it. Okay, Mark.

Mark: Not all of them. Look at the second one.

Jeannie: Sure it does—

Mr. Citerelli: Excuse me. Let's allow these two to hash this out in a two-way discussion while the rest of us listen.

Jeannie: The numbers on the second one are getting smaller; that's a pattern.

Mark: Not the last two numbers.

Jeannie: They might if we saw more decimal places. I think it has something to do with taking square roots. I played around with roots on my calculator and there's something related to roots of 46 with those numbers.

Mr. Citerelli: Excuse me. Mark, do you agree that at least some of the nonexample sequences have predictable patterns?

Mark: Sure.

Mr. Citerelli: Those that agree, raise your hands. . . . It looks like that's one thing we agree on. Bill, would you please come up to the board and help us keep track of the points on which we all agree? Mavis, do you want to modify your conjecture?

Mavis: No, but I'll withdraw it because we agree that some of the nonexamples have patterns also.

Mr. Citerelli: Thank you. Inez, read yours, and then keep it going.

Inez: You get the next number by adding something to the one before. Okay, Chico.

Chico: That's not right because look at the nonexample. You add something to get to the next one. 1+1=2, 1+2=3, 2+3=5, 3+5=8, and so on. So, if Inez is right, then that one should be on the left side. Okay, Luis.

Luis: Besides, if Inez is right that you just added something, then the numbers should all be going up, but two of 'em do [sic] down and one stays the same!

Mr. Citerelli: Excuse me. Let's hear from Inez because it's her conjecture we're discussing.

Inez: First of all, Luis, if you add negatives, they go down. Also, I'm changing my conjecture so that it's this: You get the next number by adding the same amount to each one.

The discussion continues, with more students joining in, using calculators to test hypotheses on examples and nonexamples, formulating more example sequences, reflecting on processes, generalizing from specifics, with hints from Mr. Citerelli. A follow-up discussion the next day involves students verifying and refining their conclusions (Cangelosi, 1996, pp. 89–90).

Cangelosi, James S., *Teaching Mathematics in Secondary and Middle School: An Interactive Approach,* 3rd edition, ©2003, pp. 182, 185. Adapted by permission of Pearson Education, Inc., Upper Saddle River, NJ.

How can you maintain control without overcontrolling?

Many decisions must be made when setting the ground rules to guide a discussion. Listen in on a scene from Chris Crutcher's novel *Staying Fat for Sarah Byrnes* (1993). Ms. Lemry is the teacher of a class called Contemporary American Thought, an elective course designed to help students examine their beliefs. Ms. Lemry begins by setting some ground rules and explaining her decisions:

> A number of you have chosen abortion as your topic. . . . Let me warn you, this is a topic that can get out of hand. Adults don't handle it well. I'd be surprised if there weren't people in the room who have had experience with abortion, either directly or through friends. So I'm going to keep a tight rein on things. I will feel free to remove you from the discussion, or even the room, if you're disrespectful toward other people's views. (p. 85)

If students are allowed to be a part of setting the discussion rules, they are usually quite reasonable. They understand that it makes sense:

- For one person to talk at a time.
- For speakers to feel secure about not being unkindly laughed at or put down.
- For all but the speaker to be listening carefully.

- For speakers to make an effort to project their voices in consideration of the listeners.
- For there to be no side conversations or whispering going on.
- For certain individuals or subgroups not to dominate the discussion.

You and your students may decide together that a person's right to pass on a given issue should be respected. You are responsible for walking that fine line—encouraging the quiet or shy students to participate without making them feel pressured or uncomfortable. Also, you should be aware of gender issues. Research has shown that even teachers who thought boys and girls had an equal voice in their classes are often surprised when they review a taped discussion or a scripted conversation and discover that this is not the case (Sadker & Sadker, 1994). The same holds true in terms of race, social groups, and students with disabilities or special educational needs. At times, you may find it helpful to debrief after a discussion and decide together whether some rules should be adjusted for future talk. Remain flexible.

In an effort to combat the appalling statistics showing that "American students spend, on average, three hours of a five-hour school day sitting passively while their teachers talk," Krogness (1995, p. 99) laid the groundwork for class discussions and taught her students specific techniques such as asking questions that require more than a yes/no answer and verbalizing problems in terms of what is wrong rather than who is at fault. But she also set rules for herself. "I promised not to explain or defend my point of view during this discussion, but I would keep the conversation moving, act as a monitor, and record each speaker's thoughts on a big, yellow legal pad" (p. 111).

How should the seating be arranged?

There is no one best way to have students arranged for discussion, and you have to work within the constraints of your room and its furniture. Recall when you were in classrooms where the desks were in rows and may have been bolted to the floor. The students all faced the front of the room, so they could look only at the teacher, the faces of people next to them, and the backs of a lot of heads, unless they sat in the front. When everyone faces the front, those students who sit near the back often cannot hear remarks made by those ahead of them. This situation hardly leads to fruitful, enjoyable conversation. You can't think of any group that gathers to talk whose members choose to sit that way—such a scenario is preposterous.

Perhaps the most important thing to remember is to arrange the students so that they can make eye contact with each other. Many teachers prefer a horseshoe configuration, which is fine if the teacher must be separate, perhaps to put notes on the board or project something from a computer onto a screen. Often, I ask students to move their desks or tables into a large circle when we have a whole class discussion. I sit among them, choosing a seat on the side or in the back of the room. (If I remain in the front, I find that the circle doesn't quite close in around me; the gaps tell me they still separate me as the teacher.) As the talk progresses, if students tend to look at me, I gently remind them to look at the person who last talked or to the group in general rather than at me.

What are realistic expectations for teachers new to class discussions?

Don't expect instant success and perfection at leading large group discussions from the students or from yourself. You will get better at facilitating with practice. You might audio- or video-record some of your class discussions, and analyze them later to reflect on your comments and decisions, as well as to check on whether the interactions are balanced and fair. Don't be too hard on yourself—we all can think of the "perfect" teacher comment after our class has left the room, when we don't have the pressure of making split-second decisions. In general, if the discussion is animated and shows that thinking, questioning, and new understanding are present, consider it a success. If those things are not occurring, perhaps a colleague or mentor could listen to or watch the recording, or come in and observe, and offer suggestions. Remain confident as you continue to learn through talk and listening just as you want your students to.

Small Group Discussions

Think of great discussions you've had, perhaps with your roommate late into the night in your dorm room or with a close friend in a coffee shop after a movie. Sometimes, five or six people can get into an animated discussion that's just as good, though of course different. However, if 25 people are at a party, there is not just one conversation going on, with one person talking while everyone else politely listens and waits for a turn. So, depending on your purposes, you'll find much to be gained from smaller group discussions.

Almasi (2002), based on a review of her own and others' research, offers advice for creating contexts that use peer discussion groups to promote active engagement, comprehension, and metacognitive ability:

> Such spaces must enable students to think, examine, critique, and inquire about the texts they read. This means that teachers themselves need to relinquish some of the control that they typically maintain in such contexts. Rather than asking questions and pursuing topics they feel are important for compre-

hending text, teachers must trust and value students' questions. . . . Teachers who have been successful in such endeavors often model and teach students how to monitor their understanding by using sticky notes to record things they wonder about or are confused by. . . . The peer discussion group then becomes the site in which students share and resolve such comprehension dilemmas for themselves. (p. 237)

Parr and Maguiness (2005) added an element of discussion to the traditional practice of sustained silent reading (SSR) with inner-city secondary school students in New Zealand. Some of their students were reluctant to participate in SSR for various reasons, so a science teacher, social studies teacher, and English teacher "developed and tried an instructional conversation model to support SSR practice where, through talk, teachers and students shared experiences, exchanged knowledge, and made explicit the practice of choosing and engaging in text" (p. 99). The program showed positive benefits for students, and resulted in the teachers getting to know their students better, particularly in terms of their out-of-school literacy practices.

The more authentic examples for small group discussion you can think of, the more likely you will realize that discussion is valuable and does indeed lead to insight, learning, growth, and action. Lives have been turned around as a result of attending AA meetings. Busy people come together weekly at local bookstores to talk about their reading and writing and hear about what other people are reading and writing. Town meetings are held to discuss environmental, economic, political, or educational controversies. You must point out to your students that discussion in your classroom is not just a time filler, a social break, or a frill; rather, it's an authentic way to help them grapple with the content and concepts of your course, to converse with each other over important documents or literature.

What is your role as the teacher when your students are working in small groups? It depends. At times, if you've set up guidelines and expectations, the best thing you can do is to stay out of their way. When more guidance is needed, you can:

- supply resources,
- serve as a consultant to groups that solicit your help,
- monitor interactions, and
- observe and take notes on individuals you're learning about as they contribute, struggle, or disengage.

If you find students need even more structure to be productive, then:

- assign roles within groups such as facilitator, reporter, vocabulary builder, and summarizer for a limited time,

- give optional guide questions to be used if conversation lags, or
- provide suggestions for projects, such as semantic maps, to be completed during talk.

It takes work to build a discourse community, and teachers face challenges as they teach students to learn through talking and listening. *The Professional Teaching Standards* issued by the National Council of Teachers of Mathematics (1991) identifies aspects of the teacher's role in classroom discourse, including the following:

- posing questions and assignments that challenge and engage students' thinking;
- listening carefully to their ideas;
- deciding which of the things students bring up to pursue in depth;
- monitoring participation and deciding how and when to encourage individuals; and
- deciding when to clarify issues and when to allow students to struggle with difficulties. (p. 35)

At first, students may not know how to talk to each other about literature, research articles, national news pieces in magazines, or other texts; they may be reticent or feel insecure because they are so used to, conditioned by, and dependent on the recitation format described earlier. You might have to model the procedure, perhaps by hand-picking a few students to join you in discussing a newspaper editorial and then having the class point out things that worked well and things that impeded further sharing. Bring in volunteers from the community or from among your colleagues to take part in a discussion of an event that your students could analyze and comment on before they go off in their own groups.

Teaching in action: *Language Arts.* Clarke (2007) applied critical discourse analysis to a transcript of a conversation that occurred in a fifth-grade classroom literature circle. Students were sharing responses to the novel *Shiloh* (Reynolds Naylor, 2000), but Clarke discovered that other things were happening as well. One theme that emerged was that girls' voices were noticeably missing; girls were marginalized by dominant boys who ignored or interrupted them repeatedly. Clarke gives us data:

Looking at the text as a whole, the girls only took 29 turns while the boys spoke 81 times. What was even more startling was that the boys' length of turns dramatically overwhelmed that of the girls. The girls tended to use few word responses—either to call on the boys . . . or to try to assert themselves. The girls spoke for 38 lines while the boys occupied 215. (p. 116)

Clarke assures us that the themes of this discussion reflected a general pattern in his larger analysis of many conversations. His work can serve as a reminder to us of the importance of attending to power relations and social interactions when we have our students work in small groups. His explanation of what he did after discovering the gender imbalances is helpful. He resisted the easy solution of implementing single-gendered groups. Rather, he purposely chose works to be read for future literature circles that directly addressed gender issues in order to raise awareness. He had students view recordings of their discussions, which caused them to become aware of who got to talk and who was silent, and then to create some participation rules together. He taught some mini-lessons on group processes, also.

Questions and topics can be crucial to the success of some small groups. Sometimes, I ask students to create good questions to bring with them to discussion groups, or topics they really do wonder about. I ask them not to use any questions they already know the answers to; such questions are not fruitful discussion starters. Figure 8.4 shows examples of questions my students composed to bring to their discussion groups after reading Katherine Paterson's *Jacob Have I Loved* (1980).

Probst (2007) offers an activity that involves annotating a text using sticky notes as a way to help readers create real questions, which he partially defines as "one[s] for which you would very much like an answer" (p. 50). Groups can discuss individuals' questions, and can then bring particularly intriguing questions before the whole class. Debriefing after the activity allows students to think about the process of discussion.

I decided to try this activity for myself. Armed with sticky notes, I read the first pages of Sarah Vowell's *The Wordy Shipmates* (2008) and created the questions shown in Figure 8.5 that I could ask in a literature circle. You might want to tackle a text in your discipline so that you will have a model to show your students as you introduce this activity and explain its benefits.

You'll be amazed at what you can learn about your students and their thinking by listening to them as they talk about issues and problems. In fact, when students work in small groups to solve mathematical problems, their cognitive behavior mirrors that of expert problem solvers (Artzt & Armour-Thomas, 1992; Schoenfeld, 1987; Whitin & Cox, 2003).

Teaching in action: *Math.* Artzt and Yaloz-Femia (1999) reported surprising discoveries when analyzing the dialogue of fifth graders doing mathematical problem solving in small groups. Students were given a problem showing a number line with a 0 point and a 1 point a few inches apart, with a picture of a cricket jumping from the 1 back toward the 0. The problem stated, "A cricket is on the number line at point '1.' He wants to get to point '0' but he only hop [sic] half the remaining distance each time." Several questions are asked, such as where the cricket would be on the number line after the first hop, second hop, tenth hop, nth

---

FIGURE 8.4   **Examples of student-created discussion questions based on *Jacob Have I Loved*.**

- Behaviors are modified by conditioning. Have you thought about what has reinforced each character's behavior, both before and in response?
  —*Branden Wood*

- What is the significance of the Captain's house being destroyed in the storm? Is there any symbolism attached to it?
  —*Sarah Beckwith*

- I wonder why the Captain decided to give Caroline the money to go to school off the island instead of Louise. Couldn't he tell she was unhappy there? I wonder what would have happened if Louise did get the money instead of Caroline.
  —*Christianna Hamm*

- Does Caroline have any friends? Was every child/person in town so in awe of her because of her talent or so afraid because she was frail that they didn't talk to her?
  —*Kristen Paglia*

- What are the cultural structures that impact the relationships of the women in this story?
  —*Diane Zeller*

- Do you think there was any love in the grandmother's heart for Louise?
  —*Jeremy Lahnum*

FIGURE   8.5   Sample "real questions" for a discussion of *The Wordy Shipmates* (2008).

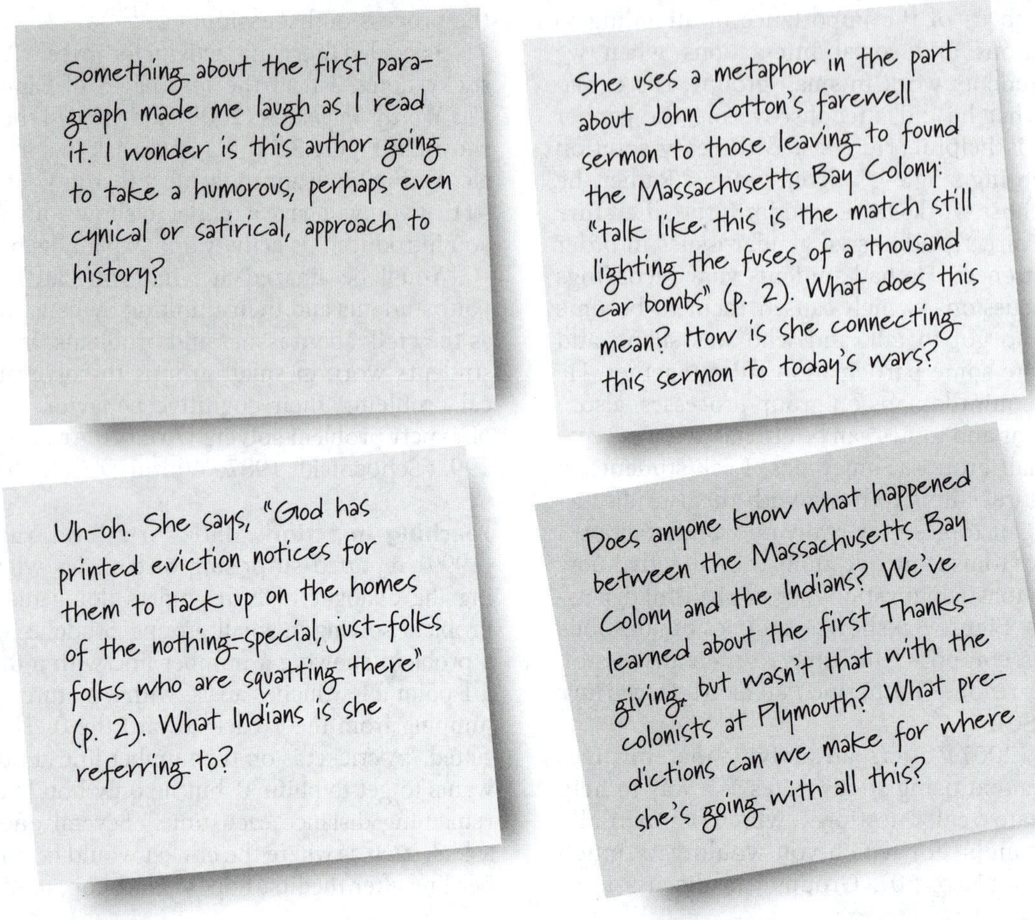

Something about the first paragraph made me laugh as I read it. I wonder is this author going to take a humorous, perhaps even cynical or satirical, approach to history?

She uses a metaphor in the part about John Cotton's farewell sermon to those leaving to found the Massachusetts Bay Colony: "talk like this is the match still lighting the fuses of a thousand car bombs" (p. 2). What does this mean? How is she connecting this sermon to today's wars?

Uh-oh. She says, "God has printed eviction notices for them to tack up on the homes of the nothing-special, just-folks folks who are squatting there" (p. 2). What Indians is she referring to?

Does anyone know what happened between the Massachusetts Bay Colony and the Indians? We've learned about the first Thanksgiving, but wasn't that with the colonists at Plymouth? What predictions can we make for where she's going with all this?

---

hop. The students are asked to explain why the cricket does or does not ever get to the point labeled 0.

One group of students tried a different tactic to figure out a pattern, and again their talk crossed disciplinary lines. They folded a piece of paper over and over, and realized that even after they were physically unable to fold it anymore, theoretically it could continue to be folded in half. Simone explains, "I can keep folding this until the Messiah comes! . . . What I'm trying to say is that it's always going to have somewhere to jump. Even if it's half of an atom. . . . I can keep on folding this until I get a million paper cuts" (pp. 122–123). Brian concludes, "It will get so tiny. Like an atom. Like a neutron. . . . It is impossible to stop folding that because it will keep on going, it is impossible for the cricket to reach the 0" (p. 123). The researchers found in the student talk evidence of abstract thinking and mathematical problem solving. They recommend that teachers require each student to write a description of the solution and supporting mathematical reasoning after working in small groups.

Alternative Discussion Formats

Inside–outside circle

One enjoyable way to get your students comfortable talking with each other about issues is to conduct an "inside–outside circle" discussion (Kagan, 1989).

Teaching in action: *Spanish.* I was introduced to this strategy when I watched a video of a Spanish class at a parents' night. Chris Paul arranged her students into two circles, with each person in the inside circle facing someone in the outside circle. She gave a prompt, such as "¿Qué hiciste durante el fin de semana?" ("What did you do over the weekend?"), and students began conversing with their partners. There were a dozen conversations in Spanish going on at once, but the students were focused on their own. After a few minutes, a timer went off, and one circle moved clockwise—a new question initiated a discussion with new pairings. The teacher explained that her students would never get the necessary amount of practice speaking and listening to the language if she used a typical seating arrangement and method of questioning one student at a time. The students loved being immersed in the language and being given so many opportunities to experiment with conversation in a nonthreatening atmosphere.

You are limited only by your own imagination once you start modifying this activity to suit your students' needs and relevant curricular topics. Read an editorial from a current newspaper about the environment, global trading, Internet abuses, economic forecasts, or cheating in and outside of schools, and set the circles to talking. Students can suggest issues they want to discuss. It is a good way to activate background knowledge and prime students for a new unit. Of course, you can use a line rather than a circle if this fits the constraints of your classroom better. Figure 8.6 illustrates a lesson using this approach.

Modified Socratic seminar

A somewhat similar method to inside–outside circle that will start your students talking is "Socratic seminar."

Teaching in action: *Math.* High school math teacher Leah Casados (Tanner & Casados, 1998) modified the "Socratic Seminar" approach (Gray, 1989; Overholser, 1992). After a homework assignment, she formed the class into an inner and an outer circle. Inner-circle students carried on a discussion focusing on the math content of the reading selection and a teacher-given question, while outer-circle students took notes on the discussion. Everyone could participate in the debriefing session, during which the teacher monitored and made improvements to the discussion guidelines for the future. As the activity was used more, students began looking at each other rather than at the teacher, began to initiate their own questions to start discussion, and could analyze group dynamics by watching videotapes of their talks. The teacher concluded, "Using the Socratic Discussion method showed me that my students can become insightful, logical mathematical problem-solvers by talking through ideas and taking ownership of them" (p. 349).

Think–pair–share

Another strategy that may help you achieve your purposes for a certain text or curricular topic is the cooperative learning activity think–pair–share (Lymon, 1981). Much research has shown the value of providing students with time to think about responses before contributing to a discussion; the quality of talk is enhanced (Gambrell, 1983; Rowe, 1974). Wait time is built into the think–pair–share strategy. Following a question, perhaps supplied by the teacher:

- All students take time to formulate their own thoughts on the issue.
- They then pair with another to share and listen.
- Then, two pairs come together in a foursome.
- Finally, students share responses in the larger group. (To keep this short, ask students to succinctly summarize highlights and refrain from repeating ideas presented by other groups.)

Teachers may use task cards to remind students of which activity segment is in progress. Baumeister (1992) found that students using this method showed increased reading comprehension and a better ability to recall information than did comparison groups.

Teaching in action: *Math.* Think about how this strategy might play out in a specific content area class. A math teacher could present the class with a conceptual problem, such as "Why does a negative number multiplied by another negative number result in a positive number?" Individually, students jot down a justifica-

---

FIGURE   8.6   A literature activity using the inside–outside circle method.

INSTRUCTIONS: We've all read Katherine Paterson's *Jacob Have I Loved,* and I'm sure we all agree that the protagonist, Louise, is an unhappy, angry adolescent. I'd like you to think about the question, "Who's to blame?" through writing and conversation. So, draw a line across your paper and label it "Culpability Continuum." Label the ends "Least Responsible" and "Most Responsible." Rank order the characters in the novel (including Louise herself) according to how much you think they were the cause of Louise's misery and place the ordered names on the continuum.

When you're done writing, form an inside and an outside circle, with each person on the inside facing a partner on the outside. When I ring my bell, talk to your partner about how you ranked the seven characters in terms of responsibility, and listen to your partner's ranking and explanation. You might change your mind, or convince your partner that your answer is better justified by textual evidence, or you might agree to disagree. When you hear the bell again, the people in the inside circle should remain where they are. Those on the outside should move clockwise past two people and face the next person you meet. Compare answers again, giving your reasons for your judgments.

tion, tentative ideas, or hypotheses. After a moment, pairs give feedback to each other, expand or eliminate conjectures, then create foursomes where further refining or arguing takes place. As groups report their thinking and theories to the whole class, a deep understanding of the math concept may replace students' earlier unquestioned acceptance of the rule they had been taught regarding multiplication of negative numbers. The teacher can add relevant information and clarify points that seem to cause confusion.

APPLICATION ACTIVITY   8.1   (SEE PAGE 252)

Discussion webs

Structuring student talk using a discussion web helps students consider multiple points of view and helps assure that a few strong voices don't dominate a discussion. Alvermann and Phelps (1998) suggest a five-step procedure, summarized here:

1. prepare for reading;
2. introduce a central question and have pairs discuss the points of view and write reasons in two support columns provided on the web outline;
3. combine pairs so that groups of four can discuss their input and reach a group conclusion (or prepare a majority and minority report);
4. give each group three minutes to present conclusions and one reason, then open the discussion to the whole group;
5. have students use their webs and the ideas they heard to write individual answers to the central question that was proposed. (p. 274)

Figure 8.7 shows a discussion web that could be used with a biology or social studies class reading Barbara Kingsolver's (2002) essay "A Forest's Last Stand."

Figure 8.8 provides suggested resources for using discussion in your instruction.

Formal and Semiformal Speaking Occasions

Public speaking, storytelling, dramatic performances, and reading aloud are all ways formal and semiformal speaking occasions can be incorporated in a content area classroom. Figure 8.9 lists resources that can help your students as you incorporate these activities into your curriculum.

Public speaking

As a content area teacher, it is not likely that you will be responsible for giving public speaking lessons. Yet, your students will be entering a world where it is

BookTalk   8.2

One topic that could spark discussion about talking is *selective mutism,* a condition that involves people *not* talking. Students can check reference materials and read informational articles about it. There are several fiction books in which characters either cannot or will not talk, often after a traumatic experience. *Silent to the Bone* (2000) by E. L. Konigsburg is one. Another is Laurie Halse Anderson's (www.writerlady.com) *Speak* (1999). Melinda, the narrator, tells no one that she has been raped at a party, but tells the reader about getting sicker and sicker and talking less and less as her ninth-grade year progresses, and she suffers exclusion by her former friends. Imagine the challenge to a writer when her narrator chooses silence! For younger students or those requiring easier reading material, Katherine Paterson's *Flip-Flop Girl* (1994) and Audrey Couloumbis's Newbery Honor Book *Getting Near to Baby* (1999) also deal with selective mutism.

necessary that they speak with competence and confidence. If all teachers took advantage of the opportunities for relatively formal speaking that fit in with other objectives, more students would get closer to meeting that goal. Some strategies are really simple. A fifth-grade teacher I observed had a podium in the front of his class. A student asked to tell about an experience he had had. He walked up to the podium and stood at it to address the class—the podium was used by speaker and listeners alike as a signal. The boy who was talking was just a bit more formal than usual in his presentation, and his classmates recognized that what he said should be attended to with respect. The teacher told me that virtually all of the students displayed poise and used good volume when standing at the podium. It was used daily, and he credited it with aiding his classroom management. And the students loved it. You could also use an aid such as a microphone (even a nonworking one) for the same purpose.

There may be times in your class when the students are working in small groups and you decide that it might be beneficial for a reporter to tell the whole class what was discovered, produced, or discussed. Using a reporter is not always necessary—if similar things occur or are discussed in the small groups, class time can better be spent moving on to something else. But when you want the groups to learn from each other, encouraging and supporting the students who report to the class is your job.

Even within smaller groups, speaking and presentation skills can come into play. My students cre-

FIGURE   8.7   An example of a discussion web.

TEACHER'S INSTRUCTIONS: We have been studying ecosystems and exploring various ways to preserve endangered environments. As you read "A Forest's Last Stand," by Barbara Kingsolver, who is a biologist, a writer, and a social activist, think about this central question: Could a cooperative farming system like the one in Mexico that Kingsolver describes work in the United States? Think about how political, social, scientific, educational, and economic forces would be involved.

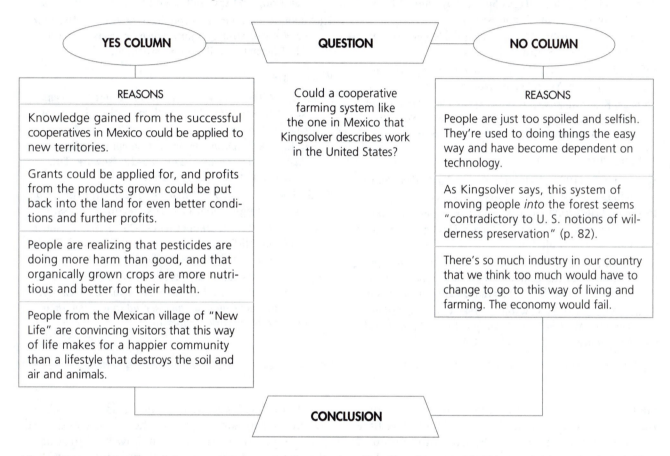

After serious consideration of the pros and cons, we conclude that, like Kingsolver, we should be optimistic and at least try to convince people that this type of cooperative farming surrounding endangered ecosystems could benefit all. In fact, we'd use her essay as the first step in our persuasive efforts. We will not let nature be destroyed!

FIGURE   8.8   Resources relating to discussion.

See more suggested titles in Appendix Figure 8.8.

Adler, M. (2005). *Building Literacy Through Classroom Discussions: Research-Based Strategies for Developing Critical Readers and Thoughtful Writers in Middle School.* New York: Scholastic.

Bolgatz, J. (2005). *Talking Race in the Classroom.* New York: Teachers College Press.

Gilmore, B. (2006). *Speaking Volumes: How to Get Students Discussing Books and Much More.* Portsmouth, NH: Heinemann.

Johnson, H., & Freedman, L. (2005). *Content Area Literature Circles: Using Discussion for Learning Across the Curriculum.* Norwood, MA: Christopher-Gordon.

Reading Group Choices 2009: Selections for Lively Book Discussions. (2008). Chester, MD: Author.

FIGURE 8.9 Resources for public speaking, storytelling, performing, and reading aloud.

See more suggested titles in Appendix Figure 8.9.

PUBLIC SPEAKING

Boyko, C., & Lolen, K. (Eds.). (2001). *Hold Fast Your Dreams: Twenty Commencement Speeches.* New York: Scholastic.

Dabrowski, K. (2005). *Teens Speak, Boys Ages 13–15.* Hanover, NH: Smith and Kraus.

Dabrowski, K. (2005). *Teens Speak, Girls Ages 16–18.* Hanover, NH: Smith and Kraus.

Safire, W. (1997). *Lend Me Your Ears: Great Speeches in History.* New York: W. W. Norton.

Shuster, K., & Meany, J. (2004). *Speak Out!: Debate and Public Speaking in the Middle Grades.* New York: International Debate Education Association Press.

STORYTELLING

Bruchac, J. B. (1997). *Tell Me a Tale: A Book About Storytelling.* San Diego, CA: Harcourt Brace.

Bruchac, J. B. (2003). *Our Stories Remember: American Indian History, Culture, & Values Through Storytelling.* Golden, CO: Fulcrum.

Champion, T. B. (2003). *Understanding Storytelling Among African American Children: A Journey from Africa to America.* Mahwah, NJ: Lawrence Erlbaum Associates.

Schiro, M. S., with D. Lawson. (2004). *Oral Storytelling & Teaching Mathematics: Pedagogical and Multicultural Perspectives.* Thousand Oaks, CA: Sage.

Spaulding, A. E. (2004). *The Wisdom of Storytelling in an Information Age: A Collection of Talks.* Lanham, MD: Scarecrow Press.

READING ALOUD

Fleischman, P. (2000). *Big Talk: Poems for Four Voices.* Cambridge, MA: Candlewick Press.

Hickman, P., & Pollard-Durodola, S. D. (2009). *Dynamic Read-Aloud Strategies for English Learners.* Newark, DE: International Reading Association.

PERFORMING

Allen, L. (2008). *Sixty Comedy Duet Scenes for Teens: Real-life Situations for Laughter.* Colorado Springs, CO: Meriwether.

Flynn, R. (2007). *Dramatizing the Content with Curriculum-Based Readers Theatre, Grades 6–12.* Newark, DE: International Reading Association.

Fredericks, A. D. (2001). *Readers Theatre for American History.* Englewood, CO: Teacher Ideas Press.

Pogrow, S. (2009). *Teaching Content Outrageously: How to Captivate All Students and Accelerate Learning, Grades 4–12.* San Francisco: Jossey-Bass.

Pugliano, C., & Chang, M. (2008). *Greek Myth Plays: 10 Readers Theater Scripts Based on Favorite Greek Myths that Students Can Read and Reread to Develop their Fluency.* New York: Scholastic.

---

ate products, such as author centers or themed units, that I want them to share. When we do not have time for every person to come to the front of the room, I sometimes organize a conference-type setting. Two or three people present their work at a time, using the front and back of the classroom and maybe a hallway. The rest of the class chooses which presentation is most beneficial for what they need to learn and play the part of the audience, interacting with the speaker, asking questions and giving feedback and suggestions. We have an agreed-upon rule that no speaker is left without an audience—if students notice that the groups are unbalanced, some move over to the person who needs listeners. Though the groups are small, the presenter is definitely in charge and has the responsibilities of a public speaker; she must be well prepared and must strive to be interesting and use strategies to engage the audience.

There are strategies you can teach your students that can enhance the presentations they give in your content area classes. Encourage them to prepare well, to outline their main ideas and to rehearse what they will say, to use notecards or visual aids when appropriate, to project their voices and speak with expression. Show them how to introduce a subject with an anecdote, a stimulating question or quotation, or a bit of humor. Students generally love to prepare PowerPoint or other computer-enhanced presentations; much thinking goes into the organization and preparation stages, and the visual format complements the speaker's words, while possibly lessening the anxiety the speaker might feel. No matter what format is being used, presenters should monitor their audience and make adjustments if they see that there is confusion or interest decreases. Following are guidelines you may share with your students for preparing and delivering formal presentations (Cooper & Morreale, 2003).

1. Take 10 to 20 seconds to get settled at the speaker's stand. This helps to establish appropriate pacing and a reasonable rate of delivery, allows the audience to focus its full attention on you, and makes for an impressive and strong beginning. It may also

prevent listeners from missing a key word or two in your opening sentences.

2. Build up to the announcement of the topic by using an example, a description, or narration that leads logically to the topic announcement. You will receive the strongest audience attention during the first seconds of the speech. This is why you need an interesting beginning and may want to use suspense before revealing the specific topic. As soon as the topic or thesis is announced, the audience's attention may wane. If the introduction is well developed and interesting, audience members are more likely to refocus attention again, quickly.

3. Preview your structure at the end of your introduction by announcing the thesis or topic and the subtopics you will cover.

4. Thoroughly detail all the major points of your speech. Without thorough detailing, a major point will be vague, unclear, and quickly forgotten by the audience.

5. Develop a definite conclusion after your last main point is covered. You might review the thesis and/or major points, suggest appropriate audience action, or give a memorable quotation that sums up the speech. You might actually say "in conclusion" or "in summary" to prevent an abrupt ending and then finish with a memorable last line.

6. Avoid common pause fillers, such as "you know." You should stop to think about what you want to say, using silence instead of filling in with these distracting expressions.

7. Use standard grammar in a public speech unless quoting someone else's actual or reconstructed dialogue.

8. Use a slow overall speaking rate, taking time to breathe properly. Otherwise, audience members will have difficulty understanding and retaining your speech materials because they don't have time to reason along with you.

9. Translate as many technical words as you can to everyday vocabulary. Those that cannot be translated should be defined carefully.

10. Use only a couple of note cards containing a brief outline rather than a total or partial manuscript. This is likely to cause a boring reading instead of a conversational presentation.

11. Don't overload with too many facts and statistics in one speech.

12. Use quotations sparingly. A speech composed largely of quoted material may sound as though you have few original ideas.

13. Provide detailed examples (a full paragraph). They add more clarity and interest than an undetailed (phrase or sentence) example. Along with good detailed examples, however, one or two undetailed ones can add extra weight of the evidence for a point or argument without taking much time to deliver.

Of course, each time you present material in class, model strategies for the students—point out techniques as you use them for the students to evaluate and consider for their own use. You may have to teach the students to make eye contact with the audience, to read or speak with clarity and expression, and to exhibit an air of authority. With practice and modeling and mentoring from you, good progress can be anticipated.

The more authentic you can make the setting and purpose of lessons and experiences involving public speaking, the better results you get. Sharon Morley's ninth-grade English classes invite parents and community members to their school each spring for a portfolio celebration. Their written work from throughout the school year is on display, and as adults ask them about particular pieces or about their writing processes, they answer them with a sophistication and seriousness appropriate for the occasion. Similarly, many schools are replacing or supplementing traditional parent–teacher conferences with student-led conferences. A report card might be available, but the student provides a context for the grades by explaining what kinds of work were done and what his self-assessment is at this point in the academic year. In a different example requiring presentation skills, students from Albany County spoke at a press conference in the New York state capital asking for support for a cause, Free the Children, an international network of children helping children that is attempting to end child labor (*The Voice*, 1999). Enhancing speaking skills should not be a goal reserved for those few students who will give graduation speeches and accept scholastic, athletic, or service awards—all of your students must know how to present themselves, their thoughts, and their work well.

Storytelling

Storytelling is a wonderful oral activity for content area classes. In *Oral Storytelling & Teaching Mathematics: Pedagogical and Multicultural Perspectives* (2004), Schiro and Lawson show how a teacher can engage students in deep thinking when math is taught through storytelling.

Teaching in action: *Math.* Doris Lawson told her sixth graders "The Egypt Story," created by Michael Steven Schiro, over the course of several sessions, and her students took on the role of mathematical anthropologists. Along the way, students made comparisons of ancient Egyptian and modern-day methods of multiplication, and asked which system works best. They worked in cooperative groups and used manipulatives to solve problems that arose in the story. Lawson found that telling math stories resulted in more enjoyable teaching and learning:

> Because when I say I'm going to tell a story, the kids immediately pay attention. . . . In fact, in my pre-algebra class where I have some kids that do struggle and it's sometimes hard to hold their attention, if I say, "I'm going to tell you a story," the class leaders will say, "Shut up! She's telling us a story." (p. 165)

Lawson, through exploring ancient Egyptian mathematics, found that she had to confront myths relating to culture and mathematics, including:

- *Myth 1:* Mathematics contains universal truths and a reasoning system that exist free of any cultural constraints.
- *Myth 2:* Contemporary mathematics is a creation of the people of Europe and North America.
- *Myth 3:* Contemporary school mathematics is consistent with the underlying social, political, religious, linguistic, and conceptual traditions of every world culture, and children from all cultures can with equal ease learn and use that mathematics. (p. 195)

She sees the value in helping students understand that many mathematical systems are in existence today, and she does that partially through storytelling.

Teaching in action: *Social Studies.* I encourage you to become known in your school as a teacher who can make her subject come alive with stories, whether factual or fictional. For example, if you're planning to be a social studies teacher, telling tidbits like the following in the context of your lecture about Henry VIII and his six wives will ensure that none of your students will leave you with the far too common belief that history is boring:

> Henry . . . had Anne [Boleyn] accused of infidelity with five men, one of them her own brother. She and all her supposed lovers were convicted of treason and condemned to death. . . . Anne did not repine at her fate and cheerfully acknowledged the boon that Henry granted her in allowing her to be decapitated by a sword instead of an ax. "The king has been very good to me," she said. "He promoted me from a simple maid to be a marchioness. Then he raised me to be a queen. Now he will raise me to be a martyr." (Fadiman, 1985, p. 69)

You don't have to memorize your content-related stories word for word—develop your own style and flair. At least some students will be inspired to join

you—have them prepare relevant stories to share at school functions or with other classes, either at their grade level or perhaps in lower grades. Their confidence and speaking skills will soar with the practice and the reinforcement and appreciation shown by audiences. Some school districts have annual schoolwide storytelling competitions or celebrations.

Grace (2004) points out that oral-based literacy skills are "often left unexplored, uninvited, and undervalued in literacy instruction" (p. 482) and recommends that they be included in the curriculum. He advocates the use of culturally conscious hip-hop, which he defines as "oral text with lyrics and messages that enlighten with social consciousness, engage with politicized messages, and empower by instilling cultural and self-awareness" (p. 484).

Social studies teachers can make use of slave narratives to help students understand "how a sense of dignity was maintained in the face of inhumanity" (p. 483). Teachers can read aloud and teach students storytelling skills by using folktales from many cultures. Figure 8.10 is an example of a storytelling assignment that might be used in a middle school or high school social studies class.

Dramatic Performances

Rasinski et al. (2005) point out how important reading fluency is at the high school as well as earlier levels. They define reading fluency as "reading with appropriate accuracy and rate but also with good and meaningful phrasing and expression" (p. 27). In general, they recommend that content area teachers throughout the school day provide opportunities for wide reading of independent-level materials and guided reading of instructional-level materials. Repeated readings can promote the practice that will lead to increased fluency and comprehension. Subject area classrooms can be the context for authentic reading practice:

> Repeated or practiced reading is best accomplished through performance activities. When students are asked to perform for others, they have a natural inclination and desire to practice the passage to a point where they can read it accurately, with appropriate rate, and especially with meaningful expression and phrasing. Texts such as poetry, scripts, oratory, and song lyrics are meant to be performed and could be incorporated into any secondary content area classroom with a bit of creative planning by the teacher. (p. 26)

Readers theatre

Readers theatre is an enjoyable way to help students actively participate in their content learning and to practice speaking and listening skills. Scripts based on other texts can be found or designed to be read by

FIGURE **8.10** A social studies storytelling assignment.

DIRECTIONS: Next week, each of you will be telling our class a story that represents a certain culture. The following steps will help you prepare to participate in this oral tradition:

1. Explore several texts and choose a story that you enjoy and that is meaningful to you. You might choose a story that represents the culture of your family and the land they came from. Or you might prefer learning to express yourself by using a story from a culture you are less familiar with. The cart in our room contains resources from the school library. They include:

- *The People Could Fly* by Virginia Hamilton
- *Lay My Burden Down: A Folk History of Slavery* by B. A. Botkin
- *The Dark-Thirty: Southern Tales of the Supernatural* by Patricia McKissack
- *The Girl Who Married a Lion, and Other Stories* by Alexander McCall Smith
- *Hold Up the Sky: And Other Indian Tales from Texas and the Southern Plains* by Jane Louise Curry
- *Red Ridin' in the Hood: And Other Cuentos* by P. Santos and Marcantonio
- *Why Goats Smell Bad and Other Stories from Benin,* translated and retold by Raouf Mama
- *Golden Tales: Myths, Legends, and Folktales from Latin America,* retold and illustrated by Lulu Delacre

- *Wise and Not So Wise: Ten Tales from the Rabbis,* selected and retold by Phyllis Gershator
- *One-Hundred-and-One Read-Aloud Asian Myths and Legends: 10-Minute Readings from the World's Best-loved Asian Literature* by Joan C. Verniero
- *Terrific Trickster Tales from Asia* by Cathy Spagnoli
- *Children of the Dragon: Selected Tales from Vietnam* by Sherry Garland
- *Lugalbanda: The Boy Who Got Caught Up in a War* by K. Henderson
- *Golem* by D. Wisniewski
- *Zen Shorts* by Jon Muth

2. Once you've chosen your story, practice it. Read it out loud, with expression, in front of a mirror or into a recorder. Try it out on your family and friends, making sure you maintain eye contact. You don't have to memorize it word for word. Make the story your own, so that you're comfortable with it.

3. Consider bringing props to enhance your story. You might want to play music or a CD of African drumming in the background as you tell your story. You might want to wear something symbolic of the culture of your story, such as kente cloth. Think about how you might use gestures or silence or movement.

4. Before you tell your story, let your listeners know if you need anything special from them. For example, you might ask for their participation by repeating a refrain with you.

---

individuals taking on the various roles of historical, scientific, artistic, or literary figures. Readers do not memorize their lines, though reading silently first is a good idea so that they read smoothly and with good expression. Allow students flexibility in terms of how they perform—where to stand, whether to use simple props, how to deliver certain lines.

Readers theatre can make your text, your subject, and your students come alive. Students can create their own scripts, full of dialogue, based on the texts they read and then present dramatic readings to an audience. Any genre, even newspaper articles or textbook passages, can be used as the stimulus text. There's no end to the number of possible creative touches students may include. Recently, a group of my social studies preservice teachers discussed Avi's (www.avi-writer.com) *Nothing But the Truth* (1991) in a literature circle, and chose to share their experience with the class in a readers theatre presentation. They used information from the book to create a dialogue between two of the many characters locked in controversy. While two group members read their parts,

the others stood just outside the classroom door humming "The Star-Spangled Banner," which thematically was very appropriate. An added benefit was that others in the class were convinced to read the book, based on this enthusiastic performance. While at an annual convention of the National Council of Teachers of English, I attended a panel session on Authors Readers Theatre, where I heard authors Katherine Paterson, Avi, Sarah Weeks, and Brian Selznick perform from each other's works; they had the rapt audience in tears. Several other children's and young adult authors are involved in the project, which you can read more about at www.authorsreaderstheatre.com. The site includes suggestions for various ways teachers at all levels can use readers theatre with their students.

Courtroom dramas

Consider holding court in your content classroom. Courtroom drama is immensely popular; books, movies, and television shows abound that take advantage of this fact, so why not join them? Your students can put book characters on trial (especially the villains or the characters they personally don't like!) through scripting and implementing a readers theatre production. They get practice speaking and listening as they take on roles, think through others' presentations and performances, and respond to the unfolding drama. They can put people's (such as Einstein's, Descartes', or Machiavelli's) theories and philosophies, as well as actions, on trial. Combine this creative activity with having them read about real trials relevant to your content areas: those of Clarence Darrow and Galileo in science; Joan of Arc, Benedict Arnold, Nathan Hale, Sacco and Vanzetti, and Nazi war criminals in social studies. If conditions are right, students at all levels show amazing creativity, sensitivity, and insight when they explore topics and create a product to share their findings.

Dramatic performances and English learners

Nolan and Patterson (2000) found that skits incorporated into programs for English learners were helpful. Because there were fixed sets of lines so that students did not have to create expressions, but could instill their own emotions and creative interpretations, both the form and communicating the message were practiced. Students rehearsed parts in a classroom with the researchers and a teacher who served as monitors and models and emphasized correct pronunciation. The skits were adapted to meet the students' needs, and choruses were added to ensure that all could take a participatory role. During final rehearsals, two surprises were noted. When a student playing a lead role was absent, others were able to step in and take over. Also, students who did not have main roles started prompting those who did, leading the researchers to conclude that many students had learned all the lines of the skit, though they had not been assigned to do so.

Data analysis based on focus group interviews showed that student perceptions concentrated on overcoming the fear of speaking English, the teamwork displayed, and communicative awareness, with statements showing that the students had learned to pay attention to the meaning, not just the words. Students also commented on contextual learning, improved pronunciation, new vocabulary, and nonverbal communication. Nolan and Patterson conclude:

> This study implies that teachers could achieve similar effects by rearranging a classroom for a short dramatization and inviting spectators from beyond the class grouping, so that students have an audience other than their classmates. When they have to dramatize a skit to an audience that has not seen it previously, the students' performance has to be accurate because it requires real communication. (p. 13)

BookTalk 8.3

What do you think Galileo sounded like as he talked to friends and foes, trying to convince them that Aristotle was wrong? How might Gregor Mendel have explained his formulation of the theory of heredity? How did conversations about radioactivity go between Marie and Pierre Curie? Storyteller Kendall Haven's (www.kendallhaven.com) *Great Moments in Science: Experiments and Readers Theatre* (1996) provides scripts that students can use to speak as famous scientists and those who learned from them. In each chapter, he gives scientific background on a topic—Benjamin Franklin's discovery of electricity in 1750, Dorothy Hodgkin's discovery of the composition of penicillin in 1943, or Maria Mitchell's discovery of a comet in 1847—then provides a script to help the scenes become real, and to help students take part in the excitement, passion, and controversy that come with breakthroughs in knowledge. The scripts are followed by instruction on conducting related experiments that enable the students to be scientists. Finally, each chapter contains a "Bridges to Books" section that gives key words, concepts, and questions to begin library exploration, and a "References for Further Reading" list. The chapters help students to see scientists as real people who use procedural knowledge in their jobs and their own learning throughout their lives. The figures in the book may pass along their intellectual curiosity to those portraying them and those watching the skits, which show how the scientists engaged in critical thinking, overcame natural and political problems, and made connections among data and disciplines. Students can participate in the hands-on, voices-on activities provided, then use the model structure to write chapters for class books on other topics, in various disciplines. This book can lead to "great moments" in your courses.

Reading Aloud

Avi, a well-known author of young adult literature, was asked at a conference what teachers can do to encourage children to read. I expected him to advise teachers to read aloud to their students, which is good, and common, advice. But he surprised me by answering that the best thing teachers could do is to take voice lessons, something he has done. He explained how important it is to read *well* to our students of all ages, and not all teachers come by that skill naturally (Avi, 1999). So, I'll use this opportunity to pass these words of wisdom along to you. Teachers can enhance their own speaking and reading skills in order to make their teaching more interesting, as well as to model techniques for students. It also helps to provide students with a purpose for listening.

You may be surprised, especially if you are preparing to teach something other than English, at the many ways you can fit various types of drama or public reading into your classes. For example, if you teach biology, you might show students how to read Paul Fleischman's *I Am Phoenix: Poems for Two Voices* (1985), which is all about birds, and *Joyful Noise: Poems for Two Voices* (1988), which contains a wealth of information on various insects.

Erickson (1996) gives tips for selecting and reading books aloud to reluctant readers. She recommends:

- Reading "hooking" chapters from whole books, though not overdoing it, since students also like to hear shorter sections in their entirety
- Reading a variety of genres, including nonfiction, magazine articles, factual newspaper accounts involving teenagers, and poetry
- Allowing students to doodle as they listen
- Inviting students to read aloud to their classmates

She lists criteria for selecting texts for read-alouds, such as choosing books that reflect authors from many cultures, and making sure the texts match listeners' social and emotional stages, though stretching students intellectually at times is good. Erickson

BookTalk 8.4

Have you ever heard of a *documentary novel?* Avi's Newbery Honor book *Nothing But the Truth* (1991) is one. There is no narrator; the multiple points of view of parents, students, the media, teachers, and administrators are represented by newspaper articles, journal entries, letters, memos, faculty room talk, and phone conversations. The story has worked its magic for years. Avi once visited Lawrence, Kansas, where the entire town had been invited to read the book. He remarked that listening to people argue about the student's suspension and the consequences for the teacher as described in the book was like listening to people fighting over something that was actually happening, not a book plot. I highly recommend this book to future teachers because, besides being a great read, it may help you reflect on how to avoid having anyone in your class, including yourself, feel backed into a corner.

offers a bibliography of texts meeting the criteria that she has used to entice her students.

Lesesne (2006) shares decades of research demonstrating the value of teachers reading aloud to students, in high school as well as elementary and middle school grades. She recommends daily read-aloud activities using materials from a variety of genres to improve skills, introduce new topics of study, and share content.

You should also have students read aloud to each other. Pair the students and they can entertain each other as they learn while having fun and practicing their oral reading. You might also choose to take the show on the road—to other classrooms or to the local mall.

Texts useful for students reading aloud are stories where multiple voices are represented. For example, *Crossing the Delaware: A History in Many Voices* (1998), by Louise Peacock, helps students understand a variety of perspectives as they read. Students might be assigned various roles and given time to practice the expressive reading of their parts so that all listeners can understand the historical setting and the complexities of human nature and social interaction involved.

APPLICATION ACTIVITY **8.2** (SEE PAGE 252)

LISTENING

E verything discussed in the last section on speaking and discussion implied that people were present and listening with interest and comprehension. Neither your presentations nor your students' formal and informal talk will work if listening is not valued and practiced. Listening is absolutely crucial for learning to occur, yet it is all too often assumed that students know how to listen, and that when they are not attending to what is being said, they are at fault or they are choosing to not listen. Actually, listening can be taught and developed; there are ways that you can help improve your own and your students' listening skills. This part discusses aspects of listening and gives you ideas for enhancing the listening that goes on in your classes.

Students' Listening

The last section talked about students and teachers together setting rules for discussion. In conjunction, it makes sense to address listening. Reasonable people agree to listen to those speaking from the standpoint of politeness, but also recognize that listening is what enables them to learn, understand, and form responses (whether they be affirmations, counterarguments,

BookTalk Online 🎙 8.5

Read It Aloud!: Using Literature in the Secondary Content Classroom (2000) by Judy Richardson is a great resource for teachers seeking effective ways to engage their students. Hear more at the Kane Resource Site.

additional examples, or requests for clarification). Listeners can help the person speaking through their nonverbal behavior, such as eye contact, head nodding, leaning forward, smiling or laughing or sighing when appropriate. One of your responsibilities as a teacher is to monitor listening behavior as students discuss in groups, giving hints and strategies when needed and reinforcement when students are listening well.

You can also help your students listen effectively as part of a class group. When your presentations are well prepared and interesting, and when you speak with expression and clarity, it is far easier for students to listen. When they start giving you signals such as looking tired, looking away, or fidgeting, you know it's time to adjust—by changing your speaking strategies, soliciting questions and interaction, or moving on to another phase of the lesson that allows them to move, talk to one another, read, or write.

BookTalk 8.6

I'm sure you've seen good interviews, and bad, live or on television. How well an interview turns out is often highly dependent on the skills of the questioner, and the genre is an interesting one for students to investigate. *The Norton Book of Interviews* (1996) is an anthology that allows your students to do just that, while learning content from the words of famous people. They can write out what they would ask Hitler during his years of rising power, then read his words (and his interviewer's description of him) in the 1932 interview with George Sylvester Viereck that appeared in *Liberty*. They can place themselves in Picasso's studio with the interviewer Jerome Seckler in 1945 as the artist talks about what his paintings mean and don't mean. They can be transported to Grand Central Station in 1926 as novelist Willa Cather tells an interviewer from *The Nebraska State Journal* about being in the process of writing a book she's called *Death Comes for the Archbishop*. Conversation becomes the medium for learning in this book of interviews, and who doesn't like to eavesdrop on a good conversation?

Guest speakers and recordings

It's helpful to give your students a variety of voices and people to listen to. Sharon Morley (1996) invites many people into her classroom to give booktalks. Colleagues, administrators, college professors, community workers, and parents come in to talk about what they like to read and to recommend new bestsellers or old favorites. "Some presenters use 5 or 10 minutes; some use the entire period, spinning the book talk into an encompassing lesson about history, about life, or about what happens when one loves to read" (p. 131). Students come to view these people in a new light after listening to them, and they come to understand that reading is not just a classroom activity, but something people in all walks of life do for entertainment and self-improvement outside school walls. They get practice asking questions of the speakers, now seen as fellow learners, and they get to listen to some of the speakers read passages that are personally meaningful and stimulating.

Students don't always need live speakers to listen to, although the more you can bring in authors and people who work in the fields you teach, the better. You can have many books on CD in your classroom library, representing both nonfiction and fiction related to your subject area. Some students may choose to borrow these because they are auditory learners and prefer comprehending through this format. Others might take them because they spend a lot of time in cars and can listen while traveling. You can also help individuals use their listening skills to learn content and absorb ideas by setting up listening centers in your classroom. These can include podcasts, audiobooks (either professional versions or those made by you and your former and present students) or CDs, mp3 players, or software programs that require learning by listening, as well as the machines necessary for listening and recording. Recordings made by students reacting to literature or issues can also be there. Have assignments, project suggestions, writing supplies, tools for student recording, and listening center rules posted at the center. Sometimes, small groups can work at the centers, while other groups are researching in the library, reading or writing silently, and conducting literature circles or collaborative investigations. Figure 8.11 lists books related to various disciplines that are available on CD, DVD, or mp3 versions and are appropriate for a classroom listening center or a classroom lending library. There are many more you will discover.

Hearing or reading aloud the words of actual speeches can make the past come alive for students. Rather than merely reading about the era of McCarthyism in our country, for example, students can listen to their science or history teacher read the words the Nobel prize–winning chemist Linus Pauling spoke to a Sen-

FIGURE 8.11

A sampling of audio versions of content-related texts.

See more suggested titles in Appendix Figure 8.11.

Collins, S. (2010). *Mockingjay*. Read by Carolyn McCormick. New York: Scholastic.

Levitt, S. D., & Dubner, S. J. (2005). *Freakonomics: A Rogue Economist Explores the Hidden Side of Nearly Everything*. Read by Stephen J. Dubner. New York: Harper Audio.

Tolkien, J. R. R. (2001). *J. R. R. Tolkien's The Lord of the Rings* (Original Soundtrack Recording). Berkeley, CA: Fantasy Records.

Tyson, N. D. (2007). *Death by Black Hole: And Other Cosmic Quandaries*. Ashland, OR: Blackstone Audiobooks.

Vowell, S. (2008). *The Wordy Shipmates*. New York: Simon & Schuster Audio.

FIGURE 8.12

Books containing interviews.

See more suggested titles in Appendix Figure 8.12.

Coan, P. M. (1997). *Ellis Island Interviews: In Their Own Words*. New York: Checkmark Books.

Lennon, J. (2001). *All We Are Saying: The Last Major Interview with John Lennon and Yoko Ono Conducted by David Sheff*, B. Golson (Ed.). New York: St. Martin's.

Pauling, L. (1995). *Linus Pauling in His Own Words: Selections from His Writings, Speeches, and Interviews*, B. Marinacci (Ed.). New York: Simon & Schuster.

Racza, B. (2010). *The Vermeer Interviews: Conversations with Seven Works of Art*. Minneapolis, MN: First Avenue Editions.

Westcott, R. (2000). *Splendor on the Diamond: Interviews with 35 Stars of Baseball's Past*. Gainesville: University Press of Florida.

ate Internal Affairs Subcommittee in 1960 when he was interrogated about his methods of collecting signatures of scientists throughout the world on an antinuclear petition that was presented to the United Nations. Students getting to know this aspect of Linus Pauling will cheer to find out that three years later he won the Nobel Peace Prize, which he valued even more highly than the Nobel he had previously won for his work in chemistry. They may very well want to hear more from this man.

Interviews

Another way to help students understand the value of listening is to introduce them to the art of interviewing. Figure 8.12 lists titles of books that contain interviews with people in a number of professions or special circumstances. Students may find that they enjoy reading this genre because it allows them to listen in as they read people's actual spoken words in answer to questions. The books also may give them ideas for their own interviewing. Encourage your students to interview each other, you, other teachers and staff members, politicians, community professionals, their own and others' parents and siblings, or people in assisted living centers who wish to share their personal histories. Your students will learn a tremendous amount about other people and their reading preferences and ideas at the same time they are practicing their own communication and literacy abilities. So, find ways whenever you can to fit interviewing into your curriculum.

One of the most talented, versatile, and well-known radio interviewers was Studs Terkel. In *Five*

Decades of Interviews with Studs Terkel (1999), you and your students can listen to the voices of those who might otherwise be merely names in a history book or on the cover of novels. You can hear writer James Baldwin and singer Mahalia Jackson speaking of Civil Rights issues in the 1960s, and ask your students to think about what they might have to say about race relations, humanity, and social justice today. Listen to renowned neurologist Oliver Sacks pondering the mystery of cases like Martin, an institutionalized patient with an extraordinary talent for music appreciation, and learn from economist John Kenneth Galbraith, writer Maya Angelou, actor Woody Allen, playwright Arthur Miller. You can hear the interviewees' laughter, and the skillful probes Terkel uses. The names that the students see in their history and literature books become live people, expressing opinions and explaining how they go about constructing knowledge in their various disciplines.

Strategies for improving students' listening skills

There are several structured approaches to helping students be active listeners and aiding listening comprehension. One way is to use an anticipation guide, just like those shown in Chapter 2 that are used before reading assignments. Such guides activate relevant schema, as well as pique students' interest in the topics and concepts they will hear about.

Set a purpose for listening. Even more simply, give your students a purpose for listening and tell them what particular information or organizational framework (e.g., cause–effect, compare–contrast) to listen for in a selection.

Teaching in action: *English.* Here is an example from an eleventh-grade New York State Regents English Exam (University of the State of New York, 2001, p. 2) excerpted from the directions given before a listening task, that gives a purpose for listening:

> **Overview:** For this part of the test, you will listen to a speech about writing effective dialogue . . . and write a response based on the situation described below. You will hear the speech twice. You may take notes . . . anytime you wish during the readings.

> **The Situation:** As a member of a class on fiction writing, you have been asked by your teacher to prepare an instructional manual for your classmates on the reasons and techniques for using dialogue to improve their writing. In preparation for writing the manual, listen to a speech by published writer Anne LaMott [sic]. Then use relevant information from the speech to write your instructional manual.

> **Your Task:** Write an instructional manual for your classmates in which you give some reasons and techniques for using dialogue to improve their writing.

Listen–read–discuss. An activity called *listen–read–discuss* (LRD) was developed by Alvermann (1987). The strategy in action might go like this:

1. The teacher lectures on a selected portion of the text.
2. Students then read the material, comparing what is written with what they heard.
3. The teacher and students discuss the content and what was learned through both routes. For example, an earth science teacher might give a mini-lecture about a trip he took to Mammoth Cave National Park in Kentucky, concentrating on the rock formations he saw, the geological history of the caves, and how it felt to him.
4. Students read information from an Internet site about the park or from the book *Mammoth Cave* (Wagoner & Cutliff, 1985). They then discuss what they learned, asking the teacher questions stimulated by their reading.

APPLICATION ACTIVITY   8.3   (SEE PAGE 252)

Teachers Listening to Students

In the spring of 2006, I attended the North Carolina Festival of the Book. There was a front porch conversation theme; in most sessions, the Southern writers sat on the stage in rocking chairs, talking with each other about their writing processes, their books, and life itself. The audiences sat in rapt attention, clearly appreciative of the privilege of being allowed to listen in, and at a certain point ask questions. We teachers could use this technique, also. An English teacher could spend part of a writing workshop day inviting a few students to sit up front, facing the class, and converse with each other about how the pieces they're working on are coming along. Social studies students could share how their research on social movements is progressing. Science students who are designing inventions for a regional contest could discuss how they're solving problems and experimenting with their creations. You can listen carefully along with the student audience members who might be waiting their turns. You can ask listening questions or offer careful probing phrases: "Tell me a little more"; "What part of the challenge has you stymied?"; "So what's the next step?"

I encourage you to have a section of your teaching journal devoted to things you hear your students say. Or start a file on your computer for interesting and thought-provoking quotes, questions, and concerns expressed by your students. Some are precious gems you'll smile or laugh over in years to come as the quotes bring back the memories and the faces; others will cause you to reflect, to examine your practices and your ideas of literacy. All will help you know and understand your students better.

ACTION RESEARCH   8.B

Be an observer–researcher at some discussion you are not a part of. It may be a literature circle in a middle school or it may be at a party where a group has informally formed because of a common interest in a topic. Being as unobtrusive as possible, listen and watch carefully to understand the dynamics. The following guide questions may help you focus:

1. Is the talking fairly evenly distributed or is it dominated by one or two people? If the latter is the case, does this seem to be all right with the others? Is a leader emerging?
2. What do the facial expressions and nonverbal communication tell you?
3. Are several divergent opinions being expressed? Is there disagreement? Are people's opinions and thoughts being listened to and valued and accepted?
4. Is any new ground being broken? Is the talk leading to new insights about the topic?

I hope you've been able to see throughout this chapter how listening and speaking are complementary and work together, often in combination with reading, writing, viewing, and hands-on exploration, toward growth of knowledge and learning. Now, I'd like to share several ideas, strategies, and stories that show many literacy components working together naturally in classroom settings.

COLLABORATIVE SPEAKING AND LISTENING PROJECTS

A business interviewee told a researcher, "We're doing more with groups and teams . . . and we'd like employees who know how to talk and negotiate and synthesize ideas. . . . The bottom line . . . is not standard English—though that is important—but critical thinking, the management of ideas" (Morris & Tchudi, 1996, p. 232). You can help students realize that they are developing skills that will be used throughout their lives at the same time they are learning content and academic skills in your class.

Jigsaw

In the cooperative learning strategy known as Jigsaw (Aronson et al., 1978), material is divided into small portions and assigned to class members. Students, working either individually or in small groups, read their assigned selection and then share information with the whole class in order for all class members to learn the information. Following are the steps in the activity.

PRE-READING

1. Identify a topic of study and its components. Then, develop a sign-up list that identifies enough portions for all members of a class to be involved.
2. Have students sign up for, or assign them, one portion of the topic/material.

DURING READING

3. Allow students ample time to read the material.
4. Students are responsible for understanding the material for which they are accountable. Instruct them to identify and learn new vocabulary and concepts. Ask them to formulate ideas for how to present the information to classmates.

POST-READING

5. Have expert groups (those who have read the same material) come together and prepare for teaching the new material. This might involve preparing visuals as well as an oral presentation. Conferencing with the teacher is acceptable.

6. Have students present their material and answer questions. (Cecil & Gipe, 2003, pp. 142–143)

Teaching in action: *Science.* I'll give an example from my own teaching of preservice secondary teachers. If a curricular goal is for middle school science students to understand the workings and interconnections of the body's organs, I divide the class (let's say 16 students) into four heterogeneous "base groups" of four. I pass out copies of the following books by Seymour Simon: *The Heart, Muscles, The Brain,* and *Bones.* Each base group decides who will become the "expert" on which subtopic, and the "experts" read the appropriate book for homework that night. The following day, the class regroups into "expert groups" so that, for example, all the students who have chosen *Muscles* meet together to discuss the text, highlight main points, ask others for clarification, and decide how best to teach the topic to their base group. *The Heart* group meets in another corner, doing the same, and so on. Then, the base groups meet once again, where each "expert" is responsible for teaching about one organ to the group. The teacher provides needed materials, facilitates the discussions, is available for consultation and troubleshooting, and encourages the presenters. At the end of the lesson, all 16 students should understand the main points from all the books and have had the opportunity to synthesize information and make connections with their peers. Their speaking and listening skills are enhanced simultaneously.

Teaching in action: *Biology/English.* Here's a second example appropriate for a high school biology or English class or for an interdisciplinary activity. All students read at least part of James Watson's *The Double Helix: A Personal Account of the Discovery of the Structure of DNA* (1980), write reactions in their learning logs, and discuss responses in terms of content and literary features. Then, the teacher assigns pairs of students (teams like Watson and Crick, the partners in the discovery) to read commentaries and reviews that followed the book's publication. *The Norton Critical Edition of The Double Helix* (1980) has about 20 of these compiled with the text itself, many with appealing, intriguing names, such as "'Honest Jim' Watson's Big Thriller about DNA," "Notes of a Not-Watson," "Honest Jim and the Tinker Toy Model," "Riding High on a Spiral," "Truth, Truth, What Is Truth (About How the Structure of DNA Was Discovered)?" and "Three Other Perspectives" written by scientists Francis Crick, Linus Pauling, and Aaron Klug. Student partners write a summary and react to this "new" information relative to the class discussion of the book itself. Each pair presents the main points of the new data or perspective they learned about, and another whole class discussion occurs relative to the book, the man, the subject, and the scientific community that responded to *The Double Helix*. The teacher should make the entire book available for optional reading. She then can give the following booktalk about a second autobiographical account:

> What must it feel like to be the discoverer of something that was previously unknown? What characteristics must a person have to persist in looking for something that has eluded great minds for ages? Students know what it means to collaborate in the classroom, but what does collaboration look like in the scientific world? Francis Crick's memoir, *What Mad Pursuit: A Personal View of Scientific Discovery* (1988), lets readers in on the thoughts and feelings of the co-discoverer of the structure of DNA; it lets the reader inside a brilliant mind. You can learn science concepts as you join Crick and Watson as they unravel a mystery through implementation of the scientific process. You'll also enjoy amusing anecdotes and personal reminiscences and reflections from this author who is a gifted popular science writer. Let yourself in on this "mad pursuit."

Survival!

"Survival!" is a collaborative project that uses some aspects of jigsaw and provides students with multiple speaking and listening opportunities.

Teaching in action: *Interdisciplinary.* To prepare students for this interdisciplinary "Survival!" unit, I supply the following prompt: "Have you ever been lost? Take a moment to close your eyes and remember the experience. Where were you? How did you feel? What decisions did you make? How did you get back to your loved ones?" I've found that virtually everyone has a story about being lost, whether in a park or shopping mall, long ago at age four or just last month. I give students a chance to recount their adventures and recall the emotions involved, then I follow this oral sharing with a writing prompt: "Imagine that you are stranded and must survive in an isolated area with no human contact. Visualize yourself in one of these settings: a small tropical island in a part of the ocean where planes rarely if ever fly, a vast dark forest, or the frozen north. Spend some time writing to anticipate problems and possible solutions. How will you survive?"

Next, I give booktalks for several novels involving a survival theme. I've used *Hatchet* (1987) by Gary Paulsen, *Julie of the Wolves* (1972) by Jean Craighead George, *The Iceberg Hermit* (1974) by Arthur Roth, *The Cay* (1991) by Theodore Taylor, *Island of the Blue Dolphins* (1990) by Scott O'Dell, *Nation* (2008) by Terry Pratchett, and *My Side of the Mountain* (1988)

by Jean Craighead George. You might also include recent nonfiction selections, such as *The Perfect Storm* (1997) by S. Junger, *Into Thin Air* (1998) by J. Krakauer, *Shipwreck at the Bottom of the World* (1998) by Jennifer Armstrong, and *Three Cups of Tea* (2009) by Greg Mortenson and S. Roth, all of which contain much science and social studies–related material. The books should represent a range in terms of style and difficulty. Students select one of the books to read, exchange e-mail addresses with classmates who make the same choice, and read and write responses to their group. After a sufficient amount of time, which varies depending on students' literacy skills and other things going on in the curriculum, I allow interest groups to meet and talk—they use the responses they've been sharing via e-mail as a starting point. While they talk, I hang up a chart the length of one wall, either in the classroom or in the hall. Down the left-hand side, I list the titles of the books. Across the top are questions for each group to answer by filling in the appropriate block on the chart. These questions include:

- What is the setting (time and place) of your story?
- How did the protagonist in your story get stranded?
- For how long was your main character in isolation?
- How did your protagonist get food?
- What tools did your protagonist find, make, or use?
- How did he or she apply math or science principles to figure out or solve problems?
- What kinds of shelter did your character use? How did he or she apply math or science principles in building a shelter?
- How did your character provide clothing for herself or himself?
- What animals did your character encounter? Were they enemies or friends? What did you learn relating to animal behavior, plants, or other biology content?
- What other humans did your protagonist encounter before being rescued?
- What struggles within herself or himself did the person deal with? How did your protagonist change or grow?
- How was the character rescued or returned to society?
- What social studies content did you learn from this book (anything about other cultures, governments, social groups, geography, history, anthropology)?
- Did you find the story believable? Give an example to show why or why not.

- How would you describe the emotional reactions your group had to reading this story?
- What content knowledge (e.g., science, math, English) did you gain from this book?
- How would you rate this book? Why should others read it or not read it?

Each cooperative learning group decides how to answer the questions and fill in the chart. If there is not consensus, they decide what to do about that. They may choose, for instance, to put down the majority opinion, or to explain the reason for division within the group. When the chart is completed and all have read and admired it, we hold a compare–contrast discussion. Students who read *Hatchet* and thought that 56 days was a long time for the fictional Brian to be alone in the woods are impressed with the information about Karana of *Island of the Blue Dolphins* (based on a true story) being isolated for 18 years. Sometimes, we stage a television "talk show," hosted by a student volunteer, where students role-play the characters getting together to talk about their harrowing adventures. Often students, after listening to other groups, decide to read several other choices for pleasure. So, talk about books continues outside the classroom long after my unit has ended.

I also provide a wall map of the world, and each group tacks a sign on the spot where their story takes place. Students can discuss how some of the problems encountered were directly related to geographical locations, climates, and seasons. They talk about what they learned about plants, animals, and the human spirit in the face of adversity. They use reference books and nonfiction trade books to research topics they found fascinating. In addition, some may choose to do an artistic interpretation of their story, responding to it in the form of a painting, diorama, drawing, mobile, or model. Students find that as they synthesize ideas through art, reading, writing, talking, listening, and working cooperatively with their groups, they not only survive the "Survival!" unit, they thrive on the experience.

Social Action and Critical Literacy Projects

Authentic, real-world activities, such as social action and critical literacy projects, can be used in the classroom to demonstrate that what students are learning in school has direct application in their own lives. Teachers in the content areas can incorporate these projects into their curriculum by being aware of issues and events in their local community that interest their students and then finding connections between the issues and events and their subject area. Once teachers identify potential projects, they can plan activities that

will not only increase their students' content knowledge but also their speaking, listening, and other literacy skills in an authentic context.

As an example, the city of Syracuse, where I live, has been debating for years over the creation of a mega-mall. Some visionaries think Destiny, USA will be the best thing that ever happened to our area, while critics and skeptics think otherwise. Teachers in area schools could take on the issue along with other community leaders and members. English teachers could have students form debate teams to argue the pro and con positions. Social studies students could talk about, and then research, and then talk about again, issues relating to economic growth and community planning. Math students could discuss projected costs, as well as architectural plans in relation to geometric principles; science students could explore the environmentally friendly energy sources planned for the mall, and talk with each other about the feasibility of remaining "green." Eventually, some students might actually add their voices to those outside the schools, for they will come to realize that they are citizens, too, and the decisions that are being made now will affect them and their future.

Teaching in action: *Multidisciplinary.* Powell, Cantrell, and Adams (2001) recount a project initiated by fourth graders in central Kentucky when they learned in class that Black Mountain, the highest peak in Kentucky, was slated to be strip mined. They were used to inquiry-based learning, and decided they wanted "to learn about the issue so that they might address it from a position of knowledge rather than ignorance" (p. 776). They employed interviewing skills as they sought the perspectives of both the miners whose livelihood depended on the coal industry and the environmentalists who opposed the destruction of the mountain. Once they had done their research, they went into a critical literacy mode—taking action to save Black Mountain:

> They wrote to individuals to solicit funds to continue their campaign and subsequently collected thousands of dollars for the project. They alerted local newspapers and television stations and arranged for press conferences to talk about the mountain's future, and they even organized a "Hands Across the Mountain" rally with students from Eastern Kentucky to raise public awareness. (p. 777)

Later, the students collaborated with eighth graders from Eastern Kentucky to speak to legislators and urge them to develop the mountain for tourism rather than strip mining. Other oral language activities included storytelling sessions, presentations to Harlan County residents, presentations at universities, and talking with families in the mountain region to learn how local activists had fought back.

Of course, much reading and writing were done simultaneously. Powell et al. point out that the struggling readers and writers may have benefitted the most because they shared perceptions of changed behavior and literacy motivation during the project, which they recognized as real and important. As the student with special needs whose letter to a professor resulted in raising $500 learned, literacy can make a difference. The authors conclude, "As with the Saving Black Mountain Project, critical literacy often leads to social action as students begin to discover and internalize the problems of society, thereby leading to more transformative uses of written and oral language" (p. 779).

APPLICATION ACTIVITY **8.4** (SEE PAGE 252)

SPEAKING AND LISTENING WITH ENGLISH LEARNERS

When there is much productive social and academic talking and listening in your classroom, English learners benefit enormously. Their teachers and peers should combine verbal and nonverbal communication as much as possible. So, when you are giving directions or instruction, use pictures, flow charts, time lines, concrete objects, and maps as often as appropriate. Use gestures, facial expressions, and movements to convey meaning. Repeat words and phrases when necessary, use simulation, and watch closely and ask questions of your English learners to determine how much scaffolding is necessary and whether the talk in your classroom at various times is within their zone of proximal development. Houk (2005) advocates teachers integrating opportunities for English language learners to use oral language in purposeful ways throughout the school day. Furthermore:

> It's critical that we are conscious of the way we talk to children. If we just grunt at kids and speak in choppy phrases all the time, our children will imitate us. If we speak clearly, using lots of descriptive and clarifying words in complete, complex sentences, our children will also replicate that precision with language. (p. 133)

Group work, where conversation occurs during hands-on activities, is ideal for your second language learners because it provides *"important elements for language acquisition—a functional communication situation, comprehensible input, and social interaction around a purposeful task"* (Peregoy & Boyle, 1997, p. 52, italics in original). Writing and talking are often going on simultaneously, so can be mutually reinforcing. You might provide your English learners with a buddy or

a home group that remains fairly stable rather than constantly putting them with different people, at least until they feel supported and comfortable.

A good example of the richness of oral language at work can be found in process-oriented science classrooms using an inquiry approach. Peregoy and Boyle explain:

> Students work in pairs or groups to define a problem, state a hypothesis, gather data, record observations, draw conclusions relating data to the hypothesis, and explain and summarize findings. . . . Scientific inquiry processes require students to use academic language to convey the thinking involved in observing, classifying, comparing, measuring, inferring, predicting, concluding, synthesizing, and summarizing. (p. 119)

The success of inquiry-based science projects for English learners is attributable to three major factors:

1. Students investigate real science problems that engage their natural curiosity about the world, such as plant growth, the solar system, electricity, and magnetism;

2. Students are actively engaged in investigations involving hands-on activities, actual observations, and lab work rather than solely reading facts and theories in a textbook; and

3. Students carry out investigations in groups that promote talking out their thinking and planning.

What we see, then, is that inquiry-based science provides many opportunities for higher-level thinking through the use of context-embedded oral language aimed at solving scientific problems, creating ideal opportunities for both language and content learning (pp. 119–120).

Hadaway, Vardell, and Young (2001) advocate scaffolding oral language development for students learning English through the use of content-related poetry. Rather than students focusing on what they don't know about the English language, they are learning about the world and academics *through* powerful language and using language to discover new concepts. They note the example of science teachers in a predominantly ESL setting beginning lessons by chanting poems about scientific topics. "Discussing poems allows students to use the language—both basic communicative and academic—that they are learning to move to higher levels of proficiency" (p. 798). (Figure 3.5 gives some sources of poetry for the content areas.)

Teachers can highlight new vocabulary, talk about the tone of a poem, and note nonverbal markers such as italics for intonation and emphasis. They can use poetry to encourage students to be problem solvers, rather than mere information receivers, as they guess at meanings and hypothesize, fill in gaps, and approximate meanings—all while enjoying the poetry. Teaching strategies include modeling with poems you enjoy personally, having the whole class read in unison, or having certain groups join in on repeated lines or refrains, groups taking turns reading stanzas with good volume and expression, individuals practicing and reciting solo lines, and innovative alternatives created by the students themselves. Of course, discussion is crucial as students examine the crafts of certain poets, explore possible interpretations and share responses, and think about creating their own content-related poems.

Hadaway et al. recommend that classrooms contain a listening center (Steinbergh, 1994) that highlights poetry and includes some of the plentiful collections of bilingual poetry available today, including *My Mexico—Mexico Mio* by Tony Johnston (1996), *This Tree Is Older than You Are* collected by Naomi Shihab Nye (1998), and *Canto Familiar* by Gary Soto (1995). They recommend exploring more creative teaching ideas at the Potato Hill Poetry website: www.potato-hill.com. They conclude:

> All students can enjoy the incredible variety of contemporary and multicultural poetry being written for young people. For English L2 learners, in particular, oral poetry sharing can provide the necessary language practice in a context that is relaxed and pleasurable, where all learners can participate as equals in enjoying the playfulness and power of language through poetry. (p. 804)

CONCLUSION

T his chapter provided ideas for profitably harnessing teens' and preteens' natural inclination toward talking, and for using listening skills well. Talking and listening can lead to learning and can connect to other components of literacy. With instruction, modeling, and both guided and independent practice, your students will recognize the importance of oral literacy and will flourish.

Your classroom should be full of productive talk. There will be opportunities for relatively formal speaking, as when students give presentations teaching others what they have learned through reading and research, and many chances for informal talking. Chandler-Olcott (2001), for example, discusses teachers choosing texts with students. The benefits of this include the opportunity to learn about the students' interests, preferences, and needs, and the chance to coach them through strategies they can use later to choose books independently. Chandler-Olcott took students to a local bookstore, where each was to choose two titles to read during a six-week summer program; she found the conversations that took place over the selection were important. If this is beyond the resources you have available, organize a similar field trip to a library. Of course, talking casually to students in your classroom, as Miller (2009) does with her sixth graders among the more than 2,000 books in their classroom library, will yield rich rewards for both you and the adolescents you teach.

WEBSITES **CHAPTER 8** Access these links using the Kane Resource Site.

Authors Readers Theatre
www.authorsreaderstheatre.com

Avi
www.avi-writer.com

Kendall Haven
www.kendallhaven.com

Laurie Halse Anderson
www.writerlady.com

Potato Hill Poetry
www.potatohill.com.

Reader's Theater Editions
www.aaronshep.com/rt/RTE.html

Reader's Theater Scripts and Plays
www.teachingheart.net/readerstheater.htm

Reading A-Z
www.readinga-z.com

APPLICATION ACTIVITIES

8.1 Select a topic in your subject area that students could talk about in small groups. Find a relevant text to stimulate their thinking and provide a starting point for discussion. Write a plan for a lesson using a small group format. Here are some questions to guide your planning:

1. What will be the best size for the groups?
2. How shall the groups be formed: randomly, self-selected, by ability, by similar interests or goals, girls and boys separated or together?
3. What guide questions or other structure should I provide?
4. What should I be doing while the groups are meeting?
5. How (if at all) will the information obtained or discussion results be shared with the whole group?
6. What potential trouble spots can I anticipate? How might I help students who are confused or seem to be getting off-track?
7. What is the most appropriate follow-up to this lesson? What comes next?
8. How can the lesson be evaluated?

Post your plan on the Kane Resource Site, or form small groups to share your plan with others, get their feedback and suggestions, and respond to other plans you hear about. Even better, if you are working with students in a practicum setting, try out your lesson. Or at least talk about it with teenagers and ask them what they think might work and what might have to be changed.

8.2 Choose a text that you think would make a good read-aloud in your content area. Read for at least 10 minutes into a recorder. Later, listen to yourself, and evaluate the clarity and expressiveness. Would you enjoy listening to a lengthy passage read by this voice? You might listen to some audio books from your public library and analyze the voices you think are particularly effective. Keep practicing, and perhaps start a collection of recordings for a listening center.

8.3 Choose a text in your subject area that you think might prove a bit difficult for students to read independently. Scaffold their learning by preparing a pre-reading lecture based on the listen–read–discuss method. Then, try the strategy by asking a student or colleague to play the role of the listener–reader. Reciprocate if a classmate needs a listener. You'll learn from participating from both perspectives.

8.4 Think about issues, perhaps involving local dilemmas such as the Kentucky children explored, that your students can investigate. Brainstorm various strategies involving talking and listening, as well as reading and writing, that your students might employ. Don't let possible constraints stop you at this point; the Kentucky example shows how youngsters can meet challenges and overcome obstacles through the power of literacy.

chapter 9

Multiliteracies: Visual, Media, and Digital

ACTIVATING PRIOR KNOWLEDGE   9.1

Recall how your past teachers used various kinds of media in content area courses. List types and examples, then think about how effective the use of media was. What worked well, and what seemed to be used just for the purpose of consuming time or controlling the class? How did students (you in particular) respond? Was the use of media the best way to learn the material? Did you respond actively to construct knowledge from films, videos, slides, and so forth? Or was your viewing within school contexts more of a passive activity? Finally, did your teachers do anything to prepare you for viewing, evaluating, and learning from the media, or did they let the material stand on its own? Write for a few moments, using specific examples whenever possible.

"*Can societal structures and school curricula accommodate and incorporate youth desires for knowledge and the new kinds of knowledge they need for negotiating the literacy demands and possibilities of a new century?*"

JABARI MAHIRI

I 'd like to begin this chapter with an e-mail message I received from my son Patrick on the morning I was beginning my Chapter 9 revisions for the third edition of this book. His daughter Molly was 26 months old at the time, and he was relating a conversation they had just had:

> **Molly:** I'm going to find it on the Internet.
>
> **Patrick:** Molly, how do you know about the Internet?
>
> **Molly:** I can know anything I want to.

Molly is a Digital Native, a native speaker "of the digital language of computers, video games, and the Internet" (Alvermann, 2007, p. 21, citing Prensky, 2001). Her father just makes it into the category of what Tapscott (1997, 2009) labeled the Net Generation (those born between 1977 and 1997), so he's close. Many of you who are reading this textbook are Digital Natives, also; you don't even remember a time when you weren't connected digitally to information sources and to other people. I, on the other hand, am what Prensky refers to as a Digital Immigrant. So, as I talk about literacy and content area teaching in relation to media and technology, you may have to forgive me for my lack of familiarity with some aspects of your digital world. And considering how fast things change and develop in the field of technology, you might be able to take some of the topics discussed here and think of new ways to apply them using your expertise with various digital tools. I think that's great!

This chapter continues to broaden the definition and boundaries of the literacy concept. In the first section, I discuss educational issues related to the use of visuals: pictures, graphs, and charts. Next, I deal with media literacy, concentrating on film and television. Finally, I examine electronic or digital literacy and discuss the content area teacher's role in helping students construct knowledge using computers, software, and the Internet. Of course, the divisions between these areas are not discrete; artwork can be seen on videos and the Internet, text and pictures are often intertwined, and examples found in one section could also apply to others. As in earlier chapters, I talk about each type of literacy separately, knowing that the boundaries are not distinct. There are opportunities for you to synthesize what you are learning as you proceed.

VISUAL LITERACY

We read many things besides written texts. We read the expressions on people's faces that convey that they are pleased, upset, or anxious. We pay attention to atmospheric conditions and make predictions about the weather; we read political and social atmospheres, too. We ponder situations where the verbal messages and nonverbal signals seem to contradict each other. So, your students should be able to understand what you mean when you speak of constructing knowledge from sources other than print.

Visual displays of information are becoming increasingly important for a number of reasons, and thus the need for what we might call *graphic literacy* is crucial. According to Weaver (1999), "Business leaders complain that new employees lack this skill. This lack of skill is probably highlighted by the increased necessity to read graphics and interpret them in the workplace" (p. vi).

You may have learned in education or psychology courses about the work of Howard Gardner, whose research demonstrates several different types of intelligence. He calls into question the way schools have typically valued linguistic and logical–mathematical ways of thinking more than the other ways, including musical, bodily–kinesthetic, interpersonal, intrapersonal, naturalist, ritualistic, and spatial–visual. According to his theory of *multiple intelligences*,

we all have some types of intelligences that are more developed than others, and we all learn differently. As a content area teacher, you should help your students learn using their preferred modes, while helping them to improve the intelligences most connected with your particular subject area (e.g., math, foreign language, physical education, or art). It's good to present concepts and curriculum through a multimodal approach. For a thorough exploration of Gardner's theories and findings, as well as ways to assess your students' strengths in the various intelligences, go to the source. Start with Gardner's groundbreaking *Frames of Mind: The Theory of Multiple Intelligences* (1983/2004), then go on to his application of the theory to education in *The Unschooled Mind: How Children Think and How Schools Should Teach* (1991/2004). This chapter focuses on how you can tap into adolescents' spatial–visual intelligence and help them use it to learn and add to their overall literacy capabilities.

We'll start with art, with pictures, and talk about how your students can learn content while reading pictures from both efferent and aesthetic stances. Recall that Rosenblatt (1978) spoke of reading for the purpose of getting information (efferent) and for the purpose of enjoyment, or living and appreciating the experience (aesthetic).

Visual Texts for Content Area Learning

This section describes types of books that are appropriate to use to enhance visual learning and literacy in the content areas, including visual trade series books, wordless picture books, cartoons and comics, and graphic novels. Also see Chapter 3 for a discussion of picture books with text.

Visual trade book series

Several popular trade book series capitalize on the visual learning modes. For example, *The Usborne Illustrated Encyclopedia: Science and Technology* (Scholastic, 1999) contains over 1,500 illustrations on fewer than 100 pages. Some books advertise even in their titles that their focus is the visual. Figure 9.1 gives an idea of the range of topics covered in such works.

Wordless picture books

If you've been surprised by the number of picture books recommended throughout these chapters as appropriate for secondary content classrooms, you may be amazed at the sophisticated books waiting to be discovered that have *no* words, or almost none. More good news is that there are dozens of

---

FIGURE 9.1   Series books and reference books focusing on visual literacy.

■ Dorling Kindersley. *Eyewitness Books*. There are dozens of beautifully illustrated books that teach about epidemics, energy, the Olympics, impressionism, amphibians, ponds and rivers, force and motion, electronics, mythology, baseball, presidents, pyramids, deserts, crime and detection, sports, crystals and gems, skeletons, Russia, the Renaissance, religion, hurricanes and tornadoes, and so much more. The series is like a library in itself.

■ Enslow Publishers. *Decades of the Twentieth Century*. Each decade in this series is presented in a manner accessible to middle grade children. The books are appealing and very informative. The chronological approach is helpful; together, the volumes cause the big picture to become very clear.

■ Grolier Educational. *The American Scene: Lives*. This encyclopedia of important Americans includes entries on people from all walks of life, including Houdini, Jesse Owens, Britney Spears, Ruth Bader Ginsburg, and Jackie Robinson.

■ Grolier. *Being Human*. There are eight volumes in this series that inform students through pictures and text about various aspects of humanity ranging from personality and behavior to communications and relationships, from the brain and senses to health and wellness.

■ Penguin Books. *The See Through History Series*. Books in this collection contain overlays for inside–outside views; their extensive listing includes works on the Industrial Revolution, ancient China, ships and submarines, tombs and treasures, and the Aztecs.

■ Kingfisher. *The Visual Factfinder Series*. Each book contains thousands of facts, figures, charts, diagrams, maps, illustrations, and photographs on such topics as science and technology and world history.

■ Scholastic. *Voyages of Discovery*. The books are beautifully designed and have overlays, stickers, and cut-away pages that make the books hands-on experiences without appearing the least bit babyish. Topics include bikes, cars, trucks, and trains; water; paint and painting; architecture and construction; and the history of printmaking.

■ Scholastic. *The National Audubon Society's First Field Guide Series*. A reader-friendly yet sophisticated set of books packed with illustrations and information about such topics as amphibians, birds, insects, mammals, the night sky, reptiles, rocks and minerals, trees, weather, and wildflowers.

■ Chelsea House Publishers. *The Encyclopedia of Musical Instruments*. Volumes in this beautiful set, authored by Robert Dearling, teach readers about percussion and electronic instruments, stringed instruments, woodwind and brass instruments, keyboard instruments and ensembles, and non-Western and obsolete instruments.

■ Carolrhoda Books. *Picture the American Past Series*. Volumes invite readers to look and learn about the lives of young people in the times of the orphan trains, the Dust Bowl days, the days of the relocation camps, and the Civil Rights era.

■ Heinemann Library. *Picture the Past Series*. Students exploring volumes in this series can be immersed in the lives of people on the Oregon Trail, on a southern plantation, in a Hopi village, on a pioneer homestead. What a literary field trip!

■ Lerner Publishing Group. *Visual Geography Series*. By exploring the books in this series, readers can learn through pictures about many countries, including Afghanistan, Israel, Germany, Saudi Arabia, Cuba, Russia, Canada, Kenya, India, China, South Africa, Egypt, Iraq, Turkey, Argentina, and Vietnam.

■ Powell's Books. *Teach Yourself Visually Series*. Readers can explore books on knitting and crocheting, computers, weight training, yoga, dog training, and digital photography, among other topics.

profitable ways you can use such resources to help the learners in your courses examine issues and try out creative approaches. Cassady (1998) recommends wordless picture books as no-risk tools for inclusive classrooms. She reminds us:

> Struggling and reluctant readers come in all ages and stages. They usually are caught in the downward spiral of failure that produces dislike and mistrust. This leads to an avoidance practice that leads to a lack of development, to further failure, and so on. In order to end this downward spiral and turn it upward toward success, which leads to pleasure, trust, and further practice, at least one truly successful activity needs to occur. (pp. 428–429)

Cassady has found that wordless picture books provide that success and enjoyment for struggling readers, and also benefit English learners. I would add that any students who learn well visually, or who are interested in art, or who enjoy the humor and puzzles and small surprises picture books so often provide, will appreciate the addition of this genre to your classroom library. Here are a few of the many ways you can use wordless books:

1. If you teach a foreign language, your students can tell the story they see in the pictures, using the foreign language vocabulary and structure as much as possible. You'll find them asking you to supply words they really want to know for their stories. Try this with *Tuesday* by David Wiesner (1991). Similarly, students with limited English proficiency can first construct the story in their primary language and then attempt it in English.

2. The books can add to your students' background knowledge and conceptual understanding. For example, *The Story of a Castle* (Goodall, 1986) shows how people of the period lived. The series consisting of *Anno's Journey* (1978), *Anno's U.S.A.* (1983b), *Anno's Britain* (1982), and *Anno's Italy* (1980) is rich with cultural symbols and historical icons.

3. Students, perhaps in English class, can use the books as writing prompts. They can add dialogue, imagine the feelings of and relationships between characters depicted, create a story line, or write a review of the book's artwork and overall quality. They can also reflect in writing about how they constructed meaning as they engaged with the pages. Some books, like Graeme Base's *The Eleventh Hour* (1989), can be pored over repeatedly, with new pieces of information discovered each time.

4. After reveling in several examples of wordless picture books, students can try their hand at the genre. They can use a variety of media and styles to create picture books relating to the topics they're learning about. If they feel insecure about their drawing or painting ability, they can experiment with a collage approach, collaborate with others whose skills are complementary, or download graphics from the Internet. They might take a book that is meant for younger students and compose a sequel or a parallel story aimed at older readers. The important thing is that they are reinforcing their own knowledge while creating a product that supplements others' learning and gives the creators a sense of artistic achievement.

Figure 9.2 lists samples of wordless (or almost wordless) picture books that work well in content areas.

ACTION RESEARCH 9.A

Find and peruse one or more wordless picture books relevant to your content area, using Figure 9.2 as a starting place. Write a journal response reflecting on what the experience of constructing meaning without text was like for you, or discussing how you might use the book(s) to teach a unit. Speculate about how you might model your reading or introduce the book to a group of students.

FIGURE 9.2

Wordless (or almost wordless) picture books for content area learning.

See more suggested titles in Appendix Figure 9.2.

Anno, M. (2004). *Anno's Spain*. New York: Philomel Books.

Blake, Q. (2003). *Tell Me a Picture*. Brookfield, CT: Millbrook Press.

Feelings, T. (1995). *The Middle Passage: White Ships/ Black Cargo*. New York: Dial Books.

Tan, S. (2008). *The Arrival*. New York: Arthur A. Levine Books.

Wiesner, D. (2006). *Flotsam*. New York: Clarion.

Cartoons and comics

Virtually everyone recognizes the fun that can be derived from cartoon art. The sadness over the retirement and death of Charles Schulz in 2000 was a striking acknowledgment of the impact a comic strip had on generations of readers around the world. Not everyone yet recognizes the additional benefit this visual art form can have on learning. Rothschild (1995) asserts that aficionados know that comics provide a rich array: "Mythology. Intensely honest autobiography. Experimentation. Character studies. Opera. Poetry. Shakespeare. History. In short, the same topics, the same elements, found in mainstream literature" (p. xiii). In this section, I hope to stimulate your thinking about how you can effectively use cartoons in your classroom.

I have a tabbed folder containing cartoons that directly relate to concepts and topics taught in various subject areas. I have "Peanuts" and "Calvin and Hobbes" cartoons about the writing process; "Far Side" cartoons about science, history, and math; "Dilbert" cartoons about technology and business. They can be used as an introduction to a lesson or a motivating tool and can rely on, reinforce, or build background knowledge.

A particular type of comic genre is the political cartoon. National and state social studies standards require that students interpret such texts. Political cartoons are found in virtually any daily newspaper—often, they are beside an editorial or letters to the editor, so you and your students can follow current events through a combination of text formats. You can ask guiding questions to help the students figure out whose perspective is being represented, what events or other texts are being alluded to, what aspects of the creation make it humorous or effective.

I encourage you to start your own file; once you start reading comics in your role as teacher, you'll be amazed at how plentiful the discipline-related cartoons are. The students can join you in your quest for additions to your collection, and can bring in content area–related cartoons they find for classroom wall displays. Cartoons also enhance the students' general and content-specific vocabulary. They have patterns of organization such as cause–effect and compare–contrast, just as other texts do, and many require critical thinking, synthesizing, taking on different perspectives, and making inferences.

Bitz (2004) reports on an after-school comic book project that involved 733 students at 33 New York City sites. The goals included building artistic and literacy skills. The project had a powerful effect, especially on students with limited English proficiency. They wrote manuscripts and drew pictures

---

BookTalk 9.3

If you were unaware of the wealth of knowledge that can be gained through comic-book form, investigate the *Beginners Documentary Comic Books* series published by Writers and Readers Publishing. Individual titles include such topics as Black history, Structuralism, Freud, Hemingway, philosophy, biology, computers, Malcolm X, psychiatry, the Black Holocaust, opera, art, the United Nations, rainforests, classical music, and many more. I read *Chomsky for Beginners* by David Cogswell and Paul Gordon (1996) and learned much information about Noam Chomsky's life, predecessors who influenced him (including Plato, Descartes, Rousseau, Karl Marx, and George Orwell), his contributions to the field of linguistics, his thinking about the media, and his views on politics. The book includes an interview with Chomsky, and quotes from this influential linguist are interspersed throughout the text. Your visual learners will love it.

BookTalk Online 9.4

The Physics of Superheroes (2005) by James Kakalios (www.physicsofsuperheroes.com) explores the scientific principles exemplified by the special powers of the X-Men, Batman, and more. Read more at the Kane Resource Site.

---

depicting their immigration to the country, as well as their current lives. The project improved motivation and writing skills, and addressed several learning standards.

Eliza Dresang (1999) notes the proliferation of comic books as respectable texts as one example of the radical change in literature. "A format that was once thought to signal mindless entertainment may in some instances require greater intellectual engagement than ordinary linear text, because readers are called upon to 'read between the frames,' themselves supplying continuity in the blank spaces left by the artist" (p. 23).

Graphic novels

Definitions of the graphic-novel format vary. Short and Reeves (2009), who tout the benefits of using graphic novels with Generation Y students (born between 1982 and 2003), offer one: "an illustrated work that involves a more mature audience in which a dramatic arc is followed where content is presented with a definite beginning, middle, and end" (p. 416). In 2008, Dresang stated that, in the decade since she published her landmark book *Radical Change: Books for Youth in a Digital Age* (1999), "no change has been more dramatic than that of the graphic novel" (p. 297). Graphic novels have been used successfully in many disciplines, including business (Short and Reeves, 2009) chemistry (McElmeel, 2008), and art (Williams, 2008). They are also recommended for special populations, such as English learners (Chun, 2009), deaf students (Smetana et al., 2009), striving readers (Knop, 2008), and Advanced Placement students (Carlson, 2008). English teachers can teach Shakespeare plays and other classics using the originals and graphic-novel versions side by side. History teachers have a wealth of choices that match their curricula. It's generally agreed that graphic novels provide motivation, stimulation, challenge, engagement, and enjoyment. What's not to like?

You can decide what place graphic novels will have in your classroom by reading some yourself, paying attention to features that might help you in your teaching and personal learning, and by trying some out with students or peers and listening closely to their reactions. Figure 9.3 lists examples of discipline-related texts in comic form and graphic novels. Figure 9.4 lists books *about* this genre.

Magazines

Students, as well as the rest of us, read many texts other than books, especially outside of school. Marc Aronson (2003) calls on those of us responsible for the literacy and learning of youngsters to be aware and accepting of this:

> First we need to open up what we mean by reading to include websites, game instructions, car manuals, and, most of all, magazines. Books are just a subset of teenagers' true reading environment. Instead of ignoring all of those materials that do not come bound with convenient Dewey listings, we must see them as opportunities. Teenagers like magazines, which generally have lively design, contemporary ideas and situations, and target a wide range of interests. (p. 95)

Figure 9.5 lists some of the many magazines available that can enhance our content area instruction.

FIGURE 9.3 Examples of graphic novels and texts in cartoon/comic format.

See more suggested titles in Appendix Figure 9.3.

Bonner, H. (2007). *When Fish Got Feet, Sharks Got Teeth, and Bugs Began to Swarm: A Cartoon Prehistory of Life Long Before Dinosaurs.* Washington, DC: National Geographic.

Edginton, I. (Adaptor). (2008). *Oscar Wilde's The Picture of Dorian Gray: A Graphic Novel.* New York: Sterling Publishing.

Sheinkin, S. (2008). *Rabbi Harvey Rides Again: A Graphic Novel of Jewish Folktales Let Loose in the Wild West.* Woodstock, VT: Jewish Lights Publishing.

Yang, G. (2006). *American Born Chinese.* New York: First Second Books.

Zinn, H., Konopacki, M., & Buhle, P. (2008). *A People's History of American Empire: A Graphic Adaptation.* New York: Metropolitan Books.

FIGURE 9.4 Examples of books *about* graphic novels and cartoons.

Abel, J., & Madden, M. (2008). *Drawing Words, Writing Pictures: Making Comics from Manga to Graphic Novels.* New York: First Second Books.

Chinn, M. (2004). *Writing and Illustrating the Graphic Novel: Everything You Need to Know to Create Great Graphic Books.* Hauppauge, NY: Barron's.

Goulart, R. (2000). *Comic Book Culture: An Illustrated History.* Portland, OR: Collectors Press.

Hamilton, J. (2009). *Graphic Novel: You Write It!* Edina, MN: ABDO Publishing.

Hart, C. (2004). *Drawing Cutting Edge Anatomy: The Ultimate Reference Guide for Comic Book Artists.* New York: Watson-Guptill.

O'Neil, D. (2001). *The DC Comics Guide to Writing Comics.* New York: Watson-Guptill Publications.

Slate, B. (2010). *You Can Do a Graphic Novel.* New York: Alpha Books.

Wolk, D. (2007). *Reading Comics: How Graphic Novels Work and What They Mean.* Cambridge, MA: Da Capo Press.

FIGURE 9.5   **Magazines that can enhance content area instruction.**

HISTORY

American History

Armchair General

America's Civil War

History Magazine

The History Channel Magazine

World War II

Military History

Military Heritage

Naval History

Vietnam

America In WWII

MHQ

Foreign Affairs

Faces

Cobblestone

Appleseeds Magazine

Calliope

LITERATURE/ENGLISH

Writer's Journal

Poets & Writers

Children's Digest

Cricket

Cicada

TeenInk

Writer's Digest

SCIENCE

Scientific American

Popular Science

Air & Space

American Scientist

Astronomy

National Geographic

SEED

Dig

Odyssey

Ranger Rick

Kids Discover Magazine

Zoobooks

Owl Magazine

Muse

Cricket

National Geographic Kids

Audubon

Biology Digest

Field and Stream

ART

American Art Review

American Artist

Artist's Magazine

Animation Magazine

Dance

MISCELLANEOUS

Consumer Reports

ESPN The Magazine

Health

Teaching Tolerance

Outdoor Life

Psychology Today

Source: List created by Grace Subik.

Readers and Writers Learning and Responding Through Art and Photography

So often, students feel that the teacher knows what a text means and their job is to discover what that elusive "right answer" is. Responding to picture books may boost our students' confidence because they may feel more secure about their ability to discuss visual stimuli and may actually teach the teacher something. Several years ago, I asked an 11-year-old artist to read some picture books with an art theme and talk to me about them. Julie's responses were truly instructive:

> Sometimes it's best to let the pen do what it wants to do. Like, a chair can't do anything but be a chair, but a pen can *do* things. . . . I found, in being an artist, and sometimes a writer, you shouldn't be bound by restrictions, the laws of physics, you could say. . . . I found that in art there's not a right or wrong way, it's just, it's kind of like, in art, there is no right or wrong, there's only *do.*

One day I visited a teacher as she was about to read aloud a chapter from Roald Dahl's *James and the Giant Peach* (1992). She passed out pieces of construc-tion paper and instructed the students to have their markers ready in case they heard something that made them want to draw. I observed that some students drew fast and furiously, using several colors and multiple sheets of paper, while others ignored the paper on their desks, listening in rapt attention with smiles or scared expressions on their faces as the scenes and the teacher's voice changed. From there, I went to another classroom where a teacher scolded a child for drawing when he was supposed to be listening to a story being read. Witnessing the juxtaposition of the two teachers' philosophies in action jarred me into examining my own beliefs about students' drawing. Since then, I have read numerous teachers' accounts of the benefits of encouraging student artwork at every stage of learning.

Nancie Atwell (1998) confesses her distress over a particular eighth-grade student who resisted her structured writing assignments and drew his way through her English class. She even quotes herself as saying regularly, "Jeff, stop drawing and *get to work*" (p. 7). He did the work, but at home, and she was frustrated because he didn't do things her way. Years later, Atwell

BookTalk   9.5

We might bemoan the fact that students today tend to shun the classics, and we might feel a bit guilty ourselves for never having made it quite to the end of *Moby Dick* or *Great Expectations*. Try out the library of "Classics Illustrated," and treat yourself to the comic-book style interpretations of Shakespeare's tragedies and such standards as *Huckleberry Finn, Gulliver's Travels,* and *Frankenstein*. These works might very well be the stepping stone to the original works.

You might start by examining *The Complete Guide to Classics Illustrated* by D. Malan (1994) or *Classics Illustrated: A Cultural History, with Illustrations* by W. B. Jones (2002) and going to the "Classics Illustrated" versions of individual classics from there.

And you might be amazed at what you learn from the adolescent artists in your class. For example, Juliana Bütz is a student who enjoys and learns from drawing. She did both scientific and imaginative drawing in her free time in high school, and did not see them as entirely separate. "I like to draw fantasy stuff, but I want to be believable, have realistic proportions. If you're going to draw a dragon, you want the joints to look as though they would really work" (personal conversation). A teacher discovered Juliana's love of and talent for drawing; he designed an independent study for her so that she could get academic credit for all the work she was doing. She researched her subjects to ensure accuracy in her art, thus learning science and art together, one reinforcing the other. She later commented on her nature drawings, "I didn't copy drawings, or use my imagination for them. I always drew from life." Figure 9.6 shows examples of Juliana's self-initiated scientific illustrations.

There are many books spanning several genres that have an art focus or theme that you can make available to your students. Some topics may fit directly into your curricular areas, while others might just be in your classroom library, ready to invite students into an artistic realm of thought and into a pleasurable, perhaps new, field of endeavor. They seem to invite response, either emotionally or with art supplies. Figure 9.7 lists sample titles that fit this category.

learned from reading the work of researcher Donald Graves (1975) that it was natural for some writers to plan and rehearse their writing through drawing, and she realized that her well-intentioned structures had actually served as constraints for Jeff. She learned to learn from her students how best to help them.

Allowing students to use art as a way to connect with your content curriculum has many benefits.

FIGURE   9.6   Sample student drawings done as an independent study.

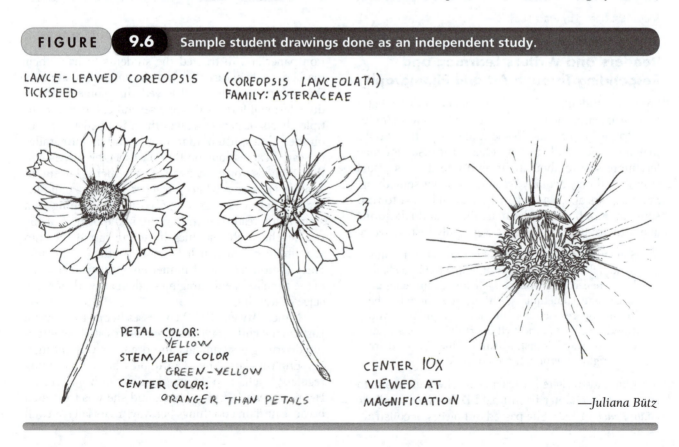

LANCE-LEAVED COREOPSIS TICKSEED

(COREOPSIS LANCEOLATA) FAMILY: ASTERACEAE

PETAL COLOR: YELLOW
STEM/LEAF COLOR GREEN-YELLOW
CENTER COLOR: ORANGER THAN PETALS

CENTER 10X VIEWED AT MAGNIFICATION

—*Juliana Bütz*

See more suggested titles in Appendix Figure 9.7.

FIGURE 9.7

Young adult books with a visual arts focus or theme.

Balliett, B. (2004). *Chasing Vermeer*. New York: Scholastic.

Creech, S. (2004). *Heartbeat*. New York: HarperCollins.

Hill, L. C. (2005). *Casa Azul: An Encounter with Frida Kahlo*. New York: Watson-Guptill.

Kudlinski, K. (2004). *The Spirit Catchers: An Encounter with Georgia O'Keefe*. New York: Watson-Guptill.

Selznick, B. (2007). *The Invention of Hugo Cabret*. New York: Scholastic.

Your students can use their own drawings or paintings, or artwork found on the Web (including photographs, drawings, diagrams, computer animations, and streaming video) to illustrate texts you've provided or texts they've composed themselves. Bruce (2000), in an article entitled "The Work of Art in the Age of Digital Reproduction," recommends using art to teach across the curriculum, providing an annotated listing of sites on the Web that offer art appropriate for content area subjects. For example, science students can explore www.SpaceArt.org and come to appreciate works focusing on images that were inspired by astronomy and space travel; they can further investigate the links to other sites about the wonders of space and about astronauts. Bruce, while pointing out that there are many art sites to help students study philosophy, history, and science, concludes that "these sites remind us of the importance of the aesthetic dimension of learning" (p. 66).

Another way to use art in the content areas is through digital photography. Bussert-Webb (2001) gave her students, all pregnant teens, disposable cameras to use as they completed a "Photo Story Project" about their present perceptions and future visions. I have loaned my digital video camera to my preservice teachers for their academic projects. They discover creative abilities they didn't realize they had!

Knowles and Smith (2005), after discussing the scholarship related to boys and literacy, make a number of suggestions for teachers and parents in hopes of increasing boys' active engagement with literacy and improve their reading and writing habits. Several of their suggestions for changing instructional strategies involve the visual realm, including using art as a way of responding to literature, using graphic organizers as a comprehension aid, using comic books and graphic novels, encouraging boys to draw out

BookTalk 9.6

Imagine a book that is part historical document, part (almost) wordless picture book, and you'll have an idea of Peter Spier's *We the People: The Constitution of the United States* (1987). The front endpapers show a map of the United States of America in 1787 as executed by Spiers. A four-page introduction gives background on the reasons why the Constitutional Convention was called, and the processes of writing the Constitution and having it ratified. Then comes the main section of the book—the only text consists of the one sentence preamble to the Constitution. For every phrase, beginning with "We, the people," there are pages of small, detailed illustrations depicting scenes from the lives of Americans and the growth of various government agencies and projects throughout the years. Finally, there is the printed version of the Constitution and its amendments, and the closing endpapers showing what the original handwritten version on parchment looks like. Students might wish to use this book as a model to make similar class books based on other famous quotations—perhaps the inscription from the Statue of Liberty, the 1848 "Declaration of Sentiments," or a collection of presidential quotes. They could also compare Spier's creation to Lynne Cheney's and Greg Harlen's take on the subject in the picture book *We the People: The Story of Our Constitution* (2008).

their thoughts and ideas before writing, and comparing books and movies that have been based on them (pp. xvii–xix).

Long (2008) developed the *full circling* methodology, a multilayered process that "uses visual media as text to be critically read, interpreted, and employed as a call to action" (p. 499). She has used photographs from the Jim Crow era, the Great Depression, and the Japanese Internment to stir her urban students' emotions and help them vocalize their awareness of many kinds of text. She and her students observe, analyze, and act on the ethical conflicts they see related to the texts; they then transmediate what has been learned through creating their own text using a different genre, such as dance, writing, art, or music. Finally, they plan some way that they can take action to address the ethical issue proactively. Long searches for deeper understanding:

> Of the ways in which visual media, when carefully considered and used as a foundation for ethical caring and action, can be very powerful tools—tools

that not only move students to feel as well as to think but also oblige them to act on the world as burgeoning advocates of human rights. (p. 507)

Reading, Using, and Creating Graphs and Charts

As stated earlier, visual literacy is becoming increasingly necessary for everyday types of reading. It's virtually impossible to open a newspaper or news magazine without finding information in chart form or in symbols of some sort. Visual displays are common in magazines, travel guides, signs along highways and in stores, textbooks, manuals, on television, and in software programs. Fortunately, the attention paid to comprehending graphs, charts, and other visual sources of information seems to be increasing in schools today. National standards in mathematics, science, English language arts, and social studies include this area of literacy, and many assessments do also. For instance, the New York State Regents exam in English required of high school students for graduation always has a major task that involves the analysis of information in graphic form, which must then be synthesized with information from a companion text. The January 2000 exam, for instance, required students to read an article about recycling taken from *Consumer Reports,* along with a chart detailing the pros and cons of recycling. The students then prepared for a debate by writing a persuasive essay, using relevant information from both documents, that agreed or disagreed with the statement that recycling is worth the effort. Similarly, the New York State Global Studies and American History Regents exams have questions involving a number of related pieces of data, including cartoons or graphs or maps, that must be interpreted, synthesized, and written about.

The book *Visual Literacy: How to Read and Use Information in Graphic Form,* by Marcia Weaver (1999), contains explanations and examples showing the wide variety of graphic formats: histograms, bar and column graphs, computer-generated flowcharts, scattergrams, fishbone diagrams, maps, organization charts, blueprints, spreadsheets, and others. It gives step-by-step lessons, suggests questions for readers to ask as they encounter various representations, and gives writing prompts, as well as a pre-test and post-test. The chapter on pie charts has several pictures of these information-filled graphics and explains:

> The unique quality of the pie chart is the fact that it shows you the overall picture of the data as well as a picture of the individual pieces of data. . . . Another characteristic is that the percent of the whole is printed right on the pie segment. There are no measurements to figure out; no hatch marks to read. (p. 120)

BookTalk   9.7

Lincoln's Gettysburg Address is powerful by itself, and the historical happenings that give it context, including the story of the consecration of the Soldiers' National Cemetery, are equally capable of evoking readers' emotions. Now, imagine the addition of quality artwork to the lines of the speech. A 1997 publication, *The Gettysburg Address,* is illustrated with black and white scratchboard drawings by Michael McCurdy. One reviewer had this to say:

> Each page provides readers an opportunity to function as participant observers—to view all that went on during this battle from different perspectives: from a panoramic view, then close up, then face-to-face. McCurdy has done a remarkable job of depicting soldiers, statesmen, and onlookers as individuals, each unique as to features, body structure, and age, and each distinctive in his or her emotional responses to the circumstances of this battle and the commemoration service. Historical details, such as the military weaponry and the clothing worn by the soldiers and civilians, are accurately portrayed. (Cianciolo, 2000, p. 162)

A perfect companion is Butzer's *Gettysburg: The Graphic Novel* (2009), which uses phrases from Lincoln's speech, along with quotes from letters and diaries, in this visual interpretation.

After providing multiple-choice questions, Weaver provides opportunities for application, giving scenarios that call for the construction of pie charts. Similar explanations and projects are found in the other chapters.

When discussing spatial–visual intelligence (one of the separate intelligences identified and made well known by Howard Gardner), Weaver quotes William James, "Whilst part of what we perceive comes through our senses from the object before us, another part (and it may be the larger part) always comes out of our own mind" (p. 191). Can you see how that connects to the theory of reader response and the philosophy of constructivism that has been present throughout this book?

Weaver and Gardner both show that visual intelligence can be increased. Encourage your students to engage in activities and take advantage of opportunities to practice their skills in this area. Fill the walls and your files with authentic materials containing all kinds of symbols and graphic displays brought in by students from newspapers, their parents' workplaces, and magazines. Add charts published by the school to share information with the public about test scores, budgets, demographics, plans for build-

| FIGURE | 9.8 | Books and games dealing with visual and spatial skills. |

See more suggested titles in Appendix Figure 9.8.

Frey, N., & Fisher, D. (2008). *Teaching Visual Literacy: Using Comic Books, Graphic Novels, Anime, Cartoons, and More to Develop Comprehension and Thinking Skills.* Thousand Oaks, CA: Corwin Press.

Long, L. (2004). *Great Graphs and Sensational Statistics: Games and Activities that Make Math Easy and Fun.* Hoboken, NJ: John Wiley.

McBride, C. (2000). *Making Magnificent Machines: Fun with Math, Science, and Engineering.* Tucson, AZ: Zephyr Press.

Tang, G. (2005). *Math Potatoes: More Mind-Stretching Math Riddles.* New York: Scholastic.

Wainer, H. (2005). *Graphic Discovery: A Trout in the Milk and Other Visual Adventures.* Princeton, NJ: Princeton University Press.

ing, and so on. There are also numerous books that provide visual puzzles, conundrums, and challenges, as well as tips for improving one's visual–spatial intelligence and memory. Figure 9.8 lists some of these books.

MEDIA LITERACY

By now, you probably can see how blurred the boundaries are between all of these special literacy terms. You might also be wondering if anything lies outside the definition of literacy; it seems to encompass everything. Here is a definition offered by high school English teacher and author Jim Burke (1999), which he culled from many others: "Literacy is the ability to access, analyze, synthesize, evaluate and communicate information and ideas in a variety of forms depending on the purpose of that occasion" (p. 204). Media literacy is a huge topic about which many books have been written. Teachers can teach units on advertising, on the news, on radio, on teen magazines; depending on your content area and the needs and interests of your students, you may explore any number of media types. I concentrate on two in this section: films and television.

Literacy and Film

ACTIVATING PRIOR KNOWLEDGE   9.2

Recall your days as a middle and high school student, as well as college courses if appropriate. What films or film clips do you remember watching in class? How were they introduced by teachers? What was their purpose? What were some follow-up activities? How did they connect to the course content? How valuable did you find them as vehicles of learning? Post your thoughts and experiences on the Kane Resource Site to find out if others have had similar experiences and reactions.

Ways to use films for learning

Too often, teachers who show films in class do not take full advantage of their potential to aid learning. Students tell me that they remember movies as fillers when there was a substitute teacher, or as rewards on Friday for good behavior during the week. I've seen movies being shown in school with no anticipation guide, no purpose-setting, and no follow-up discussion or reflection. In contrast, some teachers select and use films judiciously, leading to far-ranging benefits in their content areas. I hope that the following ideas help you increase your repertoire of ways to take advantage of the fact that adolescents, as well as much of our society, spend time watching movies. Consider viewing as a component of the language arts, right along with listening, speaking, reading, and writing.

To make a comparison to a book. The first idea that may come to mind when asked how a teacher can use film in the classroom is to have students compare a book and a movie. Some teachers are afraid, with good reason, that students will substitute watching a movie for reading a book, and so include on summer reading lists only books with no film version (Burke, 1999). But many students really enjoy analyzing both to find similarities and differences and have strong opinions about which version is more powerful, effective, or aesthetically pleasing. Your motivation, guidance, and modeling can help students hone their critical-thinking skills in this area.

Teaching in action: *Social Studies/English.* Books and movies can shape values in a positive way. For example, social studies or English teachers could have students read *Snow Falling on Cedars* (Guterson, 1995), set off the Pacific coast several years after World War II and the internment of Japanese Americans, and then watch the movie. In addition to comparing the two presentation modes and metacognitively reflecting on

BookTalk Online   9.8

We Interrupt This Broadcast by Joe Garner (1998) contains two audio CDs and many photo-essays filled with facts and human-interest stories about monumental events of the twentieth century. Read more at the Kane Resource Site.

how they constructed meaning from each, students learn important information in terms of history and geography, and can have meaningful discussions about prejudice, justice, human relations, love, and truth.

To provide background knowledge. Another wise use of film is to supply background knowledge of a difficult topic you will be teaching. If students can visualize some of the concepts and examples they will be reading about, they'll be able to meet the challenge of the text. Better comprehension and retention result. For example, ninth-grade English teacher Sharon Morley has her students watch *Shakespeare in Love* (1999) as they begin studying *Romeo and Juliet*. I know social studies teachers who bring in *Schindler's List* (1993) to help students grapple with the very difficult issues they encounter as they study the Holocaust. The video *The Death of a Star* (1987) might introduce a difficult chapter on supernovas in an astronomy course.

To improve writing skills. Movies are a natural avenue for helping your students improve their writing skills. If you require or encourage your students to keep journals, they can reflect in writing after seeing movies on their own. They may find that they discover some things about themselves and their thinking that would not have happened without this step. Also, you can start a collection of published movie reviews, inviting students to bring these obviously authentic pieces of writing to school. You can post them on a wall or have a section of your classroom library devoted to movie reviews. Students can not only discuss whether or not they agree with a reviewer's opinion of a movie, but also can evaluate the review in terms of its style, crafting, and interest level. The next logical step is for students to write their own reviews, experimenting with the various forms they've seen modeled— perhaps sending their reviews to the school or local newspaper, or debating fellow classmates about the worth or theme of a movie and the quality of the actors' performances. The writing possibilities are endless and exciting.

Finders (2000) reminds us that "critical literacy involves understanding both how to use and how

one is used by popular culture" (p. 148). One way you can foster critical viewing is to have students read reviews and critiques of films they might typically watch without consciously making judgments.

Teaching in action: *Social Studies.* As an example, show a clip from the Disney movie *Mulan,* ask the students what they think about its authenticity in terms of Chinese culture and the values it portrays, then have them read the article "A Mean Wink at Authenticity: Chinese Images in Disney's *Mulan*" (2000) by Weimin Mo and Wenju Shen. The authors give historical details backing their claims that the film is culturally inauthentic, full of distortions and stereotypes, and guilty of using racially coded language. Mo and Shen taught Chinese language and literature in China for 15 years, and with their inside knowledge of both the culture and the original story, claim that "the filmmakers of *Mulan* rob the story of its soul and in its place put jokes, songs and scary effects. Their Disney bulldozer runs over the Chinese culture, imposing mainstream cultural beliefs and values" (p. 137). Your students can look at the movie through a new lens—they can counter the article's position with their own or those of other reviewers if they wish, and apply what they learn to other movies representing various cultures.

To foster critical thinking. Movies can foster critical thinking, as well as reflection on values. Levine (1996) exhorts:

> Teenagers, for the most part, do not need protection from the realities of life. On the contrary, they need as much information and education as possible. *Dead Poets Society* deals with suicide, *Boyz N the Hood* deals with homicide, *Schindler's List* documents genocide. Responsible movies such as these do not hesitate to confront and explore the kinds of difficult topics that interest adolescents. But they provide a historical context, emphasize complexity, explore alternatives, and show teenagers the consequences of actions that may limit or even destroy future opportunities. They are important movies for teenagers to see. (p. 181)

Paul (2000) has used rap, both in video and audio form, with diverse groups of secondary students, as well as with teachers, focusing on rap as a site of critical inquiry. Using guide questions, groups or individuals could react by stating the messages they think the raps or videos convey, agreeing or disagreeing with the messages, and thinking of ways to resist the message if desired. The adolescents Paul worked with found pleasure in studying rap as poetry, and comparing the rap artists' creations to the poetry of Emily Dickinson, Edgar Allan Poe, Gwendolyn Brooks, Langston Hughes, and others. The teachers Paul worked with had some difficulty understanding the rap—which was actually beneficial for thinking about cultural points of reference and the lack of cultural synchronization shared between many teachers and their students, and for metacognitively analyzing where the difficulty in comprehension lay. The teachers discovered different genres of rap, including socially conscious rap and ghetto storytellin' or reality rap. Rap was shown to be a viable site for the practice of critical media literacy because teachers were "exposed to a new way to potentially approach students and culturally synchronize literacy instruction. Additionally, they have had a chance to critically explore significant issues attached to language, culture, and power through texts to which students relate in their everyday lives" (p. 251).

Guidelines for using film

To use film effectively in your classroom, create a comprehension guide or discussion questions for a film in the same way you would for printed material. Looking over the instructional strategies in the previous chapters, you'll find that they can be used or adapted for use with films. As with books, the most natural question to get discussion going in a classroom is the one moviegoers say to each other on the way out of the theatre, "Well, what'd ya think?" Focus questions such as the following might also assist your students as they view a film and ponder its significance; they can choose the ones they wish to pursue:

1. What (or whose) point of view is represented in this film? How might the story be told differently using another's point of view?

2. What content information did you learn from this movie? How does it connect with other things you've learned in this class or on your own?

3. What do you see as a pervasive motif, or overall theme, to this movie? Is it well developed? How did the screenwriter or director convey this theme?

4. Reflect on how you made sense of this film. Were there points of confusion for you? Did you combine what you were seeing and hearing with background information you already knew? What surprises did you become aware of as you watched?

5. Which characters are well developed? Which were simple, and which were complex? Did any characters grow or change over the course of the story?

6. What was the importance of the setting? What elements contributed to the successful portrayal of the setting?

7. What symbols, archetypes, and/or motifs did you find? Were they effective for you?

8. Discuss the use of special effects. Evaluate the film in terms of music, artistic quality, and crafting.

9. What values are portrayed in this film? Did you feel it was preachy or manipulative? In what ways? What did you learn about people, human nature, or societies?

10. If you also read the book (assuming there is one), which did you prefer? What differences did you notice? What characteristics were prominent or effective in each mode of presentation?

11. What would you say to a friend who asked you about this movie?

Film resources

An excellent resource for finding well-done films connected to your subject area is the PBS Video Catalog of Educational Resources (available from PBS Video, 1320 Braddock Place, Alexandria, VA, 22314-1698, or 1-800-344-3337). You can peruse the PBS Video Catalog of Educational Resources to see what is available that matches your curriculum and your students' interests. It's organized according to disciplinary categories and subcategories, and gives informative annotations about the videos included. For example, under the heading "Clash of Cultures," one section is devoted to videos about Native Americans—"Come to Grips with Five Centuries of Conflict: Multiple perspectives let students consider the nation's relationship with its native peoples" (p. 10). Another addresses immigration—"Melting Pot or Mosaic?: Challenge students' perceptions about identity and ethnicity" (p. 11). A third is about African Americans' "Long Road to Equality" (p. 12).

You can invite authors into your classroom via the *Famous Authors* series of video biographies available through www.FilmicArchives.com. The programs include archival documents and portraits as well as relevant social and political background to and commentary on the writers' works. Learn about James Joyce, Virginia Woolf, Mark Twain, Edgar Allan Poe, William Wordsworth, George Eliot, the Bronte sisters, Jane Austen, Walt Whitman, and more!

Perusing video/DVD rental businesses and talking to the employees might also lead you to treasures. Figure 9.9 lists films appropriate for a variety of disciplines. Many, actually, can be fruitfully used in an interdisciplinary way. You may only show relevant clips from some—appropriate instructional decision making is necessary.

APPLICATION ACTIVITY 9.1   (SEE PAGE 286)

| FIGURE | 9.9 | Samples of films for content area learning. |

ENGLISH

Shakespeare in Love, Romeo and Juliet, Hamlet, Emma, Washington Square, Little Women, To Kill a Mockingbird, Wuthering Heights, A Raisin in the Sun, A Lesson Before Dying, Beowulf, The Rime of the Ancient Mariner, The Glass Menagerie, The Color Purple, Fahrenheit 451, Jacob Have I Loved, Sense and Sensibility, Mark Twain, The Importance of Being Earnest, Sylvia.

FINE AND PERFORMING ARTS

Sister Wendy, Alexander Calder, Moon and Sixpence, Pollack, West Side Story, Tommy, Oliver, Evita, Billy Elliot, Amadeus, Sunday in the Park with George, The Agony and the Ecstacy, Ray, Girl with a Pearl Earring.

HISTORY AND GEOGRAPHY

The Crucible, Schindler's List, Not for Ourselves Alone, The Grapes of Wrath, Citizen Kane, 12 Angry Men, Secret Daughter, My Brother Sam Is Dead, Midnight Clear, Platoon, Regret to Inform, Saving Private Ryan, Slaughterhouse Five, Animal Farm, Les Miserables, Good Morning, Vietnam, Hotel Rwanda.

SCIENCE

Jurassic Park, The Hot Zone, Contact, The Elephant Man, Jane Goodall: Reason for Hope, Outbreak, Dragonheart, Galileo: On the Shoulders of Giants, March of the Penguins.

MATH

Stand and Deliver, Good Will Hunting, The Phantom Tollbooth, A Beautiful Mind, Infinity, N is a Number, Breaking the Code, Lost World, Proof, Numb3rs, Fermat's Last Tango, Copenhagen, Antonia's Line, The Mirror Has Two Faces, I.Q., Infinity.

PHYSICAL EDUCATION

Chariots of Fire, Hoop Dreams, A League of Their Own, The Field of Dreams, Space Jam, Late Bloomers, The Big Green, Like Mike.

TECHNOLOGY

Star Wars, Star Trek, Close Encounters of the Third Kind, The Dish, October Sky, Toy Story, Independence Day, Avatar, The Social Network, AI, I Robot.

Teleliteracy

Television's impact on children, as well as the rest of society, is a huge topic that has generated an enormous number of books, so somebody must still be reading! Debate continues among experts and laypeople about the connection between television watching and crime, television watching and literacy, and television watching and our general health, values, and behaviors. Statistics are constantly provided about the ever-increasing number of hours children watch television. Neil Postman (1999) asks:

> Would it not have been possible to foresee in 1947 the negative consequences of television for our politics or our children? . . . Would it not have been possible through social policy, political action, or education, to prepare for them and to reduce their severity? . . . Was it inevitable that by 1995 American children would be watching . . . 19,000 hours [of TV] by high school's end, and by age twenty would have seen 600,000 television commercials? (p. 49)

Others insist that our children actually have a *broader* attention range as a result of actively channel surfing, keeping track of many shows simultaneously, and processing visual information rapidly (Dresang, 1999; Rushkoff, 1996). Dresang depicts children of today as capable and seeking connection through mutually supportive partnerships with other youth and adults, able to handle complexity and speak up for themselves. She sees digital culture as able to provide a nurturing environment for children's capabilities (p. 58).

As educators, we must be knowledgeable about our students' viewing habits and join their conversations with opinions and suggestions. This section represents my attempt to do just that. I raise issues relevant to content area teachers and share ideas about how we can maximize the educational opportunities television provides and enhance our students' teleliteracy, including critical-viewing skills, thus minimizing television's potentially harmful effects.

Watching television as a content area teacher

You might be surprised at the number of programs on television that are educational. Because this is so, become more aware of the information you learn as you watch, perhaps taking notes to share with your students. As much as I love to read, I know that I have increased my knowledge of animals by watching television specials on ants, elephants, polar bears, and beavers. My background in art has always been limited, but Sister Wendy's series *The Story of Painting* (1997) provided an interesting overview and model of how to think about paintings, and motivated me to visit museums and continue my personal art education. I've found history documentaries, such as those shown on PBS and the History Channel, to be fascinating and thought-provoking, as well as aesthetically and emotionally rewarding. You'll find many other shows on the History Channel, as well as science-related and art-related channels, to entice students to watch television that is both educational and entertaining.

Watching television in the content area classroom

The broader and richer our knowledge, the better teachers we can be. So, watch television consciously wearing your science teacher hat, or whatever other teacher hat you've chosen, as well as your interdisciplinary hat. Then, talk with your students about what you've learned, how you reacted to or critiqued a particular show, how new discoveries or insights connect to your curriculum. Bring up language issues, social justice issues, gender issues. Stimulate debate and critical thinking about the shows and about students themselves as media consumers. Look through some education publishers' catalogs for resources to enhance your curriculum. Just as you craft and use booktalks, inform your students of upcoming worthwhile shows by giving "TV Show Alerts" (see Figure 9.10 for an example; though the television show described is from 1999, the film and companion materials are still available on PBS.org). You can share hints about what they might look for, questions to ask, and suggestions for active engagement with the information. Use reviews published in the newspaper to help you, especially if you haven't seen the show yourself.

The same motivational and instructional strategies you have been learning about and developing throughout this book can be applied to television, as well as written texts. The questions you ask and the questioning skills your students learn and develop can help them view shows and critically evaluate the substance and style. Many will welcome the increased ability to become aware of, analyze, and deconstruct purposes, methods used, and conscious and subliminal messages of television advertisements. The patterns of organization found in text, such as cause–effect, compare–contrast, and sequence are equally present in television shows. In "The Simpsons Meet Mark Twain: Analyzing Popular Texts in the Classroom" (1998), Renee Hobbs shows how her students apply the tools of textual analysis to a popular program. In one *Simpsons* episode, they found this list of targets: "the role of government in inspecting the safety of nuclear plants; the use of bribery; the methods for identifying environmental destruction; the emotional pain of lying; lack of respect for elders; Charles Darwin and the theory of natural selection; the worker–boss relationship; women's intellectual freedom in relation to their husbands; and the political campaign process" (p. 50). Quite a lot to think about!

There are also numerous ways to expand lessons based on television programs to include a variety of media available in the classroom.

Teaching in action: *Science.* Let's look in on Ms. Ahle's science class. She showed a clip from the Discovery Channel's *Mythbusters.* Students engaged with Adam Savage and Jamie Hyneman to separate truth from urban legend, using science, of course. Ms. Ahle follows this up by using the computer and LCD projector to show related information found on the *Mythbusters* website (www.dsc.discovery.com/fansites/mythbusters/mythbusters.html). When she announces that the school library has just acquired the book *Mythbusters: The Explosive Truth Behind 30 of the Most Perplexing Urban Legends of All Time* (Zimmerman, Hyneman, & Savage, 2005), no booktalk is needed; students can't wait to head to the library to get on the waiting list.

Fisherkeller (2000), based on an analysis of student talk about television, found that the young adolescents, ages 11–13, whom she studied had learned some of the rules of constructing and delivering television shows, and they understood television as a communication system with purposes and values. They noticed the storymaking craft and the plausibility of

FIGURE 9.10 Sample TV show alert.

The nineteenth century sounds so far away. Why should you care about what those people of long ago were up to? How can I help make such "ancient" history real for you? Ken Burns' *Not for Ourselves Alone* (1999) focuses on the intimate friendship of Elizabeth Cady Stanton and Susan B. Anthony, based on their passion and lifelong devotion to the struggle to obtain rights for women. The documentary itself is a work of art, full of interesting anecdotes, photographs, quotes, connections to other movements such as abolition, and voices like that of Frederick Douglass. It entertains, uplifts, inspires, and promotes reflection. It's difficult to watch this show and remain apathetic about the right and obligation to vote. A companion site, www.pbs.org/stantonanthony, provides photographs from the documentary, as well as essays and historic documents relating to the women's suffrage movement. The companion book, with the same title (1999), is available as well.

television, recognized that typical kinds of characters play off one another, and made real-world connections about the roles commercial media systems play in society. Fisherkeller recognizes the overwhelming task teachers have in finding ways to help students be "multiply literate" (p. 604), and recommends that literacy educators, media arts educators, library media specialists, and social studies teachers collaborate. "To accomplish these goals in today's complex media-saturated environment, all of us need to work together, continually and in a critical, reflective manner, to develop our knowledge and competencies as multiply literate members of the world" (p. 605).

APPLICATION ACTIVITY 9.2 (SEE PAGE 286)

Because we want our students to read, and they, for the most part, love television, we can have them read *about* this topic. There are good books that can teach them how to watch television well, know what to be suspicious of, and make wise decisions regarding the medium. Figure 9.11 lists examples of informative and provocative books to help students construct knowledge about the medium and their relationship with it. Critical thinking and reading are at work as students critique opinions and point out biases, inaccuracies, fallacies, and valid points made by researchers and authors. These texts may lead to interesting debates, position papers, letters to the editor, and other actions by your students.

It shouldn't be surprising that there are also a number of videos that deal with the topic of television and other media in terms of literacy and learning. These, too, can be helpful to ourselves and our students as we think about the values and drawbacks of television and work on improving our critical thinking in relation to

FIGURE 9.11

Books about television.

See more suggested titles in Appendix Figure 9.11.

Ali, D. (2005). *Media Madness: An Insider's Guide to the Media.* Toronto, ON, Canada: Kids Can Press.

Byrum, R. T. (2005). *Careers in Television.* Farmington Hills, MI: Lucent Books.

Lackman, R. (2003). *The Encyclopedia of 20th-Century American Television.* New York: Checkmark Books.

Lemish, D. (2007). *Children and Television: A Global Perspective.* Malden, MA: Blackwell Publishing.

Postman, N. (2006). *Amusing Ourselves to Death.* New York: Penguin Books.

FIGURE 9.12

Media on media and technology.

See more suggested titles in Appendix Figure 9.12.

Bourne, J., & Burstein, D. (2009). *Web Video: Making It Great, Getting It Noticed.* Berkeley, CA: Peachpitt Press.

Duffy, B. E., & Turow, J. (2009). *Key Readings in Media Today: Mass Communication in Contexts.* New York: Routledge.

Espejo, R. (Ed.). (2008). *Should Social Networking Sites Be Banned?* Detroit: Greenhaven Press.

Haugen, D., & Musser, S. (Eds.). (2009). *Media Violence.* Detroit: Greenhaven Press.

Schwartz, E. (2009). *YourSpace: Questioning New Media.* Mankato, MN: Capstone Press.

what we see and hear. Figure 9.12 lists examples of media teaching and preaching about media.

Students creating television

Most schools and many individual teachers have easy-to-use video cameras that can be put to good academic use, no matter what your subject area. Students can film themselves enacting a readers theatre production or dramatizing different points of view on controversial issues in government, environmental science, or art. They can try out voices, try on the personalities of literary characters they read about, manipulate messages and presentations as they learn about the media and your curricular content. Producing material can help them to think and to be creative.

Casey Hudson (Bushman & Haas, 2005) created a post-reading video project based on Nancy Farmer's (www.nancyfarmerwebsite.com) *The House of the Scorpion* (2002), a novel that has science and social studies themes throughout. The project involved students watching and evaluating clips of news reporting and commercials; researching a topic from the novel, such as the drug trade, immigration, or cloning; then producing their own news using a video camera.

Teaching in action: *Science.* As another example, when my son Patrick was in eleventh grade, his teacher in a course called Scientific Thought divided his class into groups and gave each the task of researching and then teaching the rest of the class certain scientific principles. Patrick's group was responsible for teaching about nuclear fission and fusion. After an initial few minutes of panic over the difficulty of the assignment, they decided that their

BookTalk Online 9.9

The Simpsons: A Complete Guide to Our Favorite Family, created by Matt Groening and edited by Ray Richmond and Antonia Coffman (1997), contains thousands of tidbits of information about the show and can introduce students to how to read and understand guide books. Hear more at the Kane Resource Site.

classmates would learn best by watching a television video. For the next 48 hours, they researched various sources, learned about fission and fusion, discussed how to get the main ideas across to others, and wrote a script involving a spy ring carrying out a mission to construct a nuclear bomb. They scrounged for props, background music, and costumes; made overhead transparencies of diagrams for the lecture taking place within the movie; and filmed their entertaining show, complete with a clip from a movie showing an explosion as the climax. The lesson was a great success with the fans, and most of the other groups followed suit with their own homemade video lessons on the scientific concepts they were responsible for helping their classmates understand.

You and your students can make great use of a video camera. Have your students introduce themselves and their favorite book during the first week of class as a student films the activity. Then, take the video home to learn your students' names right away. Rapport will begin to build because you can connect to them as fellow readers with particular literary interests. Mentor the students and provide instruction as they construct their videos. I certainly am not the technical expert when my class films, but I am constantly aware of opportunities for mini-lessons on curricular topics or on effective ways to present ideas and information.

DIGITAL LITERACY

Let's imagine walking together through the corridors of a school whose faculty, administration, and community have committed themselves to using technology to enhance instruction. Here's what we might see on a typical day:

- In a biology lab, groups of students are using a software program to conduct a virtual dissection of a frog.
- Students in a history class are using a publishing software program to create a class newspaper that will be distributed in the lunchroom the next day.

- Students in a chemistry lab are involved in a videoconference with preservice teachers from a local university—they're explaining the experiment they're conducting and making hypotheses based on the data they have obtained so far.
- In a math classroom, students are working at computers to solve problems with which they have been challenged.
- In English class, students are using the software program "Inspiration" to create storyboards and graphic organizers showing the relationship among characters and among plot elements of a play they've read. Next door, students in another English class, in lieu of traditional journal responses, are posting entries on a blog. They've created the blog to converse with each other and anyone else from around the world who has noticed their blog and wants to participate in the discussion of multicultural folktales. (They learned how to create their class blog by researching the site www.blogger.com.)
- In an advanced level French class, a small group of students is reading *Le Petit Prince,* by de Saint Exupéry (1943) using their electronic French–English dictionaries to aid them when they come across unfamiliar words. Meanwhile, in a beginning French class, students are completing an anticipation guide that involves going to an Internet informational site (see Figure 9.13).
- In a Humanities classroom, students are engaged in a reading–writing workshop. About half the students are reading silently from books and magazines obtained from the classroom library. Several others are at computers. One is analyzing works of fanfiction related to the *Harry Potter* book series and movies on the website Fanfiction.net for her inquiry project on gender issues. Another is updating her LiveJournal (a blogging site) account based on the political poetry she's read and written this week. Two students are talking quietly, comparing the classroom's electronic readers in order to identify advantages and drawbacks so they can give input to their teacher about which kind he should purchase more of when grant funds become available. A young man works at a computer in the corner; he's collaborating on a new anime adventure with a high school student in Japan. One student is inputting a code from game cards included in the multiplatform book he is reading so that he can participate online in solving the mystery in the book. He seems to be moving back and forth between the print and the media seamlessly.
- In a senior-level government class, students are using their laptops to participate in a WebQuest

the teachers created. The journey will take them via various links to video presentations of current happenings in the Supreme Court, Congress, the House of Representatives, and the White House.

- In the gym, physical education students are keeping track of individual and team batting averages using a spreadsheet.
- In the television production lab, a daily news show is being produced and recorded by students. (The program includes book, television show, and movie reviews.)

After school, some students head to the Media Center for Media Club activities, some of which involve projects the students themselves initiated. There, a couple of girls are reading a science e-zine on the Antarctic, while some boys are checking out Jon Scieszka's website, http://guysread.com. The school atmosphere is alive with discovery and enthusiasm. Technology is aiding and enhancing learning.

Dresang has noticed (Dresang & Kotrla, 2009) how many of our students who have grown up in the digital age approach "thinking, learning, creating, and engaging with media, including reading hand-held books" (p. 94) in a fundamentally different way than children did a few decades ago. She has studied a parallel change in the ways books have been authored and published, and is optimistic that "the

---

FIGURE 9.13 **An anticipation guide involving technology.**

DIRECTIONS: Before reading Nouveau Papillon by Pamela Hickman and Heather Collins (1997), complete this reading guide to get a better understanding of the book's vocabulary and theme.

1. Label the butterfly lifecycle using the word list below.

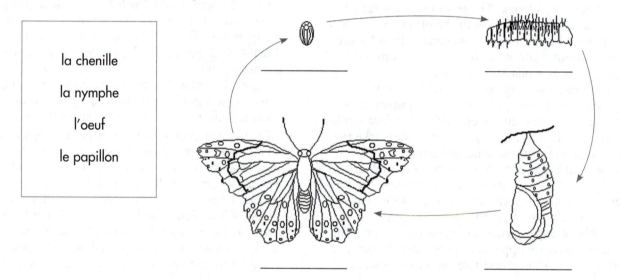

la chenille

la nymphe

l'oeuf

le papillon

©EnchantedLearning.com

2. There are many types of butterflies in France. Go to http://expopapillon.free.fr/ to find one. In 3 to 4 sentences, describe in French the colors and what the butterfly looks like, as well as any other information you learned about the particular type of butterfly. On the back of this page draw a picture of the butterfly to share with the class.

_____

_____

_____

_____

_____

_____

—*Magda Georgiadis*

combination of these readers and books can result in a unique . . . synergistic aesthetic reading experience" (p. 94).

ACTIVATING PRIOR KNOWLEDGE   9.3

Examine your own digital literacy for a few moments. When and how did you learn to use a computer for various purposes? When you use word processing for written assignments, does that change the way you compose? Does it change the quality of your thinking or your finished product? When you use the Internet to learn about topics in your classes, how does that differ from other kinds of reading and researching you do? Have you used tutorials either in school or at home to learn some subject? What software have you found particularly useful? What electronic games have you, or do you, spend time playing? What zines have you read and/or contributed to? What PowerPoint presentations or WebQuests have you created or used? What roles do Instant Messaging and text-messaging play in your life? How about blogging? How about YouTube? In general, how has technology enhanced your learning or taken away from it?

APPLICATION ACTIVITY   9.3   (SEE PAGE 286)

Technology and Learning

The dichotomies that tend to be set up by advocates and opponents of classroom computer use are rarely helpful and often are misleading. Luckily, you probably won't have to join a pro or con technology camp as you get your first job. The verdict on whether computers and the Internet hold more of a promise or a threat to your future students and to you as a teacher will not be reached easily or soon. After all, television is still viewed as a distraction by some and a fantastic educational tool by others. But real questions *are* constantly being addressed relative to the uses of technology in education because resources are indeed limited and modes of learning and thinking are changing. A school district in New York was mired in debate over whether to require all high school students to own laptops. After listening to strong public opinion, the district made having a laptop optional, at which point a third of the students signed up to buy them. A year later, virtually all students had laptops. Not surprisingly, both new opportunities and new problems and challenges resulted. Some teachers make use of the laptops and teacher stations daily, while others ignore their presence.

The same is true for phones with Internet capability (and therefore with opportunities for both distraction and educational pursuits). Literacy itself is changing rapidly relative to technology, as are teaching and the materials used in our classrooms.

It is impossible for a content area literacy textbook like this to address all facets of technology and learning. I've chosen a few areas to address in this section, and given you suggestions for further exploration of this fascinating, fast-growing field. I introduce a few well-known people who have strong opinions about where technology is leading us and our students in terms of literacy, and then show how some teachers are helping their students use technology to advance literacy, critical-thinking skills, and content area learning. We can apply the compare–contrast pattern discussed in Chapter 4 as we read varying perspectives on the future of literacy and learning in the digital age.

Voices of concern

Some predictions are cautious, some downright gloomy; educators are being warned against riding the tide of recent advances in technology and are being asked to recognize potential detrimental effects. Neil Postman, whose views on television you got a glimpse of in the previous section, cautions, "We can adapt ourselves to anything, including talking more to machines than people, but that is not an answer to anything" (1999, p. 42). Postman offers questions to help us think critically about technology:

- "What is the problem to which this technology is the solution?" (p. 42)
- "Whose problem is it?" (p. 45)
- "Which people and what institution might be most seriously harmed by a technological solution?" (p. 43)
- "What new problems might be created because we have solved this problem?" (p. 48)

Young (2009) writes of a leader at Southern Methodist University who challenged his colleagues to "teach naked"—in other words, without computers. Dean José A. Bowen asserts that PowerPoint and other computer-assisted instruction has led to boredom and lack of interaction on the part of students; he believes that lively, engaging, challenging interaction should be the hallmark of classroom instruction. Lectures can be prepared beforehand, perhaps as podcasts, so that students can watch them before they come to class. He warns that initially students might resist the change, because they have become quite comfortable, if bored, with a format that requires little but passivity from them, but that in time they come to appreciate and value the real learning and thinking that occur once the classrooms go low-tech. This is certainly something for us to think about as high school and middle school teachers.

Katherine Paterson, who became the National Ambassador for Young People's Literature in 2010, asks, "Why in a technological society do we care about literature at all?" (2000, p. 2) and follows with, "Is there anything on the World Wide Web that can nourish a child intellectually and spiritually in the sense that the best of books can?" (p. 5). We, as content area teachers, can look for answers to these crucial questions; Paterson begs us to do so: "I want those of us who care about children and their lives in the 21st century to stop long enough to notice and think . . . before we totally surrender our libraries to computer centers and our book budgets to software purchases" (pp. 1–2).

Voices of enthusiasm

Many researchers and educators are very optimistic about literacy in the digital age; they do not predict that technology will make reading or books obsolete. But they do see big changes in the recent past and on the horizon that teachers must understand and adapt to. Don Tapscott, in *Growing Up Digital: The Rise of the Net Generation* (1998), offered reassuring words to worriers:

> Everybody relax. The kids are all right. They are learning, developing, and thriving in the digital world. They need better tools, better access, more services, and more freedom to explore, not the opposite. (p. 7)

He sees children using the Internet as an active rather than a passive activity, having control and opportunities to make judgments and decisions.

Tapscott notes that by exploiting digital media, students and teachers can participate in a more powerful and effective learning paradigm. I think the following eight shifts of interactive learning may sound familiar to you at this point, because they are consistent with the kinds of opportunities we've been talking about that reading–writing workshops provide:

1. From linear to hypermedia learning
2. From instruction to construction and discovery
3. From teacher-centered to learner-centered education
4. From absorbing material to learning how to navigate and how to learn
5. From school to lifelong learning
6. From one-size-fits-all to customized learning
7. From learning as torture to learning as fun
8. From the teacher as transmitter to the teacher as facilitator (pp. 142–148)

A decade later, Tapscott offers his continuing enthusiasm and extended analysis in *Grown Up Digital: How the Net Generation Is Changing Your World* (2009).

Earlier in the chapter I alluded to the expanding views of the concept of literacy. Dresang (1999) points out that the very definition of the term *reading* has changed because of digital-age materials and digital-age youth.

> "Reading" no longer means interacting with words on a page alone. In an increasingly graphic environment, words and pictures are merging. We see this on computer monitors and television screens, and we are beginning to see it in printed books. . . . The importance of words is not questioned, but the significance of a combined presentation using both words and pictures is heightened in the digital age. (p. 65)

Author John Green (2010), in an online essay titled "The Future of Reading: Don't Worry. It Might Be Better Than You Think," tells what it was like to write an online interactive novella. He encourages us to participate in technological innovation rather than decry or ignore it, for that will allow us the power to shape the change. "Hating Twitter makes nothing happen; using Twitter to talk about something other than what you had for lunch, however,

BookTalk 9.10

What do you know about the microchip? Whatever your answer, you can add to your knowledge about and appreciation for the way microchips are changing the world by savoring *One Digital Day* (Smolen & Erwitt, 1998), from the *Day in the Life* series created by Rick Smolen. One hundred photographers went to 100 locations around the globe on a single day to capture the variety, wonder, and beauty of the microchip at work. It's a marvelous example of an interdisciplinary resource, because your future scientists, business managers, athletes, entertainers, medical workers, environmental engineers, travelers, religious leaders, historians, and clothing designers can all find information and pictures to entice them, fascinate them, and stimulate their own critical thinking and creativity. Teachers might find especially interesting the examples of students with disabilities able to keep pace with their classmates with the help of technology as well as communicate with others who share their experiences, hopes, and concerns via websites.

can make something happen." He uses the example of the 2009 Iranian election, "in which people all over the world used Twitter to help Iranians organize protests, to maintain Internet access even when the government tried to shut it down, and to disseminate evidence of militia attacks on protesters, particularly young women."

Elizabeth Birr Moje (2000) feels hope for the knowledge and skills students will have in the future, recognizing that they will be different as a result of being shaped by information technologies. But inequality of access to those technologies causes her worry. "The difference between being and not being online may be a deciding factor in the question of who has and who does not in our world of the future" (p. 128).

Where am I on the continuum?

In earlier editions I began answering this question by admitting that my feelings and opinions fluctuated, often depending on whether I had enough tech support for the goals I was trying to achieve. But as I was beginning my revisions for this edition, I reflected on how I had used technology just that afternoon. I had been reading a blog by Denise Johnson, author of a textbook on children's literature I used in a graduate class I taught last semester. I was excited to learn about a new memoir in graphic-novel format coming out by author/illustrator David Small. With a click I was brought to a book trailer where I saw some of the pictures and heard Small's voice. I also visited the site YouTube EDU (youtube.com/education), where I can access lectures by renowned professors from around the country on their areas of expertise; I was drawn to one about the science behind Dan Brown's *Angels and Demons* (2000), thinking what an addition that could be to a high school science class. After negotiating the links in a blog entry, I realized how the scales have tipped for me in terms of how I feel about the Internet as a learning and teaching tool. I remembered how my Literature, Art and Media class had been enthralled with Johnson's *The Joy of Children's Literature* (2009); they had truly experienced joy as they investigated authors' and illustrators' sites, and saw clips of readers of all ages engaging with the literature we were also reading. My students raved about sites I had yet to explore, so we were all learning from each other in our community. The bottom line is that I realize I have become a devotee of web-based inquiry in a way I had not dreamed of when I first wrote this textbook. And I feel good about it.

I next asked myself about how my philosophy has evolved regarding other forms of technology. Again, I have mostly positive things to report. I love

BookTalk Online 9.11

Adam and Eve and Pinch-Me (1994) by Julie Johnston is the story of a foster child who learns that the love of her foster parents is greater than the comfort she finds in her computer. Hear more at the Kane Resource Site.

BookTalk Online 9.12

Radical Change: Books for Youth in a Digital Age (1999) by Eliza Dresang talks about the literary boundaries and barriers that have been broken by the digital book age. Hear more at the Kane Resource Site.

my electronic reader. When I hear of a book during a conversation, I download a sample. I show my students how struggling readers, English learners, and others in their classes can download texts, change the font size, highlight phrases, read along on the screen as they use the text-to-speech option, and call up the definition of a word whenever they need to. Also, I now sign out from my public library MP3 versions of novels for my daily walking routine.

In the classrooms I now teach in, I can project covers and interior illustrations for any of the picture books I've talked about in this textbook and students can see the visuals on the large screen. Students do the same to show classmates the collages or paintings or poems they've created as responses to literature. And use of technology is not limited to the teacher's station. Gone are the days when a question would arise during class, and I'd say, "I'll get back to you tomorrow about that." Virtually any time we come up with a question we can't answer, several students will pull out their phones and in a matter of seconds they're comparing information they've found. Yes, I am a proponent of technology in the classroom, and I am grateful for the engagement and excitement it enhances! I agree with Black (2009), who, rather than dealing with technology and traditional print as an either/or choice, considers them together. Citing Warschauer's work (2007), Black says that "the shift to online and technology-mediated contexts is making traditional print-based literacy skills perhaps more crucial than they have been at any other time in history. Thus, lessons that are grounded in a 21st century mindset would necessarily involve a synthesis of traditional and new proficiencies" (p. 695). I have seen this mutually reinforcing type of learning occurring in my own students.

Content Area Teaching in the Digital Age

What does all of this mean for you as a content area teacher? You may be focusing on literacy for the first time as you read this book, and now you hear that literacy is radically changing! Will your students be reading more or less, better or not as well? Will reading be more or less necessary to gaining knowledge and skills in your content area course? Will books be more or less a part of your classroom? How much time should students be spending on computers? Where and how will students get information and grapple with concepts and issues relevant to your course?

You'll figure out answers that satisfy you and positions you're comfortable with as you talk with students, guide their reading and other ways of seeking knowledge, and watch them learn using various media. In terms of resources, things have never been better. Tapscott (1998) predicted:

> The ultimate interactive learning environment will be the Web and the Net as a whole. It increasingly includes the vast repository of human knowledge, tools to manage this knowledge, access to people, and a growing galaxy of services ranging from sandbox environments for preschoolers to virtual laboratories for medical students studying neural psychiatry. (p. 142)

More than a decade later, it's clear his predictions have come true.

Online research

In Chapter 4, you learned the importance of background knowledge as students learn content. The Internet, including online reference services, may offer virtually all the background information your students and you might need for any curricular topic, and most students will willingly and actively engage in the search for it. For example, I could ask students to find examples on the Internet of utopias and dystopias before reading Lois Lowry's *The Giver*. Afterward, I might help them find websites with reviews of the book, scholarly essays relating to the book, and information about the author. Students may in turn recommend sites to me about topics they explored for follow-up projects: memory, euthanasia, government control, near-death experiences.

Of course, you can't just tell students to do research on the Internet; this, like every other aspect of your job, requires instruction, modeling, mentoring, monitoring, and assessing, as well as creativity and decision making on your part. Your students will be simultaneously developing their technology expertise while gaining content information and strategies that will help them explore the discipline you teach. Technology supplies tools for learning, but the students and you are in a dynamic process that results in that actual learning.

Who can help you answer Bruce's (1999/2000) question, "How can [Web] searching become not only looking up, but truly productive inquiring?" (p. 351). Perhaps you can visit your school cybrarian for assistance! Online resources to guide students' website evaluations are also available. For example, a form on "Critical Evaluation of a Web Site Secondary School Level" (http://school.discoveryeducation.com/schrockguide/evalhigh.html) provides criteria for evaluating a site in categories such as accuracy, authority, objectivity, currency, and coverage. Gardner, Benham, and Newell (2000) point out that teachers have always had the responsibility of instructing students involved in the research process to check on source quality and credibility. They found that helping students navigate the huge amount of information on the Web is rewarding because their students start applying the same criteria to print sources.

Henry (2006) recommends introducing students before they begin their online searches to the way search engines are organized (e.g., text-matching categories) and the way they work (e.g., word frequency, sponsored links). She states that "once students have a good grasp of the organization of various search engines, they are more successful in conducting searches and reading information (p. 617). Henry also suggests using SEARCH, an instructional framework for locating information in print or online. The framework involves:

1. Set a purpose for searching.
2. Employ effective search strategies.
3. Analyze search-engine results.
4. Read critically and synthesize information.
5. Cite your sources.
6. How successful was your search? (p. 618)

In addition, the Internet can help you as you prepare your units and lessons. You'll have stories, interesting trivia, intriguing dilemmas, data, current research results, and visual and auditory aids that make your subject interesting and stimulate your students to question and reflect. You can find resources to help you provide well for those students who are English learners; the Center for the Study of Books in Spanish for Children and Adolescents' website at www2.csusm.edu/csb/ is one example. You can find many professional journals online—check out http://library.georgetown.edu/newjour for a comprehensive list of e-journals and other serial publications.

Many schools have literacy coaches, curriculum coordinators, librarians, media specialists, and/or technology leaders who can help you use technology to find resources and enhance your teaching, so be sure to take advantage of whatever supports are available to you. Irvin et al. (2009) describe a school with a strong culture of both technological integration and literacy. Among other things:

> The school provides a public access catalog of technological and media center holdings, including article databases with reading materials that are leveled, so that teachers, students, and family members can access resources that promote literacy and learning. This access is especially helpful when teachers need parallel texts at different reading levels. (p. 69)

The authors also point out ways that podcasts and electronic demonstrations can build prior knowledge of curricular topics, online graphic organizers can aid comprehension, and online resources can provide mentor texts and examples of various types of writing "that can be used as models or to support the teaching of minilessons related to voice, word choice, text structure, and so forth" (p. 66). There's a lot to celebrate as you prepare to teach in the digital age.

Online communities

E-mail discussions. I'm sure I don't have to sell you on the wonders and benefits of e-mail. You've probably communicated this way for years for both social and business purposes. But, you may just be starting to realize how helpful it can be in your classroom as you teach your subject and enhance your students' literacy strategies and study skills. Wolffe (1998) used e-mail journals addressed to him to help reluctant students overcome their fear of math and to expand their mathematical knowledge base. He required students to summarize what had been addressed in the day's class, then talk about an aspect of their learning experience that went well or was problematic. Students asked questions for clarification, expressed frustrations, and wrote reflections on their learning processes that often indicated an improved self-image as math students.

E-mail allows many other voices into your classroom and your lessons. You can invite parents and other community members to serve as "expert friends"—informal consultants in the game of learning. You might have a doctor, a scientist, an accountant, a city council member, a factory worker, a librarian, a machinist, a mother who is home schooling, a systems analyst, a sports commentator, and a secretary on call via e-mail. Your students can ask their parents to volunteer to share hobbies and interests. One student's parent might be a Civil War buff, another a snowmobiler, yet another a gourmet cook. Authentic reading, writing, and learning opportunities are made possible through the medium of e-mail. LISTSERV® software allows groups to grapple with problems, present new ideas, converse about activities that went on in class, and recommend and respond to texts.

We can learn much about adolescents' thoughts, interests, and e-mail writing style by corresponding with them. Here's an unsolicited example I received from a 15-year-old who seems very comfortable composing in her chosen "voice":

> Hey Aunt Sharon, 'tis I, the great and Powerful . . . Alison. Anticlimactic, yes, but impressive to a point. Ok, no it's not. Whatever.
>
> Anyway. So how ye been? I've been pretty good. I just wanted to drop you a line to tell you that come this summer, I'm gonna get me published. IN A BOOK. A real, live . . . oh, wait . . . not live, book. Thought you'd be interested to know that. It's a book o' poetry, Between Darkness and Light, and it's being published by The International Library of Poetry.
>
> If you really want to, you can see the poem that's getting published . . . on my website. You can look around if you want (and sign the guestbook), but know that there's an occasional strong word in some of my poems . . .

As shown in the above example, electronic discussions very often take on an informal tone that closely resembles what would be used in conversation. That's fine—consider that you have the best of both worlds when students "talk" through their computers. Mahiri (1998) used interactive written discourse through the use of linked computers in his classroom. Initially, students loved writing "real-time" class discussions and found it valuable to have a written record of some good class discussions for future reference. Ultimately, though, they expressed a preference for oral discussions in class (p. 74). On the other hand, Mahiri found that e-mail discussions outside the classroom enabled communication that extended teaching and learning connections.

Teaching in action: *Interdisciplinary.* The possibilities for e-mail discussion groups in all content areas are unlimited. For example, a team of middle school teachers could initiate an interdisciplinary action research project related to local environmental issues. In my community, there is a plan to extend a paved path at Onondaga Lake Park so that it loops the lake. Many skaters, bicyclists, and community leaders are thrilled; environmentalists warn of the destruction of habitats for small animals. Class teams could be formed to research the pros and cons of the plan. Members of the teams can e-mail each other and their teachers to respond to editorials they read in the paper, formulate their own positions, and write letters to business and community groups. They can hold electronic group meetings via instant messaging, noting connections to math, science, literature, and social studies as they study budget figures, research the topics of wildlife habitats and construction, read stories about environmental struggles, and exercise their right to be heard as citizens.

Book communities. Scharber (2009) offers the practice and promise of online bookclubs as a way to bridge old literacy practices (e.g., pleasure reading) with new literacies (e.g., online forums). She studied summer online book clubs for teens and preteens through a public library system, finding them to be both flexible and motivating. They used the classroom management software Moodle (www.moodle.org), which is free, safe, and easy. "Moodle's interface affords an entire environment for book clubs that includes forums for asynchronistic, threaded discussions; synchronistic (real-time) chats; and profile space for users" (p. 434). There were hyperlinks to YouTube videos and Web pages relevant to the books being discussed. The researcher discovered that the favorite component of the club was the real-time chat, where the members, who had not known each other beforehand, could now make "e-friends" (p. 435). Scharber notes how much fun the readers had and contrasted this interactive book discussion with the old "dreaded book report" (p. 436).

Teaching in action: *Language Arts.* Larson (2009) reports on a study of a semester-long case study involving a fifth-grade collaborative online learning community. Students read e-books of novels on laptops (either *Bud, Not Buddy* (1999) or *The Watsons Go to Birmingham, 1963* (1995), both by Christopher Paul Curtis, and both connecting to the fifth-grade social studies curriculum. They responded using electronic response journals and used an online message board to discuss the stories. The researcher, through analysis of written reflections and interviews, was able to conclude that students valued and respected replies from classmates, even when they offered alternative viewpoints; that they asked for clarification of ambiguous or vague postings; and that only rarely did they stray from discussing the texts. "Within the technology-rich environment, the student-constructed prompts elicited insightful and heartfelt responses and invited group members to think more deeply about the literature" (p. 648).

My own students say they benefit from belonging to electronic literature discussion groups. They like the idea of an audience who will get their thoughts soon. Sometimes, several students read the same text,

exchange e-mail addresses or create a mailing list, and discuss the text during or after reading. At times, I have required students to respond to a text just once via e-mail, only to find they have voluntarily jumped into the discussion many times. They respond to what others have contributed, either changing their minds about something they said previously or arguing or joking about a classmate's input. I ask them to copy me on the e-mail exchange, so I get to listen in, and sometimes chime in as another reader. Here are snippets of an "e-mail circle" discussion among my preservice teachers after reading *Freak the Mighty* by R. Philbrick (1993):

> I loved how the two characters combined to make a single entity. FREAK THE MIGHTY! Quite the name, eh? I mean this book shows that everyone, no matter how bad they have it, can find a friend, a lesson that I quite frankly find important to everyone from middle school to high school. The reader gains a respect and love for the characters. Our students will gain this respect as well. Maybe they will ask someone they never thought to ask before to hang out. Maybe it will change how students look at the "freaks" in their classes, in their lives. It builds social awareness.
>
> —*Jason Gibson*

> I thought to respond to this book I would try to relate it to science. I felt that the relationship between Max and Freak [Kevin] was similar to that of mutualistic relationships in animals. Both characters had some kind of strong point and both had a weak point. They used each other in a way they both found beneficial. Freak was smart and imaginative, which helped compensate for Max's lack of confidence in his own intelligence. Max was big and strong, which helped benefit Freak, who was small and weak. Together, with little Freak on Max's shoulders, they became Freak the Mighty, and they used their combined strong points to go on adventures and quests. This is a perfect mutualistic relationship where both organisms benefit from one another and no harm is done.
>
> —*Jim Knote*

Sites such as www.goodreads.com and www.shelfari.com are also available to provide forums for readers to post reactions to and evaluations of books, as well as to react to other readers' comments.

Fanfiction communities. Fanfiction, a popular hobby of Internet-savvy young people, involves using a media text as a jumping-off place for one's own creative writing. Fanfiction websites bring "fans" of a certain piece of work together to create their own story based upon it. Fans take either the story or characters (or both) of a work, whether it be a novel, television show, movie, cartoon, etc., and create their own story based on it. Sometimes people bring together characters from different works. A writer of fanfiction takes control of character, plot, and setting.

Black (2009) studied English learners as they participated in online fanfiction communities. She shares results of three case studies of girls with very different backgrounds and experiences with English-language learning, but a similar devotion to authoring fanfiction (creating texts that continue stories from popular culture or are based on characters from TV shows, movies, or books). Black shows how her subjects' participation in these online communities allowed them to practice and enhance their composition skills as knowledge of English. Fanfiction.net (FFN) offers beta-readers, who read others' online works and respond with suggestions to improve spelling and grammar as well as elements of story before they go public. Two of the girls Black reports on had each received several thousand reviews!:

> Thus, the FFN community provides ELL youths with support for the development of traditional print literacy by encouraging interactions between writers and readers, promoting confidence, and helping authors to explicitly focus on different aspects of language and composition. (p. 692)

She concludes, "popular media and new technologies can provide a basis for ELL youths to develop valuable print literacy as well as 21st century skills" (p. 696).

Blogs and wikis. A blog is a kind of website where entries are made like those in a journal or diary and that provides information and commentary on a particular subject. Wikis are contributory websites that allow individuals to collaborate, for example, on writing projects and editing a composition together.

Blogging, in particular, is very popular, both in classrooms as an instructional space, and as one part of students' out-of-school literacies. Schools must of course be aware of certain privacy and safety issues, but Patterson (2006) emphasizes the benefits of electronic conversations as powerful learning vehicles. She states her position: "We should not restrict them from engaging in computer-mediated conversations because they may read or write questionable texts. Instead, we should immerse them in an environment where they have to make good decisions about the kinds of computer-supported conversations they have, and make them accountable for bad decisions" (p. 67).

Recently a front-page article reported students in a local school who were bullying a high school girl by posting tormenting comments about her on MySpace. The targeted girl reported the incidents, and went to the press. Her picture accompanied the article. I brought the newspaper into my class, believing it would be an excellent stimulus for critical thinking, which it proved to be. I also brought in an article about blogs written by young people in Iraq. Again, I believe our students can learn a lot as they read postings by people in other countries, and teachers can take advantage of the opportunity to teach critical-reading skills by asking questions such as the following:

- What political positions are being presented?
- How credible is the person writing the blog entry?
- What gives the person credibility?

Teaching in action: *Math.* Chandler-Olcott (2009) recommends the use of content-specific blogs. She uses the authentic example of a math teacher whose blog includes:

> sample problems with solutions, uploaded slides from lectures, summaries of student course evaluations, and even poems for graduating seniors. He also asks each student to serve as class scribe on a rotating basis, and their summaries are interspersed with his postings. More than just peripheral course supplements, Darren's blogs model a wide variety of mathematical genres. (p. 86)

Chandler-Olcott also advocates teachers connecting their students to the blogs of experts in their disciplines, which can increase students' vocabulary, provide knowledge of cutting-edge ideas, and expand their conception of what the disciplines entail. In addition, teachers can involve their students in creating or posting on blogs focused on curricular topics. "A blog that invites students to respond to a piece of literature, comment on daily news headlines, or critique an image from a new gallery show offers chances for students to personalize important concepts, use content-area vocabulary in context, and explore differences in perspective" (pp. 87–88).

Zine-like writing

Guzzetti and Gamboa (2004) studied adolescent girls who wrote zines (self-published online magazines) outside of school that brought to light and resisted race, class, and gender stereotypes and that promoted principles of social justice. The informants (in this case, zinesters) recommend that teachers incorporate assignments with "'zine-likeness' that enable students to write about their own values, experiences, and ideas" (p. 433), and the authors point out their study's implications for teachers:

By familiarizing themselves with zines, teachers can become aware of their students' propensities toward creative subversion and their responses to popular culture, as well as to personal and political issues. . . . This study demonstrates that adolescents can be encouraged to . . . critically analyze texts for issues of social justice. . . . The zinesters in this study used zining to deconstruct their own experiences, to resist oppression, and to expose marginalization. Students can be encouraged to do likewise by examining the texts around them and by writing about injustices in their own worlds. (p. 433)

To learn more about zines, you might want to check out Todd and Watson's (2006) *Watcha Mean, What's a Zine?: The Art of Making Zines and Mini Comics.*

Classroom Web pages

Leu, Leu, and Coiro (2004) believe four important results are to be gained from making a classroom home page:

First, developing a home page helps your students learn. It provides a location for publishing student work and it allows you to organize safe links to Internet locations. . . . Second, developing a home page also helps others. As you develop instructional materials and links to information resources, you will find other classrooms visiting your page, benefiting from your instructional ideas. Third, developing a home page enables you to forge a tighter link between home and school. . . . Parents can use your home page to see what is taking place in your classroom and communicate with you about their children. Finally, developing a home page helps the teaching profession. As you develop a home page for your class, it projects an important image of professionalism to the public—teachers embracing new literacies and using these in powerful ways to guide students' learning. (p. 393)

The authors give an example showing the steps a certain teacher took to create a classroom Web page and the ways she now uses it. One day, she told her students of a new link that might help them with their Internet research projects, reminded them of an assignment to write to their parents via e-mail or by word processing and printing a hard copy using the classroom computer system, and announced that several messages had been posted by people from other schools who had visited their home page. She encouraged students to read and respond to these communications.

Teaching in action: *English.* Another example of a classroom Web page is shown in Figure 9.14. The figure shows a sample of "The Elizabethan Globe," created by ninth graders in Sharon Morley's class using computer software programs and the Internet.

ACTION RESEARCH   9.B

To examine a variety of classroom home pages within a particular school, go to www.oswego.org and explore by clicking on the teachers' names or subject areas. List in your learning log ideas that you think you'd like to include in a home page of your own. If you wish, post a message on the Web page of a class you'd like to know more about.

APPLICATION ACTIVITY   9.4   (SEE PAGE 286)

Internet-based inquiry projects

A WebQuest is an Internet-based inquiry activity during which learners are directed to various sites on the Web to guide and enhance their learning. It is efficient because students can spend the bulk of their time learning from and using information rather than searching for it. According to Johnson (2005), a WebQuest has five essential components:

1. The introduction describes a compelling problem or question, connects to and builds on students' prior knowledge, and prepares the learner for the quest.
2. The task explains the product or end performance that will be expected, requiring the synthesis of information or the formulation of a position.
3. The resources consist of links to websites that will enable the learner to gather information and reflect on the data obtained.
4. The process involves learners making and recognizing connections and implementing new knowledge; they might present their findings to others in class or online, also.
5. Finally, the evaluation component of a WebQuest involves learners evaluating themselves, the activity, and/or others' presentations.

As an example, a teacher of ninth-grade basic math has joined with the art teacher to create a WebQuest to get students ready to read a mystery that involves both math and art (see Figure 9.15).

Teaching in action: *Social Studies.* Damico & Baildon (2007) tell of an eighth-grade class using a Web-based inquiry curriculum to study content relating to Mexico and migration. As students investigated Internet sites, they made decisions about the credibility of sources and the relevance for their projects. The researchers conducted think-aloud sessions with pairs of students to learn about specific choices they made while engaging with websites, a strategy teachers can model and

FIGURE **9.14** "The Elizabethan Globe" created by ninth graders.

June 27, 1540
Volume 4, Issue 68

Only Two Pence

The Elizabethan Globe

"The Newspaper preferred by King Henry VIII"

Inside this issue:

The Queen's Parade	2
New Dessert at Barney's	2
Your Horoscope	3
Today's Weather	3
Shakespeare's Bio	4
New Constable	5
Classified	5

We wish a happy birthday to:

- Prince Arthur of Scotland Turns 12
- Elizabeth Baker, Turns 30
- John Blacksmith Senior Turns 40
- Anne Carpenter, Turns 28
- David Woodcutter Turns 34
- Matt Teacher Turns 20
- The Smith Twins Turned 14

The Joust of the Year

The finals of the "Masters of The Lance" will take place at 6 pm, June 30 at Wembley Castle grounds in Verona. Almost every castle in the eastern half of Europe submitted their best horse, and their best man. During the tournament started off with 100 riders, two riders remain:

After fierce and exciting, battles, Noble Christian, from London, England, and Prince Craig from the Orkney Islands in Scotland.

Here are the basic jousting rules that have been used during the tournament:
1. Only rich families are allowed to play. It is illegal for any commoners to play
2. You need two horsemen, and two horses.

3. The riders carry a shield and a spear around 10 feet long.

4. The horses run at each other and the object is to knock your opponent off his horse.

Noble Christian has been jousting for 5 years. This is his first time in the "Masters of The Lance" tournament. Christian is the under dog for the final bout. Prince Craig has been riding for 15 years. He is the 3 time defending champ. "I know this chap might be good, but he is no match for me." said the cocky Prince.

There are rumors that royalty as high as King Henry VIII will watch the bout that could go on for some time, considering they are both undefeated. So if you are interested in the greatest joust of the year, stop by. Tickets are still available.

King Henry the VIII Has a New Favorite Game

King Henry tried out the new game called 'bowls' with Peter of Scotland. At 3 on Wednesday Henry said, "I like that someone of my size could be the best at this game. Considering it doesn't involve running." When the King and Peter played together, King Henry won 100 - 85.

When we asked Peter, "Do you like this game?"

He replied, "Well I would have liked the game better if I would've won! But I had a great time in the

Kings court ."

Bowl consists of 9 pins, and an 8 inch ball that is rolled to knock the pins down.

FIGURE   9.15   Sample WebQuest.

Who Am I ?
A WebQuest Author Study

INTRODUCTION

- Real, everyday people have written the wonderful books that we have read throughout the year.
- We have read numerous books by authors such as Lois Lowry, Patricia Reilly Giff, Gary Paulsen, and others.
- Sometimes a reader can better understand a book if he or she gets to know the author. Hence, an author study.

YOUR TASK

The next book that we will be reading is a thrilling mystery!

- Use the provided websites to gather clues about the book and its author. RECORD CLUES AND ANSWERS IN YOUR NOTEPAD.
- Solve the mystery and determine the title of our upcoming book and its author, all while learning new things in the process.

THE CLUES

1. You stumble across your first clue while visiting a famous museum:
   - View the collections: www.artic.edu/aic/collections/index.php
   - View the exhibitions: www.artic.edu/aic/exhibitions/
     - Which piece of artwork was your favorite?
     - How do you think this location might be relevant to our mystery?

2. One of the museum tour guides hands you a piece of paper that reads:

   > I see you like art. Take a couple of minutes and explore the world of a magnificent artist. Who is he, you say? Find out for yourself:
   >
   > Read about his life: http://www.about-vermeer-art.com/vermeer/vermeer-biography/index.html
   >
   > View his famous artwork: http://www/about-vermeer-art.com/vermeer/vermeer-oil-paintings/index.html

   What is the artist's name?
   Why do you think he may be important to our mystery?

- You have collected and recorded all of the physical clues. Have any idea what the book might be or who the author is?
- Here are a couple more hints if you're stuck:
  - The author goes by a color name and it rhymes with "two."
  - The book has been called "The Da Vinci Code for tweens."

(continued)

FIGURE **9.15** Continued.

CONCLUSION: THE AUTHOR

■ Click here to confirm your conclusions:
http://books.scholastic.com/teachers/authorsandbooks/authorstudies/authorhome.jsp%3bjsessionid
=4JOGHC0H2E3VCCQVALDSFFAKCUBJWIWA?authorID=6148&collateralID=12772&displayName=
Biography&_requestid=95000

■ Who is the mysterious author we have been trying to track down?

■ Record three interesting facts about her.

CONCLUSION: THE BOOK

■ Balliett has written several well-known books. Using your clues, which book do you think we are going to read?

HAVE SOME FUN—YOU DESERVE IT!

■ Visit the Scholastic Flashlight Readers site and explore *Chasing Vermeer* at http://scholastic.com/titles/chasingvermeer/index.htm

■ From there, you may participate in numerous readings and activities, including pentominoes.

*** *Return to this WebQuest when you are done! ENJOY!!*

EVALUATION

■ Make sure you have accurately recorded any clues on your notepad.

■ Make sure you have answered all of the questions asked during this webquest author study on your notepad.

■ Your answers should prove that you visited each site and explored each one thoroughly, as a good detective should.

■ Hand in your notepad to the Head Detective (your teacher!).

*** *CHALLENGE:* Choose one of your favorite authors and come up with 10 clues to share with your classmates. See if they can solve your mystery!

GREAT WORK, DETECTIVE!

■ Your hard work paid off. We will soon begin reading Blue Balliett's novel titled *Chasing Vermeer*.

■ Your detective skills will be needed again as we help Petra and Calder solve their mystery.

—*Carrie Kolczynski, Bernie Dodge*

---

use during class explorations. One result of the data analysis was that the authors had new questions having to do with how readers define and refine their purposes during inquiry-based learning, whether with websites or other resources. "When or at what point in an investigation does a reader or group of readers engage with an information source? Readers, for example, often have different purposes when launching their investigation than at the end when they are preparing to present their findings" (p. 261).

Teaching in action: *History*. Hansen (2009) reports on an urban high school general track class that used multiple literacies as they engaged in year-long inquiry of topics relating to U. S. history. They made emotional connections as they studied websites about various topics in the curriculum. They used writing and drawing to make connections and to take action. For example, one student wrote a letter to the publisher of the textbook that students explored after learning from Internet sources, contesting:

The section about slavery concerns me greatly because of the lack of information. I do not think there is enough detail about the horrible journey my ancestors went through. You failed to mention how there was lack of space for the Africans to maneuver through the tightly packed ship. (p. 599)

During their study of the American Revolution, students each took on a persona of someone living at the time, using the Internet among other resources during their inquiry. The teacher assigned the task of creating a scrapbook (based on Schur, 2007) for the purpose of sharing later "when this class of elderly survivors would meet to share their memories" (p. 602). One student "became" Paul Tibbets, the pilot of the plane that dropped the atomic bomb on Hiroshima, while another became a survivor of that bomb. A girl researched the first African American woman trained as an pilot at the Tuskegee Army Air Field; there was a Buffalo Soldier, a woman whose boyfriend died in the Pacific fighting, one whose brother survived D-Day.

Students wrote letters, essays, and poems as they studied the principles of democracy and thought about what it means to be a citizen. Erika, their teacher, prepared for class by creating a DVD. "She pulled information from multiple websites and other sources, popped the disk into the projector . . . and taught from the interactive whiteboard. The students saw and heard video clips, segments of speeches, music, and old photos." All but one of the 26 students passed the state test, but, perhaps more importantly, Hansen saw a group of students who participated in an empowering classroom where the teacher's main goal—one that was met—was to connect to her students and help them recognize that, unlike the message they had heard and internalized for years, they were actually smart.

Multimedia/multimodal

Chandler-Olcott (2009) recognizes that the term *new literacies* has evolved since its introduction into the scholarly literature in the 1990s and that it continues to change. She states, "Teachers who want to address new literacies must decide on their own definition of the term, as it will drive the instruction they design" (p. 84). For instance, she extols the benefits of digital storytelling, a new literacy that exhibits multimodality by melding the human voice with various media we can obtain through the Internet and other forms of technology. She offers several ways the strategy can help students in our content area classes tell their own stories, class stories, and stories of others, as well as explain discipline-specific processes using images, soundtracks, and voice-overs to reinforce skills and content for producers and audiences.

Adams (2009) defines digital storytelling as a technique that "mixes still images (photos or artwork), voice narration, and music to tell a personal narrative, recount a historical event, or instruct . . . classes across the curriculum, from English to science, can take part" (p. 35). She explains the advantage of the medium for teachers. "Kids are drawn to technology. They also love a good story. Combining the two can be a powerful educational tool" (p. 35). As you imagine how this type of project might transform your own classes, you might want to check out the book *Digital Storytelling in the Classroom* by Jason Ohler (2008). The accompanying box suggests steps you can use to get your students started with digital storytelling.

Kajder (2007) shares several ways she and others have used new technologies to extend their students' literacy skills and content knowledge. She talks of Mrs. Abel's class, whose students maintain a class weblog that daily gets more hits than the district's website. Another teacher overcame the hurdle of not being able to listen in on all the literature circles happening simultaneously by having student groups digitally record their conversations through podcasting. Kajder's own students, using the wikibooks.org website, created a reader's guide for Camus' *The Stranger;* the students in her Virginia classroom became really engaged after finding out that students from Seattle were using their site. They had an audience! Kajder tells of the results:

Students had added videos that offered enactments of scenes. Some were podcasting their literature group discussions. Others were linking to every bit of relevant content they could find. And, in class, I'd never had more participation. By the end of our study of the novel, we'd created a reader's guide to *The Stranger* that was multimodal, completely owned by each of the students in the class, and receiving a large, and validating, number of hits each day. (p. 223)

Beach and Doerr-Stevens (2009) used online role-play to help students hone discussion skills (as well as other literacy skills) and learn how to participate in collaborative arguments, as opposed to the more traditional competitive debates they were accustomed to. Using tools including Moodle (an online course discussion platform) and a course blog, students worked toward ascertaining positions on complex issues and problem solving.

The specialists in changing libraries can teach you and your students how to utilize the technological treasures of knowledge at your disposal. Chandler-Olcott and Mahar (2003) recommend recruiting tech-savvy students to mentor their peers as they transact with digital technologies. They also suggest various ways teachers can help adolescents use multimedia technological tools:

Steps in the digital storytelling process.

To get your students started with a visual storytelling project, have them follow these steps.

Step 1: Find and clarify their stories and consider the meaning contained within them.

Step 2: Identify the emotions in the story, then decide which emotions they would like to include and how they would like to convey them to their audience.

Step 3: Find a single moment that illustrates the story's meaning by determining the moment when things changed and describing it in detail.

Step 4: Provide visuals for their stories by first describing the images that come to mind, determining what those images convey, finding or creating those images, and then deciding how best to use them to convey their intended meaning. Ways to present the images include:

- single image
- combination of multiple images within a single frame, either through collage or fading over time
- juxtaposition of a series of images over time

- movement applied to a single image, either by panning or zooming or the juxtaposition of a series of cropped details from the whole image
- use of text on screen in relation to visuals, spoken narration, or sound (p. 22)

Step 5: Provide audio for their stories. Possible audio layers include:

- recorded voice-over
- recorded voice-over in relation to sound, either music or ambient sound
- music alone or in contrast to another piece of music (p. 22)

Step 6: Assemble their stories by spreading out their notes and images, composing their script and storyboard, providing a story structure, and making the layers of visual and audio narratives work together.

Step 7: Consider the audience once more and determine the best way to present their digital stories.

Source: Adapted from www.storycenter.org/cookbook.pdf, Center for Digital Storytelling, February 2007. Retrieved March 26, 2010.

By brokering students' use of Web-based resources such as chat rooms, mailing lists, and sites like http://www.draac.com, teachers may be able to link individual students with communities of practice possessing expertise related to their interests. . . . To do this, teachers need not possess highly sophisticated technology skills themselves; instead, they must be familiar with various online resources as well as with students' needs and interests in order to connect individual adolescents with others who can support and challenge them as they compose and construct meaning with technological tools. (p. 382)

Assistive Technology for Students with Special Needs

Jeff is a seventh grader with a learning disability. Although he's intellectually curious and particularly loves science and social studies, he gets bogged down every night with his homework because he can't decode the multisyllabic words in his textbook. His mother works with him, but she's getting tired of the nightly struggles. Chen is Jeff's classmate. She reads fluently in Chinese, but most of the texts she's responsible for reading are in English, and her vocabulary is much less developed in this second lan-

guage. Chen's parents do not read English at all, so she must tackle the homework alone. Trying hard is not enough; she simply doesn't know the words.

One day their teacher produces several "Quicktionary Reading Pens" he recently acquired. Jeff, Chen, and others are allowed to use them in school and sign them out for nights and weekends. Now, when they encounter a word they don't know, they can scan it and see it displayed in large characters on the side of the pen. They can hear the word read aloud from the built-in speaker and press a button to get the definition. They are meeting with success.

The Quicktionary pen is just one example of assistive technology, which, as its name implies, helps people who are struggling with tasks for any reason. Examples of assistive technology range from computerized speech synthesizers, such as physicist Stephen Hawking uses, to screen reading programs for the visually impaired. *Computer and Web Resources for People with Disabilities: A Guide to Exploring Today's Assistive Technologies* (The Alliance for Technology Access, 2000) begins with stories of individuals who have overcome obstacles related to disabilities with the help of computers. Victor, who has cerebral palsy, used a scanning device activated by a switch to communicate; he graduated from a New York State high school with a Regents diploma. John, who also has cerebral palsy, used a computer throughout school and beyond; with a Bachelor of Fine Arts in film and video, he uses a micro-switch on his lip and a pointing device on his head to produce 3-D animation. Dusty has Down syndrome and used assistive technology such as screen magnification software in high school and college as she learned keyboarding, word processing, and the use of the Internet. Chase, who became quadriplegic from polio at the age of eight, used multiple forms of assistive technology that could be operated with a mouth stick as he went through high school, college, and law school. He now uses a speech-input program that allows him to bypass the keyboard and dictate to his computer.

This resource guide provides a wealth of Internet addresses to search in order for individuals with disabilities, their families, and educators to find out what technology is available and ways of finding financial support to acquire the assistive technology. It describes how to use various tools such as a touch screen, keyboard additions, electronic pointing devices, trackballs, word prediction programs, reading comprehension programs, writing composition programs, talking and large-print word processors, closed circuit televisions, electronic notetakers, and much more.

Teachers are finding ways to use all sorts of technology, whether labeled assistive or not, in content area classrooms with students who are having trouble succeeding. Leu, Leu, and Coiro (2004) offer a wealth of resources for teachers who are striving to include all students as they teach using Internet inquiry projects. Noting that a common concern is that students with disabilities cannot always access the information from websites because of text difficulty and/or reading disabilities, they give Web addresses for various text-to-speech readers, or screenreaders, that read text out loud from electronic documents, including Web pages. They go on to suggest resources for students who are hearing or visually challenged, students with attention deficit disorder or learning disabilities, persons with neurological disorders such as autism or Asperger's syndrome, and others.

Labbo (2002) recommends the use of CD-ROM talking books for readers with diverse language backgrounds, saying that digital resources can play a powerful role in supporting students' vocabulary, as well as comprehension of text in both their native language and texts they then reread in English. I am certainly finding it true that technology can assist with second language learning. A few years ago, as I was preparing to go to Benin, in west Africa, to teach a summer course to education leaders who spoke French, I listened to interactive instructional CDs, playing games with my fellow travelers using software programs designed to teach French, and learning to use my pocket-size electronic translator, which can take a phrase I type in and give me that phrase in five different languages. I was embracing the technology that could assist me and my students in our common endeavor—learning.

ACTION RESEARCH   9.C

Look on the Internet for book trailers relating to some of your favorite books, noticing and making judgments on the content and techniques used. Then, create a book trailer to show your class or another group of people, to entice them to read a book you find valuable. You can use iMovie or Microsoft MovieMaker if you wish; if you do it another way, be sure to let others know how you constructed and posted your trailer so they can learn something about technology as well as about books from you.

ACTION RESEARCH   9.D

One of the best places to find out what's current in the field of new literacies is, not surprisingly, online. Check out www.newliteracies.uconn.edu/index.html and see what the team there has to offer.

Kim and Kamil (2004) describe several ways computer-assisted instruction can benefit students; it can "offer students the opportunity to access customized support, to learn at a comfortable pace, and to process text actively" (p. 352). By way of example, "computers can provide students who are reading electronic texts with immediate and continuous access to vocabulary definitions, photos, videos, and links to additional information" (p. 355). But the authors warn that simply providing access to the multimedia environment and computer tools without guidance and support is not enough; instruction is necessary so that students know how to use the electronic aids, and to assure that students understand how to apply strategies for processing different types of visual information and synthesize it with the textual information.

Rose and Dalton (2002) describe the "Engaging the Text Project," which supports readers who struggle through the use of hypertext Web links. It involves multimedia and interactivity. They designed a CD-ROM that they call The Thinking Reader, which gives instruction in comprehension strategies embedded in digitized novels, and which "provides supports to scaffold students' diverse recognition, strategic, and affective networks of learning" (p. 269). This is just one example of the computer-supported literacy environments available for teachers and learners.

Of course, as with other materials, you should check out the electronic learning programs and evaluate them in terms of your students' needs and your philosophy of education. Some programs offer little more than new packaging of the drill exercises offered in standard workbooks. Others are truly innovative, inspirational, challenging, and interactive. Use all programs judiciously, and listen to your students' evaluation of them also.

CONCLUSION

There's no question that schools and modes of learning are changing rapidly along with everything else in the world, and that you must be prepared to teach much differently from the way you were probably taught. Mahiri (2001) promotes literacy practices shaped by "pop culture pedagogy" (p. 382), which uses such modes of transmission as video games, music compact discs, the Internet, television, and movies, with multitextual, multimodal, and often multicultural aspects influencing meaning making and learning. Mahiri laments the slowness of schools thus far to use pop culture as a way to help students overcome the constraints they often perceive on their school learning. He explains:

If schooling is to survive these pop culture ways of knowing and being, it too must transform. I am not advocating that teachers attempt to significantly incorporate pop culture pedagogy into schools. Pop culture works in young people's lives in context-specific ways that often could not be reproduced in the context of school. Rather I am suggesting that teachers continue to become more aware of the motives and methods of youth engagement in pop culture in terms of why and how such engagement connects to students' personal identifications, their needs to construct meanings, and their pursuit of

pleasures and personal power. Teachers should explore how work in schools can make similar connections to students' lives, but the real challenge is to make these connections to and through changing domains of knowledge, critical societal issues, and cognitive and technical skills that educators can justify their students will actually need to master the universe of the new century. (p. 382)

In this chapter, I've tried to give you, the content area teacher, some things to think about in terms of the expanding literacies of today. I hope you'll pursue the topics of media literacy, pop culture, and digital literacy much more thoroughly as you continue growing in your professional career and learning more about how adolescents interact with our rapidly changing technologies and world. The new materials and modes of presentation do not alter the fact that students will always need teachers. They need you to model, instruct, mentor, facilitate, give suggestions, listen, and learn along with them. You can help them be critical consumers of media and information derived and constructed from the media.

I'd like to let Donna Alvermann (2008) have the last word in this chapter. She believes that the ways in which adolescents are using new literacies can push the boundaries of classroom practice in exciting ways:

the most striking insight to be gained from the research on adolescents' remixing of multimodal content to create new texts is this: Those who create online content recognize that authorship is neither a solitary nor completely original enterprise. . . . Content area teachers and teacher educators who are open to considering the implications of this finding could incorporate into their regular class assignments opportunities for students to integrate subject matter texts with available online texts. . . . I propose that young people's engagement with these kinds of ideological messages and materials is central to their becoming the critical readers and writers we say we value. (p. 17)

WEBSITES | CHAPTER 9 | Access these links using the Kane Resource Site.

Astronomical Artists and Their Creations
www.spaceart.org

Blogger
www.blogger.com

Center for Digital Storytelling
www.storycenter.org

DRAAC Guide to HTML
www.draac.com/

FanFiction.net
www.fanfiction.net

Goodreads
www.goodreads.com

Howard Gardner
www.howardgardner.com

James Kakalios
www.physicsofsuperheroes.com

Jon Scieszka
http://guysread.com

Moodle
www.moodle.org

Mythbusters
www.dsc.discovery.com/fansites/mythbusters/
mythbusters.html

Nancy Farmer
www.nancyfarmerwebsite.com

New Jour
http://old.library.georgetown.edu/newjour

New Literacies Research Team
www.newliteracies.uconn.edu/index.html

Not for Ourselves Alone
www.pbs.org/stantonanthony

Oswego City School District Classroom Pages
www.oswego.org/classroompages.cfm

PBS Teacher Resources
www.pbs.org/teachers

Radical Change: Books for Youth in a Digital Age
http://ci.fsu.edu/radicalchange/FAQs

Shelfari
www.shelfari.com

The Barahona Center for the Study of Books in Spanish for Children and Adolescents
www2.csusm.edu/csb

"The Future of Reading: Don't Worry. It Might Be Better Than You Think"
www.schoollibraryjournal.com/article/CA6712772.html

University of Connecticut New Literacies Team
www.newliteracies.uconn.edu/index.html

Web site Evaluation at the Secondary Level
http://school.discoveryeducation.com/schrockguide/evalhigh.html

Wikibooks
www.wikibooks.org

You and the Mass Media
www.FilmicArchives.com

YouTube EDU
www.youtube.com.education

APPLICATION ACTIVITIES

9.1 Begin a file of films, videos, and so forth for the subject you will teach. Search catalogs, bookstores, and libraries. Watch one or more of the resources you find and write a movie review or a "Film Alert" for your students.

9.2 Marnie W. Curry-Tash (1998) asserts, "Many media educators today believe that, just as media constructs a version of world and self, viewers actively 'read' and construct a 'television text' in a way that can be oppositional or subversive" (p. 44). Watch a television show, a documentary, or a video related to a topic you might teach in your content area. Then, create a viewing guide to aid your students' understanding of and critical thinking about the piece. Help them to view actively and attentively and to construct meaning. Tap into their background knowledge. You can connect it to other texts they might have read in your class. You can use the formats that have been used all through this book—graphic organizers, anticipation guides, K-W-L-S, or Venn diagrams. Post your viewing guide on the Kane Resource Site to share and receive feedback about it.

9.3 Imagine you are being interviewed for a teaching position in your chosen subject area. The department chairperson says, "There is an ongoing dispute among our faculty. Some say computers in classrooms have really made our jobs harder. The kids don't want to do anything but play with the software, surf the Internet, and contact their friends on social networks; books are becoming obsolete. Other teachers are leading the effort to allocate even more of our limited resources to improve the technology available to teachers and students, insisting that this will result in better literacy and more content knowledge being gained. Where do you stand on the issue?" The chairperson gives no indication of how she, the principal, or the other teachers at the interview feel about the topic.

Spend a few moments writing your response to this challenge. Then, if possible, debate with someone (another candidate for the position, maybe) who has an answer different from yours.

9.4 Begin designing a Web page for your content area courses. If you already have a personal Web page, include parts of it in your new teacher Web page. Work with other prospective teachers and look at secondary teachers' Web pages to get ideas about what to include. You might post some of the things you have written while working through this book, as well as materials you've created for other classes. You might have book reviews and booktalks; sources for researching various topics within your field; pictures, quotes, and cartoons appropriate for the course; annotated bibliographies; and links to other websites. If applicable, scan in action photographs (with appropriate permissions) of you and your students, as well as projects they've completed or participated in.

10 chapter

Assessment of Content Area Literacy

When the International Reading Association (IRA) published "Adolescent Literacy: A Position Statement" in 1999, it insisted that the students in our middle and secondary schools deserve, among other things:

> Assessment that shows them their strengths as well as their needs and that guides their teachers to design instruction that will best help them grow as readers. . . . Adolescents deserve classroom assessments that bridge the gap between what they know and are able to do and relevant curriculum standards; they deserve assessments that map a path toward continued literacy growth. (p. 103)

Okay, you might be thinking, fine, who can argue with these lofty statements? But what's a content area teacher supposed to do? What does this have to do with me? And how do I learn what I have to in order to get on board and give my students what they deserve in terms of assessment?

ASSESSING ASSESSMENT

Assessment and teaching go hand in hand and must be consistent. It makes no sense to teach according to one philosophy and use assessment tools that reflect a different, perhaps opposing, one. For example, during my early teaching days, I was a seventh-grade reading teacher in a rural middle school, and our district was visited by evaluators from the State Education Department. A man came into my classroom carrying a clipboard and proceeded to go through my files. At one point he asked me, "How many of your students have mastered the skill of making inferences?" I quickly and confidently replied, "None." When he looked up with a surprised expression, I added that *I* hadn't mastered the skill either. We believed in lifelong learning and growth in this school, and I expected that as my students and I grew in experience, knowledge, and wisdom, we would get better and better at making inferences from exceedingly more difficult texts and real-world interactions. The evaluator lived by the philosophy of mastery learning and had an entire page of discrete reading skills he thought my students should have "mastered."

"One test of the correctness of educational procedure is the happiness of the child."

MARIA MONTESSORI

The chapters in this book have espoused a certain kind of teaching—one that is student-centered, one that uses authentic texts such as literature and real-world documents, and one that views learning as constructivist, where students work to make meaning through experience, talking, listening, writing, and reflection. It should come as no surprise, then, that this chapter explains and recommends several types of authentic assessments that will help you know your students' strengths and needs in both their content learning and their literacy. Furthermore, you'll learn how to connect assessment to further instruction that will help you and your students meet the standards and goals set by others and by themselves. Assessment, if properly understood and done well, is one of the best tools at teachers' and learners' disposal.

How to develop good tests related to your subject matter to find out how well your students are understanding the curriculum and skills you're teaching is a very important topic that is beyond the scope of this book. You might learn how to construct tests in an education class on instructional methods or in a course devoted to assessment and evaluation. What *is* relevant to this book is how those tests and other assessment devices connect to your students' literacy. For example, a student in your class may get a failing grade on your end-of-unit test. It might look like she did not grasp the concepts you taught, but in reality, it's possible that she could not read some of the words in the questions or misread some of the multiple-choice options. Knowing this is crucial to your decision as to what to do next with this student. Perhaps she needs to have tests read to her. Students with limited English proficiency are often at risk of not doing well on tests they have to read.

Or, perhaps you have a student like Eric in your class. His mother wrote:

> Eric's writing ability lagged far behind his reading comprehension and made the successful completion of written assignments almost impossible for him. His struggle with written expression was significant, and it negatively affected his grades in each subject throughout his school years. (Nierstheimer, 2000, p. 36)

What if Eric had the help of a scribe who could record his high-level knowledge about his school subjects? What if he were allowed to use a laptop or to record his thoughts? It might take further assessment and some trial and error before the best method of assessing and assisting Eric's learning is found, but Eric deserves those efforts on our part. So, think about literacy issues when you construct and grade tests and ask your students about how they handled the reading and writing aspects of your evaluations.

This chapter provides you with the knowledge necessary to help you learn to use assessment and instruction together to further your students' content literacy. Initially, I address several major issues relating to assessment in general. Next, I explain several literacy assessment strategies you can use in your classroom to inform instruction. Finally, I address issues relating to the self-assessment of your instruction and your growth as a content area teacher who is concerned with students' (and your own) literacy development.

I have addressed assessment issues, at least indirectly, in each of the previous chapters; it's virtually impossible to discuss instruction and learning without bringing in assessment because they are intertwined. Assessment is inherent in many of the strategies that I have explained and exemplified. Just think about K-W-L-S—the first column asks readers to list what they already know about a topic. That's assessing prior knowledge, which can help you determine what to do next instructionally. In this chapter, though, the actual focus is on assessment. The text and activities will stimulate and guide your thinking about how you as a content area teacher can and should use assessment strategies as you work toward improving and enhancing your students' content knowledge and content literacy. I invite you to jump right in by taking on the teacher/assessor role and react to the student product in Action Research 10.A.

ACTION RESEARCH 10.A

Imagine that you have been given the following poem (Lowry, 1979, pp. 11–12) by one of your students:

> hush   hush   the sea-soft night is aswim
>   with wrinklesquirm creatures
>   listen(!)
> to them   move   smooth   in the moistly dark
>   here in the   whisperwarm   wet

What is your response to this text? What do you like about it? What suggestions might you have for the writer? What grade would you give it? Is there information that would help you as you assign a grade? Reflect in your log, then discuss your response and possible questions or musings with a group of your peers or with the Kane Resource Site community.

Poem reprinted with permission.

Anastasia, a fourth grader in Lois Lowry's *Anastasia Krupnik* (1979), wrote the science-related poem in Action Research 10.A for a class assignment, taking eight days and showing a unique process. Finally, after reading and rereading her finished product, she writes this self-assessment at home: "I wrote a wonderful poem" (p. 13). Then, the day came when the class had to read their poems aloud. As you read the following excerpt, notice the different criteria that Anastasia and her teacher use in their evaluation processes:

> Mrs. Westvessel looked puzzled. "Let me see that, Anastasia," she said. Anastasia gave her the poem.
>
> "Where are your capital letters, Anastasia?" asked Mrs. Westvessel. Anastasia didn't say anything.
>
> "Where is the rhyme?" asked Mrs. Westvessel. "It doesn't rhyme at *all*." Anastasia didn't say anything.
>
> "What kind of poem is this, Anastasia?" asked Mrs. Westvessel. "Can you explain it, please?"
>
> Anastasia's voice had become very small again, the way voices do, sometimes. "It's a poem of sounds," she said. "It's about little things that live in tidepools, after dark, when they move around. It doesn't have sentences or capital letters because I wanted it to look on the page like small creatures moving in the dark."
>
> "I don't know why it didn't rhyme," she said, miserably. "It didn't seem important."
>
> "Anastasia, weren't you listening in class when we talked about writing poems? . . . when we talked about poetry in this class we simply were not talking about worms and snails crawling on a piece of paper. I'm afraid I will have to give you an F. . . ."
>
> At home, that evening, Anastasia got her green notebook out of her desk drawer. Solemnly, . . . she crossed out the word *wonderful* and replaced it with the word *terrible*.
>
> "I wrote a terrible poem," she read sadly. (pp. 12–14)

Excerpt from *Anastasia Krupnik*. Copyright © 1979 by Lois Lowry. Reprinted by permission of Houghton Mifflin Company. All rights reserved.

How willing or eager do you think Anastasia will be to write more poetry for this class, this teacher? That little scenario may have elicited a strong reaction from you or maybe a vivid memory of a moment in your school career when your own opinion of your work differed from that of an outside evaluator. Technically, the teacher did nothing wrong. She had established criteria, which Anastasia had not followed, upon which to judge the finished product. Yet, she had choices within the context of her classroom; for example, she could have chosen not to grade this poem, but let Anastasia know that she valued it in its own right, and given her another opportunity to write a poem following the formula outlined for the class. Or she could have decided to be flexible in terms of her criteria, recognizing that

this particular student's abilities, needs, and purposes did not match the somewhat arbitrary rules set up in an effort to help fledgling poetry writers. The moment certainly called for teacher decision making in terms of what the next instructional step should be to help Anastasia's growth as a writer. You'll be provided with many such opportunities as you teach and assess your students' work and processes.

ACTION RESEARCH   10.B

Before moving on, practice responding to two more pieces of student work.

Directions: Place a grade on each of the following real samples of student texts, and then write a short note to the writer.

(1) This text was written during a ninth-grade unit on mythology in response to the prompt, "If you could visit the land of the dead, whom would you look for and what would you do?" (You might want to think first about how *you* would answer the question):

> If I could visit the land of the dead, I wouldn't go because I would be too scared. Seeing dead people would make me realize that I won't live forever and I couldn't take it.

(2) The following was written by a tenth-grade student during a poetry unit:

The Dark Side

As devils mock and prey on all who know,
the secrets that will save the soul of man,
I dwell in endless thought that burns my eyes.
The searing pain from which I shall escape,
engulfs a world that soon will be just dust.
When sands of time turn into cold black mud
we all prepare to meet our hopeless end.
The gallows stand lonely with ghosts of past,
While screams pierce the silence and winds cry out,
They look for answers, all they find is pain.

Evaluation isn't easy, is it? In the first example, the ninth-grade English teacher responded, "I understand." The grade? "D." For the second example, which was written by the same student, the grade given by a tenth-grade English teacher was "100," with the comment, "Very good! Nice imagery, perfect blank verse (with a few judicious variations)." Perhaps you thought that letter or number grades shouldn't be assigned at all. If so, you're not alone. Many experts feel that grades and other outside rewards or negative consequences ultimately hurt students. According to Kohn (1999), "The evidence suggests that, all things being equal, students in a school that uses no letters or numbers to rate them will be more likely to think deeply, love learning, and tackle more challenging tasks" (p. 189).

ACTIVATING PRIOR KNOWLEDGE 10.1

Reflect on times in your academic life when your knowledge was assessed. What types of measurement instruments were used? What exactly was being evaluated? For what purposes? How accurate would you say the assessment results were? What did they tell about you? Write in your log about these or related issues.

Now, reflect on your extracurricular activities, such as sports, drama, community service, part-time jobs. How was your performance evaluated in *those* areas? What were the purposes and/or results of the assessment?

Every semester, around the middle of the term, I ask my students, "If the president of the college came in right now and announced that we were switching to a Pass/Fail system, how many of you would continue to work as hard as you have been working so far?" A few start to raise their hands, but slowly lower them again, shaking their heads. I am astounded by this. My classes are not random samples of the population; they are all preservice teachers taking a course in their education major, often immediately preceding their student teaching semester. Shouldn't they be working their hardest and learning all they can in order to become excellent teachers, regardless of what the grading system is? I believe, along with Kohn, that the system students have been raised in is responsible for their over-reliance on grades. Like Anastasia, they must have a teacher's judgment in the form of a letter grade before they can know that they've done a wonderful job.

BookTalk 10.1

Have you, like Anastasia, ever had a piece of work misjudged or not appreciated by others? For all who have ever been rejected and ridiculed, find out what good company you're in by reading *Rotten Reviews & Rejections,* edited by Bill Henderson and André Bernard (1998). You'll smile as you read the critique by *Children's Books* of Lewis Carroll's *Alice in Wonderland:* "We fancy that any real child might be more puzzled than enchanted by this stiff, overwrought story" (Henderson & Bernard, p. 27). An *Atlantic Monthly* reviewer in 1892 summarily dismissed Emily Dickinson: "An eccentric, dreamy, half-educated recluse in an out-of-the-way New England village—or anywhere else—cannot with impunity set at defiance the laws of gravitation and grammar . . . oblivion lingers in the immediate neighborhood" (Henderson & Bernard, p. 33). Read put-downs of T. S. Eliot's *The Wasteland,* F. Scott Fitzgerald's *The Great Gatsby,* J. D. Salinger's *The Catcher in the Rye,* and dozens more works that have been validated by readers over time. These reviews are laughable now, and they should give you courage to risk and endure possible rejection of your work while still valuing your self-assessment.

STANDARDIZED ASSESSMENTS AND HIGH-STAKES TESTING

The uses and abuses of standardized testing are heavily discussed at every level of society, from parents to politicians, students to songwriters. You have most likely taken a lifetime's worth of tests, perhaps starting with those measuring your reading ability at the elementary school level, and you may still be facing the GRE to determine your eligibility for certain graduate schools. Now, it's time for you to reflect on literacy assessments using the lens of a content area teacher.

How Early Are Children Aware of Assessment and Evaluation?

You've heard about and practiced the use of listening questions (Michel, 1994). Here's a quote from one of the first graders with whom Michel used listening questions: "I love it when I get an 'Excellent.' I like to look at it at my seat. Then I know I'm smart. I try to get one every day. My mom likes them too. It makes her feel happy when I do good" (p. 85). Something about that quote makes me uneasy. Will this child, or has she already, come to rely on outside reinforcement to judge the worth of her endeavors? I'd want to know how the actual *work* makes her feel, whether the *process* was rewarding. I'd want to make sure her reflection is substantive and that her sense of self-worth is not dependent on staring at an "Excellent" on the back of her hand.

A standardized test is, according to *The Literacy Dictionary:*

> 1. a test with specific tasks and procedures so that comparable measurements may be made by testers working in different geographical areas. 2. a test for which norms on a reference group, ordinarily drawn from many schools or communities, are provided. (Harris & Hodges, 1995, p. 242)

The primary purpose of standardized tests is to compare the performance of groups, rather than individuals. Raw scores, representing the actual number of correct answers, are converted to other kinds of scores, such as percentiles, so that comparisons are easier to make. These tests are sometimes used to determine whether a program or a school is effective or successful, but because other factors that the tests don't address may also be at work, it makes sense not to use test scores as the sole criterion for evaluation. It's also important to remember that norm-referenced tests are specifically designed to produce a range of scores, so it's nearly impossible for all students, or all groups, to perform at the "above average" level. But, of course, all participants want their schools or groups to perform well. Unfortunately, this can lead to "teaching to the test"—changing instructional methods or giving up instructional time to practice so students are familiar and comfortable with the test format.

Other things to consider when you analyze standardized tests or the scores your students receive include *validity* and *reliability*. In order for a test to be *valid,* it must truly test what it says it is measuring. For example, a reading comprehension test should indeed show how well students understand text. If the students you teach read well in class, but score poorly because the standardized test used passages that required prior knowledge they didn't have, the test was not valid for your group, and the scores should not be viewed as meaningful. This is often a problem for immigrant populations. Diverse students possess different background knowledge from that of majority-culture students.

For a test to be *reliable,* the scores it produces must be dependable, or stable. A group of students should receive about the same score on repeated administrations of an instrument. If your students received very high scores one week and very low scores the next, which scores could you trust? A test must produce consistent results to be considered reliable.

High-stakes tests, which are usually standardized tests, are those where the results determine such things as whether or not a child graduates, passes on to another grade, or is allowed in a certain curricular track, program, course, school, or job. The SAT test, which many of you had to take as you were applying to colleges, is an example of a standardized test, and you may well have considered the stakes high because your scores could heavily influence whether or not you were accepted by the college of your choice. Today, with growing emphasis on learning standards, the prevalence of high-stakes tests is greater than ever before. Schools that fail to show that their students are making adequate progress on these tests risk sanctions and even closures.

You must keep abreast of the debate over the uses of various standardized tests, as well as the touted benefits addressed by the proponents and the concerns addressed by the opponents of standardized, high-stakes testing. It is an area conducive to using your critical-thinking skills. For example, once you read the following statement by Peter Johnston (2000), a leading expert in the field, you might react strongly, pursue the matter, and join your voice with others to either refute the claim or work to change the system:

> We can expect high-stakes assessment to continue because the already extreme differences between rich and poor in the United States (and many other countries) continue to escalate. In this context, the combination of a competitive individualism and a meritocracy places tests as the gatekeepers to wealth and opportunity. Tests, particularly literacy tests, are the means of bloodlessly maintaining class differences. (p. 250)

Raphael and Au (2005) bemoan the fact that so many schools unintentionally lower the quality of academic experiences as they attempt to raise scores on high-stakes tests. Much time is spent on test preparation that involves little actual instruction. Also, many schools buy packaged programs that concentrate on lower-level skills rather than on critical thinking, analysis, synthesis, and other higher-level skills. The authors propose using literacy strategies, specifically question–answer relationships (QAR, explained in Chapter 5), which can prepare students in a variety of subject area classes for taking tests, while simultaneously giving instruction of high quality. They explain, "Through QAR instruction, teachers . . . are able to unpack the task demands of different types of questions and alert students to these demands as appropriate to the different tests students face" (p. 218). They give an example of a test question that required students to write an essay that included both ideas from the text and a personal connection to that text. Students who knew how to apply the QAR strategy would be able to handle that synthesis task.

Many others voice opposition to and concern about the overuse, misuse, or ill effects of standardized tests (e.g., Fink, 2008; Goldberg, 2004; Kohn, 2004; Platt, 2004; Schuster, 2004), the harm they might be doing to students' learning and emotional health (e.g., Posner, 2004; Sadker & Zittleman, 2004), and the time that might be better used for more and better instruction (e.g., Foster & Noyce, 2004; Plitt, 2004). Kylene Beers, in her 2009 NCTE Presidential Address, asserted, "High-stakes tests and packaged learning have created a generation of students who equate learning with finishing and achievement with a decent grade. . . . Testing does not improve learning; better teaching does."

The International Reading Association has taken a position that "strongly opposes high-stakes testing" (www.ira.org/positions/high_stakes.html). The National Council of Teachers of English formulated resolutions in 2000, including "On Developing a Test Taker's Bill of Rights" (www.ncte.org/resolutions/testakersrights002000.shtml) and "On Urging Reconsideration of High Stakes Testing" (www.ncte.org/resolutions/highstakes002000.shtml).

Some teachers prefer to work within the system; some join teams of item writers in order to create tests that are as good as possible for their students. There are voices of balance, such as Sheila Valencia's:

> We cannot sit back and watch as the assessment drama unfolds. We must step forward as advocates for assessments that foster better teaching practice, insist on curricular rigor, and value worthwhile student learning and engagement—all the while respecting the public mandate for accountability. (2000, p. 249)

Others advocate for a balance between standardized, high-stakes testing and other forms of more authentic assessment, such as Stiggins (2004), who declares, "we must strike a balance between standardized tests *of* learning and classroom assessment *for* learning" (p. 26).

Teaching in action: *Language Arts.* Cochran (2009) takes what I think is a sensible and successful approach to standardized testing; she teaches her eighth-grade students to analyze their own achievement data. In addition to teaching to her state's language arts standards, she teaches "'data literacy'—the ability to understand, analyze, and display information" (p. 110). She finds that using specific data helps her show individuals how they can set goals for improvement, which provides motivation and a better perception of themselves as learners who can make progress. She confers with students about their latest test results, provides instruction that targets areas that they can see need strengthening, and guides them as they develop strategies for self-monitoring. Cochran uses a workshop approach in her classroom, and allows students to choose their own practice materials:

> Now, I have created a library by standard and benchmark. It is housed in three filing cabinets. Two cabinets are full of texts from every genre

imaginable. The texts are not leveled, but rather arranged by topic, so students can select text that they find appealing. I can't imagine asking students to attack a skill they find difficult by reading text they find boring. (p. 118)

Another person who has been able to make peace with her situation is first-grade teacher Jeanne Reardon, who explains that, although she has never found standardized test results to be useful, she recognizes that they are used to judge her students, and so:

> Reading-test reading is a genre that my students must become familiar with to be literate participants in society. When it is . . . taught as a genre along with other genres, students understand this peculiar form and how it works. They become successful comprehension test-takers, and the power of the test is diminished. (1990, p. 30)

She concludes, "I cannot ignore reading tests, nor can I allow them to control my classroom. 'Putting reading tests in their place' is the alternative I use while we search for a form of reading assessment worthy of the classroom literary community" (p. 37).

You may be planning to be a high school science teacher, but you can find similar ways to work within the constraints of the mandated standardized tests your students must eventually take. The teacher's attitude and teaching methods make a huge difference.

AUTHENTIC ASSESSMENT

A major concern about standardized tests is that they are often not authentic; rather, they are artificial. If an assessment score does not really represent what a person understands about a subject or can perform in a real situation, the measurement device is flawed. When physicist Richard Feynman was a visiting lecturer in Brazil, he discovered that his students memorized very well and could pass tests, but they didn't understand the principles and could not apply them to any real situations. *Their* tests did not pass the test of authenticity, so he did not consider them valid measurements. In an address to leading Brazilian professors and government officials later in the year, he startled his audience by saying, "The main purpose of my talk is to demonstrate to you that *no* science is being taught in Brazil" (Feynman, 1985, p. 216). He finished by saying, "I couldn't see how anyone could be educated by this self-propagating system in which people pass exams, and teach others to pass exams, but nobody knows anything" (p. 218). The head of the science education program responded admirably to the criticism: "Mr. Feynman has told us some things that are very hard for us to hear, but . . . I think we should listen to him" (p. 218).

Brenner, Pearson, and Rief (2007) agree that there is often "a mismatch in what state assessments value (the ability to select the single correct answer) and what twenty-first-century workplace skills demand (the ability to formulate multiple answers to complex problems)" (p. 259). On the bright side, they also agree that "those students who are immersed in reading and writing for real reasons for real audiences, on a daily basis, do fine on any assessment. They are thinkers who can figure out what any audience needs to know and how to convey that information" (pp. 263–264). So we don't need to give up good instruction to spend inordinate amounts of time preparing students for tests.

Authentic assessment measures student learning by requiring the active construction of responses within the context of performing real tasks. The National Council for the Social Studies (1994) states, "To gauge effectively the efforts of students and teachers in social studies programs, evaluators must augment traditional tests with performance evaluations, portfolios of student papers and projects, and essays focused on higher-level thinking" (p. 285).

As content area teachers, strive to use all the resources available to you in your school to analyze test data for the purpose of designing instruction and utilizing methods that will best help your particular students. Brownlie (2009) helps us visualize this concept at work:

> In some schools, all incoming students (grade 8 or grade 9) are assessed in reading science and social studies. The responses are coded (descriptors highlighted, no grades given) by the entire staff, and the literacy committee helps examine the data and choose the goals. The results are reported to the staff and each department considers how they can support these students in achieving improved performance within their subject area—for example, How can we support learners making inferences in science, in social studies, in home economics, in information technology, in math, and in English? The students are reassessed at the end of the semester or year. The results of the teaching—the changes in learning—are reported, and new targets are set. (p. 124)

Black, Harrison, Lee, et al. (2004) emphasize that we must keep in mind the kind of assessment that relates to future learning, as opposed to that whose priority is to rank, certify competence, or hold teachers or schools accountable. They are in favor of formative assessment, in which "the evidence is actually used to adapt the teaching work to meet learning needs" (p. 10). They recommend changing expectations, as well as changing the classroom culture and environment. This can be done:

■ by changing the "classroom contract" so that all expect that teachers and students work together

for the same end: the improvement of everyone's learning;

■ by empowering students to become active learners, thus taking responsibility for their own learning;

■ by sustained attention to and reflection on ways in which assessment can support learning. (p. 20)

Afflerbach (2004) also believes in formative assessment, stating that "when done well, there is no more powerful formative assessment than that which is conducted on a daily basis by the classroom teacher. . . . Classroom contexts that support teacher questions and observation . . . must be developed to pursue the dual goals of understanding how students are learning content, and how their reading achievement is related to this learning" (p. 384).

Afflerbach (2004) finds performance assessments especially well-suited for helping teachers understand how well students in content area classes can learn from text; they are an authentic type of assessment, since they involve placing students in situations where we can "evaluate what has been learned from reading tasks that emulate and anticipate important content-domain and life performances" (p. 379). He explains:

> Performance assessment prompts are often crafted so that they result in complex tasks for students. A performance assessment might ask a student to compare and contrast information learned from two texts written on the same topic from different perspectives. . . . Performance assessment in other content domains might involve students in manipulating and applying knowledge gained from reading to write creatively or persuasively. (p. 379)

Finders and Hynds (2003) give several examples of authentic assessment they've observed in middle school settings. They tell of a ninth-grade teacher who encouraged his students to express their understandings of and reactions to text by creating cartoons. They show an example of a pamphlet students created after researching community-based agencies allowing opportunities for teen volunteers. Visuals on poster boards, oral presentations, and graphic representations in the form of charts and bar graphs are also encouraged.

Teaching in action: *Math.* Miller and Koesling (2009) describe a high school whose math faculty espouses the philosophy that ". . . problem-solving and reasoning skills, as well as content skills, can be taught best in the context of a literacy-based math curriculum" (p. 66). Koesling uses formative assessment on a daily basis. After students read through a mathematical problem, she asks them to write or talk so that she can assess whether they've understood the vocabulary and meaning of the questions involved. She then has the class read the problem a second time, and gives them a minute to reflect and chat about it with class-mates. At various points she checks for misconceptions, giving additional support to English learners as needed. The authors explain, "These informal assessments let her [Koesling] look at students' mathematical reasoning and reading and determine whether they are on target or not. She then can adjust her next instructional moves accordingly to prevent the cycle of learning shut-down that plagues many students."

CLASSROOM-BASED ASSESSMENTS

Let's turn our attention to your classroom. On a regular (actually, daily) basis, you should know how your students are understanding the content and growing in the skills of your discipline. You also should know about their literacy because their strengths and struggles in terms of reading and writing affect how (and maybe even whether) they tackle your assignments and explore your curriculum-their success in your course may be dependent on what you know about their literacy and what strategies you teach them.

Valencia (2000), in an attempt to look into the future of literacy assessment, predicts the strengthening of classroom-based assessment, much of it in the form of performance assessment. "Teachers who understand and focus on content standards, and who make links between instruction and classroom assessment, are more likely to be effective" (p. 248). Many teachers recognize that they must work within the constraints of mandated assessments coming from outside the classroom. Within your classroom, however, you have much more control over what and how you assess on a day-to-day basis. You can choose only those strategies that you find valuable and effective in informing your instruction and measuring and enhancing your students' growth. This kind of assessment is never the enemy. It's never meant to be punitive, and it never has the purpose of tricking students.

Observation

Probably the most important and valuable assessment skill you can develop is observation, which Yetta Goodman (1985) has coined *kidwatching*. You can observe your students at work, individually and in small peer groups, as well as in a whole class setting; during formal and informal activities; while they talk, listen, write, read, or explore information online. Some teachers carry notebooks or sheets of labels as they circulate and engage the students in conversation; later, they transfer any relevant notes they jotted down in terms of process or difficulties into the student's folder.

When circulating among your students, you can question the students to help them clarify what they're doing and why they're doing it. "Marietta, how did you form your hypothesis? Where will you go to obtain data to test it?" The information you gather can inform your instruction—you may slow or quicken your pace, back up to explain a concept students are having trouble applying, give a mini-lesson on research strategies. As you build rapport with your students, you'll note who is showing signs of fatigue, frustration, or excitement, and you can then proceed or react accordingly.

It's not easy to get to know over 100 students, which is the number many secondary teachers teach each school day. But over time, you get to know them as unique people, and your efforts will be worthwhile because your teaching will be aimed at where the students really are; perhaps even more important, your students will realize that you see them as individuals and care about them as learners.

Many middle schools have regular, sometimes even daily, meetings of teams of teachers who share the same cohort of students. Looking at a student's work in various subject areas can give all his or her teachers valuable insights and points to ponder. Literacy is complex, personal, local, and social (Johnston & Costello, 2005); and assessment is "a dynamic part of ongoing, goal-directed social activities and social discourses" (p. 265). For example, Monique might be struggling and seemingly noncompliant in social studies and English class, yet be perceived as an enthusiastic and model student in science and art. Teachers can talk about the difficulty of texts used, the methods of instruction usually employed, the possible impact of cooperative learning in small groups, the role that background knowledge might play, and other factors that could help everyone to meet Monique's needs. Teachers might ask themselves, individually and in the team meeting, questions such as the following, adapted from those offered by Akhaven (2004, p. 230):

- What are Monique's abilities and strengths as a reader? A speaker? A writer? A community member?
- What are her dreams, desires, work habits, likes and dislikes?
- How do I know the extent to which my instruction is making a difference?
- What should be my next steps in terms of instruction and helping Monique know my goals and set goals for herself in my course?

Michel (1994) advocates teachers using what she calls *listening questions*. She found that if a young child answered, "I don't know" to a question, either patiently waiting or asking indirect questions often resulted in the child eventually opening up and sharing more thoughts and feelings on the topic. Certainly middle school students are similar; countless times my own children informed me that they did "nothing" in response to the standard question, "What'd you do in school today?" but later, they told stories and reacted to situations if I remained available to listen and nod my head. So, listen carefully as students talk, probing for depth and details when appropriate, being comfortable with pauses, letting the student take the conversation in a chosen direction. You may refer to Figure 2.3 in Chapter 2 for an example of a teacher using listening questions.

Anecdotal Records

Roe and Smith (2005) note the value of teachers keeping anecdotal records, written accounts of particular incidents that exemplify student characteristics or progress and offer opportunities for pondering implications for instruction regarding individuals or groups. You can learn from the anecdotal records of other teachers, such as a special education teacher who is in your inclusion classroom, also. Or perhaps you have a student whose behavior or learning patterns or test results are baffling you; asking other teachers to share anecdotal information about how the student is doing in their subjects might be enlightening. Figure 10.1 contains an example of an anecdotal record.

Informal Interviews and Conferencing

If you informally interview students often as they work, asking questions about the process they are using to discover information, compose, solve problems, respond to literature, or comprehend reading material, they become comfortable talking about

---

BookTalk   10.2

Observation is a kind of reading where the text involved is very complicated and doesn't always say what it means up front. When the "text" is an adolescent, you have to read between the lines, read what isn't said as well as what is said, and read under the surface for the deep meaning. Miss Harris, the sixth-grade teacher in Katherine Paterson's (www.terabithia.com) *The Great Gilly Hopkins* (1978), is a great reader of kids. When Gilly writes a racist message intended to hurt her, Miss Harris reacts not to what has been written but rather to the writer. She sees that Gilly, underneath her tough exterior, is a vulnerable, suffering child. Having read her student correctly, she can turn the tables by responding to Gilly with respect. Miss Harris talks to her about anger, contrasting the anger that is obvious in Gilly with her own anger that she has had to bury. She serves as a role model for teachers who want to comprehend their students' needs and instruct them accordingly.

---

their thinking and working processes. This leads to increased knowledge for you about what and how to teach next, as well as to metacognitive thinking on their part. They may eventually internalize this type of questioning and ask themselves helpful questions about their thinking as they work. You can help even further by modeling and using *think-alouds*, verbalizing your thoughts as you complete a task. (Chapter 5 contains an example of a think-aloud using a biology text.) Then, ask students to do the same in conferences to assess how they are thinking.

FIGURE   10.1   A sample anecdotal record.

October 25. I was wary when I heard Mario would be in my high school biology class. He has Down syndrome, and although I read his files and saw that previous teachers had found the regular classroom to be the best setting for him, I wasn't sure what I would do if he was just not able to grasp the concepts and vocabulary of this course. Today I learned a lot about, and from, Mario himself. He gave his oral presentation (a requirement for all students, based on research of a biology-related career). Mario lectured us on what a veterinarian does. While his teaching assistant controlled the PowerPoint presentation he created with her help, Mario's talk showed he was knowledgeable and self-assured. He mentioned that some of his research had involved interviewing his uncle, a doctor. A classmate asked him how he knew about so many varieties of dogs, and he said that he has been reading dog books since he was little, and he watches dog shows (competitions) on TV. I have a new respect for Mario's knowledge and ambition. Now that I know he wants to work with dogs when he grows up, I will bring in more books on animal behavior, especially those that have good visuals, and I'll relate the concepts I'm teaching to what he already knows about dogs.

At the end of Mario's presentation, the class applauded. So did I, humbly.

Note: See about getting Mario's uncle to come in as a guest speaker.

Teaching in action: *Math.* Here's another think-aloud example using an excerpt from the biography *The Man Who Loved Only Numbers* by Paul Hoffman (1998). The reader's self-monitoring is shown in italics within brackets:

> The Fibonacci series [*uh-oh*] 1, 2, 3, 5, 8, 13, 21, 34, 55, 89, 144, 233 . . . [*I'm trying to figure out what the next number is, why the progression looks like it does—can't do it right away*] arose in a problem about sexually active bunnies but has since come up again and again in design, both natural and man-made. The seeds in a sunflower, for example, are always positioned along two interweaving spirals, one set turning clockwise, the other counterclockwise. [*I can picture that, but what does that have to do with the numbers in the last sentence?*] The number of spirals in the two sets are not the same; in fact, they are always consecutive Fibonacci numbers. So [*here comes an example—whew*], if there are 144 clockwise spirals, there are always either 89 or 233 counterclockwise spirals. [*I'm supposed to know why this is? Oh, looking back, I see that those 3 numbers are listed in the progression.*] The Fibonacci series has also come up in man-made design because as the series approaches infinity, the ratio between two consecutive terms approaches the "golden ratio" [*I don't know this term*]—the ideal proportions of a rectangle that the Greeks favored in painting and classical architecture (the Parthenon, for example) [*I can picture this—I visited the replica of the Parthenon in Nashville*]. Indeed, Fibonacci numbers have so many connections to other things that an entire journal, the *Fibonacci Quarterly*, is devoted to keeping up with them. [*Even though I still don't really get it, I want to check out this journal to find other examples. Or maybe I'll just search "Fibonacci" on the Internet.*] (pp. 208–209)

A teacher could surmise several things about the student who agreed to think aloud while reading this passage. The reader recognizes when she is confused, but doesn't panic or show too much frustration. She expects that by reading on she'll get examples and be able to make more sense of the concept under discussion. She connects new information with old by looking back at a previous sentence—something skilled readers do. She has not fully comprehended the text, yet is intellectually curious or motivated enough to want to find more examples. And she shows confidence in being able to find information on her own. There is self-assessment going on, and the teacher can use the knowledge gained to make decisions about where to go from here with this student.

During a conference or a lesson, ask a student to retell a story or text he has read. By listening carefully to the retelling, you may be able to assess the following skills or difficulties:

- Picking out main ideas
- Recalling supporting details
- Understanding relationships such as cause–effect
- Recognizing point of view
- Understanding theoretical concepts and technical terms

You can also guide the students to reflect on their study strategies, composing processes, notetaking, skimming and scanning, figuring out the meanings of new words, and other literacy skills. It's amazing how much some students can tell you about their problems and learning processes if you just ask them. Or, you might bring in a book about a topic you know a certain struggling student is crazy about—horses, snowboarding, jazz, whatever. As she looks through the book, talk with her about:

- Her independent reading
- The differences between outside reading and school requirements
- Why she does better in some subjects than others
- How teachers could best help her
- Whether she has sources of help at home
- What kind of academic difficulties frustrate or discourage her

You can also ask questions as students are writing. They can point out areas that are giving them difficulty, ideas they are excited about, what the process of revising has been like for them, and so on. They can ask you questions during these conferences, too. The work-in-progress is in front of you both to refer to as you talk about discovering, learning, and composing.

Another part of your conference with a student can involve teaching, reinforcing, or assessing the practice of self-assessment. Roe and Smith (2005) offer questions that can help students toward self-appraisal and toward becoming metacognitive as they think about the text and task they face as well as the strategies they might use. These questions are:

1. Do I understand exactly what I am supposed to do for this assignment?
2. What am I trying to learn?
3. What do I already know about this subject that will help me understand what I read?
4. What is the most efficient way for me to learn this material?
5. What parts of this chapter may give me problems?
6. What can I do so that I will understand the hard parts?
7. Now that I am finished reading, do I understand what I read? (pp. 354–355)

Prompts such as these might assist students as they communicate with you about their literacy practices relative to texts in your course.

Content Area Reading Inventories

Although observation is something that good teachers do continually, there are other measures you can use to get specific information from your students. A content area reading inventory, or CARI, is a teacher-made tool using the textbook or other materials your students will actually be using. It consists of tasks you expect them to engage in, such as interpreting pictures, graphs, and charts; using a table of contents, glossary, and index; and determining word meanings from morphological analysis and context. You can use the insights gained from the assessment results to plan appropriate instruction and select additional materials to support your lessons, provide practice, and stimulate and challenge your students.

To construct a CARI, plan on several sections. The first part consists of questions that ask the students to interact with the whole textbook to show whether they understand the components and what they are used for. Depending on the textbook, you may have questions relating to the index, preview and review questions, captions, marginal notes, highlighted definitions, or statistical charts. For the second part, you might focus on vocabulary knowledge. Ask for the meaning of specific words from the text and have the students identify whether they already knew the definition; figured it out from context; used their knowledge of prefixes, suffixes, or roots; or remain clueless about the meaning. The next section is an excerpt from the book, perhaps two or three pages long, and questions you create to tap comprehension skills at the literal, inferential, and applied levels. Recall from Chapter 5 that literal-level questions have answers that can be found directly in the text; to answer inferential-level questions, a reader must put together bits of information or grasp something that has been implied; and applied-level questions call for the reader to use background knowledge or make connections to her experience outside the text itself. You can ask students to identify key points or to outline or summarize the selection. Figure 10.2 shows a partial example of a CARI.

FIGURE 10.2 A partial content area reading inventory.

Dear Fourth Period Students,

Welcome to "Introduction to Statistics." You might be feeling a bit nervous on this first day of class because there are scary stories floating around out there about the difficulty of statistics. Not to worry! It's my favorite subject, and my goal is to make it yours too, or at least to demystify it and make it accessible and interesting to you. I'll do everything I can to help you succeed.

I expect you to do your part as well because we have to work together as a team. Please keep up with the reading, study the excellent examples in this book, work the problems I assign, and let me know if understanding ever breaks down.

For homework tonight, please complete the following questions about yourself and the textbook we'll be using. Your answers will help me know where to begin as I plan my lessons. This is not a test, and your answers will not be held against you, I promise. So relax, get ready to think, and prepare yourself for a challenging and rewarding experience this year.

PART ONE

1. Why did you sign up for this course?
2. Define *statistics*.
3. Give an example of when you might use statistics or run across them in real life (i.e., outside school).
4. Skim the table of contents in your textbook. What do you notice about the organization of the topics in each chapter?
5. What two types of information will you find in the five appendices?
6. What kinds of information will you find in blue boxes throughout the chapters? (Skim the book until you find the answer.)
7. What things do you find at the end of each chapter?
8. After looking at some examples in the book, what do you see as the difference between a graph and a table?

[Part Two might consist of questions about particular terms and concepts, while Part Three could consist of questions based on the students' reading of a few pages from the statistics textbook.]

The Cloze Procedure

Taylor (1953) first developed the *cloze assessment* that requires students to fill in blanks (while reading) to make sense of a passage by using background knowledge and syntactic and semantic cues from the text. Its purpose is to match readers with appropriate texts. You can use the cloze procedure to find out which students will have difficulty reading the class textbook, and thus will require some help; and which students will be able to handle it independently or may even need more challenging supplements or a different text. You can construct this type of informal assessment using your own classroom materials.

1. Select a passage of about 300 words, preferably from the beginning of a chapter.

2. Leave the first and last sentences intact.

3. From the remaining text, delete every fifth word and replace it with a blank space, until you have 50 blanks.

4. After modeling the process for the students (who may be unfamiliar with this type of activity) and giving them a short practice exercise with subsequent debriefing, ask them to complete the assessment—try to guess what original words were omitted.

To score the cloze, count the number of exact word replacements. Double the number of correct responses to arrive at the percentage of items the student identified. Bormuth (1968) provides the criteria in Figure 10.3 for determining a student's reading level.

The labels are fairly self-explanatory: *Independent* means the student should be able to handle the material without help, *Instructional* refers to the student who can handle the material with help, and *Frustration* means that the material is simply too hard. For those students at the frustration level, you have to decide whether to offer a more appropriate book, record sections for an audio alternative, use a teacher assistant or volunteer who can give significant help, or make other adaptations or accommodations. Too often, struggling readers are double victims—they cannot comprehend the material and then get blamed or penalized for not doing their homework or completing a reading assignment.

Some teachers prefer to allow synonym replacements because this is more consistent with their philosophy of how people construct meaning. But that takes longer to score, invalidates the scoring system given above, and could lower the reliability of the procedure. So, using the exact replacement criterion is recommended (Henk & Selders, 1984).

It is also possible to construct a modified cloze passage—students are given choices and asked to determine which word fits into each blank best in terms of meaning and syntax. Cloze passages can be used for instruction, as well as assessment, if the passage is reviewed and reasons for correct choices and thinking processes are discussed.

ACTION RESEARCH   **10.C**

To see what it's like to complete a cloze assessment, try filling in the blanks of the passage in Figure 10.4 or online at the Kane Resource Site. Then, check your answers against those on page 309, which are the words used in the actual text, and figure out the percentage of words you matched. Remember, don't worry if you know your answer makes as much sense and is as appropriate as the one used; there's a reason for not accepting synonyms.

Assure your students when giving a cloze passage that it is not a test—it is just a quick measure to learn how difficult certain subject material is likely to be for them so instruction can be better. Keep in mind that students whose first language is not English may obtain a score that underestimates their comprehension abilities because the procedure is based on a familiarity with English language patterns.

APPLICATION ACTIVITY   **10.1**   (SEE PAGE 310)

Portfolios

ACTIVATING PRIOR KNOWLEDGE   **10.2**

Have you ever put together a portfolio for an academic class or for some other purpose? What did you include to represent your work and yourself? How did you organize it? Were there ways you showed your processes, as well as the finished products? How did you feel about the portfolio? How and to whom did you present it? Reflect on these questions if applicable. If you have never worked on a portfolio, think about portfolios of others you have seen, or imagine how you might go about creating one that is representative of your work in a certain area, as well as personally valuable to you. What might it look like, especially if you were given complete freedom?

FIGURE   **10.3**

Cloze assessment reading level.

CLOZE TEST SCORES	READING LEVEL
Independent	58%–100%
Instructional	44%–57%
Frustration	0%–43%

FIGURE   10.4   Sample cloze passage.

Standardized testing is not going to go away. It is part of _____ fabric of our schools _____ our society. It is _____ business for publishers, and _____ are still used to _____ select, and place students _____—and remove them from—_____ special programs. Still, we _____ can influence how these _____ are given and used.

_____ the school district where _____ teach, pressure from first-_____ second-grade teachers and _____ responses from knowledgeable administrators _____ do away with standardized _____ in those two grades. _____-grade teachers were vocal _____ conveying what they wanted _____ the superintendent, the director of _____ education, and the board of _____. These teachers were tired _____ crying kids, wasted time, _____ an agenda that did _____ serve students first.

Now, _____ when standardized tests are _____, we treat them as _____ separate form of reading _____ I now call _reading-_____ reading_. Because our students are _____ with the format, we _____ it to them through _____ and practice tests. Sure, _____ a waste of time _____ could be better used _____ other ways, but the _____ is students will have _____ take tests throughout their _____ careers, and they need _____ learn how to do _____ successfully. To ignore this _____ is to put them _____ a disadvantage.

One of _____ big objections to standardized _____ is the emphasis on _____ "deficit model." Results are _____ to point up what _____ child can't do. Rather _____ build on the child's _____, standardized tests reinforce weaknesses. _____ to that is the _____-documented fact that standardized _____ are culturally biased toward white middle-class experiences.

If standardized tests are used in perspective, only as a set of numbers from one given day that has little relation to what we are teaching in school, I can live with them.

A portfolio is a collection of representative student work that shows progress. As a type of performance-based assessment, portfolios are extremely popular with many content area teachers. They are certainly not a new idea, at least in some arenas—artists, poets, fashion designers, photographers, and others often choose this means of presentation. Writing teachers and their students have found that a portfolio has multiple advantages: it helps students organize and categorize, make evaluative decisions, problem solve, reflect on their processes and their growth over time, and plan future projects. Presenting one's portfolio is an opportunity to point out verbally (or with the use of visuals) one's strengths, talents, and accomplishments, leading to enhanced self-esteem and confidence.

Afflerbach (2004) recommends portfolio assessment in content area classrooms, citing benefits such as their flexibility and the enhancement of organizational skills, self-assessment, and ability to reflect on personal progress inherent in the process of collecting data and analyzing evidence. Of course, teachers should model ways to use a portfolio and have an active, evolving portfolio of their own.

Portfolio contents

No one set of criteria defines a portfolio. You and your students can determine what to include for your content area, the relative worth of various components, and how it is presented or shared. You can choose a format for presentation that is right for you, whether it be formal or casual, verbal or simply visual, inside your classroom or spread throughout the halls of the school.

Teaching in action: _Math._ Knight (1992) describes her efforts at using a portfolio approach to assessment in an algebra class. Her students suggested the following items to show their efforts and learning: "daily notes, the Personal Budget long-term project, Lottery Project, scale drawing, their best tests, their worst tests, problems of the week, daily class notes, and homework" (p. 71). She found that students attached significant value to certain assignments she did not consider important. Together, teacher and students negotiated a format and structure for the portfolios. Knight decided to have peers evaluate the completed portfolios and devised a grading matrix. She found several advantages to having students grade each other's work: they received immediate, constructive feedback and they learned more as they read other introductions, reflections, and examples of problem solving. Portfolios proved to be an important tool for self-evaluation, as well as a means to celebrate much learning.

It's very important that students retain ownership of the project and are allowed to exercise their voice and creativity. The portfolios they bring in on the last day of class look quite different in terms of cover design and organization. Students enjoy talking about their own work and seeing that of their colleagues. We all have a visible sign that much professional growth and learning took place.

Teaching in action: *English.* Sharon Morley's English classes have a "Portfolio Party" after school hours on a June day. Parents and members of the community are invited to view the products and question the creators. Students are the experts as they interact with the visitors, explaining choices, accepting earned praise, talking of future endeavors, describing how they used technology tools to enhance their products. Their portfolios have a table of contents and examples of their writing in the genres they studied over the year. Their Shakespearean newspapers, which are explained in Chapter 9, are included.

In my Content Area Literacy Education class, the students work all semester toward the goal of completing a portfolio that they can share with cooperating teachers while student teaching and with potential employers later on. I insist that particular things they developed during the course be included:

- Sample reading guides showing that they can apply a variety of strategies
- A literacy autobiography
- Responses to professional journal articles
- An analysis of a textbook series
- An annotated bibliography of literature works they can use in their content area teaching
- A letter to me reflecting on their practicum experiences
- A short reflective essay in response to my prompt, "Describe yourself as a teacher of literacy in your content area, or as a teacher–reader"

My students can choose to add other components: a transcribed interview with middle school students, a list of favorite books and authors, a lesson plan or unit they've designed, photos of bulletin boards—anything that represents them as future teachers and exemplifies their emerging personal philosophy.

Figure 10.5 lists items that can be included in portfolios. Choose from among these and add others unique to your objectives and goals—tie and weave them together with a theme, reflections, unifying quotes, a purpose.

Assessing and scoring portfolios

It's vital for students to know how their portfolios will be evaluated. Depending on the content area and the teacher's purposes, criteria will vary. For example, Diehm (2004) gave his students a checklist to make his requirements and expectations clear. He included the following specific directions for electronic portfolios:

- The portfolio has an opening page that introduces the student, explains the portfolio, and shows creativity (a minimum of four aesthetic features, such as borders, photos, or music clips).
- The portfolio includes a specified number of hyperlinked pages that represent the student's best work.
- The portfolio is user friendly, leading a viewer easily from point to point; it shows exceptional effort in the number of works presented; and it is aesthetically appealing. (p. 794)

FIGURE   10.5   Potential content area portfolio inclusions.

- lab reports
- drawings and sketches
- scripts of interviews or dialogues
- poems (original or collected)
- interpretations of or responses to literature
- autobiographical essays
- favorite quotes
- samples of creative writing
- URLs for blogs or student-created websites or work posted on the Internet
- completed math, science, or technology problems with an explanation of the problem-solving process
- reflections on one's writing process
- architectural designs (perhaps for an imaginary building or city)
- compare–contrast essay on people in the discipline

- musical compositions
- outlines and plans for future projects and dreams
- correspondence with pen pals or with business representatives
- letters to the editor (possibly published!)
- book or movie reviews and/or trailers
- samples of collaborative work (could take a variety of forms)
- reflections on personal growth in a subject area
- document-based essays that show synthesis skills
- interpretation of data in graphs or charts
- memoirs
- awards or certificates for achievements
- audio, video, or computer-generated samples of student work

Teaching in action: *Multidisciplinary.* Berryman and Russell (2001) describe one school's experience using and scoring portfolios across the curriculum. Two of the required pieces had to be from a content area other than English and had to be "transactive" in nature; that is, they had to write to communicate with a real-world audience. The state's purpose was to assess schools rather than individuals, but the teachers realized over time that they could learn from scoring the portfolios how to be better teachers of writing and how to help their students be better writers across the curriculum.

The portfolios were scored using a rubric (explained in the next section) with four performance levels: *Novice, Apprentice, Proficient,* and *Distinguished.* Berryman, an English teacher, reports that, during a summer workshop, "I realized for the first time that scoring portfolio pieces could be a way to rethink teaching and learning, define weaknesses, and establish an instructional plan for a department or school-wide effort" (p. 78). When teachers in content areas other than English were trained to score the portfolios, they were surprised at how much they learned about the students by reading their writing across the disciplines. They also discovered that using writing in their classes had many benefits in terms of both assessment and instruction, without gobbling up precious time:

> The portfolio assessment was specifically designed to encourage professional development, to produce positive "washback" from assessment, rather than the all-too-common negative results of assessment, where teachers teach to the test, and valuable curriculum and teaching are crowded out.... The portfolio assessment was broad enough that it made room for new things in the curricula of various disciplines, instead of crowding things out, as external assessments often do. (p. 80)

Teachers have found that writing in all classes improves students' writing and thinking, and also functions as an informal, time-saving way for teachers to assess ongoing learning. A biochemistry teacher pointed out, "I never give tests, because I don't need to, because I have this daily written interaction with my students. I know where they are, I know what they know. We have a discourse in class all the time" (p. 81).

The use of teacher-assessed portfolios across the curriculum has helped this Kentucky school, these teachers, and their students. The portfolio scores are rising, teachers are collaborating and talking about writing projects and students, and "many teachers work seriously at assigning writing that is purposeful and meaningful in terms of teaching—not just assessing—their content" (p. 3). That's assessment at its authentic best.

Using Rubrics

Rubrics, used with performance-based activities that demonstrate learning, are scoring devices that help you assess and evaluate student work (Goodrich, 1996/1997). They consist of the following:

- a set of criteria that a score is based on (developed by the teacher alone or together with the student)
- a standard or a method to determine levels of achievement that will translate into scores.

Rubrics can be used at any level with many assessment types. The benefits of well-composed rubrics are many, including helping teachers score students' work fairly and accurately, giving students valuable information about what qualities their work should exhibit, and helping teachers talk together about goals and evaluation. Sometimes, teachers ask students to determine what criteria should be applied to certain assignments, thus guiding their thinking about the components of projects and processes. Figure 10.6 shows a rubric that an undergraduate education student made as part of a unit on Jewish refugees in the United States. A number of websites, including www.rubrics.com and rubistar.4teachers.org, provide templates that can make creating rubrics quite easy.

Teaching in action: *Math.* Carroll (1999) shows how teachers can use simple rubrics with short questions to elicit writing that can be used to develop and assess mathematical reasoning. For example, students can analyze the mistakes in their answers or in the answers of others; Carroll points out that students who are accustomed to making hypotheses, building on prior ideas, and reasoning to move toward a correct answer are not intimidated by errors.

The following problem was used to assess students' mathematical reasoning: "Sheila said, 'I can draw a triangle with two right angles.' Do you agree with Sheila? Explain your reasoning" (Carroll, p. 251). A five-level rubric was designed and refined using the students' examples.

Score

Level 0 off-task response or no response

Level 1 incorrect response with some attempt at reasoning

Level 2 correct response with unclear or incomplete reasoning

Level 3 correct response with good reasoning

Level 4 correct response with exemplary reasoning applying knowledge of triangles and angles

Carroll suggests that classroom teachers can devise even simpler rubrics, such as a three-point scale, to categorize

| FIGURE | **10.6** | A student-made presentation rubric. |

Name: _____ Date: _____

SAFE HAVEN: AMERICA'S ONLY HOLOCAUST REFUGEE SHELTER

(1) Presentation is well organized

0 Not all group members participate
2 All participate, but no organization or preparation is evident
4 Some organization apparent, but presentation is unclear
6 Organized, but presentation is not complete
8 Generally well organized with ideas logically arranged, good preparation
10 Excellent organization, all ideas are clearly ordered, well rehearsed

(2) Introduction

0 Ineffective introduction
2 Generic introduction
4 Introduction is entertaining but not relevant
6 Introduction is adequate but fails to make an impact
8 Introduction is informative but does not gain attention
10 Excellent introduction; both informative and attention getting

(3) Presentation is enhanced by visual aids

0 No visuals aids used
2 One ineffective visual aid is used
4 One visual aid is effective
6 Good visuals effectively used
8 Excellent visuals used to effectively reinforce presentation theme
10 Excellent visuals and technology effectively reinforce presentation theme

(4) Background information creates a setting in the audience's mind

0 No background information is discussed
2 Poor, irrelevant background information is discussed
4 Adequate background information, but lacking key elements
6 Adequate and accurate background information is discussed
8 Complete background information is discussed
10 Complete background information, relevant to presentation theme

(5) Presentation utilizes both assigned novels

0 No mention of either novel
2 One novel mentioned ineffectively
4 Both novels mentioned ineffectively
6 Both novels analyzed but without solid examples
8 Both novels analyzed adequately with good examples
10 Both novels incorporated fully to enhance the presentation theme

(6) Describe the living conditions at Fort Ontario

0 No discussion of the living conditions at Fort Ontario
2 Little is mentioned of the living conditions
4 Discusses only the refugees' of government's role

6 Discusses both the refugees' and government's role
8 Complete description of living conditions, but not relating to theme
10 Complete description of living conditions, relevant to presentation theme

(7) Describe the difficulties that the refugees faced in America

0 No mention of any refugee hardships
2 Little is mentioned of refugee difficulties
4 Discusses only internal/external examples
6 Discusses only political/social examples
8 Completely discusses all issues facing refugees
10 Completely discusses all issues, relevant to presentation theme

(8) Describe the relationship between Oswegonians and the refugees

0 No mention of any relationship between the townspeople and the refugees
2 Discusses only negative relationships
4 Discusses only positive relationships
6 Discusses both positive and negative relationships without examples
8 Excellent description of relationships supported by examples
10 Excellent description and examples, relevant to presentation theme

(9) Explanation for closing the Fort Ontario Emergency Refugee Shelter

0 No explanation or discussion of the fort's closure
2 Inadequate discussion of the fort's closure
4 Discussion of fort's closure is incomplete
6 Complete discussion of the events that led to the fort's closure
8 Explains closing and discusses refugees' lives
10 Explains closing, refugees' lives, relevant to presentation theme

(10) What should the federal government do in a similar situation today?

0 No discussion of your feelings
2 Plan is unacceptable
4 Plan is acceptable but lacks complete explanation
6 Good argument, but does not relate to Fort Ontario
8 Solid argument that relates to Fort Ontario
10 Persuasive argument that relates to Fort Ontario

Total Points Earned on Presentation _____

Comments: _____

_____

—*Eric Sullivan*

problem-solving responses representing *Little understanding, Making progress,* and *Good understanding.*

Using a rubric like this gives you knowledge of individuals, as well as groups. Carroll reports that this problem was given to 10 classes of fifth and sixth graders who used a curriculum that implemented the NCTM standards, emphasizing reasoning, and 10 classes that used more traditional programs—the results, not surprisingly, showed a contrast. Thirty percent of the fifth graders and 53 percent of the sixth graders using the *standards*-based curriculum scored at Level 3 or 4, while only 4 percent of the fifth graders and 13 percent of the sixth graders from traditional classes reached those levels. Try teaching a lesson or presenting a problem a certain way to your morning classes and a different way to the afternoon classes. Then, compare the students' written responses about their reasoning to assess their understanding and to give you insight as to the kinds of reasoning each method elicits.

Student-Led Conferences

Student-led conferences, or student–teacher–parent/guardian conferences, with or without portfolios, are gaining popularity and even replacing traditional parent–teacher conferences in many middle and high schools. They provide an opportunity for students to present and explain their work, as well as reflect on their progress and set new goals—to be an active participant in the assessment process. Such a conference involves a three-way (or more if another parent or invited adult is involved) discussion with the student showing her work, reflecting on her progress, and inviting and answering questions from parents or guardians. Conference preparation requires the student to synthesize ideas and work and to self-assess in terms of skills attained, content understood, desired future explorations and ambitions, and so forth. It's a wonderful chance for the student to practice presentation skills and to listen to input from adults. Together, the team sets goals, talks about ways the student can be supported at home, and celebrates the learner and her accomplishments thus far. Literacy issues (e.g., a student's outside reading habits, anxiety about speaking in front of groups, or favorite writing genres) can be addressed. McLaughlin (2000) suggests giving the parents a reaction form to complete and send to school with their child the next day. This provides an additional opportunity for the parent and child to talk, as well as a structure for getting feedback and additional comments. The form can be added to the student's portfolio.

Your job is to facilitate the conference and ensure that it remains positive—the student, parents/guardian, and teacher are all on the same side and all want the best for the student. An honest discussion of the areas in need of improvement, along with suggestions of helpful strategies and materials, need not seem threatening or disheartening. Another of your roles is to provide a comparable experience for those students without parents or whose parents/guardians cannot come to a conference. Relatives or neighbors, other teachers, or community members can volunteer to participate in a portfolio celebration or conference.

A student–teacher–parent conference may have ameliorated Eric's situation. He was a strong reader but a struggling student in junior and senior high. Eric's mother describes the numerous impersonal, demeaning, and embarrassing notices of impending failure that were sent home "To the parents of . . . " (Nierstheimer, 2000, p. 34). The reports contained code numbers representing Eric's flaws or misdemeanors—"the progress reports did not communicate with us in any personal or pleasant way and represented to us the lack of power and respect that I believe parents of struggling learners feel" (p. 34). She contrasts this with what might have been:

> As the parent of Eric, I wish that more teachers had taken the time to *know* him . . . to see his strengths, abilities, and interests, not just point out his failures. I wish more teachers had cared more about who he was as a person than how he performed as a student. (p. 35)

Are we listening?

How Is Technology Changing Assessment?

Assessment is changing along with virtually every other aspect of education, and many teachers are thrilled with the innovative ways they can conduct formative assessments as they teach their daily lessons. Quellmalz et al. (2008) describe the use of simulations that allow science students to explore relationships among variables in models of complex systems such as weather systems and ecosystems, and to investigate in ways not normally available in classrooms, such as experimenting with phenomena that are too dangerous, too expensive, or too large or small. On their computers, students can "manipulate an array of variables, observe the impact, and try again" (p. 193). The technology provides immediate feedback.

Salend (2009) describes a teacher using an interactive whiteboard as she teaches about poetic devices while her students use wireless clickers (classroom response systems) to respond to her questions. She then makes instructional decisions based on their answers to her questions. Another teacher uses assessment activities involving posting on a wiki, creating podcasts, and using presentation software.

Yet another works with a student who has cognitive disabilities to maintain a digital portfolio as an alternative to statewide testing. Salend sees advantages of technology-based assessment for students, including increased motivation, as well as advantages for teachers, who can easily monitor students and adapt instruction accordingly.

However, technology should not be used indiscriminately in assessment. Salend (2009) offers factors to consider before using technology to implement assessment, including:

- Will the assessment technique and technology allow me and my students to measure meaningful skills and instructional outcomes in a direct and complete way? . . .

- Will the assessment technique and technology allow me to accommodate my students' individual differences (e.g., disability, cultural and linguistic background, and socioeconomic status)?

- Will the assessment technique and technology help me plan, deliver, evaluate, and revise my instructional program to enhance student learning? (p. 50)

Some of the published materials designed for computers are really very traditional. For example, the Accelerated Reading program provides multiple-choice tests for students to take after reading those books for which the company has determined difficulty levels. Schmidt's (2008) research points out problematic aspects of programs such as AR, which tests comprehension by means of literal level questions only, and whose advertisement asks the question, "How could a teacher know whether students comprehended what they read?" (p. 209). She concludes that many, more-authentic means are available for teachers to assess student comprehension. She cautions:

> when schools teach children long books are worth more points than short books, and when schools teach children to consume books and regurgitate answers . . . if we continue to let AR ask the questions, we may very well lose the interest of our students and create literal readers who only want to "get points" and be done with reading. (p. 210)

One option that technology affords is that of collecting and responding to student work via e-mail and other electronic means. As students develop ideas and draft texts, teachers can quickly send feedback and suggestions to them. Attending to student work through electronic correspondence can be helpful and reinforcing to students as they are immersed in the process of research, the synthesis of ideas through essays, or creative writing. Students who might be reluctant to call on a teacher in class may

BookTalk   10.3

At the beginning of summer vacation, Allegra finds out her violin performance has been deemed worthy of allowing her to enter a competition. *The Mozart Season,* by Virginia Euwer Wolff (2000), lets the reader in on a lot of assessment: her teacher's formative assessments and subsequent changes in instruction, Allegra's sometimes painful self-assessments and crucial decisions based on them, and the final, outside evaluation given by the judges at the competition. Read *The Mozart Season* in your teacher role—Allegra and her violin teacher will help you reflect on how you can use assessment and instruction in complementary ways to help your students thrive as learners and people.

actually feel more comfortable discussing problems and learning struggles using the computer. An ongoing assessment before students turn in final papers makes sense. Continue to experiment and find new ways of using computers to assess and instruct—if you find that the two are merging, that's a good sign that your assessment is authentic, meaningful, contextualized, and helpful.

Electronic portfolios are becoming popular with students and teachers. Students can burn personal CDs, scan work, and design formats for presenting their work. They can learn to incorporate text, video, photos taken with a digital camera, voices, background music, charts, and graphs. Students are designing their own Web pages to show their work and evidence of learning. High school students can invite the admissions staffs of prospective colleges to log on to their websites to get a picture of their academic work and of their lives. Diehm (2004) created an electronic portfolio project that allowed his students to evaluate their work and put their perceived best in a Web-based collection, which could grow and evolve over students' academic careers.

Assessment of Students with Special Needs

You can learn a lot about all of your students from the many *formative* (while work or a course is in progress) and *summative* (final) assessment procedures available to you, as well as from attending to the students and their work as you teach. But you may wonder whether you should know or do anything extra for those students with special learning challenges. I believe that you should take advantage of any resource at your disposal. If some of your students have had formal evaluations to determine whether they have specific learning disabilities, for example, you may find it valuable to read the evaluation team's records and test reports to better understand those students as learners. You might find that a certain student fails your chapter tests because he has difficulty reading the exam, not because he doesn't understand the material; another might perform poorly on your essay exams because of a specific writing disability. Once you know this, you can make accommodations in terms of your forms of assessment, as well as your expectations and instruction.

There is also much to learn from talking with the reading specialists and resource teachers who work with your students. You might learn the results of a diagnostic test, such as an informal reading inventory (IRI), given to a student. An IRI consists of a series of passages of increasing difficulty that are used to determine the reader's word identification and comprehension strategies, as well as a reading level. If any assessments (other than the typical ones) were done, it makes sense for you to know about them in order to inform your instruction. For example, if testing revealed that Shannon was a word-by-word reader who focused on reading each word correctly instead of constructing and confirming meaning, the reading specialist might help Shannon realize that generating meaning should be her major consideration. Given this information, a science teacher might encourage Shannon to "self-monitor"—read a few textbook paragraphs and explain out loud what she is thinking and understanding. If Shannon can restate the ideas in her own words, she has comprehended the text.

One framework used in many schools that involves assessment and instruction integrally connected is *Response to Intervention* (RTI), which is a multi-tiered model. In the first tier, all students receive high-quality, appropriate instruction in their classrooms. This is the part of the model you, as a content area teacher, will likely be most involved in. Its focus is on creating an environment conducive to student achievement. Students who are not succeeding are evaluated to figure out what's putting them at risk for failure, and then receive targeted academic intervention of some sort to help them learn. For example, small group instruction on particular decoding or comprehension skills might occur at this level. A subsequent tier involves individualized assessment and instruction for those students for whom the instruction happening at the other levels has not adequately helped. At all stages, close monitoring of progress is essential. Proactive schoolwide screening ensures that no child's needs are unidentified or ignored. You can learn more about the RTI model and its potential application in articles written by teachers and administrators whose schools have adopted it, and through professional books such as

RTI: A Practitioner's Guide to Implementing Response to Intervention (Mellard & Johnson, 2008).

You might be the tier one teacher who initiates further testing for a student you see struggling in your science, social studies, or other content area course. You're not expected to have all of the answers, but you might be the first to suspect that there is a problem that has not yet been identified. Strive to work well with the literacy coach, reading specialist, and/or other support people in your district; everyone should want the best for the students and should work together to see that the best happens. Communication, collaboration, and consistency among all teachers working to help a student succeed in literacy and content learning are crucial.

"Everyone" should also include the students' parents or guardians. Families may have to take students for medical testing or other specialized forms of assessment, the results of which bring new information to bear on academic situations. For example, when my son Christopher was in fourth grade, his performance took a dive. Every report card he brought home looked worse in every category, and it appeared as if the problem was due to a lack of effort or laziness—although test grades remained high, his homework completion was inconsistent, his work in school left unfinished. His teacher, Chris, and his parents formed a team to solve the puzzle, but none of us alone or together could figure it out. Chris was a cooperative child who said he thought he was doing the work and didn't mean to cause trouble or get away with anything. We tried checklists, reminders, parent–teacher phone calls, planners—all to no avail. It wasn't until I took Chris to an optometrist the following summer that it was discovered he had severe perceptual problems that caused an organizational disability. Once we had the assessment, and a pair of glasses, we could work on the real problem rather than the "lack of effort" that was the easiest, but

BookTalk 10.4

Mrs. Olinski wants to put together a sixth-grade team for a state-sponsored academic competition. Her choices surprise people, but you'll discover as you read *The View from Saturday* (1996), E. L. Konigsburg's second Newbery Medal winner, the wisdom of this first assessment decision and those made throughout the months as she coaches her team to the state finals. The final performance-based evaluation will keep you, a future assessor, on the edge of your seat. You may teach differently after you experience this super example of individual excellence combining with cooperative learning under the direction of a master teacher-assessor.

inaccurate, inference based on the data from school. So, please don't give up if you can't figure out exactly what a student's problem is; persistence, creative thinking, flexibility, expert help, and patience may be necessary. And even if you never identify the cause, don't conclude that the student just wants to fail.

May (2001) debunks "The Laziness Myth," the belief that it's up to the student to learn to read well, regardless of text difficulty or quality, or, in other words, "If he'd just try harder, he'd succeed" (p. 141). He suggests ways that teachers and assistants can help students grapple with texts that are unclear, poorly written, or just plain too hard for their present capabilities. They can teach students to monitor their own reading comprehension through modeling and asking questions about meaning-making; for example, "What is my goal for reading this? How can I picture the events (or steps) the author wants me to follow? What information is missing or confusing that makes me not understand?" (p. 159). Perhaps his strongest suggestion for helping those students who are not succeeding in our classrooms concerns the selection of materials we ask them to read. "With at least 30,000 new school-age trade books being published each decade, there is very little reason for teachers and administrators to have their students stumbling along with no more motivation than to 'get through the textbook assignment'" (p. 158).

How Should English Learners Be Tested in Content Area Subjects?

Shafer Willner, Rivera, and Acosta (2009) help us understand the common misunderstandings about accommodations for the English learners, including those related to assessment, in our classrooms. For instance, they point out that often these students are given the same accommodations provided for students with disabilities, despite the differing needs of the two populations. It's inappropriate to offer an accommodation intended to lessen the effects of a physical or cognitive disability when English learners need instead measures that will address their sociocultural and linguistic needs. So, for example, some EL students might need extra time on tests to allow them to process the language of the passages and questions, or they might need to use bilingual dictionaries. Others may need to have the test read to them. Accommodations should be made on an individual basis; our EL students are at differing levels of proficiency and have unique backgrounds. The authors recommend a helpful site for teachers, the ELL Accommodations Database, at www.ells.ceee.gwu.edu.

APPLICATION ACTIVITY 10.2 (SEE PAGE 310)

ASSESSING ONE'S TEACHING AND LITERACY GROWTH

I hope you can see by now how important and integral a part assessment plays in your teaching. But it's not just students you'll be assessing. Every day, every class period, you should evaluate how your lessons went, how successful they were in terms of student learning, and then make major adjustments or fine-tune accordingly. I've heard teachers say they feel sorry for their first-period classes—each day those students get their teacher's first efforts, but with practice, the lesson gets better throughout the day. (Actually, some schools rotate class schedules, for this and other reasons.)

Figure 10.7 shows questions that might help you evaluate your lessons, especially in terms of the literacy involved. You can adapt them to suit your particular subject, students, and needs.

It's possible that at times your lessons seem to be going fine, but your long-range goals are not being accomplished as expected. Every so often, at the end of a unit, quarterly, or whenever student report cards come out, ask yourself questions similar to those presented in Figure 10.7—focus on your teaching, curriculum, and materials more generally instead of on particular lessons.

FIGURE 10.7

Questions that guide self-assessment of lessons in terms of literacy.

1. Did I open the lesson with an interesting initiating activity—a question, quote, cartoon, scenario? Did the students seem motivated by it?

2. Did I prepare thoroughly in terms of my own reading, researching, and learning about the topic I taught?

3. Were students actively engaged in listening, talking, reading, or writing? How was their thinking challenged?

4. Did I provide further resources so they can independently pursue the topic? Is my classroom library adequate for the unit we're studying? Do I have several genres of relevant materials? Do I have different perspectives represented? Have I given appropriate booktalks to entice them to read? Did I provide relevant website URLs or help them determine keywords to use for an online search?

5. In general, how well have I helped the students meet our goals and objectives for this lesson?

Ongoing Assessment

I've stressed throughout this book my conviction that you must be a reader and a writer in order to help your students develop good literacy skills and habits. No matter your starting point, you should have some way of assessing yourself as your career develops. Think now about starting a record-keeping system to track your literacy accomplishments. I keep a dated journal where I record the titles of books I read and a brief response, often indicating how the book might connect to my teaching and curriculum. You could do the same with articles you read. You might participate, along with your students, in completing a genre wheel by placing a dot in the appropriate category each time you finish a text, and setting goals to branch out to a variety of reading materials as the year goes on. See Figure 10.8 for an example of a genre wheel.

You can also keep a teaching journal where you record classroom events large and small, reflect on puzzling pedagogical issues (e.g., whether your students' current report card grades adequately reflect their growth and accomplishments), write out possible strategies to improve instruction or your relationships with the students, and record new ideas and materials you've discovered. Teachers who do this are often very glad when they read over the journal after several months and are able to see that they and their students have traveled far from their starting point and have progressed academically and socially. A colleague of mine provided this reflection: "I often feel too busy to write down what's happening in my teaching. But when I do, I love myself because when I find it later, the next time I have to teach it, I feel so thrilled that this is not uncharted territory. I've been here before and I can improve on what happened" (Jean Ann, June 2000).

Figure 10.9 contains a list of biographical or autobiographical accounts of teachers that are fascinating reflections on their own learning and growth, as well as that of their students. Figure 10.9, and Appendix Figure 10.9, also include books written by researchers who spent time in teachers' classrooms, observing change and eliciting self-assessment from those they studied.

Teacher Portfolios

Most schools have a system in place for evaluating teachers, especially new teachers, and providing feedback and suggestions for improvement and growth. Perhaps an administrator, teacher mentor, or peer coach looks over a lesson plan, observes a class, interviews the teacher, and afterward discusses what she sees and listens to the teacher's perception of

FIGURE 10.8 Sample genre wheel.

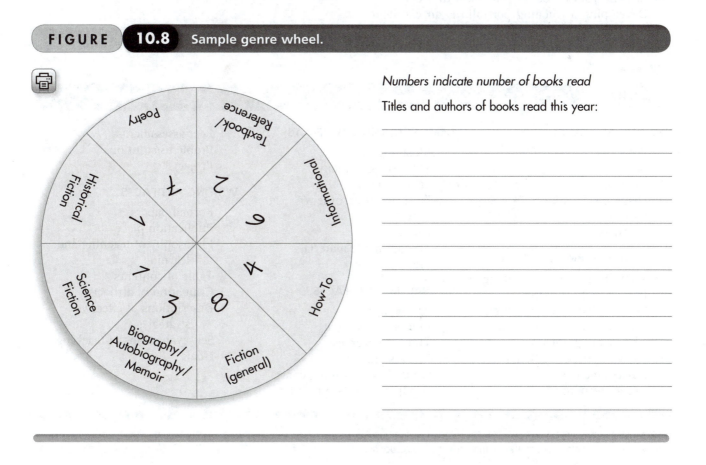

Numbers indicate number of books read

Titles and authors of books read this year:

FIGURE 10.9

Works by and about teachers.

See more suggested titles in Appendix Figure 10.9.

Atwell, N. (2007). *The Reading Zone: How to Help Kids Become Skilled, Passionate, Habitual, Critical Readers.* New York: Scholastic.

Codell, E. R. (2009). *Educating Esmé: Diary of a Teacher's First Year.* Expanded edition. Chapel Hill, NC: Algonquin Books.

Miller, D. (2009). *The Book Whisperer.* San Francisco: Jossey-Bass.

Sitomer, A. (2008). *Teaching Teens and Reaping Results: In a Wi-Fi, Hip-Hop, Where-has-all-the-sanity-gone World.* New York: Scholastic Professional.

Wilhelm, J. D. (2008). *You Gotta BE the Book: Teaching Engaged and Reflective Reading with Adolescents* (2nd ed.). New York: Teachers College Press, and Urbana, IL: National Council of Teachers of English.

the lesson. Use such opportunities to reflect on your teaching and the goals you've set for yourself and your students. Be sure to address literacy issues relating to yourself and your classes as you talk with peers.

Developing a teaching portfolio is an excellent way to understand yourself as part of the teaching profession. The process, similar to the one described

for students, involves selection, reflection, verbalizing your philosophy, making connections to others in the field, and presenting yourself to others. What avenues are you pursuing as a reader and writer? What sorts of support could you use?

Wilcox (1996) encourages prospective teachers to develop what she calls *smart portfolios,* requiring systematic self-assessment and sharing in order to experience the power of reflective thinking. She introduces five essential elements: reading, interacting, demonstrating, writing, and thinking. She has her students choose some kind of container (e.g., a three-ring binder or pocket portfolio) to organize artifacts that show evidence of thoughtfulness and growth in each of these categories. Figure 10.10 shows the examples Wilcox provides of a portfolio's contents.

Wilcox states, "Teachers who know about assessment as instruction will never be satisfied with a portfolio *just* for assessment. The smart portfolio is a powerful tool for professional development and lifelong learning" (p. 173). So, don't think of a portfolio in a passive sense, as being just a showcase for past accomplishments. Wilcox (1997) promises, "An active portfolio which can generate ideas and initiate new ways of thinking offers unlimited possibilities for enhancing teaching and learning" (p. 37). Be sure to share your thinking journal and ongoing portfolio with your students.

APPLICATION ACTIVITY 10.3 (SEE PAGE 310)

FIGURE 10.10 Contents of a smart portfolio.

READING ARTIFACTS

Book list
Book notes
Summaries
Diagrams
Overviews
Outlines

THINKING (JOURNAL) ARTIFACTS

Thinking about our thinking
Responses to prompts
Written dialogues with texts
Mind wanderings and maps
Charts and graphs
Steps in problem solving
Process memos
Reader response

DEMONSTRATING ARTIFACTS

Illustrations
Teacher assessments
Lesson plans
Feedback from others
Video
Checklists
Teacher-made materials
Presentations

INTERACTING ARTIFACTS

Photographs
Journal assessment
Thinking exercises
In-class entries
Group brainstorming charts
Group consensus products

Peer assessments
Problems/solutions
Projects

WRITING ARTIFACTS

Formal papers
Publication piece
Philosophy of teaching and learning
Table of contents
Evaluation of artifacts
Descriptions of effective strategies
Self-evaluations of teaching
Goals

From Bonita L. Wilcox (1996), "Smart Portfolios for Teachers in Training." *Journal of Adolescent & Adult Literacy, 40*(3), pp. 172–179. Reprinted with permission of the author and the International Reading Association.

Outside Assessments of Teaching

How does one distinguish good teaching from bad, excellent teaching from mediocre? As a student, you made judgments of teachers all the time, which may or may not have matched evaluations by administrators, parents, community, or even your peers. The criteria used might have been different, as were the vantage points and purposes. State education departments use certain criteria to certify teachers, often including tests, which are subject to the same concerns expressed over other types of tests. Does a perfect score on a multiple-choice exam about teaching theories and management strategies always correlate with good classroom performance? Campbell (2000) offers this critique of the "general knowledge" portion of the Praxis Series examination, which many states require teachers to pass and which he prepares future teachers to take:

> A typical standardized test. It is mostly a test of recall of information, and I treat it as a test of short-term memory. It is filled with trivia of little significance for effective teaching. This sort of test controls the future for these students. . . . I am going to propose that, if we must have such a written assessment at all, it at least be an authentic test. (p. 405)

In a move consistent with the whole field of assessment, many states have tried to devise measures that are more performance-based and authentic. For example, some teachers are required to submit videos of their teaching for outside evaluation. But is that clip reflective of the teacher's usual style and way of relating to students? Is there a way to objectively score what is seen so that there is inter-rater reliability (the likelihood that different evaluators would arrive at the same or similar scores)? Could bias play a role in such an evaluation? And what about the time involved at both ends—preparing and scoring—and the cost of evaluating the videos? Similar concerns surround portfolio evaluation and other forms of teacher evaluation, as the search continues for better ways to assess teaching.

More teachers are now taking advantage of the opportunity to become National Board certified; the voluntary certification is currently available in 24 areas. The process of applying is extensive and expensive, but one many feel is very valuable. Teachers are required to compile a portfolio according to standards and criteria set by the National Board, consisting of classroom teaching videos, lesson plans, examples of professional accomplishments, samples of student work, and written commentaries in which the teacher reflects on what he or she is doing and why. The second part consists of a day spent at one of several designated assessment centers, participating in exercises designed around challenging teacher issues. Among other things, teachers evaluate other teachers' practice, answer questions in interviews, demonstrate a knowledge of their disciplinary area, assess student needs and learning, and take exams in their fields. They give interpretive summaries of their accomplishments with families and communities and in the profession. More information can be obtained about National Board Certification at www.nbpts.org.

CONCLUSION

The assessment of literacy in a content area classroom is a major topic, one that requires your continued attention as you gain experience and get to know your students. You've been given information and some ways to think about literacy assessment in general; ways you can assess literacy in your classroom while you instruct for and encourage literacy and growth in understanding of content. I have advocated the use of performance-based, authentic assessments that contribute to, rather than detract from, the wise use of the limited instructional time you are given with your precious learners, who are developing at different rates and in different ways. I'd like to emphasize once again that your goals, your teaching, and your ways of assessing must be consistent. Zessoules and Gardner (1991) say it well:

> Rich modes of assessment cannot be activated in a vacuum. Just as standardized tests have produced a testing culture, educators interested in reform must recognize and examine the need for a classroom culture that will sustain the values, merits and practices of more authentic forms of assessment. . . . If one is going to ask students to grasp scientific principles, compose a melody, or write compelling dialogues, then one needs a curriculum that gives students frequent opportunities to investigate, test, and observe nature; to compose and experiment with many melodies; and to craft, rehearse, and revise many scenes, many times. Just as standardized testing has driven curriculum and instruction in our schools, so too the implementation of new measures must influence and shape the daily life and activities in the classroom. Unless new modes of assessment reach deep into school culture, incorporating pedagogical approaches, expectations and standards of performance, and the education of students' own capacities for self-critical judgment, new forms of testing will be as discontinuous with teaching and learning as they have ever been. (p. 50)

Answers to Action Research 10.C: the, and, big, results, sort, in, various, teachers, tests, In, I, and, thoughtful, helped, tests, First, in, to, elementary, education, of, and, not, even, required, a, that, test, unfamiliar, teach, demonstrations, it's, that, in, reality, to, school, to, so, reality, at, my, testing, the, used, the, than, strengths, Added, well, tests.

WEBSITES · CHAPTER 10 · Access these links using the Kane Resource Site.

ELL Accommodations Database
http://ells.ceee.gwu.edu

International Reading Association Position on High-Stakes Testing
www.reading.org/General/AboutIRA/Position Statements/HighStakesPosition.aspx

Katherine Paterson
www.terabithia.com

National Board for Professional Teaching Standards
www.nbpts.org

NCTE Resolution on Developing a Test Taker's Bill of Rights
www.ncte.org/positions/statements/testtakers billrights

NCTE Resolution on Urging Reconsideration of High Stakes Testing
www.ncte.org/positions/statements/highstakes testrecons

Rubrics
www.rubrics.com, rubistar.4teachers.org

APPLICATION ACTIVITIES

10.1 Try your hand at preparing a cloze passage and then have a student or a peer complete it so you can practice scoring. Share your cloze passage and receive additional feedback on the Kane Resource Site. I think you're more likely to use this assessment once you experience how simple it is to use and how useful the information can be for helping students.

10.2 Perrone (1991) considers large educational and social purposes as integral to the reconsideration of assessment. Here's what he envisions as a goal:

> [We] want our students to become *active* readers and writers—individuals who read newspapers and magazines, find beauty in a poem or love story, see Romeo and Juliet in their own lives. We want students to develop an optimistic view about the world and their place in it, to take time to really look at the trees or enjoy a sunset or study the stars. We want them to participate in politics and community life, have a vision of themselves as thoughtful mothers and fathers, understand and value work in all its dimensions, and become sensitive to the needs and values of older citizens. We want them to not only be able to locate the Republic of South Africa on a map, but to understand apartheid and feel the pain associated with it. We need to find student assessments that will help us achieve rather than thwart such purposes. (pp. 164–165)

Using this quote as a model, write a paragraph that describes your purposes for your classroom and your courses. What are some specific examples of what you want your students to become and to be able to do? When you have finished, think about the types of student assessments that might help you "achieve rather than thwart such purposes" (p. 165).

10.3 Compose a preliminary introductory page for a teaching portfolio, along with a potential table of contents showing the types of things you would eventually like to include to show the kind of teacher you hope to be. Choose a suitable container to collect your artifacts to begin a smart portfolio that will facilitate your self-assessment and professional growth.

chapter 11

Content Area Literacy: Envisioning Your Future

"How many a man has dated a new era in his life from the reading of a book."

THOREAU, WALDEN

One of the first things I asked you to do as an active reader of this textbook was to write down words you associate with the word *utopia*. Reading *The Giver* and participating in the related exercises likely enhanced your understanding of the term, the concept, and the genre of utopian/dystopian literature. At one point (Activating Prior Knowledge I.2), I asked you to imagine a utopian school, your version of educational perfection.

Now, I'd like to return to that theme. Because you've read much more, and you've learned and discussed and written about a variety of issues related to literacy in the content areas, you have more to bring to your vision and dreams of what schools and classrooms—especially *your* classroom—should be. You have made yourself part of a long tradition of educational reform and philosophy-building. There have always been critics of schools and educational practices, visionaries who promoted innovative methods, often opening alternative schools in order to teach without the constraints of the status quo. The names John Dewey, Edward Austin Sheldon, Maria Montessori, John Holt, Ivan Illich, Paulo Freire, Frank Smith, and Jonathan Kozol are familiar to many. B. F. Skinner envisioned a utopian school (which some critics consider dystopian) in *Walden Two*. Figure 11.1 lists some books you can explore to get an idea of the variety of the theories and the dedication and passion of the reformers (this list is continued in Appendix Figure 11.1). Be aware that this list includes books that may express diametrically opposed philosophies—I want you to get a variety of perspectives.

In this book, you've already met some of the experts who have spoken out against our present system of schooling and offered their versions of what schools should be. This is a time of rapid change and much talk of the future. An entire issue (January–March 2000) of the scholarly journal *Reading Research Quarterly* was devoted to the theme "Envisioning the Future of Literacy." One article, by Elizabeth Birr Moje, is entitled, "What Will Classrooms and Schools Look Like in the New Millennium?" That's an important question for you as you begin your career—you have the opportunity to be

FIGURE 11.1

Books by or about educational critics, innovators, and visionaries.

See more suggested titles in Appendix Figure 11.1.

Gruwell, E. (2008). *Teach with Your Heart: Lessons I Learned from the Freedom Writers.* New York: Broadway Books.

Kelly, F. S., McCain, T., & Jukes, I. (2009). *Teaching the Digital Generation: No More Cookie-Cutter High Schools.* Thousand Oaks, CA: Corwin Press.

Kozol, J. (2007). *Letters to a Young Teacher.* New York: Crown Publishers.

Kozol, J. (2009). *On Being a Teacher.* Oxford, England: Oneworld.

Nathan, L. F. (2009). *The Hardest Questions Aren't on the Test: Lessons from an Innovative Urban School.* Boston: Beacon Press.

Newkirk, T. (2009). *Holding On to Good Ideas in a Time of Bad Ones: Six Literacy Principles Worth Fighting For.* Portsmouth, NH: Heinemann.

Noddings, N. (2005). *The Challenge to Care in Schools: An Alternative Approach to Education* (2nd ed.). New York: Teachers College Press.

Obama, B. (2009). *The Obama Education Plan: An Education Week Guide.* San Francisco: Jossey-Bass.

Olson, K. (2009). *Wounded by School: Recapturing the Joy in Learning and Standing Up to Old School Culture.* New York: Teachers College Press.

Ravitch, D. (2010). *The Death and Life of the Great American School System: How Testing and Choice Are Undermining Education.* New York: Basic Books.

BookTalk 11.1

A murder mystery set in a high school. An English teacher as victim. Potential suspects range from the principal and a guidance counselor to fellow teachers and a myriad of students. Multiple perspectives of the teacher and multiple reactions to the death. Few to no clues; no known motive. Ready to take on the case? Read *Who Killed Mr. Chippendale?: A Mystery in Poems,* by Mel Glenn (www.melglenn.com) (1996), and keep your pad and pencil handy to note your suspicions and reflect on the problems and promises of contemporary schools and students.

a voice and a presence that can help determine the answers. Moje expresses hope as she points to more diversity among students, and eventually staff; more parent and community involvement; more access to technology (though she worries about the equality of access). Among her goals for literacy teaching are "teaching youth how to use reading and writing to construct a just and democratic society" (p. 129), and using service learning activities as

> a way to take students' projects into the community so that students will learn both to navigate multiple discourse communities and to take action in the world outside of school. As more and more students at all achievement levels report feeling disconnected from the world in the confines of a school in which the learning seems contrived, community-based projects will increase motivation and reshape schools of the future. (p. 129)

Many teachers go through a "teaching" pattern. They begin to teach one way, become dissatisfied, find a more rewarding and successful way, and write about their experiences and new approaches. Sometimes, researchers document these changes and new practices. For example, Sondra Perl and Nancy Wilson set out to find out what life was like for six teachers who were making a transition to teaching writing in a writing workshop setting in a particular school district. The authors became participant observers in the classrooms and actually lived with some of the teachers. The result was *Through Teachers' Eyes: Portraits of Writing Teachers at Work* (1986).

In another study of instructional change, Brozo and Hargis (2003) describe a concerted effort made in a high school to make reading instruction responsive to all students, no matter what their reading level. Content area teachers were surprised to learn, after testing, that there was a range of up to 15 grade levels within a single classroom. Armed with this knowledge, many teachers agreed that using the same books and methods with all students would be ineffective and/or irresponsible. A large percentage of the students were unable to comprehend the grade-level textbooks, and some were ready for more challenging materials. Three new literacy initiatives were launched school-wide: sustained silent reading; the use of young adult literature in content area classrooms; and the use of alternative texts, such as those found on Internet sites, for various disciplines. Although not all teachers participated to the fullest extent, the authors witnessed the success of many teachers in terms of making content instruction more responsive to students' literacy needs.

As a preservice or beginning teacher, you might find the teacher biography and autobiography genre helpful as you imagine both the excitement and pitfalls of teaching literacy in your content area.

We don't have to rely on nonfiction alone for visions of what school is like and what school could be. Many fictional portrayals of educational settings that are dystopian, utopian, or a combination of both contain much truth and are very thought-provoking. Read or view the materials listed in Figure 11.2, and imagine yourself in the settings, making tough decisions and having the opportunity to relate to the student characters and to envision how you might open the world of learning for them.

VISIONS OF WHAT SCHOOLS COULD BE

In "Language Education in the 21st Century: Dreaming a Caring Future" (1998), John S. Mayher tackles the challenge of creating and sharing a utopian vision for schools. He recognizes that some of his ideas will meet with objection, but decides "Any good prognosticator tries to shape as well as anticipate the future, so I will attend most directly with the schools I would like to see in the next century without being concerned about the feasibility of my dreams" (p. 156). That's the point at which I believe preservice teachers should be, and I hope you are at now. Often, my students say that they love my ideas and methods, but they don't see how these methods could work in "the real world." They are all too aware of the constraints imposed by national and state standards, state and local curricula, and department guidelines for text selection and assessment. They remind me of my son, whom I called at college to wish a happy birthday. He told me that his day was uneventful, sighing, "I realized that after 21 there are no birthdays to really look forward to." I tell my students that if they are unwilling to dream big, look beyond the boundaries, and be idealists *now,* it's unlikely they'll make much of a difference in the future. So, embrace idealism.

Mayher (1998) begins by chronicling the dystopian influences of society, which are "producing a generation of students for whom schooling has been disconnected from learning" (p. 157). Though he proclaims that "no one learns best in the schools we have" (p. 165), he doesn't stay with this grim picture for long: "I am not so naive as to believe that positive thinking alone will solve our problems, but I do know that cynicism and bitterness surely will exacerbate them" (p. 161). Mayher describes a caring learning community à la Nell Noddings, where "the message of commitment to the highest standards would be sent every day" (p. 162). His utopian school has the following characteristics:

- Multigenerational
- Inclusive
- Open almost all the time

FIGURE 11.2

Fictional works and movies about teachers, schools, and learners.

See more suggested titles in Appendix Figure 11.2.

Anderson, L. H. (1999). *Speak.* New York: Farrar, Straus & Giroux.

Crutcher, C. (2005). *The Sledding Hill.* New York: Greenwillow Books.

Flake, S. G. (2000). *The Skin I'm In.* New York: Hyperion.

Freedom Writers. (2007). Hollywood, CA: Paramount Home Entertainment.

Taylor, M. (1976). *Roll of Thunder, Hear My Cry.* New York: Dial Books.

- Multipurpose
- Beautiful
- Warm
- Friendly
- Respectful
- Safe
- Democratic
- Explicitly antiracist, antisexist, and anticlassist
- Consistent
- Meaning-based learning environment
- High quality
- Nonhierarchical
- Professional
- Learner and learning centered (pp. 162–164)

He imagines a school environment that "feeds the spirit, the heart, the body, and the mind; where all participants feel welcome and cared for; and where the business of learning and the business of living are not separate but whole" (p. 164). Mayher realizes he is fantasizing but believes the ideal school can be realized. So do I.

Daniel Liston (2004) also envisions an educational world where teachers and students alike are lured by the wonders and beauty of learning. To enter this world, or re-create this world, some changes in our present environment or attitude might be needed. "As teachers we may need to relearn how to love our subjects, to invite our students to inquire with us in those subjects, . . . and to demand that schools no longer constrain these efforts" (p. 2). Love of learning is central to his vision: "If [a teacher's] love of learning is real, it is inevitably conveyed. And if it is real, it taps and arises from the depths of a teacher's soul. Falling in love (with a text or another) is an amazing thing" (p. 12).

Liston helps us imagine what happens when teachers who love learning and who respect students' integrity teach others:

> At times, we offer clarity through the fog of cognitive dissonance and confusion and the mastery of skills that might sustain that clarity. At other times, we hold out the possibility of coming to terms with, and maybe combating, present and past inhumanity, cruelty, and injustice. And still other times, it seems simple personal delight and pleasure bring us to the classroom doors. (p. 16)

Think how these ideas would translate to a school where you teach, where all your colleagues, no matter what their discipline, passionately loved both their subject area and the art of luring their students into learning. You could be the catalyst that begins the transformation.

Another person who projected into the future and set down a visionary, though admittedly not utopian, classroom and school setting is Jabari Mahiri, in *Shooting for Excellence: African American and Youth Culture in New Century Schools* (1998). Throughout the book, he cites studies and describes the methods of teachers who exemplify the best characteristics of coaching, "modeling specific skill development, instilling self-discipline in the players, policies for fair and equal participation for all players, and a policy of multiple coaches for each team" (p. 154). His last chapter, "Imagining New Century Schools," invites readers to look through the eyes of a student at a school where literacy is central to the student-centered, exploratory approach espoused by the entire school and community. The school's philosophy is based on the premise that learners

> should leave high school with the fundamental skills to access, analyze, synthesize, and interpret information as a foundation for the continual development of their abilities to make contributions to the knowledge base. These fundamental skills included systematic and analytical thinking skills necessary for solving complex problems. In short, . . . high school should provide an experience in which students learn to learn, and learn to love learning. (p. 149)

In Mahiri's imagined school, teachers and students are very attuned to discourse and language issues. Teachers, characterized implicitly as intellectuals, learn from students and incorporate African American and youth culture in general as they motivate, instruct, and mentor in a *mutable curriculum* that celebrates diversity. One simple sentence in the author's reflection on this possible scenario stays with me: "meaningful change also means changing ourselves" (p. 159). What a challenge he's given us.

Allington (2007) offers insights based on his own and others' research on exemplary middle and high school teachers. You can use these as you develop and refine your philosophy and practice. Unique aspects of effective teachers include the following: they use multiple texts or multilevel curriculum, ensuring "that virtually all students could find texts that they were able to read accurately, fluently, and with comprehension" (p. 278); they allow student choice; they provide strategies that lead to engagement and motivation; they promote literate conversation in their classrooms; and they build connections "within lessons, across lessons, and with both in-and out-of-school applications" (p. 284). Allington urges teachers to craft curricular plans that will reduce the struggle so many students now experience.

Christenbury (2007) is a veteran teacher who has reflected on her own change and growth, and now can share her vision of a good classroom:

> In that classroom, students are taken seriously, and being intellectually curious is the norm. In that classroom, skills are taught—but never to the exclusion of creative activities and spontaneous discussions. Tests are given—but they come directly from what has been taught and what has been learned, and they are used to improve student learning and mastery, never to rank and sort and alienate or humiliate. In that classroom, reading is approached in multiple ways. . . . In this classroom, teachers teach first to students, second for curriculum mastery, and a distant third for test scores. In this classroom, activities are authentic. (p. 293)

Remember the "What if?" strategy you learned in Chapter 4? In the title of his presidential address to an NCTE convention (with the theme "Reimagining the Possibilities"), Jerome Harste asked the question, "What If English/Language Arts Teachers Really Cared?" (Harste & Carey, 1999, p. 1). He didn't find the task of envisioning the future easy, and he recognized that we can't just tinker with the curriculum and call it change because

> it is safe to say that no one can predict what kind of world our grandchildren will find upon graduation. In three generations the world experienced greater change than at any other time in history. The cultural and technological gulf between Socrates and our parents is much less than the gulf between the world our parents knew and the world our grandchildren will enter. (p. 1)

Nevertheless, Harste offers some bold thoughts, such as the following:

> We could even help children understand that they haven't really finished reading until they have taken some form of social action by mentally and physically repositioning themselves in the world. It is not enough, for example, to read about women's rights. You have to act and talk differently, too. (p. 2)

Having come to the end of this textbook and the other texts you've explored along the way, try applying Harste's definition of reading to yourself. How will you "finish reading"? How will you reposition yourself as a content area teacher? How will the adolescents in your care benefit from the changes that have occurred because of your active engagement with the topic of teaching literacy?

Given the dilemma that "what is literacy to us may not be literacy for the parents of the children we teach" (p. 5), Harste still asks the important questions: "How then, do we teach? What are our roles and responsibilities as teachers . . . ? How can multiple discourses, multiple sign systems, and multiple realities inform what we do in the millennium?" (p. 5). He answers by giving examples of teachers from around the country interacting with and encouraging literacy in innovative ways. He tells of teachers having art materials and musical instruments available, as well as a flood of writing materials and books, in their classrooms; others bringing the community into the schools by inviting parents to run discovery clubs that feature gardening, karaoke, karate, and bricklaying; teachers forming study groups; school partnerships with universities. Harste shows by reporting on wonderful ongoing projects that "what can be imagined can be done" (p. 8). He is not afraid to think utopian thoughts when it comes to schooling: "Wouldn't it be wonderful if we knew how to create spaces so that all voices could be heard in the creation of a more just, a more thoughtful, and a more democratic way of living out the imagination of our elders?" (p. 8).

Nell Noddings (1999) spins out a thought-provoking narrative illustrating the potential a stimulating topic holds for teachers willing to involve students in investigation and inquiry. She takes the question of whether evolution and creationism should both be taught in schools (and we can include intelligent design in our inquiry), and suggests that, rather than have school boards debate it and hand down a decision, the students could be encouraged to tackle the question itself. They can learn about the history of evolutionary theory, the great debates relating to it. This might lead to reading biographical information about Bishop Wilberforce, Thomas Henry Huxley, Clarence Darrow, and William Jennings Bryan, leading to other social issues and big questions such as determinism versus free will.

Noddings plays with the variety of subtopics that might arise while discussing evolution, and explains how students with different interests might choose their avenues of exploration. Those interested in animal behavior could tackle the question, "Can human language be shown to be continuous with animal communication, or is it what some scholars have called a 'true emergent'?" (p. 582). She notes that high school girls,

who, she says, often require a special intellectual interest, might be thrilled to study the two versions of creation in Genesis, along with how early feminists (e.g., Elizabeth Cady Stanton) and current women's studies scholars interpret and critique the versions. Students could read Native American, Chinese, and African creation stories. They can learn about social Darwinism. Noddings asks us to imagine her vision of what I see as the synthesis of literacy and content learning:

> Imagine how much "cultural literacy" students might gain in a unit of study such as this. Working on their own projects, listening to others, trying to fit whatever direct instruction they receive with the material they are learning on their own, they will come across names, events, and concepts that will add immeasurably to their store of knowledge. (p. 582)

APPLICATION ACTIVITY　11.1　(SEE PAGE 323)

MY VISION OF AN IDEAL SCHOOL

In this text, I set out a path to and flexible guidelines for the development of a kind of content area classroom different from the ones you most likely attended. My utopian vision is that the preservice teachers reading this book will take the ideas that fit their philosophies and goals, and make them their own as they create intellectually stimulating and literature-rich classrooms and courses. I do not wish any reader to follow exactly my ideals and priorities. Laura Thompson, a preservice teacher, said in response to reading about the wonderful classroom Nancie Atwell describes in *In the Middle* (1998), "I've never yet followed a recipe verbatim, and I don't intend to start now in my new career."

You, future teachers, will implement your adapted version of my dream as you keep reading widely and participating in other literacy activities. Read deeply in your discipline, read the works and discoveries and ideas of prominent people in your field, read professional educational journals for stories about how other teachers are helping students soar in literacy, knowledge, action, and intellectual curiosity. And read for pure enjoyment.

My hope for schools involves you bringing students to the wonders of the world, and those beyond, and bringing those things to them, sometimes through direct experience, sometimes through texts. Consider the case of students in a program in Albany, Georgia, that is designed to encourage youth with physical disabilities or learning disabilities toward careers in technology and science. They asked some "What if?" questions. What if caterpillars, which normally climb upward and use gravity as they build their cocoons downward, were launched into space? Would they

BookTalk   11.2

If I could have only one magazine subscription for my class, I might choose the interdisciplinary *Smithsonian*. It offers art, science, history, sports, current events, math, and more in an accessible and attractive format, complete with fascinating photographs. Look at some of the feature article titles in the January 2010 issue, and think about what subject areas they might be appropriate for:

- "The Truth About Lions" by Abigail Tucker (shares findings from three decades of the author's research in the Serengeti)

- "Who Wrote the Dead Sea Scrolls?" by Andrew Lawler (discusses the dispute over authorship of these important religious manuscripts)

- "Painted Dreams" by Arthur Lubow (explores the stories aboriginal people tell as part of a current art movement in Australia)

- "Sherlock Holmes' London" by Joshua Hammer (the reporter describes some of the haunts of Arthur Conan Doyle)

- "Myths of the American Revolution" by John Ferling (addresses seven commonly held beliefs about our war for independence)

Having the *Smithsonian* in your classroom for those times when students have a few minutes free, or making them available for weekend borrowing, would be a gift, a gift of learning for those minds entrusted to your care.

become disoriented? Would they adapt? "Aided by area scientists and dedicated teachers" (Wakefield, 2001, p. 32), they hypothesized, and designed an experiment to monitor five caterpillars (the "painted lady" variety) and five cocoons of varying ages that were sent into space.

The phrase "aided by area scientists and dedicated teachers" epitomizes my utopian vision for learners. The Georgia project was made possible by a Texas-based company, SPACEHAB, that brings student projects into space. Its S*T*A*R*S (Space Technology and Research Students) program uses the Internet to "Webcast" nearly real-time images of experiments to students around the world. Want to know the result of the Albany, Georgia, experiment?

> The larvae, floating and turning in the air, slowly spun silky envelopes and slipped inside. And one by one, from the crusted cocoons the students had affixed to the crossbar, emerged three-inch-wide butterflies dappled with pale orange, white, brown and black. Nature had prevailed. (p. 34)

Will your students be able to participate in experiments in outer space? I don't know—maybe. But I'm certain they can go on a literary field trip if you bring the article "The Object at Hand: Painted Ladies in Space" (Wakefield, 2001) from the *Smithsonian* magazine to class. And they can join with other student researchers by visiting the National Air and Space Museum's website. But your students might never learn of these sources if you don't introduce them. You really do possess the power to bring the world to them and launch them into the exciting world of your discipline—through literacy.

APPLICATION ACTIVITY   11.2   (SEE PAGE 323)

ENACTING THE VISION

Throughout the chapters, I've reminded you that, although it was necessary to discuss the components of literacy separately, they really are inseparable; they're a whole. Similarly, teaching literacy and teaching your content curriculum and disciplinary knowledge will be interwoven. As we bring this textbook experience to a close, I'd like to give you a picture of real teachers and students transacting with text in a high school content area classroom that demonstrates the pieces working together. You'll see motivation and vocabulary issues; background knowledge; metacognition; critical thinking; strategic uses of talking, listening, writing, and drawing. You'll see a picture that can activate your visions of what you want your classroom to be.

Teaching in action: *Math.* The vignette I'm going to summarize and comment on takes place in a high school Math Connections course in an alternative urban high school in Rochester, New York. The teacher, Judi, and two mathematics educators, Margie and Constance, who were there in the role of researchers, chose essays from the text *The Mathematical Experience* (Davis & Hersh, 1981), a book that discusses historical, political, and social dimensions of math. Margie demonstrated, modeled, and taught a technique called the "Say Something Strategy" (Harste & Short, 1988) after asking students to read the introductory paragraph. Constance recorded on newsprint the students' immediate responses about the content, the writing, and their understanding or confusion as the discussion unfolded. Margie helped the students value the process by showing them the written ideas that had developed by listening to others and voicing concerns.

> Student partners Char and Jolea selected the essay "Mathematics and War" to read together. They decided to stop after every paragraph to talk, and agreed to let Margie join their conversation. After

the first paragraph, Jolea felt stupid, but after a bit of interaction said, "I didn't understand while you were talking but now I understand. I guess a lot of the words I didn't understand" (p. 69). After the second paragraph, the partners discussed the role of astrologers in ancient times and the difference between scientists and mathematicians. As they continued reading and talking, they mentioned the strategies they were using to comprehend the text, and Char noted that, despite difficult words like *cryptography* and *econometrics,* the text was getting easier for her to read. Jolea, in the midst of reacting to the content of scientists contributing to destruction, metacognitively noted something about her reading process: "I—I got lost up here but when you walked away, I just said well I've got time now, I'll just do it over again. And I got it and I understood it." (p. 73)

Critical thinking became evident as the girls talked about whether it might be more dangerous for one country to have nuclear weapons than for two; they recognized the complexity of the issue they were reading about. Jolea spontaneously offered a reflection on the process they were using:

> I don't know if I should say this but—I don't think I'd be able to read from a book [like this] without reading and then talking about it. . . . You know, usually you have to read the whole thing, maybe you do it for homework and then the next day it's not as fresh and you forget the little things that— You remember a couple of things that confused you. But now it's—and you're doing it right away and something's right there. (Borasi & Siegel, 2000, p. 74)

When asked if she thought she could adapt the strategy to use while doing homework, Jolea answered confidently, "Yeah, I think eventually you can . . . if you do this enough to learn—Just like anything if you do something with someone enough you can usually go solo" (p. 74).

By the time they finished reading, the partners were grappling with the moral dimensions of mathematics and war and the connections between math and science, based on the text's description of World War I as the chemists' war, World War II as the physicists' war, and World War III "(may it never come)" (p. 75) as the mathematicians' war. The students were engaged in high-level thinking as a result of a thought-provoking text, a strategy that was making the text accessible, and support from a teacher in a comfortable academic environment.

For homework, students were directed to use the Sketch-to-Stretch strategy (Harste & Short, 1988; Siegel, 1984), making a sketch to show what they had learned from the text. This strategy, too, proved beneficial. Char and Jolea decided to make separate sketches because they had come away from the reading experience with different themes and wanted to draw their interpretations independently. The next day, each girl shared her drawing with the class and explained its meaning. Char's sketch had nine boxes, with one column representing the products of mathematicians' thinking at three points in time (a catapult, a bomb, Star Wars), the second representing the mathematicians' moral dilemma as they tried to balance the intellectual challenge of research and the effects on humankind, and the third showing society's positive and negative response to the products. The class compared and contrasted this with Jolea's artistic interpretation. Jolea explained her picture, the feeling underlying it, and the process of reading, discussing, and drawing.

I urge you to read the full account in Borasi and Siegel's *Reading Counts: Expanding the Role of Reading in Mathematics Classrooms* (2000). The authors reflect on what the students gained from this instructional episode involving a generative reading of the "Math and War" essay. Students came to value new connections between math and life and were exposed to information about how math, specifically in its use in warfare, has evolved and grown over time. They discussed the social role of mathematicians, as well as the moral concerns individual mathematicians have had regarding the use of their work for the purpose of war. The authors conclude:

> The extent to which Char and Jolea were able to grasp and elaborate on these themes in their "say something" conversation and their sketches was remarkable. Although these students seem to have thought little about the ethical dimensions of mathematics before reading this essay, their exploration of this issue was quite sophisticated and added new insights and connections to what was presented in the text—an impressive achievement even for adult readers of the same text! And even if some of their classmates had overlooked this issue in their own reading of the text, Char and Jolea's sharing of their sketches gave the whole class an opportunity to appreciate the meaning and importance of ethical issues in mathematics. (pp. 84–85)

The students, through literacy activities, came to a better understanding of mathematics as a discipline and are more likely to remember the information they learned because of their engagement.

Think of what can be accomplished in your courses as you provide rich texts, and opportunities to react to them and apply them to the students' lives—facilitating, modeling, and mentoring as students learn your content and discipline skills. Literacy is the key to your students' success. Strategies alone won't work, but strategies and philosophy together can work wonders.

WORKING WITH LITERACY COACHES

I have urged you to work closely with a literacy coach if one is available to you, and I have mentioned particular ways you might do so. Many resources are available to help you better understand the roles a literacy coach should play, and should not play. One particular book chapter I'd like to recommend is Egawa's (2007) "Five Things You Need to Know About Literacy Coaching in Middle and Secondary Schools" because, unlike many texts whose primary audience is the literacy coach or those aspiring to be one, this one is addressed to content area teachers. She gives examples of how definitions of the term *literacy coach* have evolved in particular schools, and explains how a coach might help you as you strive to reach the high achievement goals you have set for you and your students:

> When a content area teacher partners with the literacy coach, there are myriad ways the collaboration can play out. For instance, the two of you may decide to co-teach a lesson, with the coach taking the lead to introduce pre-reading or prewriting activities. In another class, the coach may closely watch several students who participate halfheartedly during a lesson and strategize about how to get them on board. (p. 299)

If you want to learn more about how you as a content area teacher might work with literacy leaders in your school or district, I also suggest Shanklin's article "How Can You Get the Most from Working with a Literacy Coach?" (2007). If you want to learn more about the actual role of the literacy coach, you may choose from numerous helpful books, such as Puig and Froelich's *The Literacy Leadership Team: Sustaining and Expanding Success* (2010).

NEW TEACHERS TEACHING DIFFERENTLY AND MAKING A DIFFERENCE

O ut of the blue, I received an e-mail from a former student, Chris Leahey, telling me that he was now using the strategies he had learned in my content area literacy class in his ninth-grade social studies classes and thanking me for providing him with ways to enhance his students' literacy. He also mentioned that he was about to team teach a unit with an English teacher, whom I had also taught. I knew I could learn things from them, so I visited their school, talking with them and observing a class where I interacted with their students. I'd like you to meet these third-year teachers to see how they've applied and adapted some of the principles explained in this book.

Teaching in action: *Global Studies and English.* Chris's Global Studies curriculum required that he teach colonialism in Africa. He decided he could engage his students in the topic and help them understand its complexity by having them read the novel *Things Fall Apart* by Chinua Achebe (1994). It tells the story of an African village, and of one man in particular, Okonkwo, a leader who encounters conflict both within his tribe and with outside forces of European missionaries and government officials.

Auddie Mastroleo, the English teacher, viewed Okonkwo as a model of a tragic hero and the novel as a model tragedy. Her students had just finished a unit on mythology, full of heroes, some fallen. She had also taken a course on storytelling the year before and had committed one day a week to storytelling in her class; the students, therefore, had explored many African folktales and myths. So, she saw great potential in *Things Fall Apart*. It could help her address the standards *her* curriculum is based on, too. Auddie and Chris eagerly began planning their team teaching, a new endeavor for both.

I visited them in the middle of the unit. They were wildly enthusiastic, surprising even themselves. They had provided some background knowledge, introduced value-laden issues, and discussed perspective by having the students watch *Roots*. They were now listening to students talk about *Things Fall Apart,* as well as reflect on their reading processes. As Auddie and Chris analyzed student work, both were feeling that their goals were being reached and the unit was a great success so far. I asked them to tell me more.

Chris was enamored of the book itself. Because it depicts imperialism from an African perspective, he feels it lends itself to his curriculum and the social studies standards. Beyond that, he said, "I love the book because of its language—'Proverbs are the palm oil in which words fall apart. . . .'" Last year, Chris piloted the book; his students wrote how long each chapter took and the problems they encountered. "They had problems keeping the family relationships straight, so this year we gave the kids a chart to track the family tree, and they made their own family tree. We avoided all worksheet stuff. We told them, 'We're not going to ask you to do anything that won't help you.'" The students drew symbols and animals. Chris was delighted to discover that "the kids saw things about the court case we didn't see—connections—cultural universals—a way of settling disputes." Chris taught a lesson on infant mortality after they read in the book about African babies dying. "I used charts of world mortality rates. We discussed causes of mortality." He noted that his students had written 24 essays so far in his course and were not complaining because of the way he taught. "I give kids problems to solve. The kids become global historians. They must interpret—I don't impart knowledge."

I asked Chris how he answered colleagues who think there's no time to read novels in social studies class. He answered that he didn't use literature as an extra; rather, he taught the required concepts, such as apartheid and imperialism, *through* stories. His students had also read *Sadako and the Thousand Paper Cranes* (Coerr, 1977) and *Hiroshima* (Hersey, 1946) in the context of his lessons on World War II; facts and concepts were taught in the context of the literature. He found time by making teaching through literature a priority. "Besides," Chris quipped, "the curriculum calls for teaching 5,000 years of Chinese history in six weeks. When you have an impossible task anyway. . . ." He summed up the atmosphere in his Global Studies class by saying, "We have an attitude."

Auddie was equally excited about how the team teaching was going, the learning, and the changes occurring in the students' attitudes. She felt it was the best unit she had taught in her three years as a teacher. Her students had written advice to the characters; she had used supplemental materials like an African drum CD and African photographs; they made book jackets, mobiles, and posters. Students were looking for things online that connect to the book and the issues the book raises.

Both teachers had done a lot of informal assessment along the way—Auddie noted that the students with special educational needs were handling the book just fine, with resources and assistance as needed; no one was being left behind. When I asked what the final evaluation of the unit would be, she laughed and said, "We don't know yet. We work off of what happens each day. You have to be flexible." Months later, she wrote:

> For the final assessment of the unit, we chose to assign separate tasks. In Global Studies, students continued with the unit on Africa and apartheid. They ended the unit with a document-based question in which the students could refer to the team-taught novel. In English, students analyzed and interpreted a poem and wrote a [compare–contrast] essay.

After our interview, I was invited to join Chris's class for the afternoon. He began by showing a transparency of the activity for the day, which involved small groups playing the role of white government officials, and instructed, "As a group, your task is to make a policy for handling different problems that arise in the village." Students picked up folders explaining their various tasks and roles, got in groups, then got right to work on the task. They discussed such issues as intermarriage among races, the consequences of disobeying the colonial policies that had been imposed on the Africans, taxation, building schools and churches. Almost every student contributed to the group discussions. This lesson was very organized—the students moved through nine problems quickly and had time to post answers and report on their decisions to the whole group.

Auddie later wrote a paper on the experience, in which she explained:

> My role during data collection was to simply look and listen. I became an observer of my students' behavior, quality of work, and attitude. I also, in a sense, observed myself—metacognition became key. I grew to be aware of my attitude and teaching in this unit. I became an observer, participant, and recorder of data.

As a result of Auddie's careful listening, she learned about students' attitudes:

> Students, before and after class, would often remark about their enjoyment of the activity or the novel itself. Remarks like these were to be heard: "I can't believe he would just kill his own son!" or "How do his wives put up with him?" or "I can't stand the way he is so uptight about not being like his father." Often, on the way out of class, students could be heard talking to each other about the novel. "What part are you on? I just finished reading about the court case." Such comments were the norm and they revealed a deep interest and involvement in the novel and the unit.

Chris and Auddie are both reflective teachers who are very aware of how much they are changing. Chris consciously sets one or two new goals for himself each year. He mentioned using cooperative learning effectively as one example. "We're continually evolving." Auddie, who is constantly working hard to find ways to make literature more enjoyable for and accessible to her students, has also learned to be patient with herself, stating, "I'm growing into the type of teacher I want to be." Figure 11.3 is part of the packet of reading guides the two content area teachers created to help their students interact with *Things Fall Apart*.

BookTalk 11.3

A perfect companion to Achebe's *Things Fall Apart* is Barbara Kingsolver's (www.kingsolver.com) *The Poisonwood Bible* (1998). Told from the perspectives of five female narrators (the wife and daughters of a missionary devoted to "converting the African heathens"), the story starts out in the Congo in 1960 and details the effects of colonialism on the country and society. The interrelationships are complex and often wonderful; the character development is superb; the author's use of language is exquisite. The story is a modern parable, and readers are wiser for having experienced it.

FIGURE 11.3 Reading guide packet.

Things Fall Apart

North Syracuse Junior High
Leahey/Mastroleo
Grade 9

Event	Detailed Description of Events	How is this similar to and different from events in our culture?
Ikemefuna's Fate p.		
Engagement p.		
Infant Mortality p.		
Court Case p.		

Task 1: List details from the chapter.

Task 2: Using the details listed, write one word (i.e., descriptor) that captures the overall mood or tone of each chapter.

DESCRIPTOR	DETAILS

PART I PROJECT

Choose one of the following assignments to complete for Part I of *Things Fall Apart*.

1. Write a poem about the events or the characters that you have read about in the novel for Part I. You may write more than one poem, but you must have at least 20 lines in all.

2. Create a book jacket for Part I of the novel. You must include an illustration that represents the characters or the events you have read about so far, a brief biography of the author, and a paragraph convincing someone to read this book.

3. Create a book cube for Part I of the novel. Make a 6-sided cube out of a cardboard box and cover it with paper. Illustrate 5 scenes from the novel. On the sixth side write the author's name, the title of the novel, and your name.

4. Write a letter to a character or to the author responding to Part I of the novel. Some things to consider:

   - Give advice to a character.
   - Ask questions about the story or about why a character responded in a certain way.
   - Comment on the book so far.

5. Create a mobile of the characters, scenes, objects, or symbols in the book so far. You must have at least seven ornaments.

Due Date:

FIGURE 11.3 Continued.

Model of a Tragedy	Star Wars	Things Fall Apart
SETTING		
1. Society in Turmoil		
2. Unavoidable code of ethics		
3. Enforcer(s) who oversees the code of ethics		
CHARACTER		
1. *Tragic hero:* man who seems larger than life, not average, and stronger; a special gift with language, and a mysterious birth.		
2. *Tragic flaw:*		
a) physical flaw		
b) character flaw—usually hubris		
PLOT		
1. Hero's flaw causes him to break the code of ethics.		
2. Society is put into turmoil because of the hero's choice.		
3. The enforcer tries to reveal to the hero his mistake.		
4. Hero realizes his mistake and sacrifices himself.		
5. Society is returned to order.		

ESSAY

Directions: After reading the novel *Things Fall Apart* by Chinua Achebe and the poem "The Second Coming," by William Butler Yeats, write an essay about a society or an individual in turmoil. Use ideas from both works and the questions from the poem guide to develop your essay. Show how the authors used specific literary elements or techniques to convey ideas.

Guidelines:

- Use ideas from both passages to establish the controlling idea about a society or an individual in turmoil.

- Use specific and relevant evidence from both passages to develop your ideas.

- Show how each author uses specific literary elements (conflict, theme, character, point of view, plot) or techniques (symbolism, imagery, irony, descriptive language) to show a society or an individual in turmoil.

- Organize your ideas logically.

- Use language that communicates ideas effectively.

- Follow the conventions of standard written English.

- Line 3a: What "things" could the poem be referring to?

- Line 3b: Visualize this line. What does it look like? What sounds are created?

- Line 4: Anarchy or disorder, violence, and lawlessness appear in the novel. Explain where.

- Lines 5 and 6: With words like "blood-dimmed" and "drowned" predict what the future holds—be descriptive.

 If innocence is "drowned" that means all are guilty. Guilty of what?

- Lines 7 and 8: What happens when the most noble, brave, wise, and respected people lose their strong beliefs, and the most foolish, disrespected cowards are filled with "passionate intensity"?

- Is *Things Fall Apart* an appropriate title for this novel? Explain.

THINGS FALL APART:
A CONCLUSION TO OUR CASE STUDY OF IMPERIALISM

Concept	Examples from TFA
Nationalism (i.e., intense pride in one's country and desire for independence)	
Conflict	
Religious and Cultural Differences	
Desire for Raw Materials and New Markets	
Cultural Diffusion (i.e., the exchange of goods and ideas)	
Technological Advantages	

CONCLUSION

Introducing myself to you in the Introduction was much easier than saying good-bye to you now. What final words to impart? Let's look ahead to your content area classroom. Will it be a good one in terms of literacy?

How does one know, you might wonder, when good literacy is or is not happening in schools? There are experts who would love to be your guides. William J. Bennett, for example, in *The Educated Child* (1999), offers charts with "warning signs" of weak programs in language arts, history and geography, math and science; warning signs of weak testing methods; warning signs of bad teaching. Kohn, in *The Schools Our Children Deserve* (1999), offers a "Visitor's Guide" with "Good Signs" in the left-hand column and "Possible Reasons to Worry" in the other. Reading these books simultaneously emphasized to me how much one's philosophy determines what is judged as good or bad—in many, many cases these authors gave opposing views of what a good classroom looks like, what productive learning looks like, what bad teaching looks like. For example, included in Bennett's list of "Warning Signs of a Weak Language Arts Program" is "students are often told 'there are no right or wrong answers' when analyzing literature" (1999, p. 169). On the other hand, one of Kohn's "Possible Reasons to Worry" is "emphasis on facts and right answers," while a good sign is, "emphasis on thoughtful exploration of complicated issues" (1999, p. 236).

I'd like to add my voice to the conversation. I've not tried to hide my philosophy of teaching as I've given examples and recommendations throughout the chapters, so you can probably guess the kinds of things I consider positive signs of literacy learning or evidence that it's time to be concerned. Here are a few of the questions that I might ask if I visited your content area classroom:

- Is there a classroom library with books and other materials that students can borrow and take home?
- Are current and enticing reading materials on display?
- Do the reading materials in the classroom represent varying levels of difficulty and a variety of genres?
- If I asked the students what some of their teacher's favorite books are, could they tell me?
- If I asked the students what booktalks their teacher has given lately, could they name several titles?
- Are students reading a variety of books beyond the textbook or instead of a textbook? Are they given choices in terms of what they read?
- Are students using writing to explore issues, reflect on their reading, explain ideas, and express

themselves? Do they write for real purposes and to real audiences?

- Do students talk and listen to one another about what they've read and heard, about topics being explored, about interesting vocabulary, about the subject matter, about current issues or people working in the discipline? Is it evident from the activity in the room that the teacher understands that learning is social?
- Are visual and media literacy being addressed? Are relevant websites, films, photos, illustrations, graphs, and so on explored in thoughtful ways?
- Is the teacher talking with the students while work is in progress to assess in authentic situations and facilitate and support learning?
- Does the teacher assess and provide background knowledge before teaching and providing reading materials?
- Does the teacher motivate the students to explore reading materials and to think critically about the ideas presented in them?
- Does the teacher provide reading guides and teach strategies to aid comprehension and foster thinking about texts?
- Do the teacher's demeanor and behavior show evidence of intellectual curiosity and an enjoyment of students, learning, and teaching?
- Do all students, including English learners and struggling readers and writers, feel safe, comfortable, and supported?
- Does the teacher help students make connections between their curriculum and the world outside the classroom walls?
- Is there evidence that home and community literacies and cultures are respected and valued?
- Are there activities that help the students behave like practitioners in the discipline? Have they been introduced through multiple texts to current practitioners in the field, as well as past contributors?

If the answers to these questions are all YES, I will conclude that yours is a classroom where content area literacy is taken seriously, and I will be happy.

Thoreau helped me begin my book. I'll turn to him again. Here's what he said of his reading a truly good book: "I must lay it down and commence living on its hint. . . . What I began by reading I must finish by acting" (Thoreau, 1999, p. xxxii). He pleads with the reader to be active, to move his words off the page and use them "to solve some of the problems of life, not only theoretically, but practically" (p. xxxiv). I ask you to do the same and wish you well as I join my voice with Thoreau's: "Will you be a reader, a student merely, or a seer? Read your fate, see what is before you, and walk on into futurity" (Thoreau, 1992, p. 105).

Barbara Kingsolver
www.kingsolver.com

Mel Glenn
www.melglenn.com

APPLICATION ACTIVITIES

11.1 Try your hand at what Noddings has modeled. Pick a question that is being debated in the news, or a topic required in your curriculum, and think of where students investigating it could take it. To which disciplines does it connect? How might one path of research lead to others? How might students with different talents and ways of thinking inquire about it and think about related issues? You might make a graphic organizer to picture the places you and your students could go, given free rein to explore and think.

11.2 Now it's your turn once again to join the community of dreamers. Mahiri (1998) contends that "Metaphors are an intrinsic part of theory building" (p. 23). At the 1999 NCTE conference in Denver, I heard John Noell Moore speak about his class living out the metaphor of the Van Gogh Cafe. I've asked my students to tell me what meta-phor, symbol, title, or quote captures the spirit of our class and received such varied answers as "A Field Trip to Uncharted Territory" and "Studio in the Art of Teaching Literacy."

Play with metaphor and language to help yourself envision the spirit of your future classroom. Try out quotes, titles, and allusions that might represent the community of learners you and your students will be. Or, outline some of the features of your ideal school within which to teach. What will the content area courses you teach be like? How will they be different from the kind of education you had? Where and how will literacy fit in? What books will be in the classroom library of your dreams? What other reading and writing materials will there be? Write a journal entry, or a diagram or other visual representation of your ideal classroom. Share your thoughts and illustrations on the Kane Resource Site.

resource appendix

Continuation of Chapter Bibliographic Figures

FIGURE I.1   Resources showing how teachers can use Lois Lowry's *The Giver*.

Enriquez, G. (2001). Making Meaning of Cultural Depictions: Using Lois Lowry's *The Giver* to Reconsider What Is "Multicultural" About Literature. *Journal of Children's Literature, 27*(1), 13–22.

Freedman, L., & Johnson, H. (2003). Beyond Their Own Experience: Teach Education Students' Exploration of Social Justice Issues Through Reading Newbery Winners *The Giver,* and *Out of the Dust. Journal of Reading Education, 28*(2), 16–25.

Ibbetson, K. (2002). *The Giver* as a Bridge to *Animal Farm:* Controlling Societies. ED 466803 Classroom Guide CS 511 198, www.eric.gov.

Lawrence, A. (1999). From *The Giver* to *Twenty-One Balloons:* Explorations with Probability. *Mathematics Teaching in the Middle School, 4*(8), 504–509.

Lea, S. G. (2006). Seeing Beyond Sameness: Using *The Giver* to Challenge Colorblind Ideology. *Children's Literature in Education, 37*(1), 51–67.

Lehman, B. (1998). Doubletalk: A Pairing of *The Giver* and *We Are All in the Dumps with Jack and Guy. Children's Literature in Education, 29*(2), 69–78.

Podell, T. (Producer) & Otis, S. (2003). *A Kid's Video Guide to* The Giver. Scarborough, NY: Tim Podell Productions.

FIGURE 2.1   Math titles for a classroom library.

Albert, J. (2003). *Teaching Statistics Using Baseball*. Washington, DC: Mathematical Association of America.

Balliett, B. (2004). *Chasing Vermeer*. New York: Scholastic.

Benjamin, A., & Shermer, M. (2008). *Secrets of Mental Math: The Mathemagician's Secrets of Lightning Calculation and Mental Math Tricks*. New York: Three Rivers Press.

Berlinski, D. (1999). *The Advent of the Algorithm: The Idea that Rules the World*. New York: Harcourt Brace.

Berlinski, D. (2005). *Infinite Ascent: A Short History of Mathematics*. New York: Modern Library.

Bruce, C. (2002). *Conned Again, Watson: Cautionary Tales of Logic, Math, and Probability*. Cambridge, MA: Perseus.

Cole, K. C. (1998). *The Universe and the Teacup: The Mathematics of Truth and Beauty*. New York: Harcourt Brace.

Ferrell, K. (2008). *The Great Polygon Caper*. (T. Kerr, Illus.). Hauppauge, NY: Barron's Educational Series.

Fienberg, A. (2007). *Number 8*. New York: Walker.

Gigerenzer, G. (2002). *Calculated Risks: How to Know When Numbers Deceive You*. New York: Simon & Schuster.

Halpin, B. (2008). *Forever Changes*. New York: Farrar Straus Giroux.

Hardy, G. H. (2001). *A Mathematician's Apology*. Cambridge: Cambridge University Press.

Johnson, V. (2007). *My Life as a Rhombus*. Woodbury, MN: Flux.

King, R. (2007). *The Quantum July*. New York: Delacorte Press.

Kuhn, H. W., & Nasar, S. (Eds.). (2001). *The Essential John Nash*. Princeton, NJ: Princeton University Press.

LearningExpress. (2007). *Seeing Numbers: A Pictorial Way of Learning Math*. New York: LearningExpress, LLC.

Lee, C., & O'Reilly, G. O. (2007). *The Great Number Rumble: A Story of Math in Surprising Places*. (V. Gray, Illus.). Toronto: Annick Press.

Lesmoir-Gordon, N., Rood, W., & Edney, R. (2001). *Introducing Fractal Geometry*. Lanham, MD: Totem Books.

Lichtman, W. (2007). *Do the Math: Secrets, Lies, and Algebra*. New York: Greenwillow Books.

Lichtman, W. (2008). *Do the Math #2: The Writing on the Wall*. New York: Greenwillow Books.

Long, L. (2004). *Great Graphs and Sensational Statistics: Games and Activities that Make Math Easy and Fun*. New York: John Wiley.

Mazur, J. (2004). *Euclid in the Rainforest: Discovering Universal Truth in Logic and Math*. New York: Pi Press.

McKellar, D. (2007). *Math Doesn't Suck: How to Survive Middle School Math Without Losing Your Mind or Breaking a Nail*. New York: Hudson Street Press.

Moranville, S. B. (2006). *A Higher Geometry*. New York: Henry Holt.

Nye, B. (2007). *Math, Business and Industry*. South Burlington, VT: Discovery Education. (DVD)

Ornes, S. (2009). *Sophie Germain*. Greensboro, NC: Morgan Reynolds.

Pappas, T. (1993). *Fractals, Googols, and Other Mathematical Tales*. San Carlos, CA: Wide World/Tetra.

(continued)

Paulos, J. A. (1995). *A Mathematician Reads the Newspaper*. New York: Basic Books.

Peterson, I. (2001). *Fragments of Infinity: A Kaleidoscope of Math and Art*. New York: Wiley.

Peterson, I., & Henderson, N. (2000). *Math Trek: Adventures in the Math Zone*. New York: Wiley.

Powley, L., & Weiskopf, C. (2009). *Adventures in Mathopolis: Parting Is Such Sweet Sorrow: The Story of Fractions and Decimals*. Hauppauge, NY: Barron's Educational Series.

Root, A. W. (2008). *Science, Math, Checkmate: 32 Chess Activities for Inquiry and Problem Solving*. Westport, CT: Teacher Ideas Press.

Schechter, B. (1998). "My Brain Is Open": *The Mathematical Journeys of Paul Erdös*. New York: Simon & Schuster.

Schmante-Besserat, D. (2000). *The History of Counting*. New York: Scholastic.

Singh, S. (1997). *Fermat's Enigma: The Epic Quest to Solve the World's Greatest Mathematical Problem*. New York: Walker.

Staeger, R. (2007). *Ancient Mathematicians*. Greensboro, NC: Morgan Reynolds.

Stewart, I. (2006). *Letters to a Young Mathematician*. New York: Basic Books.

West, K. (2009). *Carl Friedrich Gauss*. Greensboro, NC: Morgan Reynolds.

Wright, R. (2000). *Nonzero: The Logic of Human Destiny*. New York: Pantheon.

FIGURE 2.5 **Resources for read-alouds in middle and secondary content area classrooms.**

Braxton, B. (2007). Developing Your Reading Aloud Skills. *Teacher Librarian, 34*(4), 56–57.

Erickson, B. (1996). Read-alouds Reluctant Readers Relish. *Journal of Adolescent and Adult Literacy, 40*, 212–214.

Morgan, H. (2009). Using Read-Alouds with Culturally Sensitive Children's Books: A Strategy that Can Lead to Tolerance and Improved Reading Skills. *Reading Improvement, 46*(1), 3–8.

Pappas, C. C., & Varelas, M., with A. Barry & A. Rife. (2004). Promoting Dialogic Inquiry in Information Book Read-Alouds: Young Urban Children's Ways of Making Sense in Science. In E. W. Saul (Ed.), *Crossing Borders in Literacy and Science Instruction: Perspectives on Theory and Practice* (pp. 161–189). Newark, DE: International Reading Association and Arlington, VA: National Science Teachers Association.

Ranker, J. (2007). Using Comic Books as Read-Alouds: Insights on Reading Instruction from an English as a Second Language Classroom. *The Reading Teacher, 61*(4), 296–305.

Richardson, J. S., & Breen, M. (1996). A Read-aloud for Science. *Journal of Adolescent and Adult Literacy,* March, 504.

Richardson, J. S., & Carleton, L. (1997). A Read-aloud for Students of English as a Second Language. *Journal of Adolescent and Adult Literacy,* October, 140.

Richardson. J. S., & Forget, M. A. (1995/1996). A Read-aloud for Algebra and Geography Classrooms. *Journal of Adolescent and Adult Literacy,* Dec./Jan., 322.

Richardson, J. S., & Gross, E. (1997). A Read-aloud for Mathematics. *Journal of Adolescent and Adult Literacy,* March, 492.

Richardson, J. S., & Smith, N. S. (1996/1997). A Read-aloud for Science in Space. *Journal of Adolescent and Adult Literacy,* Dec./Jan., 308.

Scholastic. (2007). *Read-Aloud Passages and Strategies to Model Fluency: Grades 5–6*. New York: Author.

Varela, A. (2008). Reading Aloud in a High School ESL Setting. *ESL Magazine, 61*, 21–24.

Wolf, J. M. (2007). *Leveled Read-Aloud Plays: U.S. Civic Holidays*. New York: Scholastic Teaching Resources.

FIGURE 2.11 **Resources for a learning center on the Civil Rights movement.**

Allen, Z. (1996). *Black Women Leaders of the Civil Rights Movement*. Danbury, CT: Franklin Watts.

Bridges, R. (1999). *Through My Eyes*. New York: Scholastic.

Coles, R. (1995). *The Story of Ruby Bridges*. New York: Scholastic.

Crowe, C. (2003). *Getting Away with Murder: The True Story of the Emmett Till Case*. New York: Phyllis Fogelman Books.

Farris, C. K. (2008). *March On! The Day My Brother, Reverend Dr. Martin Luther King, Jr. Changed the World*. (L. Ladd, Illus.). New York: Scholastic Press.

Fradin, D. B., & Fradin, J. B. (2000). *Ida B. Wells: Mother of the Civil Rights Movement*. New York: Clarion Books.

Hampton, H., & Fayer, S. (1990). *Voices of Freedom: An Oral History of the Civil Rights Movement*. New York: Bantam Books.

Hughes, L. (1986). *The Dream Keeper and Other Poems*. New York: Knopf.

Karson, J. (2005). *The Civil Rights Movement*. Opposing Viewpoints in World History Series. Farmington Hills, MI: Greenhaven Press.

King, M. L. (1994). *Letter from Birmingham Jail*. New York: HarperCollins.

Klarnum, M. (2004). *From Jim Crow to Civil Rights: The Supreme Court and the Struggle for Racial Equality*. New York: Oxford University Press.

Levine, E. (1993). *Freedom's Children: Young Civil Rights Activists Tell Their Own Stories*. New York: Putnam.

Levy, P. B. (1992). *Let Freedom Ring: A Documentary History of the Modern Civil Rights Movement*. New York: Praeger.

Magoon, K. (2009). *The Rock and the River*. New York: Aladdin.

Marsh, C. (2005). *The Beloved Community: How Faith Shapes Social Justice, from the Civil Rights Movement to Today.* New York: Basic Books.

McWhorton, D. (2004). *A Dream of Freedom: The Civil Rights Movement from 1954–1968.* New York: Scholastic.

Meany, J. (2009). *Has the Civil Rights Movement Been Successful?* Chicago: Heinemann Library.

Meltzer, M. (2001). *There Comes a Time: The Struggle for Civil Rights.* New York: Random House.

Myers, W. D. (1993). *Malcolm X: By Any Means Necessary.* New York: Scholastic.

Shange, N. (2009). *Coretta Scott.* (K. Nelson, Illus.). New York: Katherine Tegen Books.

Sirimarco, E. (2005). *The Civil Rights Movement.* New York: Basic Books.

Taylor, M. (1976). *Roll of Thunder, Hear My Cry.* New York: Dial Press.

Taylor, M. (1992). *The Road to Memphis.* New York: Puffin Books.

Taylor, M. (2001). *The Land.* New York: Phyllis Fogelman Books.

Walt Disney Home Video. (1998). *Ruby Bridges.* Buena Vista Home Entertainment.

X, M. (1992). *The Autobiography of Malcolm X.* New York: Ballantine Books.

FIGURE 2.13 Resources relating to cooperative learning strategies and social interaction of learners.

Anderson, R. P. (2001). Team Disease Presentations: A Cooperative Learning Activity for Large Classrooms. *The American Biology Teacher, 63*(1), 40–43.

Jacobs, G. M., Power, M. A., & Loh, W. I. (2002). *The Teacher's Sourcebook for Cooperative Learning: Practical Techniques, Basic Principles, and Frequently Asked Questions.* Thousand Oaks, CA: Corwin Press.

McCafferty, S. G. (2006). *Cooperative Learning and Second Language Teaching.* New York: Cambridge University Press.

FIGURE 2.14 Professional resources dealing with a workshop approach and/or literature circles.

Brown, C. S. (1994). *Connecting with the Past: History Workshop in Middle and High Schools.* Portsmouth, NH: Heinemann.

Brownlie, F. (2005). *Grand Conversations, Thoughtful Responses: A Unique Approach to Literature Circles.* Winnipeg, Canada: Portage and Main Press.

Daniels, H., & Steineke, N. (2004). *Mini-Lessons for Literature Circles.* Portsmouth, NH: Heinemann.

Heuser, C. (2000). Reworking the Workshop for Math and Science. *Educational Leadership, 58*(1), 34–37.

Roller, C. M. (1996). *Variability Not Disability: Struggling Readers in a Workshop Classroom.* Newark, DE: International Reading Association.

Whitin, D. J. (2003). Developing a Math Workshop. In D. J. Whitin & R. Cox (Eds.), *A Mathematical Passage: Strategies for Promoting Inquiry in Grades 4–6* (pp. 109–135). Portsmouth, NH: Heinemann.

Widmer, K., & Buxton, S. (2004). *Workshops that Work: 30 Days of Mini-Lessons that Help Launch and Establish Important Routines for an Effective Reading and Writing Workshop.* New York: Scholastic.

FIGURE 3.4 Examples of picture books appropriate for teaching concepts in middle and high school disciplines.

ART AND MUSIC

Aronson, M. (1998). *Art Attack: A Short Cultural History of the Avant-Garde.* New York: Clarion Books.

Krull, K., & Hewitt, K. (1993). *Lives of the Musicians: Good Times, Bad Times (and What the Neighbors Thought).* New York: Harcourt Brace.

ENGLISH/LANGUAGE ARTS

Langley, A., & Everett, J. (1999). *Shakespeare's Theatre.* New York: Oxford University Press.

Lasky, K., & Hess, M. (1997). *Hercules: The Man, the Myth, the Hero.* New York: Hyperion Books for Children.

Truss, L. (2007). *The Girl's Like Spaghetti.* (B. Timmons, Illus.). New York: G.P. Putnam's Sons.

HISTORY/GEOGRAPHY/SOCIAL STUDIES/CULTURAL STUDIES

Begay, S. (1995). *Navajo: Visions and Voices Across the Mesa.* New York: Scholastic.

Brewster, H. (1996). *Anastasia's Album.* New York: Hyperion/Madison Press.

Cha, D. (1996). *Dia's Story Cloth: The Hmong People's Journey to Freedom.* Stitched by N. & N. T. Cha. New York: Lee & Low/Denver Museum of Natural History.

Demi. (1995). *Buddha.* New York: Henry Holt.

Guthrie, W., & Jacobsen, K. (1998). *This Land Is Your Land.* Boston: Little, Brown.

King, E. (1998). *Quinceañera: Celebrating Fifteen.* New York: Dutton.

King, M. L., Jr. (1997). *I Have a Dream.* (Paintings by 15 Coretta Scott King Award and Honor Book Artists.) New York: Scholastic.

Krull, K., & DiVito, A. (1999). *A Kids' Guide to America's Bill of Rights: Curfews, Censorship, and the 100 Pound Giant.* New York: Avon Books.

Lawrence, J. (1993). *Harriet and the Promised Land.* New York: Simon & Schuster.

McCurdy, M. (2000). *An Algonquian Year: The Year According to the Full Moon.* Boston: Houghton Mifflin.

(continued)

McElmeel, S. L. (2009). *Picture That! From Mendel to Normandy: Picture Books and Ideas, Curriculum, and Connections—for 'Tweens and Teens.* Santa Barbara, CA: Libraries Unlimited.

Ryan, P. M., & Selznick, B. (1999). *Amelia and Eleanor Go for a Ride.* New York: Scholastic.

Sis, P. (1998). *Tibet Through the Red Box.* New York: Frances Foster/Farrar.

St. George, J., & Small, D. (2000). *So You Want to Be President?* New York: Philomel Books.

Summer, L. S. (2001). *The March on Washington.* Chanhassen, MN: Child's World.

Tsuchiya, Y., & Lewin, T. (1988). *Faithful Elephants.* Boston: Houghton Mifflin.

Zhang, S. N. (1998). *The Children of China: An Artist's Journey.* Plattsburg, NY: Tundra/McClelland.

MATH

Anno, M. (1983). *Anno's Mysterious Multiplying Jar.* New York: Philomel Books.

Demi. (1997). *One Grain of Rice: A Mathematical Folktale.* New York: Scholastic.

Markle, S. (1997). *Discovering Graph Secrets: Experiments, Puzzles, and Games Exploring Graphs.* New York: Atheneum.

Mori, T., & Anno, M. (1986). *Socrates and the Three Little Pigs.* New York: Philomel Books.

Murphy, P. J. (2004). *Grace Hopper: Computer Whiz.* Berkeley Heights, NJ: Enslow Publishers.

Schmandt-Besserat, D., & Hays, M. (2000). *The History of Counting.* New York: Scholastic.

Scieszka, J., & Smith, L. (1995). *Math Curse.* New York: Viking.

Tang, G., & Briggs, H. (2001). *The Grapes of Math: Mind-Stretching Math Riddles.* New York: Scholastic.

SCIENCE

Bernardy, C. J. (1999). *Fuel.* Mankato, MN: Creative Education.

Collard, S. B., III, & Rothman, M. (2000). *The Forest in the Clouds.* Watertown, MA: Charlesbridge Publishing.

Gifford, C. (2000). *How the Future Began: Everyday Life.* New York: Kingfisher Publications.

Jackson, D. M. (1996). *The Bone Detectives: How Forensic Anthropologists Solve Crimes and Uncover Mysteries of the Dead.* Photos by C. Fellenbaum. Boston: Little, Brown.

Kaner, E., & Stephans, P. (1999). *Animal Defenses: How Animals Protect Themselves.* New York: Scholastic.

Ling, M., Atkinson, M., Greenaway, F., & King, D. (2000). *The Snake Book: A Breathtaking Close-up Look at Splendid, Scaly, Slithery Snakes.* New York: DK Publishing.

Mallory, K. (1998). *A Home by the Sea: Protecting Coastal Wildlife.* San Diego, CA: Gulliver/Harcourt Brace.

Ride, S., & O'Shaughnessy, T. (1999). *The Mystery of Mars.* New York: Scholastic.

Ride, S., & Okie, S. (1989). *To Space and Back.* New York: Lothrop, Lee & Shepard.

Settel, J. (1999). *Exploding Ants: Amazing Facts About How Animals Adapt.* New York: Atheneum.

Tanaka, S., & Barnard, A. (1998). *Graveyards of the Dinosaurs: What It's Like to Discover Prehistoric Creatures.* New York: Hyperion/Madison Press.

Wick, W. (1997). *A Drop of Water.* New York: Scholastic.

Wright-Frierson, V. (1998). *An Island Scrapbook: From Dawn to Dusk on a Barrier Island.* New York: Simon & Schuster.

Young, J. (1997). *Beyond Amazing: Six Spectacular Science Pop-ups.* New York: HarperCollins.

FIGURE 3.5   Sources of poetry for the content areas.

MATH, SCIENCE, AND TECHNOLOGY

Begay, S. (1995). *Navajo: Visions and Voices Across the Mesa.* New York: Scholastic.

Esbenson, B., & Davie, H. (1996). *Echoes for the Eye: Poems to Celebrate Patterns in Nature.* New York: HarperCollins.

Fleischman, P., & Beddows, E. (1985). *I Am Phoenix: Poems for Two Voices.* New York: Harper & Row.

Fleischman, P., & Beddows, E. (1988). *Joyful Noise: Poems for Two Voices.* New York: Harper & Row.

Nelson, M. (2001). *Carver: A Life in Poems.* Asheville, NC: Front Street.

Pappas, T. (1991). *Math Talk: Mathematical Ideas in Poems for Two Voices.* San Carlos, CA: Wide World/Tetra.

Peters, L. W. (2003). *Earthshake: Poems from the Ground Up.* New York: Greenwillow Books.

Scieszka, J., & Smith, L. (2004). *Science Verse.* New York: Viking.

Sidman, J. (2005). *Song of the Water Boatman & Other Pond Poems.* Boston: Houghton Mifflin.

Siebert, D. (1988). *Mohave.* New York: Crowell.

Siebert, D. (1991). *Sierra.* New York: HarperCollins.

Siebert, D. (2000). *Cave.* New York: HarperCollins.

Wong, J. S. (1999). *Behind the Wheel: Poems About Driving.* New York: Margaret A. McElderry Books.

ENGLISH LANGUAGE ARTS

Adoff, A. (Ed.). (1997). *I Am the Darker Brother: An Anthology of Modern Poems by African Americans.* New York: Simon & Schuster.

Atwell, N. (2006). *A Poem a Day: A Guide to Naming the World.* Portsmouth, NH: Heinemann.

Dillon, L., & Dillon, D. (1998). *To Everything There Is a Season.* New York: The Blue Sky Press.

Fletcher, R. (2005). *A Writing Kind of Day: Poems for Young Poets.* Honesdale, PA: Boyds/Wordsong.

Franco, B. (2000). *You Hear Me? Poems and Writings by Teenage Boys.* Cambridge, MA: Candlewick Press.

Janeczko, P. B. (2005). *A Kick in the Head: An Everyday Guide to Poetic Forms.* Cambridge, MA: Candlewick.

Jarrell, R. (1963). *The Bat-Poet*. New York: Macmillan.

Kherdian, D. (Ed.). (1995). *Beat Voices: An Anthology of Beat Poetry*. New York: Henry Holt.

Masters, E. L. (1996). *Spoon River Anthology*. New York: Tom Doherty Associates.

Myers, W. D. (2004). *Here in Harlem: Poems in Many Voices*. New York: Holiday House.

Okutoro, O. (Comp.). (1999). *Quiet Storm: Voices from Young Black Poets*. New York: Hyperion.

Philip, N. (Comp.). (1996). *Earth Always Endures: Native American Poems*. New York: Viking.

Shapiro, K. J. (2003). *Because I Could Not Stop My Bike: And Other Poems*. Watertown, MA: Charlesbridge.

SOCIAL STUDIES

Agard, J. (2005). *Half-Caste and Other Poems*. London: Hodder Children's Books.

Bruchac, J., & Locker, T. (1995). *The Earth Under Sky Bear's Feet: Native American Poems of the Land*. New York: Scholastic.

Carlson, L. (2005). *Red Hot Salsa: Bilingual Poems on Being Young and Latino in the United States*. New York: Henry Holt.

Carlson, L. M. (Ed.). (1994). *Cool Salsa: Bilingual Poems on Growing Up Latino in the United States*. New York: Henry Holt.

Clinton, C., & Alcorn, S. (Eds.). (1998). *I, Too, Sing America: Three Centuries of African American Poetry*. Boston: Houghton Mifflin.

Grimes, N. (2004). *Tai Chi Morning: Snapshots of China*. Chicago: Cricket Books.

Grimes, N. (2005). *Dark Sons*. New York: Hyperion.

Guthrie, W., & Jacobsen, K. (1998). *This Land Is Your Land*. Boston: Little, Brown.

Hesse, K. (1997). *Out of the Dust*. New York: Scholastic.

Holbrook, S. (2005). *Practical Poetry: A Nonstandard Approach to Meeting Content-Area Standards*. Portsmouth, NH: Heinemann.

Hopkins, L. B. (2006). *Got Geography: Poems*. New York: Greenwillow.

Hopkins, L. B., & Alcorn, S. (2000). *My America: A Poetry Atlas of the United States*. New York: Simon & Schuster.

Hopkins, L. B., & Fiore, P. M. (1994). *Hand in Hand: An American History through Poetry*. New York: Simon & Schuster.

Katz, B., & Crews, N. (2000). *We the People*. New York: Greenwillow Books.

Longfellow, H. W. (2001). *The Midnight Ride of Paul Revere*. Brooklyn: Handprint Books.

Merriam, E., & Diaz, D. (1996). *The Inner City Mother Goose*. New York: Simon & Schuster.

Myers, W. D., & Myers, C. (1997). *Harlem*. New York: Scholastic.

Nelson, M. (2005). *A Wreath for Emmett Till*. Boston: Houghton Mifflin.

Paladino, C. (1999). *One Good Apple: Growing Our Food for the Sake of the Earth*. Boston: Houghton Mifflin.

Philip, N. (2000). *It's a Woman's World: A Century of Women's Voices in Poetry*. New York: Dutton.

Philip, N., & McCurdy, M. (Eds.). (1998). *War and the Pity of War*. New York: Clarion Books.

Podwal, M. (2005). *Jerusalem Sky: Stars, Crosses, and Crescents*. New York: Doubleday.

Rottmann, L. (1993). *Voices from the Ho Chi Minh Trail: Poetry of America and Vietnam, 1965–1993*. Photos by N. T. Thanh, & L. Rottmann. Desert Hot Springs, CA: Event Horizon Press.

Shange, N. (2009). *We Troubled the Waters: Poems*. (R. Brown, Illus.). New York: HarperCollins.

Turner, A., & Moser, B. (1993). *Grass Songs: Poems of Women's Journeys West*. New York: Harcourt Brace.

Wood, N., & Howell, F. (1995). *Dancing Moons*. New York: Delacorte Press.

Young, E. (2005). *Beyond the Great Mountains: A Visual Poem About China*. San Francisco: Chronicle.

Yu, C. (2005). *Little Green: Growing Up During the Chinese Cultural Revolution*. New York: Simon & Schuster.

FINE ARTS

Adoff, J. (2002). *The Song Shoots Out of My Mouth: A Celebration of Music*. (M. French, Illus.). New York: Dutton Children's Books.

Livingston, M. C. (Ed.). (1995). *Call Down the Moon: Poems of Music*. New York: M. K. McElderry Books.

Nelson, M. (2004). *Sweethearts of Rhythm: The Story of the Greatest All-Girl Swing Band in the World*. (J. Pinkney, Illus.). New York: Dial Books.

Panzer, N. (Ed.). (1999). *Celebrate America in Poetry and Art*. New York: Hyperion.

Shange, W., Bearden, R., & Sunshine, L. (1994). *I Live in Music*. New York: Welcome Enterprises. Distributed by Stewart, Tabori & Chang.

Weatherford, C. B. (2008). *Becoming Billie Holliday*. (F. Cooper, Illus.). Honesdale, PA: Wordsong.

PHYSICAL EDUCATION

Adoff, A. (1986). *Sports Pages*. New York: Lippincott.

Janeczko, P. B. (1998). *That Sweet Diamond: Baseball Poems*. New York: Atheneum.

Knudson, R. R., & Swenson, M. (Eds.). (1988). *American Sports Poems*. New York: Orchard Books.

MISCELLANEOUS

Atkins, J. (2010). *Borrowed Names: Poems About Laura Ingalls Wilder, Madam C. J. Walker, Marie Curie, and Their Daughters*. New York: Henry Holt.

Nelson, M., & Pinkney, J. (2009). *Sweethearts of Rhythm: The Story of the Greatest All-Girl Swing Band in the World*. New York: Dial Books.

FIGURE 3.6   Stories of and by passionate practitioners and activists, some in picture book format.

Batten, M. (2001). *Anthropologist: Scientist of the People.* Boston: Houghton Mifflin.

Beckman, W. H. (2008). *Robert Cormier: Banned, Challenged, and Censored.* Berkeley Heights, NJ: Enslow.

Blue, R., & Naden, C. J. (2001). *Benjamin Banneker: Mathematician and Stargazer.* Brookfield, CT: The Millbrook Press.

Brooks, T. (2003). *Sometimes the Magic Works: Lessons from a Writing Life.* New York: Del Ray.

Christensen, B. (2001). *Woody Guthrie: Poet of the People.* New York: Knopf.

Clinton, C. (2007). *When Harriet Met Sojourner.* (S. W. Evans, Illus.). New York: HarperCollins.

Cooper, F. (1996). *Mandela: From the Life of the South African Statesman.* New York: Philomel Books.

Demi. (1998). *The Dalai Lama: A Biography of the Tibetan Spiritual and Political Leader.* New York: Henry Holt.

Dillard, A. (1974). *Pilgrim at Tinker Creek.* New York: Harper's Magazine Press.

Druggleby, J. (1995). *Artist in Overalls: The Life of Grant Wood.* San Francisco: Chronicle.

Fellows, M. (1995). *The Life and Works of Escher.* London: Parragon Book Service.

Fleischman, S. (2008). *The Trouble Begins at 8: A Life of Mark Twain in the Wild, Wild West.* New York: Greenwillow.

Gardner, H. (1993). *Creating Minds: An Anatomy of Creativity as Seen through the Lives of Freud, Einstein, Picasso, Stravinsky, Eliot, Graham, and Gandhi.* New York: HarperCollins.

Giblin, J. C. (1997). *Charles Lindbergh: A Human Hero.* New York: Clarion Books.

Goodall, J., with Berman, P. (1999). *Reason for Hope: A Spiritual Journey.* New York: Warner Books.

Greenberg, J., & Jordan, S. (1998). *Chuck Close Up Close.* New York: DK Publishing.

Hager, T. (1998). *Linus Pauling and the Chemistry of Life.* New York: Oxford University Press.

Hamilton, J. (2004). *James Watson: Solving the Mystery of DNA.* Berkeley Heights, NJ: Enslow.

Harness, C. (2001). *Remember the Ladies: 100 Great American Women.* New York: HarperCollins.

Hill, J. B. (2000). *The Legacy of Luna: The Story of a Tree, a Woman, and the Struggle to Save the Redwoods.* San Francisco: HarperSanFrancisco.

Hinton, K. (2006). *Angela Johnson: Poetic Prose.* Lanham, MD: Rowman & Littlefield.

Johnson, P. (1988). *Intellectuals.* New York: Harper & Row.

Kidder, T. (2003). *Mountains Beyond Mountains: The Quest of Dr. Paul Farmer, a Man Who Would Cure the World.* New York: Random House.

Kuklin, S. (1998). *Iqbal Masih and the Crusaders Against Child Slavery.* New York: Henry Holt.

Lang, L., with French, M. (2008). *Lang Lang: Playing with Flying Keys.* New York: Delacorte.

Lawlor, L. (2001). *Helen Keller: Rebellious Spirit.* New York: Holiday House.

Limb, P. (2008). *Nelson Mandela: A Biography.* Westport, CT: Greenwood.

Loewen, N., & Bancroft, A. (2001). *Four to the Pole!: The American Women's Expedition to Antarctica, 1992–93.* New Haven, CT: Linnet Books.

Lyons, M. E., & Garcia, M. (1999). *Catching the Fire: Philip Simmons, Blacksmith.* Boston: Houghton Mifflin.

Maddox, B. (2002). *Rosalind Franklin, the Dark Lady of DNA.* New York: HarperCollins.

Markham, L. (1997). *Jacques-Yves Cousteau: Exploring the Wonders of the Deep.* Austin, TX: Raintree Steck-Vaughn.

Matthews, T. (1998). *Light Shining Through the Mist: A Photobiography of Dian Fossey.* Washington, DC: National Geographic Society.

McKissack, P. C., & McKissack, F. L. (1998). *Young, Black, and Determined: A Biography of Lorraine Hansberry.* New York: Holiday House.

Monceaux, M. (1994). *Jazz: My Music, My People.* New York: Borzoi/Knopf.

Montgomery, S. (2004). *The Tarantula Scientist.* Boston: Houghton Mifflin.

Myers, W. D. (2008). *Ida B. Wells: Let the Truth Be Told.* New York: HarperCollins.

Myers, W. D., & Jenkins, L. (2000). *Malcolm X: A Fire Burning Brightly.* New York: HarperCollins.

Myers, W. D., & Lawrence, J. (1996). *Toussaint L'ouverture: The Fight for Haiti's Freedom.* New York: Simon & Schuster.

O'Meara, D. (2005). *Into the Volcano.* Tonawanda, NY: Kids Can Press.

Orgill, R. (2001). *Shout, Sister, Shout: Ten Girl Singers Who Shaped a Century.* New York: M. K. McElderry Books.

Partridge, E. (2005). *John Lennon: All I Want Is the Truth.* New York: Viking.

Patent, D. H. (2001). *Charles Darwin: The Life of a Revolutionary Thinker.* New York: Holiday House.

Paulsell, W. O. (1990). *Tough Minds, Tender Hearts: Six Prophets of Social Justice.* New York: Paulist Press.

Pinckney, A. D. (1998). *Duke Ellington: The Piano Prince and His Orchestra.* New York: Hyperion Books for Children.

Poole, J. (2005). *Joan of Arc.* New York: Knopf.

Porter, D. L. (2007). *Michael Jordan: A Biography.* Westport, CT: Greenwood.

Reef, C. (2001). *Sigmund Freud: Pioneer of the Mind.* New York: Clarion Books.

Roberts, J. (2005). *Bob Dylan: Voice of a Generation.* Minneapolis, MN: Lerner.

Rowley, H. (2001). *Richard Wright: The Life and Times.* New York: Henry Holt.

Russell, C. A. (2000). *Michael Faraday: Physics and Faith.* New York: Oxford University Press.

Sacks, O. (1995). *An Anthropologist on Mars: Seven Paradoxical Tales.* New York: Vintage Books.

Siegel, B. (1995). *Marian Wright Edelman: The Making of a Crusader.* New York: Simon & Schuster.

Sis, P. (1996). *Starry Messenger: Galileo Galilei.* New York: Foster/Farrar.

Spangenburg, R., & Moser, D. K. (2008). *Niels Bohr: Atomic Theorist.* Philadelphia: Chelsea House.

Spivak, D., & Demi. (1997). *Grass Sandals: The Travels of Basho.* New York: Atheneum.

Sports Illustrated. (2008). *Brett Favre: The Tribute.* New York: *Time.*

Stanley, D. (1996). *Leonardo da Vinci.* New York: Morrow.

Stanley, D. (1998). *Joan of Arc.* New York: Morrow Junior Books.

Stanley, D. (2000). *Michelangelo.* New York: HarperCollins Children's Books.

Szabo, C. (1997). *Sky Pioneer: A Photobiography of Amelia Earhart.* Washington, DC: National Geographic Society.

Venkatraman, P. (2008). *Women Mathematicians.* Greensboro, NC: Morgan Reynolds Publishing.

Weston, M. (2008). *Honda: The Boy Who Dreamed of Cars.* New York: Lee.

White, M. (2004). *C.S. Lewis: A Life.* New York: Carroll & Graf.

FIGURE 3.7   Sample titles of nonfiction books that connect to content curriculum.

SCIENCE AND MATH

Bradley, T. J. (2008). *Paleo Bugs: Survival of the Creepiest.* San Francisco: Chronicle Books.

Collard, S. B., III (2008). *Science Warriors: The Battle Against Invasive Species.* Boston: Houghton.

Dewey, J. O. (2001). *Antarctic Journal: Four Months at the Bottom of the World.* New York: HarperCollins.

Gribbin, M., & Gribbin, J. (2005). *The Science of Philip Pullman's His Dark Materials.* New York: Knopf.

Hoose, P. (2004). *The Race to Save the Lord God Bird.* New York: Farrar, Straus & Giroux.

Jackson, D. M. (2008). *Phenomena: Secrets of the Senses.* Boston: Little Brown Books for Young Readers.

Parker, B. (2003). *The Isaac Newton School of Driving: Physics and Your Car.* Baltimore: The John Hopkins University Press.

Pringle, L., & Marstall, B. (1997). *An Extraordinary Life: The Story of a Monarch Butterfly.* New York: Orchard.

Pringle, L., & Moehlman, P. D. R. (1993). *Jackal Woman: Exploring the World of Jackals.* New York: Scribner's.

Scott, E. (2008). *Mars and the Search for Life.* New York: Clarion.

Turner, P. S. (2008). *Life on Earth—And Beyond: An Astrobiologist's Quest.* Watertown, MA: Charlesbridge.

Van Meter, V., with Gutman, D. (1995). *Taking Flight: My Story.* New York: Viking.

Wainer, H. (2005). *Graphic Discovery: A Trout in the Milk and Other Visual Adventures.* Princeton, NJ: Princeton University Press.

HISTORY/SOCIAL STUDIES

Able, D. (2000). *Hate Groups.* Berkeley Heights, NJ: Enslow.

Armstrong, J. (1999). *Shipwreck at the Bottom of the World: The Extraordinary True Story of Shackleton and the Endurance.* New York: Crown.

Ashabranner, B. (2000). *A Date with Destiny: The Women in Military Service for America Memorial.* New York: 21st Century.

Ayer, E., Waterford, H., & Heck, A. (1995). *Parallel Journeys.* New York: Atheneum.

Blumenthal, K. (2005). *Let Me Play: The Story of Title IX, the Law that Changed the Future of Girls in America.* New York: Atheneum.

Brown, D. (2008). *Let It Begin Here!: April 19, 1775, the Day the American Revolution Began.* New York: Roaring Brook/Flash Point.

Budhos, M. (1999). *Remix: Conversations with Immigrant Teens.* New York: Henry Holt.

Chen, Da. (2001). *China's Son: Growing up in the Cultural Revolution.* New York: Delacorte Press.

Dash, J. (1996). *We Shall Not Be Moved: The Women's Factory Strike of 1909.* New York: Scholastic.

Giblin, J. C. (Ed.). (2000). *The Century That Was: Reflections on the Last Hundred Years.* New York: Atheneum.

Jacobs, T. A. (2000). *Teens on Trial: Young People Who Challenged the Law—and Changed Your Life.* Minneapolis, MN: Free Spirit Publishing, Inc.

Jaffe, S. H. (1996). *Who Were the Founding Fathers? Two Hundred Years of Reinventing American History.* New York: Henry Holt.

Kaufman, M. T. (2008). *1968.* New York: Roaring Brook/Flash Point.

Kuklin, S. (1996). *Irrepressible Spirit: Conversations with Human Rights Activists.* New York: Philomel.

Kurlansky, M. (2004). *1968: The Year that Rocked the World.* New York: Ballantine Books.

Levine, E. (2000). *Darkness Over Denmark: The Danish Resistance and the Rescue of the Jews.* New York: Holiday House.

Ousseimi, M. (1995). *Caught in the Crossfire: Growing Up in a War Zone.* New York: Walker.

Silvey, A. (2008). *I'll Pass for Your Comrade: Women Soldiers in the Civil War.* New York: Clarion.

Slavicek, L. C. (2008). *The Black Death.* Philadelphia: Chelsea House.

Strom, Y. (1996). *Quilted Landscape: Conversations with Young Immigrants.* New York: Simon & Schuster.

Tunnell, M. O., & Chilcoat, G. W. (1996). *The Children of Topaz: The Story of a Japanese-American Internment Camp Based on a Classroom Diary.* New York: Holiday House.

(continued)

Warren, A. (1996). *Orphan Train Rider: One Boy's True Story*. Boston: Houghton Mifflin.

Wolney, P. (2004). *The Underground Railroad: A Primary Source History of the Journey to Freedom*. New York: The Rosen Publishing Group.

Wyatt, V. (2008). *Who Discovered America?* Toronto, Canada: Kids Can Press.

FINE ARTS

Aronson, M. (1998). *Art Attack: A Short Cultural History of the Avant-Garde*. New York: Clarion Books.

Berger, M. (1989). *The Science of Music*. New York: HarperCollins.

Capek, M. (1996). *Murals*. Minneapolis, MN: Lerner Publications Company.

Carroll, C. (1996). *How Artists See the Elements: Earth, Air, Fire, Water*. New York: Abbeville Kids.

Cobb, M. (1995). *The Quilt-Block History of Pioneer Days*. Brookfield, CT: Millbrook Press.

Cobb, M. (1999). *A Sampler View of Colonial Life*. Brookfield, CT: Millbrook Press.

Collier, J. L. (1997). *Jazz: An American Saga*. New York: Henry Holt.

Cummins, J., & Kiefer, B. (1999). *Wings of an Artist: Children's Book Illustrators Talk About Their Art*. New York: Harry N. Abrams.

Ewing, P., & Louis, L. L. (1999). *In the Paint*. New York: Abbeville Kids.

Getzinger, D., & Felsenfeld, D. (2004). *Johann Sebastian Bach and the Art of Baroque Music*. Greensboro, NC: Morgan Reynolds.

Greenberg, J., & Jordan, S. (1991). *The Painter's Eye: Learning to Look at Contemporary Art*. New York: Delacorte Press.

Greenberg, J., & Jordan, S. (1998). *Chuck Close Up Close*. New York: DK Publishing.

Pekarik, A. (1992). *Painting: Behind the Scenes*. New York: Hyperion Books for Children.

HEALTH, WELLNESS, AND PHYSICAL EDUCATION

Barbour, S. (Ed.). (1998). *Alcohol: Opposing Viewpoints*. San Diego, CA: Greenhaven Press.

FIGURE 3.8   **Resources for selecting and reviewing trade books.**

Association for Library Service to Children. (2002). *The Newbery and Caldecott Awards: A Guide to the Medal and Honor Books*. Chicago: American Library Association.

Brown, J. E., & Stephens, E. C. (Eds.). (2003). *Your Reading: An Annotated Booklist for Middle School and Junior High* (11th ed.). Urbana, IL: National Council of Teachers of English.

Cianciolo, P. J. (2000). *Informational Picture Books for Children*. Chicago: American Library Association.

Damelson, K. E., & Lickteig, M. J. (2003). Finding scientific experiences and information in children's books. *School Library Media Activities Monthly, 19*(8), 36–38.

Estell, D., Satchwell, M. L., & Wright, P. S. (2000). *Reading Lists for College-Bound Students* (3rd ed.). New York: ARCO.

Gillespie, J. T. (2000). *Best Books for Young Teen Readers Grades 7–10*. New Providence, NJ: R. R. Bowker.

Hearne, B., with Stevenson, D. (1999). *Choosing Books for Children: A Commonsense Guide* (3rd ed.). Urbana: University of Illinois Press.

Johnson, H., & Freedman, L. (2005). *Content Area Literature Circles*. Norwood, MA: Christopher-Gordon.

Landrum, J. (2001). Selecting Intermediate Novels that Feature Characters with Disabilities. *The Reading Teacher, 55*(3), 252–258.

FIGURE 3.9   **Examples of documentary resources for history teachers.**

Colbert, D. (Ed.). (1997). *Eyewitness to America: 500 Years of America in the Words of Those Who Saw It Happen*. New York: Pantheon.

Compston, C., & Seidman, R. F. (Eds.). (2004). *Our Documents: 100 Milestone Documents from the National Archives*. New York: Oxford University Press.

Gershman, G. P. (2005). *Death Penalty on Trial: A Handbook with Cases, Laws, and Documents*. Santa Barbara, CA: AB-CLIO.

Greenwood, T. (2000). *The Gilded Age: A History in Documents*. New York: Oxford University Press.

Huffman, J. L. (2004). *Modern Japan: A History in Documents*. New York: Oxford University Press.

Lepore, J. (2000). *Encounters in the New World: A History in Documents*. New York: Oxford University Press.

McElvaine, R. S. (2000). *The Depression and the New Deal: A History in Documents*. New York: Oxford University Press.

Rosenfeld, S. (Ed.). (2004). *Encyclopedia of American Historical Documents*. New York: Facts on File.

Sabasteanski, A. (Ed.). (2005). *Patterns of Global Terrorism 1985–2005: U. S. Department of State Reports with Supplemental Documents and Statistics*. Great Barrington, MA: Berkshire.

Schoppa, R. K. (2004). *Twentieth Century China: A History in Documents*. New York: Oxford University Press.

FIGURE 3.11 Firsthand accounts of war.

Al-Windawi, T. (2004). *Thura's Diary: My Life in Wartime Iraq*. New York: Viking.

Bircher, W. (2000). *A Civil War Drummer Boy: The Diary of William Bircher, 1861–1865*. (S. S. Sateren, Ed.). Mankato, MN: Blue Earth Books.

Forten, C. L. (2000). *A Free Black Girl Before the Civil War: The Diary of Charlotte Forten, 1854*. (C. Steele, Ed.). Mankato, MN: Blue Earth Books.

Jones, J. B. (1993). *A Rebel War Clerk's Diary/John B. Jones*. (Earl Schlenck Miers, Annot.). Baton Rouge, LA: Louisiana State University Press.

Linklater, A. (2001). *The Code of Love: A True Story of Two Lovers Torn Apart by the War that Brought Them Together*. New York: Doubleday.

Radi, N. (2003). *Baghdad Diaries: A Woman's Chronicle of War and Exile*. New York: Vintage Books.

Roe, A. S. (1904). *The Diary of Captain Daniel Roe, an Officer of the French and Indian War and of the Revolution: Brookhaven, Long Island, During Portions of 1806–7–8*. Worcester, MA: Blanchard Press.

Ropes, H. A. (1980). *Civil War Nurse: The Diary and Letters of Hanna Ropes*. Knoxville: University of Tennessee Press.

Rosenkranz, K. (1999). *Vipers in the Storm: Diary of a Gulf War Fighter Pilot*. Atlanta, GA: Turner.

Sneden, R.–N. (2000). *Eye of the Storm: A Civil War Odyssey*. (C. F. Bryan, Jr., & N. D. Lankford, Eds.). New York: Free Press.

Watkins, S. R. (2004). *The Diary of Sam Watkins, a Confederate Soldier*. (R. Asbby, Ed.). Tarrytown, NY: Benchmark Books.

FIGURE 4.3 Books about time and sequence.

Babbitt, N. (1975). *Tuck Everlasting*. New York: Farrar, Straus & Giroux.

Chisholm, J., & Addario, S. (1998). *The Usborne Book of World History Dates*. New York: Scholastic.

Cole, K. C. (1998). *The Universe and the Teacup: The Mathematics of Truth and Beauty*. New York: Harcourt Brace.

Davis, H. (2010). *The Clearing*. Boston: Graphia.

Denman, C. (1995). *The History Puzzle: An Interactive Visual Timeline*. Atlanta, GA: Turner Publishing.

Fritz, J., Paterson, K., McKissack, P., McKissack, F., Mahy, M., & Highwater, J. (1992). *The World in 1492*. New York: Henry Holt.

George, L. (2003). *A Time Line of the American Revolution*. New York: Rosen.

Glennon, L. (Ed.). (1995). *Our Times: The Illustrated History of the Twentieth Century*. Atlanta, GA: Turner Publishing.

Goodman, S. E. (2004). *On This Spot: An Expedition Back Through Time*. New York: Greenwillow Books.

Grun, B. (1991). *The Timetables of History: A Linkage of People and Events*. New York: Simon & Schuster.

Hawking, S. (2001). *The Universe in a Nutshell*. New York: Bantam Books.

Kallen, S. A. (2009). *Time Travel*. Detroit: Kidhaven Press.

L'Engle, M. (1962). *A Wrinkle in Time*. New York: Farrar, Straus & Giroux.

Niffenegger, A. (2003). *The Time Traveler's Wife*. San Francisco: MacAdam/Cage.

Peterson, C. (2004). *Jump Back in Time: A Living History Resource*. Portsmouth, NH: Teachers Ideas Press.

Sherman, J. (2005). *How Do We Know the Nature of Time?* New York: Rosen.

Tomaselli-Moschovitis, V. (2003). *Junior Timelines on File*. New York: Facts on File.

Wells, H. G. (1988). *The Time Machine*. New York: Ace Books.

FIGURE 4.15 Books providing procedural knowledge.

Beil, K. M. (1999). *Fire in Their Eyes: Wildfires and the People Who Fight Them*. New York: Harcourt Brace.

Byman, J. (2001). *Carl Sagan: In Contact with the Cosmos*. Greensboro, NC: Morgan Reynolds.

Crick, F. (1988). *What Mad Pursuit: A Personal View of Scientific Discovery*. New York: Basic Books.

Farber, B. (1991). *How to Learn Any Language: Quickly, Easily, and on Your Own!* New York: MJF Books.

Fridell, R. (2000). *Solving Crimes: Pioneers of Forensic Science*. New York: Franklin Watts.

Goodall, J. (1999). *Reason for Hope: A Spiritual Journey*. New York: Warner Books.

Goodman, S. E. (1999). *Ultimate Field Trip 3: Wading into Marine Biology*. New York: Atheneum.

Heiligman, D. (1994). *Barbara McClintock: Alone in Her Field*. New York: Scientific American Books for Young Readers.

Jackson, D. M. (1996). *The Bone Detectives: How Forensic Anthropologists Solve Crimes and Uncover Mysteries of the Dead*. Boston: Little, Brown.

The Math Forum. (2003). *Dr. Math Gets You Ready for Algebra*. Hoboken, NJ: John Wiley & Sons.

Maze, S., & Grace, C. O. (1997a). *I Want to Be an Astronaut*. New York: Harcourt Brace.

Maze, S., & Grace, C. O. (1997b). *I Want to Be a Dancer*. New York: Harcourt Brace.

Maze, S., & Grace, C. O. (1997c). *I Want to Be an Engineer*. New York: Harcourt Brace.

(continued)

Maze, S., & Grace, C. O. (1997d). *I Want to Be a Veterinarian*. New York: Harcourt Brace.

Paulos, J. A. (2003). *A Mathematician Plays the Stock Market*. New York: Basic Books.

Pringle, L. (1997). *Elephant Woman: Cynthia Moss Explores the World of Elephants*. New York: Atheneum.

Simon, S. (2000). *From Paper Airplanes to Outer Space*. Katonah, NY: Richard Owen Publishers.

Sola, M. (1997). *Angela Weaves a Dream: The Story of a Young Maya Artist*. New York: Hyperion.

Swinburne, S. R. (1998). *In Good Hands: Behind the Scenes at a Center for Orphaned and Injured Birds*. San Francisco: Sierra Club Books for Children.

Tanaka, S. (1998). *Graveyards of the Dinosaurs: What It's Like to Discover Prehistoric Creatures*. New York: Hyperion/Madison Press.

Thimmesh, C. (2000). *Girls Think of Everything: Stories of Ingenious Inventions by Women*. Boston: Houghton Mifflin.

FIGURE 5.3   Selected examples of articles and books about discipline-based inquiry.

Alvarado, A. E. (2003). *Inquiry-Based Learning Using Everyday Objects: Hands-On Instructional Strategies that Promote Active Learning in Grade 8*. Thousand Oaks, CA: Corwin Press.

Bruck, L. B., & Towns, M. H. (2009). Preparing Students to Benefit from Inquiry-Based Activities in the Chemistry Laboratory: Guidelines and Suggestions. *Journal of Chemical Education, 86*(7), 820–822.

Encouraging Students to Think: A Special Collection of Inquiry-Based Biological Activities from the Past Decade. (2005). *Science Activities, 41*(4), 3–51.

Foster, S. (1999). Using Historical Empathy to Excite Students About the Study of History: Can You Empathize with Neville Chamberlain? *The Social Studies, 90*(1), 18–34.

Heron, A. H. (2003). A Study of Agency: Multiple Constructions of Choice and Decision Making in an Inquiry-Based Summer School Program for Struggling Readers. *Journal of Adolescent and Adult Literacy, 46*(7), 568–579.

Hynd, C. R. (1999). Teaching Students to Think Critically Using Multiple Texts in History. *Journal of Adolescent and Adult Literacy, 42*(6), 428–436.

Kuhlman, W. D. (2001). Fifth-graders' Reactions to Native Americans in *Little House on the Prairie:* Guiding Students' Critical Reading. *The New Advocate, 14*(4), 387–399.

Lederman, N. G., & Niess, M. L. (2000). Problem Solving and Solving Problems: Inquiry About Inquiry. *School Science and Mathematics,* March, 113–116.

Llewellyn, D. (2005). *Teaching High School Science Through Inquiry: A Case Study Approach*. Thousand Oaks, CA: Corwin Press.

Mayer, R. H. (1999). Use the Story of Anne Hutchinson to Teach Historical Thinking. *The Social Studies, 90*(3), 105–109.

FIGURE 6.2   A sampling of books on language.

Asimov, I. (1969). *Words of Science and the History Behind Them*. New York: New American Library.

Brook, D. (1998). *The Journey of English*. New York: Clarion Books.

Fry, B. F., Kress, J. E., & Fountoukidis, D. L. (2000). *The Reading Teacher's Book of Lists* (4th ed.). Paramus, NJ: Prentice Hall.

Gordon, K. E. (1997). *Torn Wings and Faux Pas: A Flashbook of Style, A Beastly Guide Through the Writer's Labyrinth*. New York: Pantheon Books.

Hendrickson, R. (1994). *Grand Slams, Hat Tricks, and Alley-Oops: A Sports Fan's Book of Words*. New York: Prentice Hall.

Hobbs, J. B. (2006). *Homophones and Homographs: An American Dictionary* (4th ed.). Jefferson, NE: McFarland.

Kahn, J. E. (Ed.). (1990). *Illustrated Reverse Dictionary: Find the Right Words on the Tip of Your Tongue*. Pleasantville, NY: Reader's Digest Association.

Klausner, J. (1990). *Talk About English: How Words Travel and Change*. New York: Crowell.

Lederer, R., & Dowis, R. (1999). *Sleeping Dogs Don't Lay: Practical Advice for the Grammatically Challenged*. New York: St. Martin's Press.

Lewis, T. (1990). *Et Cetera, Et Cetera: Notes of a Word Watcher*. Boston: Little, Brown.

Morris, E. (2000). *The Word Detective*. Chapel Hill, NC: Algonquin Books of Chapel Hill.

Randall, B. (1997). *When Is a Pig a Hog?: A Guide to Confoundingly Related English Words*. New York: Galahad Books.

Safire, W. (1997). *Watching My Language: Adventures in the Word Trade*. New York: Random House.

Safire, W. (1999). *Spread the Word*. New York: Random House.

Sommer, E. F., & Sommer, M. (1998). *Similes Dictionary*. Detroit, MI: Visible Ink Press.

Soukhanov, A. H. (1995). *Word Watch: The Stories Behind the Words of Our Lives*. New York: Henry Holt.

Truss, L. (2003). *Eats, Shoots and Leaves: The Zero Tolerance Approach to Punctuation*. New York: Penguin.

Walsh, B. (2000). *Lapsing into a Comma: A Curmudgeon's Guide to the Many Things that Can Go Wrong in Print—and How to Avoid Them*. Chicago: Contemporary Books.

FIGURE 6.3   Language-based games, books, and websites.

Agee, J. (1999). *Sit on a Potato Pan, Otis: More Palindromes.* New York: Farrar, Straus & Giroux.

Carroll, L. (1982). *Alice's Adventures in Wonderland.* (S. H. Goodacre, Ed.). Berkeley: University of California Press.

Farb, P. (1993). *Word Play: What Happens When People Talk.* New York: Vintage.

Fathman, A. K., & Crowther, D. T. (Eds.). (2006). *Science for English Language Learners: K–12 Classroom Strategies.* Arlington, VA: NSTA Press.

Frasier, D. (2000). *Miss Alaineus: A Vocabulary Disaster.* New York, Harcourt Brace.

Garrison, W. (1992). *Why You Say It: The Fascinating Stories Behind Over 600 Everyday Words and Phrases.* New York: MJF Books.

Gwynne, F. (1970). *The King Who Rained.* New York: Simon & Schuster.

Gwynne, F. (1976). *A Chocolate Moose for Dinner.* New York: Simon & Schuster.

Gwynne, F. (1988). *A Little Pigeon Toad.* New York: Simon & Schuster.

Heller, R. (1987). *A Cache of Jewels: And Other Collective Nouns.* New York: Scholastic.

Heller, R. (1988). *Kites Sail High: A Book About Verbs.* New York: Scholastic.

Heller, R. (1989). *Many Luscious Lollipops: A Book About Adjectives.* New York: Scholastic.

Heller, R. (1990). *Merry-Go-Round: A Book About Nouns.* New York: Scholastic.

Heller, R. (1991). *Up, Up, and Away: A Book About Adverbs.* New York: Scholastic.

Heller, R. (1995). *Behind the Mask: A Book About Prepositions.* New York: Scholastic.

Heller, R. (1997). *Mine, All Mine: A Book About Pronouns.* New York: Scholastic.

Heller, R. (1997). *Fantastic! Wow! And Unreal!: A Book About Interjections and Conjunctions.* New York: Scholastic.

Lederer, R. (1990). *The Play of Words: Fun & Games for Language Lovers.* New York: Pocket.

Lederer, R., & Dowis, R. (1999). *Sleeping Dogs Don't Lay: Practical Advice for the Grammatically Challenged.* New York: St. Martin's Press.

Lipton, J. (1991). *An Exaltation of Larks: The Ultimate Edition.* New York: Viking.

Maizels, J., & Petty, K. (1996). *The Amazing Pop-Up Book of Grammar.* New York: Penguin Books.

McQuain, J., & Malless, S. (1998). *Coined by Shakespeare: Words & Meaning First Penned by the Bard.* Springfield, MA: Merriam-Webster.

Merriam-Webster's Word Crazy: The Action Word Game on CD-ROM. Springfield, MA: Merriam-Webster.

Shepherd, R. (1991). *Playing the Language Game.* Philadelphia: Open University Press.

Stein, L., & Voskovitz, B. (1999). *The Buzzword Bingo Book: The Complete Definitive Guide to the Underground Workplace Game of Corporate Jargon and Doublespeak.* New York: Villard.

Thompson, M. C. (1990, 1991). *The Word Within the Word,* (Vols. 1 & 2). Unionville, NY: Trillium.

Thompson, M. C. (1991). *The Magic Lens.* Unionville, NY: Trillium.

Umstatter, J. (2002). *201 Ready-to-Use Word Games for the English Classroom.* Paramus, NJ: The Center for Applied Research in Education.

www.zdaily.com/word.shtml

www.gamequarium.com/spanishvocab.html

http://vocabulary.com/VUogoodlinks.html

www.memory.loc.gov/learn/features/immig/vocabulary.html

www.donquijote.org/spanishlanguage/games

A.Word.A.Day—http://wordsmith.org/words/yester.html

Word Puzzles—www.vocabulary.com

FIGURE 6.6   Content-relevant alphabet books appropriate for middle and high school students.

MATH, SCIENCE, AND TECHNOLOGY

Collison, C., & Campbell, J. (2005). *G Is for Galaxy: An Out of This World Alphabet.* Chelsea, MI: Sleeping Bear Press.

Crosbie, M. J., Rosenthal, K., & Rosenthal, S. (2000). *Arches to Zigzags: An Architecture ABC.* New York: Harry N. Abrams.

Mullins, P. (1994). *V for Vanishing: An Alphabet of Endangered Animals.* New York: HarperCollins.

Munro, R., & Maddex, D. (1986). *Architects Make Zigzags: Looking at Architecture from A to Z.* New York: Wiley.

Palotta, J. (1989). *The Yucky Reptile Alphabet Book.* Watertown, MA: Charlesbridge Publishing.

Palotta, J. (2002). *The Skull Alphabet Book.* Watertown, MA: Charlesbridge.

Poortvliet, R., & Huyben, W. (1989). *The Book of the Sandman and the Alphabet of Sleep.* New York: Harry N. Abrams.

Rosen, M. J., & Butler, D. (2000). *Avalanche.* Cambridge, MA: Candlewick Press.

Schwartz, D. M. (2001). *Q Is for Quark: A Science Alphabet Book.* Berkeley, CA: Tricycle Press.

ENGLISH AND FOREIGN LANGUAGES

Base, G. (1986). *Animalia.* New York: Harry N. Abrams.

Bourke, L. (1991). *Eye Spy: A Mysterious Alphabet.* San Francisco: Chronicle Books.

Elya, S. M. (2006). *F Is for Fiesta.* New York: G. P. Putnam's Sons.

Harley, S. (2000). *Fly with Poetry: An ABC of Poetry.* Honesdale, PA: Wordsong.

Jocelyn, M. (2005). *ABC X 3: English, Español, Français.* Plattsburg, NY: Tundra Books.

(continued)

Mannis, C. D. (2003). *The Queen's Progress*. New York: Viking.

Scillian, D. (2003). *P Is for Passport: A World Alphabet*. Chelsea, MI: Sleeping Bear Press.

Winter, J. (2004). *Calavera Abecedario: A Day of the Dead Alphabet Book*. Orlando, FL: Harcourt.

FINE ARTS

Anno, M. (1975). *Anno's Alphabet*. New York: Crowell.

Cox, P. (2001). *Abstract Alphabet: A Book of Animals*. San Francisco: Chronicle Books.

Horenstein, H. (2000). *A Is for ?: A Photographer's Alphabet of Animals*. New York: Scholastic.

J. Paul Getty Museum. (1997). *A Is for Artist: A Getty Museum Alphabet*. Los Angeles, CA: Author.

Johns, S. (1999). *The Alphabet Book: Alphabets for Design and Decoration*. London: Aurum.

Kelly, J., & Koeth, A. (Eds.). (2000). *Artist and Alphabet: Twentieth Century Calligraphy and Letter Art in America*. Boston: D. R. Godine in association with the American Institute of Graphic Arts and the Society of Scribes.

Mayers, F. C. (1988). *ABC: Musical Instruments from the Metropolitan Museum of Art*. New York: Harry N. Abrams.

Mayers, F. C. (1998). *ABC: Egyptian Art from the Brooklyn Museum*. New York: Harry N. Abrams.

Pelletier, D. (1996). *The Graphic Alphabet*. New York: Orchard.

Rubin, C. E. (Selector). (1989). *ABC: Americana from the National Gallery of Art*. Orlando, FL: Harcourt Brace/Gulliver.

Wilks, M. (1986). *The Ultimate Alphabet*. New York: Henry Holt.

SOCIAL STUDIES

Aylesworth, J. (1992). *The Folks in the Valley: A Pennsylvania Dutch ABC*. New York: HarperFestival.

Cuomo, M., & Grodin, E. D. (2009). *C Is for Ciao: An Italy Alphabet*. Chelsea, MI: Sleeping Bear Press.

Der Manuelian, P. (1995). *Hieroglyphs from A to Z*. New York: Scholastic.

Domeniconi, D. (2003). *M Is for Majestic: A National Parks Alphabet*. Chelsea, MI: Sleeping Bear Press.

Hall, F., & Oehm, K. (1998). *Appalachian ABCs*. Johnson City, TN: Overmountain Press.

Hudson, W., & Wesley, V. W. (1997). *Afro-Bets Book of Black Heroes from A to Z: An Introduction to Important Black Achievers for Young Readers*. East Orange, NJ: Just Us Books.

Johnson, T. (2008). *P Is for Piñata: A Mexico Alphabet*. (J. Parra, Illus.). Chelsea, MI: Sleeping Bear Press.

Jordan, M., & Jordan, T. (1996). *Amazon Alphabet*. New York: Scholastic.

Kreeger, C., & Cartwright, S. (1991). *Alaska ABC Book*. (Last Wilderness Adventures). Wasilla, AK: Alaska ABC Book.

Musgrove, M., Dillon, L., & Dillon, D. (1976). *Ashanti to Zulu: African Traditions*. New York: Dial Press.

Paul, A. W. (1991). *Eight Hands Round: A Patchwork Alphabet*. New York: HarperCollins.

Sanders, N. L. (2007). *D Is for Drinking Gourd: An African American Alphabet*. (E. B. Lewis, Illus.). Chelsea, MI: Sleeping Bear Press.

Yorinks, A. (1999). *The Alphabet Atlas*. Delray Beach, FL: Winslow Press.

INTERDISCIPLINARY AND MISCELLANEOUS

Ada, A. F., & Silva, S. (1997). *Gathering the Sun: An Alphabet in Spanish and English*. New York: Lothrop, Lee & Shepard Books.

Alexander, R. (1997). *Alef Is Silent: A Hebrew Alphabet*. Seattle, WA: Inksleeves.

Bruchac, J., & Goetzl, R. F. (1997). *Many Nations: An Alphabet of Native Americans*. Mahwah, NJ: Bridgewater Books.

Brustad, K., & Al-Batal, M. (1995). *Alif Baa: Introduction to Arabic Letters and Sounds*. Washington, DC: Georgetown University Press.

Edwards, M. (1992). *Alef-Bet: A Hebrew Alphabet Book*. New York: Lothrop, Lee, & Shepard Books.

Ford, J. G. (1997). *K Is for Kwanzaa: A Kwanzaa Alphabet Book*. New York: Scholastic.

Hepworth, C. (1992). *Antics!: An Alphabet Anthology*. New York: Putnam.

Herzog, B. (2003). *K Is for Kick: A Soccer Alphabet*. Chelsea, MI: Sleeping Bear Press.

Herzog, B. (2005). *P Is for Putt: A Golf Alphabet*. Chelsea, MI: Sleeping Bear Press.

Herzog, B. (2008). *A Is for Amazing Moments: A Sports Alphabet*. Chelsea, MI: Sleeping Bear Press.

Humez, A., & Humez, N. (1983). *Alpha to Omega: The Life and Times of the Greek Alphabet*. Boston: David R. Godine.

Jacobs, L., & Ohlsson, I. (1994). *Alphabet of Girls*. New York: Henry Holt.

Mayers, F. C. (1996). *Basketball ABC: The NBA Alphabet*. New York: Harry N. Abrams.

McLaren, C., & Jaber, P. (2009). *When Royals Wore Ruffles: A Funny and Fashionable Alphabet!* (C. McLaren, Illus.). New York: Schwartz & Wade Books.

Michelson, R. (2008). *A is for Abraham: A Jewish Family Alphabet*. (R. Mazzellan, Illus.). Chelsea, MI: Sleeping Bear Press.

Rankin, L. (1991). *The Handmade Alphabet*. New York: Dial Books.

Roberts, P. L. (1987). *Alphabet Books as a Key to Language Patterns: An Annotated Action Bibliography*. Hamden, CT: Library Professional Publications.

Royston, A., & Pastor, T. (1993). *The A-to-Z Book of Cars*. New York: Scholastic.

Ruiers, M. (1996). *A Mountain Alphabet Book*. Toronto, ON: Tundra Books.

Russell-McCloud, P. (1999). *A Is for Attitude: An Alphabet for Living*. New York: HarperCollins.

Young, J. (2006). *R Is for Rhyme: A Poetry Alphabet*. (V. Juhasz, Illus.). Chelsea, MI: Sleeping Bear Press.

FIGURE 6.19 Samples of visual dictionaries available for content area learning.

Ambrose, G., & Harris, P. (2007). *A Visual Dictionary of Fashion Design.* Lausanne, Switzerland: AVA Publishing.

Berger, M., & Bonner, H. (2000). *Scholastic Science Dictionary.* New York: Scholastic.

Buckley, J., Jr. (2001). *The Visual Dictionary of Baseball.* New York: Dorling Kindersley.

Carley, R. (1997). *The Visual Dictionary of American Domestic Architecture.* New York: Henry Holt.

Challoner, J. (1996). *Visual Dictionary of Chemistry.* New York: DK Children's Books.

Corbeil, J., & Archambault, A. (2000). *Scholastic Visual Dictionary.* New York: Scholastic.

Corbeil, J., & Archambault, A. (2004). *The Firefly Five Language Visual Dictionary.* Buffalo, NY: Firefly Books.

Guo, Q. (2002). *A Visual Dictionary of Chinese Architecture.* Mulgrave, Victoria, Great Britain: Images.

Kalman, B. (2008). *A Visual Dictionary of a Native Community.* New York: Crabtree Publishing.

Kalman, B. (2008). *A Visual Dictionary of the Old West.* New York: Crabtree Publishing.

Kalman, B. (2008). *A Visual Dictionary of a Pioneer Community.* New York: Crabtree Publishing.

Merriam-Webster. (2008). *Merriam-Webster's Compact Visual Dictionary.* Springfield, MA: Author.

Milner, A. (2005). *Inspirational Objects: A Visual Dictionary of Simple, Elegant Forms.* London: A. & C. Black.

Reynolds, D. W., Bies, P., Hall, N., & Ivanov, A. (1998). *Star Wars: The Visual Dictionary.* New York: Dorling Kindersley.

Stanchak, J. (2000). *Visual Dictionary of the Civil War.* New York: Dorling Kindersley.

The Visual Dictionary of Ancient Civilizations. (1994). New York: Dorling Kindersley.

FIGURE 7.2 Resources for exploring the processes of writers.

Arana, M. (2003). *The Writing Life: Writers on How They Think and Work.* New York: Public Affairs.

Brooks, T. (2003). *Sometimes the Magic Works: Lessons from a Writing Life.* New York: Ballantine Books.

Fletcher, R. (2000). *How Writers Work.* New York: HarperTrophy.

Keyes, R. (1995). *The Courage to Write: How Writers Transcend Fear.* New York: Henry Holt.

Marcus, L. S. (2000). *Author Talk.* New York: Simon & Schuster.

Murphy, B. T., & Murphy, D. L. (Eds.). (2006). *Black Authors and Illustrators of Books for Children and Young Adults.* New York: Routledge.

New York Times. (2001). *Writers on Writing: Collected Essays from the New York Times.* New York: Times Books.

Nuwer, H. (2002). *To the Young Writer: Nine Writers Talk About Their Craft.* New York: Franklin Watts.

Paterson, K. (1981). *Gates of Excellence: On Reading and Writing Books for Children.* New York: Elsevier-Dutton.

Paterson, K. (1990). *The Spying Heart: More on Reading and Writing Books for Children.* New York: Dutton Children's Books.

Paterson, K. (2001). *The Invisible Child: On Reading and Writing Books for Children.* New York: Dutton Children's Books.

FIGURE 7.3 "How-to" resources on writing and teaching writing in various genres.

Alber, M. (2001). Creative Writing and Chemistry. *Journal of Chemical Education, 78*(4), 478–480.

Bentley, N., & Guthrie, D. W. (1998). *The Young Journalist's Book: How to Write and Produce Your Own Newspaper.* Brookfield, CT: Millbrook Press.

Bomer, K. (2005). *Writing a Life: Teaching Memoir.* Portsmouth, NH: Heinemann.

Burkhardt, R. (2003). *Writing for Real: Strategies for Engaging Adolescent Writers.* Portland, ME: Stenhouse.

Chin, B. (Ed.). (2004). *How to Write a Great Research Paper.* Hoboken, NJ: J. Wiley & Sons.

Christinson, J., & Whited, A. (2005). *Nonfiction Writing Prompts for Math.* Englewood, CO: Advanced Learning Press.

Day, R. A. (1998). *How to Write and Publish a Scientific Paper.* Phoenix, AZ: Oryx Press.

Fink, C. C. (2003). *Writing to Inform and Engage: The Essential Guide to Beginning News and Magazine Writing.* Boulder, CO: Westview.

Frey, N., Fisher, D., & Hernandez, T. (2003). "What's the Gist?": Summary Writing for Struggling Adolescent Writers. *Voices from the Middle, 11*(2), 43–49.

Geffner, A. B. (1995). *How to Write Better Business Letters* (2nd ed.). Hauppauge, NY: Barron's.

Gere, A. R., Christenbury, L., & Sassi, K. (2005). *Writing on Demand: Best Practices and Strategies for Success.* Portsmouth, NH: Heinemann.

Goldberg, N. (1986). *Writing Down the Bones.* Boston: Shambahla Press.

Hand, B., Prain, V., Lawrence, C., & Yore, L. D. (1999). A Writing in Science Framework Designed to Enhance Science Literacy. *International Journal of Science Education, 21*(10), 1021–1035.

Hanley, V. (2008). *Wild Ink!: How to Write Fiction for Young Adults.* Fort Collins, CO: Cottonwood Press.

Harrison, D. L. (2004). *Writing Stories: Fantastic Fiction from Start to Finish.* New York: Scholastic Reference.

Janeczko, P. B. (2001). *How to Write Poetry.* New York: Scholastic.

Ledoux, D. (1993). *Turning Memories into Memoirs: A Handbook for Writing Lifestories.* Lisbon Falls, ME: Soleil Press.

(continued)

Magee, W. (2007). *How to Write Poems*. Laguna Hills, CA: QEB Pub.

Mirriam-Goldberg, C. (1999). *Write Where You Are: How to Use Writing to Make Sense of Your Life: A Guide for Teens*. Minneapolis, MN: Free Spirit Publishing.

Phillips, E. H. (1999). *Shocked, Appalled, and Dismayed!: How to Write Letters of Complaint that Get Results*. New York: Vintage Books.

Rosenthal, L. (Ed.). (2003). *The Writing Group Book: Creating and Sustaining a Successful Writing Group*. Chicago: Chicago Review Press.

Sheffield, C. (1999). *Borderlands of Science: How to Think Like a Scientist and Write Science Fiction*. Riverdale, NY: Baen.

Warren, C. (2007). *How to Write Stories*. Laguna Hills, CA: QEB Pub.

Zinsser, W. (2006). *On Writing Well* (7th ed.). New York: HarperPerennial.

FIGURE 7.5   Examples of descriptions of teachers or learning experiences.

Albom, M. (1997). *Tuesdays with Morrie: An Old Man, a Young Man, and Life's Greatest Lesson*. New York: Doubleday.

Ayers, W. (1993). *To Teach: The Journey of a Teacher*. New York: Teachers College Press.

Byars, B. (1991). Miss Harriet's Room. In *The Moon and I*. Englewood Cliffs, NJ: Messner.

Cisneros, S. (1991). Eleven. In *Woman Hollering Creek*. New York: Random House.

Codell, E. R. (2009). *Educating Esmé: Diary of a Teacher's First Year, Expanded Edition*. Chapel Hill, NC: Algonquin Books.

Dillard, A. (1987). *An American Childhood*. New York: HarperCollins.

Houston, G., & Lamb, S. C. (1992). *My Great Aunt Arizona*. New York: HarperCollins.

Rodriguez, R. (1983). *Hunger of Memory: The Education of Richard Rodriguez, An Autobiography*. New York: Bantam Books.

Schmidt, P. A. (1997). *Beginning in Retrospect: Writing and Reading a Teacher's Life*. New York: Teachers College Press.

FIGURE 7.6   Books featuring characters who write.

Avi. (1990). *The True Confessions of Charlotte Doyle*. New York: Orchard Books.

Avi. (1991). *Nothing But the Truth*. New York: Orchard Books.

Bantock, N. (1991). *Griffin and Sabine: A Novel Correspondence*. San Francisco: Chronicle Books.

Blos, J. W. (1979). *A Gathering of Days: A New England Girl's Journal 1830–32*. New York: Scribner's.

Codell, E. (2003). *Sahara Special*. New York: Hyperion.

Crutcher, C. (1995). *Ironman*. New York: Greenwillow Books.

Danticatt, E. (2002). *Behind the Mountains*. New York: Orchard Books.

Donnelly, J. (2003). *A Northern Light*. San Diego, CA: Harcourt.

Friedman, R. (2000). *How I Survived My Summer Vacation: And Lived to Write the Story*. Chicago: Front Street/Cricket Books.

George, J. C. (1991). *My Side of the Mountain*. New York: Puffin Books.

Henkes, K. (2003). *Olive's Ocean*. New York: Greenwillow Books.

Ives, D. (2005). *Scrib: A Novel*. New York: HarperCollins.

Little, J. (1989). *Hey, World, Here I Am!* New York: HarperCollins.

Moriarty, J. (2004). *The Year of Secret Assignments*. New York: Scholastic.

Myers, W. D. (1999). *Monster*. New York: HarperCollins.

Paterson, K. (1978). *The Great Gilly Hopkins*. New York: Crowell.

Spillebeen, G. (2005). *Kipling's Choice*. (J. Edelstein, Trans.). Boston: Houghton Mifflin.

FIGURE 7.10   Resources for obtaining documents and data related to curriculum.

CNN News: www.cnn.com

Historical Documents: http://teachers.sduhsd.K12.ca.us/tpsocialsciences/documents.htm

National Geographic Online: www.nationalgeographic.com

Beyers, A. (2004). *The Trail of Tears: A Primary Source History of the Forced Relocation of the Cherokee Nation*. New York: Rosen.

Block, H. (2000). *Herblock's History: Political Cartoons from the Crash to the Millennium*. Washington, DC: Library of Congress.

Brezina, C. (2005). *The Industrial Revolution in America: A Primary Source History of America's Transformation into an Industrial Society*. New York: Rosen.

Holzer, H. (Ed.). (2000). *Abraham Lincoln the Writer: A Treasury of His Greatest Speeches and Letters*. Honesdale, PA: Boyds Mills Press.

Kaplan, L. C. (2005). *A Primary Source Guide to Iran*. New York: PowerKids Press.

Lepore, J. (Ed.). (2000). *Encounters in the New World: A History in Documents*. New York: Oxford University Press.

Link, T. (2005). *Communism: A Primary Source Analysis.* New York: Rosen.

Mankoff, R. (Ed.). (2000). *The New Yorker Book of Political Cartoons.* Princeton, NJ: Bloomsburg Press.

Seedman, R. F. (2001). *The Civil War: A History in Documents.* New York: Oxford University Press.

Smith, B. G. (2000). *Imperialism: A History in Documents.* New York: Oxford University Press.

Smith, K. M. (Ed.), & Gross, J. L. (1999). *The Lines Are Drawn: Political Cartoons of the Civil War.* Athens, GA: Hill Street Press.

FIGURE 7.11 A sampling of Milton Meltzer's books containing multiple forms of data.

Rescue: The Story of How Gentiles Saved Jews in the Holocaust (1988). New York: Harper & Row.

Voices from the Civil War: A Documentary History of the Great American Conflict (1989). New York: Crowell.

The Bill of Rights: How We Got It and What It Means (1990). New York: Crowell.

Brother, Can You Spare a Dime?: The Great Depression, 1929–33 (1991). New York: Facts on File.

The Amazing Potato: A Story in Which the Incas, Conquistadors, Marie Antoinette, Thomas Jefferson, Wars, Famine, Immigrants, and French Fries All Play a Part (1992). New York: HarperCollins.

Lincoln, in His Own Words (Ed.) (1993). New York: Harcourt Brace.

Langston Hughes: An Illustrated Edition (1997). Brookfield, CT: Millbrook Press.

Witches and Witch Hunts (1998). New York: Blue Sky Press.

Carl Sandburg: A Biography (1999). Brookfield, CT: Twenty-first Century Books.

Driven from the Land: The Story of the Dust Bowl (2000). New York: Benchmark Books.

They Came in Chains: The Story of the Slave Ships (2000). New York: Benchmark Books.

There Comes a Time: The Struggle for Civil Rights (2001). New York: Random House.

The Day the Sky Fell: A History of Terrorism (2002). New York: Random House.

Hour of Freedom: American History in Poetry (Compiler) (2002). Honesdale, PA: Wordsong/Boyds Mills Press.

Ten Kings: And the Worlds They Ruled (with B. Anderson) (2002). New York: Orchard Books.

Ain't Gonna Study War No More: The Story of America's Peace Seekers (2003). New York: Random House.

Bound for America: The Story of the European Immigrants (2003). New York: Benchmark Books.

Great Inventors (2004). New York: Benchmark Books.

Milton Meltzer: Writing Matters (2004). New York: Franklin Watts.

Herman Melville: A Biography (2006). Brookfield, CT: Twenty-first Century Books.

Nathaniel Hawthorne: A Biography (2007). Minneapolis: Twenty-first Century Books.

FIGURE 8.1 Resources that allow you to listen to young people.

Atkin, S. B. (1993). *Voices from the Field: Children of Migrant Farmworkers Tell Their Stories.* Boston: Little, Brown.

Atkin, S. B. (1996). *Voices from the Street: Young Former Gang Members Tell Their Stories.* Boston: Little, Brown.

Bolden, T. (2001). *Tell All the Children Our Story: Memories and Mementos of Being Young and Black in America.* New York: Abrams.

Cushman, K. (2005). *What We Can't Tell You: Teenagers Talk to the Adults in Their Lives.* Providence, RI: Next Generation Press.

Ellis, D. (2009). *Children of War: Voices of Iraqi Refugees.* Toronto, ON: Groundwood.

Faber, A., & Mazlish, E. (2005). *How to Talk So Teens Will Listen & Listen So Teens Will Talk.* New York: William Morrow.

Fearnley, F. (2004). *I Wrote on All Four Walls: Teens Speak Out on Violence.* Toronto: Annick Press.

Franco, B. (Ed.). (2001). *Things I Have to Tell You: Poems and Writing by Teenage Girls.* Cambridge, MA: Candlewick Press.

Franco, B. (Ed.). (2001). *You Hear Me? Poems and Writing by Teenage Boys.* Cambridge, MA: Candlewick Press.

Gaskins, P. F. (1999). *What Are You?: Voices of Mixed-race Young People.* New York: Henry Holt.

Godfrey, R., & Godfrey, N. S. (2004). *The Teen Code: How to Talk to Us About Sex, Drugs, and Everything Else: Teenagers Reveal What Works Best.* Emmaus, PA: Rodale.

Hughes, L. (2005). *You Are Not Alone: Teens Talk About Life After the Loss of a Parent.* New York: Scholastic Press.

Mahiri, J. (2004). *What They Don't Learn in School: Literacy in the Lives of Urban Youth.* New York: P. Lang.

Okutoro, L. O. (Selector). (1999). *Quiet Storm: Voices of Young Black Poets.* New York: Jump at the Sun/Hyperion.

Philbrick, R. (2001). Listening to Kids in America. *The ALAN Review, 28*(2), 13–16.

Pipher, M. B. (1995). *Reviving Ophelia: Saving the Selves of Adolescent Girls.* New York: Ballantine Books.

Pollack, W. S., with Schuster, T. (2000). *Real Boys' Voices.* New York: Random House.

Reeves, A. R. (2004). *Adolescents Talk About Reading: Exploring Resistance to and Engagement with Text.* Newark, DE: International Reading Association.

Rosenberg, B. H. (2002). *What the Holocaust Means to Me: Teenagers Speak Out.* South River, NJ: Moshe Aaron Yeshiva Press.

(continued)

Schultz, B., & Schultz, R. (2008). *We Will Be Heard: Voices in the Struggle for Constitutional Rights Past and Present.* New York: Merrell.

Shandler, S. (1999). *Ophelia Speaks.* New York: Harper-Perennial.

Springer, J. (1997). *Listen to Us: The World's Working Children.* Buffalo, NY: Groundwood Books/Douglas & McIntyre Ltd.

Squires, B. (1995). *Listening to Children: A Moral Journey with Robert Coles.* Social Media Productions in cooperation with the Center for Documentary Studies at Duke University. PBS Video.

Turck, M. C. (2008). *Freedom Song: Young Voices and the Struggle for Civil Rights.* Chicago: Chicago Review Press.

Veljkovic, P., & Schwartz, A. J. (Eds.). (2001). *Writing from the Heart: Young People Share Their Wisdom.* Philadelphia: Templeton Foundation Press.

Weill, S. S. (2002). *We're Not Monsters: Teens Speak About Teens in Trouble.* New York: HarperTempest.

Wilhelm, J. D. (2008). *You Gotta BE the Book: Teaching Engaged and Reflective Reading with Adolescents.* New York: Teachers College Press and Urbana, IL: National Council of Teachers of English.

FIGURE 8.8 **Resources relating to discussion.**

Boyd, F. B. (1997). The Cross-aged Literacy Program: Preparing Struggling Adolescents for Book Club Discussions. In S. I. McMahon & T. E. Raphael (Eds.), *The Book Club Connection: Literacy Learning and Classroom Talk.* New York: Teachers College Press, 162–181.

California High School Speech Association's Curriculum Committee. (2004). *Speaking Across the Curriculum: Practical Ideas for Incorporating Listening and Speaking into the Classroom.* New York: International Debate Education Association Press.

Chandler, K. (1997). The Beach Book Club: Literacy in the "Lazy Days of Summer." *Journal of Adolescent and Adult Literacy, 41*(2), 104–115.

Gambrell, L. B., & Almasi, J. F. (Eds.). (1996). *Lively Discussions!* Newark, DE: International Reading Association.

Glazier, J., & Seo, J. (2005). Multicultural literature and discussion as mirror and window? *Journal of Adolescent and Adult Literacy, 48*(8), 686–700.

Spiegel, D. L. (2005). *Classroom Discussion: Strategies for Engaging All Students, Building Higher-Level Thinking Skills, and Strengthening Reading and Writing Across the Curriculum.* New York: Scholastic.

FIGURE 8.9 **Resources for public speaking, storytelling, performing, and reading aloud.**

PUBLIC SPEAKING

Desberg, P. (1996). *No More Butterflies: Overcoming Stagefright, Shyness, Interview Anxiety and Fear of Public Speaking.* Oakland, CA: New Harbinger Publications.

Donovan, S. (Ed.). (1995). *Great American Women's Speeches* (Audio Recording). New York: Harper Audio.

The Greatest Speeches of All Time (Audio Recording). (1997). Rolling Bay, WI: SoundWorks International, Inc.

Kushner, M. L. (1998). *Public Speaking for Dummies.* New York: Harper Audio.

Lamm, K. (1995). *10,000 Ideas for Term Papers, Projects, Reports, and Speeches.* New York: ARCO.

Mira, T. K. (1995). *Speak Now, or Forever Fall to Pieces.* New York: Random House.

STORYTELLING

Bruchac, J. B. (1995). Native Plant Stories. In M. J. Caduto & J. B. Bruchac, *Keepers of Life.* Golden, CO: Fulcrum Publishers.

Creeden, S. (1994). *Fair Is Fair: World Folktales of Justice.* Little Rock, AR: August House Publishers.

Gillard, M. (1996). *Story Teller, Story Teacher: Discovering the Power of Storytelling for Teaching and Living.* York, ME: Stenhouse.

Pellowski, A. (1995). *Hidden Stories in Plants.* New York: Macmillan.

Pellowski, A. (1995). *The Storytelling Handbook.* New York: Simon & Schuster.

Roe, B. D., Alfred, S., & Smith, S. (1998). *Teaching Through Stories: Yours, Mine, and Theirs.* Norwood, MA: Christopher-Gordon.

Shannon, G. (1990). *More Stories to Solve: Fifteen Folktales from Around the World.* New York: Greenwillow Books.

Storytelling: Learning and Sharing (Videorecording). (1995). Fallbrook, CA: Coyote Creek Productions.

PERFORMING

Barchers, S. I. (2000). *Multicultural Folktales: Readers Theatre for Elementary Students.* Englewood, CO: Teacher Ideas Press.

Barchers, S. I. (2001). *From Atlanta to Zeus: Readers Theatre from Greek Mythology.* Englewood, CO: Teacher Ideas Press.

Black, A., & Stave, A. (2007). *A Comprehensive Guide to Readers Theatre: Enhancing Fluency and Comprehension in Middle School and Beyond.* Newark, DE: International Reading Association.

Fredericks, A. D. (1993). *Frantic Frogs and Other Frankly Fractured Folktales for Readers Theatre.* Englewood, CO: Teacher Ideas Press.

Fredericks, A. D. (1997). *Tadpole Tales and Other Totally Terrific Treats for Readers Theatre.* Englewood, CO: Teacher Ideas Press.

Haven, K. F. (1996). *Great Moments in Science: Experiments and Readers Theatre.* Englewood, CO: Teacher Ideas Press.

Polette, N. W. (2009). *Whose Tale Is True?: Readers Theatre to Introduce and Research 49 Amazing American Women.* Westport, CT: Teacher Ideas Press.

Ratliff, G. L. (2008). *Young Women's Monologues from Contemporary Plays, #2: Professional Auditions for Aspiring Actresses.* Colorado Springs, CO: Meriwether.

Sanders, J., & Sanders, N. I. (2008). *Readers Theatre for African American History.* Westport, CT: Teacher Ideas Press.

Shepard, A. (Ed.). (2005). *Stories on Stage: Children's Plays for Readers Theatre, with 15 Play Scripts from 15 Authors.* Olympia, WA: Shepard Publications.

Smith, C. R. (2003). *Extraordinary Women from U.S. History: Readers Theatre from Grades 4–8.* Portsmouth, NH: Teacher Ideas Press.

Smith, R. W. (2008). *World History Readers' Theater: Bringing the Past to Life!* Westminster, CA: Teacher Created Resources.

FIGURE 8.11 A sampling of audio versions of content-related texts.

Ackerman, D. (1995). *A Natural History of the Senses.* Los Angeles: The Publishing Mills.

Angelou, M. (1999). *The Maya Angelou Poetry Collection.* New York: Random House Audio.

Douglass, F. (1992). *Narrative of the Life of Frederick Douglass.* Ashland, OR: Blackstone Audiobooks.

The Essential Dylan Thomas. (2005). Various readers. Franklin, TN: Naxos Audiobooks.

Goodall, J., with Berman, P. (1999). *Reason for Hope: A Spiritual Journey.* New York: Time Warner Audiobooks.

In Their Own Voices: A Century of Recorded Poetry. (1996). Los Angeles: Rhino. Word Beat.

Marshall, J. M. (2004). *The Journey of Crazy Horse.* Read by the author. Minneapolis, MN: HighBridge Audio.

McBride, J. (1996). *The Color of Water: A Black Man's Tribute to His White Mother.* Beverly Hills, CA: Dove Audio.

Miller, A. (1995). *The Crucible.* New York: Caedmon.

Moses, S. P. (2005). *I, Dred Scott.* Read by Peter Jay Fernandez. Prince Frederick, MD: Recorded Books.

Rowling, J. K., & Dale, J. (1999). *Harry Potter and the Sorcerer's Stone.* Old Greenwich, CT: Listening Library/Random House.

Shakespeare's Greatest Hits, Vol. 1. Retold by Bruce Coville. 1996, 1997, 1998, 2003. Read by Bruce Coville, Cynthia Bishop, and a full cast. Syracuse, NY: Full Cast Audio.

Watson, J. D. (2000). *The Double Helix: The Story Behind the Discovery of DNA.* Novato, CA: Soundelux Audio Publishing.

The Words and Music of World War II. (1991). New York: SONY Music Entertainment/Columbia Records.

FIGURE 8.12 Books containing interviews.

Bode, J. (1993). *Death Is Hard to Live With: Teenagers and How They Cope with Death.* New York: Delacorte Press.

Bode, J. (1996). *Hard Time: A Real Life Look at Juvenile Crime and Violence.* New York: Delacorte Press.

Bode, J. (1999). *The Colors of Freedom: Immigrant Stories.* New York: Franklin Watts.

Bode, J., & Mack, S. (1994). *Heartbreak and Roses: Real Life Stories of Troubled Love.* New York: Delacorte Press.

Bode, J., & Mack, S. (2001). *For Better, for Worse: A Guide to Surviving Divorce for Pre-teens and Their Families.* New York: Simon & Schuster.

Bode, J., & Spruce, I. M. B. (2000). *Voices of Rape.* New York: Watts.

Hatch, R., & Hatch, W. (2006). *The Hero Project: 2 Teens, 1 Notebook, 13 Extraordinary Interviews.* New York: McGraw-Hill.

Kelley, B. P. (1998). *They Too Wore Pinstripes: Interviews with 20 Glory-days New York Yankees.* Jefferson, NC: McFarland & Co.

Kline, S. (Ed.). (1999). *George Lucas: Interviews. Conversations with Filmmakers Series.* Jackson: University Press of Mississippi.

Levi, P. (2001). *The Voice of Memory: Interviews 1961–87/Primo Levi,* M. Belpoliti & R. Gordon (Eds.) (R. Gordon, Trans.). New York: New Press.

McGilligan, P. (2000). *Film Crazy: Interviews with Hollywood Legends.* New York: St. Martin's.

Robertson, J. (1996). *Twentieth Century Artists on Art.* New York: G. K. Hall.

Silvester, C. (Ed.). (1996). *The Norton Book of Interviews: An Anthology from 1859 to the Present Day.* New York: Norton.

Spielberg, S. (2000). *Steven Spielberg: Interviews,* L. D. Freedman & B. Notbohm (Eds.). Jackson: University Press of Mississippi.

FIGURE 9.2 Wordless (or almost wordless) picture books for content area learning.

Anno, M. (1978). *Anno's Journey*. Cleveland, OH: Collins-World.

Anno, M. (1980). *Anno's Italy*. New York: HarperCollins.

Anno, M. (1983). *Anno's U.S.A.* New York: Philomel Books.

Baker, J. (1991). *Window*. New York: Greenwillow Books.

Collington, P. (1987). *The Angel and the Soldier Boy*. New York: Knopf.

de Paola, T. (1979). *Flicks*. San Diego, CA: Harcourt Brace.

Goodall, J. (1976). *An Edwardian Summer*. New York: Atheneum.

Goodall, J. (1986). *The Story of a Castle*. New York: M. K. McElderry Books.

Goodall, J. (1987). *The Story of a Main Street*. New York: Macmillan.

Goodall, J. (1990). *The Story of the Seashore*. New York: M. K. McElderry Books.

Gurney, J. (1998). *Dinotopia: A Land Apart from Time*. New York: HarperCollins.

Lehman, B. (2006). *Museum Trip*. Boston: Houghton Mifflin.

Oakley, G. (1980). *Graham Oakley's Magical Changes*. New York: Atheneum.

Raczka, B. (2006). *Unlikely Pairs: Fun with Famous Works of Art*. Minneapolis, MN: Millbrook Press.

Rockhill, D. (2005). *Ocean Whisper/Susurro del Oceano*. (E. de la Vega, Trans.). Green Bay, WI: Raven Tree Press.

Rohmann, E. (1995). *Time Flies*. New York: Scholastic.

Spier, P. (1977). *Noah's Ark*. Garden City, NY: Doubleday.

Van Allsburg, C. (1984). *The Mysteries of Harris Burdick*. Boston: Houghton Mifflin.

Vincent, G. (2000). *A Day, a Dog*. New York: Front Street.

Wiesner, D. (1997). *Sector Seven*. New York: Clarion Books.

Wiesner, D. (2008). *Free Fall*. New York: HarperCollins.

FIGURE 9.3 Examples of graphic novels and texts in cartoon/comic format.

Avi. (1993). *City of Light, City of Dark: A Comic Book Novel*. Art by B. Floca. New York: Orchard Books.

Bradbury, R. (2003). *The Best of Ray Bradbury: The Graphic Novel*. New York: ibooks.

Crane, S. (2005). *The Red Badge of Courage*. New York: Puffin.

Croci, P. (2002). *Auschwitz*. New York: Harry N. Abrams.

Curry, P., & Zarate, O. (1996). *Introducing Machiavelli*. New York: Totem Books.

Factoid Books. (1999). *The Big Book of Grimm, by the Brothers Grimm as Channeled by J. Vankin and Over 50 Top Comic Artists!* New York: Paradox Press.

Giardino, V. (1997). *A Jew in Communist Prague: 1. Loss of Innocence*. New York: NBM Comics Lit.

Giardino, V. (1997). *A Jew in Communist Prague: 2. Adolescence*. New York: NBM Comics Lit.

Giardino, V. (1997). *A Jew in Communist Prague: 3. Rebellion*. New York: NBM Comics Lit.

Gonick, L. (1991). *The Cartoon History of the United States*. New York: HarperPerennial.

Gonick, L., & Criddle, C. (2004). *The Cartoon Guide to Chemistry*. New York: HarperResource.

Gonick, L., & Huffman, A. (2002). *The Cartoon Guide to Physics*. Seattle, WA: Multimedia.

Gonick, L., & Outwater, A. (1996). *The Cartoon Guide to the Environment*. New York: HarperCollins.

Gonick, L., & Smith, W. (1993). *The Cartoon Guide to Statistics*. New York: HarperPerennial.

Gonick, L., & Wheelis, M. (2005). *The Cartoon Guide to Genetics*. New York: Collins Reference.

Hale, S., & Hale, D. (2008). *Rapunzel's Revenge*. London: Bloomsbury.

Harder, J. (2004). *Leviathan*. New York: Comics Lit/NBM.

Harris, S. (1989). *Einstein Simplified: Cartoons on Science*. New Brunswick, NJ: Rutgers University Press.

Hirsch, K. D. (1997). *Mind Riot: Coming of Age in Comix*. New York: Aladdin Paperbacks.

Kubert, J. (1996). *Fax from Sarajevo: A Story of Survival*. Milwaukie, OR: Dark Horse Comics.

Lomax, D. (2004). *Gulf War Journal: A Graphic Novel*. New York: ibooks.

Martin, M. (2005). *Harriet Tubman and the Underground Railroad*. Mankato, MN: Capstone Press.

Martin, M. (2005). *The Salem Witch Trials*. Mankato, MN: Capstone Press.

Olson, K. M. (2005). *The Assassination of Abraham Lincoln*. Mankato, MN: Capstone Press.

Pomplun, T. (Ed.). (2004). *Graphic Classics: Edgar Allan Poe* (2nd ed.). Mount Horeb, WI: Eureka Productions.

Reed, G. (2005). *Mary Shelley's Frankenstein: The Graphic Novel*. New York: Penguin/Puffin.

Satrapi, M. (2003). *Persepolis: The Story of a Childhood*. New York: Pantheon Books.

Satrapi, M. (2004). *Persepolis 2: The Story of a Return*. New York: Pantheon Books.

Shakespeare, W. (2008). *Macbeth: The Graphic Novel*. Litchborough, UK: Classical Comics.

Shanower, E. (2004). *Sacrifice*. Berkeley, CA: Image Comics.

Spiegelman, A. (1991). *Maus II: A Survivor's Tale: And Here My Troubles Began*. New York: Pantheon.

Spiegelman, A. (1997). *Maus: A Survivor's Tale*. New York: Pantheon.

Spiegelman, A., & Mouly, F. (Eds.). (2000). *Little Lit: Folklore and Fairy Tale Funnies*. New York: RAW Junior.

Tan, S. (2007). *The Arrival*. New York: Arthur A. Levine Books.

Torres, A. (2008). *American Widow*. (S. Choi, Illus.). New York: Villard.

Watts, I. (2008). *Good-Bye Marianne: A Story of Growing Up in Nazi Germany*. (K. E. Shoemaker, Illus.). Toronto, ON: Tundra.

Winick, J. (2000). *Pedro & Me: Friendship, Loss, and What I Learned*. New York: Henry Holt.

FIGURE 9.7   Young adult books with a visual arts focus or theme.

Anderson, L. H. (1999). *Speak*. New York: Farrar, Straus & Giroux.

Bjork, C. (1999). *Vendela in Venice*. New York: R & S Books.

Bjork, C., & Anderson, L. (1987). *Linnea in Monet's Garden*. New York: R & S Books.

Clemesha, D., & Zimmerman, A. G. (1992). *Rattle Your Bones: Skeleton Drawing Fun*. New York: Scholastic.

Freymann-Weyr, G. (2002). *My Heartbeat*. Boston: Houghton Mifflin.

Heuston, K. (2003). *Dante's Daughter*. Asheville, NC: Front Street.

Holmes, B. W. (2001). *Following Fake Man*. New York: Knopf.

Koja, K. (2004). *Buddha Boy*. New York: Speak.

Mack, T. (2000). *Drawing Lessons*. New York: Scholastic.

Myers, W. D. (2005). *Autobiography of My Dead Brother*. New York: HarperTempest.

Park, L. S. (2001). *A Single Shard*. New York: Clarion Books.

Place, F. (2004). *The Old Man Mad About Drawing: A Tale of Hokusai*. (W. Rodarmor, Trans.). Boston: David R. Godine.

Rees, D. (2006). *The Janus Gate: An Encounter with John Singer Sargent*. New York: Watson-Guptill.

Rylant, C. (1988). *All I See*. New York: Orchard Books.

Shoup, B. (2003). *Vermeer's Daughter*. Zionsville, IN: Guild Press/Emmis.

Sills, L. (1989). *Inspirations: Stories About Women Artists: Georgia O'Keefe, Frida Kahlo, Alice Neel, Faith Ringgold*. Niles, IL: A. Whitman.

FIGURE 9.8   Books and games dealing with visual and spatial skills.

Anno, M. (1997). *Anno's Math Games*. New York: Putnam & Grosset.

Anno, M. (1997). *Anno's Math Games II*. New York: Putnam & Grosset.

Anno, M. (1997). *Anno's Math Games III*. New York: Putnam & Grosset.

Binary Arts Corporation. (1995). *Visual Brain Storms: The Smart Thinking Game*. Alexandria, VA: Binary Arts.

Block, J. R., & Yuker, H. E. (1989). *Can You Believe Your Eyes?* New York: Gardner Press.

DiSpezio, M. A. (1999). *Optical Illusion Magic: Visual Tricks and Amusements*. New York: Sterling.

Gelb, M. (1998). *How to Think Like Leonardo da Vinci: Seven Steps to Genius Every Day*. New York: Delacorte.

Hoffman, D. D. (1998). *Visual Intelligence: How We Create What We See*. New York: Norton.

Levy, J. U., & Levy, N. (1999). *Mechanical Aptitude and Spatial Relations Tests* (4th ed.). New York: Macmillan.

Markle, S. (1997). *Discovering Graph Secrets: Experiments, Puzzles, and Games Exploring Graphs*. New York: Atheneum.

Thorne-Thomsen, K. (1994). *Frank Lloyd Wright for Kids*. Chicago: Chicago Review Press.

Weber, J. A. (2000). *Architecture Everywhere: Exploring the Built Environment of Your Community*. Tucson, AZ: Zephyr Press.

FIGURE 9.11   Books about television.

Alexander, A., & Hanson, J. (Eds.). (2001). *Taking Sides: Clashing Views on Controversial Issues in Mass Media and Society*. Guilford, CT: McGraw-Hill/Dushkin.

Baker, W. F., & Dessart, G. (1998). *Down the Tube: An Inside Account of the Failure of American Television*. New York: Basic Books.

David, L., & Seinfeld, J. (1998). *The Seinfeld Scripts: The First and Second Seasons*. New York: HarperPerennial.

Grant, V. (2004). *The Puppet Wrangler*. Custer, WA: Orca.

Keirstead, P.O. (2005). *Computers in Broadcast and Cable Newsrooms: Using Technology in Television News Production*. Mahwah, NJ: Lawrence Erlbaum Associates.

McAlpine, M. (2005). *Working in Film and Television*. Baltimore: G. S. Publishing.

Nobleman, M. T. (2005). *The Television*. Mankato, MN: Capstone Press.

Pawlowski, C. (2000). *Glued to the Tube: The Threat of Television Addiction to Today's Family*. Naperville, IL: Sourcebooks.

Postman, N., & Powers, S. (2008). *How to Watch TV News*. New York: Penguin.

Roberts, R. (2004). *Philo T. Farnsworth: The Life of Television's Forgotten Inventor*. Bear, DE: Mitchell Lane Publishers.

Spangenburg, R., & Moser, D. (2003). *TV News: Can It Be Trusted?* Berkeley Heights, NJ: Enslow.

Stay, B. L. (Ed.). (1999). *Mass Media: Opposing Viewpoints*. St. Paul, MN: Greenhaven Press.

White, A. (2005). *Antarctic Survivor 2083*. New York: HarperCollins.

You and the Mass Media (www.FilmicArchives.com).

FIGURE 9.12 Media on media and technology.

Big Dream, Small Screen. (1997). Windfall Films, Ltd., PBS Video.

Does TV Kill? (1995). Frontline. Produced by Michael McLeod.

Ericsson, S., & Lewis, J. (2001). *Constructing Public Opinion: How Politicians and the Media Misrepresent the Public.* Northampton, MA: Media Education Foundation.

Gee, J. P. (2003). *What Video Games Have to Teach Us About Learning and Literacy.* New York: Palgrave/Macmillan.

Hall, J. C., et al. (2004). *The Media's Influence on the Things We Do.* Lawrenceville, NJ: Cambridge Educational.

Halper, A., Fletcher, G. P., Knight, G., et al. (1995). *Trial by Television.* Alexandria, VA: PBS Video.

Johnson, S. (2005). *Everything Bad Is Good for You.* New York: Riverhead.

Lazarus, M., & Wunderlich, R., et al. (2005). *The Strength to Resist Media's Impact on Women and Girls.* Cambridge, MA: Cambridge Documentary Films.

Magee, M. (Director). (1992). *On Television: Teach the Children.* San Francisco: California Newsreel.

McMahon, M., et al. (2005). *Truth Merchants: Public Relations and the Media.* Lawrenceville, NJ: Films for the Humanities and Sciences.

Schlessinger, A., & Valenza, J. K. (2004). *Media Literacy.* Wynnewood, PA: Schlessinger Media.

FIGURE 10.9 Works by and about teachers.

Atwell, N. (1998). *In the Middle: New Understandings About Writing, Reading, and Learning.* Portsmouth, NH: Heinemann.

Brown, C. S. (1994). *Connecting with the Past: History Workshop.* Portsmouth, NH: Heinemann.

Esquith, R. (2003). *There Are No Shortcuts.* New York: Anchor Books.

Hynds, S. (1997). *On the Brink: Negotiating Literature and Life with Adolescents.* Newark, DE: International Reading Association, and New York: Teachers College Press.

Johnson, L. (1993). *Dangerous Minds.* New York: St. Martin's.

Joseph, E. A. (2001). *The Loneliness of the Long-Distance Teacher.* Philadelphia: Xlibris.

McCourt, F. (2005). *Teacher Man: A Memoir.* New York: Scribner.

Melchior, T. (2003). *From Both Sides of the Desk.* Lake Bluff, IL: Quality Books.

Paley, V. (1997). *The Girl with the Brown Crayon.* Cambridge, MA: Harvard University Press.

Perl, S., & Wilson, N. (1986). *Through Teachers' Eyes: Portraits of Writing Teachers at Work.* Portsmouth, NH: Heinemann.

Rief, L. (1992). *Seeking Diversity: Language Arts with Adolescents.* Portsmouth, NH: Heinemann.

Smith, M. W., & Wilhelm, J. (2002). *Reading Don't Fix No Chevys: Literacy in the Lives of Young Men.* Portsmouth, NH: Heinemann.

Tompkins, J. (1996). *A Life in School: What the Teacher Learned.* Reading, MA: Addison-Wesley.

Vinz, R. (1996). *Composing a Teaching Life.* Portsmouth, NH: Boynton-Cook.

FIGURE 11.1 Books by or about educational critics, innovators, and visionaries.

ASCD. *Becoming a Great High School: 6 Strategies and 1 Attitude that Make a Difference.* Alexandria, VA: ASCD.

Bickman, M. (Ed.). (1999). *Uncommon Learning: Thoreau on Education.* Boston: Houghton Mifflin.

Bigelow, B., Harvey, B., Karp, S., & Miller, L. (2001). *Rethinking Our Classrooms, Volume 2: Teaching for Equity and Justice.* Milwaukee, WI: Rethinking Schools.

Booth, M. B., & Booth, G. M. (2003). What American Schools Can Learn from Hogwarts School of Witchcraft and Wizardry. *Phi Delta Kappan, 85*(4), 310–315.

Csikszentmihalyi, M., Rathunde, K. R., & Whalen, S. (1993). *Talented Teenagers: The Roots of Success and Failure.* New York: Cambridge University Press.

Daniels, H. (1998). *Best Practice: New Standards for Teaching and Learning in America's Schools.* Portsmouth, NH: Heinemann.

Eisler, R. T., & Miller, R. (Eds.). (2004). *Educating for a Culture of Peace.* Portsmouth, NH: Heinemann.

Eisner, E. (2005). *Reimagining Schools: The Selected Works of Elliot W. Eisner.* New York: Routledge.

Finn, P. (1999). *Literacy with an Attitude.* Albany, NY: SUNY Press.

Flood, J., & Andes, P. L. (2005). *Literacy Development of Students in Urban Schools: Research and Policy.* Newark, DE: International Reading Association.

Gill, V. (2005). *The Ten Commandments of Professionalism for Teachers: Wisdom from a Veteran Teacher.* Thousand Oaks, CA: Corwin Press.

Graves, D. H. (2004). *Teaching Day by Day: 180 Stories to Help You Along the Way.* Portsmouth, NH: Heinemann.

Holland, H., & Mazzoli, K. (2001). *The Heart of a High School: One Community's Effort to Transform Urban Education.* Westport, CT: Heinemann.

Hurd, P. D. (2000). *Transforming Middle School Science Education.* New York: Teachers College Press.

Kohn, A. (1998). *What to Look for in a Classroom: And Other Essays.* San Francisco: Jossey-Bass.

Kohn, A. (1999). *The Schools Our Children Deserve: Moving Beyond Traditional Classrooms and "Tougher Standards."* Boston: Houghton Mifflin.

Kohn, A. (2006). *The Homework Myth: Why Our Kids Get Too Much of a Bad Thing.* Cambridge, MA: Da Capo Life Long.

Mahiri, J. (Ed.). (2004). *What They Don't Learn in School: Literacy in the Lives of Urban Youth.* New York: P. Lang.

Perry, T., Steele, C., & Hilliard, A.G. (2003). *Young, Gifted, and Black: Promoting High Achievement Among African-American Students.* Boston: Beacon Press.

Schlechty, P. C. (2001). *Shaking Up the Schoolhouse: How to Support and Sustain Educational Innovation.* San Francisco: Jossey-Bass.

Tozer, S., Violas, P. C., & Senese, G. B. (2006). *School and Society: Historical and Contemporary Perspectives.* Boston: McGraw-Hill.

Waxman, H. C., & Pedrón, Y. N. (2004). *Educational Resiliency: Student, Teacher, and School Perspectives.* Greenwich, CT: Information Age.

FIGURE 11.2 Fictional works and movies about teachers, schools, and learners.

Avi. (1994). *Nothing But the Truth.* Thorndike, ME: Thorndike Press.

Codell, E. R. (2003). *Sahara Special.* New York: Hyperion Books for Children.

Cormier, R. (1974). *The Chocolate War.* New York: Pantheon.

Crutcher, C. (1993). *Staying Fat for Sarah Byrnes.* New York: Greenwillow Books.

Crutcher, C. (1995). *Ironman.* New York: Greenwillow Books.

Crutcher, C. (2001). *Whale Talk.* New York: Greenwillow Books.

Glenn, M. (1991). *My Friend's Got This Problem, Mr. Candler: High School Poems.* New York: Clarion Books.

Glenn, M. (1997). *The Taking of Room 114: A Hostage Drama in Poems.* New York: Lodestar Books/Dutton.

Hilton, J. (1934). *Good-bye, Mr. Chips.* London: Hodder & Stroughton.

Jonsberg, B. (2005). *The Crimes and Punishments of Miss Payne.* New York: Alfred A. Knopf.

Kaufman, B. (1991). *Up the Down Staircase.* New York: HarperPerennial.

Kleinbaum, N. H. (1989). *The Dead Poets Society.* New York: Bantam.

Lubar, D. (2005). *Sleeping Freshmen Never Lie.* New York: Dutton Children's Books.

Marshall, C. (2001). *Christy.* Grand Rapids, MI: Chosen Books.

Mr. Holland's Opus. (1996). Hollywood Pictures Home Videos.

October Sky. (1999). Universal City, CA: Universal Studios.

Peck, R. (2004). *The Teacher's Funeral: A Comedy in Three Parts.* New York: Dial Books.

The Breakfast Club. (1998). Universal City, CA: Universal Home Video.

The Dead Poets Society. (1992). Touchstone Pictures. Boston: DVS Home Video.

references

Abair, J. M., & Cross, A. (1999). Patterns in American literature. *English Journal, 88*(6), 83–87.

Abd-El-Khalick, F. (2002). Images of nature of science in middle grade science trade books. *The New Advocate, 15*(2), 121–127.

Abrams, S. (2000). *Using journals with reluctant writers: Building portfolios for middle and high school students.* Thousand Oaks, CA: Corwin Press.

Acronyms, initialisms & abbreviations dictionary. Detroit: Gale Research Company.

Adams, C. (2009). Digital storytelling. *Instructor, 119*(3), 35–37.

Adams, M. (1990). *Beginning to read: Thinking and learning about print.* Urbana-Champaign, IL: Center for the Study of Reading.

Afflerbach, P. (2004). Assessing adolescent reading. In T. L. Jetton & J. A. Dole (Eds.), *Adolescent literacy research and practice* (pp. 369–391). New York: The Guilford Press.

Afflerbach, P., & VanSledright, B. (2001). Hath! Doth! What? Middle graders reading innovative history text. *Journal of Adolescent and Adult Literacy, 44*(8), 696–707.

Ajayi, L. (2009). English as a second language learners' exploration of multimodal texts in a junior high school. *Journal of Adolescent and Adult Literacy, 52*(7), 585–595.

Akhaven, N. L. (2004). *How to align literacy instruction, assessment, and standards.* Portsmouth, NH: Heinemann.

Alexander, P. A., & Jetton, T. L. (2000). Learning from text: A multidimensional and developmental perspective. In P. D. Pearson, R. Barr, & M. L. Kamil (Eds.), *Handbook of reading research* (Vol. III, pp. 285–310). Mahwah, NJ: Lawrence Erlbaum Associates.

Alexander, P. A., Jetton, T. L., Kulikowich, J. M., & Woehler, C. (1994). Contrasting instructional and structural importance: The seductive effect of teacher questions. *Journal of Reading Behavior, 26,* 19–45.

Allen, C. A. (2001). *The multigenre research paper: Voice, passion, and discovery in grades 4–6.* Portsmouth, NH: Heinemann.

Allen, J. (2006). Too little or too much?: What do we know about making vocabulary meaningful? *Voices from the Middle, 13*(4), pp. 16–19.

Allen, J. (2007). Mastering the art of effective vocabulary instruction. In Beers, K., Probst, R. E., & Rief, L. (Eds.), *Adolescent literacy: Turning promise into practice* (pp. 87–104). Portsmouth, NH: Heinemann.

Alliance for Technology Access, The. (2000). *Computer and Web resources for people with disabilities: A guide to exploring today's assistive technology.* Alameda, CA: Hunter House.

Allington, R. (2007). Effective teachers, effective instruction. In K. Beers, R. E. Probst, & L. Reif (Eds.), *Adolescent literacy: Turning promise into practice* (pp. 273–288). Portsmouth, NH: Heinemann.

Allington, R. L. (2001). *What really matters for struggling readers: Designing research-based programs.* New York: Longman.

Almasi, J. F. (1995). The nature of fourth-graders' sociocognitive conflicts in peer-led and teacher-led discussions of literature. *Reading Research Quarterly, 30,* 314–351.

Almasi, J. F. (1996). A new view of discussion. In L. B. Gambrell & J. F. Almasi (Eds.), *Lively discussions! Fostering engaged reading* (pp. 2–24). Newark, DE: International Reading Association.

Almasi, J. F. (2002). Research-based comprehension practices that create higher-level discussions. In C. C. Block, L. B. Gambrell, & M. Pressley (Eds.), *Improving comprehension instruction: Rethinking research, theory, and classroom practice* (pp. 229–242). San Francisco: Jossey-Bass.

Altieri, J. L. (2009). Strengthening connections between elementary mathematics and literacy. *Teaching Children Mathematics, 15*(6), 346–351.

Alvermann, D. (2007). Multiliterate youth in the time of scientific reading instruction. In K. Beers, R. E. Probst, & L. Reif (Eds.), *Adolescent literacy: Turning promise into practice* (pp. 19–26). Portsmouth, NH: Heinemann.

Alvermann, D. E. (1986). Discussion vs. recitation in the secondary classroom. In J. A. Niles & R. V. Lalik (Eds.), *Solving problems in literacy: Learners, teachers, and researchers* (pp. 113–119). Rochester, NY: National Reading Conference.

Alvermann, D. E. (1987). Discussion strategies for content area reading. In D. Alvermann, D. R. Dillon, & D. G. O'Brien (Eds.), *Using discussion to promote reading comprehension* (pp. 34–42). Newark, DE: International Reading Association.

Alvermann, D. E. (1994). Trade books versus textbooks: Making connections across content areas. In L. M. Morrow, J. K. Smith, & L. C. Wilkinson (Eds.), *Integrated language arts: Controversy to consensus* (pp. 51–69). Needham Heights, MA: Allyn & Bacon.

Alvermann, D. E. (2002). Effective literacy instruction for adolescents. *Journal of Literacy Research, 34*(2), 189–208.

Alvermann, D. E. (2004). Multiliteracies and self-questioning in the service of science learning. In E. W. Saul (Ed.), *Crossing borders in literacy and science instruction: Perspectives on theory and practice* (pp. 226–238). Newark, DE: International Reading Association and Arlington, VA: National Science Teachers Association.

Alvermann, D. E. (2008). Why bother theorizing adolescents' online literacies for classroom practice and research? *Journal of Adolescent and Adult Literacy, 52*(1), 8–19.

Alvermann, D. E., Hinchman, K. A., Moore, D. E., Phelps, S. F., & Waff, D. R. (Eds.). (1998). *Reconceptualizing the literacies in adolescents' lives.* Mahwah, NJ: Lawrence Erlbaum Associates.

Alvermann, D. E., Hinchman, K. A., Moore, D. E., Phelps, S. F., & Waff, D. R. (Eds.) (2006). *Reconceptualizing the literacies in adolescents' lives* (2nd ed.). Mahwah, NJ: Lawrence Erlbaum Associates.

Alvermann, D. E., & Moore, D. W. (1991). Secondary school reading. In R. Barr, M. L. Kamil, P. B. Mosenthal, & P. D. Pearson (Eds.), *Handbook of reading research* (Vol. II, pp. 951–983). New York: Longman.

Alvermann, D. E., O'Brien, D. G., & Dillon, D. R. (1990). What teachers do when they say they're having discussions of content area reading assignments: A qualitative analysis. *Reading Research Quarterly, 25*, 296–322.

Alvermann, D. E., & Phelps, S. F. (1998). *Content reading and literacy: Succeeding in today's classrooms* (2nd ed.). Boston: Allyn & Bacon.

Amabile, T. M. (1983). *Motivation and creativity: Effects of motivational orientation on creative writers.* Paper presented at the 91st annual convention of the American Psychological Association. Anaheim, CA, August, 26–30.

American Educator. (2001). Religious freedom in the world: A global comparative survey sponsored by Freedom House. Author, 25(2), 18–32.

American Psychological Association Presidential Task Force on Psychology in Education. (1993). *Learner-centered psychological principles: Guidelines for school redesign and reform.* Washington, DC: American Psychological Association.

Ammon, B., & Sherman, G. W. (1996). *Worth a thousand words: An annotated guide to picture books for older readers.* Englewood, CO: Libraries Unlimited.

Anders, P. L., & Spitler, E. (2007). Reinventing comprehension instruction for adolescents. In J. Lewis, & G. Moorman (Eds.), *Adolescent literacy instruction: Policies and promising practices* (pp. 167–191). Newark, DE: International Reading Association.

Anderson, R. C., & Nagy, W. E. (Winter 1992). The vocabulary conundrum. *American Educator, 14*–18, 44–47.

Anderson, R. C., & Pearson, P. D. (1984). A schema-theoretic view of basic processes in reading. In P. D. Pearson (Ed.), *Handbook of reading research* (Vol. I, pp. 255–317). New York: Longman.

Anderson, R. C., Hiebert, E. H., Scott, J. A., & Wilkinson, I. A. G. (1985). *Becoming a nation of readers: The report of the commission on reading.* Washington, DC: National Institute of Education.

Angel, A. R., Abbott, C. D., & Runde, D. C. (2005). *A survey of mathematics with applications* (7th ed.). Boston: Pearson.

Angelillo, J. (2005). *Writing to the prompt: When students don't have a choice.* Portsmouth, NH: Heinemann.

Applebee, A. (1992). Stability and change in the high school canon. *English Journal, 81*(5), 27–32.

Applebee, A. (1994). *NAEP 1992 writing report card.* Washington, DC: Education Information Branch, OERI, U. S. Dept. of Education.

Applebee, A., Auten, A., & Lehr, F. (1981). *Writing in the secondary school: English and the content areas.* Urbana, IL: National Council of Teachers of English.

Applegate, A. J., & Applegate, M. D. (2004). The Peter Effect: Reading habits and attitudes of preservice teachers. *The Reading Teacher, 57*(6), 554–563.

Armbruster, B. B. (1984). The problem of "inconsiderate text." In G. G. Duffy, L. R. Roehler, & J. Mason (Eds.), *Comprehension instruction: Perspectives and suggestions* (pp. 202–217). New York: Longman.

Armbruster, B. B., Anderson, T. H., & Ostertag, J. (1989). Teaching text structure to improve reading and writing. *The Reading Teacher, 43*, 130–137.

Aronson, E., Blaney, N., Stephan, C., Sikes, J., & Snapp, M. (1978). *The jigsaw classroom.* Beverly Hills, CA: Sage.

Aronson, M. (2003). *Beyond the pale: New essays for a new era.* Lanham, MD: The Scarecrow Press.

Artzt, A. F., & Armour-Thomas, E. (1992). Development of a cognitive-metacognitive framework for protocol analysis of mathematical problem solving in small groups. *Cognition and Instruction, 9*, 137–175.

Artzt, A. F., & Yaloz-Femia, S. (1999). Mathematical reasoning during small-group problem solving. In L. V. Stiff (Ed.), *Developing mathematical reasoning in grades K–12: 1999 yearbook* (pp. 115–126). Reston, VA: National Council of Teachers of Mathematics.

Atkinson, T. S., Matusevich, M. N., & Huber, L. (2009). Making science trade book choices for elementary classrooms. *Reading Teacher, 62*(6), 484–497.

Atwell, N. (1987). *In the middle: Writing, reading, and learning with adolescents.* Portsmouth, NH: Heinemann.

Atwell, N. (1991). *Side by side: Essays on teaching to learn.* Portsmouth, NH: Heinemann.

Atwell, N. (1998). *In the middle: New understandings about writing, reading, and learning.* Portsmouth, NH: Heinemann.

Atwell, N. (1998). *In the middle: Reading and writing with adolescents.* Portsmouth, NH: Heinemann.

Atwell, N. (Ed.). (1990). *Coming to know: Writing to learn in the intermediate grades.* Portsmouth, NH: Heinemann.

Atwell, N. (2007). *The Reading zone: How to help kids become skilled, passionate, habitual, critical readers.* New York: Scholastic.

Avi. (1999). *If you write about mice and porcupines are you still writing out of your own experience?* Denver, CO: National Council of Teachers of English Convention.

Bailey, T. A., Kennedy, D. M., & Cohen, L. (1998). *The American pageant* (11th ed.). Boston: Houghton Mifflin.

Bakeless, J. (Ed.). (1964). *The journals of Lewis and Clark.* New York: Mentor Books.

Bakken, J. P. (2009). Improving comprehension. In B. Algozzine, D. J. O'Shea, & F. E. Obiakor (Eds.), *Culturally responsive literacy instruction* (pp. 118–139). Thousand Oaks, CA: Corwin Press.

Baldwin, R. S., & Leavell, A. G. (1992). When was the last time you read a textbook just for kicks? In E. K. Dishner, T. W. Bean, J. E. Readence, & D. W. Moore (Eds.), *Reading in the content areas: Improving classroom instruction* (3rd ed., pp. 105–111). Dubuque, IA: Kendall/Hunt.

Bamford, R. A., & Kristo, J. V. (Eds.). (2000). *Checking out nonfiction literature K–8: Good choices for best learning.* Norwood, MA: Christopher-Gordon.

Barack, L. (2010). Indianapolis trades textbooks for digital content. http://www.schoollibraryjournal.com/article/CA6715721.html?nid=2413&source=link+rid=17497973, retrieved 1/29/10.

Barley, T. (2003). Shared reading in the upper grades? You bet! *Instructor, 112*(6), 31–33.

Barnet, S., & Bedau, H. A. (2005). *Current issues and enduring questions: A guide to critical thinking and argument, with readings* (7th ed.). Boston: Bedford/St. Martin's.

Barnhart, D. K. (1991). *Neo-words: A dictionary of the newest and most unusual words of our times.* New York: Collier Books/Macmillan.

Barton, M. L., Heidema, C., & Jordan, D. (2002). Teaching reading in mathematics and science. *Educational Leadership, 60*(3), 24–28.

Baumann, J. F., & Kame'enui, E. J. (1991). Research on vocabulary instruction: Ode to Voltaire. In J. Flood, J. M. Jenson, D. Lapp, & J. R. Squire (Eds.), *Handbook of research on teaching the English language arts* (pp. 604–632). New York: Macmillan.

Baumbach, N. (2000). Van Gogh in AOL. *The New Yorker,* March 27, pp. 51–52.

Baumeister. D. (1992). *Think–pair–share: Effects on oral language, reading comprehension, and attitudes.* Dissertation, University of Maryland at College Park.

Beach, R., & Doerr-Stevens, C. (2009). Learning argument practices through online role-play: Toward a rhetoric of significance and transformation. *Journal of Adolescent and Adult Literacy, 52*(6), 460–468.

Bean, T. W. (1998). Teacher literacy histories and adolescent voices: Changing content-area classrooms. In D. E. Alvermann, K. A. Hinchman, D. W. Moore, S. F. Phelps, & D. R. Waff (Eds.), *Reconceptualizing the literacies in adolescents' lives* (pp. 149–170). Mahwah, NJ: Lawrence Erlbaum Associates.

Bean, T. W., & Readence, J. E. (1996). Content area reading: The current state of the art. In D. Lapp, J. Flood, & N. Farnan (Eds.), *Content area reading and learning: Instructional strategies* (2nd ed., pp. 15–24). Boston: Allyn & Bacon.

Bear, D. R., Invernizzi, M., Templeton, S., & Johnston, F. (2004). *Words their way: Word study for phonics, vocabulary, and spelling instruction.* Upper Saddle River, NJ: Prentice Hall.

Beck, I. L., McKeown, M. G., & Gromoll, E. W. (1989). Learning from social studies texts. *Cognition and Instruction, 6,* 99–158.

Beck, I. L., McKeown, M. G., Hamilton, R. L., & Jucan, L. (1997). *Questioning the author: An approach for enhancing student engagement with text.* Newark, DE: International Reading Association.

Beck, I. L., McKeown, M. G., Omanson, R. C., & Pople, M. T. (1984). Improving the comprehensibility of stories: The effects of revisions that improve coherence. *Reading Research Quarterly, 19*(3), 263–277.

Beers, K. (2003). *When kids can't read: What teachers can do.* Portsmouth, NH: Heinemann.

Beers, K. (2009). Presidential Address. NCTE Annual Conference, Philadelphia, November.

Bennett, S. (2009). Time to think: Using the workshop structure so students think and teachers listen. In S. Plaut (Ed.), *The right to literacy in secondary schools: Creating a culture of thinking.* New York: Teachers College Press; Newark, DE: International Reading Association.

Bennett, W. (1999). *The educated child.* New York: Free Press.

Berryman, L., & Russell, D. R. (2001). Portfolios across the curriculum: Whole school assessment in Kentucky. *English Journal, 90*(6), 76–83.

Bialynicki-Birula, I., & Bialynicki-Birula, I. (2004). *Modeling reality: How computers mirror life.* New York: Oxford University Press.

Bintz, W. P. (1997). Exploring reading nightmares of middle and secondary school teachers. *Journal of Adolescent and Adult Literacy, 41*(1), 12–24.

Bitz, M. (2004). The comic book project: Forging alternative pathways to literacy. *Journal of Adolescent and Adult Literacy, 47*(7), 574–586.

Blachowicz, C. L. Z. (1986). Making connections: Alternatives to the vocabulary notebook. *Journal of Reading, 29*(7), 643–649.

Blachowicz, C. L. Z., & Fisher, P. (2000). Vocabulary instruction. In P. D. Pearson, R. Barr, & M. L. Kamil (Eds.), *Handbook of reading research* (Vol. III, pp. 503–523). Mahwah, NJ: Lawrence Erlbaum Associates.

Blachowicz, C. L. Z., & Fisher, P. F. (2004). Keep the "fun" in "fundamental": Encouraging word awareness and incidental word learning in the classroom through word play. In J. F. Baumann & E. J. Kame'enui (Eds.), *Vocabulary instruction: Research to practice* (pp. 218–237). New York: The Guilford Press.

Black, A., & Stave, A. M. (2007). *A comprehensive guide to readers theatre: Enhancing fluency and comprehension in middle school and beyond.* Newark, DE: International Reading Association.

Black, P., Harrison, C., Lee, C., Marshall, B., & William, D. (2004). Working inside the black box: Assessment for learning in the classroom. *Phi Delta Kappan, 86*(1), 8–21.

Black, R. W. (2009). English-language learners, fan communities, and 21st century skills. *Journal of Adolescent and Adult Literacy, 52*(8), 688–697.

Blanton, W. E., Pilonieta, P., & Wood, K. W. (2007). Promoting meaningful adolescent reading instruction through integrated literacy circles. In J. Lewis and G. Moorman (Eds.), *Adolescent literacy instruction: Policies and promising practices* (pp. 212–236). Newark, DE: International Reading Association.

Block, C. C. (1999). Comprehension: Crafting understanding. In L. B. Gambrell, L. M. Morrow, S. B. Neuman, & M. Pressley (Eds.), *Best practices in literacy instruction* (pp. 98–118). New York: The Guilford Press.

Block, C. C., & Johnson, R. B. (2002). The thinking process approach to comprehension development: Preparing students for their future comprehension challenges. In C. C. Block, L. B. Gambrell, & M. Pressley (Eds.), *Improving comprehension instruction: Rethinking research, theory, and classroom practice* (pp. 54–79). San Francisco: Jossey-Bass.

Bloem, P. L., & Padak, N. D. (1996). Picture books, young adult books, and adult literacy learners. *Journal of Adolescent and Adult Literacy, 40*(1), 48–53.

Blood, R. (2002). *The weblog handbook: Practical advice on creating and maintaining your blog.* Cambridge, MA: Perseus.

Bloom, B. S., & Krathwohl, D. R. (1956). *Taxonomy of educational objectives: The classification of educational goals.* New York: McKay.

Bloom, H. (Ed.). (1998). *Women writers of children's literature.* Philadelphia: Chelsea House.

Booklist. (2003). Review retrieved from the Children's Literature Comprehensive Database 3/23/10.

Borasi, R., & Siegel, M. (2000). *Reading counts: Expanding the role of reading in mathematics classrooms.* New York: Teachers College Press.

Bormuth, J. R. (1968). Cloze test readability criterion reference scores. *Journal of Educational Measurement, 5,* 189–196.

Bowen, C. W. (2000). A quantitative literature review of cooperative learning effects on high school and college chemistry achievement. *Journal of Chemical Education, 77*(1), 116–119.

Boyce, L. N. (1996). In the big inning was the word: Word play resources for developing verbal talent. In J. VanTassel, D. T. Johnson, & L. N. Boyce (Eds.), *Developing verbal talent* (pp. 259–272). Boston: Allyn & Bacon.

Boyd, F. B. (1997). The cross-aged literacy program: Preparing struggling adolescents for book club discussions. In S. I. McMahon & T. E. Raphael (Eds.), *The book club connection* (pp. 162–181). New York: Teachers College Press.

Brad, J. (2008). Beyond the textbook: Studying Roswell in the social studies classroom. *Social Studies, 99*(3), 132–134.

Brady, M. (2000). The standards juggernaut. *Phi Delta Kappan, 81*(9), 648–651.

Brautigam, H., Hart, C. A., & Swindle, S. (2002). What books are high school students really reading for pleasure? *English Journal, 92*(2), 25–26.

Brenner, D., Pearson, P. D., & Rief, L. (2007). Thinking through assessment. In K. Beers, R. E. Probst, & L. Reif (Eds.), *Adolescent literacy: Turning promise into practice* (pp. 257–272). Portsmouth, NH: Heinemann.

Brock, C. H. (1997). Second-language learners in mainstream classrooms. In S. I. McMahon & T. E. Raphael (Eds.), *The book club connection* (pp. 141–158). New York: Teachers College Press.

Brockman, E. B. (1999). Revising beyond the sentence level: One adolescent writer and a "pregnant pause." *English Journal, 88*(5), 81–86.

Bromley, K. (2009). Vocabulary instruction in the secondary classroom. In S. R. Parris, D. Fisher, & K. Headley (Eds.), *Adolescent literacy, field tested: Effective solutions for every classroom* (pp. 58–69). Newark, DE: International Reading Association.

Brown, C. L., & Tomlinson, C. M. (1993). *Essentials of children's literature.* Boston: Allyn & Bacon.

Brown, C. S. (1994). *Connecting with the past: History workshop in middle and high schools.* Portsmouth, NH: Heinemann.

Brown, D. W. (2009). *In other words: Lessons on grammar, code-switching, and academic writing.* Portsmouth, NH: Heinemann.

Brown, J. V. (2000). Technology integration in a high school study skills program. *Journal of Adolescent and Adult Literacy, 43*(7), 634–637.

Brown, R. (1993). *Schools of thought: How the politics of literacy shape thinking in the classroom.* San Francisco: Jossey-Bass.

Brownlie, F. (2009). Adolescent literacy assessment: Finding out what you need to know. In S. R. Parris, D. Fisher, & K. Headley (Eds.), *Adolescent literacy, field tested: Effective solutions for every classroom* (pp. 117–125). Newark, DE: International Reading Association.

Brozo, W. G., & Hargis, C. H. (2003). Taking seriously the idea for reform: One high school's efforts to make reading more responsive to all students. *Journal of Adolescent and Adult Literacy, 47*(1), 14–23.

Brozo, W. G., & Simpson, M. L. (1999). *Readers, teachers, learners: Expanding literacy across the content areas.* Upper Saddle River, NJ: Merrill.

Bruce, B. (1998). Mixing old technologies with new. *Journal of Adolescent and Adult Literacy, 42*(2), 136–139.

Bruce, B. (1999/2000). Searching the web: New domains for inquiry. *Journal of Adolescent and Adult Literacy, 43*(4), 348–354.

Bruce, B. (2000). The work of art in the age of digital reproduction. *Journal of Adolescent and Adult Literacy, 44*(1), 66–71.

Bruns, J. H. (1992). They can but they don't: Helping students overcome work inhibition. *American Educator, 16*(4), 38–47.

Bryant, D. P. (Ed.). Effective instruction for struggling secondary students: A symposium. *Learning Disabilities Quarterly, 26*(2), 73–154.

Bucher, K., & Hinton, K. (2010). *Young adult literature: Exploration, evaluation, and appreciation* (2nd ed.). Boston: Allyn & Bacon.

Buckley, W. F. (1996). *The right word.* (S. M. Vaughan, Ed.). New York: Random House.

Buehl, D. (2007). A professional development framework for embedding comprehension instruction into content classrooms. In J. Lewis & G. Moorman (Eds.), *Adolescent literacy instruction: Policies and promising practices* (pp. 192–211). Newark, DE: International Reading Association.

Buikema, J. L., & Graves, M. (1993). Teaching students to use context clues to infer word meanings. *Journal of Reading, 36*(6), 450–457.

Burke, J. (1999). *The English teacher's companion.* Portsmouth, NH: Heinemann.

Burnett, B. (2002). *Cool careers without college for math and science wizards.* New York: Rosen Publishing Group.

Burnett, R. E. (2002). *Careers for number crunchers and other quantitative types.* Chicago: VGM Career Books.

Burniske, R. W. (1999). The teacher as a skilled generalist. *Phi Delta Kappan, 81*(2), 121–126.

Burns, T. R. (1995). A teacher's quest: Our mission isn't entertainment. *New York Teacher,* May 29, 2.

Bushman, J. H., & Haas, K. P. (2005). *Using young adult literature in the English classroom* (4th ed.). Upper Saddle River, NJ: Pearson/Merrill Prentice Hall.

Bussert-Webb, K. (2001). I won't tell you about myself, but I will draw my story. *Language Arts, 78*(6), 511–519.

Caine, R. N., & Caine, G. (1991). *Making connections: Teaching and the human brain.* Alexandria, VA: Association for Supervision and Curriculum Development.

Calia, C. L. (2005). *The stargazing year: A backyard astronomer's journey through the seasons of the night sky.* New York: Jeremy P. Tarcher/Penguin.

Calkins, L. (1986). *The art of teaching writing.* Portsmouth, NH: Heinemann.

Cambourne, B. (1995). Toward an educationally relevant theory of literacy learning: Twenty years of inquiry. *The Reading Teacher, 49,* 182–192.

Camilli, G., & Wolfe, P. (2004). Research on reading: A cautionary tale. *Educational Leadership, 61*(6), 26–29.

Campbell, D. (2000). Authentic assessment and authentic standards. *Phi Delta Kappan, 81*(5), 405–407.

Campbell, J. R., Voelkl, K., & Donahue, P. L. (1997). *Report in brief: NAEP 1996 trends in academic progress.* Washington, DC: National Center for Education Statistics.

Cangelosi, J. S. (1996). *Teaching mathematics in secondary and middle school: An interactive approach* (2nd ed.). Englewood Cliffs, NJ: Merrill.

Carlisle, J. (1995). Morphological awareness and early reading achievement. In L. Feldman (Ed.), *Morphological aspects of language processing* (pp. 189–209). Hillsdale, NJ: Lawrence Erlbaum Associates.

Carlisle, J. F. (1993). Selecting approaches to vocabulary instruction for the reading disabled. *Learning Disabilities Research and Practice, 8*(2), 97–105.

Carlisle, J. F., & Nomanbhoy, D. M. (1993). Phonological and morphological awareness in first graders. *Applied Psycholinguistics, 14*(2), 177–195.

Carlo, M. S., August, D., McLaughlin, B., Snow, C. E., Dressler, C., Lippman, D. N., Lively, T. J., & White, C. E. (2004). Closing the gap: Addressing the vocabulary needs of English-language learners in bilingual and mainstream classrooms. *Reading Research Quarterly, 39*(2), 188–215.

Carlsen, W. S. (1991). Questioning in classrooms: A sociolinguistic perspective. *Review of Educational Research, 61*(2), 157–178.

Carlson, I. (2008). Graphic novels in the classroom. *School Librarian's Workshop, 29*(1), 22–23.

Carr, E., & Ogle, D. (1987). K–W–L plus: A strategy for comprehension and summarization. *Journal of Reading, 30,* 626–631.

Carroll, W. M. (1999). Using short questions to develop and assess reasoning. In L. V. Stiff & F. R. Curcio (Eds.), *Developing mathematical reasoning in grades K–12: 1999 yearbook* (pp. 247–255). Reston, VA: National Council of Teachers of Mathematics.

Carter, B., & Abrahamson, R. F. (1990). *Nonfiction for young adults: From delight to wisdom.* Phoenix, AZ: Oryx Press.

Carter, C. J. (1997). Why reciprocal teaching? *Educational Leadership, 54*(6), 64–68.

Carter, K., with S. Ballard & E. Vallée. (2009). It's a Web 2.0 world: Expanding perspectives of literacy. *VOYA, 32*(2), 114–117.

Casey, H. K. (2008/2009). Engaging the disengaged: Using learning clubs to motivate struggling adolescent readers and writers. *Journal of Adolescent and Adult Literacy, 52*(4), 284–294.

Cassady, J. K. (1998). Wordless books: No-risk tools for inclusive middle classrooms. *Journal of Adolescent and Adult Literacy, 41*(6), 428–433.

Cecil, N. L. (1999). *Striking a balance: Positive practices for early literacy.* Scottsdale, AZ: Holcomb Hathaway.

Chall, J. S. (1967). *Learning to read: The great debate.* New York: McGraw-Hill.

Chamberlin, C. J. (2005). Literacy and technology: A world of ideas. In R. A. Karchmer, M. H. Mallett, J. Kara-Soteriou, & D. J. Ley, Jr. (Eds.), *Innovative approaches to literacy education: Using the Internet to support new literacies* (pp. 44–64). Newark, DE: International Reading Association.

Chambers, D. L. (1996). Direct modeling and invented procedures: Building on students' informal strategies. *Teaching Children Mathematics, 3*(2), 92–95.

Chambliss, M. J., & McKillop, A. M. (2000). Creating a print- and technology-rich classroom library to entice children to read. In L. Baker, M. J. Dreher, & J. T. Guthrie (Eds.), *Engaging young readers: Promoting achievement and motivation* (pp. 94–118). New York: Guilford Press.

Chandler-Olcott, K. (2001). Scaffolding love: A framework for choosing books for, with, and by adolescents. *The Language and Literacy Spectrum:* New York State Reading Association, 18–32.

Chandler-Olcott, K. (2009). New literacies in the secondary classroom. In S. R. Parris, D. Fisher, & K. Headley (Eds.), *Adolescent literacy, field tested: Effective solutions for every classroom* (pp. 82–93). Newark, DE: International Reading Association.

Chandler-Olcott, K., & Mahar, D. (2003). "Tech savviness" meets multiliteracies: Exploring adolescent girls' technology-related literacy practices. *Reading Research Quarterly, 38*(3), 356–385.

Chase, K. (2002). Teaching beginning learners without using textbooks. *Learning Languages, 7*(2), 11–14.

Chatton, B. (2010). *Using poetry across the curriculum: Learning to love language.* Santa Barbara, CA: Libraries Unlimited.

Chen, H. C., & Graves, M. F. (1996). Effects of previewing and providing background knowledge on Taiwanese college students' comprehension of American short stories. *TESOL Quarterly, 29,* 663–686.

Ching, S. H. D. (2005). Multicultural children's literature as an instrument of power. *Language Arts, 83*(2), 128–136.

Christenbury, L. (2007). Who is the good teacher? In K. Beers, R. E. Probst, & L. Reif (Eds.), *Adolescent literacy: Turning promise into practice* (pp. 289–293). Portsmouth, NH: Heinemann.

Christenbury, L., & Kelly, P. P. (1994). What textbooks can and cannot do. *English Journal, 83*(3), 76–80.

Christenson, L. M. (2000). Critical literacy: Teaching reading, writing, and outrage. In *Trends & issues in secondary English* (pp. 53–67). Urbana, IL: National Council of Teachers of English.

Christinson, J., & Whited, A. (2005). *Nonfiction writing prompts for math.* Englewood, CO: Advanced Learning Press.

Chun, C. W. (2009). Critical literacies and graphic novels for English-language users: Teaching *Maus. Journal of Adolescent and Adult Literacy, 53*(2), 144–153.

Cianciolo, P. J. (2000). *Informational picture books for children.* Chicago: American Library Association.

Clark, E. (1993). *The lexicon in acquisition.* Cambridge, UK: Cambridge University Press.

Clarke, L. W. (2007). Discussing *Shiloh:* A conversation beyond the book. *Journal of Adolescent and Adult Literacy, 51*(2), 112–122.

Clubb, O. (2001, March 11). Global warming: Can we change our wasteful ways? *Syracuse Herald-American,* pp. D1, D4.

Cobb, T., & Horst, M. (2004). Is there room for an academic word list in French? In P. Bogaards & B. Laufer (Eds.), *Vocabulary in a second language* (pp. 15–38). Philadelphia: John Benjamins Publishing.

Cochran, L. (2009). Self-assessment of standardized test data: Empowering students to plan and own their learning in language arts. In S. Plaut (Ed.), *The right to literacy in secondary schools: Creating a culture of think-* ing (pp. 109–121). New York: Teachers College Press; Newark, DE: International Reading Association.

Colbert, D. (Ed.). (1997). *Eyewitness to America: 500 years of America in the words of those who saw it happen.* New York: Pantheon Books.

College Entrance Examination Board. (2003). *The neglected "R": The need for a writing revolution in America's schools and colleges.* New York.

Columba, L., Kim, K. Y., & Moe, A. J. (2005). *The power of picture books in teaching math and science: Grades pre-k–8.* Scottsdale, AZ: Holcomb Hathaway.

Commeyras, M., Bisplinghoff, B. S., & Oson, J. (Eds.). (2003). *Teachers as readers: Perspectives on the importance of reading in teachers' classrooms and lives.* Newark, DE: International Reading Association.

Compton's pictured encyclopedia. (1931). (Vol. 2). Chicago: F. E. Compton & Company.

Conley, M. W. (1995). *Content reading instruction: A communication approach* (2nd ed.). New York: McGraw-Hill.

Conner, L., & Gunstone, R. (2004). Conscious knowledge of learning: Accessing learning strategies in a final year high school biology class. *International Journal of Science Education, 26*(12), 1427–1443.

Connor, J. J. (2003). "The textbooks never said anything about . . .": Adolescents respond to *The Middle Passage: White Ships/Black Cargo. Journal of Adolescent and Adult Literacy, 47*(3), 240–246.

Connor, U. (1997). Contrastive rhetoric: Implications for teachers of writing in multicultural classrooms. In C. Severino, J. C. Guerra, & J. E. Butler (Eds.), *Writing in multicultural settings* (pp. 198–208). New York: Modern Language Association of America.

Considine, D., Horton, J., & Moorman, G. (2009). Teaching and reading the millennial generation through media literacy. *Journal of Adolescent and Adult Literacy, 52*(6), 471–481.

Cooper, J. D., Boschken, I., McWilliams, J., & Pitochini, L. (2000). A study of the effectiveness of an intervention program designed to accelerate reading for struggling readers in the upper grades. In T. Shanahan & F. V. Rodriguez-Brown (Eds.), *49th Yearbook of the National Reading Conference* (pp. 477–486). Chicago: National Reading Conference.

Cooper, P., & Morreale, S. (Eds.). (2003). *Creating competent communicators: Activities for teaching speaking, listening, and media literacy in grades 7–12.* Scottsdale, AZ: Holcomb Hathaway.

Cope, B., & Kalantzis, M. (2000). *Multiliteracies: Literacy learning and design of social futures.* New York: Routledge.

Copeland, B. S., & Messner, P. A. (2003). *Linking picture books to standards.* Westport, CT: Libraries Unlimited.

Cox, C., & Zarillo, J. (1993). *Teaching reading with children's literature.* New York: Macmillan.

Coxhead, A. (2000). A new academic word list. *TESOL Quarterly, 34,* 213–238.

Crafton, L. (1983). Learning from reading: What happens when students generate their own background information. *Journal of Reading, 26,* 586–593.

Cramer, E. H., & Castle, M. (Eds.). (1994). *Fostering the love of reading: The affective domain in reading education.* Newark, DE: International Reading Association.

Crystal, D. (1995). *The Cambridge encyclopedia of the English language.* New York: Cambridge University Press.

Csikszentmihalyi, M. (1991). Literacy and intrinsic motivation. In S. R. Graubard (Ed.), *Literacy* (pp. 115–140). New York: Noonday.

Csikszentmihalyi, M. (1993). *The evolving self.* New York: HarperCollins.

Csikszentmihalyi, M. (1996). *Creativity: Flow and the psychology of discovery and invention.* New York: Harper-Collins.

Cuban, L. (1991). History of teaching in social studies. In J. Shaver (Ed.), *Handbook of research on social studies teaching and learning* (pp. 197–209). New York: Macmillan.

Cummins, J. (1994). The acquisition of English as a second language. In K. Spangenberg-Urbschat & R. Pritchard (Eds.), *Kids come in all languages: Reading instruction for ESL students* (pp. 36–62). Newark, DE: International Reading Association.

Cunningham, A. E., & Stanovitch, K. E. (1998). What reading does for the mind. *American Educator,* Spring/Summer, pp. 8–15.

Curran, M. J ., & Smith, E. C. (2005, November). The imposter: A motivational strategy to encourage reading in adolescents. *Journal of Adolescent & Adult Literacy, 49*(3), 186–190.

Curry-Tash, M. W. (1998). The politics of teleliteracy and adbusting in the classroom. *English Journal, 87*(1), 43–48.

Damico, J. S. & Baildon, M.C. (2007). Examining the ways readers engage with web sites during think aloud sessions. *Journal of Adolescent and Adult Literacy, 51*(3), 254–263.

Daniels, H. (2006). What's the next big thing with literature circles? *Voices from the Middle, 13*(4), 10–15.

Darling-Hammond, L., Ancess, J., & Falk, B. (1995). *Authentic assessment in action.* New York: Teachers College Press.

Davenport, S., with Charbauski, S., Kim, J., & Ramsey, B. (1999). Review of Gary Paulsen's *Soldier's Heart:* Being the story of the enlistment and due service of the boy Charley Goddard in the First Minnesota Volunteers (1998, Delacorte Press). *Journal of Adolescent and Adult Literacy, 43*(2), 204–206.

Davis, J. H. (2005). Redefining Ratso Rizzo: Learning from the arts about process and reflection. *Phi Delta Kappan, 87*(1), 11–17.

Davis, P., & Hersh, R. (1981). *The mathematical experience.* Boston: Houghton Mifflin.

Dawkins, R. (Ed.). (2008). *The Oxford book of modern science writing.* New York: Oxford University Press.

Dean, D., & Grierson, S. (2005). Re-envisioning reading and writing through combined-text picture books. *Journal of Adolescent and Adult Literacy, 48*(6), 456–468.

Deci, E. L., Koestner, R., & Ryan, R. M. (2001). Extrinsic rewards and intrinsic motivation in education: Reconsidered once again. *Review of Educational Research, 71*(1), 1–27.

Diaz-Gemmati, G. M. (2000). "And justice for all": Using writing and literature to confront racism. In *Trends & issues in secondary English* (pp. 76–97). Urbana, IL: National Council of Teachers of English.

Diehm, C. (2004). From worn-out to Web-based: Better student portfolios. *Phi Delta Kappan, 85*(10), 792–794.

DiGisi, L. L., & Willett, J. B. (1995). What high school biology teachers say about their textbook use: A descriptive study. *Journal of Research in Science Teaching, 32,* 123–142.

Donahue, P., Voelkl, K., Campbell, J., & Mazzeo, J. (1990). *NAEP 1998 reading report card for the nation and states.* Washington, DC: U.S. Department of Education.

Dreazen, Y. (1998). What if . . . ?: New issues would arise if a cure for cancer is found. Knight Ridder Newspapers, *Syracuse Herald-Journal,* Tuesday, June 16, p. A8.

Dresang, E. (1999). *Radical change: Books for youth in a digital age.* New York: H. W. Wilson.

Dresang, E. T. (2008). Radical change revisited: Dynamic digital age books for youth. *Contemporary Issues in Technology and Teacher Education, 8*(3), 294–304.

Dresang, E. T., & Kotrla, B. (2009). Radical change theory and synergistic reading for digital age youth. *The Journal of Aesthetic Education, 43*(2), 92–107.

Duffy, G., Roehler, L., & Hermann, B. A. (1988). Modeling mental processes helps poor readers become more strategic readers. *The Reading Teacher, 42,* 762–767.

Duffy, T. M., Higgins, L., Mehlenbacher, B., Cochran, C., Wallace, D., Hill, C. et al. (1989). Models for the design of instructional text. *Reading Research Quarterly, 24*(4), 434–457.

Duke, N. K., Pressley, M., & Hilden, K. (2006). Difficulties with reading comprehension. In C. A. Stone, E. R. Silliman, B. J. Ehren, & K. Apel (Eds.), *Handbook of language and literacy: Development and disorders* (pp. 501–520). New York: The Guilford Press.

Dunn, M. A. (2000). Closing the book on social studies: Four classroom teachers go beyond the text. *The Social Studies,* May/June, 132–136.

Durkin, D. (1978/79). What classroom observations reveal about reading comprehension instruction. *Reading Research Quarterly, 14,* 481–533.

Eanet, M. G., & Manzo, A. V. (1976). REAP—A strategy for improving reading/writing/study skills. *Journal of Reading, 19,* 647–652.

Ebbers, M. (2002). Science text sets: Using various genres to promote literacy and inquiry. *Language Arts, 80*(1), 40–50.

Ebbers, S. M., & Denton, C. A. (2008). A root awakening: Vocabulary instruction for older students with reading difficulties. *Learning Disabilities Research and Practice, 32*(2), 90–102.

Edwards, C. (2008). The how of history: Using old and new textbooks in the classroom to develop disciplinary knowledge. *Teaching History, 130,* 39–45.

Edwards, E. C., Font, G., Baumann, J. F., & Boland, E. (2004). Unlocking word meanings: Strategies and guidelines for teaching morphemic and contextual analysis. In J. F. Baumann & E. J. Kame'enui (Eds.), *Vocabulary instruction: Research to practice* (pp. 159–176). New York: The Guilford Press.

Egawa, K. (2007). Five things you need to know about literacy coaching in middle and high schools. In K. Beers, R. E. Probst, & L. Reif (Eds.), *Adolescent literacy: Turning promise into practice* (pp. 295–302). Portsmouth, NH: Heinemann.

Eisner, E. (2002). The kind of schools we need. *Phi Delta Kappan, 83*(8), 576–583.

Ellermeyer, D. A., & Chick, K. A. (2003). *Multicultural American history through children's literature.* Portsmouth, NH: Teacher Ideas Press.

Elley, W. B. (1992). *How in the world do students read?* Newark, DE: International Reading Association.

Elliott, J. L. (2008). *Using the writer's notebook in grades 3–8.* Urbana, IL: NCTE.

Elster, H. (1999). *The big book of beastly mispronunciations: The complete opinionated guide for the careful speaker.* Boston: Houghton Mifflin.

Emig, J. (1971). The composing processes of twelfth graders. *NCTE Research Report No. 13.* Urbana, IL: National Council of Teachers of English.

Enriquez, G. (2001). Making meaning of cultural depictions: Using Lois Lowry's *The Giver* to reconsider what is "multicultural" about literature. *Journal of Children's Literature, 27*(1), 13–22.

Erdsneker, B., Haller, M., & Steinberg, E. (1998). *Civil service arithmetic and vocabulary* (13th ed.). New York: Macmillan.

Erickson, B. (1996). Read-alouds reluctant readers relish. *Journal of Adolescent and Adult Literacy, 40*(3), 212–214.

Estes, T. H., & Vasquez-Levy, D. (2001). Literature as a source of information and values. *Phi Delta Kappan, 82*(7), 507–512.

Eva-Wood, A. L. (2008). Does feeling come first?: How poetry can help readers broaden their understanding of metacognition. *Journal of Adolescent and Adult Literacy, 51*(7), 564–576.

F. E. Compton & Company. (1931). *Compton's Pictured Encyclopedia.* Chicago: Author.

Fabos, B. (2000). ZAPME! zaps you. *Journal of Adolescent and Adult Literacy, 43*(8), 720–725.

Fadiman, C. (1985). *The Little, Brown book of anecdotes* (C. Fadiman, Ed.). Boston: Little, Brown.

Farnan, N., Flood, J., & Lapp, D. (1994). Comprehending through reading and writing: Six research-based instructional strategies. In K. Spangenberg-Urbschat & R. Pritchard (Eds.), *Kids come in all languages: Reading instruction for ESL students* (pp. 135–157). Newark, DE: International Reading Association.

Fecho, B. (1998). Crossing boundaries of race in a critical literacy classroom. In D. E. Alvermann, K. A. Hinchman, D. W. Moore, S. F. Phelps, & D. R. Waff (Eds.), *Reconceptualizing the literacies in adolescent lives* (pp. 75–101). Mahwah, NJ: Lawrence Erlbaum Associates.

Ferguson, C. (2002). Using the revised taxonomy to plan and deliver team-taught, integrated, thematic units. *Theory into Practice, 41*(4), 238–243.

Fernsten, L. A. (2008). Writer identity and ESL learners. *Journal of Adolescent and Adult Literacy, 52*(1), 44–52.

Feynman, R. P. (1985). *"Surely you're joking, Mr. Feynman!": Adventures of a curious character.* New York: Norton.

Feynman, R. P. (1988). *"What do you care what other people think?": Further adventures of a curious character.* New York: Norton. .

Finders, M. J. (2000). "Gotta be worse": Negotiating the pleasurable and the popular. *Journal of Adolescent and Adult Literacy, 44*(2), 146–149.

Finders, M. J., & Hynds, S. (2003). *Literacy lessons: Teaching and learning with middle school students.* Upper Saddle River, NJ: Merrill Prentice Hall.

Fink, R. (1995/1996). Successful dyslexics: A constructivist study of passionate interest reading. *Journal of Adolescent and Adult Literacy, 39*(4), 268–280.

Fink, R. (2006). *Why Jane and John couldn't read—and how they learned: A new look at striving readers.* Newark, DE: International Reading Association.

Fink, R. (2008). High-interest reading leaves no child behind. In R. Fink & S. J. Samuels (Eds.), *Inspiring reading success: Interest and motivation in an age of high-stakes testing* (pp. 19–61, 98–116). Newark, DE: International Reading Association.

Fisher, D., & Frey, N. (2003). Writing instruction for struggling adolescent readers: A gradual release model. *Journal of Adolescent and Adult Literacy, 46*(5), 396–405.

Fisher, D., & Frey, N. (2008). *Word wise and content rich, grades 7–12: Five essential steps to teaching academic vocabulary.* Portsmouth, NH: Heinemann.

Fisher, D., Frey, N., & Lapp, D. (2008). Shared readings: Modeling comprehension, vocabulary, text structures, and text features for older readers. *The Reading Teacher 61*(7), 548–556.

Fisherkeller, J. (2000). "The writers are getting kind of desperate": Young adolescents, television, and literacy. *Journal of Adolescent and Adult Literacy, 43*(7), 596–606.

Flanagan, K. (2007). Effective content vocabulary instruction in the middle: Matching pupils, purposes, words, and strategies. *Journal of Adolescent and Adult Literacy, 51*(3), 226–238.

Flavell, J. H. (1976). Metacognitive aspects of problem-solving. In L. B. Resnick (Ed.), *The nature of intelligence* (pp. 231–235). Hillsdale, NJ: Lawrence Erlbaum Associates.

Flesch, R. (1955). *Why Johnny can't read.* New York: Harper.

Fletcher, R. (1996). *A writer's notebook: Unlocking the writer within you.* New York: Avon Books/HarperCollins.

Fletcher, R. (2007). *How to write your life story.* New York: Collins.

Fletcher-Spear, K., Jenson-Benjamin, M., & Copeland, T. (2005, Winter). The truth about graphic novels: A format, not a genre. *ALAN Review, 32*(2), 37–44.

Flower, L., & Hayes, J. (1984). Problem solving strategies and the writing process. In R. Graves (Ed.), *Rhetoric and composition: A sourcebook for teachers and writers* (2nd ed., pp. 269–283). Upper Montclair, NJ: Boynton-Cook.

Ford, D. J. (2001). *What constitutes a good science trade book? Reviewing the reviewers' choices.* Paper presented at the annual meeting of the National Association of Research in Science Teaching, St. Louis, MO.

Ford, M. P., & Opitz, M. F. (2002). Using centers to engage children during guided reading time: Intensifying learning experiences away from the teacher. *The Reading Teacher, 55*(8), 710–717.

Forsten, C., Grant, J., & Hollis, B. (2003). Reading to learn: Are textbooks too tough? *Principal, 83*(2), 28–33.

Forsten, C., Grant, J., & Hollis, B. (2003). *Differentiating textbooks: Strategies to improve student comprehension and motivation.* Peterborough, NH: Crystal Springs Books.

Foster, D., & Noyce, P. (2004). The mathematics assessment collaborative: Performance testing to improve instruction. *Phi Delta Kappan, 85*(5), 367–374.

Fox, D. L., & Short, K. G. (2003). *Stories matter: The complexity of cultural authenticity in children's literature.* Urbana, IL: National Council of Teachers of English.

Franks, L. (2001). Charcoal clouds and weather writing: Inviting science to a middle school language arts classroom. *Language Arts, 78*(4), 319–324.

Freedman, R. (1988). Newbery Medal acceptance. *The Horn Book Magazine, 64*(4), 444–451.

Frey, N., Fisher, D., & Hernandez, T. (2003). "What's the Gist?": Summary writing for struggling adolescent writers. *Voices from the Middle, 11*(2), 43–49.

Fried, R. L. (2001). *The passionate learner: How teachers and parents can help children reclaim the joy of discovery.* Boston: Beacon Press.

Fry, E. (1977). Fry's readability graph: Clarifications, validity, and extension to Level 17. *Journal of Reading, 21*(3), 242–252.

Fulwiler, T. (1986). The politics of writing across the curriculum. In T. Fulwiler & A. Young (Eds.), *Writing across the disciplines: Research into practice.* Upper Montclair, NJ: Boynton/Cook.

Galda, L., & Liang, L. A. (2003). Literature as experience or looking for facts: Stance in the classroom. *Reading Research Quarterly, 38*(2), 268–275.

Gallagher, K. (2009). *Readicide: How schools are killing reading and what you can do about it.* Portland, ME: Stenhouse Publishers.

Gallas, K. (2001). "Look, Karen, I'm running like Jell-O": Imagination as a question, a topic, a tool for literacy research and learning. *Research in the Teaching of English, 35*(4), 457–492.

Gambrell, L. B. (1983). The occurrence of think-time during reading comprehension instruction. *Journal of Educational Research, 77*(2), 77–80.

Gambrell, L. B. (1987). Children's oral language during teacher-directed reading instruction. In J. E. Readence

& R. S. Baldwin (Eds.), *Research in literacy: Merging perspectives* (pp. 195–200). Rochester, NY: National Reading Conference.

Gambrell, L. B. (1996). Creating classroom cultures that foster reading motivation. *The Reading Teacher, 50,* 14–25.

Gambrell, L. B., & Almasi, J. F. (1994). Fostering comprehension development through discussion. In L. M. Morrow, J. K. Smith, & L. C. Wilkinson (Eds.), *Integrated language arts: Controversy to consensus* (pp. 71–90). Boston: Allyn & Bacon.

Gambrell, L. B., & Almasi, J. F. (1996). *Lively discussions!: Fostering engaged reading.* Newark, DE: International Reading Association.

Gambrell, L. B., Pfeiffer, W. R., & Wilson, R. M. (1985). The effects of retelling upon reading comprehension and recall of text information. *Journal of Educational Research, 78*(4), 216–220.

Ganske, K., Monroe, J. K., & Strickland, D. S. (2003). Questions teachers ask about struggling readers and writers. *The Reading Teacher, 57*(2), 118–128.

Garber-Miller, K. (2006). Playful textbook previews: Letting go of familiar moustache monologues. *Journal of Adolescent and Adult Literacy, 50*(4), 284–288.

Gardner, H. (1983/2004). *Frames of mind: The theory of multiple intelligences.* New York: Basic Books.

Gardner, H. (1991/2004). *The unschooled mind: How children think and how schools should teach.* New York: Basic Books.

Gardner, H. (1993). *Creating minds: An anatomy of creativity as seen through the lives of Freud, Einstein, Picasso, Stravinsky, Eliot, Graham, and Gandhi.* New York: Basic Books.

Gardner, H. (2006). *Five minds for the future.* Boston: Harvard Business School Press.

Gardner, H. (2006). *Multiple intelligences: New horizons.* New York: Basic Books.

Gardner, S., Benham, H. H., & Newell, B. M. (2000). Oh, what a tangled Web we've woven!: Helping students evaluate sources. In *Trends & issues in secondary English* (pp. 28–39). Urbana, IL: National Council of Teachers of English.

Garner, R., & Reis, R. (1981). Monitoring and resolving comprehension obstacles: An investigation of spontaneous text lookbacks among upper-grade good and poor comprehenders. *Reading Research Quarterly, 16*(4), 569–581.

Gaskins, I. W. (2008). Ten tenets of motivation for teaching struggling readers—and the rest of the class. In R. Fink & S. J. Samuels (Eds.), *Inspiring reading success: Interest and motivation in an age of high-stakes testing* (pp. 98–116). Newark: DE: International Reading Association.

Gauch, P. L. (1997). In the belly of the whale. *The Horn Book Magazine,* May/June, 294–299.

Gazzaniga, M. S. (1985). *The social brain: Discovering the networks of the mind.* New York: Basic Books.

Gee, J. (2000). Discourse and sociocultural studies in reading. In P. D. Pearson, R. Barr, & M. L. Kamil (Eds.),

Handbook of reading research (Vol. III, pp. 195–207). Mahwah, NJ: Lawrence Erlbaum Associates.

Genthe, H. (1998). The incredible sponge. *Smithsonian, 29*(5), 50–58.

Georghiades, P. (2004). From the general to the situated: Three decades of metacognition. *International Journal of Science Education, 26*(3), 365–383.

Gere, A. R., Christenbury, L., & Sassi, K. (2005). *Writing on demand: Best practices and strategies for success.* Portsmouth, NH: Heinemann.

Germann, P. J., Haskins, S., & Auls, S. (1996). Analysis of nine high school biology laboratory manuals: Promoting scientific inquiry. *Journal of Research in Science Teaching, 33*(5), 475–499.

Giovanni, N. (2007). *On my journey now: Looking at African-American history through the spirituals.* Somerville, MA: Candlewick Press.

Glandon, S. (2000). *Caldecott connections to science.* Englewood, CO: Fulcrum Publishing.

Glazer, E. M., & McConnell, J. W. (2002). *Real-life math: Everyday use of mathematical concepts.* Westport, CT: Greenwood Press.

Goldberg, J. (2008). *McGraw-Hill's careers for geniuses and other gifted types.* New York: McGraw-Hill. (electronic resource)

Goldberg, M. F. (2004). The test mess. *Phi Delta Kappan, 85*(5), 361–366.

Goldman, S. R., & Rakestraw, J. A., Jr. (2000). Structural aspects of constructing meaning from text. In P. D. Pearson, R. Barr, & M. L. Kamil (Eds.), *Handbook of reading research* (Vol. III, pp. 314–335). Mahwah, NJ: Lawrence Erlbaum Associates.

Goodman, K. S. (1967). Reading: A psycholinguistic guessing game. *Journal of the Reading Specialist, 6,* 126–135.

Goodman, Y. (1985). Kidwatching: Observing children in the classroom. In A. Jaggar & M. T. Smith-Burke (Eds.), *Observing the language learner* (pp. 9–18). Newark, DE: International Reading Association.

Goodrich, H. (1996/1997). Understanding rubrics. *Educational Leadership, 54*(4), 14–17.

Gorman, M. (2003). *Getting graphic!: Using graphic novels to promote literacy with preteens and teens.* Worthington, OH: Linworth Pub.

Gottfried, S. S., & Kyle, W. C., Jr. (1992). Textbook use and the biology education desired state. *Journal of Research in Science Teaching, 29,* 35–49.

Gough, P. B. (1985). One second of reading. In H. Singer & R. Ruddell (Eds.), *Theoretical models and processes of reading* (3rd ed., pp. 661–686). Newark, DE: International Reading Association.

Grabill, J. T., & Hicks, T. (2005). Multiliteracies meets methods: The case for digital writing in English education. *English Education, 37*(4), 301–311.

Grace, C. M. (2004). Exploring the African American oral tradition: Instructional implications for literacy learning. *Language Arts, 81*(6), 481–490.

Graesser, A. C., Golding, J. M., & Long, D. L. (1991). Narrative representation and comprehension. In R. Barr, M. L. Kamil, P. B. Mosenthal, & P. D. Pearson (Eds.), *Handbook of reading research* (Vol. II, pp. 171–205). White Plains, NY: Longman.

Graesser, A. C., McNamara, D. S., & Louwerse, M. M. (2003). What do readers need to learn in order to process coherence relations in narrative and expository text? In A. P. Sweet & C. E. Snow (Eds.), *Rethinking reading comprehension* (pp. 82–98). New York: The Guilford Press.

Graham, A. (1988). Casey's daughter at the bat. In R. R. Knudson & M. Swenson (Eds.), *American sports poems* (p. 42). New York: Orchard Books.

Graham, P. W. (1999). *Speaking of journals: Children's book writers talk about their diaries, notebooks, and sketchbooks.* Honesdale, PA: Boyds Mills Press.

Graham, S., & Perrin, D. (2007). *Writing next: Effective strategies to improve writing of adolescents in middle and high schools.* Washington, DC: Alliance for Excellent Education.

Grandgenett, N. F., Hill, J. W., & Lloyd, C. V. (1999). Connecting reasoning and writing in student "how to" manuals. In P. A. House & A. F. Coxford (Eds.), *Connecting mathematics across the curriculum* (pp. 142–146). Reston, VA: National Council of Teachers of Mathematics.

Graves, D. (1993). *A fresh look at writing.* Portsmouth, NH: Heinemann.

Graves, D. H. (1975). The child, the writing process, and the role of the professional. In W. Petty (Ed.), *The writing processes of students.* New York: State University of New York.

Graves, M. (2006). *The vocabulary book: Learning and instruction.* New York: Teachers College Press; Newark, DE: International Reading Association.

Graves, M. F. (2004). Teaching prefixes: As good as it gets? In J. F. Baumann & E. J. Kame'enui (Eds.), *Vocabulary instruction: Research to practice* (pp. 81–99). New York: The Guilford Press.

Graves, M. F., Prenn, M., & Cooke, C. (1985). The coming attraction: Previewing short stories. *Journal of Reading, 28,* 594–599.

Gray, D. (1989). Putting minds to work. *American Educator, 13*(3), 15–22.

Green, T. M. (1994). *The Greek and Latin roots of English* (2nd ed.). New York: Ardsley House.

Gregory, M. R. (2002). Constructivism, standards, and the classroom community of inquiry. *Educational Theory, 52*(4), 397–408.

Grolier encyclopedia of knowledge. (1991). Vol. 3. Danbury, CT: Grolier.

Groopman, J. E., & Folger, T. (Eds.). (2008). *The best American science and nature writing of 2008.* Boston: Houghton Mifflin.

Guillen, M. (1995). *Five equations that changed the world: The power and poetry of mathematics.* New York: Hyperion.

Gunderson, L. (2000). Voices of the teenage diasporas. *Journal of Adolescent and Adult Literacy, 43*(8), 692–706.

Gunderson, L. (2008). The state of the art of secondary ESL teaching and learning. *Journal of Adolescent and Adult Literacy, 52*(3), 184–188.

Gunning, T. G. (1996). *Creating reading instruction for all children* (2nd ed.). Boston: Allyn & Bacon.

Guthrie, J. T., & Anderson, E. (1999). Influences of concept-oriented reading instruction on strategy use and conceptual learning from text. *Elementary School Journal, 99*(4), 343–366.

Guthrie, J. T., Cox, K., Anderson, E., Harris, K., Mazonni, S., & Rach, L. (1998). Principles of integrated instruction for engagement in reading. *Educational Psychology Review, 10*(2), 177–199.

Guthrie, J. T., & Wigfield, A. (2000). Engagement and motivation in reading. In P. D. Pearson, R. Barr, & M. L. Kamil (Eds.), *Handbook of reading research* (Vol. III, pp. 403–422). Mahwah, NJ: Lawrence Erlbaum Associates.

Guzzetti, B., & Gamboa, M. (2004). Zines for social justice: Adolescent girls writing on their own. *Reading Research Quarterly, 39*(4), 408–436.

Hadaway, N. L., Vardell, S. M., & Young, T. A. (2001). Scaffolding oral language development through poetry for students learning English. *The Reading Teacher, 54*(8), 796–806.

Haggard, M. R. (1985). An interactive strategies approach to content reading. *Journal of Reading, 29*(3), 204–210.

Hahn, M. L. (2002). *Reconsidering read-aloud.* Portland, ME: Stenhouse.

Hairston, M. (1994). What happens when people write? In R. Eschholz & C. Eschholz (Eds.), *Language awareness* (pp. 471–472). New York: St. Martin's.

Hansen, J. (2009). Multiple literacies in the content classroom: High school students' connections to U.S. history. *Journal of Adolescent and Adult Literacy, 52*(7), 597–606.

Hargrove, T. V., & Nesbit, C. (2003). *Science notebooks: Tools for increasing achievement across the curriculum.* Columbus, OH: ERIC Clearinghouse for Science, Mathematics, and Environmental Education. ED 482720.

Harmon, J. M. (1998). Vocabulary teaching and learning in a seventh-grade literature-based classroom. *Journal of Adolescent and Adult Literacy, 41*(7), 518–529.

Harmon, J. M. (2000). Assessing and supporting independent word learning strategies of middle school students. *Journal of Adolescent and Adult Literacy, 43*(6), 518–527.

Harmon, J. M., Wood, K. D., & Hedrick, W. B. (2009). Interactive word walls: More than just reading the writing on the walls. *Journal of Adolescent and Adult Literacy, 52*(5), 398–408.

Harmon, J. M., Wood, K. D., Hedrick, W. B., & Gress, M. (2008). "Pick a word—Not just any word": Using vocabulary self-selection with expository texts. *Middle School Journal, 40*(1), 43–52.

Harris, T. L., & Hodges, R. E. (Eds.). (1995). *The literacy dictionary: The vocabulary of reading and writing.* Newark, DE: International Reading Association.

Harste, J. C. (1986, December). *What it means to be strategic: Good readers as informants.* Paper presented at the annual meeting of the National Reading Council, Austin, TX.

Harste, J. C. (2003). What do we mean by literacy now? *Voices from the Middle, 10*(3), 8–12.

Harste, J. C., & Carey, R. F. (1999). *Curriculum, multiple literacies, and democracy: What if English/Language arts teachers really cared?* Presidential Address, National Council of Teachers of English, Denver, CO.

Harste, J. C., & Short, K. G., with Burke, C. (1988). *Creating classrooms for authors: The reading–writing connection.* Portsmouth, NH: Heinemann.

Harvey, S. (1998). *Nonfiction matters: Reading, writing and research in grades 3–8.* York, ME: Stenhouse Publishers.

Harvey, S. A. (2002). Out of the art room and into the world. *Phi Delta Kappan, 83*(10), 796–797.

Harwayne, S. (1992). *Lasting impressions: Weaving literature into the writing workshop.* Portsmouth, NH: Heinemann.

Hatch, E., & Brown, C. (1995). *Vocabulary, semantics, and language education.* Cambridge, England: Cambridge University Press.

Haugen, H. H. (2001). Suckers for science. *Science Teacher, 68*(1), 50–51.

Haury, D. L. (2000). *High school biology textbooks do not meet national standards.* ERIC Digest ED 463949. ERIC Publications.

Haven, K. F. (1996). *Great moments in science: Experiments and readers theatre.* Englewood, CO: Teacher Idea Press.

Healy, J. (2000). Failure to connect: How computers affect our children's minds—for better or worse. *Phi Delta Kappan, 81*(5), Supplement, 1–10.

Heitman, J. (2004). *Teach writing to older readers with picture books: Every picture tells a story.* Worthington, OH: Linworth.

Helman, L. (2008). English words needed: Creating research-based vocabulary instruction for English learners. In A. E. Farstrup & S. J. Samuels (Eds.), *What research has to say about vocabulary instruction* (pp. 211–237). Newark, DE: International Reading Association.

Helman, L. A. (2004). Building on the sound system of Spanish: Insights from the alphabetic spellings of English language learners. *The Reading Teacher, 57*(5), 452–460.

Henk, W. A., & Selders, M. L. (1984). A test of synonymic scoring of cloze passages. *The Reading Teacher, 38,* 282–287.

Hennings, D. G. (2000). Contextually-relevant word-study: Adolescent vocabulary development across the curriculum. *Journal of Adolescent and Adult Literacy, 44*(3), 268–279.

Henry, L. A. (2006). SEARCHing for an answer: The critical role of new literacies while reading on the Internet. *The Reading Teacher, 59*(7), 614–627.

Herber, H. (1978). *Teaching reading in content areas* (2nd ed.). Upper Saddle River, NJ: Prentice Hall.

Hershberger, K., Zembal-Saul, C., & Starr, M. L. (2006). Evidence helps the KWL get a KLEW. *Science & Children, 43*(5), 50–53.

Hesse, K. (1998). Newbery Medal acceptance. *The Horn Book Magazine, 74*(6), 422–427.

Hibbing, A. N., & Rankin-Erickson, J. L. (2003). A picture is worth a thousand words: Using visual images to improve comprehension for middle school struggling readers. *The Reading Teacher, 56*(8), 758–770.

Hidi, S., & Harackiewicz, J. M. (2000). Motivating the academically unmotivated: A critical issue for the 21st century. *Review of Educational Research, 70,* 151–180.

Hidi, S., & Renninger, K. A. (2006). The four-phase model of interest development. *Educational Psychologist, 41*(2), 111–127.

Hill, M. (1991). Writing summaries promotes thinking and learning across the curriculum—but why are they so difficult to write? *Journal of Reading, 34,* 536–539.

Hill, R. S. (2009). The new literacy equation: Books + computers = multiplatform. *VOYA, 32*(2), 111–113.

Hillocks, G. (2006). Middle and high school composition. In P. Smagorinsky (Ed.), *Research on composition: Multiple perspectives on two decades of change* (pp. 48–77). New York: Teachers College Press.

Hinchman, K. A., & Zalewski, P. (1996). Reading for success in a tenth-grade global studies class: A qualitative study. *Journal of Literacy Research, 28,* 91–106.

Hirsch, E. D. (2006). *The knowledge deficit: Closing the shocking education gap for American children.* Boston: Houghton Mifflin.

Hirsch, E. D. (2009). *The making of Americans: Democracy and our schools.* New Haven: Yale University Press.

Hirsch, E. D., Jr. (1996). *The schools we need and why we don't have them.* New York: Doubleday.

Hoad, T. F. *The Concise Oxford Dictionary of English Etymology.* Oxford: Oxford University Press.

Hobbs, R. (1998). The Simpsons meet Mark Twain: Analyzing popular texts in the classroom. *English Journal, 87*(1), 49–51.

Hoetker, J., & Ahlbrand, W. P. (1968). The persistence of recitation: A review of observational studies of teacher questioning behavior. Occasional Paper Series, Number 3.

Hoffer, W. W. (2009). Thinking, not shuffling: Expecting all students to use their minds well. In S. Plaut (Ed.), *The right to literacy in secondary schools: Creating a culture of thinking* (pp. 140–151). New York: Teachers College Press and Newark, DE: International Reading Association.

Hoffman, J. V., McCarthy, S. J., Abbott, J., Christian, C., Corman, L., Curry, C., Dressman, M., Elliot, B., Matherne, D., & Stahle, D. (1994). So what's new in the new basals?: A focus on first grade. *Journal of Reading Behavior, 26*(1), 47–73.

Hollie, S. (2001). Acknowledging the language of African American students: Instructional strategies. *English Journal, 90*(4), 54–59.

Holmes, B. C. (1983). The effect of prior knowledge on the question answering of good and poor readers. *Journal of Reading Behavior, 15,* 1–18.

Holt, J. (1989). *Learning all the time.* Reading, MA: Addison-Wesley.

Holt, J. C. (1981). *Teach your own: A hopeful path for education.* New York: Delacorte Press/Seymour Lawrence.

Holt, J. C. (1982). *How children fail.* New York: Delacorte Press/Seymour Lawrence.

Hopkins, G., & Bean, T. W. (1998/1999). Vocabulary learning with the verbal–visual word association strategy in a Native American community. *Journal of Adolescent and Adult Literacy, 42*(4), 274–281.

Horn Book Guide. (2004). Review retrieved from the Children's Literature Comprehensive Database 3/23/10.

Houk, F. A. (2005). *Supporting English language learners: A guide for teachers and administrators.* Portsmouth, NH: Heinemann.

House, P. A. (1996). Try a little of the write stuff. In P. C. Elliot & M. J. Kenney (Eds.), *Communication in mathematics, K–12 and beyond.* Reston, VA: National Council of Teachers of Mathematics.

Howard, P. J. (2000). *The owner's manual for the brain: Everyday applications from mind-brain research.* Austin, TX: Bard Press.

Howell, D. D., & Howell, D. K. (2003). *Digital storytelling: Creating an estory.* Worthington, OH: Linworth.

Howes, E. V., Hamilton, G. W., & Zaskoda, D. (2003). Linking science and literature through technology: Thinking about interdisciplinary inquiry in middle school. *Journal of Adolescent and Adult Literacy, 46*(6), 494–504.

Hoyt, L., & Therrialt, T. (2003). Understanding text structures. In L. Hoyt, M. Mooney, & B. Parkes (Eds.), *Exploring informational texts: From theory to practice* (pp. 52–58). Portsmouth, NH: Heinemann.

Hughes, H. (2009). Multigenre research projects. *Middle School Journal, 40*(4), 34–43.

Hughes, W. (2000). *Critical thinking: An introduction to the basic skills.* Peterborough, Ont.: Broadview Press.

Hurst, B. (2005). My journey with learning logs. *Journal of Adolescent and Adult Literacy, 49*(1), 42–46.

Hynd, C. R. (1999). Teaching students to think critically using multiple texts in history. *Journal of Adolescent and Adult Literacy, 42*(6), 428–436.

Hynd, C. R., McNish, M. E., Guzzetti, B., Lay, K., & Fowler, P. (1994). *What high school students say about their science texts.* Paper presented at the annual meeting of the College Reading Association, New Orleans, LA.

International Reading Association. (1999). *Adolescent literacy: A position statement.* Newark, DE: Author.

Irvin, J. L., Meltzer, J., Mickler, M. J., Phillips, M., & Dean, N. (2009). *Meeting the challenge of adolescent literacy: Practical ideas for literacy leaders.* Newark, DE: International Reading Association.

Ivey, G., & Broaddus, K. (2001). 'Just plain reading': A survey of what makes students want to read in middle school classrooms. *Reading Research Quarterly, 36*(4), 350–377.

Jackson, K. (2005). *Sporting News presents Saturday shrines: College football's most hallowed grounds.* St. Louis, MO: Sporting News Books.

Jackson, Y., & Cooper, E. (2007). Building academic success with underachieving adolescents. In K. Beers, R. E. Probst, & L. Reif (Eds.), *Adolescent literacy: Turning promise into practice.* Portsmouth, NH: Heinemann.

Jacobs, G. E. (2004). Commentary: Complicating contexts: Issues of methodology in researching the language and literacies of instant messaging. *Reading Research Quarterly, 39*(4), 394–406.

Jacobson, F. F. (Ed.). (1997). *Library trends* (Vol. 45). Urbana, IL: University of Illinois Graduate School of Library and Information Science.

Jenkins, J. R., Antil, L. R., Wayne, S. K., & Vadasy, P. F. (2003). How cooperative learning works for special education and remedial students. *Exceptional Children, 69*(3), 279–292.

Jesness, J. (2004). *Teaching English language learners K–12*. Thousand Oaks, CA: Corwin Press.

Johnson, A. P. (2000). *Up and out: Using creative and critical thinking skills to enhance learning*. Boston: Allyn & Bacon.

Johnson, D. (2009). *The joy of children's literature*. Boston: Houghton Mifflin Harcourt.

Johnson, D. D. (2001). *Vocabulary in the elementary and middle school*. Boston: Allyn & Bacon.

Johnson, D. D., Johnson, B. V. F., & Schlichting, K. (2004). Logology: Word and language play. In J. F. Baumann & E. J. Kame'enui (Eds.), *Vocabulary instruction: Research to practice* (pp. 179–200). New York: The Guilford Press.

Johnson, D. D., & Pearson, P. D. (1984). *Teaching reading vocabulary* (2nd ed.). Fort Worth, TX: Holt, Rinehart & Winston.

Johnson, D. W., & Johnson, R. J. (1999). *Learning together and alone* (5th ed.). Englewood Cliffs, NJ: Prentice Hall.

Johnson, H., & Freedman, L. (2001). Talking about content knowledge at the middle level: Using informational trade books in content-area literature circles. *The Language and Literacy Spectrum, II*, 52–62.

Johnson, H., & Freedman, L. (2005). *Content area literature circles: Using discussion for learning across the curriculum*. Norwood, MA: Christopher-Gordon.

Johnson, N. J., & Giorgis, C. (2002). Pleasure reading. *The Reading Teacher, 55*(8), 780–788.

Johnston, P. (2000). How will literacy be assessed in the next millennium? *Reading Research Quarterly, 35*(2), 249–250.

Johnston, P., & Costello, P. (2005). Principles for literacy assessment. *Reading Research Quarterly, 40*(2), 256–267.

Jones, M. M. (2009). Engaging classroom communities: Belonging, rigor, and support as three pillars of a thinking classroom. In S. Plaut (Ed.), *The right to literacy in secondary schools: Creating a culture of thinking* (pp. 127–139). New York: Teachers College Press and Newark, DE: International Reading Association.

Jonsberg, S. D. (2001). What's a (white) teacher to do about Black English? *English Journal, 90*(4), 51–53.

Josten, D. (1996). Students rehashing historical decisions— and loving it! *Journal of Adolescent and Adult Literacy, 39*(7), 566–574.

Kagan, S. (1989). *Cooperative learning resources for teachers*. San Juan Capistrano, CA: Resources for Teachers.

Kajder, S. B. (2007). Unleashing potential with emerging technologies. In K. Beers, R. E. Probst, & L. Reif (Eds.), *Adolescent literacy: Turning promise into practice* (pp. 213–229). Portsmouth, NH: Heinemann.

Kallos, J. (2004). *Because netiquette matters!: Your comprehensive reference guide to e-mail etiquette and proper technology use*. Philadelphia: Xlibris.

Kane, S. (1995). Literary characters who write: Models and motivators for middle school writers. In M. R. Sorenson & B. Lehman (Eds.), *Teaching with children's books* (pp. 49–57). Urbana, IL: National Council of Teachers of English.

Kane, S. (2007). Does the imposter strategy pass the authenticity test? *Journal of Adolescent and Adult Literacy, 51*(1), 58–64.

Kane, S. (2008). *Integrating literature in the content areas*. Scottsdale, AZ: Holcomb Hathaway.

Kapinus, B., Gambrell, L. B., & Koskinen, P. S. (1991). The effects of retelling upon the reading comprehension of proficient and less proficient readers. *Journal of Educational Research, 6*, 356–362.

Kapitzke, C. (2001). Information literacy: The changing library. *Journal of Adolescent and Adult Literacy, 44*(5), 450–456.

Kaywell, J. (Ed.). (2007). *Dear author: Letters of hope*. New York: Philomel.

Kear, D. J., Coffman, G. A., McKenna, M. C., & Ambrosio, A. L. (2000). Measuring attitude toward writing: A new tool for teachers. *The Reading Teacher, 54*(1), 10–23.

Keehn, S., Harmon, J., & Shoho, A. (2008). A study of readers theater in eighth grade: Issues of fluency, comprehension, and vocabulary. *Readers and Writers Quarterly, 24*(4), 335–362.

Keene, E. O. (2002). From good to memorable: Characteristics of highly effective comprehension teaching. In C. C. Block, L. B. Gambrell, & M. Pressley (Eds.), *Improving comprehension instruction: Rethinking research, theory, and classroom practice* (pp. 80–105). San Francisco: Jossey-Bass.

Keene, E. O. (2003). From good to memorable: Characteristics of highly effective comprehension teaching. In A. P. Sweet & C. E. Snow (Eds.), *Rethinking reading comprehension* (p. 85). New York: The Guilford Press.

Keene, E. O. (2007). The essence of understanding. In K. Beers, R. E. Probst, & L. Rief (Eds.), *Adolescent literacy: Turning promise into practice* (pp. 27–38). Portsmouth, NH: Heinemann.

Kelley, M., & Clausen-Grace, N. (2008). From picture walk to text feature walk: Guiding students to strategically preview informational text. *Journal of Content Area Reading, 7*(1), 5–28.

Kim, H. S., & Kamil, M. L. (2004). Adolescents, computer technology, and literacy. In T. L. Jetton & J. A. Dole (Eds.), *Adolescent literacy research and practice* (pp. 351–368). New York: The Guilford Press.

Kim, J. S. (2008). Research and the reading wars. *Phi Delta Kappan, 89*(5), 372–375.

Kingsolver, B. (2002). A forest's last stand. In *Small wonder: Essays* (pp. 75–87). New York: HarperCollins.

Klentschy, M. P., & Molina-De La Torre, E. (2004). Students' science notebooks and the inquiry process. In E. W. Saul (Ed.), *Crossing borders in literacy and science instruction: Perspectives on theory and practice* (pp. 340–354). Newark, DE: International Reading Association, and Arlington, VA: National Science Teachers' Association.

Kliman, M., & Kleinman, G. (1992). Life among the giants: Writing, mathematics, and exploring Gulliver's world. *Language Arts, 69* (Feb.), 128–136.

Kneeshaw, S. (1999). Using reader response to improve student writing in history. *OAH Magazine of History, 13*(3), 62–65.

Knight, P. (1992). How I use portfolios in mathematics. *Educational Leadership, 49*(8), 71–72.

Knop, K. (2008). Graphic novels: Join the club! *Library Media Connection, 27*(3), 40–41.

Knowles, E., & Smith, M. (2005). *Boys and literacy: Practical strategies for librarians, teachers, and parents.* Westport, CT: Libraries Unlimited.

Kohn, A. (1998). *What to look for in a classroom . . . and other essays.* San Francisco: Jossey-Bass.

Kohn, A. (1999). *The schools our children deserve: Moving beyond traditional classrooms and "tougher standards."* Boston: Houghton Mifflin.

Kohn, A. (2001). Fighting the tests: A practical guide to rescuing our schools. *Phi Delta Kappan, 82*(5), 348–357.

Kohn, A. (2004). Test today, privatize tomorrow: Using accountability to "reform" public schools to death. *Phi Delta Kappan, 85*(8), 568–563.

Kolloff, P. B. (2002). Why teachers need to be readers. *Gifted Child Today Magazine, 25*(2), 50–54, 64.

Konold, K. E., Miller, S. P., & Konold, K. B. (2004). Using teacher feedback to enhance student learning. *Teaching Exceptional Children, 36*(6), 64–69.

Konopak, B., Martin, M., & Martin, S. (1987). Reading and writing: Aids to learning in the content areas. *Journal of Reading, 31*, 109–117.

Konopak, B., Martin, S., & Martin, M. (1990). Using a writing strategy to enhance sixth-grade students' comprehension of content material. *Journal of Reading Behavior, 22*, 19–38.

Koretz, M. (1999, June 6). Books for young readers. *Syracuse Herald-American, Stars Magazine*, p. 17.

Kovacs, D., & Preller, J. (1991). *Meet the authors and illustrators.* New York: Scholastic.

Kozol, J. (1991). *Savage inequalities: Children in America's schools.* New York: Crown.

Kozol, J. (2000). *Ordinary resurrections: Children in the years of hope.* New York: Crown.

Kozol, J. (2005). *The shame of the nation: The restoration of apartheid schooling in America.* New York: Crown.

Krashen, S. (1981). The case for narrow reading. *TESOL Newsletter, 15*, 23.

Krashen, S. (1989). We acquire vocabulary and spelling by reading: Additional evidence for the input hypothesis. *Modern Language Journal, 73*, 440–463.

Krashen, S. (2004). False claims about literacy development. *Educational Leadership, 61*(6), 18–21.

Krathwohl, D. R., Bloom, B. S., & Masia, B. B. (1964). *Taxonomy of educational objectives, Handbook II: Affective domain.* New York: McKay.

Krogness, M. M. (1995). *Just teach me, Mrs. K: Talking, reading, and writing with resistant adolescent learners.* Portsmouth, NH: Heinemann.

Kuhlman, W. D. (2001). Fifth-grader's reactions to Native Americans in *Little House on the Prairie:* Guiding students critical reading. *The New Advocate, 14*(4), 387–399.

Kuhn, T. S. (1996). *The structure of scientific revolutions* (3rd ed.). Chicago: University of Chicago Press.

L'Engle, M., with C. F. Chase. (1996). *Glimpses of grace.* San Francisco: HarperSanFrancisco.

Labbo, L. D. (2002). Computers, kids, and comprehension. In C. C. Block, L. B. Gambrell, & M. Pressley (Eds.), *Improving comprehension instruction: Rethinking research, theory, and classroom practice* (pp. 275–289). San Francisco: Jossey-Bass.

Lambert, S. E., & DeCotis, R. J. (2006). *Great jobs for math majors.* New York: McGraw-Hill.

Lamott, A. (1994). *Bird by bird: Some instructions on writing and life.* New York: Pantheon Books.

Langer, J. (1986). *Children's reading and writing: Structures and strategies.* Norwood, NJ: Ablex.

Langer, J. A. (1992). Rethinking literature instruction. In J. A. Langer (Ed.), *Literature instruction: A focus on student responses* (pp. 35–53). Urbana, IL: National Council of Teachers of English.

Langer, J. A., & Applebee, A. N. (1987). *How writing shapes thinking: A study of teaching and learning.* Urbana, IL: National Council of Teachers of English.

Lapp, D., Fisher, D., & Grant, M. (2008). "You can read this text—I'll show you how": Interactive comprehension instruction. *Journal of Adolescent and Adult Literacy, 51*(5), 372–383.

Larson, L. C. (2008). Electronic reading workshop: Beyond books with new literacies and instructional technologies. *Journal of Adolescent and Adult Literacy, 52*(2), 121–131.

Larson, L. C. (2009). Reader response meets new literacies: Empowering readers in online learning communities. *The Reading Teacher, 62*(8), 638–648.

Lasley, T. J., II, Matczynski, T. J., & Rowley, J. B. (2002). *Instructional models: Strategies for teaching in a diverse society* (2nd ed.). Belmont, CA: Wadsworth/Thomson Learning.

Laverick, C. (2002). B–D–A strategy: Reinventing the wheel can be a good thing. *Journal of Adolescent and Adult Literacy, 46*(2), 144–147.

Lawrence, D. (1999). The community as text: Using the community for collaborative Internet research. *English Journal, 89*(1), 56–62.

Lawrence, S. A., McNeal, K., & Yildiz, M. N. (2009). Summer program helps adolescents merge technology, popular culture, reading, and writing for academic purposes. *Journal of Adolescent and Adult Literacy, 52*(6), 483–494.

Le Patner, M., Ruthven, R., Matuk, F. N., & Whited, A. (2005). *Nonfiction writing prompts for social studies.* Englewood, CO: Advanced Learning Press.

Learner-Centered Principles Revision Work Group. (1995). *Learner-centered psychological principles: A framework for school redesign and reform.* Unpublished document. Washington, DC: American Psychological Association.

Lee, C. (2001). Is October Brown Chinese? *American Educational Research Journal, 38*(1), 97–142.

Lee, C. C. (2001). Culturally responsive school counselors and programs: Addressing the needs of all students. *Professional School Counseling, 4*(4), 257–261.

Leggo, C., & Sakai, A. (1997). Knowing from different angles: Language arts and science connections. *Voices from the Middle, 4*(2), 26–30.

Leonhardt, D. (2000, May 28). Spotlight on common sense. *Syracuse Herald-American,* p. D1.

Lesesne, T. S. (2006). Reading aloud: A worthwhile investment? *Voices from the Middle, 13*(4), 50–54.

Lesesne, T. (2007). Getting lost in a book: Unconscious delight and lifelong readers. *Voices from the Middle,* March, 53.

Lester, J. H., & Cheek, E. H., Jr. (1997/1998). The "real" experts address textbook issues. *Journal of Adolescent and Adult Literacy, 41*(4), 282–291.

Leu, D. J., Jr., & Kinzer, C. K. (1999). *Effective literacy instruction, K–8* (4th ed.). Upper Saddle River, NJ: Merrill.

Leu, D. J., Jr., & Leu, D. D. (1999). *Teaching with the Internet: Lessons from the classroom.* Norwood, MA: Christopher-Gordon.

Leu, D. J., Jr., Mallette, M. H., Karchmer, R. A., & Kara-Soteriou, J. K. (2005). Contextualizing the new literacies of information and communication technologies in theory, research, and practice. In R. A. Karchmer, M. H. Mallette, J. Kara-Soteriou, & D. J. Leu, Jr. (Eds.), *Innovative approaches to literacy education: Using the Internet to support new literacies* (pp. 1–10). Newark, DE: International Reading Association.

Leu, D. J., Leu, D. D., & Coiro, J. (2004). *Teaching with the Internet K–12: New literacies for new times* (4th ed.). Norwood, MA: Christopher-Gordon.

Levine, M. (1996). *Viewing violence: How media affects your child's and adolescent's development.* Garden City, NY: Doubleday.

Lewis, J. P. (2007). *The Brothers' War: Civil War voices in verse.* Washington, D.C.: National Geographic.

Liang, L. A., & Dole, J. A. (2006). Help with teaching reading comprehension: Comprehension instructional frameworks. *The Reading Teacher, 59*(8), 742–753.

Lindaman, D., & Ward, K. R. (2004). *History lessons: How textbooks from around the world portray United States history.* New York: New Press.

Lipson, M. Y. (1982). Learning new information from text: The role of prior knowledge and reading ability. *Journal of Reading, 14,* 243–261.

Lipstein, R. L., & Renninger, K. A. (2007). "Putting things into words": The development of 12–15-year-old students' interest for writing. In G. Rijlarsdaam (Series Ed.) and P. Boscolo & S. Hidi (Volume Eds.), *Studies in Writing, Volume 19: Writing and Motivation* (pp. 113–140). Oxford: Elsevier.

Liston, D. (2004). The lure of learning in teaching. *Teachers College Record, 106*(3), 459–486.

Lloyd, C. V. (1998). Engaging students at the top (without leaving the rest behind). *Journal of Adolescent and Adult Literacy, 42*(3), 184–191.

Loewen, J. (2010). *Teaching what really happened: How to avoid the tyranny of textbooks and get students excited about doing history.* New York: Teachers College Press.

Long, T. W. (2008). The full circling process: Leaping into the ethics of history using critical visual literacy and arts-based activism. *Journal of Adolescent and Adult Literacy, 51*(6), 498–508.

Lovrich, D. (2004). A ladder of thinking. *Science Teacher, 71*(4), 56–59

Lowry, L. (1990, July/August). Newbery Medal acceptance. *The Horn Book Magazine, 66,* 412–421.

Lowry, L. (1994, July/August). Newbery Medal acceptance. *The Horn Book Magazine, 70,* 414–422.

Lubliner, S. (2001). *A practical guide to reciprocal teaching.* Bothell, WA: Wright Group/McGraw-Hill.

Luce-Kapler, R. (2007). Radical change and wikis: Teaching new literacies. *Journal of Adolescent and Adult Literacy, 51*(3), 214–223.

Lundberg, I., & Lynnakyla, P. (1993). *Teaching reading around the world: IEA study of reading literacy.* Hamburg, Germany: International Association for the Evaluation of Educational Achievement.

Lyga, A. A. W., with B. Lyga (2004). *Graphic novels in your media center: A definitive guide.* Westport, CT: Libraries Unlimited.

Lymon, F. (1981). The responsive classroom discussion. In A. S. Anderson (Ed.), *Mainstreaming digest* (pp. 109–113). College Park: University of Maryland, College of Education.

Mader, C. E. (2009). "I will never teach the old way again": Classroom management and external incentives. *Theory Into Practice, 48*(2), 147–155.

Maggio, R. (1997). *Talking about people: A guide to fair language.* Phoenix, AZ: Oryx Press.

Mahiri, J. (1998). *Shooting for excellence: African American and youth culture in new century schools.* Urbana, IL: National Council of Teachers of English, and New York: Teachers College Press.

Mahiri, J. (2001). Pop culture pedagogy and the end(s) of school. *Journal of Adolescent and Adult Literacy, 44*(4), 382–385.

Mahiri, J. (Ed.). (2004). *What they don't learn in school: Literacy in the lives of urban youth.* New York: Peter Lang.

Maida, P. (1995). Reading and notetaking prior to instruction. *Mathematics Teacher 88*(6), 470–473.

Malloy, M. E. (1999). Ein Riesen-Spafs! (Great fun!): Using authentic picture books to teach a foreign language. *The New Advocate, 12*(2), 169–184.

Mandel, S. M. (2003). *Cooperative work groups: Preparing students for the real world.* Thousand Oaks, CA: Corwin Press.

Manuel, J. (1998). Reviewing talking and listening in the secondary English curriculum. In W. Sawyer, K. Watson, & E. Gold (Eds.), *Reviewing English* (pp. 264–276). Sydney, Australia: St. Clair Press.

Manzo, A. V. (1969). The ReQuest procedure. *Journal of Reading, 11,* 123–126.

Manzo, A. V., & Manzo, U. (1997). *Content area literacy: Interactive teaching for active learning.* Upper Saddle River, NJ: Merrill.

Marzano, R. J. (2004). The developing vision of vocabulary instruction. In J. F. Baumann & E. J. Kame'enui (Eds.), *Vocabulary instruction: Research to practice* (pp. 100–117). New York: The Guilford Press.

Masingila, J. O., & Prus-Wisniowska, E. (1996). Developing and assessing mathematical understanding in calculus through writing. In P. C. Elliot & M. J. Kenney (Eds.), *Communication in mathematics, K–12 and beyond* (pp. 95–104). Reston, VA: National Council of Teachers of Mathematics.

Mason, L. R. (2004). Explicit self-regulated strategy development versus reciprocal questioning: Effects on expository reading comprehension among struggling readers. *Journal of Educational Psychology, 96*(2), 283–296.

Massey, D. D., & Heafner, T. L. (2004). Promoting reading comprehension in social studies. *Journal of Adolescent and Adult Literacy, 48*(1), 26–40.

Maxwell, R. J., & Meiser, M. J. (1997). *Teaching English in middle and secondary schools* (2nd ed.). Upper Saddle River, NJ: Merrill.

May, F. B. (2001). *Unraveling the seven myths of reading: Assessment and intervention practices for counteracting their effects.* Boston: Allyn & Bacon.

May, N. (2003). *We are the people: Voices from the other side of American history.* New York: Thunder's Mouth Press.

Mayher, J. (1998). Language education in the twenty-first century: Dreaming a caring future. In J. S. Simmons & L. Baines (Eds.), *Language study in middle school, high school, and beyond* (pp. 154–166). Newark, DE: International Reading Association.

Mazer, N. F. (1997). *When she was good.* New York: Arthur A. Levine Books.

McCollin, M., & O'Shea, D. J. (2009). Improving fluency. In Algozzine, B., O'Shea, D.J., & Obiakor, F.E. *Culturally responsive literacy instruction* (pp. 76–101). Thousand Oaks, CA: Corwin Press.

McCombs, B. L. (1989). Self-regulated learning and academic achievement: A phenomenological view. In B. J. Zimmerman & D. H. Schunk (Eds.), *Self-regulated learning and achievement: Theory, research, and practice* (pp. 51–82). New York: Springer-Verlag.

McDonough, J., & Shaw, C. (2003b). *Materials and methods in ELT: A teacher's guide* (2nd ed.). Malden, MA: Blackwell Publishing.

McElmeel, D. L. (2008). The chemistry of graphic novels. *Library Media Connection, 27*(3), 38–38.

McElvaine, R. S. (2000). *The Depression and the New Deal: A history in documents.* New York: Oxford University Press.

McGinley, W. (1992). The role of reading and writing while composing from sources. *Reading Research Quarterly, 27*(3), 226–248.

McIntyre, E., & Pressley, M. (1996). *Balanced instruction: Strategies and skills in whole language.* Norwood, MA: Christopher-Gordon.

McKeown, M. G., & Beck, I. L. (2004). Direct and rich vocabulary instruction. In J. F. Baumann & E. J. Kame'enui (Eds.), *Vocabulary instruction: Research to practice* (pp. 13–27). New York: The Guilford Press.

McKeown, R. G. (2007). Think-aloud strategy: Metacognitive development and monitoring comprehension in the middle school second-language classroom. *Journal of Adolescent and Adult Literacy, 51*(2), 136–147.

McKool, S. S. (2007). Factors that influence the decision to read: An investigation of fifth grade students' out-of-school reading habits. *Reading Improvement, 44*(3), 111–131.

McLaughlin, M. (2000). Assessment for the twenty-first century: Performance, portfolios, and profiles. In M. McLaughlin & M. Vogt (Eds.), *Creativity and innovation in content area teaching* (pp. 301–327). Norwood, MA: Christopher-Gordon.

McLeod, S. H. (2001). *WAC for the New Millennium: Strategies for continuing writing-across-the-curriculum.* Urbana, IL: National Council of Teachers of English.

McMahon, S. I. (1996). Book club: The influence of a Vygotskian perspective on a literature-based reading program. In L. Dixon-Krauss (Ed.), *Vygotsky in the classroom: Mediated literacy instruction and assessment* (pp. 59–76). New York: Longman.

Mellard, D. F., & Johnson, E. (2008). *RTI: A practitioner's guide to implementing response to intervention.* Thousand Oaks, CA: Corwin Press.

Met, M. (2004). Improving students' capacity in foreign languages. *Phi Delta Kappan, 86*(3), 214–218.

Meyer, C. A. (1992). What's the difference between "authentic" and "performance" assessment? *Educational Leadership, 49*(8), 39–40.

Michaels, J. R. (2001). *Dancing with words: Helping students love language through authentic vocabulary instruction.* Urbana, IL: National Council of Teachers of English.

Michel, P. (1994). *The child's view of reading: Understandings for teachers and parents.* Boston: Allyn & Bacon.

Miller, D. (2002). *Laura Ingalls Wilder and the American frontier: Five perspectives.* Lanham, MD: University Press of America.

Miller, D. (2009). *The book whisperer: Awakening the inner reader in every child.* San Francisco: Jossey-Bass.

Miller, L. D. (1993). Making the connection with language. *Arithmetic Teacher, 40*(6), 311–316.

Miller, P., & Koesling, D. (2009). Mathematics teaching for understanding: Reasoning, reading, and formative assessment. In S. Plaut (Ed.), *The right to literacy in secondary schools: Creating a culture of thinking* (pp. 65–80). New York: Teachers College Press; Newark, DE: International Reading Association.

Miller, T. (1998). The place of picture books in middle-level classrooms. *Journal of Adolescent and Adult Literacy, 41*(5), 376–381.

Miner, A. C., & Reder, L. M. (1996). A new look at the feeling of knowing: Its metacognitive role in regulating question answering. In J. Metcalfe & A. P. Shimamura (Eds.), *Metacognition: Knowing about knowing.* Cambridge, MA: MIT Press.

Mlodinow, L. (2008). *The drunkard's walk: How randomness rules our lives.* New York: Pantheon.

Mo, W., & Shen, W. (2000). A mean wink at authenticity: Chinese images in Disney's Mulan. *The New Advocate, 13*(2), 129–142.

Moffett, J. (1968). *Teaching the universe of discourse.* Boston: Houghton Mifflin.

Moje, E. B. (1996). I teach students, not subjects: Teacher–student relationships as contexts for secondary literacy. *Reading Research Quarterly, 31,* 172–195.

Moje, E. B. (2000). What will classrooms and schools look like in the new millennium? *Reading Research Quarterly, 35*(1), 128–129.

Moje, E. B., Ciechanowski, K. M., Kramer, K., Ellis, L., Carillo, R., & Collazo, T. (2004). Working toward third space in content area literacy: An examination of everyday funds of knowledge and discourse. *Reading Research Quarterly, 39*(1), 38–70.

Monseau, V. (1996). *Responding to young adult literature.* Portsmouth, NH: Boynton/Cook.

Montapert, A. A. (1982). *Inspiration and motivation.* Englewood Cliffs, NJ: Prentice Hall.

Moore, B. N., & Parker, R. (1995). *Critical thinking* (4th ed.). Mountain View, CA: Mayfield.

Moore, D. W. (2000). How will literacy be assessed in the next millennium? *Reading Research Quarterly, 35*(2), 246–247.

Moore, D. W., Bean, T. W., Birdyshaw, D., & Rycik, J. A. (1999). Adolescent literacy: A position statement (for the Commission on Adolescent Literacy of the International Reading Association). *Journal of Adolescent and Adult Literacy, 43*(1), 97–111.

Moore, D. W., Moore, S. A., Cunningham, P. M., & Cunningham, J. W. (1994). *Developing readers and writers in the content areas K–12* (2nd ed.). White Plains, NY: Longman.

Moore, J. N. (1999). *Imagining the Van Gogh Cafe: Designing instruction for multiple literacies in the English classroom.* NCTE Conference, Denver, CO.

Moreau, J. (2003). *Schoolbook nation: Conflicts over American history textbooks from the Civil War to the present.* Ann Arbor: University of Michigan Press.

Morley, S. (1996). Faculty book talks: Adults sharing books and enthusiasm for reading with students. *Journal of Adolescent and Adult Literacy, 40*(2), 130–132.

Morris, D., & Hartas, L. (2003). *Game art: The graphic art of computer games.* New York: Watson-Guptill Publications.

Morris, P. J., & Tchudi, S. (1996). *The new literacy: Moving beyond the 3Rs.* Portland, ME: Calendar Island Publishers.

Morrow, L. M. (1996). *Motivating reading and writing in diverse classrooms.* (NCTE Research Rep. No. 28.) Urbana, IL: National Council of Teachers of English.

Morrow, L. M. (2003). Motivating voluntary lifelong readers. In J. Flood, D. Lapp, J. R. Squire, & J. M. Jensen (Eds.), *Handbook of research on teaching the English language arts* (pp. 857–867). Mahwah, NJ: Lawrence Erlbaum Associates.

Moss, B. (1991). Children's nonfiction trade books: A complement to content area texts. *The Reading Teacher, 45,* 26–32.

Moss, B. (2003). *Exploring the literature of fact.* New York: The Guilford Press.

Moss, B., & Hendershot, J. (2002). Exploring sixth graders' selection of nonfiction trade books. *The Reading Teacher, 56*(1), 6–17.

Mountain, L. (2007/2008). Synonym success—Thanks to the thesaurus. *Journal of Adolescent and Adult Literacy, 51*(4), 318–324.

Mowder, L. (1992). Domestication of desire: Gender, language, and landscape in the *Little House* books. *Children's Literature Association Quarterly, 17,* 15–19.

Mulcahy-Ernt, P., & Stewart, J. P. (1994). Writing and reading in the integrated language arts. In L. M. Morrow, J. K. Smith, & L. C. Wilkinson (Eds.), *Integrated language arts: Controversy to consensus* (pp. 105–132). Boston: Allyn & Bacon.

Mundy, J., & Hadaway, N. (1999). Children's informational picture books visit a secondary ESL classroom. *Journal of Adolescent and Adult Literacy, 42*(6), 464–475.

Murphy, E. (2001). In search of literature for the twenty-first century. *English Journal, 90*(3), 111–115.

Murray, D. (1985). *A writer teaches writing* (2nd ed.). Boston: Houghton Mifflin.

Mydans, S. (2001). Left-behind mines pose risk for animals. New York Times News Service. *Syracuse Herald-American,* March 11, p. A5.

Myhill, D. (2000). Misconceptions and difficulties in the acquisition of metalinguistic knowledge. *Language and Education, 14*(3), 151–163.

Nadis, S. (1994). Fantastic voyage: Traveling the body in microbiotic style. *OMNI Magazine,* Winter, p. 9.

NAEP framework for reading assessment plan for 2009, www.naepreading.org. Retrieved 8/12/06.

Nagy, W. E. (1989). *Teaching vocabulary to improve reading comprehension.* Newark, DE: International Reading Association.

Nagy, W. E., & Scott, J. A. (2000). Vocabulary processes. In P. D. Pearson, R. Barr, & M. L. Kamil (Eds.), *Handbook of reading research* (Vol. III, pp. 269–284). Mahwah, NJ: Lawrence Erlbaum Associates.

Nagy, W., & Anderson, R. C. (1984). How many words are there in printed school English? *Reading Research Quarterly, 19,* 304–330.

Nagy, W., Anderson, R., & Herman, P. (1987). Learning word meanings from context during normal reading. *American Educational Research Journal, 24,* 237–270.

Nagy, W., Herman, P., & Anderson, R. (1985). Learning words from context. *Reading Research Quarterly, 20,* 233–253.

Nasar, S., & Cohen, J. (Eds.). (2008). *The best science writing of 2008.* New York: HarperPerennial.

Nathanson, S., Pruslow, J., & Levitt, R. (2008). The reading habits and literacy attitudes of inservice and prospective teachers. *Journal of Teacher Education, 59*(4), 313–321.

Nathenson-Mejia, S., & Escamilla, K. (2003). Connecting with Latino children: Bridging cultural gaps with children's literature. *Bilingual Research Journal, 27*(1), 101–116.

National Academy of Sciences. (1996). *National science education standards.* Washington, DC: National Academy Press.

National Council for the Social Studies. (1994). *Expectations of excellence: Curriculum standards for social studies.* Washington, DC: Author.

National Council of Teachers of English & International Reading Association. (1996). *Standards for the English language arts.* Urbana, IL, and Newark, DE: Authors.

National Council of Teachers of Mathematics. (1990). *Curriculum and evaluation standards for school mathematics.* Reston, VA: Author.

National Council of Teachers of Mathematics. (1991). *The professional teaching standards.* Reston, VA: Author.

National Council of Teachers of Mathematics, Commission on Standards for School Mathematics. (1989). *Curriculum and evaluation standards for school mathematics.* Reston, VA: National Council of Teachers of Mathematics.

National Research Council. (1994). *National science education standards: An enhanced sampler.* Washington, DC: National Academy of Sciences.

National Writing Project, & Nagin, C. (2006). *Because writing matters: Improving student writing in our schools* (Rev. ed.). San Francisco: John Wiley & Sons.

Negroponte, N. (1995). *Being digital.* New York: Knopf.

Nell, V. (1988). *Lost in a book: The psychology of reading for pleasure.* New Haven, CT: Yale University Press.

New London Group. (1996). A pedagogy of multiliteracies: Designing social futures. *Harvard Educational Review, 66*(1), 60.

Nierstheimer, S. L. (2000). "To the parents of . . .": A parent's perspective on the schooling of a struggling reader. *Journal of Adolescent and Adult Literacy, 44*(1), 34–36.

Nikolajeva, M., & Scott, C. (2001). *How picturebooks work.* New York: Garland.

Niles, O. S. (1985). Integration of content and skills instruction. In T. L. Harris & E. J. Cooper (Eds.), *Thinking and concept development: Strategies for the classroom* (pp. 177–194). New York: College Entrance Examination Board.

Noddings, N. (1992). *The challenge to care in schools: An alternative approach to education.* New York: Teachers College Press.

Noddings, N. (1999). Renewing democracy in schools. *Phi Delta Kappan, 80*(8), 579–583.

Nolan, R. E., & Patterson, R. B. (2000). Curtains, lights: Using skits to teach English to Spanish-speaking adolescents and adults. *Journal of Adolescent and Adult Literacy, 44*(1), 6–14.

Nolan, T. E. (1991). Self-questioning and prediction: Combining metacognition strategies. *Journal of Reading, 35*(2), 132–138.

Northwest Regional Educational Laboratory. (1998/1999). *Assessment and accountability program.* Portland, OR: Northwest Regional Educational Laboratory.

Norton, D. (1999). *Through the eyes of a child: An introduction to children's literature.* Upper Saddle River, NJ: Merrill.

O'Brien, D. G., Stewart, R. A., & Moje, E. B. (1995). Why content literacy is difficult to infuse into the secondary school: Complexities of curriculum, pedagogy, and school culture. *Reading Research Quarterly, 30*(3), 442–463.

Oczkus, L. D. (2003). *Reciprocal teaching at work: Strategies for improving reading comprehension.* Newark, DE: International Reading Association.

Ogle, D. (2009). Creating contexts for inquiry: From KWL to PRC2. *Knowledge Quest, 38*(1), 56–61.

Ogle, D. (2009). Reading comprehension across the disciplines: Commonalities and content challenges. In S. R. Parris, D. Fisher, & K. Headley. *Adolescent literacy, field tested* (pp. 34–46). Newark, DE: International Reading Association.

Ogle, D. M. (1986). K–W–L: A teaching model that develops active reading of expository text. *The Reading Teacher, 39*(6), 564–570.

Ohanian, S. (2001). News from the test resistance trail. *Phi Delta Kappan, 82*(5), 363–366.

Ohler, J. (2008). *Digital storytelling in the classroom.* Thousand Oaks, CA: Corwin Press.

Ohlhausen, M. M., & Jepson, M. (1992). Lessons from *Goldilocks:* Somebody's been choosing my books but I can make my own choices now. *The New Advocate, 5*(1), 31–46.

Oldfather, P. (1993). What students say about motivating experiences in a whole language classroom. *The Reading Teacher, 46*(8), 672–681.

Oldfather, P., & Dahl, K. (1994). Toward a social constructivist reconceptualization of intrinsic motivation for literacy learning. *Journal of Reading Behavior, 26,* 139–158.

Olson, C. B. (1992). *Thinking writing: Fostering critical thinking through writing.* New York: HarperCollins.

Orr, D. W. (2000/2001). Verbicide. *American Educator,* Winter, 26–29, 48.

O'Shea, D. J., Katsafanas, J., & Lake, K. (2009). Improving decoding and structural analysis skills. In B. Algozzine, D. J. O'Shea, & F. E. Obiakor (Eds.), *Culturally responsive literacy instruction* (pp. 46–75). Thousand Oaks, CA: Corwin Press.

Overholser, J. C. (1992). Socrates in the classroom. *Social Studies, 83*(2), 77–82.

Pace, B. G., & Townsend, J. S. (1999). Gender roles: Listening to classroom talk about literary characters. *English Journal, 88*(3), 43–49.

Padak, N., Newton, E., Rasinski, T., & Newton, R. M. (2008). Getting to the root of word study: Teaching Latin and Greek word roots in elementary and middle grades. In A. E. Farstrup & S. J. Samuels (Eds.), *What research has to say about vocabulary instruction* (pp. 6–31). Newark, DE: International Reading Association.

Palincsar, A. S., & Brown, A. L. (1984). Reciprocal teaching of comprehension-fostering and comprehension-monitoring activities. *Cognition and Instruction, 1,* 117–175.

Palmer, R. G., & Stewart, R. A. (1997). Nonfiction trade books in content area instruction: Realities and potential. *Journal of Adolescent and Adult Literacy, 40,* 630–641.

Pappas, C. C., & Varelas, M., with Barry, A., & Rife, A. (2004). Promoting dialogic inquiry in information book read-alouds: Young urban children's ways of making sense in science. In E. W. Saul (Ed.), *Crossing borders in literacy and science instruction* (pp. 161–189). Newark, DE: International Reading Association, and Arlington, VA: National Science Teachers Association.

Paris, S. G., & Winograd, P. (1989). How metacognition can promote academic learning and instruction. In B. F. Jones & L. Idol (Eds.), *Dimensions of thinking and cognitive instruction* (Vol. 1, pp. 15–52). Hillsdale, NJ: Lawrence Erlbaum Associates.

Parr, J. M., & Maguiness, C. (2005). Removing the silent from SSR: Voluntary reading as social practice. *Journal of Adolescent and Adult Literacy, 49*(2), pp. 98–107.

Paterson, K. (2000). The future of literature: Asking the question. *The New Advocate, 13*(1), 1–15.

Patterson, N. (2006). Computers and writing: The research says YES! *Voices from the Middle, 13*(4), 64–68.

Paul, D. G. (2000). Rap and orality: Critical media literacy, pedagogy, and cultural synchronization. *Journal of Adolescent and Adult Literacy, 44*(3), 246–252.

Pauling, L. (1995). *Linus Pauling in his own words: Selections from his writings, speeches and interviews.* (B. Marinacci, Ed.). New York: Simon & Schuster.

Paulos, J. A. (1988). *Innumeracy: Mathematical illiteracy and its consequences.* New York: Farrar, Straus & Giroux.

Paulos, J. A. (1991). *Beyond numeracy: The ruminations of a numbers man.* New York: Knopf.

Paulson, E. J. (2005). Viewing eye movements during reading through the lens of chaos theory: How reading is like the weather. *Reading Research Quarterly, 40*(3), 338–358.

Pavonetti, L. (2001). Celebrating diversity through children's literature: An interview with Leo and Diane Dillon. *Journal of Children's Literature, 27*(2), 45–51.

Pearson, M. B. (2005). *Big ideas in small packages: Using picture books with older readers.* Worthington, OH: Linworth.

Pearson, M. B. (2005). *Using picture books with older readers.* Worthington, OH: Linworth.

Pearson, P. D. (2004). The reading wars. *Educational Policy, 18*(1), 216–252.

Pearson, P. D., & Gallagher, M. C. (1983). The instruction of reading comprehension. *Contemporary Educational Psychology, 8,* 317–344.

Peck, R. (1994). *Life and death at the mall: Teaching and writing for the literate young.* New York: Delacorte.

Peregoy, S. F., & Boyle, O. F. (1997). *Reading, writing, and learning in ESL: A resource book for K–12 teachers* (2nd ed.). New York: Longman.

Perfetti, C., Britt, M., Rouet, J. F., Georgi, M., & Mason, R. (1994). How students learn and reason about historical uncertainty. In M. Carretero & J. Voss (Eds.), *Cognitive and instructional processes in history and the social sciences* (pp. 257–284). Hillsdale, NJ: Lawrence Erlbaum Associates.

Perl, S. (1979). The composing process of unskilled writers. *Research in Teaching English, 13,* 5–22.

Perl, S., & Wilson, N. (1986). *Through teachers' eyes: Portraits of writing teachers at work.* Portsmouth, NH: Heinemann.

Perrone, V. (1991). Moving toward more powerful assessment. In V. Perrone (Ed.), *Expanding student assessment* (pp. 164–166). Alexandria, VA: Association for Supervision and Curriculum Development.

Pescatore, C. (2007/2008). Current events as empowering literacy: For English and social studies teachers. *Journal of Adolescent and Adult Literacy, 51*(4), 326–339.

Pescatore, C. (2008). Current events as empowering literacy: For English and social studies teachers. *Journal of Adolescent and Adult Literacy, 51*(5), 326–339.

Peters, C. W. (1996). Reading in social studies: Using skills and strategies in a thoughtful manner. In D. Lapp, J. Flood, & N. Farnan (Eds.), *Content area reading and learning: Instructional strategies* (2nd ed., pp. 181–207). Boston: Allyn & Bacon.

Peterson, D., & VanDerWege, C. (2002). Guiding children to be strategic readers. *Phi Delta Kappan, 83*(6), 437–439.

Peterson, R., & Eeds, M. (1990). *Grand conversations: Literature groups in action.* New York: Scholastic.

Piaget, J. (1952). *The origins of intelligence in children.* New York: International University Press.

Pikulski, J., & Tobin, A. (1982). The cloze procedure as an informal assessment technique. In J. Pikulski & T. Shanahan (Eds.), *Approaches to the informal evaluation of reading* (pp. 42–62). Newark, DE: International Reading Association.

Platt, R. (2004). Standardized tests: Whose standards are we talking about? *Phi Delta Kappan, 85*(5), 381–382, 387.

Plitt, B. (2004). Teacher dilemmas in a time of standards and testing. *Phi Delta Kappan, 85*(10), 745–748.

Posner, D. (2004). What's wrong with teaching to the test? *Phi Delta Kappan, 85*(10), 749–751.

Postman, N. (1995). *The end of education: Redefining the value of schools.* New York: Knopf.

Postman, N. (1999). *Building a bridge to the eighteenth century: How the past can improve our future.* New York: Knopf.

Powell, R., Cantrell, S. C., & Adams, S. (2001). Saving Black Mountain: The promise of critical literacy in a multicultural democracy. *The Reading Teacher, 54*(8), 772–781.

Powell-Brown, A. (2003/2004). Can you be a teacher of literacy if you don't like to read? *Journal of Adolescent and Adult Literacy, 47*(4), 284–288.

Prensky, M. (2001). "Digital Natives, Digital Immigrants." *On the Horizon 9*(5). Retrieved [by Alvermann] Nov. 1, 2005, from www.marcprensky.com/writing/default.asp.

Pressley, M. (1995). More about the development of self-regulation: Complex, long-term, and thoroughly social. *Educational Psychologist, 30,* 207–212.

Pressley, M. (2000). What should comprehension instruction be the instruction of? In P. D. Pearson, R. Barr, & M. L. Kamil (Eds.), *Handbook of reading research* (Vol. III, pp. 545–561). Mahwah, NJ: Lawrence Erlbaum Associates.

Pressley, M., El-Dinary, P. B., Gaskins, I., Schuder, T., Bergman, J., Almasi, L., & Brown, R. (1992). Beyond direct explanation: Transactional instruction of reading comprehension strategies. *Elementary School Journal, 92,* 511–554.

Pressley, M., Wharton-McDonald, R., Hampson, J. M., & Echevarria, M. (1998). The nature of literacy instruction in ten grade-4/5 classrooms in upstate New York. *Scientific Studies of Reading, 2,* 159–194.

Probst, R. E. (2007). Tom Sawyer, teaching, and talking. In K. Beers, R. E. Probst, & L. Rief (Eds.), *Adolescent literacy: Turning promise into practice* (pp. 61–80). Portsmouth, NH: Heinemann.

Pugalee, D. K. (2004). A comparison of verbal and written descriptions of students' problem solving processes. *Educational Studies in Mathematics, 55*(1–3), 27–47.

Puig, E. A., & Froelich, K. S. (2010). *The literacy leadership team: Sustaining and expanding success.* Boston: Allyn & Bacon.

Quellmalz, E. S., Debarger, A. H., Haertel, G., Schank, P., Buckley, B. C., Gobert, J., Horwitz, P., & Ayala, C. C. (2008). Technology-based simulations in science assessment: The Calipers Project. In J. Coffey, & R. Douglas (Eds.), *Assessing science learning: Perspectives from research and practice* (pp. 191–202). Arlington, VA: NSTA Press.

Quinn, A. E. (2001). Moving marginalized students inside the lines: Cultural differences in classrooms. *English Journal, 90*(4), 44–50.

Quintana, C. C. (2001). The development and description of an inventory to measure the reading preferences of Mexican immigrant students. *Bilingual Research Journal, 25*(4), 563–581.

Raffaele, P. (2005). Born into bondage. *Smithsonian, 36*(6), 64–73.

Raham, G. (2004). *Teaching science fact with science fiction.* Portsmouth, NH: Teacher Ideas Press.

Raphael, T. E. (1984). Teaching learners about sources of information for answering comprehension questions. *Journal of Reading, 27*(4), 303–311.

Raphael, T. E., & Au, K. H. (2005). QAR: Enhancing comprehension and test-taking across grades and content areas. *The Reading Teacher, 59*(3), 206–221.

Rasinski, T. (2008). Teaching fluency artfully. In R. Fink & S. J. Samuels (Eds.), *Inspiring reading success: Interest and motivation in an age of high-stakes testing.* Newark, DE: International Reading Association.

Rasinski, T. V., & Padak, N. (2008). *From phonics to fluency: Effective teaching of decoding and reading fluency in the elementary school.* Boston: Pearson Allyn & Bacon.

Rasinski, T. V., Padak, N. D., McKeon, C. A., Wilfong, L. G., Friedauer, J. A., & Heim, P. (2005). Is reading fluency a key for successful high school reading? *Journal of Adolescent and Adult Literacy, 49*(1), 22–27.

Ravitch, D. (1995). *National standards in American education: A citizen's guide.* Washington, DC: The Brookings Institute.

Ravitch, D., & Finn, C. (1987). *What do our 17-year-olds know?: A report on the first national assessment of history and literature.* New York: Harper & Row.

Readers Theatre: www.readinga-z.com, www.aaronshep.com/rt/RTE.html.

Reardon, J. (1990). Putting reading tests in their place. *The New Advocate, 1*(1), 29–37.

Reed, J. H., Schallert, D. L., Beth, A. D., & Woodruff, A. L. (2004). Motivated reader, engaged writer: The role of motivation in the literate acts of adolescents. In T. L. Jetton & J. A. Dole (Eds.), *Adolescent literacy research and practice* (pp. 251–282). New York: The Guilford Press.

Reeves, D. L., with Clasen, L. (2007). *Career ideas for kids who like math and money.* (N. Bond, Illus.). New York: Ferguson.

Reid, S. (2002). *Book bridges for ESL students: Using young adult and children's literature to teach ESL.* Lanham, MD: Scarecrow Press.

Resnick, L. B. (1987). *Education and learning to think.* Washington, DC: National Academy Press.

Richards, J. C., & Anderson, N. A. (2003). What do I see? What do I think? What do I wonder? (STW): A visual literacy strategy to help emergent readers focus on story book illustrations. *The Reading Teacher, 56,* 442–444.

Richardson, J. (1994). Coordinating teacher read-alouds with content instruction in secondary classrooms. In G. Cramer & M. Castle (Eds.), *Fostering the life-long love of reading: The affective domain in reading education* (pp. 209–217). Newark, DE: International Reading Association.

Richardson, J. (2000). *Read it aloud! Using literature in the secondary content classroom.* Newark, DE: International Reading Association.

Richey, V. H., & Puckett, K. E. (1992). *Wordless/Almost wordless picture books.* Englewood, CO: Libraries Unlimited.

Rieck, B. J. (1977). How content teachers telegraph messages against reading. *Journal of Reading, 20*(8), 646–648.

Rief, L. (1992). *Seeking diversity: Language arts with adolescents.* Portsmouth, NH: Heinemann.

Rings, L. (2002). Novice-level books for reading pleasure in the second language classroom. *Die Unterrichtspraxis/Teaching German, 35*(2), 166–173.

Ripley, C. P. (1992). *The black abolitionist papers: 1985–1992.* Chapel Hill: University of North Carolina Press.

Robb, L. (2003). *Teaching reading in social studies, science, and math: Practical ways to weave comprehension strategies into your content area teaching.* New York: Scholastic.

Robb, L. (2004). *Nonfiction writing: Writing from the inside out.* New York: Scholastic.

Robinson, F. P. (1946). *Effective study.* New York: Harper & Row.

Roe, B. D., & Smith, S. H. (2005). *Teaching reading in today's middle schools.* Boston: Houghton Mifflin.

Roller, C. M. (1996). *Variability not disability: Struggling readers in a workshop classroom.* Newark, DE: International Reading Association.

Roller, K. (1990). The interaction of knowledge and structure variables in the processing of expository prose. *Reading Research Quarterly, 25,* 79–89.

Romano, T. (2000). *Blending genre, altering style: Writing multigenre papers.* Portsmouth, NH: Heinemann.

Romano, T. (2007). Teaching writing from the inside. In K. Beers, R. E. Probst, & L. Rief (Eds.), *Adolescent literacy: Turning promise into practice* (pp. 179–188). Portsmouth, NH: Heinemann.

Romines, A. (1997). *Constructing the Little House: Gender, culture, and Laura Ingalls Wilder.* Amherst: University of Massachusetts Press.

Rose, D., & Dalton, B. (2002). Using technology to individualize reading instruction. In C. C. Block, L. B. Gambrell, & M. Pressley (Eds.), *Improving comprehension instruction: Rethinking research, theory, and classroom practice* (pp. 257–274). San Francisco, Jossey-Bass.

Rosenblatt, L. M. (1938/1995). *Literature as exploration* (5th ed.). New York: Modern Language Association.

Rosenblatt, L. M. (1978). *The reader, the text, the poem: The transactional theory of the literary work.* Carbondale & Edwardsville: Southern Illinois University Press.

Rosenblatt, L. M. (2005). Literature—S.O.S.! *Voices from the Middle, 12*(3), 34–38.

Rosenthal, N. (1995). *Speaking of reading.* Portsmouth, NH: Heinemann.

Ross, D., & Frey, N. (2009). Real-time teaching: Learners need purposeful and systematic instruction. *Journal of Adolescent and Adult Literacy, 53*(1), 75–78.

Rothschild, D. A. (1995). *Graphic novels: A bibliographic guide to book-length comics.* Englewood, CO: Libraries Unlimited.

Routman, R. (1996). *Literacy at the crossroads: Crucial talk about reading, writing, and other teaching dilemmas.* Portsmouth, NH: Heinemann.

Routman, R. (2000). *Conversations.* Portsmouth, NH: Heinemann.

Rowe, M. B. (1974a). Reflections on wait-time: Some methodological questions. *Journal of Research in Science Teaching, 11*(3), 263–279.

Rowe, M. B. (1974b). Relation of wait-time and rewards to the development of language, logic, and fate control: Part II—Rewards. *Journal of Research in Science Teaching, 11*(4), 291–308.

Ruddell, M. R. (1993). *Teaching content reading and writing.* Boston: Allyn & Bacon.

Ruddell, M. R., & Shearer, B. A. (2002). "Extraordinary," "tremendous," "exhilarating," "magnificent": Middle school at-risk students become avid word learners with the Vocabulary Self-Selection Strategy (VSS). *Journal of Adolescent and Adult Literacy, 45*(5), 352–363.

Ruddell, R., & Unrau, N. (1994). Reading as a meaning-making construction process: The reader, the text, and the teacher. In R. Ruddell, M. R. Ruddell, & H. Singer (Eds.), *Theoretical models and processes of reading* (pp. 996–1056). Newark, DE: International Reading Association.

Rumelhart, D. (1976). *Toward an interactive model of reading* (Report No. 56). La Jolla: University of California, San Diego, Center for Human Information Processing.

Rumelhart, D. (1981). Schemata: The building blocks of cognition. In J. Guthrie (Ed.), *Comprehension and teaching: Research reviews* (pp. 3–26). Newark, DE: International Reading Association.

Rushkoff, D. (1996). *Playing the future: How kids' culture can teach us to survive in an age of chaos.* New York: HarperCollins.

Ryan, L. T. (2005). Henry Petroski: Engineer by day; author by night. *Syracuse Post Standard, Stars Magazine,* October 9, pp. 4–6.

Ryan, M. (1994). The day they threw out the textbooks. *Parade Magazine,* February 20, pp. 10–11.

Rycik, J. A., & Irvin, J. L. (2005). *Teaching reading in the middle grades: Understanding and supporting literacy development.* Boston: Pearson.

Ryder, R. J., & Graves, M. F. (1998). *Reading and learning in content areas* (2nd ed.). Upper Saddle River, NJ: Merrill.

Ryder, R. J., & Graves, M. F. (2002). *Reading and learning to read in the content areas* (3rd ed.). Upper Saddle River, NJ: Merrill.

Sadker, D., & Zittleman, K. (2004). Test anxiety: Are students failing tests—or are tests failing students? *Phi Delta Kappan, 85*(10), 740–744, 751.

Sadker, M., & Sadker, D. (1994). *Failing at fairness: How America's schools cheat girls.* New York: Scribner's.

Salend, S. J. (2009). Technology-based classroom assessments. *Teaching Exceptional Children, 41*(6), 48–58.

Sampson, M. B. (2002). Confirming a K-W-L: Considering the source. *The Reading Teacher, 55*(6), 528–532.

Sanacore, J. (1998). Promoting the lifelong love of writing. (Reading Leadership). *Journal of Adolescent and Adult Literacy, 41*(5), 392–396.

Santa, C., & Havens, L. (1995). *Creating independence through student-owned strategies: Project CRISS.* Dubuque, IA: Kendall-Hunt.

Saul, W., Reardon, J., Schmidt, A., Pearce, C., Blackwood, D., & Bird, M. D. (1993). *Science workshop.* Portsmouth, NH: Heinemann.

Savage, J. F. (1994). *Teaching reading using literature.* Iowa: RIE Document CS011590.

Scardamalia, M., Bereiter, C., & Goelman, H. (1982). What writers know: The language process and structure of written discourse. In M. Nystrand (Ed.), *The role of production factors in writing ability.* New York: Academic Press.

Schallert, D. L., & Roser, N. L. (1996). The role of textbooks and trade books in content area instruction. In D. Lapp, J. Flood, & N. Farnan (Eds.), *Content area reading and learning: Instructional strategies* (2nd ed., pp. 27–38). Boston: Allyn & Bacon.

Scharber, C. (2009). Online book clubs: Bridges between old and new literacies practices. *Journal of Adolescent and Adult Literacy, 52*(5), 433–437.

Schatz, E. I., & Baldwin, R. S. (1986). Context clues are unreliable predictors of word meanings. *Reading Research Quarterly, 21,* 439–453.

Schellings, G. L. M., & van Hout-Wolters, B. H. A. M. (1995). Main points in an instructional text, as identified by students and their teachers. *Reading Research Quarterly, 30,* 742–756.

Scherer, M. J. (2004). *Connecting to learn: Educational and assistive technology for people with disabilities.* Washington, DC: American Psychological Association.

Schiro, M. (2004). *Oral storytelling and teaching mathematics: Pedagogical and multicultural perspectives.* Thousand Oaks, CA: Sage.

Schmidt, R. (2008). Really reading: What does accelerated reading teach adults and children? *Language Arts, 85*(3), 202–211.

Schoenbach, R., Braunger, J., Greenleaf, C., & Litman, C. (2003). Apprenticing adolescents to reading in subject-area classrooms. *Phi Delta Kappan, 85*(2), 133–138.

Schoenfeld, A. H. (1987). What's all the fuss about metacognition? In A. H. Schoenfeld (Ed.), *Cognitive science and mathematics education* (pp. 189–215). Hillsdale, NJ: Lawrence Erlbaum Associates.

Schoonen, R., vanGelderen, A., de Glopper, K., Hulstijn, J., Simis, A., Stevenson, M. et al. (2003). First language and second language writing: The role of linguistic knowledge, speed of processing, and metacognitive knowledge. *Language Learning, 53*(1), 165–202.

Schulz, C. (1995). Peanuts. In *Syracuse Herald-American,* August 27, 1995, Comics Section, unpaged.

Schumaker, J., & Lenz, K. (1999). *Adapting language arts, social studies, and science materials for the inclusive classroom.* Reston, VA: Council for Exceptional Children.

Schur, J. B. *Eyewitness to the Past: Strategies for Teaching American History in Grades 5–12.* New York: Stenhouse.

Schuster, E. H. (2004). National and state writing tests: The writing process betrayed. *Phi Delta Kappan, 85*(5), 375–378.

Scott, J. A., & Nagy, W. E. (2004). Developing word consciousness. In J. F. Baumann & E. J. Kame'enui (Eds.), *Vocabulary instruction: Research to practice* (pp. 201–217). New York: The Guilford Press.

Scott, J. A., Nagy, W. E., & Flinspach, S. L. (2008). More than merely words: Redefining vocabulary learning in a culturally and linguistically diverse society. In A. E. Farstrup & S. J. Samuels (Eds.), *What research has to say about vocabulary instruction* (pp. 182–210). Newark, DE: International Reading Association.

Segal, E. (1977). Laura Ingalls Wilder's America: An unflinching assessment. *Children's Literature in Education, 8,* 63–70.

Severance, J. B. (2001). *Einstein: Visionary scientist.* New York: Clarion Books.

Sewall, G. T. (2008). *Islam in the classroom: What the textbooks tell us.* New York: American Textbook Council.

Shade, R. (1991). Verbal humor in gifted students and students in the general population: A comparison of spontaneous mirth and comprehension. *Journal for the Education of the Gifted, 14*(2), 134–150.

Shafer, G. (1997). Reader response makes history. *English Journal, 86*(7), 65–68.

Shafer, G. (2001). Standard English and the migrant community. *English Journal, 90*(4), 37–43.

Shafer Willner, L., Rivera, C., & Acosta, B. D. (2009). Ensuring accommodations used in content assessments are responsive to English Language Learners. *The Reading Teacher, 62*(8), 696–698.

Shagoury, R. (2007). The need to write, the need to listen. In K. Beers, R. E. Probst, & L. Rief (Eds.), *Adolescent literacy: Turning promise into practice* (pp. 39–41). Portsmouth, NH: Heinemann.

Shanahan, T., & Tierney, R. (1991). Research on the reading–writing relationship: Interactions, transactions, and outcomes. In R. Barr, M. L. Kamil, P. Mosenthal, & P. D. Pearson (Eds.), *Handbook of reading research* (Vol. II, pp. 246–280). New York: Longman.

Shanahan, T., & Tierney, R. J. (1990). Reading–writing connections: The relations among three perspectives. In J. Zutell & S. McCormack (Eds.), *Literacy theory and research: Analysis from multiple paradigms* (pp. 13–34). Chicago, IL: National Reading Conference.

Shanklin, N. (2007). How can you get the most from working with a literacy coach? *Voices from the Middle, 14*(4), 44–47.

Short, D. (1999). *New ways in teaching English at the secondary level.* Alexandria, VA: Teachers of English to Speakers of Other Languages.

Short, J. C., & Reeves, T. C. (2009). The graphic novel: A "cool" format for communicating to Generation Y. *Business Communication Quarterly, 72*(4), 414–430.

Short, K. G., Harste, J., & Burke, C. (1996). *Creating classrooms for authors and inquirers.* Portsmouth, NH: Heinemann.

Shriver, M. (2000). *Ten things I wish I'd known—Before I went out into the real world.* New York: Warner Books.

Siegel, M. (1984). Reading as signification. *Dissertation Abstracts International, 45,* 2824A (Indiana University).

Siler, T. (1996). *Think like a genius.* New York: Bantam Books.

Silin, J. G. (2003). Reading, writing, and the wrath of my father. *Reading Research Quarterly, 38*(2), 260–267.

Silver, S., & Smith, C. (1996). Building discourse communities in mathematics classrooms: A worthwhile but challenging journey. *Communication in Mathematics, K–12 and Beyond*. National Council of Teachers of Mathematics Yearbook, 20–28.

Simmons, J. S., & Deluzain, H. E. (1992). *Teaching literature in middle and secondary grades*. Boston: Allyn & Bacon.

Simpson, M., & Nist, S. L. (2000). An update on strategic learning: It's more than just textbook strategies. *Journal of Adolescent and Adult Literacy, 43*(6), 528–541.

Simpson, M. L. (1986). PORPE: A writing strategy for studying and learning in the content areas. *Journal of Reading, 29*(5), 407–414.

Sincich, T. (1990). *Statistics by example* (4th ed.). San Francisco: Dellen.

Singer, B. D., & Bashir, A. S. (2006). Developmental variations in writing composition skills. In C. A. Stone, E. R. Silliman, B. J. Ehren, & K. Apel (Eds.), *Handbook of language and literacy: Development and disorders* (pp. 559–582). New York: The Guilford Press.

Sippola, A. E. (1995). K–W–L–S. *The Reading Teacher, 48*(6), 542–543.

Slapin, B., & Seale, D. (1992). *Through Indian eyes: The Native experience in children's books*. Philadelphia: New Society Publishers.

Slavin, R. E. (1986). *Jigsaw II: Using student team learning* (3rd ed.). Baltimore: John Hopkins University, Center for Research on Elementary and Middle Schools.

Smetana, L., Odelson, D., Burns, H., & Grisham, D. L. (2009). Using graphic novels in the high school classroom: Engaging deaf students with a new genre. *Journal of Adolescent and Adult Literacy, 53*(3), 228–240.

Smith, C. C., & Bean, T. W. (1980). The guided writing procedure: Integrating content reading and writing improvement. *Reading World, 19*, 290–298.

Smith, F. (1985). *Reading without nonsense* (2nd ed.). New York: Teachers College Press.

Smith, F. (1988). *Joining the literacy club: Further essays into education*. Portsmouth, NH: Heinemann.

Smith, F. (2003). *Unspeakable acts, unnatural practices: Flaws and fallacies in "scientific" reading instruction*. Portsmouth, NH: Heinemann.

Smith, F., & Goodman, K. S. (2008). "On the psycholinguistic method of teaching reading" revisited. *Language Arts, 86*(1), 61–65.

Smith, J. K. (1994). Standardized testing versus authentic assessment: Godzilla meets Winnie-the-Pooh. In L. S. Morrow, J. K. Smith, & L. C. Wilkinson (Eds.), *Integrated language arts: Controversy to consensus* (pp. 215–229). Boston: Allyn & Bacon.

Smith, M. (1991). Constructing meaning from text: An analysis of ninth-grade reader responses. *Journal of Educational Research, 84*, 263–271.

Smitherman, G. (1997). Moving beyond resistance: Ebonics and African American youth. *Journal of Black Psychology, 23*(3), 227–232.

Smokes, S. (2001, March 11). Teen dramas played out in shades of black and white. *Syracuse Herald-American*, pp. D1, D5.

Smolen, R., & Erwitt, J. (Creators). (1998). *One digital day: How the microchip is changing our world*. New York: Times Books/Random House in association with Against All Odds Productions.

Smolkin, L. B., & Donovan, C. A. (2004). How not to get lost on *The Magic School Bus*: What makes high science content read-alouds? In E. W. Saul (Ed.), *Crossing borders in literacy and science instruction* (pp. 291–314). Newark: DE: International Reading Association, and Arlington, VA: National Science Teachers Association.

Snodgrass, M. E. (1995). *Encyclopedia of utopian literature*. Santa Barbara, CA: ABC-CLIO.

Snow, C. E., Griffin, P., & Burns, M. S. (2005). *Knowledge to support the teaching of reading: Preparing teachers for a changing world*. San Francisco: Jossey-Bass.

Soares, M. B. (1992). Literacy assessment and its implication for statistical measurement. Paper prepared for the Division of Statistics, UNESCO, Paris.

Sober, E., & Wilson, D. S. (1998). *Unto others: The evolution and psychology of unselfish behavior*. Cambridge, MA: Harvard University Press.

Spalding, E. (2000). Performance assessment and the new standards project: A story of serendipitous success. *Phi Delta Kappan, 81*(10), 758–764.

Spandel, V. (2008). *Creating writers through 6-trait writing: Assessment and instruction* (5th ed.). Boston: Pearson.

Spears, R. A. (1998). *NTC's American English learner's dictionary: The essential vocabulary of American language and culture*. Lincolnwood, IL: National Textbook Company.

Spector, K., & Jones, S. (2007). Constructing Anne Frank: Critical literacy and the Holocaust in eighth-grade English. *Journal of Adolescent and Adult Literacy, 51*(1), 36–48.

Spörer, N., Brunstein, J. C., & Kieschke, U. (2009). Improving students' reading comprehension skills: Effects of strategy instruction and reciprocal teaching. *Learning & Instruction, 19*(3), 272–286.

Sprague, M., & Cotturone, J. (2003). Motivating students to read physics content. *Science Teacher, 70*(3), 24–29.

Spretnak, C. (1997). *The resurgence of the real*. Reading, MA: Addison-Wesley.

Spufford, F. (2002). *The child that books built: A life in reading*. New York: Metropolitan Books.

Stahl, S., Hynd, C., Britton, B., McNish, M., & Bosquet, D. (1996). What happens when students read multiple source documents in history? *Reading Research Quarterly, 31*, 430–456.

Stahl, S. A., Hynd, C. R., Glynn, S. M., & Carr, M. (1996). Beyond reading to learn: Developing content and disciplinary knowledge through texts. In L. Baker, P. Afflerbach, & D. Reinking (Eds.), *Developing engaged readers in school and home communities* (pp. 139–164). Mahwah, NJ: Lawrence Erlbaum Associates.

Stahl, S. A., & Shanahan, C. (2004). Learning to think like a historian: Disciplinary knowledge through critical analysis of multiple documents. In T. L. Jetton & J. A. Dole (Eds.), *Adolescent literacy: Research and practice* (pp. 94–115). New York: The Guilford Press.

Stanovitch, K. E. (1980). Toward an interactive-compensatory model of individual differences in the development of reading fluency. *Reading Research Quarterly, 16*, 32–71.

Stanovitch, K. E. (1986). Matthew effects in reading: Some consequences of individual differences in the acquisition of literacy. *Reading Research Quarterly, 21*, 360–407.

Stauffer, R. G. (1980). *The language experience approach to the teaching of reading.* New York: Harper & Row.

Steinbergh, J. (1994). *Reading and writing poetry: A guide for teachers.* New York: Scholastic.

Stepans, J. (2003). *Targeting students' science misconceptions: Physical science concepts using the conceptual change model.* Tampa, FL: Showboard.

Stephens, E. C., & Brown, J. E. (2000). *A handbook of content literacy strategies: 75 practical reading and writing ideas.* Norwood, MA: Christopher-Gordon.

Sterrett, A. (2002). *101 careers in mathematics.* Washington, DC: Mathematical Association of America.

Stevens, R., & Slavin, R. (1995). The cooperative elementary school: Effects on students' achievement, attitudes, and social relations. *American Educational Research Journal, 32*(2), 321–351.

Stevens, R. J. (2003). Student team reading and writing: A cooperative learning approach to middle school literacy instruction. *Educational Research and Evaluation, 9*(2), 137–160.

Stiggins, R. (2004). New assessment beliefs for a new school mission. *Phi Delta Kappan, 86*(1), 22–27.

Stix, G., & Lacob, M. (1999). *Who gives a gigabyte?: A survival guide for the technologically perplexed.* New York: Wiley.

Stoskopf, A. (2001). Reviving Clio: Inspired history teaching and learning (without high-stakes tests). *Phi Delta Kappan, 82*(6), 468–473.

Strachan, J. (2000). Minding the DBQs. *New York Teacher, XLI*(11), 24.

Straczynski, J. M., & Romita, J., Jr. (2001). *The amazing spiderman,* Vol. 2, No. 36. Marvel Comics.

Street, B. (1995). *Social literacies: Critical approaches to literacy development, ethnography, and education.* New York: Longman.

Street, B. (2003). What's "new" in new literacy studies? Critical approaches to literacy in theory and practice. *Current Issues in Comparative Education, 5*(2), 1–14.

Street, C. (2002). Expository text and middle school students: Some lessons learned. *Voices from the Middle, 9*(4), 33–38.

Sweet, A. P., & Snow, C. (2002). Reconceptualizing reading comprehension. In C. C. Block, L. B. Gambrell, & M. Pressley (Eds.), *Improving comprehension instruction: Rethinking research, theory, and classroom practice* (pp. 17–53). San Francisco: Jossey-Bass.

Swinehart, J. (2009). Metacognition: How thinking about their thinking empowers students. In S. Plaut (Ed.), *The right to literacy in secondary schools: Creating a culture of thinking* (pp. 25–35). New York: Teachers College Press and Newark, DE: International Reading Association.

Syracuse Herald-Journal. Canary in the mine shaft: Cornell bioengineering study. (Editorial). Author, May 24, 1999, A6.

Szabo, S. (2006). KWHHL: A student-driven evolution of the KWL. *American Secondary Education, 34*(3), 57–67.

Taba, H. (1967). *Teachers' handbook for elementary social studies.* Reading, MA: Addison-Wesley.

Taboada, A., Guthrie, J. T., & McRae, A. (2008). Building engaging classrooms. In R. Fink and S.J. Samuels (Eds.). *Inspiring Success: Reading Interest and Motivation in an Age of High-Stakes Testing.* Newark, DE: International Reading Association.

Tanner, M. L., & Casados, L. (1998). Promoting and studying discussions in math classes. *Journal of Adolescent and Adult Literacy, 41*(5), 342–350.

Tapscott, D. (1997). *Growing up digital.* New York: McGraw-Hill.

Tapscott, D. (1998). *Growing up digital: The rise of the Net generation.* New York: McGraw-Hill.

Tapscott, D. (2009). *Grown up digital: How the net generation is changing your world.* New York: McGraw-Hill.

Tatum, A. W. (2009). *Reading for their life: (Re)building the textual lineages of African American adolescent males.* Portsmouth, NH: Heinemann.

Taylor, R. T., & McAtee, R. (2003). Turning a new page to life and literacy. *Journal of Adolescent and Adult Literacy, 46*(6), 476–480.

Taylor, W. L. (1953). Cloze procedure: A new tool for measuring readability. *Journalism Quarterly, 30*, 415–433.

The Norton book of interviews. (1996). New York: Norton.

Thompson, M. C. (1996a). Formal language study for gifted students. In J. VanTassel, D. T. Johnson, & L. N. Boyce (Eds.), *Developing verbal talent* (pp. 149–173). Boston: Allyn & Bacon.

Thompson, M. C. (1996b). Mentors on paper: How classics develop verbal ability. In J. VanTassel, D. T. Johnson, & L. N. Boyce (Eds.), *Developing verbal talent* (pp. 56–74). Boston: Allyn & Bacon.

Thoreau, H. D. (1999). *Uncommon learning: Henry David Thoreau on education* (M. Bickman, Ed.). Boston: Houghton Mifflin.

Tierney, R., Soter, A., O'Flahavan, J., & McGinley, W. (1989). The effects of reading and writing upon thinking critically. *Reading Research Quarterly, 24*, 134–173.

Todd, M., & Watson, E. (2006). *Watcha mean, what's a zine?: The art of making zines and mini comics.* Boston: Houghton Mifflin.

Tower, C. (2005). What's the purpose? Students talk about writing in science. *Language Arts, 82*(6), 472–483.

Trofanenko, B. (2002). Images of history in middle-grade social studies trade books. *The New Advocate, 15*(2), 129–132.

Tuccillo, D. P. (2001). Happily ever after? Teens and fairy tales. *The ALAN Review, 28*(2), 66–68.

Tukey, L. (2002). Differentiation. *Phi Delta Kappan, 84*(1), 63–64, 92.

Turner, J. C. (1995). The influence of classroom contexts on young children's motivation for literacy. *Reading Research Quarterly, 30*, 410–441.

U. S. Department of Education. (1999). *1998 NAEP Reading report card for the nation.* nces.ed.gov/naep

University of the State of New York. (2001). Regent's High School Examination: Comprehensive Examination in English, Session One, January.

Unrau, N. (2008). *Content area reading and writing: Fostering literacies in middle and high school cultures* (2nd ed.). Upper Saddle River, NJ: Pearson.

Urbanski, C. D. (2006). *Using the workshop approach in the high school English classroom.* Thousand Oaks, CA: Corwin Press.

Usnick, V., & McCarthy, J. (1998, March). Turning adolescents onto mathematics through literature. *Middle School Journal,* pp. 50–54.

Valencia, S. W. (2000). How will literacy be assessed in the next millennium? *Reading Research Quarterly, 35*(2), 247–249.

Van de Walle, J. A. (1998). *Elementary and middle school mathematics: Teaching developmentally* (3rd ed.). New York: Longman.

VanCleave, J. (1991). *Astronomy for every kid: 101 experiments that really work.* New York: John Wiley & Sons.

Vardell, S. M., Hadaway, N. L., & Young, T. A. (2006). Matching books and readers: Selecting literature for English learners. *The Reading Teacher, 59*(8), 734–741.

Vaughan, W. (2002). Effects of cooperative learning on achievement and attitude among students of color. *Journal of Educational Research, 95*(6), 364–369.

Veccia, S. H. (2004). *Uncovering our history: Teaching with primary sources.* Chicago: American Library Association.

Vellutino, F. R. (2003). Individual differences as sources of variability in reading comprehension in elementary school children. In A. P. Sweet & C. E. Snow (Eds.), *Rethinking reading comprehension* (pp. 51–81). New York: The Guilford Press.

Vermette, P. J. (1998). *Making cooperative learning work.* Upper Saddle River, NJ: Prentice Hall.

Victor, E., & Kellough, R. D. (1997). *Science for the elementary and middle school* (8th ed.). Upper Saddle River, NJ: Merrill.

Voice, The. (1999). Kids for kid's sake. Vol. 27(3) Albany, NY: United University Professors, 13.

VOYA. (2009). Review retrieved from the Children's Literature Comprehensive Database 3/23/10.

Vygotsky, L. (1962). *Thought and language* (E. Hanfmann & G. Vakar, Eds. and Trans.). Cambridge, MA: MIT Press.

Vygotsky, L. (1978). *Mind in society: The development of higher psychological processes* (M. Cole, V. John-Steiner, S. Scribner, & E. Souberman, Eds.). Cambridge, MA: Harvard University Press.

Wade, S. E., & Moje, E. B. (2000). The role of text in classroom learning. In M. L. Kamil, P. B. Mosenthal, P. D. Pearson, & R. Barr (Eds.), *Handbook of reading research* (Vol. III, pp. 609–627). Mahwah, NJ: Lawrence Erlbaum Associates.

Wahlgren, G. F. (1997). Creating a Mathematical Storybook. *Mathematics Teaching in the Middle School, 3*(2), 126–127.

Wakefield, J. (2001). The object at hand: Painted ladies in space. *Smithsonian, 33*(3), 30–34.

Walczyk, J. J., & Hall, V. C. (1989). Is the failure to monitor comprehension an instance of cognitive impulsivity? *Journal of Educational Psychology, 81*(3), 294–298.

Walker, N. T., & Bean, T. W. (April, 2003). *Multiple uses of texts in content area teachers' classrooms.* Paper presented at the annual meeting of the American Educational Research Association, Chicago, IL.

Warschauer, M. (2007). The paradoxical future of digital learning. *Learning Inquiry, 1*(1), 41–49.

Watson, T. (2000). Misconceptions and mistakes. *Education in Science, 189,* 16.

Weaver, C. (1994). *Reading process and practice: From sociopsycholinguistics to whole language* (2nd ed.). Portsmouth, NH: Heinemann.

Weaver, M. (1999). *Visual literacy: How to read and use information in graphic form.* New York: Learning Express.

Webb, J. (2001). Should we leave Okinawa? *Parade Magazine,* March 11, pp. 4–6.

Webster's encyclopedic unabridged dictionary of the English language. (1996). New York: Random House.

Weir, C. (1998). Using embedded questions to jump-start metacognition in middle school remedial readers. *Journal of Adolescent and Adult Literacy, 41*(6), 458–467.

Wells, M. C. (1996). *Literacies lost: When students move from a progressive middle school to a traditional high school.* New York: Teachers College Press.

Wentzel, K. R. (1996). Social and academic motivation in middle school: Concurrent and long-term relations to academic effort. *Journal of Early Adolescence, 16,* 390–406.

Wentzel, K. R. (1997). Student motivation in middle school: The role of perceived pedagogical caring. *Journal of Educational Psychology, 89*(3), 411–419.

Wenze, G. T. (2003). Teaching through trade books: Life cycle science. *Science and Children, 40*(7), 14–16.

White, E. M. (1999). *Assigning, responding, evaluating: A writing teacher's guide* (3rd ed.). New York: St. Martin's.

White, S. (2007). "That's online writing, not boring school writing": Writing with blogs and the Talkback Project. *Journal of Adolescent and Adult Literacy, 51*(2), 92–96.

Whitelaw, J., & Wolf, S. A. (2001). Learning to "see beyond": Sixth-grade students' artistic perceptions of The Giver. *The New Advocate, 14*(1) 57–67.

Whitin, D. J., & Cox, R. (2003). *A mathematical passage: Strategies for promoting inquiry in grades 4–6.* Portsmouth, NH: Heinemann.

Whitin, D. J., & Whitin, P. E. (1996). Fostering metaphorical thinking through children's literature. In P. C. Elliot & M. J. Kenney (Eds.), *Communication in mathematics, K–12 and beyond* (pp. 60–65). Reston, VA: National Council of Teachers of Mathematics.

Wilcox, B. L. (1996). Smart portfolios for teachers in training. *Journal of Adolescent and Adult Literacy, 40*(3), 172–179.

Wilcox, B. L. (1997). Writing portfolios: Active vs. passive. *English Journal, 86*(6), 34–37.

Wilhelm, J. (2002). *Action strategies for deepening comprehension*. New York: Scholastic.

Wilhelm, J., & Smith, M. W. (2006). What teachers need to know about motivation. *Voices from the Middle, 13*(4), 29–31.

Wilhelm, J. D. (1997). *"You gotta BE the book": Teaching engaged and reflective reading with adolescents*. New York: Teachers College Press, and Urbana, IL: National Council of Teachers of English.

Wilhelm, J. D. (2001). *Improving comprehension with think-aloud strategies*. New York: Scholastic.

Williams, R. M. (2008). Image, text, and story: Comics and graphic novels in the classroom. *Art Education, 61*(6), 13–19.

Willingham, D. (2007). Critical thinking: Why is it so hard to teach? *American Educator, 31*(2), 8–19.

Willingham, D. T. (2006/2007). The usefulness of *brief* instruction in reading comprehension strategies. *American Educator, 30*(4), 39–45.

Wilson, E. O. (2002). The power of story. *American Educator, 26,* Spring, 8–11.

Wilson, W. (2004). *Critical thinking using primary sources in world history*. Portland, ME: Walch.

Wily, J. P. (1998). Coming to terms. *Smithsonian*, December, 28–30.

Winograd, P. N., Wixson, K. K., & Lipson, M. Y. (Eds.). (1989). *Improving basal reading instruction*. New York: Teachers College Press.

Winters, R. (2009). Interactive frames for vocabulary growth and word consciousness. *The Reading Teacher, 62*(8), 685–690.

Wolf, V. L. (1988). A comparison of characters in children's classics. *Children's Literature Association Quarterly 13*(3), 135, 137.

Wolffe, R. (1998). Math learning through electronic journaling. In D. Reiss, D. Selfe, & A. Young (Eds.), *Electronic communication across the curriculum* (pp. 273–281). Urbana, IL: National Council of Teachers of English.

Wood, S. N. (2001). Bringing us the way to know: The novels of Gary Paulsen. *English Journal, 90*(30), 67–72.

Worthy, J. (1998). On every page someone gets killed!: Book conversations you don't hear in school. *Journal of Adolescent and Adult Literacy, 41*(7), 508–517.

Wyman, R. (2005). *America's history through young voices: Using primary sources in the K–12 social studies classroom*. Boston: Pearson/Allyn & Bacon.

Yager, R. E., & Penick, J. E. (1990). Science teacher education. In W. R. Houston (Ed.), *Handbook on research in teacher education* (pp. 657–673). New York: Macmillan.

Yenika-Agbaw, V. (1997). Taking children's literature seriously: Reading for pleasure and social change. *Language Arts, 74*(6), 446–453.

York, S. (2008). *Booktalking authentic multicultural literature: Fiction, history, and memoirs for teens*. Santa Barbara, CA: Linworth.

Young, J. P. (1998). Discussion as a practice of carnival. In D. E. Alvermann, K. A. Hinchman, D. W. Moore, S. F. Phelps, & D. R. Waff (Eds.), *Reconceptualizing the literacies in adolescents' lives* (pp. 247–264). Mahwah, NJ: Lawrence Erlbaum Associates.

Young, J. R. (2009). When computers leave classrooms, so does boredom. *Chronicle of Higher Education, 55*(42), A1.

Young, T. A., & Vardell, S. (1993). Weaving readers theatre and nonfiction into the curriculum. *The Reading Teacher, 46,* 396–406.

Zahar, R., Cobb, T., & Spada, N. (2001). Acquiring vocabulary through reading: Effects of frequency and contextual richness. *Canadian Modern Language Review, 57*(4), 541–572.

Zenkov, K., & Harmon, J. (2009). Picturing a writing process: Photovoice and teaching writing to urban youth. *Journal of Adolescent and Adult Literacy, 52*(7), 575–584.

Zessoules, R., & Gardner, H. (1991). Authentic assessment: Beyond the buzzword and into the classroom. In V. Perrone (Ed.), *Expanding student assessment* (pp. 47–71). Alexandria, VA: Association for Supervision and Curriculum Development.

Zinsser, W. (1994). Simplicity. In P. Eschholz, A. Rosa, & V. Clark (Eds.), *Language awareness* (pp. 486–489). New York: St. Martin's.

Ziv, A., & Gadish, O. (1990). Humor and giftedness. *Journal for the Education of the Gifted, 13*(4), 332–345.

Zuidema, L. A. (2005). Myth education: Rationale and strategies for teaching against linguistic prejudice. *Journal of Adolescent and Adult Literacy, 48*(8), 666–675.

Zwiers, J. (2008). *Building academic language: Essential practices for content classrooms*. San Francisco: Jossey-Bass; Newark, DE: International Reading Association.

Zywica, J., & Gomez, K. (2008). Annotating to support learning in the content areas: Teaching and learning science. *Journal of Adolescent and Adult Literacy, 52*(2), 155–164.

trade books cited

Abbott, E. (1963). *Flatland: A romance of many dimensions* (5th ed., Rev.). New York: Barnes & Noble.

Achebe, C. (1994). *Things fall apart*. New York: Anchor Books.

Adoff, J. (2002). *The song shoots out of my mouth*. New York: Dutton.

Afzal-Khan, F. (Ed.). (2005). *Shattering the stereotypes: Muslim women speak out*. Northampton, MA: Olive Branch Press.

Aliki. (1998). *Marianthe's story: Painted words; Spoken memories*. New York: Greenwillow Books.

Allport, A. (2005). *Immigration policy*. Philadelphia: Chelsea House.

Ambrose, S. E. (2001). *The good fight: How World War II was won*. New York: Atheneum Books for Young Readers.

Anderson, L. H. (1999). *Speak*. New York: Farrar, Straus & Giroux.

Anderson, L. H. (2000). *Fever: 1793*. New York: Simon & Schuster Books for Young Readers.

Anno, M. (1978). *Anno's journey*. Cleveland, OH: Collins-World.

Anno, M. (1980). *Anno's Italy*. New York: HarperCollins.

Anno, M. (1982). *Anno's Britain*. New York: Philomel Books.

Anno, M. (1983a). *Anno's mysterious multiplying jar*. New York: Philomel Books.

Anno, M. (1983b). *Anno's U.S.A.* New York: Philomel Books.

Anonymous. (1982). *Go ask Alice*. New York: Avon Books.

Armour, R. (1969). *On your marks: A package of punctuation*. New York: McGraw-Hill.

Armstrong, J. (1998). *Shipwreck at the bottom of the world*. New York: Scholastic.

Armstrong, J. (2005). *Photo by Brady: A picture of the Civil War*. New York: Atheneum Books.

Arnold, N. (1997). *Nasty nature*. New York: Scholastic.

Aronson, M. (2008). *Unsettled: The problem of loving Israel*. New York: Ginee Seo Books/Athenaeum Books for Young Readers.

Ash, R. (1999). *The top 10 of everything 1999*. New York: DK Publishing.

Ashby, R. (2009). *Young Charles Darwin and the Voyage of the HMS Beagle*. Atlanta: Peachtree.

Asimov, I. (1966). *The fantastic voyage: A novel*. Boston: Houghton Mifflin.

Atwood, M. (1986). *The handmaid's tale*. Boston: Houghton Mifflin.

Avi. (1991). *Nothing but the truth*. Thorndike, ME: Thorndike Press.

Babbitt, N. (1975). *Tuck everlasting*. New York: Farrar, Straus & Giroux.

Babbitt, N. (2000). *Tuck everlasting*. New York: Farrar.

Ballard, R. (1988). *Exploring the Titanic: How the greatest ship ever lost was found*. New York: Scholastic.

Balliett, B. (2004). *Chasing Vermeer*. (B. Helquist, Illus.). New York: Scholastic.

Balliett, B. (2006). *The Wright 3*. (B. Helquist, Illus.). New York: Scholastic.

Balliett, B. (2008). *The Calder game*. (B. Helquist, Illus.). New York: Scholastic.

Banks, R. (1998). *Cloudsplitter*. New York: HarperFlamingo.

Baréma, J. (2005). *The test: Living in the shadow of Huntington's disease*. New York: Franklin Square Press.

Barnes, P. W., & Barnes, C. S. (1996). *House mouse, Senate mouse*. New York: Scholastic.

Barrett, R., & Beard, H. (1993). *The way things really work (And how they actually happen)*. New York: Viking.

Base, G. (1986). *Animalia*. New York: Harry N. Abrams.

Base, G. (1989). *The eleventh hour*. New York: Harry N. Abrams.

Bayer, E. (2000). *Elie Wiesel: Spokesman for remembrance*. New York: Rosen Publishing Group.

Benet, R., & Benet, S. V. (1961). *A book of Americans*. New York: Henry Holt.

Berne, E. C. (2008). *Laura Ingalls Wilder*. Edina, MN: ABDO.

Blasingame, J. B. (2007). *Gary Paulsen*. Westport, CT: Greenwood Press.

Bledsoe, L. J. (2003). *Antarctic scoop*. New York: Holiday House.

Bloor, E. (1997). *Tangerine*. San Diego, CA: Harcourt Brace.

Bober, N. S. (2001). *Countdown to independence: A revolution of ideas in England and her American colonies: 1760–1776*. New York: Atheneum Books for Young Readers.

Bodanis, D. (2001). *E=MC2: A biography of the world's most famous equation*. New York: Berkley Books.

Bolden, T. (2001). *Tell all the children our story: Memories and mementos of being young and black in America*. New York: Harry N. Abrams.

Bolles, E. B. (Ed.). (1997). *Galileo's commandment: An anthology of great science writing*. New York: Freeman.

Born, M. (2005). *The Born–Einstein letters 1916–1955: Friendship, politics and physics in uncertain times*. New York: Macmillan.

Brenner, B. (1978). *Wagon wheels.* New York: Harper & Row.

Bridges, R. (1999). *Through my eyes.* New York: Scholastic.

Brockman, J. (2004). *Curious minds: How a child becomes a scientist.* New York: Pantheon Books.

Bronte, C. (1943). *Jane Eyre.* New York: Random House.

Brothers Grimm, The. (1972). *Snow White and the seven dwarfs.* (R. Jarrell, Trans.). New York: Farrar, Straus & Giroux.

Brown, D. (2000). *Angels and demons.* New York: Pocket Books.

Brown, D. (2003). *The Da Vinci code.* New York: Doubleday.

Bruce, C. (1998). *The Einstein paradox: And other science mysteries solved by Sherlock Holmes.* New York: Basic Books.

Bruce, C. (2001). *Conned again, Watson: Cautionary tales of logic, math and probability.* Cambridge, MA: Perseus Publishing.

Bruce, C. (2004). *Schrödinger's rabbits: The many worlds of the quantum.* Washington, DC: The National Academies Press.

Bryant, J. (2008). *Ringside 1925: Views from the Scopes trial.* New York: Alfred A. Knopf.

Bunting, E. (1991). *Fly away home.* New York: Clarion Books.

Bunting, E. (1994). *Smoky night.* New York: Harcourt Brace.

Bunting, E. (1998). *So far from the sea.* New York: Scholastic.

Burchard, P. (1999). *Lincoln and slavery.* New York: Atheneum Books for Young Children.

Burke, J. (1999). *I hear America reading: Why we read what we read.* Portsmouth, NH: Heinemann.

Butzer, C. M. (2009). *Gettysburg: The graphic novel.* New York: Bowen Press/Collins.

Byars, B. (1977). *The pinballs.* New York: HarperCollins.

Byars, B. (1996). *The Moon and I.* New York: Beech Tree Books.

Cabot, M. (2008). *Airhead.* New York: Point.

Canfield, J., & Hansen, M. V. (1993). *Chicken soup for the soul: 101 stories to open the heart and rekindle the spirit.* Deerfield Beach, FL: Health Communications.

Canfield, J., Hansen, M. V., & Kirberger, K. (1997). *Chicken soup for the teenage soul: 101 stories of life, love and learning.* Deerfield Beach, FL: Health Communications.

Capra, F. (2000). *The Tao of physics: An explanation of the parallels between modern physics and eastern mysticism.* Boston: Shambhala.

Carlson, L. M. (Ed.). (1995). *Cool salsa: Bilingual poems about growing up Latino in the United States.* New York: Fawcett Jupiter.

Carroll, A. (Ed.). (1997). *Letters of a nation: A collection of extraordinary American letters.* New York: Broadway Books.

Carroll, L. (1963). *Alice in Wonderland and Through the looking glass.* New York: Macmillan.

Carton, E. (2006). *Patriotic treason: John Brown and the soul of America.* New York: Free Press.

Cavendish, M. (Ed.). (1995). *War diary 1939–1945.* Secaucus, NJ: Chartwell Books.

Cheney, E. D. (1995). *Louisa May Alcott: Life, letters, and journals.* New York: Gramercy Books.

Cheney, L. (2008). *We the people: The Constitution of the United States.* (G. Harlen, Illus.). New York: Simon & Schuster Books for Young Readers.

Cherry, L. (1990). *The great kapok tree: A tale of the Amazon rain forest.* San Diego, CA: Harcourt Brace.

Cherry, L. (1992). *A river ran wild.* San Diego, CA: Harcourt Brace.

Chesebrough, D. B. (1991). *"God ordained this war": Sermons on the sectional crisis, 1830–1865.* Columbia: University of South Carolina Press.

Choldenko, G. (2004). *Al Capone does my shirts.* New York: Putnam.

Choldenko, G. (2009). *Al Capone shines my shoes.* New York: Dial Books for Young Readers.

Chrisp, P. (2008). *One million things: A visual dictionary.* New York: Dorling Kindersley.

Clavell, J. (1989). *The children's story: But not just for children.* New York: Dell.

Coerr, E., & Himler, R. (1977). *Sadako and the thousand paper cranes.* New York: Putnam.

Coerr, E., & Young, E. (1993). *Sadako.* New York: Putnam.

Cogswell, D., & Gordon, P. (1996). *Chomsky for beginners.* New York: Writers and Readers Publishers.

Cohen, R. (2002). *Dear Mrs. Roosevelt: Letters from children of the Great Depression.* Chapel Hill: University of North Carolina Press.

Cole, J., & Degen, B. *The magic school bus series.* New York: Scholastic.

Cole, K. C. (1998). *The universe and the teacup: The mathematics of truth and beauty.* New York: Harcourt Brace.

Coles, R. (1995). *The story of Ruby Bridges.* New York: Scholastic.

Collins, S. (2008). *The hunger games.* New York: Scholastic.

Collins, S. (2009). *Catching fire.* New York: Scholastic.

Colman, P. (2003). *Girls: A history of growing up female in America.* New York: Scholastic Reference.

Conroy, P. (1980). *Lords of discipline.* Boston: Houghton Mifflin.

Conroy, P. (1986). *The prince of tides.* Boston: Houghton Mifflin.

Conroy, P. (1987). *The water is wide.* New York: Bantam Books.

Conroy, P. (1996). *Beach music.* London: Black Swan.

Cooper, M. L. (2002). *Remembering Manzanar: Life in a Japanese relocation camp.* New York: Clarion Books.

Cormier, R. (1977). *I am the cheese.* New York: Pantheon Books.

Cormier, R. (1986). *The chocolate war.* New York: Dell.

Couloumbis, A. (1999). *Getting near to baby.* New York: Putnam.

Creech, S. (1994). *Walk two moons.* New York: HarperCollins.

Crick, F. (1988). *What mad pursuit: A personal view of scientific discovery.* New York: Basic Books.

Crowe, C. (2003). *Getting away with murder: The true story of the Emmett Till case.* New York: Phyllis Fogleman Books.

Crutcher, C. (1986). *Stotan!* New York: Greenwillow Books.

Crutcher, C. (1993). *Staying fat for Sarah Byrnes.* New York: Greenwillow Books.

Crutcher, C. (1995). *Ironman.* New York: Greenwillow Books.

Cummings, J. M. (2008). *The night I freed John Brown.* New York: Philomel Books.

Cummings, P., & Cummings, L. (Eds.). (1992). *Talking with artists.* Volume 1. New York: Bradbury Press.

Cummings, P., & Cummings, L. (Eds.). (1995). *Talking with artists.* Volume 2. New York: Simon & Schuster Books for Young Readers.

Cummings, P., & Cummings, L. (Eds.). (1998). *Talking with adventurers.* Washington, DC: National Geographic Society.

Cummings, P., & Cummings, L. (Eds.). (1999). *Talking with artists.* Volume 3. New York: Clarion Books.

Curtis, C. P. (1995). *The Watsons Go to Birmingham, 1963.* New York: Delacorte Press.

Curtis, C. P. (1999). *Bud, Not Buddy.* New York: Delacorte Press.

Cushman, K. (1995). *The midwife's apprentice.* New York: HarperTrophy.

Dahl, R. (1988). *Matilda.* New York: Scholastic.

Dahl, R. (1992). *James and the giant peach.* New York: Cornerstone Books.

Dakos, K. (1990). Call the periods, call the commas. In K. Dakos, *If you're not here, please raise your hand: Poems about school* (p. 46). New York: The Trumpet Club.

Davis, J. (1994). *Why Greenland is an island, Australia is not—and Japan is up for grabs: A simple primer for becoming a geographical know-it-all.* New York: Quill.

Davis, K. C. (1999). *Don't know much about history.* New York: Avon Books.

de Saint Exupéry, A., & Woods, K. (1943). *The little prince.* New York: Harcourt, Brace & World.

Deedy, C. A. (2000). *The yellow star: The legend of King Christian X of Denmark.* Atlanta, GA: Peachtree.

Denman, C. (1995). *The history puzzle: An interactive visual timeline.* Atlanta, GA: Turner.

Dewdney, A. K. (1997). *Yes we have no neutrons: An eye-opening tour through the twists and turns of bad science.* New York: Wiley.

Dickens, C. (1998). *Oliver Twist.* New York: Tor.

Dickens, C. (1999). *Great expectations.* Wickford, RI: North Books.

Dickens, C., & Goodrich, C. (1996). *A Christmas carol.* New York: Morrow.

Dickinson, P. (1988). *Eva.* New York: Delacorte.

Dillard, A. (1987). *An American childhood.* New York: HarperCollins.

Dillard, A. (1998, 2000). *Pilgrim at Tinker Creek.* Thorndike, ME: Thorndike Press.

Dillon, L., & Dillon, D. (1998). *For everything there is a season.* New York: The Blue Sky Press.

Duncan, A. F. (1995). *The National Civil Rights Museum celebrates everyday people.* Mahwah, NJ: Bridgewater Books.

Ekeland, I. (1993). *The broken dice: And other mathematical tales of chance.* Chicago: University of Chicago Press.

Elster, C. H. (1999). *The big book of beastly mispronunciations: The complete opinionated guide for the careful speaker.* Boston: Houghton Mifflin.

Elster, C. H., & Elliot, J. (1994). *Tooth and nail: A novel approach to the new SAT.* San Diego, CA: Harcourt Brace.

Erdrich, L. (2005). *The game of silence.* New York: HarperCollins.

Erdrich, L. (2008). *The porcupine year.* New York: HarperCollins.

Erickson, P. (1998). *Daily life on a southern plantation 1853.* New York: Lodestar Books.

Everett, G. (1993). *John Brown: One man against slavery.* New York: Rizzoli International Publications.

Farmer, N. (2002). *The house of the scorpion.* New York: Atheneum Books for Young Readers.

Feelings, T. (1995). *The middle passage: White ships/Black cargo.* New York: Dial Books.

Fine, A. (1997). *The tulip touch.* Boston: Little, Brown.

Fine, E. H. (2004). *Cryptomania: Teleporting into Greek and Latin with the Kryptokids.* (K. Doner, Illus.). Berkeley, CA: Tricycle Press.

Fitzhugh, L. (1964). *Harriet the spy.* New York: Harper & Row.

Fleischman, P. (2001). *Seek.* Chicago: Cricket Books.

Fleischman, P., & Beddows, E. (1985). *I am Phoenix: Poems for two voices.* New York: Harper & Row.

Fleischman, P., & Beddows, E. (1988). *Joyful noise: Poems for two voices.* New York: Harper & Row.

Fleischman, P., & Frampton, D. (1993). *Bull Run.* New York: HarperCollins.

Forbes, E. (1996). *Johnny Tremain.* New York: Putnam Doubleday Books for Young Readers.

Fowles, J. (1969). *The French lieutenant's woman.* Boston: Little, Brown.

Fox, H. (2004). *Eager.* New York: Wendy Lamb Books.

Fox, H. (2006). *Eager's nephew.* New York: Wendy Lamb Books.

Frank, A. (1952). *The diary of a young girl.* New York: Modern Library.

Freedman, R. (1987). *Lincoln: A photobiography.* Boston: Houghton Mifflin.

Freedman, R. (2000). *Give me liberty!: The story of the Declaration of Independence.* New York: Holiday House.

Fried, R. L. (2001). *The passionate learner: How teachers and parents can help children reclaim the joy of discovery.* Boston: Beacon Press.

Fried, R. L. (2001). *The passionate teacher: A practical guide.* Boston: Beacon Press.

Fritz, J. (1983). *The double life of Pocahontas.* New York: Putnam.

Fritz, J. (1987). *Shh! We're writing the Constitution!* New York: Putnam.

Fritz, J., Paterson, K., McKissack, P., McKissack, F., Mahy, M., & Highwater, J. (1992). *The world in 1492.* New York: Henry Holt.

Garner, J. (1998). *We interrupt this broadcast.* Naperville, IL: Sourcebooks.

Gelb, M. J. (1998). *How to think like Leonardo da Vinci: Seven steps to genius every day.* New York: Delacorte.

Gelb, M. J. (2003). *Discover your genius: How to think like history's ten most revolutionary minds.* New York: Quill.

George, J. C. (1972). *Julie of the wolves.* New York: Harper & Row.

George, J. C. (1988). *My side of the mountain.* New York: Dutton.

George, J. C. (1991). *Who really killed Cock Robin?: An ecological mystery.* New York: HarperCollins.

George, J. C. (1992). *The missing gator of Gumbo Limbo: An ecological mystery.* New York: HarperCollins.

George, J. C. (1996). *The case of the missing cutthroats: An ecological mystery.* New York: HarperCollins.

George, J. C. (2008). *And the wolves came back.* New York: Dutton Children's Books.

Ghigna, C. (2003). *A fury of motion: Poems for boys.* Honesdale, PA: Wordsong/Boyds Mills Press.

Giblin, J. C. (1988). *Let there be light: A book about windows.* New York: Crowell.

Giblin, J. C. (1990). *The riddle of the Rosetta Stone: Key to ancient Egypt.* New York: Crowell.

Giblin, J. C. (1995). *When plague strikes: The Black Death, Smallpox, AIDS.* New York: HarperCollins.

Giblin, J. C. (1999). *The mystery of the mammoth bones: And how it was solved.* New York: HarperCollins.

Giblin, J. C. (Ed.). (2000). *The century that was: Reflections on the last one hundred years.* New York: Atheneum Books for Young Readers.

Giblin, J. C. (2005). *Good brother, bad brother: The story of Edwin Book and John Wilkes Booth.* New York: Clarion Books.

Giblin, J. C. (2007). *The many rides of Paul Revere.* New York: Scholastic.

Giblin, J. C. (2008). *Did Alexander rescue Winston?: A research puzzle.* New York: Henry Holt.

Gibson, W. (1957). *The miracle worker.* New York: Knopf.

Gladwell, M. (2007). *Blink: The power of thinking without thinking.* New York: Little, Brown.

Glaser, J. (2006). *John Brown's raid on Harpers Ferry.* (A. Milgom, B. Anderson, & C. Barnett III, Illus.). Mankato, MN: Capstone Press.

Glenn, M. (1996). *Who killed Mr. Chippendale?: A mystery in poems.* New York: Lodestar Books.

Goldish, M. (2008). *Gray wolves: Return to Yellowstone.* New York: Bearport.

Goodall, J. (1986). *The story of a castle.* New York: M. K. McElderry Books.

Goodall, J. (2000). *Africa in my blood: An autobiography in letters: The early years.* (Dale Peterson, Ed.) Boston: Houghton Mifflin.

Goodall, J. (2001). *Beyond innocence: An autobiography in letters: The later years.* (Dale Peterson, Ed.) Boston: Houghton Mifflin.

Goodall, J., with Berman, P. (1999). *Reason for hope: A spiritual journey.* New York: Warner Books.

Gordon, K. E. (1997). *Torn wings and faux pas: A flashbook of style, a beastly guide through the writer's labyrinth.* New York: Pantheon Books.

Gould, S. J. (1996). *Full house: The spread of excellence from Plato to Darwin.* New York: Three Rivers Press.

Govenar, A. (Ed.). (2000). *Osceola: Memories of a sharecropper's daughter.* (S. Evans, Illus.). New York: Hyperion Books for Children.

Graham, A. (1988). Casey's daughter at the bat. In R. R. Knudson & M. Swenson (Eds.), *American sports poems* (p. 42). New York: Orchard Books.

Graham, L. (1980). *John Brown: A cry for freedom.* New York: Crowell.

Granfield, L. (1999). *High flight: A story of World War II* (M. Martchenko, Illus.). Plattsburgh, NY: Tundra Books.

Granfield, L. (2001). *Where poppies grow: A World War I companion.* New York: Stoddart Publishing.

Graves, D. (1998). *How to catch a shark: And other stories about teaching and learning.* Portsmouth, NH: Heinemann.

Green, J. (2006). *An abundance of Katherines.* New York: Dutton.

Greene, B. (2000). *Summer of my German soldier.* New York: Scholastic.

Greene, M. (2004). *Into the land of freedom: African Americans in Reconstruction.* Minneapolis: Lerner Publications.

Groening, M. (2009). *Bart Simpson: Son of Homer.* New York: Harper.

Groening, M., & Gimple, S. M. (1999). *The Simpsons forever!: A complete guide to our favorite family . . . continued.* New York: HarperPerennial.

Groening, M., & McCann, J. L. (2005). *The Simpsons one step beyond forever!: A complete guide to our favorite family—Continued once again.* New York: Harper.

Groening, M. (Creator), Richmond, R., & Coffman, A. (Eds.). (1997). *The Simpsons: A complete guide to our favorite family.* New York: HarperPerennial.

Guterson, D. (1995). *Snow falling on cedars.* New York: Vintage Books.

Haddix, M. P. (2000). *Among the hidden.* New York: Aladdin Paperbacks.

Hager, T. (1995). *Force of nature: The life of Linus Pauling.* New York: Simon & Schuster.

Hager, T. (1998). *Linus Pauling and the chemistry of life.* New York: Oxford University Press.

Hakim, J. (2003). *Freedom: A history of US.* New York: Oxford University Press.

Hansberry, L. (1959). *A raisin in the sun: A drama in three acts.* New York: Random House.

Harris, S. (1977). *What's so funny about science?* Los Altos, CA: William Kaufman.

Harris, S. (1982). *What's so funny about computers?* Los Altos, CA: William Kaufman.

Harris, S. (1989). *Einstein simplified: Cartoons on science.* New Brunswick, NJ: Rutgers University Press.

Hawking, S. (1988). *A brief history of time: From the big bang to black holes.* New York: Bantam Books.

Hawking, S. (1993). *Black holes and baby universes.* New York: Bantam Books.

Heiligman, D. (2009). *Charles and Emma: The Darwins' leap of faith.* New York: Henry Holt.

Henderson, B., & Bernard, A. (Eds.). (1998). *Rotten reviews & rejections.* Wainscoot, NY: Pushcart Press.

Herbst, J. (1993). *Star crossing: How to get around in the universe.* New York: Atheneum.

Herron, C. (1997). *Nappy hair.* (J. Cepeda, Illus.). New York: Knopf.

Hersey, J. (1946). *Hiroshima.* New York: Knopf.

Hesse, K. (1992). *Letters from Rifka.* New York: Henry Holt.

Hesse, K. (1996). *The music of dolphins.* New York: Scholastic.

Hesse, K. (1997). *Out of the dust.* New York: Scholastic.

Hesse, K. (2001). *Witness.* New York: Scholastic.

Hiaasen, C. (2004). *Hoot.* New York: Knopf/Random House.

Hiaasen, C. (2005). *Flush.* New York: Alfred A. Knopf/Random House.

Hiaasen, C. (2009). *Scat.* New York: Alfred A. Knopf.

Hickam, H. H. (1999). *October sky.* New York: Dell.

Hill, J. B. (2000). *The legacy of Luna: The story of a tree, a woman, and the struggle to save the redwoods.* San Francisco: HarperSanFrancisco.

Hine, A. (Ed.). (1965). *This land is mine: An anthology of American verse.* Philadelphia: Lippincott.

Hines, S. W. (Ed.). (2006). *Writings to young women from Laura Ingalls Wilder.* Nashville, TN: Tommy Nelson.

Hines, S. W. (Ed.). (2007). *Laura Ingalls Wilder, farm journalist: Writings from the Ozarks.* Columbia: University of Missouri Press.

Hinton, S. E. (1967). *The outsiders.* New York: Bantam Doubleday Dell.

Hoffman, P. (1998). *The man who loved only numbers: The story of Paul Erdős and the search for mathematical truth.* New York: Hyperion.

Hoose, P. (2001). *We were there, too: Young people in U. S. history.* New York: Farrar, Straus & Giroux.

Houston, J. W., & Houston, J. D. (1995). *Farewell to Manzanar: A true story of Japanese American experience during and after the World War II internment.* New York: Bantam Books.

Hunt, I. (1964). *Across five Aprils.* Chicago: Follett.

Jackson, L. B. (1997). *I have lived a thousand years: Growing up in the Holocaust.* New York: Simon & Schuster Books for Young Readers.

Jarrell, R. (1996). *The bat-poet.* New York: HarperCollins.

Jiang, J. (1997). *Red scarf girl: A memoir of the cultural revolution.* New York: HarperCollins.

Johnson, A. (2005). *A sweet smell of roses.* (E. Velasquez, Illus.). New York: Simon & Schuster.

Johnston, J. (1994). *Adam and Eve and pinch-me.* Boston: Little, Brown.

Johnston, T. (1996). *My Mexico—Mexico Mio.* New York: Putnam.

Jonas, A. (1990). *Aardvarks, disembark!* New York: Greenwillow Books.

Jones, C. F. (1991). *Mistakes that worked: 40 familiar inventions and how they came to be.* New York: Delacorte.

Jones, C. F. (1996). *Accidents may happen: Fifty inventions discovered by mistake.* New York: Delacorte.

Jones, E. D. (1948). *Lincoln and the preachers.* New York: Harper.

Jones, W. B. (2002). *Classics Illustrated: A cultural history, with illustrations.* Jefferson, NC: McFarland.

Joyce, J. (1992). *Ulysses.* New York: Modern Library.

Junger, S. (1997). *The perfect storm: A true story of men against the sea.* New York: Norton.

Juster, N. (1961). *The phantom tollbooth.* New York: Scholastic.

Kadohata, C. (2004). *Kira-Kira.* New York: Atheneum.

Kakalios, J. (2005). *The physics of superheroes.* New York: Gotham.

Karson, J. (2005). *The Civil Rights Movement. Opposing viewpoints in World History Series.* Farmington Hills, MI: Greenhaven Press.

Kaufman, M. T. (2008). *1968.* New York: Roaring Brook Press.

Keller, E. F. (1983). *A feeling for the organism: The life and work of Barbara McClintock.* San Francisco: Freeman.

Kidder, T. (2003). *Mountains beyond mountains: The quest of Dr. Paul Farmer, a man who would cure the world.* New York: Random House.

King, S. (2000). *On writing: A memoir of the craft.* New York: Pocket Books.

Kingsolver, B. (1988). *The bean trees.* New York: Harper & Row.

Kingsolver, B. (1995). *High tide in Tucson: Essays from now or never.* New York: HarperCollins.

Kingsolver, B. (1998). *The poisonwood bible.* New York: HarperFlamingo.

Klarnum, M. (2004). *From Jim Crow to civil rights: The Supreme Court and the struggle for racial equality.* New York: Oxford University Press.

Kluger, S. (2008). *My most excellent year: A story of love, Mary Poppins, and Fenway Park.* New York: Dial Books.

Knowles, J. (1960). *A separate peace.* New York: Macmillan.

Kodama, T. (1995). *Shin's tricycle.* New York: Walker.

Koestler-Grack, R. (2009). *Elie Wiesel: Witness for humanity.* Pleasantville, NY: Gareth Stevens.

Kolata, G. B. (1999). *Flu: The story of the great influenza pandemic of 1918 and the search for the virus that caused it.* New York: Farrar, Straus & Giroux.

Konigsburg, E. L. (1993). *T-Backs, t-Shirts, COAT, and suit.* New York: Atheneum.

Konigsburg, E. L. (1996). *The view from Saturday.* New York: Atheneum Books for Young Readers.

Konigsburg, E. L. (2000). *Silent to the bone.* New York: Atheneum Books for Young Readers.

Krakauer, J. (1998). *Into thin air.* New York: Anchor Books.

Krull, K. (1993). *Lives of the musicians: Good times, bad times (and what the neighbors thought).* San Diego, CA: Harcourt Brace.

Krull, K. (1994). *Lives of the writers: Comedies, tragedies (and what the neighbors thought).* New York: Harcourt Brace.

Krull, K. (1995). *Lives of the artists: Masterpieces, messes (and what the neighbors thought).* San Diego, CA: Harcourt Brace.

Krull, K. (1997). *Lives of the athletes: Thrills, spills (and what the neighbors thought).* San Diego, CA: Harcourt Brace.

Krull, K. (1998). *Lives of the presidents: Fame, shame (and what the neighbors thought).* San Diego, CA: Harcourt Brace.

Krull, K. (2000). *Lives of extraordinary women: Rulers, rebels (and what the neighbors thought).* San Diego, CA: Harcourt Brace.

Kupperberg, P. (2006). *A primary source history of the colony of New York.* New York: Rosen.

L'Engle, M. (1962). *A wrinkle in time.* New York: Farrar, Straus & Giroux.

L'Engle, M. (1972). *A circle of quiet.* New York: Harper & Row.

L'Engle, M. (1973). *A wind in the door.* New York: Bantam Doubleday Dell.

L'Engle, M. (1980). *A ring of endless light.* New York: Bantam Doubleday Dell.

Landau, S. (2001). *Dictionaries: The art and craft of lexicography.* New York: Cambridge University Press.

Lasky, K. (2009). *One beetle too many: The extraordinary adventures of Charles Darwin.* Cambridge, MA: Candlewick Press.

Lee, H. (1995). *To kill a mockingbird.* New York: HarperCollins.

Lemieux, M. (1999). *Stormy night.* Toronto, Canada: Kids Can Press.

Levine, E. (2000). *Darkness over Denmark: The Danish Resistance and the rescue of the Jews.* New York: Scholastic.

Levitt, S. D., & Dubner, S. J. (2005). *Freakonomics: A rogue economist explores the hidden side of everything.* New York: William Morrow.

Levitt, S. D., & Dubner, S. J. (2009). *Superfreakonomics: Global cooling, patriotic prostitutes, and why suicide bombers should get life insurance.* New York: William Morrow.

Lichtman, W. (2007). *Do the math: Secrets, lies and algebra.* New York: Greenwillow Books.

Lichtman, W. (2008). *Do the math #2: The writing on the wall.* New York: Greenwillow Books.

Lincoln, A., & McCurdy, M. (1997). *The Gettysburg Address.* Boston: Houghton Mifflin.

Lionni, L. (1968). *The alphabet tree.* New York: Pantheon.

Little, J. (1986). After English class. In J. Little (Ed.), *Hey, world, here I am!* (p. 28). New York: Harper & Row.

Locker, T. (1997). *Water dance.* San Diego, CA: Harcourt Brace.

Loewen, J. (2004). *Rethinking our past: Recognizing facts, fictions, and lies in American history.* Prince Frederick, MD: Recorded Books.

Loewen, J. W. (1995). *Lies my teacher told me: Everything your American history textbook got wrong.* New York: The New Press.

Loewen, J. W. (2000). *Lies across America: What our historic sites get wrong.* New York: Simon & Schuster.

Lowry, L. (1979). *Anastasia Krupnik.* Boston: Houghton Mifflin.

Lowry, L. (1984). *Anastasia, ask your analyst.* Boston: Houghton Mifflin.

Lowry, L. (1989). *Number the stars.* Boston: Houghton Mifflin.

Lowry, L. (1993). *The giver.* Boston: Houghton Mifflin.

Lowry, L. (2000). *Gathering blue.* Boston: Houghton Mifflin.

Lowry, L. (2004). *Messenger.* Boston: Houghton Mifflin.

Lowry, L. (2006). *Gossamer.* Boston: Houghton Mifflin.

Lutz, W. (1990). *Doublespeak: From revenue enhancement to terminal living: How government, business, advertisers, and others use language to deceive you.* New York: HarperPerennial.

Lutz, W. (1996). *The new doublespeak: Why no one knows what anyone's saying anymore.* New York: HarperPerennial.

Lyons, M. E., & Branch, M. M. (2000). *Dear Ellen Bee: A Civil War scrapbook of two Union spies.* New York: Scholastic.

Macaulay, D. (1973). *Cathedral.* Boston: Houghton Mifflin.

Macaulay, D. (1975). *Pyramid.* Boston: Houghton Mifflin.

Macaulay, D. (1977). *Castle.* Boston: Houghton Mifflin.

Macaulay, D. (1987). *Unbuilding.* Boston: Houghton Mifflin.

Macaulay, D. (1993). *Ship.* Boston: Houghton Mifflin.

Macaulay, D. (2003). *Mosque.* Boston: Houghton Mifflin.

Macaulay, D., with Ardley, D. (1998). *The new way things work.* Boston: Houghton Mifflin.

Madonna. (2003). *The English Roses.* (J. Fulvimari, Illus.). New York: Calloway.

Malan, D. (1994). *The complete guide to Classics Illustrated.* St. Louis, MO: Malan Classical Enterprises.

Malkin, M. (2004). *In defense of internment: The case for "racial profiling" in World War II and the war on terror.* Washington, DC: Regnery Publishers.

Manning, M. (2009). *What Mr. Darwin saw.* London: Frances Lincoln.

Maran, R. (1998). *Teach yourself computers and the Internet visually* (2nd ed.). Foster City, CA: IDG Books Worldwide.

Marsh, C. (2005). *The beloved community: How faith shapes social justice, from the Civil Rights Movement to today.* New York: Basic Books.

Martin, J. B. (1998). *Snowflake Bentley.* Boston: Houghton Mifflin.

Maruki, T. (1980). *Hiroshima no pika*. New York: Lothrop, Lee & Shepard.

Mass, W. (2008). *Every soul a star*. New York: Little Brown Books for Young Readers.

Mathis, S. B. (1975). *The hundred penny box*. New York: Viking.

McCloud, S. (1994). *Understanding comics: The invisible art*. New York: HarperPerennial.

McDonald, S. P. (1936). Casey—Twenty years later. In H. Felleman (Ed.), *The best loved poems of the American people* (p. 286). Garden City, NY: Doubleday.

McKissack, P., & McKissack, F. (1994). *Christmas in the big house, Christmas in the quarters*. New York: Scholastic.

McLynn, F. (Ed.). (1993). *Famous letters: Messages and thoughts that shaped our world*. Pleasantville, NY: Reader's Digest Association.

McWhorter, D. (2004). *A dream of freedom: The Civil Rights movement from 1954 to 1968*. New York: Scholastic.

Meltzer, M. (1997). *Langston Hughes: An illustrated edition*. Brookfield, CT: Millbrook Press.

Meltzer, M. (2001). *There comes a time: The struggle for civil rights*. New York: Random House.

Melville, H. (2001). *Moby Dick, or, The whale*. New York: Penguin Books.

Merriam, E., & Smith, L. (1995). *Halloween ABC*. New York: Macmillan.

Meyer, S. (2005). *Twilight*. New York: Little, Brown and Co.

Miller, M. (1999). *Words that built a nation: A young person's collection of historic American documents*. New York: Scholastic.

Mills, C. (1998). *Standing up to Mr. O*. New York: Scholastic.

Mochizuki, K. (1993). *Baseball saved us*. New York: Lee & Low.

Monk, R. C. (Ed.). (1994). *Taking sides: Clashing views on controversial issues in race and ethnicity*. Guilford, CT: Dushkin.

Montgomery, S. (2004). *The Tarantula scientist*. Boston: Houghton Mifflin.

Moranville, S. B. (2006). *A higher geometry*. New York: Henry Holt.

Morgan, A. H. (1930). *The field book of ponds and streams*. New York: Putnam.

Mori, T., & Anno, M. (1986). *Socrates and the three little pigs*. New York: Philomel Books.

Morimoto, J. (1990). *My Hiroshima*. New York: Viking.

Morpurgo, M. (1990). *Waiting for Anya*. New York: Scholastic.

Morrison, T. (1987). *Beloved*. New York: Knopf.

Morrison, T. (2004). *Remember: The journey to school integration*. Boston: Houghton Mifflin.

Mortenson, G., & Roth, S. L. (2009). *Three cups of tea: Young person's edition*. Adapted by S. Thomson. New York: Puffin.

Motz, L., & Weaver, J. H. (1995). *The story of astronomy*. New York: Basic Books.

Munteanu, N. (2007). *Darwin's paradox*. Calgary, Canada: Dragon Moon Press.

Murray, K. M. E. (2001). *Caught in the web of words: James A. H. Murray and the Oxford English Dictionary*. New Haven, CT: Yale University Press.

Myers, W. D. (1991). *Now is your time!: The African American struggle for freedom*. New York: HarperCollins.

Myers, W. D. (1999). *Monster*. New York: Scholastic.

Myers, W. D. (2004). *Here in Harlem: Poems in many voices*. New York: Holiday House.

Nasar, S. (1998). *A beautiful mind: A biography of John Forbes Nash, winner of the Nobel Prize in economics*. New York: Simon & Schuster.

Nash, O. (1953). *The moon is shining bright as day*. New York: Lippincott.

Naslund, S. J. (1999). *Ahab's wife, or the star gazer: A novel*. New York: Morrow.

Neuschwander, C., & Geehan, W. (1997). *Sir Cumference and the first round table: A math adventure*. Watertown, MA: Charlesbridge.

Newton, L. H., & Ford, M. M. (Eds.). (1994). *Taking sides: Clashing views on controversial issues in business ethics and society*. Guilford, CT: Dushkin.

Ng, W. (2002). *Japanese American internment during World War II: A history and reference guide*. Westport, CT: Greenwood Press.

Nielsen, S. (2008). *Word nerd*. New York: Random House.

Nolan, H. (1997). *Dancing on the edge*. San Diego, CA: Harcourt Brace.

Nye, N. S. (Collector). (1998). *This tree is older than you are: A bilingual gathering of poems and stories from Mexico with paintings by Mexican artists*. New York: Aladdin Paperbacks.

Nye, N. S. (2005). *A maze me: Poems for girls*. (T. Maher, Illus.). New York: Greenwillow Books.

O'Dell, S. (1990). *Island of the blue dolphins*. Boston: Houghton Mifflin.

O'Dell, S. (1997). *Sing down the moon*. New York: Dell.

O'Meara, D. (2005). *Into the volcano*. Tonawanda, NY: Kids Can Press.

Oates, S. B. (1984). *To purge this land with blood: A biography of John Brown* (2nd ed.). Amherst: University of Massachusetts Press.

Olds, B. (1995). *Raising holy hell*. New York: Henry Holt.

Paley, V. (1997). *The girl with the brown crayon*. Cambridge, MA: Harvard University Press.

Park, B. (1995). *Mick Harte was here*. New York: Knopf.

Park, R. (2000). *Voodoo science: The road from foolishness to fraud*. New York: Oxford University Press.

Parker, S., & Kelly, J. (1996). *Shocking science: 5,000 years of mishaps and misunderstandings*. Atlanta, GA: Turner.

Parker, S., & West, D. (1993). *Brain surgery for beginners: And other major operations for minors*. New York: Scholastic.

Partridge, E. (2002). *Restless spirit: The life and work of Dorothea Lange*. New York: Scholastic.

Patent, D. H. (2008). *When the wolves returned: Restoring nature's balance in Yellowstone*. Photographs by D. & C. Hartman. New York: Walker.

Paterson, K. (1977). *Bridge to Terabithia.* New York: Dell.

Paterson, K. (1978). *The great Gilly Hopkins.* New York: HarperCollins.

Paterson, K. (1980). *Jacob have I loved.* New York: Crowell.

Paterson, K. (1994). *Flip-flop girl.* New York: Dutton.

Paulsell, W. O. (1990). *Tough minds, tender hearts: Six prophets of social justice.* New York: Paulist Press.

Paulsen, G. (1987). *Hatchet.* New York: Bradbury Press.

Paulsen, G. (1993). *Nightjohn.* New York: Delacorte.

Paulsen, G. (1998). *Soldier's heart.* New York: Delacorte.

Paulsen, G. (2000). *The beet fields: Memories of a sixteenth summer.* New York: Delacorte.

Paulsen, G. (2001). *Guts: The true stories behind Hatchet and the Brian books.* Thorndike, ME: Thorndike Press.

Paulsen, G. (2009). *Mudshark.* New York: Wendy Lamb Books.

Peacock, L., & Krudop, W. (1998). *Crossing the Delaware: A history in many voices.* New York: Atheneum Books for Young Readers.

Pearson, M. E. (2008). *The adoration of Jenna Fox.* New York: Henry Holt.

Pederson, T., & Moss, F. (1998). *Make your own web page!: A guide for kids.* New York: Price Stern Sloan.

Pennac, D. (1994). *Better than life.* Toronto, Canada: Coach House Press.

Pennac, D. (2008). *The rights of the reader.* (Q. Blake, Illus.). Cambridge, MA: Candlewick Press.

Perl, L., & Lazan, M. B. (1996). *Four perfect pebbles: A Holocaust story.* New York: Scholastic.

Philbrick, R. (1993). *Freak the mighty.* New York: Blue Sky Press.

Polacco, P. (1994). *Pink and Say.* New York: Philomel Books.

Potter, R. R. (1995). *John Brown: Militant abolitionist.* Austin, TX: Steck-Vaughn.

Pratchett, T. (2008). *Nation.* New York: HarperCollins.

Preston, R. (1994). *The hot zone.* New York: Random House.

Provenson, A. (1997). *The buck stops here: The presidents of the United States.* New York: Harper & Row.

Rapoport, R. (2000). *See how she runs: Marion Jones and the making of a champion.* Chapel Hill, NC: Algonquin Books.

Raskin, J. B. (2000). *We the students: Supreme Court cases for and about students.* Washington, DC: CQ Press.

READ Magazine. (1995). *Dear author: Students write about the books that changed their lives.* Berkeley, CA: Conari Press.

Rees, D. (1997). *Lightning time.* New York: DK Publishing.

Reynolds, D. S. (2005). *John Brown, Abolitionist: The man who killed slavery, sparked the Civil War, and seeded civil rights.* New York: Knopf.

Reynolds Naylor, P. (2000). *Shiloh.* New York: Aladdin.

Rinaldi, A. (1998). *Mine eyes have seen.* New York: Scholastic.

Rodriguez, R. (1983). *Hunger of memory: The education of Richard Rodriguez: An autobiography.* New York: Bantam Books.

Roth, A. (1974). *The iceberg hermit.* New York: Scholastic.

Roth, P. (2004). *The plot against America.* Boston: Houghton Mifflin.

Roth, P. (2004). *The plot against America.* Read by Ron Silver. Prince Frederick, MD: Recorded Books.

Ryan, P. M. (2004). *Becoming Naomi León.* New York: Scholastic.

Sachar, L. (1998). *Holes.* New York: Farrar, Straus & Giroux.

Salinger, J. D. (1951). *Catcher in the rye.* Boston: Little, Brown.

Sanborn, F. B. (1969). *The life and letters of John Brown: Liberator of Kansas, and martyr of Virginia.* New York: Negro University Press.

Santiago, E. (1994). *When I was Puerto Rican.* New York: Vintage Books.

Sasson, J. (2001). *Princess: A true story of life behind the veil in Saudi Arabia.* Van Nuys, CA: Windsor-Brooke Books.

Say, A. (1993). *Grandfather's journey.* Boston: Houghton Mifflin.

Say, A. (2004). *Music for Alice.* Boston: Houghton Mifflin.

Schanzer, R. (2004). *George vs. George: The American Revolution as seen from both sides.* Washington, DC: National Geographic.

Schanzer, R. (2009). *What Darwin saw: The journey that changed the world.* Washington, DC: National Geographic.

Schmandt-Besserat, D., & Hays, M. (2000). *The history of counting.* New York: Morrow Junior.

Scholastic. *Dear America series.* New York: Author.

Scholastic. *My name is America series.* New York: Author.

Scholastic. *Royal diaries series.* New York: Author.

Scholastic. (1999). *The Usborne illustrated encyclopedia: Science and technology.* New York: Author.

Schomp, V. (2004). *World War II (letters from the battlefront).* New York: Benchmark Books.

Schultz, C. (1980). *Charlie Brown, Snoopy and Me, and all the other Peanuts characters.* Garden City, NY: Doubleday.

Schwartz, D. M. (1985). *How much is a million?* New York: Lathrop, Lee & Shepard.

Schwartz, D. M. (1998). *G is for googol: A math alphabet book.* New York: Scholastic.

Schwartz, D. M., & Doner, K. (2001). *Q is for quark: A science alphabet book.* Berkeley, CA: Tricycle Press.

Scieszka, J., & Smith, L. (1995). *Math curse.* New York: Viking.

Scieszka, J., & Smith, L. (2004). *Science verse.* New York: Viking.

Seife, C. (2000). *Zero: The biography of a dangerous idea.* New York: Viking.

Selznick, B. (2007). *The invention of Hugo Cabret.* New York: Scholastic.

Sendak, M. (1963). *Where the wild things are.* New York: Harper & Row.

Sendak, M. (1993). *We are all in the dumps with Jack and Guy.* New York: HarperCollins.

Seuss, Dr. (1971). *The lorax.* New York: Random House.

Seuss, Dr. (1984). *The butter battle book.* New York: Random House.

Shaffer, M. A., & Barrows, A. (2008). *The Guernsey Literary and Potato Peel Pie Society.* New York: The Dial Press.

Shakespeare, W. (2001). *Romeo and Juliet.* New York: Oxford University Press.

Sheinkin, S. (2005). *King George: What was his problem?: Everything your schoolbooks didn't tell you about the American Revolution.* (T. Robinson, Illus.). New York: Roaring Book Press.

Sheinkin, S. (2008). *Two miserable presidents: Everything your schoolbooks didn't tell you about the Civil War.* (T. Robinson, Illus.). New York: Roaring Book Press.

Shepherd, J. (1999). Winter green. *Alaska, 65*(1), 34.

Sickels, A. (2007). *Laura Ingalls Wilder.* New York: Chelsea House.

Siebert, D., & Minor, W. (1988). *Mojave.* New York: Crowell.

Siebert, D., & Minor, W. (1989). *Heartland.* New York: Crowell.

Siebert, D., & Minor, W. (1991). *Sierra.* New York: HarperCollins.

Simon, S. (1997). *The brain: Our nervous system.* New York: Morrow Junior Books.

Simon, S. (1997). *The heart: Our circulatory system.* New York: Morrow Junior Books.

Simon, S. (1998). *Muscles: Our muscular system.* New York: Morrow Junior Books.

Simon, S. (1998). *Bones: Our skeletal system.* New York: Morrow Junior Books.

Sis, P. (1996). *Starry messenger: A book depicting the life of a famous scientist, mathematician, astronomer, philosopher, physicist, Galileo Galilei.* New York: Farrar, Straus & Giroux.

Skinner, B. F. (1948, 1990). *Walden two.* New York: Macmillan.

Slife, B. (Ed.). (1996). *Taking sides: Clashing views on psychological issues.* Guilford, CT: Dushkin.

Smith, M. W., & Wilhelm, J. D. (2002). *Reading don't fix no Chevys: Literacy in the lives of young men.* Portsmouth, NH: Heinemann.

Sophocles. (1989). *Antigone.* (R. E. Braun, Trans.). New York: Oxford University Press.

Soto, G. (1995). *Canto Familiar.* San Diego, CA: Harcourt Brace.

Speare, E. (1958). *The witch of Blackbird Pond.* New York: Dell.

Spears, R. A. (1998). *NTC's American English Learners Dictionary: The essential vocabulary of American language and culture.* Lincolnwood, IL: NTC Publishing Group.

Spier, P. (1987). *We the people: The constitution of the United States.* Garden City, NY: Doubleday.

Spinelli, J. (1990). *Maniac Magee.* Boston: Little, Brown.

St. George, J. (1992). *Dear Dr. Bell . . . Your friend, Helen Keller.* New York: Putnam.

Standing Bear, L. (1983). *My people, the Sioux.* Boston: Houghton Mifflin.

Stanley, D. (1996). *Leonardo da Vinci.* New York: Morrow Junior Books.

Stanley, J. (1994). *I am an American: A true story of Japanese internment.* New York: Scholastic.

Stein, R. C. (1999). *John Brown's raid on Harpers Ferry in American history.* Berkeley Heights, NJ: Enslow.

Steinberg, L. (2003). *Thesaurus Rex.* Cambridge, MA: Barefoot Books.

Stephenson, T. (2009). *Swine flu/H1N1: The facts.* Philadelphia: Jessica Kingsley.

Stewart, I. (2001). *Flatterland: Like Flatland only more so.* Cambridge, MA: Perseus.

Stille, D. R. (1997). *Extraordinary women of medicine.* New York: Children's Press.

Stolley, R. B. (Ed.). (2000). *LIFE: Our century in pictures for young people.* Boston: Little, Brown.

Streissguth, T. (1999). *John Brown.* Minneapolis, MN: CarolRhodaBooks.

Swinburne, S. R. (1999). *Once a wolf: How wildlife biologists fought to bring back the gray wolf.* Boston: Houghton Mifflin.

Tamplin, R. (Ed.). (1995). *Famous love letters: Messages of intimacy and passion.* Pleasantville, NY: Reader's Digest Association.

Tan, A. (1989). *The Joy Luck Club.* New York: Putnam.

Tashjian, J. (2001). *Multiple choice.* New York: Scholastic Signature.

Tatlock, A. (2002). *All the way home.* Minneapolis, MN: Bethany House.

Taylor, M. (1976). *Roll of thunder, hear my cry.* New York: Dial Books.

Taylor, T. (1991). *The cay.* New York: Avon Books.

Ten Boom, C., with Sherrill, J., & Sherrill, E. (1971). *The hiding place.* Washington Depot, CT: Chosen Books.

Terkel, S. (1999). *Voices of our time: Five decades of Studs Terkel interviews.* St. Paul, MN: Highbridge Company (Sound Recording).

Thayer, E. L. (2000). *Casey at the bat.* (C. Bing, Illus.). New York: Scholastic.

Thomas, R. (1996). *Rats saw God.* New York: Simon & Schuster.

Thoreau, H. D. (1969). *Civil disobedience.* Boston: D. R. Godine.

Thoreau, H. D. (1992). *Walden, or life in the woods.* New York: Knopf.

Tolkien, J. R. R. (1987). *The hobbit, or, there and back again.* London: Unwin Hyman.

Tompkins, J. (1996). *A life in school: What the teacher learned.* Reading, MA: Addison-Wesley.

Tsuchiya, Y. (1988). *Faithful elephants.* Boston: Houghton Mifflin.

Twayne's United States author series: Young adult authors. Boston: Twayne Publishers.

Tyson, N. D. (2007). *Death by black hole: And other cosmic quandaries.* New York: W. W. Norton & Company.

Tyson, N. D. (2009). *The Pluto files: The rise and fall of America's favorite planet.* New York: W. W. Norton.

Van Allsburg, C. (1991). *The wretched stone.* Boston: Houghton Mifflin.

VanVoorst, J. F. (2009). *Rise of the thinking machines: The science of robots.* Mankato, MN: Compass Points Books.

Vincent, G. (2000). *A day, a dog.* Asheville, NC: Front Street.

Vinz, R. (1996). *Composing a teaching life.* Portsmouth, NH: Boynton/Cook.

Vowell, S. (2003). *Partly cloudy patriot.* New York: Simon & Schuster.

Vowell, S. (2005). *Assassination vacation.* New York: Simon & Schuster.

Vowell, S. (2008). *The wordy shipmates.* New York: Riverhead Books.

Wagoner, J. J., & Cutliff, L. D. (1985). *Mammoth Cave.* Arlington, VA: Interpretive Publications.

Ward, G. C. (1999). *Not for ourselves alone: The story of Elizabeth Cady Stanton and Susan B. Anthony: An illustrated history.* New York: Knopf.

Washington, G., & Yoder, C. P. (2003). *George Washington, the writer: A treasury of letters, diaries, and public documents.* Honesdale, PA: Boyds Mills Press.

Watson, J. (1980). The double helix: A personal account of the discovery of the structure of DNA. In G. S. Stent (Ed.), *Norton critical edition: Text, commentary, reviews, original papers.* New York: Norton.

Watson, J. (2001). *The double helix: A personal account of the discovery of the structure of DNA.* New York: Touchstone.

Whelan, G. (2008). *Homeless bird.* New York: HarperCollins.

White, B. (1993). *Mama makes up her mind: And other dangers of southern living.* Reading, MA: Addison-Wesley.

White, E. B. (1945). *Stuart Little.* New York: Harper & Row.

White, E. B. (1952). *Charlotte's web.* New York: Harper Trophy.

White, T. H. (1958). *The once and future king.* New York: Putnam.

Whiteknact, S. (2006). *A primary source history of the colony of Virginia.* New York: Rosen.

Whitman, W. (1992). *Leaves of grass, the deathbed edition.* New York: Quality Paperback Book Club.

Wiesel, E. (2000). *Night, and related readings.* New York: Glencoe/McGraw-Hill.

Wiesner, D. (1991). *Tuesday.* New York: Clarion Books.

Wiesner, D. (2008). *Flotsam.* New York: Clarion.

Williams, W. F. (2000). *The encyclopedia of pseudoscience: From alien abductions to zone therapy.* Chicago: Fitzroy Dearborn.

Wilson, E. O. (1998). *Consilience: The unity of knowledge.* New York: Knopf.

Wilson, J. (1936). Casey's revenge. In H. Felleman (Ed.), *The best loved poems of the American people* (p. 284). Garden City, NY: Doubleday.

Winchester, S. (1998). *The professor and the madman: A tale of murder, insanity, and the making of the Oxford English Dictionary.* New York: HarperCollins.

Winter, J. (1988). *Follow the drinking gourd.* New York: Trumpet Club.

Wise, E. (2005). *Robotics demystified.* New York: McGraw-Hill.

Wolf, W. J. (1959). *The almost chosen people: A study of the religion of Abraham Lincoln.* Garden City, NY: Doubleday.

Wolff, V. E. (1998). *Bat 6.* New York: Scholastic.

Wolff, V. E. (2000). *The Mozart season.* New York: Scholastic Signature.

Worsley, D., & Meyer, B. (1989). *The art of science writing.* New York: Teachers and Writers Collaborative.

Wright-Frierson, V. (2002). *An island scrapbook: From dawn to dusk on a Barrier island.* New York: Aladdin Paperbacks.

Writers and Readers Publishers. *Beginners Documentary Comic Books* (series). New York: Author.

Wurman, R. S. (1989). *Information anxiety.* Garden City, NY: Doubleday.

Yolen, J. (1990). *The devil's arithmetic.* New York: Puffin Books.

Youngson, R. M. (1998). *Scientific blunders: A brief history of how wrong scientists can sometimes be.* New York: Carroll & Graf.

Zimmerman, K., Hyneman, J., & Savage, A. (2005). *Mythbusters: The explosive truth behind 30 of the most perplexing urban legends of all time.* New York: Simon Spotlight Entertainment.

Zoller, K., & Preston, K. (2007). *You did what?: The biggest mistakes professionals make.* Wyomissing, PA: Tapestry Press.

Zusak, M. (2006). *The book thief.* New York: Alfred A. Knopf.

OTHER MEDIA

Burns, K. (1999). *Not for ourselves alone: The story of Elizabeth Cady Stanton and Susan B. Anthony.* PBS Home Video.

Death of a star. (1987). Boston: WGBH Educational Foundation.

Mulan. (2000). Burbank, CA: Walt Disney Home Video.

My bodyguard. (1980). Beverly Hills, CA: Twentieth Century Fox Home Entertainment/CBS Fox Video.

Outbreak. (1995). Burbank, CA: Warner Home Video.

PBS video catalog. 1320 Braddock Place, Alexandria, VA 22314-1698

Roots. (1977). New York: ABC.

Ruby Bridges. (1998). Buena Vista Home Entertainment.

Schindler's list. (1993). Universal Pictures. Universal City, CA: MCA Universal Home Video.

Shakespeare in love. (1999). Burbank, CA: Miramax Films/Universal Pictures/The Bedford Falls Company.

Snow falling on cedars. (1999). Universal City, CA: Universal.

Sister Wendy series. (1997). *The story of painting.* Beverly Hills, CA: CBS/Fox Video; BBC video.

Viola, K., & Ellison, H. (performer). (1989). *The masters of comic book art.* Santa Monica, CA: Rhino Home Video.

author & title index

subject index